CW00796668

Refugee Imaginaries

Contents

Notes on Contributors

Hakim Abderrezak is an associate professor at the University of Minnesota. His research focuses on cinematic, literary and musical representations of clandestine crossings of the Mediterranean Sea.

Btihaj Ajana is Senior Lecturer at the department of Digital Humanities, King's College London. She teaches and researches the field of digital culture. She is the author of *Governing through Biometrics: The Biopolitics of Identity* (2013) and editor of *Self-Tracking: Empirical and Philosophical Investigations* (2018) and *Metric Culture: Ontologies of Self-Tracking Practices* (2018).

Anna Bernard is Senior Lecturer in English and Comparative Literature at King's College London. She is the author of *Rhetorics of Belonging: Nation, Narration, and Israel/Palestine* (2013) and co-editor of *Debating Orientalism* (2013) and *What Postcolonial Theory Doesn't Say* (2015). She is currently working on a book called *International Solidarity and Culture: Nicaragua, South Africa, Palestine, 1975–1990*.

Norbert Bugeja is Senior Lecturer in Postcolonial Studies at the Mediterranean Institute, University of Malta. His monograph *Postcolonial Memoir in the Middle East* appeared from Routledge in 2012. Since then, he has published and lectured extensively on life writing and literary politics in the Mediterranean region. He is General Editor of the *Journal of Mediterranean Studies*, and has lectured at the universities of Warwick, Kent and Malta. He is also a published poet.

Byron Caminero-Santangelo is Professor of English and Environmental Studies at the University of Kansas. He is the author of *Different Shades of Green: African Literature, Environmental Justice, and Political Ecology* (University of Virginia Press, 2014) and *African Fiction and Joseph Conrad: Reading Postcolonial Intertextuality* (SUNY Press, 2005). He also co-edited *Environment at the Margins: Literary and Environmental Studies in Africa* (Ohio University Press, 2011).

Lilie Chouliaraki is Professor of Media and Communications at the London School of Economics. Her research interests revolve around human vulnerability as a problem of communication and her theoretical and empirical work encompasses disaster news, war and conflict reporting, humanitarian communication and representations of migration. She is the author of, among others, *The Spectatorship of Suffering* (Sage, 2006) and *The Ironic Spectator. Solidarity in the Age of Post-humanitarianism* (Polity, 2013; ICA Outstanding Book Award 2015).

Liam Connell teaches English Literature at the University of Brighton, where he is part of the Refugee and Migration Network. He co-edited, with Nicky Marsh, *Literature and Globalization: A Reader* (Routledge, 2010) and is the author of *Precarious Labour and the Contemporary Novel* (Palgrave, 2017).

Emma Cox is Reader in Drama and Theatre at Royal Holloway, University of London. She is the author of *Performing Noncitizenship: Asylum Seekers in Australian Theatre, Film and Activism* (Anthem, 2015), *Theatre & Migration* (Palgrave, 2014), and the edited play collection *Staging Asylum* (Currency, 2013).

Ned Curthoys is a Senior Lecturer in English and Literary Studies at the University of Western Australia. His books include *Edward Said: the Legacy of a Public Intellectual* (Melbourne University Press, 2007), co-edited with Debjani Ganguly, and *The Legacy of Liberal Judaism: Ernst Cassirer and Hannah Arendt's Hidden Conversation* (Berghahn, 2013).

Jonathan Darling is Assistant Professor in Human Geography at Durham University. He is co-editor of *Sanctuary Cities and Urban Struggles: Rescaling Migration, Citizenship, and Rights* (Manchester University Press, 2019) and *Encountering the City: Urban Encounters from Accra to New York* (Routledge, 2016). He is currently working on a monograph examining the UK's asylum dispersal system.

Sudeep Dasgupta is Associate Professor in Media Studies, University of Amsterdam. His research interests and publications cover the fields of visual culture, globalisation and migration, gender and queer studies and postcolonial studies.

Sam Durrant is Associate Professor of Postcolonial Literature at the University of Leeds. He is the author of *Postcolonial Narrative and the Work of Mourning* (State University of New York Press, 2004) and co-editor of *Essays in Migratory Aesthetics* (Rodopi, 2007) and *The Future of Trauma Theory: Contemporary Literary and Cultural Criticism* (Routledge, 2014), He is currently working on a monograph on animist ecologies in contemporary African literature.

David Farrier is Senior Lecturer in Modern and Contemporary Literature at the University of Edinburgh. He is the author of *Anthropocene Poetics*

(University of Minnesota Press, 2019) and *Postcolonial Asylum* (Liverpool University Press, 2011).

Elena Fiddian-Qasmiyeh is Professor of Migration and Refugee Studies and Co-Director of the Migration Research Unit at UCL. Her research draws on critical theoretical frameworks to explore experiences of and responses to displacement in the context of the Middle East, including through the ongoing AHRC-ESRC funded Refugee Hosts project (www.refugeehosts.org) and ERC Horizon 2020 funded Southern Responses to Displacement project (www.southernresponses.org).

Peter Gatrell teaches history at the University of Manchester, where he is also affiliated to the Humanitarian and Conflict Response Institute. His latest book, *The Unsettling of Europe*, a history of migration in and to Europe since 1945, will appear with Penguin Books and Basic Books in August 2019.

Myria Georgiou is Professor in the Department of Media and Communications, London School of Economics and Political Science (LSE). Her research examines how media and communications advance or hinder inclusion and participation of refugees, migrants and other marginalised communities in transnational contexts, especially across urban societies. She is the author and editor of five books, including two monographs: *Diaspora, Identity and the Media* (Hampton Press, 2006) and *Media and the City* (Polity, 2013).

Anthony Good is Emeritus Professor of Social Anthropology at the University of Edinburgh, and has acted as a country expert witness in over 500 asylum appeals. He is the author of *Anthropology and Expertise in the Asylum Courts* (Routledge-Cavendish, 2007) and co-editor (with Nick Gill) of *Asylum Determination in Europe: Ethnographic Perspectives* (Palgrave Macmillan, 2018).

André Grahle is Assistant Professor in philosophy at LMU Munich. He is the co-editor of *The Moral Psychology of Admiration* (Rowman and Littlefield, 2019) and the author of *Ideals and Meaningfulness*, forthcoming with the same publisher. André's current research project focuses on the ethics of testimony in contexts of refugee arrival. He was involved in the production of *Newcomers* (2018), a refugee testimony film by Syrian director Ma'an Mouslli.

Daniel Hartley is Assistant Professor in World Literatures in English at Durham University. He is the author of *The Politics of Style: Towards a Marxist Poetics* (Brill, 2017), and has published widely on Marxist theory and contemporary literature.

Madelaine Hron is an Associate Professor in the Department of English and Film Studies at Wilfrid Laurier University in Canada. She is the author of *Translating Pain: Immigrant Suffering in Literature and Culture* (University of Toronto Press, 2009), and of various articles related to migration, human rights issues, African literature, Rwanda post-genocide, trauma and violence.

Mariam Issa is an author, storyteller, intercultural facilitator, dedicated community builder, social cohesion champion, social entrepreneur and motivational public speaker and co-founder of the not-for-profit organisation and community garden RAW (Resilient Aspiring Women).

Alison Jeffers is a senior lecturer in Applied Theatre and Contemporary Performance at the University of Manchester. Her research concerns questions around migration and performance with specific emphasis on theatre made with and about refugees and asylum seekers in the UK.

Rosanne Kennedy is Associate Professor of Literature and Gender, Sexuality and Culture at the Australian National University. Her research interests include cultural memory, trauma and testimony; literature, law and human rights; gender studies and feminist theory; and environmental humanities. She has published widely in journals including *Memory Studies, Comparative Literature Studies, Studies in the Novel, Biography, Signs, Australian Feminist Studies* and many others.

Hannah Lewis is Vice Chancellor's Fellow in Sociological Studies, University of Sheffield. She is co-editor of *The Modern Slavery Agenda: Policy, Politics and Practice in the UK* (2019) and co-author of *Precarious Lives: Forced Labour, Exploitation and Asylum* (2014) and has published on themes of refugee integration, leisure and community and migrant labour exploitation in a range of journals.

Paul Long is Professor of Media and Cultural History in the Birmingham Centre for Media and Cultural Research, Birmingham City University. He researches popular music history, heritage and archives as well as histories of creative industries. He is currently writing *Memorialising Popular Music Culture: History, Heritage and the Archive* (Rowman and Littlefield) for publication in 2020.

Mary Mitchell is a PhD researcher at Royal Holloway investigating co-created media with Palestinian refugees in Lebanon. She holds an MSc from Oxford University in Forced Migration and has a decade of experience as a practitioner working on communications strategies in the private, public and third sectors.

Maureen Moynagh is a Professor in English at St. Francis Xavier University where she teaches postcolonial literature and theory. Her book publications include *Political Tourism and its Texts* (University of Toronto Press, 2008) and *Documenting First Wave Feminisms, 2 Vols.* (University of Toronto Press, 2012, 2013). Recent articles have appeared in *Research in African Literatures, Interventions, Biography* and *Comparative Literature.*

Misha Myers is a Senior Lecturer and Course Director of Creative Arts at Deakin University, Melbourne. Her work is all about telling stories of place through digital, interactive and located media, often in collaboration with specific communities or cultural groups.

Parvati Nair is Professor of Hispanic, Cultural and Migration Studies at Queen Mary University of London and Special Adviser on Migration at the United Nations University. Her research is located on the nexus of migration and culture, with particular emphasis on visual representations, especially photography, of human mobility, forced or otherwise.

Mariangela Palladino is Senior Lecturer in English at Keele University. Her research interests lie at the intersection of postcolonial literatures and cultural studies, with a particular focus on the study of representations of contemporary migration between Africa and Europe.

Joseph Pugliese is Professor of Cultural Studies at Macquarie University. With Professor Suvendrini Perera, he is working on *Deathscapes: Mapping Race and Violence in Settler States*, a transnational digital project that maps Indigenous deaths in custody and refugee deaths at the border.

Yousif M. Qasmiyeh is a doctoral researcher at the University of Oxford's English Faculty, where he is examining conceptualisations of time and containment in both Arabic and English literary texts which trace the journeys of refugees or would-be refugees, within the context of the burgeoning field of Refugee Writing. In addition to teaching Arabic literature at the University of Oxford, he is Writer-in-Residence for the AHRC-ESRC funded Refugee Hosts research project, the Arabic language researcher on the Prismatic Translation strand of the OWRI-funded Creative Multilingualism project, and the 'Creative Encounters' editor for the *Migration and Society* journal.

Douglas Robinson is Chair Professor of English at Hong Kong Baptist University. His books include *Translation and Empire* (St. Jerome, 1997; Routledge, 2015) and *Displacement and the Somatics of Postcolonial Culture* (Ohio State University Press, 2013).

Arthur Rose is a Vice Chancellor's Fellow in English at the University of Bristol. His publications include *Literary Cynics: Borges, Beckett, Coetzee* (2017), *Theories of History* (2018), co-edited with Michael J. Kelly, and *Reading Breath in Literature* (2019), co-edited with Stefanie Heine, Naya Tsentourou, Peter Garratt and Corinne Saunders.

Mireille Rosello works on globalised mobility and queer thinking at the University of Amsterdam (Amsterdam School for Cultural Analysis). More specifically her research focuses on the racialisation and criminalisation of precarious refugees and the cultural and political uses of the Trans* moment.

Dima Saber is a Senior Research Fellow at the Birmingham Centre for Media & Cultural Research (BCU). Her research is focused on media depictions of conflict in the Arab region. She is also responsible for leading and delivering projects in partnership with grassroots media collectives in the MENA, looking at the relations between digital media literacy and social impact in post-revolutionary and in conflict settings.

Lyndsey Stonebridge is Interdisciplinary Professor of Humanities and Human Rights at the University of Birmingham, UK. Her recent books include *Placeless People: Writing, Rights, and Refugees* (Oxford University Press, 2018), winner of the Modernist Studies Association Best Book Prize, 2019; and *The Judicial Imagination: Writing after Nuremberg* (Edinburgh University Press, 2011), winner of the British Academy Rose Mary Crawshay Prize. Her other books include *The Destructive Element* (1998), *Reading Melanie Klein* (with John Phillips, 1998), *The Writing of Anxiety* (2007), and *British Fiction after Modernism* (with Marina MacKay, 2007). *Writing and Righting: Literature in the Age of Human Rights* is out with Oxford University Press in 2020. She is currently writing a book on the relevance of Hannah Arendt for our times, *Thinking Like Hannah Arendt*, which will be published by Jonathan Cape in 2022, and collaborating on a large project with refugee and host communities in Lebanon, Jordan, and Turkey, *Refugee Hosts*. A regular media commentator, she has written for *The New Statesman*, *Prospect*, and *The New Humanist*.

Louise Waite is Professor of Human Geography at the University of Leeds. Her books include *Modern Slavery in the UK: Politics, Policy and Practice* (with G. Craig, A. Balch and H. Lewis, Policy Press, 2018), *Vulnerability, Exploitation and Migrants: Insecure Work in a Globalised Economy* (with H. Lewis, G. Craig and K. Skrivankova, Palgrave, 2015) and *Precarious Lives: Forced Labour, Exploitation and Asylum* (with H. Lewis, S. Hodkinson and P. Dwyer, Policy Press, 2014).

Gillian Whitlock is Professor Emerita in Communication and Arts at the University of Queensland and a Fellow of the Academy of the Humanities. She is author of *The Intimate Empire* (Cassell, 2000), *Soft Weapons. Autobiography in Transit* (University of Chicago Press, 2006), and *Postcolonial Life Narrative: Testimonial Transactions* (Oxford University Press, 2015), as well as numerous chapters and articles on life writing. Her recent research project on 'The Testimony of Things' focuses on archives of refugee testimony from the Nauru camp.

Agnes Woolley is Lecturer in Transnational Literature and Migration Cultures at Birkbeck, University of London. Her books include *Contemporary Asylum Narratives: Representing Refugees in the Twenty First Century* (Palgrave, 2014).

Introduction

Emma Cox, Sam Durrant, David Farrier, Lyndsey Stonebridge and Agnes Woolley

Emigration does not only involve leaving behind, crossing water, living amongst strangers, but, also, undoing the very meaning of the world . . .

John Berger

Most newcomers agree that Hamra is the most hospitable district of Beirut. Known for its openness to trade, today multinational chain stores compete with small businesses, some established for years, many opened by Syrians over the past eight years. The restaurant and ice-cream trades are buoyant. Histories of displacement and resistance, living and being, have long been trodden into Hamra's streets. Its enviable excess of bookshops is testimony to the role that thinking and creativity have played in those histories: collections by the poet exiles, Mahmoud Darwish and Adonis, nestle next to translations of George Orwell's *Nineteen Eighty-Four*; books on Che Guevara and Bin Laden brush shoulders with Donald Trump's *The Way to the Top*. World literature has come of geopolitical age in the bookshops of Hamra as, indeed, have the realities of trying to live in a time when who you are allowed to be is brutally dependent on the caprices of whichever – and whatever kind of – nation-state you happen to have been born in, forced to leave, barred entry to, detained in, tolerated by, or, at best, welcomed into on the most contested and fragile of terms. On the walls in the women's bathrooms of the politics department in nearby St Joseph's University, someone has added to the traditional plea for communal responsibility when it comes to the matter of sharing the work of dealing with our human waste: '*Laissez l'état-nation dans les toilettes où vous l'avez trouvé*' – leave the nation-state in the toilets where you found it.

In May 2018 a team of researchers from the UK-based project *Refugee Hosts*,[1] including one of the editors of and two of the contributors to this volume, were looking at old photographs of Hamra with a group of young Syrians living there, several of whom were writers and artists. Some of these photos were so old that they showed Hamra Street when it was still a cacti orchard. Others displayed the district in all its French mandate elegance: looking good, but beginning to lose the light of the Mediterranean as it grew. A final set were in the faded colours of the pre-civil war boulevards: fast cars and short dresses, all about to bleed into the shades of smashed concrete and brick that would flicker across TV screens throughout the 1980s. Relative strangers all of us – save for the Palestinian poet Yousif M. Qasmiyeh, who lived and taught in nearby Shatila refugee camp for several years and for whom Hamra is a familiar place – we pored over the images trying to map the past on to the buildings, streets and vistas we had lately been walking through. Art can do this: it can tell us how histories look through new eyes; how places are made through the perceptual labour and insights of different generations of people, coming from different places, looking sometimes awry but always with the intensity that comes with newness and uncertainty. This is one of the reasons why refugee stories are always more than the histories of those forced on the move – and why Refugee Studies needs to take the patient work of narrative and interpretation, perceiving and feeling, creating and de-creating, seriously.

There were several different ways in which it was possible for Syrians to come to Beirut after the war broke out in 2010. You could register as a refugee with UNHCR (United Nations High Commissioner for Refugees), but then you would have to agree not to work. If you were rich enough you could buy a residence permit, which would allow you to work, but only with the sponsorship of a Lebanese citizen. Or you could decide that your best bet was to lose your passport at the border and pass like a ghost into one of the legal and political twilight communities of the displaced that are now a permanent feature not only in Lebanon and the Middle East, but across the world. We have become accustomed to calling this type of existence precarious, but this does not always do justice to how deeply mass migration has transformed ideas about political and ethical belonging and responsibility, not just for the displaced, but for everybody.

Citizenship is the universal mark of belonging somewhere; it is also, as Hannah Arendt once wrote, a mask that we put on in order to be legally and politically visible. When the refugees of the last century first fell through the cracks of the nation-state, they discovered that as they fell the masks of citizenship dropped from their faces too. Arendt was one of the first to predict that the more the world globalised, the more people would be thrown into an existence where all they had left was their 'humanity' to bargain with. Now 'humanity', as the legal scholar and human rights lawyer Itamar Mann has argued recently, is itself a mask in the world trade in migrants; a cut-price form of citizenship offered, usually grudgingly, to those currently navigating their way through law and poverty, bureaucracy and survival. And, just as most people do not like to be called refugees, not many of us care to be defined as an example of a generically pitiable humanity, no matter that that definition might buy us some minimal humanitarian support. 'I made', a Palestinian playwright from Syria insisted at the Hamra workshop, 'choices.' Yes, agreed a young woman film-maker who had made her choices too, 'but there was a war'.

This situation puts pressure on easy claims about the 'humanising' qualities of art, literature and narrative. When 'humanity' itself is a category – the only visibility left to refugees – then calling on it uncritically and unhistorically is as likely to make those already in the twilight less, not more, visible. At worst, it requires performances of suffering in order to validate not just the humanity of refugees, but of the rights-rich too. 'Each story I hear from a refugee helps me feel, bone-deep, my immutable connection to its teller as a fellow human', wrote the American-Afghani novelist Khaled Hosseini, after a refugee story-gathering tour of Sicily and Lebanon. By contrast, when we talk about refugee imaginaries in this book, as we explain below, we are talking neither simply of imaginings about people who find themselves in the category of 'refugees', immutably human or otherwise, nor only of the imaginings of people forced on the move, but about the whole complex set of historical, cultural, political, legal and ethical relations that currently tie all of us – citizens of nation-states and citizens of humanity only – together.

The thing about black-and-white photographs of places, we agreed in our workshop, is the way the monotone invites forms of repose that may, or may not, have little to do with the actuality of either when the photographs were taken or now. The wide, relatively car-free streets of the 1940s, opened up to the light and the air, remarked one woman, made Hamra look like a very safe place. A war-widow from Damascus with two small children, she knew everything there was to know about keeping your family safe; from the war, from the insane traffic system in Beirut which is every parent's nightmare, from the pollution, from the suspicious and sometimes hostile looks her hijab attracted. The film-maker explained that she had used black and white in her own film about Witwet, a small mixed neighbourhood in Beirut, because its minimalism helped mark a pause, a time, in the timeline of now. The film is a group portrait of different generations of men, some creating (musical instruments, food, music, drama), some bored, many sad, all – this is a particular gaze – made beautiful by their transience. This delicate transience is achieved as much as by what the film does not do as by what it does. Silences, time lapses and running scenes in reverse all demand a stillness and attention. Rain falls against the window; tomatoes are chopped in a regular rhythm; a model dervish whirls. The playwright complains that there is no story. The film-maker replies that there are no heroes in her film. Each character has his own perceptions, his own relationship to her camera. 'Life in Beirut', she later explained, 'is a living thing in itself.' Creative work like this, often done on hope and shoestrings, adds to the archive of statelessness that has been growing steadily since the middle of the last century. More than ever, we need to recognise that this is not so much – or at least not only – work from the margins as from the vanguard of the arts and human sciences, made by people who know at first hand how our current political morality turns on what is seen and not seen. In the words of the film-maker from Hamra: 'We spend so much time in life worshipping what we know about living . . . but what we really know can disappear in a blink of an eye.'

The humanities as an expanded field

This collection places refugees at the centre of interdisciplinary exchange, demonstrating vital new perspectives and topical concerns available to the humanities by bringing together leading researchers from a range of disciplines. Our aim is to clarify and enrich understandings of how the humanities are responding to and contributing to an understanding of refugees today, and to recognise the ways in which imaginative work is implicated in such understanding. The book is situated at the cross-currents of growing and cognate fields: refugee and migration studies; literary, performance, art and film studies; digital and new media; postcolonialism and critical race theory; transnational and comparative cultural studies; anthropology; and cultural politics. It is part of a move towards an expanded terrain for what is broadly conceived of as the critical humanities. We aim not merely to set up a juxtaposition of approaches, but to engage in working and thinking across disciplines, in order to explore what comes of conversations between forms, geographies, histories and theories when dealing with such a complex, multivalent topic as refugee displacement. Such conversations include the ways in which artistic, social and legal work is cross-pollinating in response to changes in refugee history, and are concerned with how, in the process, this work is itself pushing at conventional boundaries.

The volume shows that the humanities can and do engage with what is happening now, but that they do so in a way that draws on thick description (detailed, contextual, and often engaging narrative as a knowledge base), on qualitative methodologies, and on valuing partial or open-ended knowledges. The humanities are invested in representations and concepts (which may stand at something of a remove from refugees' lives), but what this book seeks to demonstrate is that the work of representation and conceptualisation is also, and crucially, entangled in what it means to be a refugee. Issues relating to performance, the documentation of self and testimony are frequently continuous in administrative and artistic contexts. Hyper-visibility in the news media, likewise, is continuous with social media practices in which refugees now engage. Narratives may become dominant, but they may also be shared, brokered cross-culturally or contested. The bureaucratisation of movement itself can become the basis for strategies of resistance for refugees who enter into public or virtual spaces with the knowledge that their words and bodies are to be rendered into text and image. Attentive to such dynamics, humanities research can do 'real world' work without flattening the world into blocs of stakeholders.

Imaginaries, practices, aesthetics

Our core interest in this volume is refugee *imaginaries*. These are broadly conceived, on the one hand, as ways in which refugees are figured and interact in various social spheres – including media and social media platforms; ceremonial, memorial and burial practices; legal judgments and their ideological contexts; activism; acts of home-making – and on the other, as artistic imaginaries – literary, theatrical and cinematic work by and about refugees. The analyses presented throughout the book show very clearly the artistic practices that are imbricated within the social and the social practices that are embedded within the artistic; indeed, one of the cumulative effects of the book's diversity of contributions is to complicate conventional distinctions between the representational and the social, the symbolic and the actual. In this way, a legal judgment may be understood to intervene in public discourse and daily lives just as much as a documentary film project, not just in terms of what each *means*, but also in term of the processes, relationships, encounters and negotiations engendered in and through each. In other words, the work of reimagining refugees' worlds and the world's relation to refugees comes to constitute a practice in itself.

At the same time, a still-prominent feature of traditional humanities is a deep association with the arts; specifically, with the critical elucidation of artistic products (not always recognised sufficiently as *practices*). The relationships that exist between the artistic product, its makers and its audiences present a series of complex questions regarding the different kinds of process and transactions involved in, say, the participatory dynamics of theatrical work, or the activist effects embedded in the production of documentary cinema. Given that refugee-responsive artistic practice has increased significantly in recent decades, and even more markedly in recent years (to a large extent as a consequence of the high profile afforded to the 'refugee crisis', an act of critical reframing that denotes a crisis for the Global North), it has never been more urgent to ask what the relationship is between audiences and consumers, or whose interests are served by the audiencing of refugee arts. As John Fiske argued a long time ago, an audience is a social formation, bound by norms and interests that may be more implicit than explicit (Fiske 1992). The same, of course, although to a lesser degree, may be said of critical scholarship. What, then, are 'we' asking of aestheticised engagements with, say, maritime transit, encampment or resettlement? How are we to reconcile the fact that the empathetic, imaginative engagement sought by a good deal of artistic work may be short-lived (albeit intense) and institutionally circumscribed, if such artistic work is somehow to be allied with a project of sustained political mobilisation? Do certain modes, tropes and emotional registers become expected or recognisable in narrative works, and are more complicated characterisations harder to come by? To what extent is narrative representation yoked to a humanitarian paradigm concerned with demonstrating the fundamental value of the other's humanity, but which may obviate other ways of perceiving (politically, economically, ecologically) the other's predicament?

Issues such as these are complicated, inevitably, by the multiplicity of refugee imaginaries in circulation. The gulf generated by conflicting refugee imaginaries – between refugees in very real forms of existential and material crisis and those in which the Global North represents itself as the victim of crises that originate far away – is broad (and this is before we even approach the fine-grained differences that set apart any one given refugee experience from any other). It is vital that we distinguish between the imaginaries of refugees themselves, shaped by their hopes and despairs, their fear and bravery, their losses and their desires, and the imaginaries generated in and by the Global North about refugees, shaped by xenophobia, fear and anxiety as well as by humanitarian concern. These two imaginaries overlap, of course, but also compete for territory: the humanitarian figure of the refugee as victim – embodied by the iconic but non-threatening image of Alan Kurdi (the three-year-old boy whose body was washed up on a Turkish beach in September 2015[2]) – perpetually competes with the more threatening image of the refugee as (bogus) asylum seeker, as economic migrant, as tide or swarm or terrorist; and both radically limit the space for a refugee imaginary that is based in the experiences of actual people.

These competing imaginaries also have their material incarnations, realised in a set of institutional and juridical contexts – extraterritorial processing, the criminalisation of forced migration, the detention estate – that are, conversely, effaced by what Nicholas De Genova calls 'the Border Spectacle' (De Genova 2013: 1181). As it is visualised and spoken about in popular and political discourse, the border spectacle achieves a particular unity of effects: to efface structural or material conditions; to erase individual histories; and, consequently, to dehumanise. What links these effects is often the utilisation of a kind of liquidity – the capacity to manipulate flows, to saturate or dissolve. From Australia's 'Pacific Solution' to the juxtaposed border controls between the UK and France, the Western detention estate is to a significant degree characterised by the successful co-option of flexible formations. For instance, the European 'hotspot approach' is designed to allow frontline member states to concentrate resources wherever there is 'a specific and disproportionate migratory pressure at their external borders'. This 'pre-emptive frontier' (as Glenda Garelli and Martina Tazzioli put it) is part of a fluid formation through which the apparatus of the border – fingerprinting, surveillance, expulsion orders – can flow to wherever the integrity of the border is most directly challenged (Garelli and Tazzioli 2016). Hotspots are not simply reactive, however, but active in constructing the illegality of migrants and refugees; they are performances of a manufactured crisis. This is the crux of the 'border spectacle' – a process of 'naturalising' the particular refugee imaginary that casts unsanctioned movement as an inherently illicit act.

What the border spectacle effaces is that forced migrants and refugees are *by design* caught in a relation of inclusive exclusion. 'Exclusion', Étienne Balibar writes, 'is the very essence of the nation-form' (Balibar 2004: 23); but this exclusion is also, to borrow from Giorgio Agamben, a form of capture. Western states *need* the migrants and refugees they seek to exclude, as a source of labour and of legitimation – both to highlight the rights enjoyed by the citizen and to reinforce the limitation placed upon these rights.

Discursive formations are also part of the work of border spectacle. In particular liquid metaphors – of flows, floods, swamping, inundation, etc. – not only reinforce negative perceptions, feeding particular refugee imaginaries, but also determine what appears and what is obscured in the 'border spectacle'. First, liquid imagery inevitably has a quality of effortlessness to it; when applied to the dangerous crossings from Libya to Lampedusa, it can easily obscure the risk such journeys involve. Even when this is countered by the now-familiar images of overcrowded boats, the notion of flows suggests a mobility that is at odds with the stop-start nature of most journeys, marked by delays and obstacles as well as hazards. Liquid imagery also dehistoricises migrants and refugees. Typically, they emerge from the sea 'washed clean' of the specific histories that forced them to flee, remade as generic 'migrants' in the terms of the governing imaginary. Whether it is the 'sea of death' pronounced by former Italian Prime Minister Enrico Letta following the drowning of more than 350 people on 3 October 2013, or journalistic references to 'the flow of desperate individuals [that] is a drop in the sea of African poverty', too often the stories of migrants and refugees are dissolved in the medium they move through; and it is a relatively short step from images of flows and floods to something even more troubling – the reduction of those who don't survive the journey to what Joseph Pugliese calls mere 'bodies of water' (Pugliese 2006). Just as the detention estate in effect makes detainees incarnate the border, the distinction between the drowned and their marine environment is liquefied; and as with the naturalisation of migration as illegal, the 'naturalisation' of 'bodies of water' naturalises vulnerability, and does not account for the structural (geopolitical, economic, legal) factors that produce it.

While those refugee imaginaries that seek to reinforce territorial control arise from pre-existing, combative social formations, consciously or otherwise they also elude closure. The narrative in which the Global North claims the crisis as its own is an anxious narrative, in need of constant reassertion. This performance of territoriality creates gaps that, with skill and patience, might be expanded. Many of the topics covered in *Refugee Imaginaries* offer ways of thinking into these gaps; grappling with questions of engagement and audiencing, enabling by their very form deeper appreciation of the ways in which aesthetic work is imbricated in other events, interactions and interventions in the world. One example is the discussion by Alison Jeffers of Theatres of Sanctuary in the 'Asylum' section. These initiatives – contiguous with the better-known Cities of Sanctuary movement – place political and ethical pressure on what it means to occupy and indeed to aestheticise public space. When theatres and cities are designated as carrying out comparable interventions, whereby a space becomes explicit in its symbolism, space itself is clarified: members of the public may see, from within a context of a limited geography, something new about the way spaces adjudicate behaviours (between belonging and non-belonging, citizen and non-citizen) more widely. With these kinds of preoccupations, and an approach to audiencing/spectating/participating that aims to be self-reflexive, *Refugee Imaginaries* situates its readership as standing alongside rather than separated from the audiences of the works, events and practices examined in the book.

Defining 'the refugee'

Refugee Imaginaries offers an expanded vision of both commonly and formally understood notions of what a refugee is, and of what refugee mobility consists in. Common understandings of refugeedom tend to demand a particular semiotics of suffering – associating forced movement with poverty, and refugee status with amorphous notions of moral deservingness and abject need – so that refugees who own smartphones or laptops, for instance, or who find ways to pay extortionate sums of money to people smugglers, are condemned in much mainstream media discourse. At the same time, even ostensibly more favourable notions of refugeedom have their limitations: disarticulated from political or historical conditions, the refugee can come to stand in for an all-too-generalised notion of exile that is as much psychological as political (wherein anyone may conceivably be a 'refugee'). In formal, statist terms, the figure of the refugee is tied to a multi-pronged but nonetheless specific conception of persecution: as article 1 of the United Nations Convention Relating to the Status of Refugees 1951 stipulates, a refugee is a person who has a 'well-founded fear of being persecuted for reasons of race, religion, nationality, membership of a particular social group or political opinion' (UNHCR 1951: 14). The touchstone constituted by the Convention (along with the 1967 Protocol) both assures and curtails contemporary refugee claims. First of all, persecution can be and generally is interpreted narrowly or evaluated from a vantage of administrative suspicion, and moreover, precludes many forms of war displacement, and increasingly will preclude the vast numbers of 'climate refugees' anticipated in coming years. The question of whether the UN's refugee adjudication framework is still fit for purpose is the subject of growing debate and unease (see, for example, Ethics Centre 2017). While critical enquiry across the humanities requires that both common and formal notions of refugeedom are accounted for, a particular capacity of humanities scholarship is not just to identify but to contribute to the shaping of alternative, resistant or emergent conceptions of the refugee. This may involve finding a space between eternal or universalist archetypes (of exile or wandering) and the jurisdictional terms of UN-framed refugeen-ess. It may mean foregrounding the refugee without foregrounding the UN; it may mean approaching the twentieth and twenty-first centuries not through the lens of nation-state relations, but through the visions and stories of those who exist temporarily or permanently on the outside.

In this volume, we have sometimes used the term refugee in accordance with the UN definition but at other times sought to broaden or trouble it. To insist on the UN definition would be to deny the complexities of our current political moment and to implicate ourselves in the increasingly narrow distinc-tions made by states in order to deny entry to those who seek refuge. Impos-ing strict definitions would also suggest a desire on our part for the kinds of stable categories that thick description so often exposes as oversimplified. We are wary, for example, of reinforcing the kind of hierarchies that emerged during the current 'refugee crisis', in which Syrians are understood as 'good' refugees and Africans continue to be stigmatised as economic migrants, chan-cers or opportunists. Less spectacularised conflicts in Africa and elsewhere generate migrants who are much less able to lay claim to refugee status, while the idea of the refugee as someone who has experienced persecution struggles to comprehend the 'persecuting' force of global capitalism and the forms of 'slow violence' (Nixon 2013) that routinely render certain places uninhabit-able. The UN definition also centres refugeeness on an individual's fear of persecution and fails to cope with the kinds of mass production of refugees that we have seen in recent years, from the Congo to Venezuela. The common distinction between forced and voluntary migrants is also problematic in so far as it elides the ways in which there remains a degree of agency in acts of 'forced migration'; conversely, 'voluntary migration' is never, of course, freely chosen and is often a response to various forms of privation.

Finally, part of the thrust of this volume is also to highlight the thin line that separates not simply various forms of migrancy but also the distinction between citizen and non-citizen. As Agamben writes: 'the citizens of advanced industrial states demonstrate . . . an evident propensity to turn into denizens, into noncitizen permanent residents, so that citizens and denizens – at least in certain social strata – are entering an area of potential indistinction' (Agamben 2008: 94). As the demographics of Brexit in the UK and other similarly overde-termined ideological assertions across the globe suggest, the rise of nationalist xenophobia is a response to the economic and political forms of disenfranchise-ment that render certain citizens all too proximate, in a psychically disavowed sense, to the stateless.

Book structure and rationale

This collection is organised by an understanding that refugees are displaced in space and time. Part I provides an account of the histories and genealogies of forms of refugee experience that have shaped refugee imaginaries, providing a theoretical and historical grounding for the sections that follow, which present eight different 'scenes' of displacement: 'Asylum', 'The Border', 'Intra/Extra Territorial Spaces', 'The Camp', 'Sea Crossings', 'Digital Territories', 'Home' and 'Open Cities'. Together, these sections offer an alternative conceptual and political cartography of a field that is more commonly defined in terms of national and geopolitical spaces, which cast the refugee experience as incidental to larger histories. Our aim is consciously to place refugee identity and movement – rather than nation-states – at the centre of modernity.

Refugee Imaginaries aims to serve as a tool for navigating a rapidly changing field, and to open up imaginative, conceptual and practical spaces for future work. The range of authors included offers a wide variety of approaches for scholars, refugee community workers, policy makers, artists and arts audiences. Ultimately, the volume demonstrates that the humanities, in all of their intersections with Refugee Studies, are buoyantly interdisciplinary, but bound by an impulse to question as much as answer, to open up space as much as to mark it out. We endeavour to make space to examine refugee imaginaries, not only as a public discourse in need of transformation but also as a transformatory aesthetic, or reworlding, that seeks to change the terms through which the refugee comes into being, thereby reconfiguring distinctions between the refugee and the migrant, the refugee and the citizen, statelessness and the nation-state.

Note

1. Refugee Hosts: Local Community Experiences of Displacement from Syria: Views from Lebanon, Jordan, and Syria, PI Elena Fiddian Qasmiyeh, CO-I Lyndsey Stonebridge, Poet-in-Residence Yousif M. Qasmiyeh, https://refugee-hosts.org/. Funded by the AHRC and ESRC, grant no. AH/P005438/1.
2. According to the BBC, "his name has been spelt 'Aylan' by much of the media [but] this was a Turkish version of the name given by Turkish officials – his Kurdish name was Alan." https://www.bbc.co.uk/news/world-europe-34141716 (accessed 20 September 2019).

Bibliography

Agamben, Giorgio (2008), 'Beyond human rights', *Open. Cahier on art and the public domain*, 15: 86–9.
Arendt, Hannah (1951), *Origins of Totalitarianism* (New York: Schocken Books, 2004).
Arendt, Hannah (1963), *On Revolution* (Harmondsworth: Penguin, 1965).
Balibar, Étienne (2004), *We, The People of Europe? Reflections on Transnational Citizenship* (Princeton: Princeton University Press).
De Genova, Nicolas (2013), 'Spectacles of migrant "illegality": the scene of exclusion, the obscene of inclusion', *Ethnic and Racial Studies*, 36.7: 1180–98.

Ethics Centre (Sydney) (2017), 'IQ2 debate: the refugee convention is out of date', http://www.ethics.org.au/events/past-event-gallery/iq2-debate-the-refugee-convention-is-out-of-date (accessed 14 May 2019).

Fiske, John (1992), 'Audiencing: a cultural studies approach to watching television', *Poetics*, 21.4: 345–59.

Garelli, Glenda, and Martina Tazzioli (2016), 'The EU hot spot approach to Lampedusa', *Open Democracy*, 26 February, https://www.opendemocracy.net/can-europe-make-it/glenda-garelli-martina-tazzioli/eu-hotspot-approach-at-lampedusa (accessed 14 May 2019).

Hosseini, Khaled (2018), 'Refugees are still dying. How do we get over our news fatigue?', *The Guardian*, 18 August, https://www.theguardian.com/books/2018/aug/17/khaled-hosseini-refugees-migrants-stories?CMP=Share_iOSApp_Other (accessed 14 May 2019).

Mann, Itamar (2018), 'Humanity as mask', paper given at 'We Refugees – 75 Years Later. Hannah Arendt's Reflections on Human Rights and the Human Condition', ZfL, Berlin, March 2018.

Nixon, Rob (2013), *Slow Violence and the Environmentalism of the Poor* (Cambridge, MA: Harvard University Press).

Pugliese, Joseph (2006), 'Bodies of water', *Heat*, 12: 13–20.

UNHCR (1951), 'The 1951 Refugee Convention', https://www.unhcr.org/uk/1951-refugee-convention.html (accessed 26 June 2019).

Part I
Refugee Genealogies

Refugee Genealogies: Introduction

Lyndsey Stonebridge

Few groups can claim to be quite so thoroughly 'made' by modern geopolitical history as refugees. People have always been on the move. There have always been wars, disasters, poverty and persecutions to flee from. Principles of asylum and hosting were core to the formation of communities, religions and city-states long before they were codified in any written law or international agreement. But the modern refugee, as she is imagined today, is a direct consequence of European, colonial and postcolonial nation-state formations, implosions, conflicts and failures that began in the last century, and the changing meanings of home, exile, belonging and community that followed, and follow still, from those convulsions. 'Only a world of sovereign states that had categories of people called "citizens" and were intent on regulating population flows could produce a legal category of "refugees"', the historian Michael Barnett writes in his study of the United Nations High Commission for Refugees (UNHCR) (Barnett 2001: 251). The modern refugee is the negative of the modern citizen, which is another way of saying that refugee history is everybody's history.

This opening section gives an overview of refugee history and of thinking, theorising, writing and imagining by and about refugees from the twentieth century through to the present. The ways in which refugees have been made to mean – described here as refugee genealogies – run like thin red lines across our contemporary global cultural politics. As refugee historian Peter Gatrell shows in his opening chapter, refugees are not just the unfortunate by-products of wars, revolutions, colonialisation, decolonialisation – the politics of moving people are central to modern history.

Suppressing that history is also part of the modern refugee story: more often than not, if they are seen at all, refugees are seen as victims of circumstance rather than of political decision-making; unfortunate others in a humanitarian crisis to be solved, rather than fellow citizens in transit. Yet as far back as the 1930s, the American journalist Dorothy Thompson argued that when it came to refugees, humanitarianism would never be enough. Doing refugee history is not neutral: it is also a resistance against the idea that once you slip between nation-states you cease to exist as a political, historical and critical person in the world. As Ned Curthoys argues in his chapter on theories of the modern refugee, the refugee is not simply 'an object of pity, but a theoretical perspective on a shattered world'.

In the *Origins of Totalitarianism* (1951), Hannah Arendt, herself a stateless person for eighteen years, wrote one of the most important post-war theoretical perspectives on that shattered world. Curthoys's chapter traces Arendt's theoretical legacy for contemporary thinking about refugees, migration and political citizenship. Her prognosis in the middle of the last century was bleak. Refugees revealed a bitter truth about so-called universal human rights: those cast out of the protection of their nations were in effect cast out of humanity itself. The world, Arendt wrote, found 'nothing sacred in the abstract nakedness of being human' (2004: 380).

Modern refugees were 'new kinds of human being': the superfluous people, those who were put in refugee camps by their friends and concentration camps by their enemies, as Arendt described it in her biting and brilliant 1943 essay, 'We Refugees'. To be made by geopolitical history, managed by humanitarianism, theorised, thought about, pitied and feared, she wrote in that essay, was at the same time to be deprived of a place to think, be or to speak for oneself in the public realm. As well as a juridical, political and social category to be squeezed into, 'refugeedom' (a term first coined by the Russian-Jewish scholar Avram Kirzhnits in the 1920s as Gatrell informs us) is an existential and psychical, or, as Arendt would say, a 'human' condition. The mismatch between being confined in a category and experiencing the human condition of displacement is often where refugee imaginaries – writing, art, speech, advocacy, protest – properly begin.

'Exile', Edward Said wrote of this mismatch in 'Reflections on Exile', is 'strangely compelling to think about but terrible to experience' (2000: 173). As the two final essays in this section demonstrate, for refugee writing, negotiating the passage between thought and experience is a matter of style and genre as well as of history and politics. Arthur Rose also opens his argument with Arendt's 'We Refugees'. 'In the first place, we don't like to be called refugees' (2007: 264): Arendt begins her essay with her characteristic ironic style, double-voicing the parvenus who want to fit in and not be seen as refugees, but thereby exposing the actual groundlessness of the refugee condition. This negative identification with the category of the refugee, Rose argues, is a now a distinguishing feature of refugee style across both fictional and non-fictional writing. A second feature is the 'cruel optimism' that motivates not only the poor refugee parvenu but also those who struggle to escape the refugee category into another kind of political future. Refugee style, Rose concludes, refuses the terms of refugeedom even as it voices them.

As Anna Bernard shows in her chapter on the genres of refugee writing, that refusal is also a way of imagining different terms for recognition and justice. The humanitarian imaginary requires evidence of passivity and pathos – there has, after all, to be someone to be helped. Demands that we 'give voice' to refugees, as welcome as they can be, are often also seasoned with the requirement, frequently legal as well as cultural, of a persuasive demonstration of authentic worthiness. But 'what kind of realism requires that its subjects be saints?' Bernard asks. Her essay identifies three key genres for refugee writing: poetry (which can move, with people, relatively easily), verbatim theatre (for its self-consciously problematic advocacy) and graphic narratives. These genres not only testify to refugee experience, they also push that experience back into politics and history. A life cannot, of course, be lived in art and literature alone, certainly not by those who, pushed out of place, time and history, struggle simply to live at all. But it is, we suggest, within these more explicitly confrontational refugee imaginaries that questions of complicity, responsibility and human connectedness can begin to be worked through afresh.

Bibliography

Arendt, Hannah (2004 [1951]), *The Origins of Totalitarianism* (New York: Schocken Books).

Arendt, Hannah (2007), 'We refugees', in *The Jewish Writings*, ed. Jerome Kohn and Ron. H. Feldman (New York: Schocken Books), 264–74.

Barnett, Michael (2001), 'Humanitarianism with a sovereign face: UNHCR in the global undertow', *International Migration Review*, 35.1: 244–77.

Said, Edward (2000 [1984]), 'Reflections on exile', in *Reflections on Exile and Other Essays* (London: Granta), 173–86.

Thompson, Dorothy (1938), *Refugees: Anarchy or Organization?* (New York: Random House).

Chapter 1

Refugees in Modern World History

Peter Gatrell

At the time of writing (December 2017) the news media paints a dismal but highly selective and frequently ahistorical portrait of mass population displacement across the globe. The prolonged civil war in Syria has been at the forefront of international politics, but media reports never mention the country's history as a refugee-hosting state between the wars, when it was home to Armenian refugees, and after 1948 when it sheltered Palestinian refugees (White 2017; Gatrell 2013: 59–60, 133). Depictions of the suffering of refugees from Syria briefly gave way to stories from the border between Myanmar/Burma and Bangladesh where, after years of neglect, attention was suddenly lavished on Rohingya Muslims who fled from Rakhine State to escape the violence inflicted on them by the Myanmar military, whose actions gave rise to accusations of 'ethnic cleansing'. The war of words was simultaneously stoked by the Myanmar regime, which labels the Rohingya as 'terrorists'. But this was no sudden 'crisis'; it stretched back at least three decades (Elahi 1987; Gatrell 2013: 203–4). The ongoing 'refugee crisis' in the Mediterranean continues to garner attention, particularly migrant crossings between Libya and Italy. Reports in autumn 2017 indicated that the Italian government did a deal with tribal leaders in the south of Libya to dissuade them from people trafficking by offering financial inducements – a 'solution' that speaks rather to the interests of Italian politicians and their voters than to those of migrants and asylum seekers in Libya.[1] The Rohingya crisis points to the importance of history – how else can one make sense of their predicament or position within the complex politics of modern Myanmar and Bangladesh? Likewise, Italy's stance reflects not only its position as a destination country but its history as an imperial power that exercised authority over Libya until the end of the Second World War. We need to keep these connections and entanglements in mind (Ballinger 2016; Gatrell 2017).

Then, of course, there are sites of displacement that no longer figure or hardly figured on the radar of international news reporting. In Italy, to take just one example, the current crisis has entirely effaced other histories – the arrival of Albanian migrants in the 1990s, but also the crisis of displacement after the Second World War, not only on the doorstep of Italy (the Julian Marches) but in decolonisation and displacement (Ballinger 2018). Refugees have been hidden from history, but some refugees lived or live in the shadows more than others – the protracted displacement of Sahrawi refugees is a case in point (Fiddian-Qasmiyeh 2014; Chatty 2010).

Refugees were not epiphenomenal but central to the history of the twentieth century. They were not just the unfortunate by-product of wars, revolutions and state formation, but the direct outcome of targeting those who are deemed not to belong to the nation-state. In addition to violent conflict, international diplomatic agreements contributed to the creation of refugees. This chapter outlines briefly the major episodes and some of the less well-known 'crises' in Europe, the Middle East, the Indian subcontinent, the Far East and sub-Saharan Africa, locating their origin in world war, revolution, decolonisation and state formation. In asking how and for whom refugees in different contexts were construed as a distinct category and a specific 'problem', this chapter alludes to relief efforts, and 'durable solutions' including repatriation and 'homecoming' in a variety of settings.

I should at the outset make two disclaimers. The first is that a short survey such as this cannot possibly hope to mention all episodes of mass population displacement in the twentieth century: even the most dramatic and significant events get relatively short shrift in this chapter. The reader is referred to major surveys (Marrus 1985; Kushner and Knox 1999; Gatrell 2013), and specialised studies, some of which are mentioned below. Constraints of space also mean that many important issues warrant barely a mention, including the cultural representations of population displacement in the past and the extent to which refugees were able to voice their own aspirations. Other contributions to this volume help to fill these gaps.

Secondly, I do not wish to labour the issue of definition ('who is a refugee?'), except to make the important point that the history of refugees is in part a history of categorisation and labelling (Shacknove 1985; Zetter 1991; Soguk 1999; Bakewell 2008; Shaw 2012; Persian 2012). As the director of the Inter-Governmental Committee for European Migration (ICEM), put it in 1969:

> Many persons have grappled with the problem of defining a 'refugee'. Personally, I am convinced that 'refugee' is a generic term. There are refugees from fire, from floods, hurricanes, earthquakes, invasions, hostilities, persecutions, oppressions, denial of human rights and so forth. By his own decision and by the fact of moving away from what he fears or considers an area of danger, a person becomes a refugee or perhaps a displaced person. (J. F. Thomas, quoted in Tabori 1972: 293)

It is worth adding that there is also a contextualised history in which displaced people insist on their status as refugees, in other words that 'being a refugee' is a core part of their identity and claims for redress or repatriation, as is the case with many Palestinian refugees.

This chapter argues for the multiple mainsprings of population displacement, directing the reader's attention to the fact that most episodes and sites were to be found beyond Europe. It highlights the creation of an international refugee regime that excluded refugees while protecting others. It speaks to the importance of local and regional regimes of assistance. It discusses the implications of displacement and the refugee regime for a variety of interests and actors, refugees included.

States make refugees, refugees make states

World wars, revolutions, decolonisation and civil wars brought about population displacement at various times in the twentieth century. Civilians have been forced to flee in order to save their skin. But mass displacement was also the result of being targeted by one's own government. Minorities were particularly vulnerable. It was not so much the conduct of non-core groups in conditions of 'total war' that was the issue (although ethnic minorities were sometimes accused of colluding with the enemy), but their very existence that led to them being singled out for internal deportation, outright expulsion or worse. In addition to the obvious exposure of Jews in Nazi Germany and Nazi-occupied Europe to persecution and then extermination during the Second World War, one can point to Ottoman policy towards Armenians during the First World War (Mandel 2003; Mylonas 2012). States make refugees (Zolberg 1983).

International diplomatic agreements also contributed to mass population displacement – here I have in mind the process whereby states agreed or were encouraged to pursue a mutual transfer of population, or whereby states engaged in unilateral expulsions. In the one case, displacement was justified as a prophylactic measure; in the other, displacement had a primarily punitive purpose. The best-known instance of the former was the compulsory Greek–Turkish population exchange in 1923 (see below). The clearest example of the latter in twentieth-century Europe was the expulsion of ethnic Germans from Poland and Czechoslovakia under terms agreed at Potsdam in 1945. What was at stake here was a combination of state formation, communist revolution and outright revenge, along with a desire to turn new states into ethnically more homogeneous entities.

My second proposition is that refugees can make states; in other words the causal connection identified by Zolberg can be reversed: refugees also contribute to nation-state making. A clear illustration of this was the refugee crisis in Tsarist Russia during the First World War when displacement generated not only a widespread sense of persecution and loss among non-Russian minorities, but also provided the means whereby those minorities could mobilise in support of greater autonomy and ultimately for independence. Political leaders among Latvian, Lithuanian, Jewish, Ukrainian, Polish and Armenian displaced populations undertook sustained cultural, educational, religious and welfare work on their behalf (Gatrell 1999). The different offices within refugee relief bodies that were organised on a national basis constituted an embryonic civil service. Many leaders of these wartime refugee organisations subsequently became prominent political figures in the successor states. Later in this chapter we shall see how displacement helped to constitute the state by challenging governments to come up with answers about 'integration' and 'development'.

Refugeedom in the era of the First World War

During the First World War, millions of European civilians were 'on the move'. In fact, it is misleading to suppose that mass displacement had been absent from Europe before the war. In particular, political upheavals in the Balkans and in Anatolia unleashed a refugee crisis whose ramifications spread into the 1920s. One might say that refugees created refugees, in so far as conflicts in the Balkans in the later nineteenth century led to the resettlement of Muslims from Bulgaria and Greece in Ottoman Anatolia, a legacy that contributed to animosity between Muslim refugee settlers and Armenian Christians and helps explain the genocide in 1915. During the war, the refugee crisis in Belgium and in Serbia generated considerably publicity. But there, as elsewhere, including in Russia, the wartime crisis faded into obscurity (Kulischer 1948; Gatrell and Zhvanko 2017).

Writing in the *Soviet Historical Encyclopedia* ten years after the Russian Revolution, a leading Russian Jewish scholar by the name of Avram Kirzhnits (1888–1940) was the first scholar to summarise for a wide audience the scale of population displacement in the Russian Empire (Kirzhnits 1927). Kirzhnits pointed out that civilians quit their homes in Russia's western borderlands not only on account of enemy invasion in the first phase of the war, but also as a result of the concerted actions of the Tsarist army in deporting civilians from this huge region in 1915. In his words, this amounted to a 'bacchanalia of forced migration' (*bakkhanaliia vysleneniia*) that ensnared Poles, Jews, Latvians, Lithuanians, Belarusians and Ukrainians, who were targeted on account of their presumed disloyalty to the empire; Jews in particular suffered from widespread antisemitism. One of the unexpected consequences of their deportation was the dissolution of the Pale of Settlement, although according to Kirzhnits the presence of Jews in the Russian interior did little to lessen the prejudice they faced as refugees. Kirzhnits relied upon official and semi-official accounts to paint a picture of the scale of the refugee crisis – around seven million people were displaced in Russia between 1914 and 1917 – and the most notable organisations involved in relief work, including the assistance provided by trade unions in provincial cities of the empire. He summarised displacement as 'refugeedom' (*bezhenstvo*), a term that had already gained currency during the war. It drew attention to the constitution of a new 'element' that disturbed conventional categories in Russian society. As indicated above, it also licensed patriotic politicians and intelligentsia to make the case for 'national' recognition (Gatrell 1999).

The resolution of this crisis proved to be protracted and complex. In the first place, the homes to which many of the internally displaced refugees returned when Russia left the war were now located in new states such as Poland and Lithuania. But, in the second place, this repatriation coincided with the outbreak of more fighting as the new Bolshevik regime confronted its enemies in different theatres of war. Matters were further complicated by the war between Soviet Russia and Poland. Refugees who were repatriated or repatriated themselves – some remained in the Soviet Union – underwent a rigorous screening process to weed out communist sympathisers. This also enabled the state to dismiss the claims of minority groups, Jews above all, to citizenship.

The political scientist Aristide Zolberg (1931–2013) drew attention to state-building activity in peacetime that targeted minorities for persecution and excision. His evidence derived in part from the formation of successor states in post-war Europe out of the wreckage of the big continental empires. The peace settlement conceded self-determination on the basis of nationality, but simultaneously exposed non-nationals who did not 'belong'. Minority treaties provided relatively little protection to these 'non-core' groups, and indeed antagonised the new governments of Eastern Europe rather than encouraging them to adopt more benign policies towards minorities (Zolberg 1983; Baron and Gatrell 2004).

Refugees' voices occasionally surface from the abundant official documentation. In the words of a farmer's wife from West Flanders who had been forced out by the German advance in 1914:

> those people who had fled their home, were always called refugees. I heard it many times: 'it's a refugee'. And I sometimes hated people for saying so . . . such an odd label, 'refugee'. You are not to blame, you are destitute, and still they call you a 'refugee' . . . We had become nobodies. (Elfnovembergroep 1978: 47)

Refugee survey and 'the refugee problem'

So-called 'White Russians' who opposed Bolshevik rule and who had been defeated militarily and politically now appeared in Constantinople, Prague, Berlin and Paris, as well as in Harbin and Shanghai. Estimates of their total number have been put at around one million. In 1921 member states of the new League of Nations affirmed that those Russian refugees who had 'lost the protection of the Soviet Government and not acquired another nationality' deserved to be recognised as refugees and assisted by a dedicated High Commissioner, the polar explorer Fridtjof Nansen. In 1926 the delegates to the League agreed that refugees were those displaced 'as a consequence of the war and of events directly connected with the war'. This included Armenian refugees who had survived the genocide in the Ottoman Empire. Refugees were a temporary aberration; they were expected to be slotted in somewhere (Skran 1995: 269; Chatty 2010).

With only a tiny office under the aegis of the League of Nations, assisting Russian refugees became a story of self-help and private philanthropy, in which the Russian Red Cross and Zemgor (a continuation of the leading wartime public organisation in Tsarist Russia for the relief of civilian victims of war) played the lead role in providing schooling, vocational training, basic medical treatment and assistance for children and the elderly. A Russian Aid Society supported indigent White Russian exiles; so too did the Russian Orthodox Church and the American Red Cross. They faced an immense task. Sir John Hope Simpson's wide-ranging survey of the 'refugee problem' concluded that, particularly in the Far East, 'things could scarcely be worse from the refugee standpoint, and unless steps of some kind are taken the mass of the emigration will sink into a condition of moral degradation and economic misery which will disgrace Western civilisation' (Simpson 1939: 513).

Simpson's magisterial survey, conducted in 1937–38 under the auspices of the Royal Institute of International Affairs, focused on Russian and Armenian refugees, with a sideways glance at refugees from the Spanish Civil War, at Italian refugees, and at Jewish refugees from Nazi Germany. He was mainly concerned with their legal status in countries of refuge, including countries in the Middle East and South America. There is nothing in his book about Greek and Turkish refugees (see below). Nor did he devote any attention to population displacement brought about by colonial wars (Sequeira 1939; Wilkin 1980).

Two years before Simpson began work on his survey, the well-known historian of central Europe Carlile Macartney (1895–1978) wrote the entry on 'refugees' in the first edition of the *Encyclopedia of the Social Sciences* (Macartney 1935). Macartney began by pointing out that the 'individual political refugee' was a familiar figure who was 'legally able to return to his state' but who chose not to do so, lest this 'expose him [sic] to disagreeable consequences'. He referred to large-scale refugee movements in the era of the Roman Empire as well as the Middle Ages when 'the persons involved were more or less at the mercy of those receiving them'. In more recent times, he wrote, the Balkan Wars, the First World War and the Russian Revolution were the main driving forces behind large-scale refugee flows. Macartney drew attention to the assistance afforded Russian and Armenian refugees by the Nansen Office, but also mentioned the results of the Lausanne Convention in 1923. Without going into details, this agreement brokered by the League of Nations provided for 'the compulsory exchange of Turkish nationals of the Greek Orthodox religion established in Turkish territory, and of Greek nationals of the Moslem religion established in Greek territory'. There were bitter arguments about the status and attributes of the newcomers, whose credentials as 'nationals' were called into question. Institutional designation quickly caught up with customary usage: thus the League's Refugee Settlement Commission had responsibility not only for Greek refugees who fled during the war in 1922 but for the new transferees. Refugees, so to say, were made by popular parlance (Gatrell 2013: 63–72).

Macartney concluded:

> It is clear that the refugee problem has been affected profoundly by modern conditions of life. In the increasing complexity of present day society a man is less easily able than ever before to dispense with the normal protection of his state . . . The position of the refugee who has no mother country is miserable indeed. (Macartney 1935: 204)

This seemed to point to a lack of 'mercy'. Noting that the economic depression had made it difficult to 'absorb' refugees in large numbers, Macartney made a heartfelt plea to prospective host countries:

> Where repatriation has proved impossible, naturalisation is the only final solution . . . Historical evidence indicates that while refugee movements have usually occasioned great suffering among the refugees themselves, they have often enriched the countries which have granted hospitality and have almost uniformly impoverished those from which they fled. (Macartney 1935: 205)

Setting aside the reference to a 'final solution', which soon acquired a different and far more devastating association, Macartney's insistence on the contribution that refugees were likely to make to host countries represented a voice of sanity in harsh times.

The aftermath of the Second World War: a global refugee 'problem'

Some 23 million people were 'uprooted' in Europe alone during the final stages of the Second World War and thereafter, as a result of repatriation, territorial readjustment and population transfer. Those who had been brought to Nazi-occupied Europe to work as forced labourers were expected to return to their homes, and their repatriation became the responsibility of the United Nations Relief and Rehabilitation Administration. A significant minority resisted repatriation: these refugees, 'Displaced Persons' in official parlance, remained in camps in Germany, Austria or Italy until they could be resettled in a third country. The DP camp became a key site for refugees' self-expression and political activism (Wyman 1998; Hilton 2009). Beyond Europe – in the Middle East, the Indian subcontinent and South-East Asia – the numbers amounted to around 20 million. By the end of the 1950s one estimate put the global total of refugees at 40 million (Gatrell 2013).

We now know a good deal about the radical consequences of civil war in Greece, the murderous conflicts in the Polish-Ukrainian borderlands and the settling of wartime scores in the frontier region between Italy and Slovenia. Another vindictive piece of post-war reckoning took place in Bulgaria, where in 1950–51 the new Communist government followed in the footsteps of its pre-war predecessor and expelled around 140,000 ethnic Turks in pursuit of a mono-ethnic polity. Population displacement in Europe was not a by-product but rather a constitutive element in post-war reconstruction. At Potsdam the Allies punished the German inhabitants of Poland and Czechoslovakia irrespective of age and gender, but the agreement to launch a massive transfer of population not only had a punitive purpose; it also corresponded to politically accepted ideas about humanitarian 'population politics' – humanitarian, because relocating people and creating ethnically more homogeneous nation-states would eliminate the 'problem of minorities' that had bedevilled European politics in the interwar years.

The hasty implementation of Partition in the Indian subcontinent in 1947 unleashed an enormous cross-border movement of refugees that continued for years, directly affecting around 15 million people who moved from West and East Pakistan to India and vice-versa. (Of course, not everyone moved, and it is important to remember this.) Population displacement was also the result of revolution in China where the victory of the Communist Party in 1949 caused 700,000 Chinese to flee to Hong Kong; by 1956 one-third of its population was made up of refugees. Additionally, in the late 1950s the projection of Chinese power in Tibet prompted the flight of as many as 100,000 refugees to India and Nepal. Elsewhere decolonisation was the main motor of refugeedom. A different imperial retreat took place when Japan's lengthy occupation of Korea came to an end. Here the consequences were equally momentous, because East–West rivalry culminated in a war that divided the country and displaced around nine million people. By 1960 there were still three million registered refugees in South Korea, making up one-quarter of its total population.

Likewise the division of Vietnam following the Geneva Accords in 1954 forced nearly 900,000 refugees to flee from the Communist North across the 17th Parallel. President Diem gained the backing of American officials and NGOs such as the Catholic Relief Services for a programme of economic development, by settling refugees in the Mekong Delta and inviting them to become self-sufficient and 'modern'. In Korea the similarly authoritarian government of Syngman Rhee claimed refugees from the North as 'national refugees', along with those internally displaced in South Korea. Refugees imbibed this rhetoric in order to seek welfare payments and housing from the Republic, which was heavily backed by US economic and military assistance. However, in the short and medium term they benefited little from their status as national refugees or from external largesse, and regularly experienced displacement as discrimination and contempt on the part of the locally ensconced population.

Jews who survived the Holocaust looked to Palestine as a place of safety, and their future was closely bound up with that of its indigenous Arab population. The implications for Palestinians were well understood by leading figures in the Zionist movement long before the state of Israel came into being. The formation of the state of Israel in 1948 gave rise to the displacement of around 700,000 Palestinian refugees. As one elderly Palestinian refugee put it in 1957, 'we have become refugees on the borders of our own country to make room for other refugees from many parts of the world' (Anderson 1957: 23).

But who is/was recognised as a 'refugee'? The prevailing view among Western diplomats in 1950 was that the UN mandate should not extend to 'a person who has the same rights and obligations as the nationals of the country in which he has taken residence'. This narrow interpretation was chiefly designed to exclude from the mandate any international responsibility for ethnic Germans who had been unceremoniously expelled from Poland and Czechoslovakia and who therefore had to rely on government resources supplemented by funds and other assistance contributed by private relief agencies. In 1951 signatories to the United Nations Refugee Convention formally acknowledged that the chief criterion for legal recognition of the refugee should be that of demonstrating a 'well-founded fear of being persecuted for reasons of race, religion, nationality, or membership of a particular social group or political opinion'. The protection to which recognised refugees were entitled was the responsibility of the new UN High Commissioner for Refugees. But this office lacked the funds and the mandate to function as an 'operational' agency. Like the predecessor organisation under the League of Nations, UNHCR therefore relied upon non-governmental organisations to provide assistance to refugees in situ (Loescher 2017).

The 1951 Refugee Convention betrayed a partial if highly influential understanding of the character, scale and scope of displacement. Separate provision had already been made for Palestinian refugees, and for Korean refugees. Others excluded from the provisions of the Refugee Convention included 420,000 Karelian refugees who fled to Finland from the Soviet Union in 1940 and 1944, and some 175,000 members of the Turkish minority in Bulgaria who found asylum in Turkey after having been expelled from Bulgaria. In 1956 Hungarian refugees crept into the orbit of UNHCR thanks to some clever footwork on the part of the High Commissioner. Refugees in Tibet were not protected by the Convention, and instead threw themselves on private charities and NGOs active in India and Nepal. Millions of others, including so-called 'repatriates' from former European colonies in North Africa, sub-Saharan Africa and the Dutch East Indies, as well as repatriants from Japan's empire in East Asia, were not officially refugees, but regularly faced discrimination in a 'homeland' to which they had little attachment

(Smith 2003; Watt 2009). Regional refugee regimes were constituted, each with their own imperatives and distinctions (Peterson 2015). In India, for example, the process of assistance and rehabilitation required a bureaucratic labelling that saw the circulation of multiple terms to characterise displacement: refugees, evacuees, displaced persons, infiltrees and aliens (Roy 2012; Zamindar 2007).

Several major studies on refugees saw the light of day in the years immediately following the Second World War. Jacques Vernant and Joseph Schechtman both demonstrated how the world had been turned upside down: mass displacement was a global phenomenon. Vernant (1912–83), a lawyer by training, authored a mammoth survey of refugees on behalf of the newly created UNHCR, taking account of new sites of displacement in South Asia and East Asia, including Korea. Confronting issues of definition, he argued that German expellees, although 'treated as self-respecting individuals and not to be dealt with by bureaucracy as beings belonging to an inferior category', were 'nonetheless refugees in the wider sociological sense, because their social and economic integration into the national community which has accepted them is far from complete' (Vernant 1953: 142). Unlike Vernant, Schechtman (1891–1970), intervened regularly in political debate in support of the Zionist cause. Schechtman concentrated on what he termed 'permanent constructive solutions rather than palliative measures', organised population transfer being one possible 'solution'. He nailed his colours to the mast by arguing that resettlement and integration rather than repatriation offered the best way forward. He was particularly dismissive of Palestinian claims to a right of return (Schechtman 1963; Ferrara 2011).

Cold War, decolonisation and development

When Louise Holborn (1898–1975) contributed an entry on 'world problems' to the now-renamed *International Encyclopedia of Social Sciences*, she described the 'refugee problem' as characteristic of a world whose closed frontiers imposed hardship and insecurity on stateless people. Holborn was something of a UN insider. Author of several articles before and after the Second World War on 'the refugee problem', she is best remembered for substantial surveys of the International Refugee Organisation and UNHCR (Holborn 1938; Holborn 1939; Holborn 1952; Holborn 1956; Holborn 1975). In her words, the 'refugee problem' in the 1950s had become 'universal, continuing, and recurring'. But she insisted on a distinction between political and economic refugees. Holborn offered a rather upbeat assessment of external aid in supporting the integration of refugees in the host country and the role of UNHCR as the embodiment of 'impartiality and prestige required for a humane and effective solution of these problems', even if its mandate did not extend to all refugees (Holborn 1968: 361, 371).

In the same volume, the medical sociologist Judith Shuval (b. 1926) wrote on refugees' 'adjustment and assimilation' and addressed the psychological 'strain of prolonged displacement' that encouraged 'apathy' and 'dependency': 'Observers have noted a certain detachment from the past and a feeling of lack of continuity resulting from constant interruption of stable patterns.' She concentrated on the factors that influenced 'a satisfactory outcome of the adjustment process', including their 'social homogeneity' (that is, heterogeneity is more likely to enable refugees to 'move smoothly into the appropriate segments of the host society'). According to Shuval, refugees are 'less predisposed to change', a formulation that she repeats several times, as part of a general argument that 'absorption of the refugees turns into a major national problem', particularly where the numbers are large in proportion to the size of the host country's population (Shuval 1968: 373, 376).

Holborn spoke of 'international refugees' as distinct from 'national refugees' (those who would now be called internally displaced persons); they 'lacked diplomatic protection'. In other words, she followed the pre-war emphasis on something that the refugee had forfeited, rather than on the persecution to which refugees had been subjected, and which became a cornerstone of the 1951 Refugee Convention. In addition, she adopted a bureaucratic approach focusing mainly upon intergovernmental organisations. Shuval's approach represented a departure in the social science literature, quite distinct from Macartney's emphasis on refugees' capability. Her interpretation was nevertheless at odds with more informed studies, such as Stephen Keller's economic anthropology of Partition-era refugees which established that they were adaptable and entrepreneurial (Keller 1975). Her focus on 'detachment' from the past is at odds with evidence of refugees' preoccupation with their history.

For most of these observers, the Cold War was implicit rather than explicit. Certainly it loomed large in accounts of displacement during the third quarter of the twentieth century. The Cold War meant that some refugees were more deserving of recognition and attention than others. To take one example, the influential US Committee for Refugees, mindful in part of the consequences of revolution in Cuba, pointed to millions of people 'trapped' as stateless persons, half of them 'escapees from communist-controlled countries . . . a needless waste of humanity [that] may have a powerful and dangerous impact on the society which has failed to assimilate them' (USCR 1960). The discourse around refugees as a real or potential 'security threat' was not new, but it resonated powerfully in the post-war world.

To minimise these risks, host governments continued to scrutinise the claims of asylum seekers prior to deciding on whom to admit. By the 1960s, signatories to the UN Refugee Convention, together with NGOs, spoke of 'durable solutions': local integration, resettlement or repatriation. Integration locally encouraged greater attention to issues of development, partly in order to find jobs for refugees but also to minimise friction between refugees and the host population, particularly in low-income countries where the majority of the world's refugees lived. A clear-cut illustration of the complex interplay between refugees and 'national' development emerged in the flight of (mostly) Tutsi refugees to the Ngara District of Tanzania in the context of a dual decolonisation – of Rwanda and Tanzania. Tanzanian officials entertained the possibility of attracting international aid to develop remote districts whose land could be made available to refugees who constituted a ready-made supply of labour. Julius Nyerere and those around him hoped that refugees could be made to 'feel psychologically' citizens of the new state. Displacement, decolonisation and development were thus inextricably linked in the official mind. Refugees, of course, did not necessarily see things the same way. Tutsi leaders, far from envisaging their permanence as refugees in Tanzania, planned to return to Rwanda at some stage. Nor did local residents look kindly on refugees, whom they regarded as warriors whose presence posed a threat to their security – a view that some government officials shared. By the mid-1960s the experiment of resettlement had turned sour. The local Tanzanian population declared refugees to be 'illegal immigrants' whose presence was no longer desirable. Once again, the search for a 'solution' became bound up with ideas of entitlement and exclusion (Rosenthal 2015).

Post-Cold War developments: transnational refugees?

The most dramatic manifestations of mass population displacement in the late twentieth and early twenty-first centuries were associated with the collapse of communism in Europe, notably the disintegration of Yugoslavia, and with conflicts in parts of the Middle East, in sub-Saharan Africa and in Latin America. Civilians in the Global South sought to 'escape from violence', but the response from developed countries was limited and inhospitable. Politicians in the Global North turned to history, not to make the links between the colonial past and the colonial present (Gregory 2004), but rather to trumpet the 'proud tradition of welcome' that demonstrated a commitment to providing sanctuary but that also required other countries to do their bit (Kushner 2006).

Critical voices in Refugee Studies made the point that the international refugee regime now supported repatriation or local integration, not resettlement in the countries of the Global North (Chimni 2004). Decisions in 2017 to repatriate long-standing refugee populations in Kenya and Bangladesh support this interpretation. It had already become evident in Cambodia and Rwanda, in both cases following genocidal violence, that UNHCR was prepared to back organised repatriation. Resettlement seemed to belong to the era of the Cold War.

Yet this shift in policy does not exhaust the questions that the historian will wish to ask. There remain issues around refugees and state formation. What conditions enable refugees to constitute themselves as a state-in-exile? Refugee camps are particularly significant, giving activists a ready-made constituency, a captive audience to mobilise on behalf of the persecuted 'nation', and usually significant material resources to do so. Space permits only a brief illustration. Eritrean refugees displaced by the war with Ethiopia spent extended periods in exile in adjacent states such as Sudan and elsewhere, where refugee camps afforded an opportunity to train 'refugee warriors', to recast 'traditional' social relations based on clan, kin and ethnic ties, and to crystallise a strong sense of Eritrean national identity (Kibreab 2000). Eritrea's recent history is even more complex and contested. Eritrean refugees who subsequently moved to Europe have sustained a discourse of a relentlessly oppressive Eritrean dictatorship that propels tens of thousands of people to seek a means of escape. But this stance overlooks the fact that many refugees may be more akin to 'economic migrants' who look for opportunities in countries such as Israel in order to send remittances to Eritrea to sustain impoverished households (Müller 2016). But are they impoverished because of globalisation or because of the exactions levied by the state?

Conclusion: why 'crisis'? Why 'refugeedom'?

As this chapter has pointed out, many of those who have no choice but to flee their homes did not and do not fall within the mandate of intergovernmental organisations. The international refugee regime has always been selective. In interwar Europe it left hundreds of thousands of people in the cold. After 1945, refugees in many parts of the world likewise fell outside the new international refugee regime: refugees in South Asia, in East Asia and German expellees, together with internally displaced persons wherever they might be. Historians need not and should not fall into the same exclusionary trap. We need an extended canvas and a more generous vision.

Thinking about refugees historically also invites us to reflect on the durability of refugee crises, whether in Palestine or Tibet, Cyprus or the Horn of Africa. The legacy of displacement persists, irrespective of a 'durable solution'. The book is never entirely closed on this history. Renée Hirschon established this in relation to Greek refugees from Asia Minor, more than half a century after the Greek–Turkish population exchange: in her ethnography of Piraeus she found that displacement was inscribed in place and in everyday life (Hirschon 1989). The scars of Partition-era displacement persist in Pakistan and India (Butalia 2001; Virdee 2013). Palestinian refugees are acutely conscious of the history of the *Nakba* in 1948 (Hammer 2005; Allan 2013). Displacement is a living history.

This chapter has also stressed the need for a contextualised approach to mass population displacement. By implication, it invites us to reflect on what is at stake in depicting refugee movements as 'unprecedented' or to portray them as a 'crisis' that requires immediate attention, an approach that validates intervention by states and humanitarian aid organisations that seek to regulate and manage refugees, with no opportunity for refugees to hold those in authority to account (Nyers 2006; Malkki 1996). Paying close attention to the formulation of 'solutions' to a refugee 'problem' takes us into broader questions, such as how refugees are connected in the minds of states and other actors to notions of security and 'development'. A history of refugees, in other words, is never just about refugees.

This brings me to my final reflections. A history of refugees is also a history of refugeedom, a term that is worth reviving, because it directs attention to the 'experience' of displacement, but also encompasses the process of labelling and categorisation, the umbrella of protection and thus those who are not protected. It points to techniques of rule by states, intergovernmental and non-governmental actors. It is difficult to generalise about the constitution and operation of these actors that come in different shapes and sizes, except to say that many organisations were ruthless in speaking on behalf of refugees from a lofty standpoint, claiming to know best. To be sure, some NGOs adopted a more reflective stance, as in the case of an American Quaker aid worker during the Korean War:

> It bothered me in spirit that the first thing we did was to get settled in billets behind barbed wire in a guarded compound and this in a sovereign nation. This brought to mind a whole flow of memories associated with post-war Europe. There is a kind of grim and tragic monotony to this century's stereotype of large-scale relief and reconstruction and refugee aid: Spanish refugees, Jewish and political refugees, displaced persons, expellees, escapees, Pakistan, Palestine, Korea, South Vietnam. Where next do the vast governmental and the small voluntary agencies trek in the wake of these problems?[2]

The trek is never-ending.

As mentioned above, the term refugeedom is a coinage from Russia's First World War. Its effects were neatly encapsulated in the remarks of an eyewitness in autumn 1915, about whom nothing is known other than her name (E. Vystavkina) and gender. Vystavkina contributed to a short-lived publication, 'The Refugee's Guide' (*Sputnik bezhentsa*), with a brief article entitled 'Their souls'. I doubt it has ever been bettered as an eloquent and insightful statement of refugeedom:

> Not so long ago, these people lived a full and independent working life. They had the right to be just like us, that is, indolent, rude and ungrateful. Now they have lost this prerogative; their poverty and helplessness oblige them to be meek and grateful, to smile at people they don't like, to answer each and every question without the right to ask questions of their own, to submit to the authority of people they don't respect and have no wish to know, to accept disadvantageous terms from those who wish to exploit their mishaps and destitution. (Gatrell 1999: 206)

More than a century later, her comments about stereotypes, expectations and status still stand.

Notes

1. The Italian Minister of the Interior Marco Minniti announced pompously that 'On 31 March [2017] the tribes came to my office here in Rome'; https://www.theguardian.com/world/2017/sep/07/italian-minister-migrants-libya-marco-minniti (accessed 9 September 2017).
2. American Friends Service Committee Archives, Foreign Service 1954 – Country reports – Korea – Visitors – Louis Schneider, Schneider to Frank and Julia Hunt, confidential, 11 November 1954.

Bibliography

Allan, Diana (2013), *Refugees of the Revolution: Experiences of Palestinian Exile* (Stanford: Stanford University Press).

Anderson, Per-Olow (1957), *They Are Human Too: A Photographic Essay on the Palestine Arab Refugees* (Chicago: Henry Regnery).

Bakewell, Oliver (2008), 'Research beyond the categories: the importance of policy irrelevant research into forced migration', *Journal of Refugee Studies*, 21.4: 432–53.

Ballinger, Pamela (2016), 'Colonial twilight: Italian settlers and the long decolonization of Libya', *Journal of Contemporary History*, 51.4: 813–38.

Ballinger, Pamela (2018), 'A sea of difference, a history of gaps: migrations between Italy and Albania, 1939–1992', *Comparative Studies in Society and History*, 60.1: 90–118.

Baron, Nicholas P., and Peter Gatrell (eds) (2004), *Homelands: War, Population and Statehood in the Former Russian Empire, 1918–1924* (London: Anthem Books).

Butalia, Urvashi (2001), 'An archive with a difference', in Suvir Kaul (ed.), *The Partitions of Memory* (Delhi: Permanent Black), 74–110.

Chatty, Dawn (2010), *Displacement and Dispossession in the Modern Middle East* (Cambridge: Cambridge University Press).

Chatty, Dawn (ed.) (2010), *Deterritorialized Youth: Sahrawi and Afghan Refugees at the Margins of the Middle East* (New York: Berghahn Books).

Chimni, B. S. (2004), 'From resettlement to involuntary repatriation: towards a critical history of durable solutions to refugee problems', *Refugee Survey Quarterly*, 23.3: 55–73.

Elahi, K. Maudood (1987), 'The Rohingya refugees in Bangladesh: historical perspectives and consequences', in John R. Rogge (ed.), *Refugees: A Third World Dilemma* (Totowa, NJ: Rowman and Littlefield), 227–32.

Elfnovembergroep (1978), *Van den grooten oorlog* (Kemmel: Malegijs).

Ferrara, Antonio (2011), 'Eugene Kulischer, Joseph Schechtman and the historiography of forced migrations', *Journal of Contemporary History*, 46.4: 715–40.

Fiddian-Qasmiyeh, Elena (2014), *The Ideal Refugees: Islam, Gender, and the Sahrawi Politics of Survival* (Syracuse: Syracuse University Press).

Gatrell, Peter (1999), *A Whole Empire Walking: Refugees in Russia during World War I* (Bloomington: Indiana University Press).

Gatrell, Peter (2013), *The Making of the Modern Refugee* (Oxford: Oxford University Press).

Gatrell, Peter (2017), 'Refugees – what's wrong with history?', *Journal of Refugee Studies*, 30.2: 170–89.

Gatrell, Peter, and Liubov Zhvanko (eds) (2017), *Europe on the Move: Refugees in the Era of the Great War, 1912–1923* (Manchester: Manchester University Press).

Gregory, Derek (2004), *The Colonial Present: Afghanistan, Palestine, Iraq* (Oxford: Blackwell).

Hammer, Juliane (2005), *Palestinians Born in Exile: Diaspora and the Search for a Homeland* (Austin: University of Texas Press).

Hilton, Laura J. (2009), 'Cultural nationalism in exile: the case of Polish and Latvian Displaced Persons', *The Historian*, 71.2: 280–317.

Hirschon, Renée (1989), *Heirs of the Greek Catastrophe: The Social Life of Asia Minor Refugees in Piraeus* (New York: Berghahn Books).

Holborn, Louise W. (1938), 'The legal status of political refugees', *American Journal of International Law*, 32.4: 680–703.

Holborn, Louise W. (1939), 'The League of Nations and the refugee problem', *Annals of the American Academy of Political and Social Science*, 203: 124–35.

Holborn, Louise W. (1952), 'The United Nations and the refugee problem', *Yearbook of World Affairs*, 6: 124–48.

Holborn, Louise W. (1956), *The International Refugee Organization: A Specialized Agency of the United Nations, its History and Work, 1946–1952* (London: Oxford University Press).

Holborn, Louise W. (1968), 'Refugees: world problems', in *Encyclopedia of the Social Sciences* (New York: Macmillan), 361–73.

Holborn, Louise W. (1975), *Refugees: A Problem of Our Time. The Work of the United Nations High Commissioner for Refugees, 1951–1972*, 2 vols (Metuchen, NJ: Scarecrow Press).

Keller, Stephen L. (1975), *Uprooting and Social Change: The Role of Refugees in Development* (Delhi: Manodar Books).

Kibreab, Gaim (2000), 'Resistance, displacement, and identity: the case of Eritrean refugees in Sudan', *Canadian Journal of African Studies*, 34.2: 249–96.

Kirzhnits, A. (1927), 'Bezhenstvo', *Sovetskaia istoricheskaia entsiklopediia (Soviet Historical Encyclopedia)*, vol. 5 (Moscow), cols. 176–7.

Kulischer, Eugene M. (1948), *Europe on the Move: War and Population Changes, 1917–1947* (New York: Columbia University Press).

Kushner, Tony (2006), *Remembering Refugees: Then and Now* (Manchester: Manchester University Press).

Kushner, Tony, and Katharine Knox (1999), *Refugees in an Age of Genocide: Global, National and Local Perspectives during the Twentieth Century* (London: Frank Cass).

Loescher, Gil (2017), 'UNHCR's origins and early history: agency, influence, and power in global refugee policy', *Refuge*, 33.1: 77–86.

Macartney, Carlile A. (1935), 'Refugees', in *Encyclopedia of the Social Sciences* (New York: Macmillan), vol. 13, 200–5.

Malkki, Liisa H. (1996), 'Speechless emissaries: refugees, humanitarianism, and dehistoricization', *Cultural Anthropology*, 11.3: 377–404.

Mandel, Maud S. (2003), *In the Aftermath of Genocide: Armenians and Jews in Twentieth-Century France* (Durham, NC: Duke University Press).

Marrus, Michael (1985), *The Unwanted: European Refugees in the Twentieth Century* (Oxford: Oxford University Press).

Müller, Tanja (2016), 'Representing Eritrea: geopolitics and narratives of oppression', *Review of African Political Economy*, 43.150: 658–67.

Mylonas, Harris (2012), *The Politics of Nation-Building: Making Co-nationals, Refugees, and Minorities* (Cambridge: Cambridge University Press).

Nyers, Peter (2006), *Rethinking Refugees: Beyond States of Emergency* (New York: Routledge).

Persian, Jayne (2012), 'Displaced Persons and the politics of international categorization', *Australian Journal of Politics and History*, 58.4: 481–96.

Peterson, Glen (2015), 'Sovereignty, international law, and the uneven development of the international refugee regime', *Modern Asian Studies*, 49.2: 439–68.

Rosenthal, Jill (2015), 'From "migrants" to "refugees": identity, aid, and decolonisation in Ngara district, Tanzania', *Journal of African History*, 56.2: 261–79.

Roy, Haimanti (2012), *Partitioned Lives: Migrants, Refugees, Citizens in India and Pakistan, 1947–65* (New Delhi: Oxford University Press).

Schechtman, Joseph B. (1963), *The Refugee in the World: Displacement and Integration* (New York: A. S. Barnes).

Sequeira, James H. (1939), 'The Ethiopian refugees in Kenya', *Journal of the Royal African Society*, 38.152: 329–33.

Shacknove, Andrew (1985), 'Who is a refugee?', *Ethics*, 95.2: 274–84.

Shaw, Caroline (2012), 'The British, persecuted minorities and the emergence of the refugee category in the nineteenth century', *Immigrants and Minorities*, 30.2–3: 239–62.

Shuval, Judith (1968), 'Refugees: adjustment and assimilation', in *Encyclopedia of the Social Sciences* (New York: Macmillan), 373–7.

Simpson, John Hope (1939), *The Refugee Problem: Report of a Survey* (Oxford: Oxford University Press).

Skran, Claudena M. (1995), *Refugees in Inter-War Europe: The Emergence of a Regime* (Oxford: Clarendon Press).

Smith, Andrea L. (ed.) (2003), *Europe's Invisible Migrants* (Amsterdam: Amsterdam University Press).

Soguk, Nevzat (1999), *States and Strangers: Refugees and Displacements of Statecraft* (Minneapolis: University of Minnesota Press).

Tabori, Paul (1972), *The Anatomy of Exile: A Semantic and Historical Study* (London: Harrap).

United States Committee for Refugees (1960), *World Refugee Year* (Washington, DC: USCR).

Vernant, Jacques (1953), *The Refugee in the Post-War World* (London: Allen and Unwin).

Virdee, Pippa (2013), 'Remembering Partition: women, oral histories and the Partition of 1947', *Oral History*, 41.2: 49–62.

Watt, Lori (2009), *When Empire Comes Home: Repatriation and Reintegration in Postwar Japan* (Cambridge, MA: Harvard University Press).

White, Benjamin Thomas (2017), 'Refugees and the definition of Syria, 1920–1939', *Past and Present*, 235: 141–78.

Wilkin, David (1980), 'Refugees and British administrative policy in Northern Kenya, 1936–1938', *African Affairs*, 79.317: 510–30.

Wyman, Mark (1998), *DPs: Europe's Displaced Persons, 1945–1951* (Ithaca: Cornell University Press).

Zamindar, Vazira Fazila-Yacoobali (2007), *The Long Partition and the Making of Modern South Asia: Refugees, Boundaries, and Histories* (New York: Columbia University Press).

Zetter, Roger (1991), 'Labelling refugees: forming and transforming a bureaucratic identity', *Journal of Refugee Studies*, 4.1: 39–62.

Zolberg, Aristide (1983), 'The formation of new states as a refugee-generating process', *Annals of the American Academy of Political and Social Science*, 467: 282–96.

Zolberg, Aristide R., Astri Suhrke and Sergio Aguayo (1989), *Escape from Violence: Conflict and the Refugee Crisis in the Developing World* (New York: Oxford University Press).

Chapter 2

Theories of the Refugee, after Hannah Arendt

Ned Curthoys

Arendt: perplexities in the 'rights of man'

The fundamental deprivation of human rights is manifested first and above all in the deprivation of a place in the world which makes opinions significant and actions effective . . . We became aware of the existence of a right to have rights (and that means to live in a framework where one is judged by one's actions and opinions) and right to belong to some kind of organized community. (Arendt 1994: 296)

The challenge is then to cultivate strategies by which some sort of shared situation is understood to transcend the chasm conventionally formed between citizen and stranger. (Franke 2011: 42)

The refugee catastrophe of the mid-twentieth century and the ongoing problem of mass statelessness exposed the deathly frailty of the Western political and human rights project. Today more than 21 million people lead a vulnerable and marginalised existence in refugee camps and settlements. With the enormous growth of a dispersed population deprived of basic legal entitlements, theorists have seized on the figure of the refugee to think about: 1) the enduring reality of the nation-state and the limited privilege of citizenship it affords as a problematic basis for the instantiation of human rights; 2) the extent to which stateless people and undocumented migrants can obtain political and civic rights, recognition and dignity as claimants of human rights; and 3) the forms of political community and affective conceptions of global citizenship that are capable of sustaining the rights of stateless people.

The most influential response to the modern tragedy of mass statelessness is the German Jewish political theorist Hannah Arendt's essay 'The Decline of the Nation State and the End of the Rights of Man', the ninth chapter of her germinal analysis of the antecedents of the rise of fascism and Stalinism, *The Origins of Totalitarianism* (1951). Arendt herself was a stateless person for a number of years. Arrested as an 'enemy alien' in France, she narrowly avoided Auschwitz when she escaped the French detention camp of Gurs in 1940. Arendt's essay's pithy formulation of a 'right to have rights', in conjunction with her pessimistic realism about the failure of the putatively innate existence of human rights to guarantee political and civic rights, has helped to structure a difficult but productive conversation about our capacity to guarantee and extend human rights into the future. In her chapter, Arendt seems to argue that human rights has exhausted its generative possibilities: the calamity of the rightless is not a specific deprivation of freedom or due process but that they are no longer a recognised subject of rights, since 'they no longer belong to any community whatsoever' (Arendt 1994: 295). However, I will argue in this chapter that Arendt's essay moves beyond its apparently dystopian premise.

In her essay, Arendt wanted to know why the inspirational articulation of natural rights that helped to inspire the French Revolution, *The Declaration of the Rights of Man and the Citizen* of 1789, had ultimately revealed the concept of 'inalienable human rights' it proclaimed to be a fallacious abstraction. Arendt's answer was that the twentieth century since the First World War had witnessed an enormous increase in refugees and stateless peoples who could no longer find a meaningful place in the world from which to speak and act. Human rights were meant to rest upon the 'nature' or essence of 'man' as such, independent of historical circumstances or any form of social contract. Yet at a moment of historical crisis, when the concept was most needed to protect the displaced and vulnerable and rebuke the totalitarian assault on human plurality, human rights were anything but self-evident. As Arendt eloquently observes, the world found 'nothing sacred in the abstract nakedness of being human' (Arendt 1994: 299).

Arendt shares with subsequent commentators a profound concern about the destruction of the stateless person's 'legal personality' and political status, and their access to a public realm that recognises and validates them as a subject of rights. As she caustically reminds us, the fate of the stateless person is actually worse than that of a criminal, who is at least entitled to legal process, or a slave who has lost specific rights but not a recognised place within a social hierarchy that keeps them within the 'pale of humanity'. For the stateless person, often deliberately denaturalised by their country of origin, the loss of a place in the world, the loss of a capacity for speech and action that involves them in 'common human responsibilities', did not prompt recognition of their common humanity but instead left them bereft of the 'very qualities which make it possible for other people to treat him as a fellowman' (Arendt 1994: 300). A disillusioned Arendt thus notes the 'pragmatic soundness' of Edmund Burke's withering critique of the French Constituent Assembly's *Declaration of the Rights of Man and the Citizen* (1789) as positing a meaningless abstraction in comparison to the historically derived, customary rights that are a transmissible entailment of the nation, the only sort of rights that can possibly be understood as a 'source of law'. In a striking concretisation of the political basis of human rights, Arendt suggests that the post-war 'restoration of human rights' such as indicated by the then recent establishment of the state of Israel had been achieved 'so far only through the restoration or establishment of national rights' (Arendt 1994: 299). As a solution to the 'Jewish question', Arendt notes that Israel as a 'colonized and then conquered territory' then created a new category of refugees, increasing the number of 'stateless and rightless' by another 700,000–800,000 people (Arendt 1994: 290). The repetition of the logic of partition on a much larger scale in India and Pakistan demonstrates, Arendt laments, a 'deadly sickness' in which even newly formed nation-states can no longer demonstrate equality before the law, granting rights and privileges on the basis of ethnicity and social privilege that may herald the deprivation of 'all citizens of legal status' and the rule of an 'omnipotent police' (Arendt 1994: 290). At the end of her essay Arendt warns that disqualifying denaturalised refugees from the ranks of humanity, from the 'world' as a created artifice, threatens an atavistic return to 'barbarism' in which millions of rightless people, confined to a purely private existence, are thrown back into a 'peculiar state of nature', the 'conditions of savages' (Arendt 1994: 300). If many millions are to be denied the public status and legal personality afforded by nationality, we are witnessing nothing less, Arendt warns, than the precondition for a 'possible regression from civilization' that will not be the result of external invasions but an artefact of a 'global, universally interrelated civilization' (Arendt 1994: 302).

Arendt's fear that the once marginal phenomenon of statelessness was a harbinger of the collapse of representative democracy and the rule of law pivots between a robust critique of statelessness as a transnational phenomenon that threatens emancipatory politics, and what Jacques Rancière has described as Arendt's 'archipolitical position' (Rancière 2004: 299) and the anthropological anxieties it generates about the fate of Western culture, in which 'ever-increasing numbers [of refugees] threaten our political life, our human artifice' (Arendt 1994: 302). On the one hand, Arendt fears that the nation-state and its policing agencies will become increasingly totalitarian due to the power they assume over stateless people and refugees. This is one of the reasons, she notes, that the Nazis had met with 'so disgracefully little resistance from the police in the countries they occupied' (Arendt 1994: 289). On the other hand, as Michael Rothberg has demonstrated in *Multidirectional Memory* (Rothberg 2009: 40), throughout *The Origins of Totalitarianism* Arendt is preoccupied with the figure of the 'savage without culture', memory or history, who cannot contribute to the artificial creation of a common world, a form of bare life whose very existence on the African continent helped to generate the kind of degenerative race thinking that crystallised into Nazi imperialism. It is thus a colonial trope with a Eurocentric developmental narrative, as Rothberg points out, that provides the 'metaphorical grounding' for the central characters that map out Arendt's analysis in *The Origins of Totalitarianism*: the African 'savage without culture', the refugee as the naked human being deprived of culture, and the stateless concentration camp inmate stripped of the right to have rights (Rothberg 2009: 40).

Arendt, then, provides a transnational genealogy of the gradual diminution of the nation by ethno-nationalist imperatives, for which the figure of the refugee without a guaranteed place in the world is emblematic; as such, she also is a theorist of the present human condition and the ethical and epistemological challenges it poses to customary ways of thinking. Here and in other writings that ally themselves to rethinking contemporary history by reference to memory, experience and anecdote, she encourages a *thinking without banisters*[1] that is not bound to the obligatory authority of political, religious and ethical traditions. In 'The Decline of the Nation State and the End of the Rights of Man' she suggests that in the twentieth century we are too alienated from 'nature' and its frighteningly destructive potentialities, and too aware of the vicissitudes of 'history' without a progressive teleology, to be able to deduce law and right from those hypostatised terms. The 'essence of man' is no longer recognisable through appeals to historical or natural categories. In the twentieth century humanity is no longer a regulative ideal as it was for Kant, a source of moral reasoning and a guiding prospect for increasing human commerce in a future of republican federated states, but rather an immanent reality of global politics, an 'inescapable fact'. Arendt wonders whether 'humanity', as a sometimes frightening and urgent condition of intensifying interdependency, can supplant the role of nature and history in articulating and then 'guaranteeing' the 'right to have rights', the right of every individual to 'belong to humanity':

> This new situation, in which 'humanity' has in effect assumed the role formerly ascribed to nature or history, would mean in this context the right to have rights, or the right of every individual to belong to humanity, should be guaranteed by humanity itself. It is by no means certain that this is possible. (Arendt 1994: 298)

Acknowledging the precariousness of this claim ('it is by no means certain whether this is possible'), its irreducibility to any specific legislative proposal or legal regime, Arendt maintains that it is unclear whether such a framework of constitutive rights is realisable in the present sphere of international law, which operates in terms of agreements and treaties between sovereign states. At this juncture Arendt reminds us of the presuppositions of her book as a whole. Just as the emergence of totalitarian governments is a 'phenomenon within, not outside, our civilization', a global and interrelated civilisation may 'produce barbarians from its own midst' which are in fact, the 'conditions of savages' (Arendt 1994: 302).

In recent years, writers and thinkers have responded to the questions Arendt left in her analysis. In her cynicism about the normative foundation of human rights, is Arendt confirming the validity of existing political communities and their delimited conception of popular sovereignty? What are the two forms of 'rights' that Arendt is talking about in her formulation of the 'right to have rights' (moral or legal?) and what is to be their philosophical, political and legal foundation? Does Arendt actually exclude refugees, who are arguably reduced to symptoms of a crisis in political organisation, from making an active contribution to present civilisation, and from past accomplishment and future world making (Rothberg 2009: 56)? Or does her conception of the refugee deprived of a place in the world offer phenomenological insights into other categories of person, such as prisoners, women, exploited migrants and working people who also lack access to the dignity and legal persona afforded by citizenship?

Some perplexities about the right to have rights

Seyla Benhabib, one of the most prominent interpreters of Arendt and a renowned theorist of human rights and international law, has theorised the legal prospects for human rights in light of Arendt's formulation on multiple occasions. In *The Rights of Others: Aliens, Residents, and Citizens*, Benhabib argues, as do a number of theorists in this section, that Arendt was insufficiently sanguine about the possibilities of universal moral rights, assuming that such rights were politically and juridically circumscribed by the sovereign privilege and demographic exclusions of the territorially defined nation-state, a political space that 'cannot be limited or trumped by other norms and institutions' (Benhabib 2004: 66–7). Where Arendt, according to Benhabib, posited the human right to membership of a political community as an abstract moral 'ought' implicitly at the mercy of stronger states, Benhabib understands these rights as increasingly incorporated into existing rights regimes through various discourse practices and networks of institutions (Benhabib 2004: 142), such as the international treaties and conventions that bind states, including today's imperial hegemon the United States, to observe civil, economic and political rights.

In other respects, Benhabib's account of how the right to have rights might be given democratic legitimacy and juridical form is influenced by Arendt's formulation understood as an attempted mediation between popular sovereignty (rights of the citizen) and cosmopolitan universalism. In 'The Perplexities of the Rights of Man' Arendt critiques a future world-government as nightmarishly authoritarian, unelected and unaccountable to a culturally diverse global constituency. Yet throughout her corpus Arendt sharply criticises the conquest of the state and its legal framework by the ethnocentric 'nation', and theorises the advantages of a federated system of polities that respects the diversity of peoples. Benhabib appropriates Arendt to seek an alternative to the position of 'democratic sovereigntists' such as John Rawls and Michael Walzer on the one hand, and on the other global constitutionalists who seek to bind states to enforceable cosmopolitan norms. Benhabib puts her faith in the 'jurisgenerativity of law' to instantiate human rights norms and empower local initiatives (Benhabib 2004: 176–83). Critiquing legal formalism, Benhabib has recently made the point that in its response to a global human rights culture, the symbolic sphere of the law can develop an 'extralegal normative universe by developing new vocabularies for public claimmaking' (Benhabib 2018: 28). The law can do so by 'encouraging new forms of subjectivity to engage with the public sphere', and by 'interjecting existing relations of power with anticipations of justice to come' (Benhabib 2018: 121, 29).

Benhabib places empirical confidence in the 'vernacularization' of human rights claims by a process of 'democratic iterations' (Benhabib 2018: 28; 2011: 138–66). She defines democratic iterations as complex processes of public argument, deliberation and exchange through which universalist rights claims are 'contested and contextualized, invoked and revoked, posited and positioned throughout legal and political institutions as well as in the associations of civil society' (Benhabib 2004: 179). Echoing Arendt's suspicion that world government cannot be representative, Benhabib stresses the importance of democratic legitimacy, in which human rights norms cannot be imposed by legal and political elites on recalcitrant peoples. Rather, such norms must become elements in the public culture of democratic peoples through their own processes of interpretation, articulation and iteration. As with other theorists of constitutional patriotism, such as Jürgen Habermas, Jan-Werner Müller and Craig Calhoun, Benhabib assumes that a process of rational and cooperative public deliberation guided by enlightened legal precedent and an informed civil society can gradually transform the ethnopolitics of many nation-states. The result would be respect for the rights-claims of stateless individuals and asylum seekers who are seeking new lives or temporary protection within the national territory. Benhabib demonstrates fealty to Arendt's insistence that only organised, legitimately representative and dynamically evolving political communities can guarantee human rights when she writes that:

> The liberal defence of human rights, understood as placing limits on the publicly justifiable exercise of power needs to be complemented by the civic-republican vision of rights as constituent of a people's exercise of public autonomy. (Benhabib 2013: 46)

Jacques Rancière, in his much-cited 2004 essay 'Who is the Subject of the Rights of Man?', is more perturbed than Benhabib by the inadequacies of Arendt's insistence on the absolute disjuncture between the rights of 'man' and 'citizen', and between the existential conditions of citizen and refugee, since he feels that this distinction is a manifestation of Arendt's interpretation of the political as a specific 'sphere' of human self-realisation that needs to be vigilantly separated from the realm of 'necessity', of private, social, apolitical life. Criticising the 'archi-political' thrust of Arendt's writing which judges the worth of human beings by their capacity for political action, Rancière argues that Arendt voids the subject of rights in the *Declaration of the Rights of Man and the Citizen* of its productive ambiguity. Rancière is dismayed that, for Arendt, the 'rights of man are the rights of the unpoliticized person' who has no rights, which 'amounts to nothing' (Rancière 2004: 302). For Arendt, according to Rancière, the 'rights of man are the rights of the citizen' of a constitutional state or nothing at all. Rancière, perhaps overlooking the ironic undertow of Arendt's essay, harshly critiques Arendt for positing a factitious quandary which adjudges the 'rights of man' as tautological and thus the rights of a subject 'who does not exist': the rights of a 'single subject' who would be at once the source and the bearer of rights, a self-cancelling entity who would only use the rights he or she already possesses (Rancière 2004: 302).

According to Rancière, the 'Rights of Man are the rights of those who have not the rights they have and have the rights that they have not' (2004: 302). The subject of rights is the 'process of subjectivisation' itself, which challenges the disjuncture of 'man' and 'citizen' by performatively claiming the abeyant rights of those deprived of such rights (for example, the rights to equality of French women during the French Revolution as claimed and enacted by the political activist Olympe de Gouges), and claiming the 'rights they have not' through performative tactics. Rancière's example of the latter claim is the *sans-papiers* political movement of undocumented North African migrants claiming work and residency rights based on their existing, contributory presence in the French polity. For Rancière, the ongoing cleavage between abstract 'man' and de facto 'citizen' is not a sign of rights as either void or tautologically redundant but an 'interval for subjectivization' (2004: 304). The essence of human rights does not precede political naming but opens up a space of testing, enlargement, verification and comprehension, a contested space of 'dissensus' that destabilises sovereign dictates over processes of inclusion and exclusion. As James Ingram notes of Rancière's position, human rights are an always-available resource for those who have been denied rights they can plausibly claim. Where Arendt seems to argue that only an existing polity can achieve a consensus about rights as belonging to 'definite or permanent subjects', Rancière counters that the politicisation of human rights involves precisely the opposite – agonistic conflicts about their meaning, application and extension. Rancière insists that the *politics* of human rights consists precisely in the activity of claiming them.

While essentially agreeing with Rancière's agonistic conception of human rights as an opening to political contestation, Étienne Balibar (2013) and James Ingram (2008) find considerably more promise in Arendt's 'right to have rights' understood as the *right to politics*. Arendt's seemingly groundless claim of a right to political community is a reminder that the politics of human rights are effective only when people invent and maintain them through an often conflictual political practice, for which there can be no extrapolitical or ontological guarantee. Resisting the normative anxieties of thinkers such as Benhabib, Balibar suggests that Arendt's inference of the right to have rights is not a formulation aspiring to a '*higher level* of abstraction' from which concrete rights could be deduced, but is best interpreted as an 'immanent practical problem' oriented towards the effective realization of 'justice within rights' (Balibar 2013: 21). Like Rancière, Balibar regards the overlap of 'man' and 'citizen' in the French and American Rights Declarations positively, rather than as an insoluble impasse between the ideal and the real, as Arendt feared. For Balibar, the overlap of man and citizen affirms 'a universal right to political activity for every individual, in all the domains in which the problem of collectively organized possession, power, and knowledge is posed' (Balibar 1994: 212). Claude Lefort makes a similar point in *The Political Forms of Modern Society* (1986) where he argues that the 'democratic achievement of the declaration of the rights of man lies precisely in the indeterminacy that the separation of right and power introduces into the political association' (quoted in Schaap 2013: 16).

Balibar, then, suggests that Arendt's theory of the right to have rights is prophetic, that it does show the way to a community to come. The 'community of citizens' which Arendt's rights formulation calls for is no longer an *existing* community or an *existing form of community* to be ideally located in the past. It becomes a 'community to come', or *a community without a model*, which is bound to appear first as a 'non-community', but is *virtually there* in the struggles themselves (Balibar 2013: 25). As Andrew Schaap points out, the always yet to be achieved claim of universal human rights disrupts political rationality, including Marx's utopian positing of a final historical goal of human emancipation from the political, thus affirming the symbolic effectivity of human rights as a condition of possibility for democratic politics (Schaap 2013: 3).

Arendtian politics and its significance for theories of the refugee

In the next section we move from a debate about the political implications of Arendt's critique of human rights to a discussion of those theorists who defend her analysis in Arendt's own terms. In her recent book *Rightlessness in an Age of Rights: Hannah Arendt and the Contemporary Struggles of Migrants* (2015), Aten Gündoğdu critiques Rancière's assumption that Arendt was intent on 'shaming' the exclusions and limitations of human rights discourses (Gündoğdu 2015: 27). By contrast, Gündoğdu reads Arendt's discussion of the perplexities of the 'rights of man' as productively 'aporetic' on the model of Socrates' dialectical inquiries into foundational concepts (Gündoğdu 2015: 28). Like Socrates,

Arendt examines the shortcomings of conventional opinions, in this case about the meaning and efficacy of human rights. She does not then feel the need to ground human rights in a new moral or institutional order (Gündoğdu 2015: 28) (as we have seen, her critics often angst over the normative justification and formalisation of the 'rights to have rights') but instead examines how political vocabularies of rights have achieved a new meaning with the rise of stateless-ness, thus alerting us to the 'manifold, protean, and indeterminate trajectories of these rights' (Gündoğdu 2015: 29).

In this respect Arendt's critique of the dangerously anti-political, because absolutist, implications of rights as inherent properties of being human fore-shadows more recent criticisms of human-rights based humanitarian proj-ects, often involving military intervention, that transform human rights into the 'rights of the absolute victim' (Gündoğdu 2015: 80). In an innovative analysis, Gündoğdu argues that Arendt's conceptions of labour and action in *The Human Condition* (1958) and other writings offer a critical phenom-enology of the particular kinds of 'worldlessness' suffered by refugee popula-tions dispersed into camps and detention centres, strengthening the argument that the rights to which they need to be entitled are positive guarantees of a place in the world, that is, civil and political covenants. She also makes a fascinating case for the subtleties of Arendt's argument for human beings to be guaranteed a protected 'legal persona' through which they can engage in communicative and political action (Gündoğdu 2015: 105). Arendt's insis-tence on a right to legal personhood, a right to be a 'who' rather than a 'what', offers a prism through which to discuss the application of human rights law to refugee claimants in various supra-national forums such as the European Court of Human Rights, since claimants are often subject to prac-tices of unlawful deportation and punitive detention tantamount to a kind of civil death (Gündoğdu 2015: 107–25).

Pragmatism, cultural representation and human rights

Many pragmatist theorists of human rights are also quite happy with the kind of productive groundlessness that Arendt's formulation of a right to have rights entails; but, unlike Benhabib, Balibar and Gündoğdu, this is because they understand human rights as a necessary but undemonstrable fiction best inculcated by affective means. The pragmatist philosopher Richard Rorty's classic essay 'Human Rights, Rationality, and Sentimentality' does not explic-itly evoke Arendt's theory of human rights, but it responds to the ongoing perplexity as to how to introduce a seemingly groundless 'absolute' such as human rights into the uncertain world of human affairs. Like Arendt, Rorty doesn't believe that one can instantiate human rights by an appeal to the 'natural' rights of human beings as having certain innate capacities that make them an ontologically distinct category from animals. For Rorty, pragmatism is a philosophical discourse more preoccupied with ethical self-fashioning and imaginative redescriptions of existing vocabularies than with making epistemological progress. In a manner comparable to Arendt's historicised, post-metaphysical inquiry into the political prospects of human rights, Rorty recommends that we substitute the question 'What can we make of ourselves?' for 'What is our nature?' Rather than grounding the transcendental moral claims of human rights in 'rationality' and thus posing the genuinely aporetic question as to whether those rights are real and justifiable, we should admit that the human rights culture emergent in the West since the eighteenth century helps to summarise 'culturally influenced intuitions about the right thing to do in various situations' (Rorty 2010a: 354). It follows that instead of engaging in a rational critique of those individuals and societies that stubbornly refuse to recognise our common human nature, we should forego transcultural universals that are themselves a survival of the rationalist faculty psychology of the Enlightenment (Rorty 2010a: 356).

From this perspective, the question of human rights is no longer based on ontological questions about the specific nature of humanity or stern Kantian precepts about our moral obligations to others, but is rather a promise of social cooperation, in which we are capable of making ourselves into whatever we are 'clever and courageous enough to imagine ourselves becoming' (Rorty 2010a: 358). Rorty jettisons any *a priori* ontology of the human and instead suggests that rights questions are best suited to an interdisciplinary philosophical anthropology guided by the promise that human beings can 'feel *for each other* to a much greater extent than [animals] can' (2010a: 358). Hearing 'sad and sentimental stories' about the plight of others has stimulated the human rights project much more than 'moral knowledge' in the form of arguments about a human essence worthy of dignity and respect (2010a: 355). Rorty thus recommends the 'sentimental education' of the young across the globe by a process of 'manipulating sentiments' (2010a: 358). Rather than impressing ahistorical facts upon nationalists and xenophobes, it is sufficient that more and more people become other-respecting by empathising with a variety of narratives and subject positions, a process that needs to be accompanied by the amelioration of scarcity, want and inequality. This acculturating process of thickening and expanding our imaginative identifications is necessary and sufficient to achieve what Rorty calls an 'Enlightenment utopia' of rights-respecting individuals (2010a: 355, 361).

Rorty tends to imply that as the human rights project is a province of the affluent West, a degree of 'moderate ethnocentrism' is justified because the leisured and reflective populations of countries indebted to Enlightenment liberalism have shown the way in establishing a global moral community. His reliance on the production of empathic reasoning manipulated by a 'sentimental education' has little to say about cultural plurality or a world in which millions of people have been effectively excluded from social visibility. As opposed to the agonistic politics of human rights claims articulated by

Rancière, Balibar and others, Rorty imagines a rather condescending, cross-cultural conversation in which a rights-respecting Western interlocutor no longer engages in the fruitless task of trying to rationally prove to a member of a traditional non-Western society that at bottom we are all equal. He rather argues *from the civilising effects* of treating distinctions between people as arbitrary, of respecting the demarcation between Church and state, and of promoting the rule of law and its equal application (Rorty 2010b: 443).

Despite affinities with Rorty's post-foundational approach to human rights in which Western political forms are privileged as an antidote to the political barbarism that produces refugees, Arendt rejects a rescue narrative in which the marginalised other awaits incorporation into existing genres of sentimental narration. I want to end this chapter by arguing that Arendt offers an alternative account of how the 'rights of others' might ultimately be respected and provide the basis for human flourishing beyond the existing system of ethnic majority nation-states.

Arendt's early essays on Jewish politics provide considerable resources for theorising the stateless person as an *insurgent subjectivity* whose plight is a microcosm of increasing numbers of human beings. As Patricia Owens reminds us, it was precisely during this period (1942–44) that Arendt was offering 'concrete proposals to undermine the establishment of a monoethnic/religious Jewish state to prevent Palestinians suffering a similar fate as European Jews' (Owens 2017: 42). We might, then, regard Arendt's projection of statelessness as articulating with diasporic Jewish history and its ethical traditions as advancing a pluralistic, querulous political position beyond any conventional national imaginary.

In essays such as 'We Refugees' (1943) and 'The Jew as Pariah' (1944) Arendt was interested in how emancipated Jews who had an ambiguous and tenuous relation to a nation of origin that did not recognise their admission to the ranks of human *qua* Jews had developed a pariah consciousness as a basis for the struggle for human rights. 'K' in Kafka's *The Castle* was a particular focus. In 'The Jew as Pariah' Arendt argues that K speaks for the 'average small-time Jew who really wants no more than his rights as a human being: home, work, family, and citizenship' (Arendt 2007: 291). Arendt argues that K's struggles are representative of the dramas of 'assimilation' of a person who might have some rights as a citizen but is yet to be granted a place in the world as a speaking and acting being. In chasing such rights, K ends up entirely 'alone', parting company with those who are like him but who do not wish to press for the positive freedom for self-realisation. K directs his desire towards all things in which human beings have a 'natural right' such as home, family, work, the right to be useful, the right to be a member of society, citizenship, all the prerequisites of human existence. In other words, K claims the right to have rights as immanent to his dignity as a human being rather than as granted piecemeal by the patronage of the powers that be. According to Arendt, in *The Castle* K embarks on an 'experiment' that demonstrates that in the contemporary world his aspirations are, in reality, 'exceptional' and 'magnificent' (Arendt 2007: 294); far from depending on assimilation to his milieu, K's aspiration for rights is no longer to be realised by 'simple, natural methods' (Arendt 2007: 293). In shattering the mythos of the legitimate power of constituted authorities, which can only defer and offer excuses before his energetic claims, K demonstrates to the villagers themselves that the 'rule of the castle', the bureaucratic state, can be attacked and that 'human rights are worth fighting for' (Arendt 2007: 295). Those rights demonstrate the inadequacies of a world in which the struggle of 'one simple man' to live like a normal human being reveals the absurdity and inadequacy of an existing order based on inherited privilege, perhaps an allegory for a world in which citizenship has become a privilege that needs to be urgently interrogated.

Arendt contends that as an allegory, Kafka's *The Castle* suggests that the arrival of the stateless person as an overwhelming political reality will be transformative. Like the plight of K, mass statelessness reveals a world in which there is no protection against bare murder, in which a human being can be driven from the 'streets and broad places open to all', so that, as Kant predicted of an interdependent geopolitical order, 'social isolation is no longer possible' (Arendt 2007: 296). In her earlier essay, 'We Refugees', Arendt also privileges the consciousness of the refugee who tells the truth of her or his situation and fights for a place in the world. The refugee is not the excrescence of a system of nation-states, or the by-product of dysfunctional cultures that have yet to join the human rights project. Rather, refugees driven from country to country represent the 'vanguard of their peoples' as long as they continue like K to strive for their positive rights, since they signal the imminent collapse of an inherited international order of positive rights unless their aspirations are respected, just as the 'comity of European peoples went to pieces when, and because, it allowed its weakest member to be excluded and persecuted' (Arendt 2007: 274).

For Arendt, the stateless person is not an object of pity, but a theoretical perspective on a shattered world, since the deprivation of the right to have rights threatens a crisis of civilisation and is a harbinger of fascism.[2] Sympathetic interpreters of Arendt's analyses of the ironic dissonance between the condition of statelessness and the effectiveness of human rights as either claimed or enacted would agree that Arendt has contributed to the challenge of cultivating 'strategies by which some sort of shared situation is understood to transcend the chasm conventionally formed between citizen and stranger' (Franke 2011: 42). At the very least, as we have seen in this chapter, her writing and the debates it has provoked articulate their own 'dissensus', which is the need to think the situation of refugees as a problem for a world in need of a locally active, opinion-forming citizenry that holds government accountable but also as a complication of emplaced subjectivity and the political system that encourages its structural disavowal of the vulnerable stranger.

Notes

1. A metaphor now considered emblematic of Arendt's philosophical project of thinking in the absence of normative philosophical or ethical traditions; see her explanation in 'Hannah Arendt on Hannah Arendt' (Arendt 2018: 473).

2. Arendt's claims to pariahdom foreshadow Judith Butler's recent defence of diasporic Jewish identities in *Parting Ways: Jewishness and the Critique of Zionism* (2012). Critiquing the settler-colonial and nationalistic project of political Zionism, Butler idealises the hybrid condition of diaspora as a continuing departure from self-identity that is subtended by self-formation in the culture of the non-Jew. In the figure of the diasporic Jewish subject Butler reprises the attempt to make one's way, like K, in a world of heterogeneity while insisting on the protestation of one's own distinctive difference. Thus diaspora as conditioned by historical experiences of exile and transnational mobilities becomes a critical prism of recent theorists of statelessness who do not wish to regard statelessness merely as a contemporary geopolitical problem or as symptomatic of the ills of globalisation and neo-colonialism, as argued by Slavoj Žižek in *Against the Double Blackmail: Refugees, Terror and Other Troubles with the Neighbours* (2016), who complacently laments that 'refugees are the price humanity is paying for the global economy'. Butler reminds us that it was Edward Said himself who felt a great affinity for the 'unhoused and diasporic character of Jewish life' which aligns it with 'our age of vast population transfers', with 'refugees, exiles, expatriates, and immigrants', a condition celebrating heterogeneity and multiple historical genealogies that might evoke relational sympathies with dispossessed Palestinians (Butler 2012: 49).

Bibliography

Arendt, Hannah (1994), *The Origins of Totalitarianism* (San Diego: Harcourt).

Arendt, Hannah (2007), *The Jewish Writings*, ed. Jerome Kohn and Ron H. Feldman (New York: Schocken Books).

Arendt, Hannah (2018), *Essays in Understanding 1953–1975: Thinking Without a Banister* (New York: Schocken Books).

Balibar, Étienne (1994), *Masses, Classes, Ideas: Studies in Political Philosophy Before and After Marx*, trans. James Swenson (New York: Routledge).

Balibar, Étienne (2013), 'On the politics of human rights', *Constellations*, 20.1: 18–26.

Benhabib, Seyla (2004), *The Rights of Others: Aliens, Residents, and Citizens*, vol. 5 (Cambridge: Cambridge University Press).

Benhabib, Seyla (2011), *Dignity in Adversity: Human Rights in Turbulent Times* (Cambridge: Polity Press)

Benhabib, Seyla (2013), 'Reason-giving and rights-bearing: constructing the subject of rights', *Constellations*, 20.1: 38–50.

Benhabib, Seyla (2018), *Exile, Statelessness and Migration: Playing Chess with History from Hannah Arendt to Isaiah Berlin* (Princeton: Princeton University Press).

Brown, Wendy (2004), '"The most we can hope for. . .": human rights and the politics of fatalism', *The South Atlantic Quarterly*, 103.2: 451–63.

Butler, Judith (2012), *Parting Ways: Jewishness and the Critique of Zionism* (New York: Columbia University Press).

Franke, Mark F. N. (2011), 'The unbearable rightfulness of being human: citizenship, displacement and right not to have rights', *Citizenship Studies*, 15.1: 39–56.

Gündoğdu, Ayten (2014), 'A revolution in rights: reflections on the democratic invention of the rights of man', *Law, Culture and the Humanities*, 10.3: 367–79.

Gündoğdu, Ayten (2015), *Rightlessness in an Age of Rights: Hannah Arendt and the Contemporary Predicament* (Oxford: Oxford University Press).

Ingram, James D. (2008), 'What is a "right to have rights"? Three images of the politics of human rights', *The American Political Science Review*, 102.4, 401–16.

Krause, Monica (2008), 'Undocumented migrants: an Arendtian perspective', *European Journal of Political Theory*, 7.3: 331–48.

Owens, Patricia, 'The international origins of Hannah Arendt's historical method', *International Origins of Social and Political Theory*, 34: 37–62.

Rancière, Jacques (2004), 'Who is the subject of the rights of man?', *The South Atlantic Quarterly*, 103.2: 297–310.

Rorty, Richard (2010a [1990]), 'Human rights, rationality, and sentimentality', in *The Rorty Reader*, ed. Christopher J. Voparil and Richard J. Bernstein (Chichester: John Wiley and Sons), 351–65.

Rorty, Richard (2010b), 'Justice as a larger loyalty', in *The Rorty Reader*, ed. Christopher J. Voparil and Richard J. Bernstein (Chichester: John Wiley and Sons), 433–43.

Rothberg, Michael (2009), *Multidirectional Memory: Remembering the Holocaust in the Age of Decolonization* (Stanford: Stanford University Press).

Said, Edward W. (2012), *Representations of the Intellectual* (London: Vintage).

Schaap, Andrew (2013), 'Human rights and the political paradox', *Australian Humanities Review*, 55: 1–22.

Žižek, Slavoj (2016), *Against the Double Blackmail: Refugees, Terror, and Other Troubles with the Neighbours* (Harmondsworth: Penguin).

Chapter 3

A Genealogy of Refugee Writing

Arthur Rose

This genealogy of refugee writing offers style as a means to approach the problem of writing for, about and by refugees. Edward Said famously differentiated 'the age of the refugee' from earlier experiences of exile as a matter of scale, arguing that this 'large, impersonal setting' was a context against which 'exile cannot be made to serve notions of humanism' (Said 2002: 174). In this chapter, I argue that style is a key way of understanding this transition, first by comparing E. M. Cioran's caustic parody of exile writing, 'The Advantages of Exile' (1952), with Hannah Arendt's equally caustic reflection on refugee coping strategies in 'We Refugees' (1943). I then turn to more recent texts that indicate moments when previous stylistic models become unsustainable. Economic optimism, under the sign of a coherent, if partisan, global order, takes centre stage in Jonny Steinberg's memoir *A Man of Good Hope* (2014), published just before the 2015 'explosion' of refugee narratives in the Western media. By contrast, Viet Thanh Nguyen's *The Refugees* (2017) and Mohsin Hamid's *Exit West* (2017) suggest a more fragmented, more chaotic attitude to this optimism, no longer stabilised by any coherent narrative of fairness or justice. In each of my examples, I return to the stylistic functions of two salient features of modern refugee writing: negative identification and cruel optimism.

Arendt and refugee style

Hannah Arendt's key essay (discussed by Ned Curthoys in the previous chapter) begins: 'In the first place, we don't like to be called refugees. We ourselves call each other "newcomers" or "immigrants"' (Arendt 1994: 110). Here Arendt combines two forms of negative identification as it relates to the refugee: the refugee's own desire to dis-identify or not 'be called [a] refugee', as well as subtraction of the refugee from other categories, whether 'newcomer' or 'immigrant', but equally exile or émigré. But the sentence gestures towards a larger problem for writing about refugees, which often struggles to figure the refugee as a person, rather than as a category or a type. At best, these categories may be inclusive, like Arendt's 'we'. More commonly, though, they are associated with morally negative images of flow: the metaphors might relate to water – 'streams' or 'floods' of refugees – or they may be insectile, 'swarms' or 'plagues'.[1] Alternatively, when individual refugees do acquire an exemplary status, as identifiable characters, actors or representatives, this frequently involves exceptionalism; they can be named, voiced and counted, even as their fellow refugees cannot.[2] When a refugee is the protagonist of the narrative, like Arendt, her narrative personhood often comes at the expense of her identity as a refugee.

With these equivocations, Arendt's essay prefigures many of the features and problems that attend writing by, for and about refugees since. Eight paragraphs into the essay, Arendt formalises the distinction between 'I' and 'we' when she abruptly switches from the first-person plural to the first-person singular. 'In spite of our outspoken optimism' and with 'all sorts of magical tricks to conjure up the spirits of the future', Arendt confesses, 'I don't know which memories and which thoughts nightly dwell in our dreams. I dare not ask for information, since I, too, had rather be an optimist' (Arendt 1994: 112). Pronominal matters of person, time and place are subject to what Roman Jakobson called 'shifting'. Deictic markers 'shift' according to the subjects and objects they are intended to designate. The result is a productive, if tense, ambiguity. The inclusive 'we' and the exclusive 'I' are demonstrably mobile identities that slip between successive, often antithetical, priorities that obtain in particular places ('here' as opposed to 'there') and times ('now' as opposed to 'then'). They work by leaving the refugee herself under-represented.

Of course, Arendt qualifies, it is often argued that 'we' should, as generous, easy-going people, be good to refugees, who are, in 'themselves', unimpeachable; the difficulty lies in discerning the difference between the true refugee and the false. This is resolved through negative identification: by defining those who aren't refugees, rather than those who are, 'where' 'they' are from, and 'how long' 'they' will stay. Writing that attempts to adequately represent the refugee often inverts this process: instead of hollowing her out, such descriptions of the refugee infuse her with a rich and complex inner life. The risk posed by such writing is that it again undoes the position of the refugee as category. Even if this undoing offers to validate the individual experiences of particular refugees, the ambiguity caused by linguistic shifting threatens to turn the exemplar into the exception. How can we understand this?

Developing her theory of refugee style, Lyndsey Stonebridge argues that Arendt uses irony to mediate between refugee as category and refugee as individual. While she notes that Arendt's switch to the first-person singular is apparently the essay's first non-ironic passage, she argues that it, too, conforms to Arendt's ironic style. The voice 'is doubled not only against itself, but also against the conditions of its own disentitlement' (Stonebridge 2011: 109). 'Irony', in Stonebridge's reading, 'produces puzzles, or perplexities, because it un-houses the voice; with irony we think we recognise what is being said, but we do not quite, because it is being said somehow differently' (2011: 105). But it also registers the difficulty of speaking, as a refugee, on behalf of refugees; assuming that, as a refugee, it is possible to explain the 'darkest speculations' of other refugees, the shift in Arendt's 'voice' coming, as it does, straight after the recognition of the large number of suicides in the refugee 'community'.

There is, then, a tension between the authoritative, public 'we', claiming to speak for all refugees, and the doubting, intellectual 'I' that registers the impossibility of this claim. This tension subverts Giorgio Agamben's confident assertion, in his 1993 essay on 'We Refugees', that Arendt 'turns the condition of the countryless refugee [. . .] upside down in order to present it as the paradigm of a new historical consciousness' (Agamben 2008: 90). Stonebridge qualifies Agamben's claim as historically problematic, since, in 1943, the paradigm is rather a matter of historical unconsciousness: the stateless being either 'unmentioned' altogether or relegated to a 'temporary category'. Nevertheless, Agamben does have a point by 1993 when he claims that the refugee has become a paradigm for a certain style of thought. Work by anthropologists such as Liisa Malkki (1995) and E. Valentine Daniel (Daniel 2002; Daniel and Knudsen 1996) confirms how after 1945 and the 1951 UN Conventions on the refugee, there was a growing awareness of the refugee as a juridico-political category. For Agamben himself, the refugee fits conveniently into the larger project of his *Homo Sacer* series (1995–present), since the elimination of the refugee's rights, together with her becoming stateless, renders her life 'bare' or *zoē*. This reading is not incompatible with the views put forward in either 'We Refugees' or *The Origins of Totalitarianism* (1951). In this regard, there is historical continuity in thinking about the refugee as an extra-national identity that presents itself as a 'limit-concept' that 'brings a radical crisis to the principles of the nation-state' (Agamben 2008: 94). For Arendt, those refugees who insist on telling the 'indecent' truth understand that 'history is no longer a closed book to them and politics is no longer the privilege of Gentiles' (Arendt 1994: 119). By 1993, for Agamben, this awareness of their position as 'vanguard of their peoples' is the basis for a profound rethinking of extraterritorial agreements, from 'the *ius* (right) of the citizen' to 'the *refugium* (refuge) of the singular', wherein the *topographical* sum of a nation might be perforated *topologically* to develop a new, extraterritorial space. But Agamben misses the implications that the refugee's conflicted identity has for style, particularly the 'indecency' of this truth. The troubled 'I' is all too easily imagined as either opposing the 'we' or being absorbed by it, where the shift in stylistic register means that it sits, in uneasy relation, alongside it.

To understand the stakes of this relation, we need to return to the moment when Arendt changes the narrative person from plural to singular: 'In spite of our outspoken optimism, we use all sorts of magical tricks to conjure up the spirits of the future.// I don't know which memories and which thoughts nightly dwell in our dreams. I dare not ask for information, since I, too, had rather be an optimist' (Arendt 1994: 112). The transition arises in response to the problem of optimism. In general, the text treats optimism with a vicious, euphemistic irony: 'those odd optimists among us who, having made a lot of optimistic speeches, go home and turn on the gas or make use of a skyscraper in quite an unexpected way' (Arendt 1994: 112). Clearly, she is not referring to an actual feeling of optimism. Rather, she refers to a discursive deployment of optimism, akin to what Lauren Berlant has called 'cruel optimism': 'a relation [that] exists when something you desire is actually an obstacle to your flourishing' (Berlant 2011: 1). Crucial for Berlant and, I would suggest, Arendt, optimism is not strictly the feeling of optimism but the underlying attachment that invests in a particular understanding of the good life: 'optimism manifests in attachments and the desire to sustain them: attachment is a *structure* of relationality' (Berlant 2011: 13). For Arendt's refugees, this optimism emerges out of the fantastical attachment to the idea that the good life might be possible, if only they were better able to merge into the host nation and/or return to the state of undifferentiated private citizen.

Arendt's essay problematises the simplicity of the concept of a refugee – a person in search of refuge – by demonstrating the aesthetic and political complexities associated with writing by, for and about refugees. But how, then, might we account for the development of the category of the refugee since 1943? Is the refugee always to be caught in the bind of the same cruel optimism? One way of bringing more nuance to these kinds of perplexities is to develop a genealogy of refugee writing.

What is a genealogy?

For E. Valentine Daniel, all refugee narratives are genealogies: 'gray, scribbled over by a mess of memories and experiences, differently valued, variously arranged, and shaded over by a range of emotions that keep shifting like the sand beneath the tide' (Daniel 2002: 282). These narratives cannot be thought of as straightforward histories of cause and effect, even if that might better suit the needs of aid workers and government agencies. They are stories that must be read 'against the grain' of the larger juridico-political discourses they inhabit, with attention to their 'local events and histories' (Daniel 2002: 282). Such attention might, Daniel argues, give rise to an alternative version of the refugee; less a sovereign individual, in the juridico-political sense, than a 'dividuated' person, whose divisions are registered less at the personal than at the modal and may extend beyond the apparent limits of their own skin.

Genealogies are conventionally understood as a subversive form of history, whereby a subterranean continuity underwrites 'normal' patterns of historical events. The great exponent of the 'subversive' genealogy, Friedrich

Nietzsche, famously called for the value of values themselves to be called into question: good/bad and good/evil. In unpacking these rival oppositions, he showed that the apparently ahistorical category, 'the good', became historically contingent in relation to rival categories of bad (where the antonym 'good' is synonymous with strength) and evil (where the antonym 'good' is opposition to strength).

In the case of refugee writing, this often entails weak – or lazy – genealogies. The most frequently touted 'universal' refugee discourses often assume that the receiving population would, in the cynical terms of J. M. Coetzee's *Diary of a Bad Year*, like to see themselves as 'a decent, generous, easy-going people' (Coetzee 2007: 111). The citizens in Coetzee's essay, 'On Asylum in Australia', mitigate their disavowed distaste for refugees by employing a means-test of worthiness, not so much of the refugees but of themselves. Their morality arguments contrast their own, 'decent' responses to refugees with those of other, 'less decent' people. 'Plenty of Third World societies', he ventriloquises, 'treat lepers with equal heartlessness' (Coetzee 2007: 111). Even as they may acknowledge the need, even the wish, to treat people humanely, Coetzee's citizens willingly blind and deafen themselves to the heartlessness and grim callousness of the 'system of deterrences, and indeed spectacle of deterrences' carried out in their name (Coetzee 2007: 112). Morality-based subversion is contingent on a competition of decencies obtaining across cultural contexts. Those who insist most on their generosity are likely to be least generous. This may come from the sense of having something to lose. As one character in Mohsin Hamid's *Exit West* wryly remarks, in a conversation comparing the poor treatment of refugees in Europe with the comparative indifference expressed in their own, non-European city, '[our situation] was different. Our country was poor. We didn't feel we had as much to lose' (Hamid 2017: 162). Whether refugees are recast as 'economic migrants' or 'terrorists' often depends on the local crisis of the moment (financial or identitarian) for the nation in question, but it evokes the same shoring up of moral capital: profuse regrets about the necessity of security measures mediated by the unforgivably worse treatment by less decent people in other parts of the world.

The historian Peter Gatrell's *The Making of the Modern Refugee*, and his essay in this volume, provide a compelling counterpoint to genealogies constructed in this weak sense. Gatrell argues convincingly that the making of the modern refugee, through war, revolution and state building, was itself absolutely integral to the formation of states, fomenting revolution and causing wars, which, in turn, generated new forms of becoming a refugee. According to Gatrell, there are 'many ways to become a refugee' (2015, 13). As he argues, because these conditions, structures and epistemologies have different configurations, while large-scale refugee crises could often trace back their unfolding to common events, the ways in which particular localities responded to these events were often quite different.

Similarly, Daniel's anthropological reading of the refugee narrative finds, in these revisions, inconsistencies and complications of 'dividuated' refugee tales, narrative devices for 'reading against the grain'. For instance, he observes in the obfuscations of refugee narratives a generic crisis of trust: 'the moment the nation-state that is supposed to protect fails to do so, or even worse, colludes in inflicting suffering on a person in its care, the germ that constitutes a refugee is formed' (Daniel 2002: 279). In his 'crisis of trust', Daniel is also describing an evolution of cruel optimism: the suspension of the refugee's comfort in 'being in the world' forces her to 'see the world differently' (2002: 279). For Daniel, a person becomes a refugee the moment she realises that a gap has opened up between her habitual existence and the state apparatus that, previously, invisibly supported it. Although he suggests that the refugee narrative might be read 'as a story in a novel', Daniel imagines that to do so would be 'to "read" refugee discourse poorly'. Instead of the novel's 'straightforward history of causes and effects', he proposes a genealogy of refugee discourse in which 'events are selectively remembered and forgotten, and interpretations selected out and selected in. And the agent that does the selecting is usually not the individual but culture and history' (Daniel 2002: 282). For all that it relies on a straw man, where 'the novel' simply presents narrative in a sequential fashion, Daniel's point is compelling precisely because his description of genealogy is so congruent with the non-sequential, episodic style that characterises novels, short stories and memoirs that recount refugee experience.

I want to suggest that a coherent genealogy of refugee writing emerges when it is understood as an intervention into refugee discourses as a problem of style. Refugee writings demonstrate historical and stylistic features, whose regulative conditions within a long tradition manifest as an intervention into discursive constructions of the refugee. Simply put, writing the refugee requires the conscientious writer, irrespective of their biographical relation to refugeedom, to pay careful attention to three features that I have been outlining here: negative identification, pronominal shifting and cruel optimism.

Exile or refugee?

The rise of refugee writing is tied to the waning of another genre: the exile memoir. Of course, it follows that not all exiles are refugees and not all refugees are exiles. At first glance, the refugee and the exile appear to occupy different metaphysical categories, since the exile is defined by the place they have left, whereas the refugee is positioned by their search for a 'place of refuge'. In popular representation, the exile may turn her placelessness into art, whereas the placelessness of the refugee is more precarious, less a resource for artistic development than an impediment to flourishing. In other words, the exile remains a Romantic, cosmopolitan figure, thriving in her individuality, whereas the refugee is more prosaic and more abject. Needless to say, the exile, as a literary figure, frequently enjoys privileges that the refugee, again in a literary sense, does not, not least the basic needs of a writer (food, shelter and a space to write). She retains the poetic authority of the 'extraterritorial': 'poets unhoused and wanderers across language. Eccentric, aloof, nostalgic, deliberately untimely. . .' (George Steiner, quoted in Said 2002: 174).

I began this chapter by recalling Said's attempt to override prior distinctions between the exile and the refugee, whereby the aesthetic connotations of exile fall away in refugee writing as a matter of scale: 'our age – with its modern warfare, imperialism, and the quasi-theological ambitions of totalitarian rules – is indeed the age of the refugee, the displaced person, mass immigration' (Said 2002: 174). 'Against this large, impersonal setting', Said continues, 'exile cannot be made to serve the notions of humanism' (2002: 174). Perhaps for this reason, the origins of refugee style have a close relationship to latter-day exile writing.[3] This is evident when Arendt's 'We Refugees' is compared to E. M. Cioran's polemic, 'Advantages of Exile' (1952).

Cioran was a Romanian exile writer who lived much of his life in Paris. Like Samuel Beckett, whom he much admired, Cioran became a linguistic exile, writing all but his earliest works in French. A caustic pessimist, Cioran wrote 'Advantages of Exile' as an evisceration of the fantasies that characterised internal economies of exchange of exile communities, wherein exile writers, writing in their home languages, peddle their experiences of exile to audiences of other exile writers, who buy this work in anticipation of peddling back their own experiences of exile. Both Arendt and Cioran insist on the historical determinism of the refugee/exile experience: 'It is not easy to be *nowhere*, when no external condition obliges you to do so [. . .] The exile achieves it without turning a hair, by the cooperation – i.e., the hostility – of history' (Cioran 1987: 76). Both draw on the image of exiles/refugees desperately asserting their parallel identities through the small distribution publications disseminated in their communities: 'No matter how scanty the number of *emigres*, they form groups, not to protect their interests but to get up subscriptions, to bleed each other white in order to publish their regrets, their cries, their echoless appeals' (Cioran 1987: 75). Both use irony to demonstrate how behind masks of either complacency or eagerness the exile/refugee hides a desperate desire to belong. 'Soon, resigned to anonymity and even intrigued by his mediocrity, [Cioran's exile] will assume the mask of a bourgeois from *nowhere in particular*. Thus he reaches the end of his lyrical career, the most stable point of his degeneration' (Cioran 1987: 78).

As if in anticipation of Cioran's examples, however, Arendt's essay subtracts refugee writing from its origins in the exile genre. Her first sentence, remember, declares the desire *not* to identify as a refugee, in stark contrast to Cioran's exiles, who seem all too pathologically committed to their exile identity. This rejection of identification is emphasised in a further difference: though similar magazines are drawn up for the refugee as for the exile 'to bleed each other white', the refugees mark theirs as for 'Americans of German Language' rather than German exiles (Arendt 1994: 110).

Cioran's exiles turn cruel optimism into a form of savage activation: 'the more we are disposed the more intense our appetites and our illusions become' (Cioran 1987: 74). For Arendt, this optimism disguises a fatalistic passivity: 'our proclaimed cheerfulness is based on a dangerous readiness for death' (Arendt 1994: 112). If Cioran can sneer at the exile who becomes the bourgeois from nowhere in particular, the pathos of Arendt's exemplary refugee, Mr Cohen, is that he will never become that bourgeois, despite his desperate attempts, his desperate desire, to do just that.

Refugee writing here subtracts itself from a longer tradition of exile writing in the refugee's desire not to exist as a refugee. Paradoxically, non-fiction writing by non-refugees about refugees risks achieving this evacuation of the identity when it sets up its refugee protagonists as either exemplars of a condition or its exceptions, such as in the South African non-fiction writer Jonny Steinberg's *A Man of Good Hope* (2014). Steinberg's memoir tells the story of a Somalian refugee who makes his way to South Africa to start a business, is exposed to numerous acts of xenophobia, and eventually relocates to the USA. The book climaxes in the realisation that

> it has taken this long to see him properly, I think, because the language with which he describes himself is misleading. When he told me his story he did so in the words of a refugee, for these are the words he must use, always, at every border post he approaches, at every government office outside which he queues. (Steinberg 2014: 312)

For Steinberg, Asad's story emerges as an exception against a background of refugee language. By rendering Asad's story exceptional, Steinberg reproduces an exemplary quality of the refugee narrative: the exemplar as exception.

The pathos of privilege

The stylistic practice in the essays of Arendt and Cioran might usefully explain Steinberg's problematic distinction between the exemplary refugee and the exceptional refugee in genealogical terms. Refugee writing has a relation to the narratives of cosmopolitanism, exile and counter-exile that precede it. But it also eschews the particular pathos of privilege in these prior forms, which too often foreground privileged writers mourning their statelessness. It replaces this pathos of privilege with a pathos of agency – as is mapped out in Steinberg's memoir. The pathos of agency is particularly placeless. Unlike the 'world state' welcomed by the cosmopolitan, or the lost nation-state mourned by the exile and transcended by the counter-exile, the statelessness of the refugee is 'a political and legal wilderness' (Stonebridge 2011: 102). Under these conditions, the refugee is not just 'a paradigm of what it means to be deprived of rights, politics and culture, but a person who enacts that deprivation in her speaking being' (Stonebridge 2011: 109).

Similarly, for Judith Butler, when writing of the refugee, 'we cannot presume a movement from an established state to a state of metaphysical abandonment; these movements are more complex and require a different kind of description' (Butler and Spivak 2007: 8). But, according to Butler, this description does not appear in the Arendt of *The Origins of Totalitarianism*, who 'restricts her understanding of the refugee to that of the exile' (Butler and Spivak 2007: 17). *Pace* Butler, Arendt does not restrict her treatment of the refugee to the exile in 'We Refugees', for reasons that I have already shown. But between Stonebridge and Butler, we can make a few axiomatic claims. First, mere movement cannot serve to distinguish the refugee category from the exile. There must be some concomitant loss of agency attendant on an appeal to hospitality. Second, the political terms of refugee and exile are necessarily differentiated as a matter of privilege.

Stonebridge rightly identifies privilege in the irony that Arendt is able to bring to bear on her situation, in the 'I' moments of the essay. But she measures her recognition, and explication, of Arendt's use of irony in her text against two external political features: Arendt's own situation as a refugee from Nazi Germany and the later work she would produce on statelessness in *The Origins of Totalitarianism* (1951). In concert with these 'external' features, there are complex stylistic dynamics within the essay, particular in the use of deictic 'shifters' to develop the 'different type of description' distinctive to forms of refugee writing: the We–I relation. In a narrative continuity that connects Arendt to Steinberg's Asad, the political need to be defined as a refugee does not prevent the refugee from attempting to evade, in private confession, the refugee label. Neither does the desire to evade the label, and the concomitant associations with metaphysical abandonment raised by Butler, mean, as Steinberg assumes, that the label should be discarded. If anything, Arendt's essay explicitly states that the disavowal of refugee status (except as a judicial category) may be a constitutive feature of the refugee as such.

The first line of 'We Refugees' frames Arendt's disavowal as dislike, which is also a sustained point of interest in Mohsin Hamid's *Exit West* (2017). *Exit West* traces the movement of Saeed and Nadia from their unnamed city to Greece, the UK and the USA. Although Hamid opens the novel 'in a city swollen by refugees', for the most part the novel treats Saeed and Nadia as 'migrants'. At one moment 'migrant' is made synonymous with refugee, but only in retrospect: while living in London, Saeed recalls his 'fellow refugees' at the 'migrant camp' in Mykonos (Hamid 2017: 129). Even then, their initial encounter with the camp has it only looking 'like a refugee camp' (2017: 100). The majority of the implicitly 'refugee' spaces that Saeed and Nadia move through (together with the camps, there are squats and other housing projects) are likened to transitory locations not usually associated with refuge. So, the camp in Mykonos is likened to 'a trading post in an old-time gold rush' (2017: 101), the squat in London to 'a university dormitory' (2017: 128), and the shanty town in Marin produces 'sounds like a festival' (2017: 205). The refugees who people the streets of the unnamed city at the beginning of the novel may pitch tents, erect lean-tos and sleep rough like Saeed and Nadia (2017: 23), but they do not acquire the richness of 'non-refugee' experience that Hamid will grant his two protagonists.

This recalls Arendt's essay, yet the novel is firmly contemporary. Although the city of origin is left markedly unmarked, characters' names, matters of dress and cultural practice encourage a Western reader to imagine a predominantly Islamic city in central or southern Asia or the Middle East. Those familiar with Hamid's earlier works, such as *Moth Smoke* (2000) or *The Reluctant Fundamentalist* (2007), might surmise that the location is Lahore, Pakistan. The succession of locations (Greece, London, USA) through which Saeed and Nadia pass has a more recent, and poignant, trajectory in the projected route taken by refugees from the Syrian civil war (2011–present). In fact, the stark contrast between the unmarked city of origin and the marked places of arrival indicts 'native' responses to refugees: it matters not where they come from, what matters is the disruptive force of their arrival.

In order to anonymise the city, while at the same time exploring multiple trajectories of global exchange, Hamid adopts a similar linking device to that used by Colson Whitehead in *The Underground Railroad* (2016): a quasi-magical means of transition between two geographically separate locations. By removing, or reducing, accounts of travel between locations (as in the case of Narnian wardrobes, travel between the doors is instantaneous), Hamid erases any travel-related clues that might identify the city of origin. He also opens up the possibility of understanding the refugee crises as necessarily having unintended, global consequences. Thus, brief vignettes about unnamed characters in Sydney, Rio de Janeiro, Vienna and Amsterdam illustrate the unpredictable nature of the doors (no one knows where they might lead), and also facilitate a slow collapse of borders: 'without borders nations appeared to be becoming somewhat illusory' (Hamid 2017: 155). This collapse breeds conflict between 'migrants and nativists' (2017: 155).

Arendt's refugees pick up the markers of new locations quickly: 'after four weeks in France or six weeks in America, we pretended to be Frenchmen or Americans' (Arendt 1994: 111) – hence poor Mr Cohen who, in Agamben's words, 'after having been 150 percent German, 150 percent Viennese, 150 percent French, must bitterly realize in the end' that Arendt's conclusion to 'We Refugees' is correct: '*on ne parvient pas deux fois* [one fails twice – and one cannot pass twice]' (Agamben 2008: 90). In *Exit West*, however, the characters do not blend, nor are they given the opportunity to: even as they change to assume the habits of the 'natives', so 'their very presence here meant that its people and manners and ways and habits were undergoing considerable change' (Hamid 2017: 178). In its insistence on the mutual plasticity of migrants and natives,

Hamid's novel asserts a strange relationship between past, present and future. No longer comfortable with 'forgetting more efficiently' like Arendt's refugees, or Steinberg's 'suspension' between a belonging past and a belonging future, Hamid writes a prose that registers the changes in feelings, identities, paths from the past into the present in preparation for the future. Consider this sentence, for example:

> Saeed's father then summoned Nadia to his room [. . .] and said that he was entrusting her with his son's life [. . .] and he hoped she would one day marry his son [. . .] but this was up to them to decide [. . .] and she sat there with him in silence and the minutes passed, and in the end she promised, and it was an easy promise to make because she had at that time no thoughts of leaving Saeed [. . .] (Hamid 2017: 93)

'Then' and 'at that time' gesture to the difference between times of narrative (the story) and narration (telling the story). But there is also prolepsis, the time of 'hope', and iteration, the time taken by 'ands'. Already, we have the suggestion that the proleptic hope will be frustrated (it is only 'at that time' that she has no thoughts of leaving Saeed), while the time that the conversation takes, in that present, is marked by 'silence' and 'minutes passed'. These features of Hamid's style etiolate Arendt's 'spirit' of the future by presumptively curtailing its possibility. The effect is not to restrict the complex possibilities of refugee experience. If anything, he takes what was for Arendt a vanguard, and for Agamben a paradigm, and turns it into a universal condition. In what is perhaps a triumph of cruel optimism, his narrator comments, somewhat sententiously, 'everyone migrates, even if we stay in the same houses our whole lives, because we can't help it. We are all migrants through time' (Hamid 2017: 209).

Yet Hamid's universalising of migrant/refugee experience may have uncomfortable consequences. The novel's focus – the lived realities of a refugee couple – suggests that these sententious asides are meant to be treated with some irony. Arendt calls this disavowal of circumstance 'forgetting'. Hamid prefers 'nostalgia'. In each case, the imperfect censure of the past provokes 'ghosts' or 'spirits', which arise in response to attempts to efface the concrete in the name of the metaphysical.

The nostalgia of ghosts and spirits

In refugee writing, the figure of the ghost, a trope that frequently represents memory and forgetting, can act as objective correlative for Berlant's cruel optimism, since the ghost acts both as reminder of a good life now past and obstruction to a good life to come. In the collection of short stories *The Refugees*, by academic and Pulitzer prize-winning author Viet

Thanh Nguyen, ghosts, both literal and metaphorical, come to stand in for, and in the way of, fantasies of the good life. In the opening story, 'Black-eyed women', the narrator, a 'ghost-writer', is visited by her dead brother. Ghosts like her brother are 'pallid creatures, more frightened of us than we are of them' (Nguyen 2017: 21). For the refugees in Nguyen's stories, ghost stories are 'historical accounts from reliable sources' (2017: 6). Thus the brother provides an oblique, troubling link back into the narrator's child-hood trauma as a 'boat person', the term for South-East Asian refugees who took to the sea after the Vietnam War ended in 1975. Nguyen's sensitive treatment of the brother's death and the narrator's rape suggests that the narrator herself is ghost-like: 'You died too', the brother says, 'you just don't know it' (2017: 17). More importantly, it opens up the possibility of reading the rest of the stories in the collection as those stories the mother tells to the narrator, stories that may 'happen all the time' and yet need to be told so as 'to be found, garments shed by ghosts' (2017: 20, 21).

If Nguyen does not avoid the refugee label, neither should his active endorsement of it (he mentions his refugee experience several times) fully detach from the structure of negative identification. Even as he identifies with his refugee identity, he disidentifies with a total immersion in that identity. What changes, from Arendt to Nguyen, is how refugee intellectuals approach assimilation: taken as an optimistic ideal, albeit with some irony, by Arendt, aspirational assimilation becomes, for Nguyen, a hurdle overcome during his academic career. Turning back to the memories of refugee experience, then, he develops a more nuanced response to the nostalgia that seems so toxic in Arendt.[4]

In an earlier essay on tensions in the treatment of refugees between South-East Asian studies, South-East Asian American studies and Asian American studies, Nguyen diagnoses two kinds of refugee nostalgia. Restorative nostalgia, as Svetlana Boym argues, means that 'the past can be recovered wholly and the lost homeland can be restored authentically' (Nguyen 2012: 912). Reflective nostalgia, on the other hand, 'regards the past with more ambivalence, tolerating shadowy ambiguity, fearing not so much an other but the absolute truth' (Nguyen 2012: 912). In both, the loss of homeland gives memories potential, 'which is of course how our greatest nostalgias are born' (Hamid 2017: 204). But while the former paints a false image of the future, in which the past may be brought, whole and unimpeached, to replace a troubled present, the latter acknowledges, with all Arendt's indecency, the terrible losses of the present.

Nguyen departs from the standard refugee narrative by recalling that many 'former' refugees from Vietnam, living in the United States, actually enjoy privileges that far exceed those of their former compatriots, who were never refugees. In the final story of *The Refugees*, 'Fatherland', a returnee's story is told from the perspective of a half-sister, who remained in Vietnam. The reader follows the excitement of the family in Vietnam as they are showered with gifts by the returnee, Vivien, who is apparently a doctor. The *volta* happens when the half-sister, Phuong, tells Vivien that she wants to go to America. Vivien confesses that she is actually an unemployed receptionist to excuse her more blatant betrayal: she won't help Phuong to leave Vietnam or go to America. Later, Phuong decides to use lingerie that Vivien gave her, as a provocative admonition 'to be bad', to prostitute herself. In symbolic recognition of this decision to sacrifice her fantasy – that the good life might be found in America – Phuong also burns the photographs of the trip, the better to efface memories of their encounter. Here, we find in practice what in his critical work Nguyen called the 'double edged' discourse about refugees: 'If it critiques nation-states, it must also be unsentimental in critiquing refugee aspirations to national belonging, even when those refugees are far from elite' (Nguyen 2012: 931). The *longue durée* in Nguyen's *The Refugees* offers a firm riposte to relations between refugees and states. Against the nation-state's arbitrarily granted or withdrawn sanctuary, Nguyen contemplates how the affective concerns of privileged refugees may, over time, have a greater influence over the obstruction or flourishing of fellow refugees.

There are more than merely generic differences between *A Man of Good Hope*, *Exit West* and *The Refugees*. Their geographical diversity testifies to a proliferation of refugee stories about displacements over the past seventy years in locations across the globe: the trajectory of *A Man of Good Hope* runs from Somalia to South Africa, in *Exit West* the characters move from an unnamed Islamic state to the UK, while *The Refugees* connects Vietnam and the US. Underneath more recent shifts and changes, however, there lies a striking continuity, from Arendt to Nguyen, in the literary treatment of refugee optimism. Arendt's 'We Refugees' took as its target the optimism of refugees. Rather than the oppressors who caused people to flee, the physical hardships of the journeys, the bureaucratic processes at their conclusion, Arendt focused on an 'optimism' 'based on a dangerous readiness for death' (1994: 112).

Optimism is what Cioran derides in the exile, what carries Asad to South Africa in *A Man of Good Hope*, what drives the characters in *Exit West* and *The Refugees*. In each case, this optimism is, to use Berlant's words, an 'obstruction to their flourishing'. Berlant concludes *Cruel Optimism* with a double bind: 'even with an image of a better good life available to sustain your optimism, it is awkward and it is threatening to detach from what is already not working' (2011: 263). Nguyen finds in his *Refugees* a similar obstruction. It is not enough to say that Steinberg and Hamid simply miss the necessity of awkward and threatening detachment; rather, refugee writing must navigate a choice all too easy to render rhetorically, all too difficult to actualise, between awkward detachment and just about managing. This may be the challenge for a genealogy of refugee writing in the present.

Notes

1. E. Valentine Daniel noted the 'hydrophobic' tendency in the collective nouns colloquially used for refugees in 2002. More than ten years later, the UK's then Prime Minister, David Cameron, exploited a similar 'entomophobia' when he referred to 'swarms of refugees'.
2. Representing the refugee repeats the paradox that Gayatri Chakravorty Spivak associates with representing the subaltern: when the subaltern is given a voice, they cease to be subaltern (Morris and Spivak 2010). Certainly, many of the structural features of subalternity – material loss of agency, rhetorical subordination, political marginalisation – obtain in the case of the refugee. The philosophical equation of the refugee with the subaltern fails when forms of refugee writing are subjected to historical scrutiny, particularly in light of the critical role that refugees have had in the formation of modern nation-states (Gatrell 2015). Refugee metaphors of the past, which paralleled those of the exile and the émigré, today give way to the more dehumanising 'flow' metaphors for reasons that have at least as much to do with political censure as with aesthetic development.
3. See further Stonebridge (2018).
4. In a *PMLA* special issue on Nguyen's work, Yogita Goyal asks 'how might centering the refugee reframe existing classifications of ethnicity, race, and national origin and serve as the ethical optic through which current worlds become legible?' (2018: 383). Similarly, Caroline Rody asks, 'why should [the writing] not display a dislocated, refugee-immigrant subject's virtuosic juggling of disparate, unwieldy sets of forces and sources, or his urgent search for answering faces and voices in his new "super" nation home, while he seeks to forge an articulate, literary "I"?' (2018: 399). Nguyen himself responds to the first question by dubbing it a 'refugee optic', and pointing this optic towards the second question: 'Dislocation is my location, one that has been inhabited by many others before me' (Nguyen 2018: 432).

Bibliography

Agamben, Giorgio (2008), 'Beyond human rights', *Social Engineering*, 15: 90–5.

Arendt, Hannah (1958), *The Origins of Totalitarianism*, 2nd edn (Cleveland, OH: Meridian).

Arendt, Hannah (1994), 'We refugees', in Marc Robinson (ed.), *Altogether Elsewhere: Writers on Exile* (Boston, MA: Faber and Faber), 110–19.

Berlant, Lauren (2011), *Cruel Optimism* (Durham, NC: Duke University Press).

Butler, Judith, and Gayatri Chakravorty Spivak (2007), *Who Sings the Nation-State? Language, Politics, Belonging* (Oxford: Seagull Books).

Cioran, E. M. (1987), *Temptation to Exist*, trans. Richard Howard (London: Quartet Books).

Coetzee, J. M. (2007), *Diary of a Bad Year* (London: Harvill and Secker).

Daniel, E. Valentine (2002), 'The refugee: a discourse on displacement', in Jeremy MacClancey (ed.), *Exotic No More: Anthropology on the Front Lines* (Chicago: University of Chicago Press), 270–86.

Daniel, E. Valentine, and John Chr. Knudsen (eds) (1996), *Mistrusting Refugees* (Berkeley: University of California Press).

Gatrell, Peter (2015), *The Making of the Modern Refugee*, 2nd edn (Oxford: Oxford University Press).

Goyal, Yogita (2018), 'Un-American: refugees and the Vietnam War', *PMLA*, 133.2: 378–83.

Hamid, Mohsin (2017), *Exit West* (London: Hamish Hamilton).

Koopman, Colin (2013), *Genealogy as Critique: Foucault and the Problems of Modernity* (Bloomington: Indiana University Press).

Morris, Rosalind C., and Gayatri Chakravorty Spivak (2010), *Can the Subaltern Speak? Reflections on the History of an Idea* (New York: Columbia University Press).

Nguyen, Viet Thanh (2012), 'Refugee memories and Asian American critique', *positions: asia critique*, 20.3: 911–42.

Nguyen, Viet Thanh (2017), *The Refugees* (London: Corsair).

Nguyen, Viet Thanh (2018), 'Dislocation is my location', *PMLA*, 133.2: 428–36.

Rody, Caroline (2018), 'Between "I" and "we": Viet Thanh Nguyen's interethnic multitudes', *PMLA*, 133.2: 396–405.

Rose, Arthur (2013), 'Insomnia and exile: Cioran's separate man', in Axel Englund and Anders Olsson (eds), *Languages of Exile: Migration and Multilingualism in Twentieth-Century Literature* (Oxford: Peter Lang), 101–18.

Said, Edward (2002 [2000]), 'Reflections on exile', in *Reflections on Exile and Other Essays* (Cambridge, MA: Harvard University Press), 137–49.

Shaw, Caroline Emily (2012), 'The British, persecuted foreigners and the emergence of the refugee category in nineteenth-century Britain', *Immigrants and Minorities*, 30.2–3, 239–62.

Steinberg, Jonny (2014), *A Man of Good Hope* (Johannesburg: Jonathan Ball).

Stonebridge, Lyndsey (2011), *The Judicial Imagination: Writing after Nuremberg* (Edinburgh: Edinburgh University Press).

Stonebridge, Lyndsey (2018), *Placeless People: Writings, Rights, and Refugees* (Oxford: Oxford University Press)

Whitehead, Colson (2016), *The Underground Railroad* (New York: Doubleday).

Chapter 4

Genres of Refugee Writing

Anna Bernard

The Palestinian novelist Ghassan Kanafani's early short story 'Al-qamīs al-masrūq' ('The Stolen Shirt', 1958) features a young father, Abu Al-Abd, whom the reader encounters preparing to stay up all night to dig a channel in the mud to divert the rain from his family's tent in an unnamed refugee camp (Kanafani 2015). Abu Al-Abd is worrying about his ill and malnourished son and his wife's insistence that he find work. He fantasises about stealing one of the sacks of flour provided by the 'International Relief Agency' (the story's name for UNRWA) and reselling it on the black market, which is the only way he can think of to make money. He encounters a fellow camp resident, Abu Sameer, who tells him that he has been carrying out this very act, selling the sacks via 'the blond American at the agency' who is in charge of their distribution. This is why the next shipment of flour has been delayed. Abu Sameer invites Abu Al-Abd to join the operation, but the enraged Abu Al-Abd, filled with an 'awesome violence', brings down his shovel on Abu Sameer's head and kills him instantly. His wife pulls him away from the corpse. He returns to the tent 'drenched in water and mud', embraces his son, remembers his desire to buy him a new shirt, and begins to cry.

Kanafani's story won the Kuwait Literary Prize the year he wrote it (Al-Nakib 2015: 91), but it was not published until 1982, a decade after his assassination in Beirut. To date, there is no English translation in print, in contrast with the relatively wide international circulation of Kanafani's later fiction. One reason for the story's neglect may be its rejection of the enduring demand that writing about refugees adopt a 'politics of innocence' by presenting its protagonists as virtuous individuals who exhibit no anger, deceit or violence (Cox 2015: 29). 'The Stolen Shirt' conveys the dishonesty of this stipulation, and instead asks: what kind of realism requires that its subjects be saints? Might the irate refugee be more real than the smiling refugee? The criminal adult male more real than the innocent young boy? By giving his short story this aphoristic quality, Kanafani links it to the fable, a form that issues 'a direct address [. . .] to the other as at once the you who reads and who might be lured into an identification' (Keenan 1997: 56–7). This generic association converts a narrative that initially seems like a documentary account of life in the camp into a moral tale (Rangan 2017: 192). The story asks the reader to consider not only what she might feel in Abu Al-Abd's position, but also what she might do.

This emphasis on the event and the scene – as Edward Said wrote of Kanafani's best-known work *Rijāl fī al-shams* (*Men in the Sun*, 1963) – is one of several conventions of the modern short story form that are mobilised by 'The Stolen Shirt' (Kanafani 1978 [1963]; see Said 2002: 51–4). It relies on a spare, stripped-down descriptive style; its characters' behaviours and motives are sketched quickly, not developed over the course of a longer plot; and it ends abruptly and inconclusively, soliciting the reader's engagement by inviting her to imagine what happens next. It is an advocacy narrative, in so far as it asks the reader to apprehend the plight of the residents of the Palestinian refugee camps, but it does not specify an action for the reader to perform. Instead, it leaves the crisis that it depicts unresolved, and for the protagonist, considerably worse by the end of the story. 'The Stolen Shirt' thus sets out a role for literature that is at once restrained and ambitious. On the one hand, Kanafani denies the reader the consolation of the idea that the act of reading will make any difference to the real situation described in the text. On the other, he insists that the lives of Palestinian refugees must be rendered with clarity and commitment, combining 'a critical power' with 'a devotion to what must not be destroyed', as he would later put it (Kanafani 1990: 139).

'The Stolen Shirt' reminds us that our thinking about the value and impact of refugee writing is inseparable from the question of literary craft, and therefore from the question of literary genre. The genres of refugee writing are the genres of writing itself: they are literary and extraliterary, fictional and non-fictional, single-authored and collaborative. While some genres are more commonly associated with the representation of refugee experience than others, because they lend themselves more readily to activism or can be produced more easily in difficult circumstances, the full range of writing by and about refugees spans poetry, short fiction, novels, drama, graphic narrative, children's literature, letters, theory, journalism, legislation and human rights reporting.[1] Unlike the spaces that refugees traverse or in which they are trapped, there are no hard borders between these genres. They share settings, characters and points of reference: the camp, the detention centre, the border guard, the smuggler, the shipping container or raft (Farrier 2012a: 1). They take inspiration from older modes of narrating migration, exile and pilgrimage, invoking ancient and medieval works such as Homer's *Odyssey*, Chaucer's *Canterbury Tales* or Ibn Battuta's *Riḥla* (*Travels*) (Cox 2014: 11). They draw on other forms – testimony, elegy, homily, soliloquy, adventure – that have been transformed by the proliferation of refugee stories in the twentieth and twenty-first centuries, and that cannot now be conceived in isolation from the age of mass displacement and statelessness.[2]

Among the recent examples of this body of work in English-language circulation, three genres are especially conspicuous: poetry, verbatim theatre and graphic narrative. While these works share thematic and political preoccupations, the properties of each genre frame refugee experience differently, and they ask different kinds of imaginative engagement from their audiences. Poetry is a major genre of refugee writing in part because of the relative ease of its production and circulation: it can be written in detention or in transit, it lends itself to writing workshops, and it can be published in pamphlets or anthologies and on websites. However, it is also significant for its association with both rousing public recitation and the lyric 'I', which emphasise the reader's role as the text's recipient and highlight the tension between collective and individual narratives of refugee experience. Verbatim theatre is also among the more prominent forms of contemporary refugee advocacy, with companies such as the UK-based ice&fire, which I discuss below, performing their work in various educational and community venues. Although these productions are based on refugee testimony, they are often edited and performed by non-refugee artists for an implied audience of other non-refugees. They thus foreground the problems of voice, substitution and identification that underlie all depictions of refugee experience, situating the performers as a point of liaison between the audience and the real people that the protagonists represent (Cox 2015: 23–60; Farrier 2011: 182–93). More recently, graphic narrative has become a key genre of refugee writing, especially for accounts of refugees' journeys from the Middle East and Africa to Europe, with numerous works published in English and English translation from French, German, Arabic and other languages in the last decade. The form is notable for its synthesis of visual and narrative conventions for representing the figure of the refugee, and for its reliance on the quest narrative, which both endorses and interrogates the idea of the refugee's ultimate redemption as a citizen of the host country. A number of the examples of these genres that I will discuss are, like 'The Stolen Shirt', by and about Palestinian refugees. This selection reflects my own academic background, but it also indicates the long duration of Palestinian statelessness and displacement, and the centrality of this struggle to any discussion of contemporary refugee experience.

Approaching refugee writing through the prism of genre compels critical analysis to go beyond the itemisation of themes and information that the overt politics and didactic messaging of these texts can sometimes encourage. These works stage an appeal to the reader, mirroring and yet often undermining the 'bureaucratic performance' (Jeffers 2012: 35–42) that refugees and asylum seekers are compelled to enact at the borders, courtrooms and visa application centres of their host countries. They proffer the idea that literature provides an alternative site for refugees' claims for recognition and justice, a site where such claims might be received with openness rather than suspicion, and where the reader might be willing to act as an ally rather than a judge. To take this proposition seriously, we must consider not just what these texts say, but how they say it, and understand advocacy as a driver of aesthetic innovation as well as a political project.

'I was once like you': poetry as testimony, accusation, elegy

Poetry's ability to mimic a direct communication from speaker to reader lends itself especially well to advocacy. The reader may be addressed in the second person; the poem may include intimate details or thoughts that make it seem like a private address; the speaker may insinuate or spell out their desired response to the text. This characteristic links the poetry of advocacy to activist uses of testimony, which also privilege the speaker–recipient relationship and anticipate that the recipient will not only believe the testimony, but be transformed by it. In anthologies of poetry by and about refugees, paratextual materials often attribute this capacity to the works they include. For instance, *Are You Happy With That?* (2013), a collection of poems by refugee and non-refugee activists based in Wales, includes a list of activist websites at the beginning and end of the anthology, along with a combative postscript that repeatedly demands, through the use of anaphora, whether the reader is 'happy with' the injustices of the British asylum system that the poems depict (People Seeking Sanctuary in Wales 2013: 196). Similarly, *Mediterranean* (2018), a compilation by the online US magazine *Warscapes*, brings together poetry and other art forms about African and Arab migrants' journeys to Europe. It enjoins the reader to read beyond the text by providing a 'starter syllabus' of recommended works of literature, film, art and theory in an appendix (Shingarpure et al. 2018: 89–91). These addenda endorse an instrumentalist understanding of poems by and about refugees, suggesting that the encounter between poem and reader will have failed if the reader does not take further action. At the same time, the editors' assumption that the encounter with the poems will be transformative ascribes to poetry an intrinsic relational value that does not depend on what the reader does next.

The British-Somali poet Warsan Shire's celebrated prose poem 'Conversations About Home' (2011) presumes an intimacy between the refugee speaker and the non-refugee reader by integrating the voice of a lyric 'I' whose testimony does not satisfy the demand for legal evidence into the structure of the asylum interview. The poem is set 'at the Deportation Centre', and it begins, as the title suggests, as if in the middle of a conversation:

> Well, I think home spat me out, the blackouts and the curfews like tongue against loose teeth. God, do you know how difficult it is, to talk about the day your own city dragged you by the hair, past the old prison, past the school gates, past the burning torsos erected on poles like flags? [. . .] No one leaves home unless home is the mouth of a shark. (Shire 2011: loc. 306)

The speaker responds to the bureaucratic demand to 'talk about the day' by shifting to the second person, urging the reader to imagine what it would be like to receive this request. She transposes the meaning of the mouth, turning it from the site of production of speech (and thus legal testimony) into a site of physical vulnerability and violence. This emphasis on the mouth persists throughout the poem: 'I tore up and ate my own passport'; 'I'm bloated with language'; 'Look at all these borders, foaming at the mouth'; 'my mouth becomes a sink full of blood'; 'men who look like my father, pulling out my teeth and nails'; 'his manhood in my mouth' (Shire 2011: loc. 306–22). This trope signals the speaker's experience of displacement, torture and sexual violence without satisfying the juridical demand for details. The first references to the mouth metaphorise the speaker's social and legal precarity as physical danger; later references indicate actual physical assault. Alongside this figurative sequence, the speaker alludes to the devastating losses of her children and her mother, again without providing details, and laments her exile in Britain.

However, in the final stanza the intimacy of the speaker's testimony gives way to a more antagonistic address:

> Do they not know that stability is like a lover with a sweet mouth upon your body one second; the next you are a tremor lying on the floor [. . .] All I can say is, I was once like you, the apathy, the pity, the ungrateful placement and now my home is the mouth of a shark, now my home is the barrel of a gun. (Shire 2011: loc. 322)

Here the connotation of the mouth shifts, designating not only the speaker's lack of safety, but also the contingency of the reader's own sense of security. The juxtaposition of the lover's mouth with the shark's names a shared precarity between speaker and addressee that the speaker's deporters refuse to acknowledge. The return to the second person implicates the reader alongside the speaker's other persecutors, withdrawing their comfortable status as a presumed ally. This shift to a more accusatory, jeremiadic register mobilises poetry's association with public recitation and thus with public political speech, asserting the reader's civic as well as moral responsibility for the speaker's story.

Yet although Shire's poem subverts the documentary requirements of official testimony, it does not disrupt the broader analogy between poetry and personal testimony. This conjunction distinguishes it from poetry by and about refugees that is more self-consciously modernist, such as the work of the leading Palestinian poet Mahmoud Darwish. Darwish generally eschews the simulation of testimony, instead employing a non-narrative and non-referential aesthetic that gives the impression of 'attending to the negative, of seeing what is both there and not there' (Stonebridge 2015: 1335). In 'The Earth is Closing on Us' ('*Taḍīqu binā al-arḍ*', 1984), the lyric 'I' is replaced with a lyric 'we', affirming a shared history of dispossession but also challenging the assumption that the Palestinian 'I' automatically represents other Palestinians. The collective experience of statelessness is conveyed through a series of evocative but opaque figures of displacement and exclusion:

> The earth is closing on us [. . .] and
> we tear off our limbs to pass through.
> [. . .] We saw the faces of those who'll
> throw our children
> Out of the windows of this last space. [. . .]
> Where should we go after the last frontiers? Where should the birds
> fly after the last sky? [. . .]
> We will die here, here in the last passage. Here and here our blood
> will plant its olive tree. (Darwish 2005: 13)

Like Shire, Darwish evades the juridical demand for detail by metaphorising social and legal injury as physical harm, while also evoking actual physical violence against Palestinians. He pushes the metaphor further than Shire does, conveying the magnitude of the Palestinian dispossession by describing it as a massacre. Denying citizenship to children is like throwing them out of a window; allowing refugees to die in exile is like amputating their limbs or spilling their blood.

However, instead of holding the reader to account for this violence, the poem dwells on its subjects' losses in an elegiac mode that refuses the possibility of redemption. It thus adopts the disconsolate mode of mourning that Jahan Ramazani claims is 'inextricable' from modern poetry (Ramazani 1994: 1–2). The speaker mourns the future as much as the past and present: she or he mourns the deaths that are to come, and an ongoing exile whose end has become unimaginable. The speaker's rhetorical questions prompt grief rather than anger, pointing out that there is still no answer to the question of where the Palestinians should go, only an intransigent ban on their movement. The repetition of the word 'here' (*hunā*) at the end of the poem reiterates their entrapment in the 'last space' of non-citizenship. The poem seeks to transform its subjects' relationship to the reader not by documenting their suffering, but by demanding that the reader apprehend the enormity of their dispossession.

Testimony in performance: substitution and identification in verbatim theatre

This demand for recognition of the severity and injustice of the hardships that refugees have endured is also a key feature of verbatim and other documentary theatre based on refugee testimony. Like testimonial poetry, verbatim theatre values speech as a medium for conveying a true account of historical events and personal experience. As Derek Paget has put it, 'the very fact that *someone has said it* adds to the power of these words' (Paget 2010: 185; see also Cox 2015:

30). The use of verbatim testimony also promises to resolve some of the anxieties about appropriation and 'parasitism' (Jeffers 2012: 13) that can arise in creative productions about refugees by non-refugee artists and activists, since it does not invent or imagine refugees' experiences, but presents them as a 'direct' transmission from the protagonists. The genre is most often associated with appeals for solidarity with refugees among Western audiences, but it has also been used in other contexts, notably in the Ramallah-based Ashtar Theatre's staging of *The Syrian Monologues* in 2015–16.[3]

The promise of immediacy notwithstanding, there are in fact various forms of mediation involved in the theatrical performance of refugee testimony. Producers, directors and actors must make decisions about the editing of transcripts, selection and ordering of testimonies, use of monologue and dialogue, casting, staging and characterisation. Formats range from the rehearsed reading to fictional dramatisation, although they often share a plot structure in which information about the refugee protagonists is gradually revealed, with the apparent aim of slowly bringing the uninformed viewer onside.[4] Each of these decisions is part of verbatim theatre's particular form of 'innovation and experimentation', which is driven by the need to produce a 'strong and immediate impact' on the audience (Jeffers 2012: 149). The impulse of this theatre is reactive, arguably to a greater extent than the other genres I am considering.[5] It seeks to counter the public demonisation of refugees by providing information about detention practices, asylum policies and procedures, and the extreme circumstances in which people decide to migrate, emphasising the potential for empathetic identification with the protagonists.

The UK-based theatre company ice&fire has been a visible and prolific producer of verbatim theatre about refugees, with a repertoire that includes *Asylum Monologues* (2006), *Asylum Dialogues* (2008), *Palestine Monologues* (2008), *The Illegals* (2008), *On a Clear Day You Can See Dover* (2010, about the migrant camp in Calais), *Afghan Monologues* (2011) and *This Is Who I Am* (2017, about LGBT+ refugees).[6] On their website, ice&fire emphasise their address to the audience: 'We put human rights at the core of everything we do to make accessible theatre for a wide range of audiences across the UK [. . .] We believe that through theatre we can bring unparalleled understanding and empathy to some of the world's most urgent issues.'[7] The website offers some formal indicators of audience response, including an external evaluation of the success of *The Illegals* in raising audience awareness of the situation of undocumented migrants in London. The report praises the production for 'successfully put[ting] across' five 'key messages' about the experiences of this demographic, as measured by the responses of post-performance focus groups (Charity Doctor LLP 2008: 4).

Critics of ice&fire and other producers of verbatim theatre about refugees express concerns about the genre's didacticism; its reliance on imaginative substitution, which can reproduce the distinction between protagonist and viewer instead of subverting it; and its tendency to represent characters as types rather than complex individuals (Farrier 2012b: 433; Farrier 2011: 186; Cox 2015: 58). These are valid objections, and yet they risk overlooking the productions' deliberate privileging of utility over 'art', which promotes a pedagogic emphasis on 'breadth of content' rather than conventional character and plot development (Paget 2010: 181). These plays also tend to be self-conscious about the limits of their representations (Woolley 2014: 3). In particular, the invitation to imaginative substitution is often more reflective than it might first appear. For instance, Sonja Linden's fictional plays *I Have Before Me a Remarkable Document Given to Me By a Young Lady from Rwanda* (2003) and *Crocodile Seeking Refuge* (2005), which are drawn from refugee testimony and listed in ice&fire's repertoire, cast doubt on non-refugee characters' responses to refugee characters. In *I Have Before Me*, the British writer Simon's recommendation that the Rwandan refugee Juliette write a 'personal story that will make people really understand what went on' is presented as a tone-deaf dismissal of Juliette's own intentions for her book. At the end of the play, Juliette departs from his script, asking a live audience to read her book 'so the people who were killed will not be forgotten'. She and Simon then read the first lines of her book aloud together, he in English and she in Kinyarwanda (Linden 2003: loc. 367–80). While this conclusion celebrates the possibility that refugee testimony can be effectively communicated through the combined efforts of refugee and non-refugee artists and activists, it insists that refugees must take the lead in deciding how their stories will be told.[8] It also suggests that imaginative substitution is an impulse rather than a realisable goal, and that the viewer's desire to 'really understand what went on' cannot be satisfied by the mere consumption of refugees' testimony.

Performances of verbatim refugee testimony by non-refugee actors foreground these tensions. The actors are positioned as liaison figures between the audience and the real protagonists whose speech is being performed, particularly when the actor's native language and/or ethnic background reflects that of members of the audience rather than the character they are playing.[9] The scripts themselves sometimes also include characters who perform this function. *I Have Before Me* and *Crocodile Seeking Refuge* include white, middle-class, British characters whose lives are profoundly changed by their encounters with refugees (not always unequivocally for the better; in *Crocodile*, one of the protagonists, an asylum lawyer, loses her marriage because of her work). *Citizen X: Letters From Detention* (2003), a verbatim play based on letters from detainees in Australian centres, includes an anguished monologue from a nurse about the living conditions in Woomera. ice&fire's *Asylum Dialogues* features the stories of two white British men: Rob Lawrie, who was prosecuted for smuggling an Afghan child out of Calais, and John Catley, an advocate for asylum seekers from Jamaica. Their play *Palestine Monologues* begins with testimonies from Israeli soldiers from the activist group Breaking the Silence, and ends with a statement from an Israeli activist who is the son of an Auschwitz survivor.[10] Alongside a partial identification with the refugee characters, then, the audience is invited to identify more fully with the non-refugee characters (most of them real people) who have risked their own comfort or safety to ally themselves with refugees. The characters sometimes make this invitation explicit. At the end of *Asylum Dialogues*, for instance, John addresses the audience directly: 'take courage and try – like me, you may be just lucky enough to help a desperate fellow human being. If a Black Country lad like me can do it, anyone can.'[11]

The inclusion of such characters could be read as diminishing a non-ref-ugee audience's engagement with refugee testimonies by discouraging them from attempting to imagine situations and experiences that are profoundly different from their own. However, the use of these liaison figures can also be understood as a way of facilitating the desired impact of the work, by making it clear that listening to refugees' stories is an important but incom-plete response. Audience members are encouraged to admire the non-refugee characters' examples, and like them, to translate the performance's invitation to solidarity into action.[12] This approach is in keeping with Alison Jeffers's suggestion that the most impactful encounter at theatrical performances of refugee testimony is between members of the audience:

> [W]e cannot assume that simply by being there or by holding the gaze of the refugee actor it is possible to somehow bridge any gap that might exist between performer and audience, or between citizen and refugee [. . .] we stand shoulder-to-shoulder in the act of considering how to respond to the face-to-face interaction of the performance both in the moment and after-wards. (Jeffers 2013: 306–7)

This assessment, like the productions themselves, emphasises theatre's capac-ity to serve as an event in which members of the audience not only feel together, but think together, and thus rehearse the collective response that the plays demand from citizens of host countries.

Graphic narrative: visuality, physicality and the quest

Verbatim theatre might seem a more obvious vehicle for refugee advocacy than graphic narrative. Yet the best-known contemporary graphic narratives tell stories of refugees: Art Spiegelman's *Maus* (1991–2), Joe Sacco's *Pales-tine* (1993) and Marjane Satrapi's *Persepolis* (2000–3). The prevalence of this theme reflects graphic journalism's influence on the wider genre, which has meant that many works privilege non-fictional content and, in the US context, the explanation of non-US events to US audiences (Worcester 2017: 137, 143). Yet it also demonstrates the generative capacity of graphic narra-tive's 'medium-specificity' (Baetens and Frey 2015: 117) – its combination of text and image – as a vehicle for refugee advocacy. Recent examples include Shaun Tan's *The Arrival* (2006), which narrates the story of a migrant's arrival in an unfamiliar city using only images; Matt Huynh's *Ma* (2013), about the author's parents' journey to Australia by boat; Bessoura and Barroux's *Alpha: Abidjan to Gare du Nord* (2014); Mana Neyestani's *An Iranian Metamorphosis* (2014); Leila Abdelrazaq's *Baddawi* (2015); Safdar Ahmed's *Villawood: Notes from an Immigration Detention Centre* (2015); Reinhard Kleist's *An Olympic Dream: The Story of Samia Yusuf Omar* (2015), about the Olympic sprinter from Somalia who drowned crossing the Mediterranean in 2012; Eoin Colfer, Andrew Donkin and Giovanni Rigano's *Illegal* (2017); and Kate Evans's *Threads from the Refugee Crisis* (2017), about the author's visits to the Calais camp. These works are often released by activist publishers and sometimes receive endorsements or funding from NGOs. *Alpha*, notably, carries an endorsement from Amnesty International and was translated from French with support from Arts Council England and English PEN. The book is supplemented by a website providing more background information and pedagogical materials, including a board game in which each player assumes the identity of an 'illegal' migrant.[13]

Two features of graphic narrative particularly lend themselves to refugee advocacy. The first is the multiple narrative sequencing possibilities that emerge from its distinctive combination of image and text, in which the interdependence of separate images and passages determines their meaning.[14] This generic property invites an active readerly engagement, since the reader must work to interpret the relationship between various forms of visual and textual information, including the layout of images on the page; the juxtaposition of images, narration and dialogue; and the use of intermediality (Baetens and Frey 2015: 127). For example, Abdelrazaq's *Baddawi*, which tells the story of the author's father's childhood in the Palestinian refugee camp Baddawi in Lebanon, solicits the reader's engagement by moving between layouts that promote different kinds of reading practice. The book foregrounds the dialectic between linearity (the movement from one image to the next) and tabularity (the appearance of the page).[15] Some parts of the narrative use a conventional comic strip format in which the panels are regularly sized and presented in sequence, such as the scene in which the protagonist Ahmad first attends an UNRWA school (Abdelrazaq 2015: 22–3). When Ahmad and his friends imagine the beatings that take place in the Lebanese army headquarters near the school, however, the strip format gives way to a half-page horizontal panel in the shape of a thought cloud, in which the boys envision monstrous two-dimensional figures attacking a seated person wearing a keffiyeh (2015: 27). Abdelrazaq also often uses full-page images to recount historical events, including the 1948 *Nakba* (2015: 16–19; see also 35, 44, 66, 73, 80), and to indicate key moments in Ahmad's life: he fires a gun, loses a friend to shelling, and contemplates the choice between studying in the US or staying in Lebanon (2015: 87–9, 99–100, 113).

The use of the strip as the basic narrative format reinforces the linear chronology of the coming-of-age story, but each departure from this layout introduces a more complex temporality (Baetens and Pylyser 2017: 308) and relationship between the protagonist and his sociohistorical context, through the juxtaposition of past and present, private and public, and real and irreal (cf. Deckard 2017). *Baddawi* also demonstrates the genre's capacity for visual intertextuality and intermediality. The book incorporates folkloric art into documentary images by framing them with patterns from Palestinian *tatreez* (embroidery), and its cover invokes one of the most iconic characters of twentieth-century Palestinian visual art, the Palestinian cartoonist Naji al-Ali's Handala, by depicting Ahmad with his back to the reader and his hands clasped behind him. The accretion of these diverse forms of representation exhorts the reader to work out the relationships between them, and to develop an understanding of the camp as a dynamic site of sociality, creativity and culture as well as exploitation and violence.

The second feature of graphic narrative that lends itself to refugee advocacy is its approach to characterisation. Characters are introduced and developed through the representation of the body, particularly the face, in contrast to the novel's 'excessively disembodied' emphasis on their thinking (Baetens and Frey 2015: 174–5). In Kleist's *An Olympic Dream*, for instance, the protagonist's facial expressions are often the focal point of the panel. Samia's expressions of determination, fear, frustration and exhaustion are presented in close-up, complementing and sometimes overriding the information provided by her speech and fictionalised Facebook posts. At the end of the book, the author includes an appendix of 'studies' of Samia that show her from the front and in profile, each with the same watchful expression. This attention to the protagonist's physicality emphasises the effort to commemorate Samia's life by recovering the evidence of her physical existence from the documentary record. The attention to her face indicates the complexity of her interior life, but foregoes the assumption of full knowledge of her motivations and emotions. Other graphic narrative accounts of refugee journeys similarly privilege the face of the protagonist, as well as those of the other refugees that he or she encounters en route. In *Illegal*, a fictional account of the young Ebo's journey from his village in Niger to Sicily, other occupants of the raft in which he crosses the Mediterranean are presented in static portraits, with a caption in which each person explains why she or he is making the journey (Colfer, Donkin and Rigano 2017: 72). *Illegal* also includes an appendix of studies of Ebo and his siblings, along with sketches of the raft and the other travellers, foregrounding the creative experimentation and decision making that has gone into the representation of their stories.

These works' emphasis on the artistic depiction of the protagonists' active and expressive bodies complements their focus on the practical difficulties and dangers of refugees' journeys. The texts often borrow from the genre of the quest narrative (or, as David Farrier notes, the road movie; Farrier 2011: 196), featuring a heroic protagonist who must surmount various material and logistical obstacles to reach his or her destination. This association relies on graphic narrative's genealogical relationship to superhero comics, but in these works the characters' heroism lies in their survival. The protagonists travel from their home towns by truck and boat, possessing little money or information; they are robbed, assaulted and imprisoned; their fellow travellers disappear or die. While the goal of arriving in Europe (an arbitrary destination; Farrier 2011: 196) is motivated by the promise of safety and eventual citizenship, these texts rarely confirm the desire for a redemptive narrative arc (Stonebridge 2015: 1333). In *An Olympic Dream*, Samia dies; in *Alpha*, Alpha is arrested in Paris and deported back to Abidjan, and he never finds his wife and son; in *Illegal*, although Ebo is reunited with his sister Sisi in Italy, the reunion takes place after their brother Kwame has drowned during the crossing. The protagonists' heroism is thus closely aligned with their martyrdom; their 'fierce determination' is all the more admirable because their situation is 'seemingly hopeless' (Morpurgo 2016: n.p.).

In *Threads*, in a sequence called 'Fairy Tale', Evans as author-narrator invokes this plotline by imagining a happy ending for the Calais resident Hoshyar: she smuggles him on to the ferry to Dover, they pass through the checkpoints without detection, and she drops him off at his uncle's house in England. But then she considers the more likely scenario – that she would be caught and imprisoned – and imagines her children left with their grandmother, and her easel and chair left darkened and empty (Evans 2017: 146–51). The implication is not simply that Evans is unwilling to lose her family and her art, but that her work as an artist and advocate matters, and that the non-refugee reader's advocacy matters too. Evans often addresses the reader didactically, asking her to 'linger' on the image of policemen confiscating bread from refugee children and to imagine 'leaving someone you care about stuck in a place like this' (Evans 2017: 109, 134). The book ends with a short essay laid out in newspaper clippings against a lace background, in reference to Calais's industrial history as a site of lace production. An iPhone at the top of each page presents the arguments against asylum: 'If we give refuge to anyone that needs it, where are these never-ending resources, space, jobs, homes going to come from?' The essay, entitled 'Hope', challenges such claims – 'Mathematical modelling shows that removing all national barriers to migration would *double* global GDP' – and asserts the UK's responsibility for the crisis as the world's second-largest exporter of arms (Evans 2017: 175). The tabular image juxtaposes an industrial and DIY aesthetic with print and online media, producing a twenty-first-century homily that drives home the book's message. Evans invites the implied reader, a UK citizen, to begin her own journey by taking responsibility for what she has read and demanding the opening of her country's borders.

Reading and responsibility

Literature is distinguished from other forms of advocacy by its foregrounding of the demand with which Evans ends: that the reader share responsibility for the story. As David Herd puts it in his afterword to the collection *Refugee Tales*, a collaborative adaptation of the *Canterbury Tales* by refugees and non-refugee writers:

> What perhaps it means is that a story that belongs to one person now belongs, also, to other people; that other people acknowledge the experience that constitutes the story, but also that in making that acknowledgement they register responsibility. These are tales, in other words, that call for and generate a collective; tales that need to be told and re-told so that the situation they emerge from might be collectively addressed. (Herd and Pincus 2016: loc. 1998; see also Farrier 2011: 124–5, 151–2; Keenan 1997)

The works I have discussed also exhibit this belief in literature's capacity to generate a shared sense of responsibility among non-refugees, one that is 'built up through the common act of listening to these stories and working out among "us" the best way to respond' (Jeffers 2013: 306). These works engage and subvert genre conventions both instrumentally and prefiguratively: they seek to encourage and sustain solidarity activism now, while also fostering the future cross-border community that the catastrophe demands.[16] They are clear, however, that writing and reading about refugees is not a sufficient form of action in itself. It should instead be understood as 'an insertion into a wider ecology of activism' (Paget 2010: 190), in which we are all invited to take part.

Acknowledgements

I would like to thank Christine Bacon of ice&fire for granting me access to scripts; Sharae Deckard and Charlotta Salmi for sharing work in progress; Omid Tofighian for a thought-provoking conversation about his work as a translator and the question of genre; and Lyndsey Stonebridge for her example and her support.

Notes

1. See David Farrier's account of the 'Nauru epistolarium' (Farrier 2011: 16).
2. I thank Lyndsey Stonebridge for this insight.
3. See 'The Syrian Monologues', Ashtar Theatre, n.d., http://www.ashtar-theatre.org/the-syrian-monologues.html (accessed 10 July 2018).

4. For a discussion of the false opposition between an 'ignorant' and 'informed' audience, see Jeffers (2013: 301, 306).
5. See, for example, the opening scene of ice&fire's *The Illegals* (2008), in which the characters describe themselves with terms used to denigrate undocumented migrants.
6. 'Previous Work', ice&fire, http://iceandfire.co.uk/previous-work/ (accessed 10 July 2018).
7. 'About Us', ice&fire, http://iceandfire.co.uk/about-us/ (accessed 10 July 2018).
8. On the capacity of participatory theatre projects to work towards this goal, see Balfour and Woodrow (2013: 27).
9. On ice&fire's ethnic casting decisions, see Farrier (2012b: 436).
10 Sonja Linden, *Palestine Monologues* (2008), script provided by Christine Bacon.
11. Sonja Linden and Christine Bacon, *Asylum Dialogues* (2008), script of 2016 performance provided by Christine Bacon.
12. At the end of performances I have attended, ice&fire has also provided a pamphlet listing 'ten things you can do'. See also Paget (2010: 187).
13. Alpha website, http://www.thealphabook.org/ (accessed 4 July 2018).
14. Thierry Groensteen calls this property of graphic narrative 'iconic solidarity' (Groensteen 2007: 17–20).
15. Fresnault-Deruelle 2014: 121–38. Sharae Deckard names this relationship as a dialectic in her paper 'Speculations on world-literary graphic narratives' (Deckard 2017).
16. See Cox's distinction between instrumental and civic sociality (Cox 2015: 4).

Bibliography

Abdelrazaq, Leila (2015), *Baddawi* (Charlottesville, VA: Just World Books).
Ahmed, Safdar (2015), *Villawood: Notes from an Immigration Detention Centre*, Medium, 5 March, https://medium.com/shipping-news/villawood-9698183e114c (accessed 5 July 2018).
Al-Nakib, Mai (2015), 'Kanafani in Kuwait: a clinical cartography', *Deleuze Studies*, 9.1: 88–111.
Baetens, Jan, and Hugo Frey (2015), *The Graphic Novel: An Introduction* (Cambridge: Cambridge University Press).
Baetens, Jan, and Charlotte Pylyser (2017), 'Comics and time', in Frank Bramlett, Roy T. Cook and Aaron Meskin (eds), *The Routledge Companion to Comics* (Abingdon: Routledge), pp. 303–10.
Balfour, Michael, and Nina Woodrow (2013), 'On stitches', in Michael Balfour (ed.), *Refugee Performance: Practical Encounters* (Bristol: Intellect), 15–34.
Bessoura and Barroux (2016 [2014]), *Alpha: Abidjan to Gare du Nord*, trans. Sarah Ardizzone (Edinburgh: Bucket List)
Charity Doctor LLP (2008), 'Evaluation report: *The Illegals*', ice&fire, December, http://iceandfire.co.uk/wp-content/uploads/2015/06/The-illegals-Evaluation-Report.pdf (accessed 11 July 2018).
Colfer, Eoin, Andrew Donkin and Giovanni Rigano (2017), *Illegal* (London: Hodder and Stoughton).

Cox, Emma (2014), *Theatre and Migration* (Basingstoke: Palgrave Macmillan).

Cox, Emma (2015), *Performing Noncitizenship: Asylum Seekers in Australian Theatre, Film and Activism* (London: Anthem).

Darwish, Mahmoud (2005 [1984]), 'The Earth is Closing on Us', in *Victims of a Map*, trans. Abdullah al-Udhari (London: Saqi).

Deckard, Sharae (2017), 'Speculations on world-literary graphic narratives', paper presented to the American Comparative Literature Association Annual Meeting, 8 July.

Evans, Kate (2017), *Threads from the Refugee Crisis* (London: Verso).

Farrier, David (2011), *Postcolonial Asylum: Seeking Sanctuary Before the Law* (Liverpool: Liverpool University Press).

Farrier, David (2012a), 'Editorial', *Moving Worlds*, 12.2: 1–2.

Farrier, David (2012b), 'Everyday exceptions', *Interventions*, 14.3: 429–42.

Fresnault-Deruelle, Pierre (2014 [1976]), 'From linear to tabular', in Ann Miller and Bart Beaty (eds), *The French Comics Theory Reader* (Leuven: Leuven University Press), 121–38.

Groensteen, Thierry (2007), *The System of Comics*, trans. Bart Beaty and Nick Nguyen (Jackson: University Press of Mississippi).

Herd, David, and Anna Pincus (eds) (2016), *Refugee Tales* (Manchester: Comma Press), Kindle edition.

Huynh, Matt (2013), *Ma*, http://www.matthuynh.com/macomic (accessed 5 July 2018).

Jeffers, Alison (2012), *Refugees, Theatre and Crisis: Performing Global Identities* (Basingstoke: Palgrave Macmillan).

Jeffers, Alison (2013), 'Hospitable stages and civil listening: being an audience for participatory refugee theatre', in Michael Balfour (ed.), *Refugee Performance: Practical Encounters* (Bristol: Intellect), 297–310.

Kanafani, Ghassan (1978 [1963]), *Men in the Sun*, trans. Hilary Kilpatrick (Boulder: Lynne Riener).

Kanafani, Ghassan (1990 [1968]), 'Thoughts on change and the "blind language"', trans. Barbara Harlow and Nejd Yazidji, *Alif*, 10: 137–57.

Kanafani, Ghassan (2015), 'The Stolen Shirt', trans. Michael Fares, Jadaliyya, 31 March, http://www.jadaliyya.com/pages/index/21243/ghassan-kanafanis-the-stolen-shirt (accessed 5 July 2018). Originally published in *Al-qamīs al-masrūq wa qisas ukhrā* (Beirut: Mu'assassat al-Abhath al-'Arabiyya, 1982).

Keenan, Thomas (1997), *Fables of Responsibility: Aberrations and Predicaments in Ethics and Politics* (Stanford: Stanford University Press).

Kleist, Reinhard (2016 [2015]), *An Olympic Dream: The Story of Samia Yusuf Omar*, trans. Ivanka Hahnenberger (London: SelfMadeHero).

Linden, Sonja (2003), *I Have Before Me a Remarkable Document Given to Me By a Young Lady from Rwanda* (Twickenham: Aurora Metro), Kindle edition.

Linden, Sonja (2005), *Crocodile Seeking Refuge* (Twickenham: Aurora Metro).

Mamouney, Don (2003), *Citizen X: Letters From Detention*, https://www.safecom.org.au/citizenx.htm (accessed 11 July 2018).

Morpurgo, Michael (2016), preface to Bessoura and Barroux, *Alpha: Abidjan to Gare du Nord*, trans. Sarah Ardizzone (Edinburgh: Bucket List), n.p.

Neyestani, Mana (2014), *An Iranian Metamorphosis*, trans. Ghaal Mosadeq (Minneapolis: Uncivilized Books).

Paget, Derek (2010), 'Acts of commitment: activist arts, the rehearsed reading, and documentary theatre', *New Theatre Quarterly*, 26.2: 173–93.

People Seeking Sanctuary in Wales (2013), *Are You Happy With That?*, ed. Tom Cheesman (Swansea: Hafan Books).

Ramazani, Jahan (1994), *The Poetry of Mourning* (Chicago: University of Chicago Press).

Rangan, Pooja (2017), *Immediations: The Humanitarian Impulse in Documentary* (Durham, NC: Duke University Press).

Said, Edward (2002 [1983]), 'Arabic prose and prose fiction after 1948', in *Reflections on Exile* (Cambridge, MA: Harvard University Press), 41–60.

Shingarpure, Bhakti, et al. (eds) (2018), *Mediterranean* (Storrs, CT: Warscapes and UpSet Press).

Shire, Warsan (2011), 'Conversations About Home', in *Teaching My Mother How to Give Birth* (London: flipped eye publishing), Kindle edition.

Stonebridge, Lyndsey (2015), 'Statelessness and the poetry of the borderline: André Green, W. H. Auden and Yousif M. Qasmiyeh', *Textual Practice*, 29.7: 1331–54.

Tan, Shaun (2006), *The Arrival* (Sydney: Hachette).

Woolley, Agnes (2014), *Contemporary Asylum Narratives: Representing Refugees in the Twenty-First Century* (Basingstoke: Palgrave Macmillan).

Worcester, Kent (2017), 'Journalistic comics', in Frank Bramlett, Roy T. Cook and Aaron Meskin (eds), *The Routledge Companion to Comics* (Abingdon: Routledge), 137–45.

Part II

Asylum

Asylum: Introduction

Agnes Woolley

Asylum is an ambivalent term, freighted with a set of often contradictory interpretations. As Alison Jeffers notes in this volume, it is a less localised, more abstract concept than its cognates 'sanctuary' and 'refuge', which suggest geographic specificity. Where these have retained predominantly positive associations, asylum has a more uneven history; from its earliest uses as a place of sanctuary where fugitives from the law were sheltered from its power (from the Greek *asylos* meaning that which is inviolable), the nineteenth-century asylum movement in the English-speaking world engendered popular understandings of asylums as spaces negatively associated with madness and deviance. Now asylum occupies a precarious position in the cultural imaginary, especially as it relates to migration. As both Jeffers and Anthony Good point out in these pages, a popular commitment to the *idea* of asylum continues, despite ever-increasing hostility to its practice. Perhaps in part a Victorian hangover, in the UK asylum seekers are readily associated with state dependency and aberrant behaviour; cast as one of Stanley Cohen's 'folk devils', as Good notes in his chapter. More recently, Imogen Tyler (2013) has used the notion of 'revolting subjects' to describe the ways in which groups such as asylum seekers are figured as socially abject in mainstream media representations, which are largely responsible for that enduring opposition between 'fraudulent' or 'bogus' asylum seekers and an idealised, 'genuine' refugee.

But contemporary asylum is not only a scandal in the journalistic sense. As David Farrier has argued, it is also a 'scandal' for those critical discourses that have overlooked the legal and economic conditions of asylum seekers and refugees in their endorsement of the unhampered mobility of the cosmopolitan migrant. The national and supranational legal context in which asylum seeking exists today is crucial to a nuanced understanding of the ways in which asylum and refugeedom differ from voluntary migration. The idea of asylum as a universal, individual and claimable legal right is a twentieth-century phenomenon formalised in the 1951 UN Refugee Convention and the 1967 Protocol, and remains the prevailing mechanism for adjudicating asylum claims.[1] While the lived experience of migration emerges from a broad spectrum of circumstances, the international legal instruments designed to adjudicate the basis on which someone might be granted refuge are narrow, developed in the immediate aftermath of the Second World War to address the numbers of refugees crossing between European countries. In answer to Farrier's question 'What is the place of the asylum seeker before the law?' (2011: 10), the chapters in this section tackle both the written letter of the law and the culturally conditioned social laws governing interactions between individuals in societies and communities.

Through case studies, both Anthony Good and Sudeep Dasgupta engage in detail with current legal mechanisms for determining refugee status, probing the limits and legacies of legal systems in Europe and the Global North. Dasgupta's rigorous discussion shows how asylum claims based on gender identity and sexual orientation both register and challenge conventional or normative understandings of the tripartite relationship between sex, gender and desire. Importantly, Dasgupta focuses on the writing and the reading of the law: both how it is constituted through language, and how it is 'read' by decision makers on asylum. As he points out, the narrative basis of the asylum adjudication process – its dependence on a credible, but also narratively teleological, account of persecution – has implications which extend to the shaping of an idealised legal subject. In the case of sexual and gender identity, for example, 'coming out' is read exclusively as 'an emotionally affirmative act of self-valuation', which results in a 'fully realised sexual and gender identity'. However, for Dasgupta, asylum claims based on sexuality and gender also work to 'queer global space' by registering 'unstable desires' that pull against those national laws that seek to read bodies straightforwardly. This means that it is the global space in which the deregulation of sexuality becomes possible.

Good approaches the legal workings of asylum through the lens of morality, interrogating the interaction between lay and legal understandings of the morality of asylum. Despite the principle that common law judges should not appeal to 'general, non-legal moral precepts', Good shows how 'asylum decision making lends itself to the making of such judgements in practice, because of the central role played by credibility'. This is truer still of non-common law countries such as France, where a judge must appeal to their 'intimate [or innermost] conviction' (*intime conviction*) when making a decision. Although decisions on asylum in both the UK and France are based on adherence to the 1951 Refugee Convention, the historical and cultural contexts of these national legal systems lead to distinct approaches to decision making at appeals stage. What is more, lacunae in the original Convention, such as gender and sexuality, are dealt with differently according to the national context. Troubling the law in this way, both Good and Dasgupta participate in a critical reassessment of the legal mechanisms governing asylum, one that is increasingly pressing given the geopolitical and climatic upheaval currently producing record numbers of displaced people.

The rigorous analyses of the law in the first two chapters of this section provide a useful counterpoint to the final chapter by Alison Jeffers, which takes up Good's sense of a general moral approach to the issue of asylum by considering the 'lore' surrounding culturally and historically inflected understandings of duties and obligations to one another in communities. Jeffers looks to alternative spaces of determination – cities and, specifically, theatres of sanctuary – popular movements that exist outside state apparatuses of asylum and offer ways of acting 'under the conditions whereby fundamental ideas about protection and asylum cannot keep pace with contemporary realities'. Focusing on the *Queens of Syria* project, in which a group of Syrian women residing in Jordan take part in a production and reinterpretation of Euripides' *The Trojan Women*, Jeffers assesses what she calls the 'politics of the empty gesture'. Productions such as *Queens of Syria*, she argues, stick to the letter of the UN Convention by 'evoking sanctuary practices based on the traditional power of Church and city to shelter strangers on a more human scale'; they are faithful to the Convention, where nation-states seek to evade its conditions. As well as 'redefin[ing] a sense of what is possible in terms of a response to refugees in this historical moment', Jeffers's chapter returns to the sense of hope and possibility embedded in the earliest uses of the term 'asylum'.

Note

1. There are important refugee-receiving countries which have not signed up to the Convention: Jordan, Lebanon, India, Bangladesh and Pakistan to name a few. Given that Africa is the continent that receives the most refugees, it is also worth noting that the African Union has its own definition of a refugee that is more expansive than the UN's.

Bibliography

Farrier, David (2011), *Postcolonial Asylum: Seeking Sanctuary Before the Law* (Liverpool: Liverpool University Press).
Tyler, Imogen (2013), *Revolting Subjects: Social Abjection and Resistance in Neoliberal Britain* (London: Zed Books).

Chapter 5

Sexual and Gender-Based Asylum and the Queering of Global Space: Reading Desire, Writing Identity and the Unconventionality of the Law

Sudeep Dasgupta

The asylum seeker is located between the category of the refugee and a space of sanctuary. In sexual and gendered asylum cases – that is, specific cases dealing with sexual identity and orientation, as well as gender identity – gays, lesbians and trans-persons become the objects of law as well as agents in the transformation of law. Cases of sexual asylum conjoin time and space in particular configurations in which national interests and international instruments give form to sexual identity through shifting cultural norms. The tripartite relation between biological *sex*, cultural notions of *gender* and sexual *desire* are implicated in cases of sexual asylum. The heteronormative understanding of the relation between these three assumes that sex (male/female) is determined by biology, leading to corresponding cultural notions of masculinity and femininity, and this sex–gender relation is lived through sexual desire for the opposite sex. Feminist and queer theory has powerfully critiqued the assumed naturalness of this relation, and sexual asylum cases provide important vantage points from which the stabilisation of this tripartite relation is being undone. The Refugee Convention of 1951 and other international instruments such as the 1967 Protocol Relating to the Status of Refugees are works-in-progress which often have both regressive *and* emancipatory effects for those seeking asylum based on sexual orientation or gender identity. Through inscriptions and altered reiterations they register both the conventional understandings of class, nation and race and the unconventional trajectories of sexual desire narrativised by displaced bodies. Asylum law and advocacy on sexual orientation or gender identity register this charged conjunction between conventions and unconventionality.

This chapter first analyses how the asylum seeker is written into being through laws and conventions that produce a queer subject shuttling between the poles of normalisation and critical destabilisation. By analysing specific court judgments in different countries, I argue that heteronormative understandings of the sex–gender–desire relation restrict access to refuge in sexual asylum cases. At the same time, I show how the application of the law also destabilises these heteronormative understandings, opening up such restrictive understandings of sexuality and gender. Some parenthetical remarks on the implications of my analyses below are in order here. The different national contexts in which these court judgments are made limit their concrete effects. The cases analysed below do not have universal relevance across all nations. At the same time, these judgments have repercussions in international law, as I will show in relation to the UK and the European Court of Justice. My argument does not aim at a comprehensive picture of sexual and gender-based asylum cases across the world. Neither is my argument a comparative one in which laws in specific countries are related to each other. The focus is on how *specific* sexual asylum cases across different countries serve as exemplars that provide a broad sketch of shifts at a global level in the way sexual and gender identity are being understood. By analysing sexual and gender-based asylum cases in a number of countries, and their real and potential consequences beyond these countries, my argument identifies specific shifts in certain jurisdictions as well as the possibilities for deploying their legal arguments more widely.

The second part of the chapter analyses the ways in which the testimony of sexual and gender-based asylum seekers is interpreted during court proceedings in order to make status determinations. This legal interpretation of asylum seekers' speech in specific cases I term 'reading'. The dialectic of sexual normalisation and deregulation in cases of sexual and gender asylum is exacerbated by the protocols of reading (by the law) which demand a *linear narrative* of sexual identity from the asylum seeker. An exposition of sexual identity assumes an essential and stable form of gender identity and sexual desire whose gradual realisation is narrativised teleologically, such that at the time of demanding sexual asylum a clear, non-contradictory and fully realised sexual and gender identity has been formed. The assumption that this form of narrative exposition is the right form of 'evidence' of sexual identity is, as we shall see below, found in many court judgments. By reading *for* such narrative evidence of sexual identity, the law is unable to countenance the decentred, ambivalent and contradictory forms through which sexual desire is *lived* by asylum seekers. The stability of sexual identity is queered when the renderings of sexual desire in asylum seekers' speech and the reading strategies by the law which attempt to convert them into clear narratives of sexual identity intersect.

The United Nations High Commissioner for Refugees (UNHCR) states that 'An asylum seeker is someone whose request for sanctuary has yet to be processed. Every year, around one million people seek asylum. National asylum systems are in place to determine who qualifies for international protection.'[1] The 'has yet to be' temporality of the asylum seeker produces a

subject-in-the-making in the transient space of the 'as yet'. When this subject is to be defined in terms of sexual identity (or orientation), the success of asylum claims depends on the appropriate rendering of sexual self-identity in terms readable by judging officials according to categories and descriptions written into laws and conventions. The stark inequality in power relations between the self whose identity is expressed and the decision maker (individual, agency, state) which determines the legibility and legitimacy of the expression of sexual orientation or gender identity marks the temporality of the interval between the refugee and the asylum seeker. As Jacqueline Bhabha describes it,

> most refugees fleeing to safety in developed states do not arrive with a ready guarantee of access to enduring human rights. Rather, they enter as 'asylum seekers' – a temporary and increasingly disenfranchised category of non-citizen who need to establish their eligibility for refugee status before they can enjoy the prospect of long-term safety and nondiscriminatory treatment. (Bhabha 2002: 155)

Both the determining power of the law in writing sexual identity and the unstable rendering of sexual desire by asylum seekers intersect in the 'no guarantees' temporality of the 'as yet'. The inscriptions and reiterations of the law meet the reading of sexual desire, and in this conjunction the writing of the sexual subject into case judgments striates the global space produced by bodies on the move. Rather than moving across national borders under international protection to a place of sexual and social sanctuary, the trajectories of individual sexual desire *produce* global space queerly through the experience of forced displacement.

In *Mourning Becomes the Law: Philosophy and Representation*, Gillian Rose describes 'the work' of the philosophy of law as a social and historical process which registers the ongoing confrontation between diverse national, cultural, political and humanitarian practices. The law is not a 'text' which establishes the final comprehensibility of the concept it expresses – be that refugee, sexual identity, desire. The 'texts' of the law can be read 'deterministically' as 'fixed, closed conceptual structures, colonising being with the garrison of thought' (Rose 1996: 8). Legal texts can also be read as 'works . . . implying the *labour* of the concept' that expresses 'the difficulty which . . . conceptuality represents by leaving gaps and silences in the mode of representation' (Rose 1996: 8, emphasis added). The law can be read as the garrisoning by thought of a (sexual) being by colonising its (failure at consistent) self-representation and turning it into a text when an asylum case is decided. The work of the concept exposes the law's inability to comprehensively grasp the reality it expresses, and sexual asylum law and asylum seekers' speech registers the productivity of these failures for reworking the law unconventionally. A conceptual understanding of both forms of representation as 'works' represents the gaps, failures, stutterings and contradictions that attend any form of representation. Cases of sexual asylum reveal that both the law and the asylum seeker's speech are involved in working through and transforming the meaning of sexual identity as it is lived differentially by specific individuals. It is in this sense that 'the labour of the concept' refers to the *transformative* work that both writing and reading sexual identity perform for thinking gender and sexual identity unconventionally. Both the representation by the law *of the* asylum seeker and the representation by the asylum seeker *to* the representative of the law register this labour of the concept. Writing and reading about the politics of sexual asylum is not about the verification of the givenness of the law but an acknowledgement of 'a multiplicity of eventualities' (Rose 1996: 8) in the time of the interval which exemplify 'the creative involvement of actions in the configuration of power and the law' (Rose 1996: 12).

The work of the law and the writing of identity

The refugee as an object of discourse emerges as the effect of political conjunctures at specific moments. The 1951 Convention Relating to the Status of Refugees came into force in 1954 and is the primary instrument through which protection to refugees is granted by nation-states and international bodies such as UNHCR. The inscription of the Convention was followed in 1967 by the Protocol Relating to the Status of Refugees, which expanded the reach of the Convention beyond events in Europe in the post-war period. The concern over refugees, however, predated 1951 when the International Refugee Organization was founded in 1946 to address the displacements produced by the Second World War. This early focus on the refugee was caught up in fears around preserving the sovereignty of the nation-state rather than protecting the individual fleeing persecution (Goodwin-Gill 2008: 1). The refugee began to emerge as the point of tension between a universal category of the 'human' for UNHCR and the attempts by nation-states to limit its scope. According to the 1951 Convention, refugees were defined as those affected only by events that took place *in* Europe before 1951. However, UNHCR's ambit was universal, 'unconstrained by geographical or temporal limitations, while the definition forwarded to the Conference by the General Assembly' restricted the category of refugee 'to those who became refugees by reason of events occurring before 1 January 1951' (Goodwin-Gill 2008: 2). Nation-states were given the option of retaining the temporally and geographically specific restrictions of the 1951 Convention.

  This brief snapshot of the tensions between particular national interests and the more expansive understanding of human rights resonates in the shifting inscriptions of the law produced by sexual asylum cases. Writing the refugee into the law is precisely the work of managing the gaps, tensions and failures that attend any attempt at inscribing the complex social reality of displaced populations in an international frame. These gaps and complexities are identifiable in the shifting meanings attached to forms of social identity such as gender and sexuality. Article 1(A) of the Convention and the Protocol together define the refugee as 'any person who is outside their country of origin and unable or unwilling to return there or to avail themselves of its protection, on account of a well-founded fear of persecution for reasons of race, religion, nationality, membership of a particular social group, or political opinion' (Goodwin-Gill 2008: 3). Gender and sexual identity are not stated explicitly and most often fall under the category of 'membership of a particular social group'.

For sexual and gender asylum seekers, the individual realities of living one's shifting gender and sexual identity are intrinsically bound up with processes of forced displacement caused by persecution. How these realities are garrisoned in thought is discernible in the mode of writing gays, lesbians and transgender persons into the category of 'membership of a particular social group'. Bhabha notes that 'it is increasingly the case that the asylum seeker's flight is tortuous; it is likely to be indirect, facilitated by commercial intermediaries and false documents . . . Questions of identity may be problematic – who exactly is the applicant and what is his or her nationality?' (2002: 156). Beyond national identity, identifying the 'social group' they belong to becomes problematic when their identities are continually, and often forcibly, transformed by the power dynamics involved in the process of displacement. Conventional stereotypes of gender, age and sexuality come into conflict with the transformations in identity produced through culturally specific locations and their traversal through displacement. Bhabha argues that such conventional understandings

> narrow the scope for advancing asylum claims on behalf of claimants who do not fit the prevailing stereotype. Thus, if women from a particular region are categorized as submissive, voiceless victims, then a woman who flees persecution on the basis of her political activism . . . will face the additional hurdle of persuading the decision-maker that her political opinions, as a woman in that country, are taken sufficiently seriously to count as a threat. (Bhabha 2002: 162–3)

The conventionality of refugee law and its instantiation in asylum cases is undone by the continual appearance of unconventional figures whose trajectories come into contradiction with the politics of nation-state sovereignty and the cultural presuppositions that layer over social identity and thus impinge on the consistency of the 'human' in human rights discourse. Identity emerges as the contingent effect of the displaced body's forced trajectories. Elsewhere I have argued that in the condition of 'scattered subalternities' (Dasgupta 2017), the bodies of displaced peoples do not move through a stable global cartography of readable spaces. Rather, their bodies are writing instruments that inscribe shifting borders and spatial coordinates through which national, cultural and social identity get rewritten. The scattered subaltern's (un)readability is both cause and effect of heterogeneous global space and its outmoded cartography.

Martin Manalansan (2006) has rightly argued for extending Adrienne Rich's (1986) insistence on a politics of location for understanding the intersection of gender and sexuality in migration.[2] *Forced* migration exacerbates the need for an intersectional analysis of sexual asylum given that the cultural presumptions of the law seek to stabilise a heterogeneous global space according to conventional stereotypes of gender and sexual identities. Expanding on Eric Santner's analysis of the embodiment of (national) political sovereignty in relation to the body of 'the people', I argue that asylum seekers' bodies exhibit what Santner describes as 'biopolitical animation' where 'biological life is amplified and perturbed by the symbolic dimension of relationality at the very heart of which lie problems of authority and authorization' (Santner 2001: 30). The authorisation executed through the granting of asylum is based on the inscription of an identity whose bodily integrity must be readable to an authority (the immigration service, for example) according to the cultural, political and symbolic protocols of a Convention. Yet the Convention's conceptual vocabulary exposes the unstable relation between an authorising inscription and the being whose desire must be read. When sexual and gender identity is at issue, this failure of inscription is an effect of the fact that 'the flesh' is a 'fantasy construct, charged with [. . .] human desires, fears, and values, a virtual reality that has gathered around bodies' (Goodman 2016: 7).

By seeking to make sense of sexual and gender identity in the wake of global displacements, the sensory perception of the world itself is deranged. 'Sense' perceives itself, argues Jean-Luc Nancy 'as a world of separation, and of pain . . . the world of exteriority from which life withdraws giving way to an endless displacement from one term to the next that can neither be sustained nor gathered in an identity of meaning' (2002: 3). A politics of *dislocation* emphasises how forced movement to flee persecution results in the asylum seeker as the operator of a queering of sexuality. The effect of bodily displacement exacerbates the errancy of sexual desire, undermining the fixing of identity by the law of the sexual subject fleeing homophobic or gender-based violence. At this point, it is crucial to insist that intersectional understandings of bodily displacement are not mere examples of an abstract theory of sexuality or sexual identity based on fluidity and fragmentation. Forced migration caused by persecution on the basis of sexual and gender identity concretises abstract notions of fluid sexuality and gender by exposing the specific operations that discipline sexualities through the stabilisation by the law of 'the shifting line between legal and illegal status' (Luibhéid 2008: 289). The application for asylum is the moment when *specific* intersections of multiple power-relations such as gender and sexual relations give form to an individual, thus throwing into question the relation between a desiring body's identity and the possibility of ascribing it membership 'in a particular social group' (Landau 2004: 102). An emphasis on the 'authorising' power that seeks to contain 'bodily animation' interrogates the prevailing intellectual focus on the global 'power of flows' (Castells 2000: 500) to help identify where and how 'flows of power' intersect (Ampuja 2011: 287).

Some specific legal examples will help to contextualise the foregoing discussion. Joseph Landau has argued that crucial legal shifts in US court rulings exemplify how sexual asylum starts to produce unconventional understandings of gender and sexual identity. The decision in 2004 of the Ninth Circuit Court in the US to honour 'an asylum seeker's expression of gendered traits, including a person's hairstyle, clothing, demeanor, use of makeup, and choice of names' as the 'true and honest depiction of identity and self-determination' undid any 'natural' (i.e. biological) basis for establishing gender identity (Landau 2004: 102).[3] The decision exemplified the long-standing critique in queer and feminist theory of the biological basis for establishing sex, as well as the naturalised link between sex and gender. By acknowledging that the behaviour and bodily traits 'exhibited' by a person are legitimate grounds for determining gender identity, a performative understanding of gender identity and existing social perceptions of gender were combined.

Conventional understandings of the relation between sex, gender and sexual desire produce a 'heterosexual matrix' (Butler 1999a: 194) in which biological sex implies a corresponding gender and the opposite sexual object of sexual desire. By delinking gender from the body's sex, the Ninth Circuit Court's ruling has consequences not just for transgender identity, but by implication for the determination of sexual orientation too.[4] Whether or not transgender asylum seekers identified as homosexual, the social assumption that their *sexuality* (rather than their gender) was being manifest through their outward appearance and behaviour was marshalled as evidence to successfully claim homophobic persecution. The theory of 'imputed gay identity' (Landau 2004: 102) produced by the law expanded the non-biological understanding of gender by redefining homosexuality as a question of social perception rather than self-affirmation. Further, the imputation argument of the law linked an individual affirmation of gender identity to social perceptions of sexuality. In effect, a non-biological inscription of gender identity by the law produced an imputed sexually desiring body on the basis of potential social legibility.

The sexually desiring gendered body literally *comes into being* through the process of seeking asylum and legal decision making. Crucially, the meaning of *belonging* to a social group is uncoupled from a biological and individual ascription of identity. This albeit geographically limited development in the US of a 'soft immutability theory of identity' and 'imputed gay identity' (Landau 2004: 103) has global implications since the national courts' rulings are based on the international ambit of the Refugee Convention. These two understandings of identity uncoupled the link between sex, gender and desire by framing the individual through the social. But the place of the 'social' is not unambiguous. The very possibilities that social perception open up for fleeing sexual persecution can also close it down in other interpretations of international law.

In 1985 the US Board of Immigration Appeals defined a 'particular social group' as based 'solely on the existence of an "immutable" characteristic', one that 'an individual either cannot change or should not be required to change because it is fundamental to identity or conscience' (quoted in Marouf 2008: 48). This ruling emphasised individual characteristics within a defined group rather than social perception as the basis for granting asylum. In 2002, however, UNHCR issued guidelines to Convention signatories which expanded the basis of defining a 'social group' to include 'social perception' (Marouf 2008: 63, 65) in deciding asylum cases. The increasing reliance on social visibility, Marouf argues, led 'to incoherent, inconsistent decisions that have no basis in the 1951 Refugee Convention and its 1967 Protocol' (2008: 49). Marouf shows that

> [W]ith respect to sexual orientation, the United States and international authorities have rejected the notion that gays and lesbians who remain 'discreet' – and therefore 'invisible' – are not protected by the refugee definition . . . Under the 'social visibility' test, however, their claims may well be denied. Indeed, even claims brought by 'out' gays and lesbians may be rejected if they come from societies that do not recognise homosexuals as a group or homosexuality as a social identity. (2008: 50)

The visibility (being out) of sexual identity undermines sexual and gender asylum claims since 'social perception' is deemed impossible in societies where the category of 'homosexual' is considered non-existent. The reliance on social visibility turns the asylum seeker doubly invisible both in the home country and the place of desired sanctuary through the use of prevailing cultural stereotypes. 'Soft immutability' of gender and 'imputed gay identity' (Landau 2004: 101) loosened the understandings of the gendered and sexually desiring body by inserting the social while writing the sexual asylum seeker into law. 'Social perception' (Marouf 2008: 63) based on the culturally stereotypical assumptions of non-Western societies, on the other hand, shut down the chances for successful asylum claims. The unconventionality of the Convention emerges precisely here in the normative inscriptions of the sexual asylum seeker and the selective deployment of legal alternatives for establishing its culturally normed body.

Sexual determination and the indeterminate reading of the asylum seeker

> [H]uman sexuality . . . is inherently perverse, inherently in excess of teleological function . . . [it] emerges on the basis of a constitutive swerve . . . from a norm that is established only retroactively. (Santner 2016: 48)

What happens to the 'virtual reality' (Goodman 2016: 7) of the desiring body when the speaking subject confronts the sexual determination by the law of its identity? Reading the writing of the sexual asylum seeker exposes the unconventionality inherent in the inscriptions of the sexual subject when sexual identity is to be determined in actual asylum cases. Linearity, consistency and transparency guide the law's demand for a narrative of sexual identity, yet this demand is confounded by the silences, contradictions and fractured renderings of an asylum seeker's sexuality, particularly when transformed by the traumatic consequences of the experience of displacement and persecution. Testimonies solicited in the asylum hearing reverse the temporality of Santner's description of sexuality by testing the swerving constitution of sexuality against a norm established before the asylum seeker has arrived at the desired place of sanctuary. The fraudulent telos of a narrative of sexual identity is exposed precisely when the complex experiences of the globally displaced are tested at the culmination of their journeys. The narrative of sexual identity in the West culminating in the event of 'coming out' fails to successfully overlap with the moment of sexual determination by the law of the asylum seeker's testimony. The heterogeneous global space produced by sexual and gender asylum seekers is doubly critical: it exposes both the universalist pretensions of a linear and progressive narrativisation of sexual identity, and calls into question the straightforward and stereotypical readings of forcibly displaced queer global subjects.

The demand for asylum is 'the point of acute confrontation' between 'the fraught and adversarial insistence on a shared universe of rights and resources that the disenfranchised and persecuted peoples of the developing world import through their physical presence on the territory of developed states and through their claim to asylum' and 'the imperative of a new architecture of cosmopolitan democracy that takes human rights claims at face value' through an ideological discourse of 'the free flow of ideas across the globe' (Bhabha 2002: 180) that accompanies transnational capitalism. When the medium of individual life stories is tested by immigration officials, the narrative assumptions of teleological normalcy, consistency and transparency are confounded by transitory articulations of the contradictory experiences of sexual desire. The sexual and gender asylum seeker's writing of alternative cartographies of desire contradicts the stabilisation of global space through the identification of sexual identity and cultural difference.

The law's desire to identify and fix the sexual identity of the asylum seeker is countered by the desire for recognition by the asylum seeker. Both desire and recognition undermine the logic of identification. Judith Butler has convincingly argued that for 'subjects of desire' (1999b) the outwardly propulsive dynamic of desire, including the desire for recognition, is accompanied by the inadequacy of self-knowledge and incomplete knowledge of the other and *its* desire (Butler 2015). This argument is particularly relevant for sexual and gender asylum seekers whose stories are tentatively articulated in culturally incomprehensible contexts through the mediation of advocates who themselves translate faltering speech into narrative testimony for authorising interlocutors. The desire for recognition involves both the affirmation of an existing identity and the futural actualisation of its existence through the assent of an inadequately knowable other (Düttmann 2000).

The regulation of sexuality takes place between an affirmation and its confirmation in the 'as yet' temporality between the experience of unruly desire and the moment of recognition by the law. That is why an abstract theory of sexual fluidity inadequately expresses the power dynamics involved in the regulation of sexuality. Carl Stychin warns that 'mobility should not be "celebrated"' as the unproblematic basis for the constitution of a lesbian or gay identity (2000: 606). His illuminating analysis of transnational mobility in the context of same-sex relationships highlights the deployment of normative demands of sexual behaviour (monogamy rather than promiscuity), financial security and commitment in reviewing immigration requests. In the case of the forced migration of sexual asylum seekers, however, the legal demand for proof of homosexuality in the context of persecution rather than that of class-based, heteronormative norms of homosexual love reveals both the regulation and deregulation of transnational sexualities.

When the self-assertion of sexual identity is experienced as a problem rather than a given, and when its forced narrativisation at the point of granting or denying asylum is determined by the interlocutor who will confer this identity, the narratives demanded of sexual asylum seekers by the law fail the test of legibility. The 'swerving' (Santner 2016: 48) of sexuality in life trajectories was clearly identifiable in a Ukrainian lesbian's testimony before a Canadian tribunal in 2007 (Berg and Millbank 2007: 213). Having ended a relationship with a woman when she was young, the fear of homophobia led her to marry a man, after whose death she entered into a relationship with a woman. The immigration officials argued that since she stated she had been happy in her marriage, and she failed to sexually interact with her close women friends, her testimony was insufficiently credible to support an ascription of lesbian identity. The incredible assumption that proximity to women implies a (missed) opportunity to sexualise this proximity reveals a deliberate refusal to acknowledge the explicitly stated fear of homophobic violence that led her into a heterosexual marriage in the first place. When a narrative model of sequential decisions leading to self-realisation is expected, the testimony of lesbian sexuality swerving between fear and desire cannot be read.

Further, the endpoint of the narrative of sexual identity is assumed to be reached when self-realisation of one's sexuality is qualitatively understood as an affirmative articulation of desire. This assumption was exposed in a Pakistani man's repeated characterisation of homosexuality as a 'problem' (Berg and Millbank 2007: 200) in an asylum case in Australia. The initial judgment by the Australian immigration service (later overturned) argued that the use of this word showed that he did not see his homosexuality as a positive aspect of his personal identity. His words were read thus: 'Whilst claiming to view expression of homosexuality as a right, the Applicant thus also depicted it as a kind of deficiency or defect' (quoted in Berg and Millbank 2007: 200). The possibility that 'the problem' of homosexuality might be the difficulty of living as a gay man in a homophobic society, or indeed that the claimant saw his homosexuality as a *social* problem of homophobia rather than a personal one of internalised self-hatred, was not entertained in the judgment. The positive casting of 'coming out' as an emotionally affirmative act of self-valuation here denies the reality that coming out is a process rather than an act in a potentially hostile environment, and one fraught with fears and desires deriving from the uncontrollability of the effects it can generate in situations beyond one's individual control. *Narrative* resolution reduces this complex and ambivalent process to a single act, the culminating telos of a social, sexual and political trajectory ending in the confirmation of a sexual identity.

The failure of a determining reading practice that confers recognition on a sexual and gender asylum seeker's speech is most starkly seen in the inability to read the meaning-laden moments of silence; both the involuntary incapacity to articulate as well as the deliberate refusal to speak. Forced sexual and gender migration involves experiences of violence including physical assault and rape as well as emotional persecution such as social ostracisation. Toni A. E. Johnson explains that

> [T]he asylum hearing becomes a venue where 'unspeakable' occurrences stemming from persecutory experience must be given voice. However, the production of voice [. . .] is often stilted, filled with the gaps and omissions of the things [which] often pertain to violent and violative acts and the space of the courtroom does not induce individuals to be open about their experience, even though it is that openness that may well assist the granting of asylum. (2011: 67)

Narrativising a sexual identity on the basis of personal testimonies of past experiences is not just difficult, but also the occasion for encountering past traumas again in the painfully power-laden context of the encounter between a demand and the conferral of recognition. It is widely acknowledged both in psychological research and studies of jurisprudence that the experience of trauma fundamentally alters a person's ability to adequately, consistently and clearly articulate details of such experiences. Yet repeatedly in asylum claims, applicants have been rejected because their silences have been read as proof of the absence of evidence.

Just as coming out is not an act but a continual process, the declaration of sexual identity from the compromised position of a traumatised claimant confronting the state cannot be seen as a one-time expression of transparently readable sexual reality. Debora Singer of Asylum Aid, UK, describes the complexity of the interview situation thus: 'your own feelings about your sexuality, your reluctance for it to be known publicly, your lack of words related to sexual issues (in English or your own language) all come into play. Plus having to relive the trauma of how you were persecuted' (Singer 2015). Such expressions cannot be read if the interview is seen as the culminating moment for the transparent expression in words of one's identity. As Berg and Millbank rightly argue 'the development of their sexual identity [. . .] may still be in a state of flux or uncertainty at the time of the claim' (2007: 201). Autobiographical narratives by asylum claimants suffering post-traumatic stress and depression have consistently exhibited discrepancies, but the latter can only be cast as problems for reading if the former conditions are ignored.

In the 2002 case of *Mahmood* in Canada analysed by Berg and Millbank, the 25-year-old male claimant's solicited testimony was deemed unreliable precisely because initial silences were deemed to contradict information provided voluntarily. The silence involved the claimant's inability to provide explicit details of a gang-rape perpetrated on him when he was 15. He acknowledged 'pain and bleeding' (Berg and Millbank 2007: 202) due to the rape only when explicitly asked, but failed to describe these details voluntarily. This initial silence was contrasted to his ability to describe consensual sex with male partners as he grew older. No distinction was made by the tribunal between consensual and forced sex, with the corresponding assumption that the psychic consequences of publicly recounting both forms of sex were comparable, indeed the same. The experience of trauma, the difficulty of articulating it, and the intimidating official situation in front of (male) strangers were completely disregarded. The meaning of silence was rendered unreadable.

A decontextualised liberal notion of individual agency comes into play in the following example, which interprets the meaning of silence prior to an asylum claim rather than in the temporality of its making. The example registers how cultural blindness and assumptions of individual agency affect asylum decisions. In the case of *Re BYU* in 2003, a Canadian tribunal ruling, upheld by the federal court, stated that the claimant's failure to report a rape by four police officers *to the police* showed inadequate attempts to seek state protection (Berg and Millbank 2007: 203). This despite the fact that the hospital treating the claimant had reported the crime to the police. The impossibility (indeed the perversity) of demanding justice from a state that had violated the claimant was disregarded by the tribunal. The fact that the rape was reported by those who medically treated the victim was deemed of no consequence. The victim's silence in the past was interpreted as proof that insufficient recourse to state protection had been made. In effect, a state's violation of its own citizen's rights paradoxically became the alibi for negatively judging the claimant's past silence while in effect silencing the reporting of the crime.

The interview is the time of multiple times across culturally incommensurate places, and silence during testimony eloquently expresses their coexistence in the moment. Silences expose time 'as an inner redivision of time, as the production of gaps which are not manifestations of ignorance and belatedness but positive ruptures away from the normal logic of the division of temporalities' (Rancière 2017: 33). Silences rupture the temporal plotting of events according to a narrative of sexual resolution coinciding with the interview-based judgment. These silences are indeed often read as signs of belatedness ('the homosexual "problem"' of the insufficiently emancipated Pakistani gay man). Against this temporal plotting of progress, the testimony when narrativised in the moment of an interview constructs time 'as a milieu' (Rancière 2017: 33) of the coexistence of multiple times, events, affects and experiences. Silences, seeming contradictions, non-teleological affirmations articulate an injured self's experiences, which remain unreadable according to the demands of clear narrative articulations of sexual identity. When silence is read as muting or denying testimonies of oppression, asylum advocates are forced to explain them through 'derogatory characterizations of asylum seekers' countries of origin, as areas of barbarism or lack of civility in order to present a clear-cut picture of persecution' (Bhabha 2002: 162). Silences become read as civilisational signals of the 'belatedness' of other countries and cultures while simultaneously exposing the particularistic assumptions of universalist understandings of human rights. The logic behind both the excitation to discourse and the reading of silence 'might be described as "the worse the better" – the more oppressive the home state, the greater the chances of gaining asylum in the host state' (Bhabha 2002: 162). The readability of degrees of oppression, however, founders on the asylum seeker's inability to articulate past traumas, particularly in cases of repeated sexual assault. Silence interrupts a narrative viewpoint, turning 'the worse, the better' into the worse, the worse.[5] Thus precisely when derogatory notions of 'cultural difference' could be deployed for successful asylum applications according to a sliding scale of oppression, the readability of silences, contradictions and so-called 'evasions' in sexual asylum narratives undermines the determination by the law of a person's sexual identity.

It is precisely this vicious circle that is slowly being broken in recent court judgments around interview procedures for sexual and gender asylum seekers. In 2014 the European Court of Justice ruled that the requirement of proof of homosexuality had to be removed from asylum interview procedures. In 2016 the UK Home Office issued guidelines to caseworkers basing its advice on the EU Charter of Fundamental Rights. These clearly state that the interrogation of details of sexual experiences and demanding proof of sexual activity (such as photographs) violated the right to respect for private life.[6] Further, the court ruled that requiring knowledge of places such as gay clubs and other establishments perpetuated stereotypes of gay men and lesbians against which asylum seekers were being illegitimately tested.[7] Ignorance of homosexual, mainly urban, life in the West could not be used as evidence in deciding a claimant's sexuality. The universal right to respect for privacy enabled asylum seekers from different countries to maintain silence without being judged negatively qua the provision of evidence of sexuality, while the rejection of stereotypical assumptions of homosexual behaviour acknowledged the culturally specific circumstances of the asylum seeker.

While sexual determination at the time of the asylum claim seeks to convert the reading of desire into the writing of sexual identity, European and international law deploys a range of universal discourses (respect for privacy and human dignity) to paradoxically acknowledge the cultural specificity of asylum seekers' social and sexual experiences. This universal deployment of the defence of the particular is not a contradiction. Rather, as Rancière argues, the universal 'is not the law ruling over the multiple and the particular. It is the principle at work in the operation which calls into question the distribution of the sensible separating universal matters from particular matters' (2009: 282–3). The deployment of cultural difference across nation-states in Europe as a crucial element in the reading of sexual identity folds the universal into the particular in a specific way, thus undoing a clear separation between the universal category of the 'human' and the particularities of lived sexuality.

Conclusion

Applying the law is inseparable from putting the failures of the law to work for unconventional reconceptualisations of the meaning of justice. Gillian Rose argues that 'unaddressable oppositions between morality and legality [. . .] good will and natural desire and inclination, force and generality, can be traced to an historically specific legal structure which establishes [. . .] the juridical fiction of persons, things and obligations' (1984: 2–3). Sexual and gender asylum expands Rose's understanding of the paradoxes of civil society and underlines the relation between morality and legality as the legal fiction of persons and their sexual identity is determined. The continual transformation of this relation by practices of writing and reading sexual asylum cases registers how (inter)national obligations towards those needing sanctuary must keep positing oppositions and identities that cannot be permanently sustained. The hetero/homo and male/female oppositions that undergird sexual asylum cases are both reinforced *and* reworked in the different cases analysed in this chapter. 'The juridical opposition between free subjects and subjected things', Rose argues, 'characterizes [. . .] the relation of the individual to itself in modern states' (1984: 2–3). Sexual asylum cases demonstrate that asylum seekers are individuals who are both subject to the state while also capable of exposing the limitations of the law and altering their relation to the state in transformative ways. Subjects become subjected things before the law just as their objecthood can be converted into agency through the law. Sexual asylum displaces this opposition by revealing how agency and its absence emerge continually in 'the historical production and reproduction . . . of illusory contraries' (Rose 1984: 2–3).

The politics of sexual and gender asylum exposes the force-field between unstable desires writing global space queerly, and national laws seeking to read bodies straightforwardly. The desiring body queerly rewrites global space as the paradoxical place where universality and particularity intersect and are redefined. The claims around sexual asylum also further a reconsideration of the category of the human in the tension between human rights conventions and sexual asylum cases. They put pressure on conventional inscriptions of sexual identity by demonstrating how forced migration in circumstances of extreme persecution centralises the global as the crucial space for deregulating sexuality. The asylum seeker's body configures the global into the national through international law and deranges conventional understandings of both sexual identity and cultural difference.

Notes

1. http://www.unhcr.org/asylum-seekers.html (accessed 17 May 2019).
2. Manalansan's focus is primarily on employment migration and the heteronormative assumptions of gender in migration studies. My focus is specifically on *the law's* characterisation of gendered and sexual bodies in refugee law and sexual asylum cases.
3. The 2004 decision applied only to male-to-female (MTF) transgender persons.
4. In the US, gays and lesbian were recognised as belonging to 'a particular social group' (Refugee Convention 1951) in 1990.
5. The gendered dimensions of this failure of narrative are also crucial, since in some research a consistently high level of physical assault of lesbians is discernible while percentages vary for gay men across different countries (Berg and Millbank 2007: 202).
6. http://www.bbc.com/news/30290532 (accessed 17 May 2019). The ECJ's judgment against the Dutch government's demand for proof of homosexuality was made applicable to all EU nations. Its impact outside the Netherlands is discernible in the fact that one UK immigration official stated that *one out of ten* asylum claims were turned down on the basis of inadequate proof.
7. Sabine Jansen provides numerous examples of the application of stereotypes to sexual asylum seekers, including knowledge of authors, social venues including bars, and expressions of linear sexual identity development. On reviewing such cases, she observes, 'It seems that a gay male asylum seeker is someone who visits gay venues regularly, who reads gay classics like Oscar Wilde, who is familiar with rainbow flags and pink triangles, who had a difficult coming-out process and a serious psychological struggle connected to it, who on the other hand can elaborate extensively on his coming-out process, and who is very interested in developing his sexual identity instead of just practising same-sex sexual acts' (Jansen 2014: 2).

Bibliography

Ampuja, Marko (2011), 'Globalization theory, media-centrism and neoliberalism: a critique of recent intellectual trends', *Critical Sociology*, 38.2: 281–301.

Berg, Lauri, and Jenni Millbank (2007), 'Constructing the personal narratives of lesbian, gay and bisexual asylum claimants', *Journal of Refugee Studies*, 22.1: 195–223.

Bhabha, Jacqueline (2002), 'Internationalist gatekeepers? The tension between asylum advocacy and human rights', *Harvard Law Journal*, 15: 155–81.

Butler, Judith (1999a), *Gender Trouble: Feminism and the Subversion of Identity* (London: Routledge).

Butler, Judith (1999b), *Subjects of Desire: Hegelian Reflections in Twentieth-Century France* (New York: Columbia University Press).

Butler, Judith (2015), *Senses of the Subject* (New York: Fordham University Press).

Castells, Manuel (2000), *The Information Age: Economy Society and Culture. Volume I: The Rise of the Network Society* (Oxford: Blackwell).

Dasgupta, Sudeep (2017), 'The aesthetics of indirection: intermittent adjacencies and subaltern presences at the borders of Europe', *Cinéma & Cie*, 17.28: 41–50.

Duffy, Nick (2016), 'Home Office bans caseworkers from asking LGBT asylum seekers for "proof" of gay sex', *Pink News*, 8 August, http://www.pinknews. co.uk/2016/08/08/home-office-bans-caseworkers-from-asking-lgbt-asylum-seekers-for-proof-of-gay-sex/ (accessed 20 September 2017).

Düttmann, Alexander García (2000), *Between Cultures: Tensions in the Struggle for Recognition* (London: Verso).

Goodman, Kevis (2016), 'Introduction', in Kevis Goodman, with Bonnie Honig, Peter E. Gordon and Hent de Vries (eds), *The Weight of All Flesh: On the Subject Matter of Political Economy* (Oxford: Oxford University Press), 1–19.

Goodwin-Gill, Guy S. (2008), 'Convention Relating to the Status of Refugees (1951) and the Protocol Relating to the Status of Refugees (1967)', *United Nations Audiovisual Library of International Law*, http://legal.un.org/avl/ha/prsr/prsr. html (accessed 5 July 2017).

Jansen, Sabine (2014), 'Credibility, or how to assess the sexual orientation of an asylum seeker?', paper given at the EDAL Conference 2014: 'Reflections on the Current Application of the EU Asylum Acquis Workshop Sexual Orientation, Gender Identity and Human Dignity', http://www.asylumlawdatabase.eu/sites/ www.asylumlawdatabase.eu/files/aldfiles/Credibility%20of%20sexual%20 orientation%2C%20%20presentation%20Sabine%20Jansen%20at%20 EDAL%20conference%20Jan%202014.pdf (accessed 30 April 2018).

Johnson, Toni A. M. (2011), 'On silence, sexuality and skeletons: reconceptualizing narrative in sexual asylum hearings', *Social and Legal Studies*, 20.1: 57–78.

Landau, Joseph (2004), '"Soft immutability" and "imputed gay identity": recent developments in transgender and sexual-orientation-based asylum law', *Fordham Law Journal*, 32.2: 101–26.

Luibhéid, Eithne (2008), 'Sexuality, migration and the shifting line between legal and illegal status', *GLQ: A Journal of Lesbian and Gay Studies*, 14.2–3: 289–315.

Manalansan IV, Martin F. (2006), 'Queer intersections: sexuality and gender in migration studies', *The International Migration Review*, 40.1: 224–49.

Marouf, Fatma E. (2008), 'The emerging importance of "social visibility" in defining a "particular social group" and its potential impact on asylum claims related to sexual orientation and gender', *Yale Law and Policy Review*, 27.1: 47–106.

Nancy, Jean-Luc (2002), *Hegel: The Restlessness of the Negative* (Minneapolis: University of Minnesota Press).

Rancière, Jacques (2009), 'The method of equality: an answer to some questions', in *Jacques Rancière: History, Politics, Aesthetics*, ed. G. Rockhill and P. Watts (Durham, NC: Duke University Press), 273–88.

Rancière, Jacques (2017), *Modern Times: Essays on Temporality in Art and Politics* (Zagreb: Multimedijalni institut).

Rich, Adrienne (1986), *Blood, Bread, Poetry: Selected Prose, 1979–1985* (New York: Norton).

Rose, Gillian (1984), *Dialectic of Nihilism: Post-Structuralism and Law* (London: Basil Blackwell).

Rose, Gillian (1996), *Mourning Becomes the Law: Philosophy and Representation* (Cambridge: Cambridge University Press).

Santner, Eric E. (2001), *The Psychotheology of Everyday Life: Reflections on Freud and Rozenzweig* (Chicago: University of Chicago Press).

Santner, Eric E. (2016), *The Weight of All Flesh: On the Subject Matter of Political Economy*, ed. K. Goodman (Oxford: Oxford University Press).

Singer, Debora (2015), 'How do you prove you are gay? A culture of disbelief is traumatizing asylum seekers', *The Guardian*, 24 November, https://www.theguardian.com/commentisfree/2015/nov/24/gay-asylum-seekers-sexuality-home-office (accessed 15 September 2017).

Stychin, Carl F. (2000), '"A stranger to its laws": sovereign bodies, global sexualities and transnational citizens', *Journal of Law and Society*, 27.4: 601–25.

Chapter 6

Morality and Law in the Context of Asylum Claims

Anthony Good

The 1951 Refugee Convention is often depicted as a recognition of the special moral claims of refugees as persons suffering persecution because of their beliefs or ethnicity, and British politicians are fond of extolling our 'proud tradition' of welcoming refugees.[1] In fact, it has been argued that the Convention's purpose is rather different, and that its continued observance, despite perceived popular antipathy towards asylum seekers, is a paradoxical confirmation of the legitimacy of immigration controls in a modern democracy. There is an irreconcilable tension between the need for liberal democracies to portray themselves as representing shared communities with common values, including recognition of basic human rights such as the right not to suffer persecution, and the discretionary right asserted by all modern states to decide who can enter and reside in their territory. This accounts for what Gibney (2014: n.p.) terms the 'schizophrenic response' of European states, whereby they 'continue to embrace asylum but spurn the asylum seeker' and offer protection only grudgingly. From this perspective, indeed, 'the asylum seeker' becomes every bit as much of an abstraction as the notion of asylum itself, a tendency encouraged by the widespread use of dehumanising metaphors – likening asylum seekers to a 'flood' or 'torrent', potentially 'swamping' the recipient society (Charteris-Black 2006: 570–2).

Countering this dominant official and popular discourse are eruptions of activism and resistance that come to the fore particularly at moments of 'crisis' such as the mass influx of Syrian refugees into Europe. These reflect tensions between two competing approaches to refugee issues: an instrumental security model emphasising control of refugees on the basis of the balance between the perceived risks they pose and the opportunities they offer to receiving countries; and an individual rights model focusing on asylum seekers as unique individuals whose applications must be considered on their own merits (Goodwin-Gill 2001: 14–15). Right across Europe, administrative and legal systems strike their own balances between these two tendencies (Gill and Good 2019).

Writings on asylum often take as their starting point one of the classic texts of post-war British sociology, Stanley Cohen's *Folk Devils and Moral Panics*, first published in 1972. Cohen characterised the media reporting of confrontations between teenage 'mods' and 'rockers' during 1964 as an example of a 'moral panic', arising when a 'condition, episode, person or group of persons emerges to become defined as a threat to societal values and interests' (2002: 1). In his introduction to the third edition, Cohen looked at further examples of 'moral panics' that had arisen in the years following the book's first appearance, including the case of refugees and asylum seekers (2002: xxii–xxvi). He characterises such panics as focused on issues that are actually new forms of older worries and concerns (2002: vii–viii), and in these terms the asylum panic seems a particular manifestation of a long-running, perhaps eternal, fear of strangers (Simmel 1950). Indeed, the policies of refugee-receiving states in the Global North display both of the classic responses to outsiders identified by Zygmunt Bauman (1995: 2). 'Anthropophagy' – 'devouring' strangers and 'metaphorically transforming them into a tissue indistinguishable from one's own' – is evident in Home Office requirements that would-be citizens should first display mastery of British culture and language, while 'anthropoemy' – 'vomiting' out strangers and 'banishing them from the limits of the orderly world' – is exemplified by the increasing use of detention in the UK, the fences erected along Eastern European borders in response to the Syrian refugee 'crisis', and Australian policies of marooning asylum applicants on remote islands.

Public concern regarding asylum differs from most other moral panics, however. First, it has been long-drawn-out rather than focused on 'specific newsworthy episodes' – for example, in the *Daily Mail*'s 'deliberate and ugly . . . campaign of vilification' (Cohen 2002: xxiii). This seems a rare example of a moral panic that is chronic rather than acute in nature. Secondly, it is more directly political; the main political parties have 'not only led and legitimated public hostility, but spoken with a voice indistinguishable from the tabloid press' (Cohen 2002: xxiii). Thirdly, there are marked differences between people's views on asylum (and immigration generally) in the abstract, and their responses at a personal level, when the asylum seekers are their neighbours or fellow parents at their children's school (Finney and Peach 2004: 22). In such contexts empathy and tolerance may become more evident. This seems at first sight a reversal of the state-level schizophrenia mentioned above, in that popular animosity manifests itself towards asylum seekers considered in the abstract, whereas individuals may experience greater goodwill in practice. Yet this apparent paradox resolves itself in the other half of Cohen's title. The trope of the asylum seeker as 'folk devil' can only be sustained in the abstract, for it is necessarily a caricature – one of a panoply of stereotyped 'devils' that jostle continually for public attention: the terrorist, the religious fundamentalist, the paedophile, the drug addict and so on.

With or without such caveats, Cohen's characterisation of public and media attitudes towards asylum seekers as a form of 'moral panic' has frequently been echoed by other writers over the following decade (for example, Welch and Schuster 2005; Martin 2015), to the extent that describing asylum in this way risks becoming a dead metaphor that has lost much of its explanatory bite. This chapter approaches the link between refugees and morality in a slightly different way, looking particularly at the legal and administrative processes through which asylum seekers attempt to obtain recognition of their status as refugees in two different national contexts: the United Kingdom and France.

Popular and official reactions induced by moral panics are usually 'out of all proportion to the actual threat offered' (Hall et al. 1978: 16), and 'the moral barricades are manned by editors, bishops, politicians and other right-thinking people' (Cohen 2002: 1). These 'moral entrepreneurs' (Becker 1963: 147) include both 'rule creators' who spearhead crusading campaigns aimed at influencing public opinion, and 'rule enforcers' who feel obliged to reflect changed public attitudes in their enforcement behaviour, either to enhance or retain public respect for their role, or simply because they see rule enforcement as a defining feature of their job, irrespective of the content of the rules themselves (Becker 1963: 156). One particular set of 'rule enforcers' are the immigration judges who hear asylum appeals in France and the UK. Examining their role requires us to look more broadly at the relationships between law and morality, as seen by both legal professionals and lay litigants.

Asylum decision making in France and the United Kingdom

Both France and the UK base their asylum decisions on Article 1A(2) of the 1951 UN Refugee Convention – which defines a 'refugee' as someone having a 'well-founded fear of being persecuted for reasons of race, religion, nationality, membership of a particular social group or political opinion' – but the administrative and legal procedures adopted by each nation-state for determining whether an individual satisfies this definition involve complex processes of cultural and linguistic translation and interpretation, reflecting the different legal cultures into which they are embedded. For example, the five 'reasons' listed in that definition were undefined in the Convention itself, and the list does not fully reflect contemporary situations and understandings, particularly in its failure to address persecution for reasons of gender and sexuality (Crawley 2000; Spijkerboer 2013). Each national legal system has developed its own ways of addressing such lacunae. In both countries, too, the administrative and legal entities involved in asylum decision making have undergone frequent organisational and terminological changes.[2] Fortunately, however, the elements most relevant to the present discussion, the structures of asylum appeal hearings themselves and the nature of the decision making that takes place there, have not significantly altered in form. The following discussion uses the nomenclature applicable at the time of writing.

In the UK, asylum claims are administered by UK Visas and Immigration, a branch of the Home Office. Soon after receiving a claim, UKVI conducts a screening interview to establish the applicant's identity and collect basic personal information. A more lengthy substantive interview with a UKVI case-owner takes place a few weeks later. This focuses on the chronology of the applicant's narrative, its internal credibility, and its consistency with Country of Origin Information (COI) about their home country, particularly the level of risk that persons of their background are said to face.[3] At both interviews interpreters hired by UKVI are generally present.[4] If the case-owner decides that the claim is valid, the applicant is notified that they are to be granted refugee status or another form of protection, but no specific reasons are given. Most claims are refused, however, so the case-owner writes a detailed Reasons for Refusal Letter (RFRL) explaining and justifying this decision. Most RFRLs claim that the applicant's story lacks credibility because of alleged inconsistencies or because aspects of their narrative are deemed inconsistent with the COI.

Most such refusals carry rights of appeal to the First-tier Tribunal (Immigration and Asylum Chamber), whose immigration judges sit in at several hearing centres across the UK. There are marked differences in procedure – and in outcomes – between different hearing centres and different judges (Gill et al. 2018). A solicitor assembles the documents for the appeal, but (in England and Wales though generally not in Scotland) the advocate who actually represents the appellant in court is normally a barrister. UKVI is usually represented in court by a Home Office Presenting Officer (HOPO), a civil servant rather than a professional lawyer. Interpreters are provided by the Court Service.[5]

Appeal hearings begin with the appellant's 'examination-in-chief'. This is usually very short; appellants are merely asked by their counsel to confirm that the contents of their asylum interview transcript and witness statement are true and that they wish to submit these as evidence. The HOPO then cross-examines the appellant, asking detailed questions in the hope of eliciting replies that seem inconsistent with the appellant's previous statements, thereby casting doubt on their credibility. Very occasionally other witnesses are called to corroborate the appellant's story or give expert evidence. Expert evidence is usually presented only in written form, however, and is always adduced by the appellant rather than the Home Office. It is mostly medical in nature: skin experts give evidence on causes of scarring, or psychiatrists testify regarding the incidence of PTSD. Somewhat less commonly there is evidence from 'country experts' with specialised knowledge of the appellant's country of origin.[6]

The HOPO then makes closing submissions, arguing that the refusal of asylum should be upheld. These generally involve attacks on the credibility of the appellant's narrative, as well as 'objective evidence' in the form of COI about the situation in their home country. The appellant's barrister then attempts to rebut the credibility points and offers rival interpretations of the COI. After the hearing, the judge takes away the entire 'bundle' of documentary evidence, and over the next few days produces a written determination announcing and justifying his or her decision. This must assess the credibility of the appellant's account; indicate how much weight was given to each significant piece of evidence, which usually involves assessing and weighing the COI and expert evidence; and provide a reasoned explanation of how the decision was arrived at. Subsequent appeals to higher courts are limited to matters of law. Although the boundary between law and fact is often hazy in asylum claims, there is usually no fresh witness testimony at these later hearings.

In France, would-be refugees must obtain asylum application forms from their local Préfecture, and submit these, along with written statements in French, to the Office français de protection des réfugiés et apatrides (OFPRA), a public institution working under the Ministry of the Interior. An OFPRA caseworker (*officier de protection*) from the appropriate geographical division interviews the applicant. An interpreter is provided if necessary. The caseworker first collects basic personal information on the applicant and then focuses on their narrative and reasons for seeking asylum. The caseworker forwards a proposal to accept or reject the application to their Head of Section, who signs the final decision. The applicant is then sent a letter informing them of the outcome. OFPRA caseworkers often cite COI in the 'Establishment of the Facts' section of the case file, but only the actual decision and interview transcript are sent to the applicant. French rejection letters are far shorter than British RFRLs: one or two paragraphs summarise the applicant's reasons for applying for refugee status, and a few further paragraphs give rather generic reasons of law and fact why the application has been refused. The full OFPRA file can, however, be accessed by applicants and their advocates at the appeal stage.

Appeals against OFPRA decisions are heard by panels of three judges at the National Asylum Court (Cour nationale du droit d'asile; CNDA) on the outskirts of Paris. The chair (*président*) – a magistrate – is flanked by a 'UNHCR assessor' (*assesseur HCR*) nominated by UNHCR and approved by the vice-president of the Council of State, and an 'administration assessor' (*assesseur de l'administration*) nominated by a minister on OFPRA's governing board. Appellants are entitled to be assisted by a barrister (*conseil*) and interpreter. Prior to the hearing, a CNDA *rapporteur* – a functionary who has no equivalent in common law systems – writes a report based on the case file, including an opinion (*avis*) on whether the appeal should be accepted or rejected. Only the *président* has the right to see the case file in advance, though not all do so (Valluy 2004).

In any one morning or afternoon session, a panel may decide up to thirteen different appeals.[7] Each begins with the *rapporteur* reading the report they have prepared on that case. The panel then questions the applicant: some chairs ask the initial questions themselves, while others invite the two assessors to go first. The barrister's oral pleadings (*plaidoiries*) come at the end.

The length of the judges' questioning depends on the nature and complexity of the case, but the time taken to hear each appeal – including the reading out of the *rapporteur*'s report and the barrister's statement – is generally little more than 30 minutes.[8]

After all the appeals have been heard the room is cleared, and the judges discuss all the cases that have come before them, deciding whether to annul OFPRA's original decision (and therefore grant refugee status or subsidiary protection) or to reject the appellant's appeal. Although the case files are available to them, the time pressures that judges are under mean that they have little opportunity to consult them, and they rely heavily on the *rapporteur*'s summaries, both during the hearings and when reaching their decisions. The *rapporteur* takes notes of their deliberations and afterwards writes drafts of each decision, which are sent to the panel chair for signature. When the panel annuls the original OFPRA decision, the letter to the appellant simply states that they have been granted refugee status or subsidiary protection, without indicating reasons. Unsuccessful appellants receive a decision letter, usually only two or three pages long, which summarises the arguments (*moyens*) developed at the appeal and the reasons for rejection. Common reasons are that the applicant's responses were 'contradictory', 'confused', 'unconvincing' or 'lacking in personal details' (*pas personnalisées*). These letters have been disparagingly described by a former UNHCR assessor as 'a terse summary of the story in ten lines, ending with a stereotyped phrase stating the positive or negative conclusion' (Valluy 2004).

Law, morality and culture: professional and lay discourses

Professional discourses

Is law a distinct, autonomous domain, or is it embedded in the broader moral discourses and cultures of the society within which it is located; and if so, to what degree? Law is clearly culturally embedded to the extent of being normative, but is it *moral*? Answers to this question vary according to context. In this discussion, I use 'ethics' to refer to sets of rules associated with specific professional identities or institutional contexts, whereas 'morality' relates to fundamental principles of right and wrong, operating primarily at a personal level. For simplicity I discuss only cases where decisions are made by professional judges and assessors, rather than by lay juries who might be expected to be more directly swayed by cultural and media influences external to the legal sphere itself. That limitation is appropriate anyway, because this is what happens at asylum appeals in both countries.

The legal anthropologist Lawrence Rosen, studying *qadi* courts in Morocco, takes a cultural approach to law resembling Geertz's (1965) account of religion. Rosen argues that law, like religion, serves as a 'metasystem which creates order in a universe that is often experienced in a more disorderly way'

(1989: 17). He recognises, however, that his approach is only partly applicable to common law systems since whereas 'law and morality are seen as entirely consonant' in Islamic legal systems, there is in common law 'a fundamentally problematic aspect' to this relationship. For *qadi* courts 'culture is not outside of the law but integral to it' (1989: 72), whereas common law judges 'are not supposed to bring their own moral values into their decisions' (Rosen 2006: 26). If common law judges are to appeal to moral propositions, 'their views may have to be couched indirectly . . . through a claim that they accord with such deep, shared sentiments of society as to be almost invisible in the process' (Rosen 2006: 27).[9]

In common law countries, 'the dominant view in both the teaching and practice of law [is] that most cases are decided by a value-neutral process of rule selection and application' (Conley and O'Barr 1990: 60). Students are required to concentrate on 'the structures of text and authority that give legal opinions power', rather than the 'attendant moral and social contexts' (Mertz 2002). In brief, legal ethics can be seen as predominantly Kantian, as deontological rather than consequentialist in character; that is, virtue consists in doing one's duty by taking decisions in closest possible adherence to the rules rather than decisions leading to the most desirable or useful outcomes.[10]

Although common law may inhibit overt judicial appeals to public morality, it does place limits on the extent to which legal decision making can *depart* from the moral standards of society at large. For example, Home Office caseworkers used to be told in their office manual (Immigration and Nationality Directorate 2002: ¶14.1, Annex A) that they should only appeal tribunal decisions if there were strong grounds for thinking that the judge had made a legal error or that the decision was 'Wednesbury unreasonable' (a reference to *Associated Provincial Picture Houses Ltd v Wednesbury Corporation* [1948] 1 KB 223). They were referred to Lord Diplock's gloss that this meant a decision 'so outrageous in its defiance of logic or of accepted moral standards that no sensible person . . . could have arrived at it' (*Council of Civil Service Unions v Minister for the Civil Service* [1984] UKHL 9). True to its positivist slant, however, English law has since tended to resile from Diplock's evocation of moral standards. For example, Lord Carnwath asked:

> how [can] 'outrage' . . . ever be an appropriate or acceptable part of the judicial armoury? [. . .] And how do 'moral standards' come into this formulation? There may be many ways in which the conduct of public authorities can be morally objectionable . . . Such activities may be illegal, but not because . . . judges find them outrageous. (2013: 4)

As illustrated by a recent key asylum decision – *R (on the application of Mohibullah) v Secretary of State for the Home Department* [2016] UKUT 00561 (IAC) – courts often prefer the criterion of 'conspicuous unfairness' rather than 'moral outrage'.

Common law, then, addresses matters relating to public policy (*ordre public*) rather than matters of morality (*bonnes moeurs*). Seen in that way, common law systems appear almost as the antithesis of the Moroccan courts studied by Rosen, while continental, code-based legal systems seem to occupy a middle ground. German law, for example, uses the term '*gute Sitten*' – 'good morals' or 'good manners' – which is understood to encompass both public order and morality (Alexidze 1981: 239). As Rosen puts it, German judges are 'personally authorised to look for "good moral precepts"' (2006: 27).

French law also deals directly with personal morality through the notion of the 'intimate conviction' (*intime conviction*) required of judges when coming to their decisions. Whereas British and American judges are enjoined to decide cases by weighing the evidence and seeing whether the appropriate standard of proof has been met – 'a reasonable degree of likelihood' in asylum cases – French judges must examine their consciences and reach decisions according to their 'innermost conviction'. This is a founding principle of post-Revolutionary French law (Inchauspé 2015: 604), and in French criminal cases Art. 353 of the *Code de procédure pénale* is read out to judges and jurors before they retire to consider their verdict. It ends: 'The law asks them but this single question, which encloses the full scope of their duties: have you an inner belief?' (trans. Kobelinsky 2019: 54). CNDA judges explicitly invoke this same principle in reaching their decisions (Belorgey 2003; Valluy 2004). Such a requirement seems to offer far greater scope for judges to draw on personal moral convictions and broader societal moral codes.

Lay discourses: 'legal consciousness'

We now turn from the approaches to law internalised by legal professionals to what Merry terms 'legal consciousness' (1990: 5), the understandings of the legal system displayed by members of the public who come intermittently into contact with it. For example, Conley and O'Barr (1990) studied language-use in small claims and magistrates courts in the United States, where litigants present their own cases rather than hiring lawyers. They found that the ways in which lay persons present their problems in court lie along a continuum. At one extreme, some adopt a *rule-oriented* approach, relating their problems to specific laws or regulations that have allegedly been violated. This is potentially quite a successful strategy because it chimes with the perspectives of legal professionals themselves. There is a good chance that people presenting their problems in this way will be fully understood.

At the other extreme, a *relational orientation* is characterised by 'fuzzier' definitions of issues, whereby rights and responsibilities are predicated on 'a broad notion of social interdependence' rather than on obeying rules (Conley and O'Barr 1990: 61). Such testimony stresses issues that reflect the litigant's general social situation 'but are irrelevant to the court's more limited and rule-centered agenda'. Lawyers tend to view such testimonies as illogical and unstructured, because they conform to a logic so different from that of the legal system as to be largely incomprehensible to those trained in formal legal analysis. It is fundamentally a moral discourse. Consequently, the courts 'often fail to understand their cases, regardless of their legal merits' (Conley and O'Barr 1990: 61).

In her own work on lower courts in the USA, Merry focuses on the role of court officials rather than litigants, and identifies three types of legal discourse – legal, moral and therapeutic – rather than Conley and O'Barr's bipolar continuum. Court officials know from bitter experience how messy cases involving close relatives or neighbours often become when addressed through strict legal procedures (among themselves, they label these 'rubbish cases'), and do their best to persuade would-be litigants that their problem is not legal at all, but a failure of interpersonal relations that should be resolved through mediation or counselling. Many aspiring litigants are open to such a reframing; after all, Merry's 'moral discourse', being 'a discourse of relationships, of moral obligations' (1990: 113), resembles Conley and O'Barr's 'relational orientation'. Court officials themselves, however, assume a clear distinction between law and morality, whereby issues are 'deemed trivial in a legal sense, though important in terms of the morality of interpersonal relationships' (Merry 1990: 179). The gatekeepers to the American legal system, then, see problems of interpersonal morality as 'unworthy of court attention' (Merry 1990: 130).

In the particular case of asylum, the scope for applicants to chose their own styles of discourse – let alone to change them strategically according to their evolving perceptions of their effectiveness as the case proceeds – is virtually nil, partly because they usually lack even a folk-appreciation of the British or French legal systems, but mainly because their personal discourses are suppressed by the mediation of legal representatives and court interpreters. In practice, the presentation of their asylum claims is done by legal professionals and almost inevitably takes on a rule-oriented form. Even when asylum seekers appear in court without legal representation, their unfamiliarity with court procedure and their need to work through an interpreter are likely to place severe limits on the discursive scope of their presentation.

Narratives of persecution

Despite what was said earlier about the impropriety in principle of common law judges appealing to general, non-legal moral precepts, asylum decision making lends itself to the making of such judgments in practice, because of the central role played by credibility. Most asylum seekers, because of the circumstances under which they fled from their countries of origin, cannot provide evidential support to the extent normally expected in a court of law. They cannot call witnesses or produce documents and often the only evidence they have – on which the all-important credibility decision will largely be based – is their personal history, their individual narrative of persecution. The basic requirement is that their story be 'coherent and plausible' and 'not run counter to generally known facts' (UNHCR 1992: para 204), but there is no standard means of carrying out such assessments, which depend almost entirely on unique individual circumstances.

On several occasions during the course of their asylum application, would-be refugees in the UK tell their stories to interlocutors of various kinds: UKVI case-owners, their own solicitors, medical experts, and so on. These interviews differ in terms of the purposes and motives of the questioners, and the techniques and strategies followed, though they all depart from normal conversational modes because of the artificially rigid question-and-answer format employed in legal processes (Atkinson and Drew 1979). Moreover – although lawyers largely discount this unless a fairly disastrous breakdown in communication occurs – these are actually trialogues involving interpreters too (Gibb and Good 2014). There are, no doubt, personal differences in interviewing style among UKVI case-owners and immigration solicitors.[11] Even so, there are clear generic differences between the two kinds of interview. One does not even have to read the two transcribed extracts below to notice these differences; their appearances on the page are quite distinct.[12]

The first extract comes from a UKVI asylum interview with Mr P, a young Tamil man from Sri Lanka.[13] The early stages of the interview ran as follows:

Case-owner: I'm interested in the problems that caused you to leave Sri Lanka. When did these start?

Mr P: November. I was arrested by the army. [Interpreter checks] They told me that I was being arrested on suspicion . . . [*Interpreter*: What suspicion?] Suspicion that I was supporting the . . . [*Interpreter*: Who?] the LTTE.
[46-second pause]

Case-owner: Did the army offer any evidence for suspecting you?

Mr P: No.
[14-second pause]

Case-owner: Who arrested you?

Mr P: Sri Lankan army.
[31-second pause]

Case-owner: Do you know the names or the rank of any of the army men?

Mr P: No.
[15-second pause]

Case-owner: How many men arrested you?

Mr P: Seven army personnel, but this was during a round-up.
[27-second pause]

Case-owner: Who else was arrested during this round-up?

Mr P: Two others.
[11-second pause]

Case-owner:	Who were the two others arrested?
Mr P:	Two men . . . men from my village . . . my friends. One person's name is Re— . . . and Ra—.
	[11-second pause]
Case-owner:	And the other?
Interpreter:	I said. Re— is one and Ra— is the other.
Case-owner:	Ah sorry, yeah; Re— . . .
	[38-second pause]
Case-owner:	At what time of day were you arrested?
Mr P:	Eight in the morning.
	[37-second pause]

The second extract comes from a statement-taking interview between a solicitor and Mrs A, a Somali woman who had fled to Ethiopia before coming to the UK with her children.[14] The interview began with two hours of detailed discussion about Mrs A's clan membership. This was crucial because if it was accepted that she was indeed a member of the Ashraf minority clan, she was very likely to gain asylum. She was then asked about the origins of the civil war in Somalia, the arrival of UN forces in B, her home town, and its takeover by the Habr Gedir clan after the UN left. The interview continued as follows:

Solicitor:	And what happened to you and your family?
Mrs A:	Then we were living like that, until the RRA took control of B from the Habr Gedir.
Interpreter:	The RRA is a Rahanweyn militia. I think R stands for Rahanweyn and A for army; probably it's an English abbreviation.
Mrs A:	So they made this organisation to fight with the majority clans. It took them many, many years to recoup the region from the Habr Gedir.
Solicitor:	Do you remember when they did?
Mrs A:	I would say either the end of 1995 or 1996.
Solicitor:	And what were things like when they took control?
Mrs A:	Well, they were militia, and they started persecuting minorities such as Ashraf, which is my clan. [. . .]
Solicitor:	And were you yourself attacked during this period?
Mrs A:	Let me come to the main incident. One day – it was before early morning prayers – a group of armed militia men attacked our home. Our house was big, and they forced their way by breaking the main gate. They started shooting at us. My father was killed. They sprayed bullets in the house, killing my father and brother, and my cousin on my mother's side was wounded. My mother was also wounded. I panicked and I tried to flee. I don't know what happened, but someone hit me on the head with something. I was pregnant at the time. I became unconscious. In the morning after sunrise, the neighbours came for our rescue. I, my

> mother and our two daughters were taken to a house within the neighbourhood. I was also bleeding. I thought I would die. I was told what happened, and I was informed of the death of my brother and father. My mother was injured, but from that day she was not the same person because of the shock. And that's when my father was buried, the same day. And we only remained in B for two weeks and we left for Ethiopia.

Solicitor:	I know this is very painful no doubt to talk about, but I just have to clarify, did you lose the baby?
Mrs A:	Yes the girl is alive, but I have been bleeding until I give birth.
Solicitor:	But do you think the bleeding was because of the injury to the head?
Mrs A:	I don't know if I was hit here, I only know I was hit on the head. If I was hit on the stomach, I don't know.
Solicitor:	And you don't believe that you were sexually assaulted?
Mrs A:	I don't believe, no.
Solicitor:	Okay, so you then went to Ethiopia. What year was this?
Mrs A:	It was March 1997 when we left.

UKVI interviews are interrogative in form, displaying almost no narrative give-and-take and a preponderance of short, factual questions that often elicit only monosyllabic answers. The excruciatingly long pauses further inhibit the interviewee's ability to supply a coherent narrative. By contrast, statement taking by solicitors involves a flow whereby one question leads to another, motivated by the previous answer rather than determined in advance, and the applicant is granted far more scope to develop nuanced, lengthy responses. Although there are again pauses to allow for interpretation these do not inhibit the performance of the narrative to anything like the same degree.

The solicitor's task – made far easier in this case by Mrs A's unusually thoughtful and analytical answers – is to convert the asylum seeker's account into rule-oriented form and thereby maximise its intelligibility for the judge. This part of the interview, supplemented by clarifications at a meeting some weeks later, was rendered in the statement as follows:

> 41. However, by late 1995/early 1996, the Rahanweyn had regrouped and formed the RRA, having gained considerable outside support. I do not remember what RRA stood for exactly but it was something like Rahanweyn Army. [. . .] They seriously persecuted minorities, not sparing anyone. [. . .]

> 43. I do remember clearly the main incident which caused us to leave Somalia. On 1st March 1997 very early in the morning, before early morning prayers the Rahanweyn militia attacked our home. They forced their way in breaking the main gate. They started shooting spraying bullets all over the place. I panicked and tried to flee. As I did so I was hit over the head by something. I think I probably fell on the ground and injured my knee at the same time. I was pregnant at the time. I fell unconscious. The next thing I remember was in

the morning when neighbours came. Me, my mother and two daughters were taken the neighbours [*sic*]. My husband was at his mother's house at the time. I was losing blood. It was a very frightening experience. I thought that I was going to lose the baby and that I was even going to die myself. I do not know why I was bleeding, whether I was also hit on the stomach or whether it was just from the head injury. I did not lose the baby thankfully. I found out that my father and brother had been shot dead. My maternal cousin who was also with us was also wounded. My mother was wounded in her leg. My mother was in shock. My mother has never been the same since.

44. My father and brother were buried in B. Two weeks later we left Somalia.

At the appeal hearing itself these various narratives are targeted by the HOPO's cross-examination. Any apparent discrepancies across the multiple versions of the applicant's account will be used by the HOPO to cast doubt on their credibility, yet it is arguable that the very different interviewing styles may themselves facilitate such 'discrepancies'; for example, appellants may fail to mention something at their asylum interview because they were given no scope to do so.

As the French procedure does not involve formal witness statements it is harder to compare the strategies of lawyers and OFPRA caseworkers. The latter do, however, vary in how they conduct the second, substantive part of the asylum interview: some begin with an open question ('Why did you leave your country?') and continue with a series of follow-up questions; others prefer to ask more closed questions from the outset; and some vary their strategy depending on the person they are interviewing. Applicants will already have told their story in their written application, but most caseworkers appreciate the problems posed for non-francophone or poorly educated applicants by the requirement to provide this written statement in French, so they tend to attach more importance to what is said at interview, especially the extent to which it involves circumstantial and personal details.

Morality and refugee status determinations

Most legal processes are concerned with attributing blame or responsibility for past events, but asylum decisions are future-oriented. It is the risk that the asylum seeker might suffer persecution on return that is crucial, given the ban on *réfoulement* imposed by the Refugee Convention.[15] Although it is generally necessary in practice for asylum seekers to demonstrate that they have experienced persecution in the past, this serves merely as a proxy indicator of future risk. Given the importance of the notion of 'risk on return' in asylum decision making, it is worth noting that the extensive broader discourse on risk is entirely ignored in legal reasoning. While this lacuna is striking, it is not at all surprising, given the prevalence of solipsism in legal thought.

Drawing on Beck's (1992) notion of 'risk society', Cohen notes that its 'global scope . . . its self reflective quality and its pervasiveness create a new backdrop for standard moral panics' (2002: xxxi). There are of course different ways of understanding risk (Jasanoff 1993); 'artefactual' approaches assume that risks are objectively knowable, while 'constructivist' approaches see them as socially constructed. Virtually all academic writers are constructivists at least to the extent of recognising that the notion of 'risk' itself has undergone historical evolution, but legal approaches remain firmly artefactual.

Douglas and Wildavsky (1982: 5) put forward the strong constructivist position that choices between risky alternatives (here, the risk that asylum applicants will suffer persecution on return, versus the 'risk' of undermining immigration policy by allowing them to remain) are always political, cultural and indeed moral decisions, because they require a degree of consensus over the relative desirability of possible outcomes. No absolute or objective risk calculations are possible, but that does not mean the risks are not real. As Douglas herself made clear, the argument 'is not about the reality of the dangers, but about how they are politicised' (1992: 29).

Asylum claims evoke multiple associations between risk, morality and otherness. Above all, there is the appellant's fear of mistreatment by the dominant 'other' if forced to return: most Sri Lankan Tamil asylum seekers, for instance, claim to be at risk of detention and torture by the security forces of the Sinhalese-dominated state. Yet appellants risk a more radical, double 'othering' by those in power, whereby they are stigmatised as 'terrorists' by their country of origin, and as 'bogus welfare scroungers' by politicians, media and public in their country of refuge. Judges are avowedly concerned only with the first two aspects: information regarding the individual helps them to identify the nature of the appellant's fear, while expert evidence and COI helps them to assess whether that fear is 'well-founded'. The third aspect of risk, the stigmatisation of appellants as dangerous outsiders to British society, ostensibly plays no part in their decisions except in those rare cases where such dangers are deemed severe enough to bring into play Article 1F, the Convention's 'exclusion clause'.[16]

Fassin and Kobelinsky (2012) analyse procedures in the French asylum courts in terms of the notion of a 'moral economy'. Whereas E. P. Thompson (1971) applied this term to the exchange of material goods and services, they use it more broadly to designate the allocation of rights and responsibilities that are becoming increasingly scarce – in France, as in the UK, the increase in numbers of asylum applicants has been more than matched by the decreasing percentage of applicants who succeed in their claims. This moral economy is characterised by three fundamental moral dimensions, all of which display internal paradoxes (Fassin and Kobelinsky 2012: 685). The most basic of these concerns the right to asylum itself: the paradox here is that, given the prevailing political context, the court's decisions simultaneously promote the concept of asylum while making it ever more difficult to achieve in practice – a version of Gibney's point above. The second moral dimension reflects the notions of justice held by judges and court officials. Justice is seen by them in terms of both accuracy – that is, their decision should correctly reflect the situation of the appellant – and fairness – that is, there should be no discrepancies between the decisions of different judges when confronted with similar cases. The paradox here is that most of those involved in the process believe that certain judges are far more likely than others to grant favourable decisions.[17] The final moral dimension concerns the judges' personal emotional responses to the stories told by the applicants appearing before them. These are usually negative: as noted earlier, French judges typically hear thirteen appeals one after another and have been known to make audible derogatory comments such as 'it is the tenth time we've heard the same thing' (Kobelinsky 2015: 172). Occasionally, however, their emotional response is positive: in court, or during their deliberations afterwards, judges express empathy, respect or even admiration towards an applicant who in their opinion embodies the ideal qualities of a persecuted political refugee (Kobelinsky 2015: 174–9). While this final feature might at first glance seem more likely under the French system, because of the importance accorded to subjectivity in the guise of the judge's *intime conviction*, than in common law jurisdictions with their central fiction of objectivity, the broad conclusions drawn by Fassin and Kobelinsky seem applicable to the UK too, not least because in practice this contrast is not absolute but only a matter of degree (Clark 1963: 2–3).

Bruno Latour's comments on the highest French court, the Conseil d'Etat, are, I would argue, applicable to legal procedures more generally, in the UK as well as in France: 'The strange thing about legal objectivity is that it quite literally is objectless, and is sustained entirely by the production of a mental state' (Latour 2004: 107). Cultivation of this mental state depends, he argues, on adherence to those very features of legal procedure so widely derided by outsiders: fancy clothes, archaic language and – particularly relevant in the present case – arcane rules of procedure. Such criticisms, he says, fail to recognise that

> this respect for appearances is a form of objectivity . . . [J]udges can become 'objective' only by constructing an intricate and complex institution which detaches and isolates their consciences from the ultimate solution. (2004: 107–8)

In both countries the paradoxical nature of these various moral dimensions is not formulated as such by most legal actors in the process, who tend to focus more on ethical than on moral issues. What is more, and here above all Fassin and Kobelinsky's analysis seems directly applicable to British courts too, many immigration judges do indeed seem to operate on the basis of deontological rather than utilitarian or consequentialist ethics. That is, justice consists in taking decisions that are demonstrably in accordance with the rules rather than decisions leading to the most useful or most desirable outcomes;

see, for example, the strong emphasis in the UK on procedural consistency and fairness as indices of justice (Thomas 2008; 2011). Such a response is particularly understandable given the peculiar difficulties of asylum decision making – the dearth of evidence, the centrality of credibility assessment, the focus on possible futures – as well as the potentially extreme consequences of getting it wrong, of sending an appellant back to face torture or even death.

One should beware of over-generalising, however. Judges are to a large degree, as one British judge told me, 'sovereigns in their own courtroom'. While statutes and procedural rules do circumscribe this autonomy, within those limits they enjoy considerable freedom to adopt distinctive, individual stances. It is certainly the case, for example, that some immigration judges experience moral qualms; their faithful adherence to procedure notwithstanding, they worry about the consequences of their decisions for particular appellants. Knowing my own status as a 'country expert' witness in Sri Lankan asylum appeals, several British judges told me about some particularly tricky Sri Lankan cases they had recently dealt with, asking me, 'Do you think I did the right thing?' Needless to say I was never able to supply this reassurance – partly because I had not seen the actual case documents, but more basically because outcomes are no more predictable for experts than for judges. How much easier, one imagines, is the sleep of those other judges seemingly untroubled by such moral doubts, who are able, as Fassin and Kobelinsky put it 'to substitute their deontological concern, that is to say, their consciousness of duty done' (2012: 685, my translation).

Notes

1. This chapter derives from a paper given at an ESRC seminar on 'Morals in the moral panic' at Glasgow Caledonian University in 2014. I am grateful for Agnes Woolley's advice on reconfiguring that paper to fit this volume. Research was supported by ESRC Research Grant R000223352 and AHRC Grant AH/E50874X/1 under its Diasporas, Migration and Identities Programme (jointly with Robert Gibb, University of Glasgow).
2. In the UK, for example, the Immigration and Nationality Directorate metamorphosed briefly into the Border and Immigration Agency, then the UK Border Agency, and is now UK Visas and Immigration (UKVI).
3. On the complexities involved in credibility assessments, see Good (2011a; 2015b); on the role of COI, see Gibb and Good (2013) and Good (2015a). For discussions of these issues from a more strictly legal perspective, see Thomas (2006; 2008; 2011) and Sweeney (2009).
4. Rycroft (2005) contrasts these two kinds of interview from an interpreter's perspective.
5. 'Interpretation' is normally understood as the oral transfer of meaning between languages, whereas 'translation' is the equivalent process for written text. Legal professionals in both France and the UK use these terms differently, however; for

them, 'interpretation' refers above all to the judicial process of determining the 'true meaning' of a legal text or document (Colin and Morris 1996: 16; Cornu 2007: 510). Consequently, they tend to speak of court interpreters 'translating' rather than 'interpreting' a speaker's utterances.

6. On the role of expert witnesses, and the epistemological problems posed for them by positivist legal understandings of facts, proof and causation, see Good (2007; 2008).
7. By contrast, in the UK it would be unusual to hear more than two asylum appeals in one day, and the decision making occurs later.
8. Note the more inquisitorial role played by French judges as compared to the convention that British judges should seek to avoid 'entering the fray' by questioning witnesses.
9. By contrast, Cotterrell argues that common law traditionally required judges 'to create legal principle out of diverse moral and social experience', but this view lost ground to a more powerful image of 'enacted positive law, handed down "from above", in the form of statutes and other law produced from non-judicial sources' (Cotterrell 2000: 13–14).
10. For a detailed exposition of deontological ethics in law (though focusing on advocates rather than judges), see D'Amato and Eberle (2010).
11. Personal differences may be even more pronounced among solicitors, who all told me that they had received little or no training in taking statements and had rarely, if ever, observed colleagues doing so.
12. For longer extracts from these interviews, see Good (2011a: 106–12; 2011b: 84–7).
13. I was not allowed to attend such interviews, but Mr P permitted me to transcribe the tape of his interview. The precise words attributed to him are, of course, in fact those of the interpreter; where the interpreter does more than just interpret, this is made explicit.
14. This transcript is based on my own written notes, assisted by the pauses for interpretation.
15. *Réfoulement* refers to the forcible return of asylum seekers or refugees to their country of origin where they are at risk of persecution. The practice violates one of the fundamental principles of international law and refugee conventions.
16. Article 1F states that the provisions of the Refugee Convention do not apply to persons who have 'committed a crime against peace, a war crime, or a crime against humanity'; 'committed a serious non-political crime outside the country of refuge'; or 'been guilty of acts contrary to the purposes and principles of the United Nations'.
17. Detailed research in the United States has revealed huge disparities between individual judges (Ramji-Nogales et al. 2009). No such data are available for France or the UK.

Bibliography

Alexidze, Levan A. (1981), 'Legal nature of *jus cogens* in contemporary international law', *Academie de Droit International. Recueil Des Cours, Collected Courses*, 172: 219–70.

Atkinson, J. Maxwell, and Paul Drew (1979), *Order in Court: The Organisation of Verbal Interaction in Court Settings* (London: Macmillan).

Bauman, Zygmunt (1995), 'Making and unmaking of strangers', *Thesis Eleven*, 43: 1–16.

Beck, Ulrich (1992), *Risk Society: Towards a New Modernity* (London: Sage).

Becker, Howard S. (1963), *Outsiders: Studies in the Sociology of Deviance* (New York: Free Press).

Belorgey, J. M. (2003), 'Le contentieux du droit d'asile et l'intime conviction du juge', *La Revue administrative*, 336: 619–22.

Carnwath, Lord (2013), 'From judicial outrage to sliding scales – where next for Wednesbury?', https://www.supremecourt.uk/docs/speech-131112-lord-carnwath.pdf (accessed 16 April 2018).

Charteris-Black, J. (2006), 'Britain as a container: immigration metaphors in the 2005 election campaign', *Discourse and Society*, 15.5: 563–81.

Clark, Charles E. (1963), 'The limits of judicial objectivity', *American University Law Review*, 12.1: 1–13.

Cohen, Stanley (2002 [1972]), *Folk Devils and Moral Panics: The Creation of the Mods and Rockers*, 3rd edn (London: Routledge).

Colin, Joan, and Ruth Morris (1996), *Interpreters and the Legal Process* (Winchester: Waterside Press).

Conley, John M., and William M. O'Barr (1990), *Rules versus Relationships: The Ethnography of Legal Discourse* (Chicago: University of Chicago Press).

Cornu, Gérard (2007), *Vocabulaire juridique*, 8th edn (Paris: Quadrige/Presses Universitaires de France).

Cotterrell, Roger (2000), 'Common law approaches to the relationship between law and morality', *Ethical Theory and Moral Practice*, 3.1: 9–26.

Crawley, Heaven (2000), 'Gender, persecution and the concept of politics in the asylum determination process', *Forced Migration Review*, 9: 17–20.

D'Amato, Anthony, and Edward J. Eberle (2010), 'Three models of legal ethics', *Northwestern University School of Law: Faculty Working Papers*, 73, http://scholarlycommons.law.northwestern.edu/facultyworkingpapers/73 (accessed 16 April 2018).

Douglas, Mary (1992), *Risk and Blame: Essays in Cultural Theory* (London: Routledge).

Douglas, Mary, and Aaron Wildavsky (1982), *Risk and Culture* (Berkeley: University of California Press).

Fassin, Didier, and Carolina Kobelinsky (2012), 'Comment on juge l'asile: l'institution comme agent moral', *Revue française de sociologie*, 53.4: 657–88.

Finney, Nissa, and Esme Peach (2004), *Attitudes towards Asylum Seekers, Refugees and Other Immigrants* (London: ICAR), https://web.archive.org/web/20140516161007/http://www.icar.org.uk/asylum_icar_report.pdf (accessed 16 April 2018).

Geertz, Clifford (1965), 'Religion as a cultural system', in Michael Banton (ed.), *Anthropological Approaches to the Study of Religion* (London: Tavistock), 1–46.

Gibb, Robert, and Anthony Good (2013), 'Do the facts speak for themselves? Country of Origin Information in French and British refugee status determination procedures', *International Journal of Refugee Law*, 25.2: 291–322.

Gibb, Robert, and Anthony Good (2014), 'Interpretation, translation and intercultural communication in refugee status determination procedures in the UK and France', *Language and Intercultural Communication*, 14.3: 385–99.

Gibney, Matthew (2014), 'Asylum: principled hypocrisy', in Bridget Anderson and Michael Keith (eds), *Migration: A COMPAS Anthology* (Oxford: COMPAS), http://compasanthology.co.uk/asylum-principled-hypocrisy/ (accessed 11 April 2018).

Gill, Nick, and Anthony Good (eds) (2019), *Asylum Determination in Europe: Ethnographic Perspectives* (Basingstoke: Palgrave Macmillan).

Gill, Nick, Rebecca Rotter, Andrew Burridge and Jennifer Allsopp (2018), 'The limits of procedural discretion: unequal treatment and vulnerability in Britain's asylum appeals', *Social and Legal Studies*, 27.1: 49–78.

Good, Anthony (2007), *Anthropology and Expertise in the Asylum Courts* (London: Routledge/Clarendon).

Good, Anthony (2008), 'Cultural evidence in courts of law', *Journal of the Royal Anthropological Institute* (N.S.), S47–S60.

Good, Anthony (2011a), 'Witness statements and credibility assessments in the British asylum courts', in Livia Holden (ed.), *Cultural Expertise and Litigation: Patterns, Conflicts, Narratives* (London: Routledge), 94–122.

Good, Anthony (2011b), 'Tales of suffering: asylum narratives in the refugee status determination process', *West Coast Line*, 68: 80–9.

Good, Anthony (2015a), 'Anthropological evidence and Country of Origin Information in British asylum courts', in Benjamin N. Lawrance and Galya Ruffer (eds), *Adjudicating Refugee and Asylum Status: The Role of Witness, Expertise and Testimony* (New York: Cambridge University Press), 122–44.

Good, Anthony (2015b), 'The benefit of the doubt in British asylum claims and international cricket', in Daniela Berti, Anthony Good and Gilles Tarabout (eds), *Of Doubt and Proof: Ritual and Legal Practices of Judgment* (Farnham: Ashgate), 119–40.

Goodwin-Gill, Guy (2001), 'After the Cold War: asylum and the refugee concept move on', *Forced Migration Review*, 10: 14–16.

Hall, Stuart, Charles Critcher, Tony Jefferson, John Clarke and Brian Roberts (1978), *Policing the Crisis: Mugging, the State, and Law and Order* (London: Macmillan).

Immigration and Nationality Directorate (2002), *Asylum Policy Instructions*, http;//www.ind.homeoffice.gov.uk/default.asp?PageId=711 (accessed 15 April 2002).

Inchauspé, D. (2015), 'L'intime conviction en droit français et dans la tradition juridique anglo-saxonne', *Annales Médico-Psychologiques*, 173.7: 603–5.

Jasanoff, Sheila (1993), 'Bridging the two cultures of risk analysis', *Risk Analysis*, 13.2: 123–9.

Kobelinsky, Carolina (2015), 'Emotions as evidence; hearings in the French asylum court', in Daniela Berti, Anthony Good and Gilles Tarabout (eds), *Of Doubt and Proof: Ritual and Legal Practices of Judgment* (Farnham: Ashgate), 163–82.

Kobelinsky, Carolina (2019), 'The "inner belief" of French asylum judges', in Nick Gill and Anthony Good (eds), *Asylum Determination in Europe: Ethnographic Perspectives* (Basingstoke: Palgrave Macmillan), 53–68.

Latour, Bruno (2004), 'Scientific objects and legal objectivity', in Alain Pottage and Martha Mundy (eds), *Law, Anthropology, and the Constitution of the Social: Making Persons and Things* (Cambridge: Cambridge University Press), 73–114.

Martin, Greg (2015), 'Stop the boats! Moral panic in Australia over asylum seekers', *Journal of Media and Cultural Studies*, 29.3: 304–22.

Merry, Sally Engle (1990), *Getting Justice and Getting Even: Legal Consciousness among Working-Class Americans* (Chicago: University of Chicago Press).

Mertz, Elizabeth (2002), 'Performing epistemology: notes on language, law school, and Yovel's legal-linguistic culture', *Stanford Agora* 3, http://agora.stanford.edu/agora/volume2/mertz.shtml (accessed 16 April 2018).

Ramji-Nogales, Jaya, Andrew I. Schoenholtz and Philip G. Schrag (2009), *Refugee Roulette: Disparities in Asylum Adjudication and Proposals for Reform* (New York: New York University Press).

Rosen, Lawrence (1989), *The Anthropology of Justice: Law as Culture in Islamic Society* (Cambridge: Cambridge University Press).

Rosen, Lawrence (2006), *Law as Culture: An Invitation* (Princeton: Princeton University Press).

Rycroft, Roxana (2005), 'Communicative barriers in the asylum account', in Prakash Shah (ed.), *The Challenge of Asylum to Legal Systems* (London: Cavendish), 223–44.

Simmel, Georg (1950 [1921]), 'The stranger', in *The Sociology of Georg Simmel*, ed. and trans. Kurt H. Wolff (Glencoe, NY: Free Press), 402–8.

Spijkerboer, Thomas (ed.) (2013), *Fleeing Homophobia: Sexual Orientation, Gender Identity and Asylum* (London: Routledge).

Sweeney, James A. (2009), 'Credibility, proof and refugee law', *International Journal of Refugee Law*, 21.4: 700–26.

Thomas, Robert (2006), 'Assessing the credibility of asylum claims: EU and UK approaches examined', *European Journal of Migration and Law*, 8: 79–96.

Thomas, Robert (2008), 'Consistency in asylum adjudication: Country Guidance and the asylum process in the United Kingdom', *International Journal of Refugee Law*, 20: 489–532.

Thomas, Robert (2011), *Administrative Justice and Asylum Appeals: A Study of Tribunal Adjudication* (Oxford: Hart Publishing).

Thompson, E. P. (1971), 'The moral economy of the English crowd in the eighteenth century', *Past and Present*, 50: 76–136.

UNHCR (1992), *Handbook on Procedures and Criteria for Determining Refugee Status* (Geneva: UNHCR).

Valluy, Jérome (2004), 'La fiction juridique de l'asile', *Plein Droit*, 63, https://www.gisti.org/doc/plein-droit/63/fiction.html (accessed 13 April 2018).

Welch, Michael, and Liza Schuster (2005), 'Detention of asylum seekers in the UK and USA: deciphering noisy and quiet constructions', *Punishment and Society*, 7.4: 397–417.

Chapter 7

The Politics of the Empty Gesture: Frameworks of Sanctuary, Theatre and the City

Alison Jeffers

Less than seventy years ago, when the 1951 Refugee Convention came into being after the Second World War, it was deemed important to create firm legal distinctions whereby people deserving of protection in a foreign state were granted the label 'refugee'. In 2017, in what seems like an entirely different age, this term has transmuted and evolved to reflect changing understandings of refugees and what they represent. In 2007 Roger Zetter, revisiting his ideas about the labelling of refugees formulated for the 1970s and 1980s, concluded that a fundamental 'fractioning' of the label had taken place whereby the 'refugee label has become *politicised* [. . .] by [being embedded in] the wider political discourse of resistance to migrants and refugees' (Zetter 2007: 172, emphasis in original). Tony Kushner and Katharine Knox suggested in the last year of the twentieth century that 'the concept of asylum [might] not last into the next century' (1999: 397), calling it 'remarkable' that the 'popular attachment to the concept of asylum [had] remained strong *in spite of* the atmosphere created by successive governments and the popular press' (1999: 402, emphasis in original). The concept of asylum *has* continued, but in a shape that perhaps few who saw the need for it in the middle of the last century would recognise. In the face of a worsening atmosphere around migration in general, and asylum in particular, popular movements do continue to emerge and two in particular are examined here – Cities and, more particularly, Theatres of Sanctuary, both of which investigate how to act while the concept and practices of asylum continue to be severely compromised.

In recent years images of refugees desperately trying to get to northern Europe, crowded into unseaworthy boats, stuck at militarised border fences, camping in train stations and at roadsides, have induced a sense of despair among those who would help or support these forced migrants. 'What is to be done?' asks Slavoj Žižek when all possible solutions seem so hopeless to the problem of 'hundreds of thousands of people who, desperate to escape war and hunger, wait in north Africa or on the shores of Syria trying to cross the Mediterranean to find refuge in Europe' (Žižek 2016: 7). In these circumstances the apparatus by which the labels 'migrant', 'refugee' and 'asylum seeker' are granted feel woefully inadequate, with so many millions of people fleeing the world's 'failing states' to seek sanctuary in other places where their chances of simply surviving seem much stronger.[1]

This chapter will examine how we might act under the conditions whereby fundamental ideas about protection and asylum cannot keep pace with contemporary realities. I will argue that one possible path through this complex and shifting territory might be to pay attention to initiatives that work outside of, and even challenge, the statist politics of asylum by enacting models of sanctuary 'beyond the limits of its current international institution and national implementation' (Squire and Darling 2013: 60). In initiating the City of Sanctuary movement, its organisers and supporters stick to the letter of the UN Convention by accepting the challenges of offering sanctuary and the hospitality that it introduces, in effect 'calling the bluff' of their governments and enacting the terms of the 1951 Refugee Convention when the state refuses to do so. The analysis will be carried out by discussing the Theatre of Sanctuary movement that has emerged from City of Sanctuary and discussing the production of the play *Queens of Syria* which toured the UK in 2016.[2] Through examining the potential power of what Žižek (2008: 30) calls 'the empty gesture', that is the gesture that is not supposed to be accepted, in the context of ideas about sanctuary I hope to show the ways in which both the City and Theatre of Sanctuary movements redefine a sense of what is possible in terms of a response to refugees in this historical moment.

To do this I will first investigate Žižek's question 'What is to be done?' to show how the fulfilment of the empty gesture makes it easier to conceive of change by grasping the opportunity of the smaller-scale actions of the city and the theatre. I will look at certain historical precedents where sanctuary has been offered, tying together sacred and secular sites of sanctuary in the church and the theatre. Following that I will outline the City of Sanctuary movement, thinking about civic performances of sanctuary in offering protection to refugees, aligning City of Sanctuary with earlier campaigns in British cities to make them nuclear-free and Fairtrade zones. This is followed by an examination of the *Queens of Syria* project, specifically focusing on a performance in 2016 in West Yorkshire Playhouse in Leeds, a Theatre of Sanctuary within a City of Sanctuary, before concluding that the locally fulfilled 'empty gesture' of offering sanctuary has some power in speaking back to failed statist notions of asylum.

Sanctuary and the power of fulfilling the empty gesture

Drawing on Žižek's ideas, Jenny Hughes and Simon Parry alert us to the radical possibilities of thinking about the power of political gestures – corporeal and symbolic – and to the way in which empty gestures might offer 'some means of eluding control' (2015: 308). In his essay 'The Seven Veils of Fantasy' Žižek suggests that political systems require two levels of support in order to function – one he calls the 'public text', which Hughes and Parry translate as the 'observance of written laws' (2015: 308); the other is the 'phantasmic support of the public symbolic order' or 'the unwritten rules' (Žižek 2008: 37). In asking where these two things interact, Žižek comes up with the paradoxical notion of the empty symbolic gesture: 'a gesture which is meant to be rejected' because 'it is the proper thing to do' (Žižek 2008: 36, 37). In making the empty gesture, and rejecting it, both the one who offers and the one who rejects gain a sense of solidarity and the normal order of things is restored. However, to 'call the bluff' of the one who offers and to actually accept their empty gesture is described as 'catastrophic', heralding 'the dissolution of the social link' (Žižek 2008: 37). This leads Žižek to suggest that

> [s]ometimes, at least – the truly subversive thing is not to disregard the explicit letter of the law on behalf of the underlying fantasies, but to stick to this letter against the fantasy that sustains it. In other words, the act of taking the empty gesture (the offer to be rejected) literally – to treat the forced choice as a true choice – is, perhaps, one of the ways [. . .] to suspend the phantasmic frame of the unwritten rules. (2008: 38–9)

In the situation under consideration here, the empty gesture is that of asylum and the protection of the state offered to refugees by all the states that have signed the Refugee Convention of 1951. When it was passed under international law it was arguably genuine – a gesture intended to 'provide the foundations for dealing with international refugee problems' (Kushner and Knox 1999: 10). However, by the 1980s there was 'a growing unwillingness to provide shelter for [refugees] especially within the countries of western Europe' (Kushner and Knox 1999: 335), and what had begun as a gesture of hospitality and protection had become increasingly 'empty', with many more asylum seekers refused than accepted: the very term 'asylum seeker' had to be coined in the 1990s when there was felt to be a need to distinguish between 'genuine' refugees and those who might be 'claiming asylum' when they were actually economic migrants (see Whittaker 2006). Vicki Squire and Jonathan Darling go so far as to suggest that activists claim that 'asylum is no longer a helpful term given its increasingly derogatory use both in the media and more widely' (2013: 61). I suggest that the City of Sanctuary movement mobilises the increasingly empty statist gesture of hospitality and protection for asylum seekers and refugees and, in doing so, alters not only life for those who require sanctuary, but also for those who make the offer and the ways in which they imagine themselves and where they live.

Some of the weight of my argument hinges on the specificities of the term *sanctuary* which is more grounded in a sense of place than asylum (discredited or not). It is part of the word grouping around the verb 'to sanctify', or to make holy, originally signifying a building set apart for the purposes of holy worship – the sanctuary. It later came to indicate the space immediately surrounding the altar in a religious building, seen as its heart, and became known as a space where civic laws did not pertain (Hoad 1996: 416). Traditionally, those seeking the sanctuary of the Church cannot be arrested by the state – divine law superseding the secular. So, in contemporary common usage *asylum* has become more closely linked to ideas of the state that decides whether or not claims on it to provide asylum are justified. *Sanctuary* has a more localised feel, less formal and less bound up with the letter of the law, suggesting a sense of autonomy from larger state processes.

One famous sanctuary seeker was Viraj Mendis, a Sri Lankan political refugee who took refuge in the Church of the Ascension in Hulme, Manchester in 1986. Supported by the priest, the Revd John Methuen, and a large group of well-wishers, Mendis lived in the church for 760 days until the authorities snapped and the police raided the church, arresting him and deporting him to Sri Lanka (Shifrin 2004). Mendis had taken literally the traditional gesture of sanctuary offered by the church and the church supported his actions despite the negative publicity and inconvenience that must have emerged through someone living in the building for over two years. Even though the state ultimately violated the sanctuary, the church's gesture was a strong way of indicating the powerful potential of offering protection in the face of hostility from the authorities, challenging their reluctance to offer what was in their gift – political asylum. In taking up the implied invitation of sanctuary in a holy place, Mendis revealed the 'underlying fantasy' of protection for refugees, in this case with the blessing of the Church.

A further example of refugees enacting the Church's offer of sanctuary took place in Paris in 1996 when a large group of men, women and children took refuge in Saint Bernard's church. After two months of living there, the French police removed 98 men, 54 women and 68 children.[3] Arianne Mnouchkine's theatre company, Théâtre du Soleil, welcomed some of the undocumented migrants into their theatre space, La Cartoucherie, after their expulsion from the church, an experience that inspired their production *Et Soudain, Des Nuits D'Éveil* (*And Suddenly, Nights of Awakening*) (Ringer 1998). This example, continuing the tradition of sheltering those who need protection when the state refuses to offer it, draws together theatre and the Church. Both concern themselves with immediate need over wider imperatives, at a local level pitting themselves against what they see as the unsympathetic and remote bureaucracy of national asylum apparatus. I will now move on to consider the British City of Sanctuary movement and the more recent Theatres of Sanctuary initiative in order to investigate how the politics and ethics of sanctuary might illustrate the possibility of finding spaces and modes of belonging for both refugees and citizens.

Performing sanctuary

In discussing the setting up of the City of Sanctuary movement in Sheffield in 2005, Darling (Darling 2010) reiterates its inception as 'a gesture that sought to instill a spirit of "welcome and hospitality towards asylum seekers and refugees"' (2010: 125). The 'gesture' of becoming a City of Sanctuary can be seen as a response to the empty gesture of welcome or hospitality made by the state. In fulfilling the empty gesture, City of Sanctuary represents an attempt to (re) frame the city as a place of sanctuary, promoting itself as 'a movement to build a culture of hospitality for people seeking sanctuary in the UK'.[4] By 2017 City of Sanctuary had approximately 90 locations listed as part of the movement, including not only cities but small towns and even more rural areas with no concentrated populations. In this it has fulfilled its earlier ambition to become a network of key local initiatives which 'join' the movement though a series of activities accompanied by pledges of support from local politicians, businesses and other organisations. Streams of Sanctuary is a further development whereby interest groups and organisations can apply for recognition, and of particular interest here is the Arts Stream through which certain theatres have achieved 'sanctuary status' as discussed below.[5]

Importantly, although City of Sanctuary is now a large national network which describes itself as a 'mainstream, grassroots movement', it lies outside what Ash Amin and Nigel Thrift might call 'the formal structures of municipal affairs' (2005: 17). Indeed, the paradoxical positioning of City of Sanctuary within the mainstream *and* the grassroots chimes with Amin and Thrift's idea of the 'various urban knowledges and practices' that spawn social movements 'not so much based around formal goals as they are around developing agendas' (2005: 17). City of Sanctuary runs according to a set of 'values' that focus on inclusiveness, openness, participation, inspiration and integrity rather than a strict set of goals, rules or policies. It is described by Squire (2011: 296) as 'a dispersed, "bottom-up" approach to political change' that works on a local level to focus on developing relationships rather than lobbying or campaigning. Operating in this way, it '*exceeds* the statist limits of the hospitable' through 'localized activities and informal encounters' (Squire and Darling 2013: 61, emphasis in original).

Emphasising the possibilities engendered by the fluid, paradoxical framework of the City of Sanctuary movement shows how it can advocate 'outward looking, yet place-based moments of political responsibility' (Darling 2010: 126). The denial of any absolute positions entails thinking of the City of Sanctuary movement as relational but also strongly located. The rejection of any 'either/or' positionality in favour of a more inclusive 'both/and' approach suggests that it is possible to maintain a level of localism at the same time as looking beyond the possibly small-scale, insular or parochial to identify the need to offer hospitality to asylum seekers and refugees '"within" the city', partly because the city is aware of its role in the 'national framing of asylum politics "beyond" the city' (Darling 2010: 126). This double framing created by the rejection of binary thinking about the local/national nexus is particularly relevant to the Theatre of Sanctuary movement which has emerged from City of Sanctuary, and which I will examine below. But before that I would like to conclude this section by examining two further links between sanctuary and performance.

Being alert to the theatrical metaphors used in connection with the sanctuary movement draws attention to the frequent use of casting and recasting. Darling (2010) frequently uses the term 'recasting' to explore the reimagining of the city as a spatial entity by which it starts to perceive of itself, and to be perceived, as a hospitable space, altering the geographical self-imagination of the location. To recast a play in the theatre is to place someone into a role in which they were not originally cast, potentially changing the audience's perception of that actor, the role and the play. When a city is recast, or reframed, both it and the discourse within which it is recast have to change. As Fiona Jenkins suggests, once the 'token gesture' of tolerance has been superseded by that of generosity in relation to immigrant 'others', a 'certain social solidarity [. . .] an affirmation of a risky "connection"' has been offered and the hosts cannot imagine themselves to be left 'just as we are' (Jenkins 2002); something shifts once the city has been recast and the City of Sanctuary label becomes attached, potentially reframing the location both from within and from the outside.

Secondly, Amin and Thrift use a performance metaphor to discuss the effect of labelling a place: '[a] city named in a certain way also *becomes* that city through the practices of people in response to the labels. *They perform the labels*' (Amin and Thrift 2002: 23, emphasis added). Thus, the city of Sheffield might imagine itself, or be imagined, as the erstwhile centre of a declining steel industry, languishing in a post-industrial depression, or as the home of the City of Sanctuary movement which is spreading its influence across the country and beyond. The city becomes 'a site of international influence' (Amin and Thrift 2005: 14) meaning that we can see it not just as the *site* of politics 'but as part of politics itself', because the hierarchy of 'urban, national, international and global' has been destabilised (Amin and Thrift 2005: 15). Cities are not 'passive players in a global game played out among and between nations and national actors [. . .] but simultaneously sites of both issue and response, influencing what happens around the world' (Amin and Thrift 2005: 17). By taking up the challenge of fulfilling the empty gesture of hospitality the city becomes active – a site of both 'issue and response', asserting its importance and authority despite operating on a much smaller scale but also reflecting back the possibilities of operating according to different goals and agendas.

In many ways, the City of Sanctuary initiative is similar to the Nuclear Free Zones that surfaced in the 1980s. Manchester City Council was the first local authority in the UK to declare itself a Nuclear Free Zone in 1980 and, as more cities followed suit, the Nuclear Free Local Authorities Network developed.[6] Darling also points to connections between the City of Sanctuary movement and the movement to declare cities and towns Fairtrade zones, drawing attention to Alice Malpass and her colleagues' work on this subject when they report that '[s]ince 2000, more than 100 towns and cities in Britain have been awarded certification as Fairtrade Towns/Cities and more than 200 other places are currently campaigning for Fairtrade status' (Malpass et al. 2007: 3). Thus Garstang, a small and otherwise unremarkable Lancashire town, becomes *recast* as the first British town to declare itself a Fairtrade zone (Malpass et al. 2007). Similarly, Manchester is *recast* as a Nuclear Free Zone and Sheffield is reframed as the first city in the UK to be formally recognised for its welcome to refugees and asylum seekers. There is a sense, perhaps, of pride in these labels through being 'the first', but in none of these cases is it the goal to be 'the only', as the longer-term aim is to be the beginning of a network or movement.

Theatres of Sanctuary

In 2014 West Yorkshire Playhouse (WYP) in Leeds became the UK's first Theatre of Sanctuary. Ruth Hannant, creative education manager for WYP, explained that the initiative had grown out of a production of *Refugee Boy* in 2013, a play based on the novel by Benjamin Zephaniah and adapted for the stage by the poet Lemn Sissay.[7] The production was accompanied by special events and workshops 'for, with and about refugees and asylum seekers' (Brining 2016). The theatre received money from Arts Council England to tour *Refugee Boy* to Glasgow, Ipswich, Nottingham, Birmingham, London and Manchester – trying to partner with City of Sanctuary groups and the local refugee council in each location. Individuals involved in Leeds City of Sanctuary acknowledged the efforts of the theatre staff and suggested that they apply to be a Theatre of Sanctuary. Following their recognition as such, Asmarina Voices, a women's singing group, emerged, made up of women from some of Leeds's refugee communities. This and a free ticketing scheme, a youth arts group, a men's programme and instrumental lessons coalesced into a portfolio of creative activities aimed at supporting refugees and asylum seekers in and around the city as well as encouraging them to form a relationship with the theatre.

Other theatres have followed suit and Theatre of Sanctuary status was granted to the Young Vic Theatre in London in 2016, while SBC Theatre Company became a Theatre Company of Sanctuary, also in 2016.[8] When the Young Vic was granted Theatre of Sanctuary status, its artistic director David Lan stated

> I think the function of theatre is to lead. It's not to ask people What should we be doing? What do you want to see? But to take decisions about what really matters. And what really matters in the world today is the extraordinary convulsions of population across the world.[9]

James Brining, the artistic director of WYP, takes a more situated approach when he says, 'Great cities should enable these kinds of activities to thrive' (Brining 2016), emphasising a civic response rather than a broad humanitarian one. If, as Amin and Thrift suggest, the city is more like a process than a location, and places 'are best thought of not so much as enduring sites but as moments of encounter [. . .] variable events, twists and fluxes as inter relations' (2002: 26), then the theatre is one place where this is made manifest. The transient nature of the place provides a sense of 'light sociality' (Amin and Thrift 2002: 43), a palimpsestic place where roles and identities can be explored, tested, made manifest or discarded.

The Young Vic theatre co-produced *Queens of Syria* in 2016 with Developing Artists and Refuge Productions (Figs 7.1 and 7.2). It involved a group of thirteen female refugee performers who had fled from the war in Syria to Aaman in Jordan. This production was based on an earlier project with the same title established in 2013 which had been created by Charlotte Eager, Georgina Paget and William Stirling of Refuge Productions in Aaman. The project started out with sixty women in what was described as 'drama therapy workshops geared towards a performance of Euripides' ancient play *Trojan Women*'.[10] A documentary on the original project in Aaman (directed by Yasmin Fedda) is useful in contextualising the production that was seen on British stages in 2016, and shows early acting and voice workshops, the women working on the text (translated into Arabic) under the guidance of the Syrian theatre director Omar Abusaada and two unnamed female theatre professionals who ran acting and voice workshops.[11] The film concludes with scenes from the women's performances in Aaman (twenty-five women remained to perform from the larger original group of sixty) and their curtain call to audience applause.

The original piece created with the group in Aaman was made up of extracts from *Trojan Women* staged though choric chant and projected close-ups of the women's faces as they speak lines from the text in Arabic (subtitled into English). This is interspersed with accounts using a storytelling style of direct audience address in which the women tell their harrowing stories of living through and escaping a civil war. The piece uses filmed interviews with some of the participant actors[12] showing the women making connections between their own experience and that of the Trojan women in the play as they await their fate at the end of the war with the Greeks: as one woman says in the video, 'We are talking about the play but these things are real. They exist. It's not just about Troy. This is what happened for real. It's happened to us even' (Fedda 2016).

The version that was created to tour the UK used the same style of performance, the screened interviews with the performers offering a commentary on the relationship of the original play to their lives, now supplemented with interviews about the impact on them of taking part in the project. Visually, the staging was rather austere, with simple benches down each side of the

Figure 7.1 *Queens of Syria* performed at the Young Vic Theatre, London, 2016 (photograph: Vanja Karas)

Figure 7.2 *Queens of Syria* performed at the Young Vic Theatre, London, 2016 (photograph: Vanja Karas)

stage on which the women sat when they were not performing. A large screen upstage showed filmed close-ups of the women speaking and was also used for the English translations of the Arabic text. As in the original production, individual voices were amplified by microphones on stands that were positioned and removed by members of the company with smooth precision. The performers wore floor-length traditional dress, all with hair covered and some showing only their eyes. Their costumes had the visual effect of making their faces and hands very prominent, highlighted against the dark clothing and the stark blackness of the set. The performance that I saw ran for one night in the 300-seat Courtyard Theatre of the WYP and was sold out despite worries on the part of the theatre management that the piece might not be popular enough to fill the theatre.[13]

The mythopoetics of *Queens of Syria*

To provide a more critical account of this theatrical encounter (and the wider project within which is it located) it is helpful to draw on what Emma Cox has called the 'mythopoetics' of theatre and migrants, whereby we should consider 'not just the stories that are (re)told but also the way artists are positioned and perceived, whether by their own volition or by the desires of collaborators, audiences, critics and sponsors', what she calls the 'politics of myth-making' (2014: 22). As a project spanning over four years, *Queens of Syria* is unusually well documented, which makes reading its mythopoetics a little easier than it might be for other theatre projects that have received less attention and that have not been so well supported financially and otherwise. Indeed, the wealth of documentation is itself an indicator of some of the 'politics of mythmaking' surrounding this project, giving audiences a sense of what the producers see as the weight of its importance, its 'uniqueness' and its potential to inform and educate. There exists not only the professionally produced documentary from the previous iteration of the project in Aaman, but also a dedicated website for the UK tour and a classroom resource, sponsored by the British Council, also one of the sponsors of the original project and Fedda's film. As well as lesson plans and activities to help pupils better understand aspects of forced migration and the war in Syria, the online classroom resource makes it possible to access videos of some of the actor participants talking about their experiences of the war in Syria and why they felt they had to leave.[14]

Although this mythopoetic reading of *Queens of Syria* focuses more on the latter part of Cox's definition (the way the artists are positioned and perceived), it is useful to briefly consider the first part (the story that is being retold). *Trojan Women*, written by Euripides in fifth-century Athens, focuses on 'the plight of women enslaved at the end of the Trojan war' (Wiles 2003: 60), an ancient tale of female persecution and one of the many tragedies with the 'running theme' of 'the lack of a good reason for fighting the Trojan War' (Wiles 2003: 98). There have been other well-known productions of the play that have taken up the cause of the victims of war, and LaMaMa theatre in New York initiated a project in 2016 based on a famous production of the piece from the 1970s by composer Elizabeth Swados and director Andrei Serban. In an ongoing project, the artists at LaMaMa revisited the work to 'engage with communities where there is a recent history of conflict, and a desire on the part of these communities to use theater' as a way to address 'war, displacement, violence against women and children, genocide'.[15] Developing Artists, who produced the UK tour of *Queens of Syria*, call the play 'Euripides' anti-war tragedy',[16] and much of the literature surrounding the project ensures that audiences will make links between the Trojan wars and the war in Syria, with the producers pointing out that all of the women who participated 'identified only too closely with the characters in the play'.[17] Euripides' template provided a mythopoetic frame of recognition for audiences, but it also functioned as a valuable base on which the participant actors could build a sense of self-recognition which they felt validated their experiences. Although there are questions around the nature and extent of the input of the participant actors, I will interpret them as 'the artists' from Cox's definition above, looking first at how they were positioned and perceived by collaborators, sponsors and audience members before turning the spotlight to look at how audiences were being imagined in this project.

Three key sets of emphases about the artists emerge from the literature surrounding the project. The first is the fact that they are non-professional actors, something that was stressed initially in the film of the original project in Aaman and frequently reintroduced into the narrative of the project. Secondly, their experiences of being refugees included pain and trauma to the extent that they were in need of some kind of therapeutic intervention; the labelling of the original project as 'drama therapy' (which has already been mentioned in a footnote as misguided) is evidence of this. The language surrounding the UK tour has been somewhat moderated, but there is still an insistence that the therapeutic element of the project had 'empowered' the women involved and transformed them from 'a group struggling to express themselves and their traumas, to confident women who had found their voices again';[18] the project was thought to have provided the women with an opportunity for self-expression and exploration of their experiences through creative means. Both of these aspects warrant further investigation, and readers who may be troubled at some of the overly casual links between trauma, testimony and empowerment might like to consult James Thompson's work on this subject (Thompson 2009).

However, it is the third claim about the 'ordinariness' of the women that is most useful to consider here. It seems to be assumed that the participant actors' ordinariness will hold the key to some of the main goals of the project 'to inform and educate the UK public about the realities on the ground in Syria, and also, crucially, to develop their understanding of the realities of life as a refugee'.[19] The producers were at pains to point out that 'These were not the voices of partisans, journalists or political commentators, but of ordinary Syrian women whose lives had been turned upside down by the turmoil of previous years.'[20] The women's stories are said to get behind the 'statistics and panoramic images of human outlines [to] hear the first-hand testimonies of those who have lived them'.[21] Stressing the non-partisan ordinariness of the women seems to be a strategy not only to individuate them but to give their stories legitimacy in an attempt to remove them from the taint of propaganda or media interference, in effect 'humanising' them to make the audience receptive to them as survivors of war and as refugees.

After the performance of *Queens of Syria*, the audience was given the opportunity to participate in a 'post-show Q&A'. These post-performance encounters often 'get a really bad press' (Walton 2013) and playwright David Mamet has even tried to ban them in relation to his work (Billington 2017). They have become wearingly ubiquitous in British theatres, to the point where they could be seen as an empty (micro-)gesture on the part of theatre establishments, offered with limited expectations of them being taken up or with little sense of anything valuable emerging from the encounter. However, on this occasion the invitation to stay and talk was taken up by the vast majority of the audience and the Q&A provided a glimpse of the 'real' women behind the performances when they came across as individuated, engaged, passionate and funny women, laughing about getting five-star reviews in the newspapers, a strong contrast to the rather severe onstage personas required for the ensemble playing of this production. On this occasion, the lively participation in the Q&A outside the formal theatrical frame illustrated the way in which the small-scale, local gesture of setting up an encounter between some of the citizens of Leeds and the refugee participant actors of the play might offer a simple example of Žižek's notion of 'eluding control' over attitudes to refugees, something that I will take up in more detail below.

The mythopoetics of the audience

Cox's mythopoetics outlines the relationship between collaborators, sponsors, audiences and artists in theatre of migration. Within these complex patterns of influence or impact I would like to consider specifically the impact of the beliefs of the collaborators, sponsors (and, to a lesser extent) the artists on the audience – showing how they are hailed as 'subjects and as members of a social entity' (Cox 2014: 32); in what ways do they constitute a forum that 'positions them as active collaborators, rather than recipients of meaning' (Cox 2014: 30)? I suggest there are two issues in play here. One of the main aims of Refuge Productions is to 'publicise and humanise the Syrian refugee crisis',[22] so we may conclude that one of the main assumptions is that the audience needs to be told about the war in Syria and about refugees more broadly. The inclusion of the Schools' Education Programme alongside the tour, and the fact that the participant actors visited local schools in the places where they performed, adds to the strong educational thrust of the project overall.[23] The other issue focuses on the challenge for audiences to see beyond media representations which serve to distance suffering and perpetuate stereotypes and which fail to individuate the performers. The participant actors were said by the producers to provide 'a refreshingly different perspective that undermined the prevalent stereotypes about the Syrian conflict challenging assumptions about conservative Muslim women and even about refugees'.[24] In his writing about the ethical and political challenges posed by the 'distant suffering' of others Luc Boltanski outlines the challenges of being

> confronted with suffering [when] all moral demands converge on the single imperative of action. Commitment is commitment to action, the intention to act and orientation towards a horizon of action. But what form can this commitment take when those called upon to act are thousands of miles away from the person suffering, comfortably installed in front of the television set in the shelter of the family living-room? (2004: xv)

This is an important aspect of the mythopoetics of audiences for refugee theatre – the fact that we usually view the suffering of those fleeing wars at a distance through news media, thus thwarting our ambition to act, to 'do something'. Even the small number of refugees out of the total across the world who do manage to travel to Europe, and the vastly smaller number that make it to the UK, will probably be viewed from a distance by most people rather than encountered face to face. Boltanski agrees that 'the multi-plication of victims, their distance in time and space, the difficulty of count-ing them and above all of bringing them together under the same rubric [. . .] tends to exhaust the reserves of indignation' and give way to 'indifference and apathy' (2004: 53). One partial answer might be to

> commit oneself through speech; by adopting the stance, even when alone in front of the television, of someone who speaks to somebody else about what they have seen. But to be an acceptable response to the shocking spectacle of distant suffering [. . .] speech must at the same time report to the other both what was seen and how this personally affected and involved the spectator. (Boltanski 2004: xv)

The liveness of the act of theatre is important partly in countering the dis-tancing effect of media presentations of the refugee experience. In the the-atre, Boltanski's 'speaking' moves out of the domestic space of the living room and into the civic arena. Equally important is the 'localness' of the encounter because thinking about the civic arena emphasises the importance of scale. Bringing us back to the distinction drawn between Lan's language of global humanitarianism and Brining's local emphasis, we in the audience are not being asked to address overwhelming humanitarian questions but simply to consider the questions posed by the women on the stage in front of us in the small civic space of the theatre. This conversation may be fleeting but it should serve to catalyse speech among ourselves as audience members through which gestures of sanctuary and resistance become possible.

    This became clear during the Q&A session at the end of the play; in answer to one of the most urgent questions from the audience, 'What can we do?', the firm response came back from the figures on the stage: 'Join City of Sanctuary'. Although it is possible that this was simply a propagandist opportunity for City of Sanctuary, more importantly it served to demonstrate that the audience's relationship was *not* with the Syrian refugees on stage; they may be the respondents but they are not the subject of the conversation. Placing the participant actors within the frame of Theatre of Sanctuary denies the audience the opportunity to sympathise, because the play is presented within structures that demand action in Leeds, or Manchester, or Edinburgh, or wherever the play is presented in the UK. The women in the play are not supplicants, not victims to be pitied, but agents of change that will continue after they have left, offering the scope for 'minor acts' in which 'asylum seek-ers and irregular migrants claim a rightful presence in the city' (Squire 2011: 302). Watching the performance and speaking to the participant actors pro-vides a bridge to action, but it is not the action.

    The politics of the empty gesture, the concept of sanctuary and the mytho-poetics of *Queens of Syria* can all be linked by thinking about some of the paradoxes around framing. The *double framing* of the City of Sanctuary movement advocates the rejection of simple national/local binaries, allowing the movement to embrace the small-scale at the same time as looking beyond the locatedness of this position. Thus, citizens examine values both within the city 'gates' and beyond, resulting in subtle shifts that occur as a result of framing a particular city as a space of sanctuary as opposed to other, perhaps less desirable narratives that may have been imposed upon it. The *rhetorical framing* of *Queens of Syria* did not allow empathy to spill over into sympathy or pity, denied to the audience by the propinquity of the participant actors who were also, and at the same time, distant. While the participant actors perform in front of us, they are also distant in that their suffering is distant to a British audience, and usually accessed only through the news media. The power of accepting and acting on the empty gesture lies in evoking sanctuary practices based on the traditional power of Church and city to shelter strangers on a more human scale. The *paradoxical framing*, therefore, of taking up the empty gesture of sanctuary made to refugees by the state suggests that the only thing that we can 'do' for refugees, 'the truly subversive thing', is to enact hospitality at a local level. Taking up the empty gesture offered by the sanctuary movement, whether through theatre or other means, shows how intimate gestures of hospitality and protection might animate the small-scale and the local in a gesture of defiance towards an indifferent, and often hostile, state.

Notes

1. There are currently approximately 65.5 million displaced people in the world, with just under one-third of these (22.5 million) being classed as refugees. 55 per cent of the world's refugees come from Syria, South Sudan and Afghanistan; approximately 5.5 million people have fled Syria while a total of 3.9 people have fled the other two states. http://www.unhcr.org/uk/figures-at-a-glance.html (accessed 31 July 2017).
2. It is important to stress that this analysis treats *Queens of Syria* as a theatre project which is multiply situated and which extends over several years and various iterations. The production under discussion here is but one manifestation of this larger theatrical project.
3. https://migration.ucdavis.edu/mn/more.php?id=1029 (accessed 31 July 2017).
4. https://cityofsanctuary.org/about/ (accessed 1 August 2017).
5. There are various streams supported by City of Sanctuary through which groups and organisations across a city might be thematically linked. As well as the arts, there are streams that focus on women, health, destitution, faith and many more. See https://cityofsanctuary.org/streams/ (accessed 1 August 2017).
6. http://www.nuclearpolicy.info/about/about-nfla/ (accessed 19 April 2017).
7. Ruth Hannant, creative education manager at the West Yorkshire Playhouse, interview with the author, 27 April 2017.
8. http://www.sbctheatre.co.uk/theatre-company-of-sanctuary (accessed 3 August 2017).
9. https://www.youtube.com/watch?v=K81boZg1TU8 (accessed 16 May 2019).
10. *Queens of Syria*, programme note.

11. A number of issues emerge from the documentary that are important but that go beyond the scope of this essay. The use of the term 'drama therapy' is misleading and misguided; while the work with the female participants may have had a therapeutic effect on them as individuals, there was no evidence in the film of any formal drama therapy being carried out. In fact, difficult issues are raised by the women, including the emotional distress caused by them having to remember the circumstances of their lives during the war in Syria and the details of their flight to Jordan. In the video they also voice serious concerns for their families back in Syria if they are seen publicly to be opposing the regime, something which they think that their involvement in the play implies. The director is often shown as rather unsympathetic to these concerns and there is no evidence of any support structures being provided for the women involved.

12. I use the term 'participant actors' to reflect the participatory nature of the project and to remind readers that the women are not trained actors.

13. Ruth Hannant, creative education manager at the West Yorkshire Playhouse, interview with the author, 27 April 2017.

14. https://docs.wixstatic.com/ugd/ed7be1_da0c0e34138b4e83bb9316e3f6ef67fa.pdf (accessed 20 April 2017).

15. http://lamama.org/the-trojan-women-project/ (accessed 20 April 2017).

16. http://www.developingartists.org.uk/our-projects/queens-of-syria:-jordan (accessed 2 August 2017).

17. *Queens of Syria*, programme note.

18. https://www.queensofsyriatour.com/ (accessed 20 April 2017).

19. http://www.developingartists.org.uk/our-projects/queens-of-syria:-jordan (accessed 2 August 2017).

20. *Queens of Syria*, programme note.

21. Oliver King, artistic director of Developing Artists, *Queens of Syria*, programme note.

22. *Queens of Syria*, programme note.

23. Ruth Hannant, creative education manager at the West Yorkshire Playhouse, interview with the author, 27 April 2017.

24. *Queens of Syria*, programme note.

Bibliography

Amin, Ash, and Nigel Thrift (2002), *Cities: Reimagining the Urban* (Cambridge: Polity Press).

Amin, Ash, and Nigel Thrift (2005), 'Citizens of the world. Seeing the city as a site of international influence', *Harvard International Review*, 27: 14–17.

Billington, Michael (2017), 'David Mamet's move to punish theatres for debating his work is absurd', *The Guardian*, 10 July, https://www.theguardian.com/stage/theatreblog/2017/jul/10/david-mamet-theatres-debating-blog (accessed 5 March 2018).

Boltanski, Luc (2004), *Distant Suffering: Morality, Media and Politics* (Cambridge: Cambridge University Press).

Brining, James (2016), 'James Brining: proud to stand centre stage for diversity', *The Yorkshire Post*, 20 October.

Cox, Emma (2014), *Theatre and Migration* (Basingstoke: Palgrave Macmillan).

Darling, Jonathan (2010), 'A City of Sanctuary: the relational re-imagining of Sheffield's asylum politics', *Transactions*, 35: 125–40.

Fedda, Yasmin (2016), *Queens of Syria*, DVD Special UK Tour Edition.

Hoad, T. F. (ed.) (1996), *Concise Dictionary of English Etymology* (Oxford: Oxford University Press).

Hughes, Jenny, and Simon Parry (2015), 'Introduction: gesture, theatricality and protest – composure at the precipice', *Contemporary Theatre Review*, 25: 300–12.

Jenkins, Fiona (2002), 'Gesture beyond tolerance: generosity, fatality and the logic of the state', *Angelaki*, 7: 119–29.

Kushner, Tony, and Katharine Knox (1999), *Refugees in an Age of Genocide: Global, National and Local Perspectives during the Twentieth Century* (London: Frank Cass).

Malpass, Alice, Paul Cloke, Clive Barnett and Nick Clarke (2007), 'Fairtrade urbanism? The politics of place beyond place in the Bristol Fairtrade city campaign', *International Journal of Urban and Regional Research*, 31: 633–45.

Ringer, Loren (1998), '*Et Soudain, Des Nuits D'Éveil (and Suddenly, Nights of Awakening)*. A collective work in harmony with Hélène Cixous. Le Théâtre du Soleil, Paris. 25 January 1998', *Theatre Journal*, 50.4: 529–31.

Shifrin, Tash (2004), 'Mendis returns to Manchester', *The Guardian*, 22 September, https://www.theguardian.com/society/2004/sep/22/asylum.guardiansociety supplement (accessed 2 July 2019).

Squire, Vicki (2011), 'Community cohesion to mobile solidarities: the City of Sanctuary network and the Stranger into Citizens campaign', *Political Studies*, 59: 290–307.

Squire, Vicki, and Jonathan Darling (2013), 'The "minor" politics of rightful presence: justice and relationality in City of Sanctuary', *International Political Sociology*, 7: 59–74.

Thompson, James (2009), *Performance Affects: Applied Theatre and the End of Effect* (Basingstoke: Palgrave Macmillan).

Walton, John (2013), 'Post-show theatre discussions: presenting your "DVD extras" menu', *The Guardian*, 11 October, https://www.theguardian.com/culture-professionals-network/culture-professionals-blog/2013/oct/11/post-show-theatre-discussions (accessed 5 March 2018).

Whittaker, David, J. (2006), *Asylum Seekers and Refugees in the Contemporary World* (London: Routledge).

Wiles, David (2003), *Greek Theatre Performance: An Introduction* (Cambridge: Cambridge University Press).

Zetter, Roger (2007), 'More labels, fewer refugees: remaking the refugee label in an era of globalization', *Journal of Refugee Studies*, 20: 172–92.

Žižek, Slavoj (2008), *The Plague of Fantasies* (London: Verso).

Žižek, Slavoj (2016), *Against the Double Blackmail: Refugees, Terror and other Troubles with the Neighbours* (Harmondsworth: Penguin).

Part III

The Border

The Border: Introduction

Emma Cox

Borders have a peculiar dual quality of being at once arbitrary and fundamental. In a territorial sense, this can mean that the work of an insistently linear political demarcation overlaps with the ancient topographical limits and thresholds mapped by mountain ranges, rivers and coastlines. Perhaps most pertinently, though, and as humanities scholars have recognised, borders also function as symbolic or aestheticised *spaces*. In recent years, a range of scholarship in the humanities has pursued notions of borders and border politics defined not in terms of linearity but spatiality, wherein human encounter and appearance are uniquely charged, and often representational (see, for example, Pugliese 2010; Nield 2008; Rajaram and Grundy-Warr 2007). Such theorisations have shaped an idea of borders not merely as sites of biopolitical pivoting from one condition of emplacement to another, but as things that engender aesthetic work and interventionist politics. Chapters in this section trace, in different ways, an understanding of the border as both productive and coercive, inscribing its own ambivalence even as it distinguishes *here* from *there*, *then* from *now*.

In a chapter that thinks deeply not just about representations of borders, or their ontologies, but also about the generative functions of border art – that is, art that has interconnected aesthetic and activist consequences – Agnes Woolley offers a fine-grained reading of the Italian documentary film *On the Bride's Side* (2014), situating it as a 'staged intervention into, and a public disavowal of, a politics of asylum in contemporary Europe'. This chapter is attentive to histories of transit across clandestine routes, particularly those hugging Europe's Mediterranean fringes, and in so doing it locates *On the Bride's Side* in the context of earlier displacements that shadow it, and of the topographies of memory forged by these. Woolley's discussion is instrumental, illuminating documentary film as a form of engagement with refugee narratives, as well as border art as a 'claim on public space [. . .] made through the power of the aesthetic relation'. She shows, moreover, that *On the Bride's Side*'s 'articulation of an expansive border space projects a broader conception of what it means to be European, one that accommodates and acknowledges commonalities and shared histories', linking this purpose with Europe's insufficient reckoning with its own 'Enlightenment ideals of hospitality and freedom, which have operated so unevenly'.

Liam Connell also engages with film as a medium for refugee narratives, offering close analyses of two narrative films, Marc Forster's *World War Z* (2013) and Philippe Lioret's *Welcome* (2009). This chapter picks up on what is perhaps the most significant conceptual paradigm for theorising refugee embodiment, that derived from Giorgio Agamben's concept of biopolitics as the 'biopolitical paradigm of the modern' (1998: 119), and identifies a tendency for this conceptualisation of refugeehood to collapse everything into biopolitics, to foreclose on modes of embodied communication that operate independently of its frame. Drawing on Judith Butler's performative theory of assembly in order to set out an expanded notion of what political 'speech' might entail, Connell asks important questions about how we might reconcile the biopolitical body of the refugee with the representation of somatic refugee embodiment on screen. In the context of the zombie apocalypse narrative of *World War Z*, Connell points out that '[t]he film's representation of refugees and zombies as congruent marries with recent political discourse that has undermined the rights to asylum by linking refugees to threats to civic integrity and indeed health'. In his analysis of *Welcome*, Connell is attentive to how this social realist film instantiates the refugee's 'body as a biopolitical and as a natural entity', presenting bodily exertion that is an act of preparedness for crossing maritime borders, and ultimately, death produced through the violence of covert border crossing. This chapter is invaluable for thinking through embodiment both within and beyond the confines of the state. In this regard, Connell identifies something in narrative film that is broadly continuous with what Woolley is concerned with in her discussion of documentary film as activist intervention: in both analyses, bordering emerges not merely as political framing – integral though this may be – but, as Woolley puts it, as a process that operates on 'multiple levels [. . .] social, psychological, material, discursive, aesthetic'.

Lilie Chouliaraki and Myria Georgiou's chapter investigates digital bordering, drawing on fieldwork research on the use of digital technologies by humanitarian and aid organisations. Coming from a communication studies perspective, this chapter emphasises new and emerging modes of communication between refugees that work with and within, rather than necessarily resist, a securitisation/humanitarianism matrix. The chapter also notes the persistence of pre-electronic forms of communication (maps, signs, notices, leaflets and even word of mouth), recognising these as functioning side by side with social media communications networks. Chouliaraki and Georgiou's discussion is invaluable for the detail it offers on what is taking place 'on the ground' where refugees are arriving, and for the insights it provides into processes of administering arrival. The chapter explicates what the authors term 'compassionate solidarity' networks – primarily locally organised groups – that use social media in ways that are distinct from the more mainstream mediatisation of communication via military securitisation, on the one hand, and securitised care, on the other. From this, Chouliaraki and Georgiou propose a 'physicality of care' within activist groups that is constituted by a 'feedback loop [between] the digital [and] the physical'; as they write: '[d]igital technology may have produced what we earlier called new biometric epistemologies of the border, yet it appears that these epistemologies continue to be undercut by technologies of co-presence – bodies, gazes, spoken words'.

This enmeshment of the technological and the somatic – and the possibilities for hospitality to work in and through both – finds echoes in both Woolley's and Connell's analyses. Common to all three chapters in this section, then, is a recognition that, however technologised and mediatised bordering and border crossing has become, it is the corporeal encounter between peoples and the fragile ontology of embodiment per se that is perpetually at work when attempts are made to negotiate the border's coercive logic. Notwithstanding their identification of potentiality and creativity of/ at the border, the chapters in this section remain cognisant of the founding political assumptions and current trajectories of governmental border work; they recognise that an understanding of borders as productive or 'thickened' spaces – or indeed as sites of intervention – comes hand in hand with global increases in militarisation and surveillance. Both of these aspects have contributed to rendering totemic the psycho-geographical power of the border as a zone in which refugees' arrivals and departures continue to be administered tortuously, over prolonged periods.

Bibliography

Agamben, Giorgio (1998), *Homo Sacer: Sovereign Power and Bare Life*, trans. D. Heller-Roazen (Stanford: Stanford University Press).

Nield, Sophie (2008), 'The Proteus cabinet, or "we are here but not here"', *Research in Drama Education: The Journal of Applied Theatre and Performance*, 13.2: 137–45.

Pugliese, Joseph (2010), *Transmediterranean: Diasporas, Histories, Geopolitical Spaces* (Brussels: P. I. E. Peter Lang).

Rajaram, Prem Kumar, and Carl Grundy-Warr (2007), *Borderscapes: Hidden Geographies and Politics at Territory's Edge* (Minneapolis: University of Minnesota Press).

Chapter 8

Docu/Fiction and the Aesthetics of the Border

Agnes Woolley

During the first few months of the German occupation of France in 1940, Lisa Fittko, an Austro-Hungarian Jew exiled in France, became an accidental people smuggler. In her 1985 memoir, *Escape Through the Pyrenees*, Fittko describes the 'apocalyptic atmosphere' of Marseilles and south-eastern France at the time, where every day there were new stories of 'absurd escape attempts; plans involving fantasy boats and fictitious captains, visas for countries not found on any map, and passports issued by nations that no longer existed' (Fittko 2000: 105). In this fevered atmosphere, with the Gestapo watching many of the routes out of France, Fittko encountered the sympathetic mayor of Banyul-Sur-Mer, who pointed her to an 'ancient smugglers' path' (Fittko 2000: 109) called *la route Lister*, which navigated a high mountain pass before dropping down to the Spanish port town of Portbou. Fittko began helping refugees across to Spain from where many would move on to the United States. One of the first to pass with her using this route was the German-Jewish philosopher Walter Benjamin, whose journey across the border and subsequent death in Portbou is now the stuff of legend. Extensively memorialised, *la route Lister* is no longer a clandestine border crossing, but has become a pilgrimage route of sorts for those retracing the philosopher's last journey and a site where historical narratives of exile, asylum and hospitality shed light on the more recent journeys of refugees moving into, rather than out of, Europe.

Concealed crossing points, as *la route Lister* was, can still be traced across Europe's shifting borders and, over 500 kilometres to the north of the Pyrenees, dividing France and Italy, lies a similarly treacherous mountain pass at the Italian village of Grimaldi. For at least the last hundred years, border crossers here have included Italian anti-fascists, Jews fleeing antisemitism, Yugoslavs escaping genocide and war and, more recently, Tunisians displaced by the tumult of the Arab Spring and Syrians fleeing the civil war. In 2013, seventy-five years after European citizens and refugees worked together to outrun the Nazis, a group of Italian activists and Syrian and Palestinian refugees dressed up as a wedding party and defied European border controls by crossing the Grimaldi pass. They documented the journey, and the resulting film, *On the Bride's Side* (2014), follows the wedding party's multiple border-crossing journey from Italy to Sweden. The film, and the acts of border crossing it documents, is a staged intervention into, and a public disavowal of, a politics of asylum in contemporary Europe that emerged in response to the displacements of the Second World War, yet is no longer capable of addressing the multiple and myriad refugee movements of the twenty-first century. Since the UNHCR's pronouncement in 2014 that the number of forcibly displaced people worldwide had exceeded fifty million for the first time since the Second World War (Edwards 2014), parallels between post-War refugee movements and the current so-called refugee crisis have been hastily drawn. My aim in bringing together these two moments of border crossing by way of introduction is not to assert historical equivalence, but to chart how acts of solidarity stretch across time and build on one another: where Lisa Fittko shepherded scores of refugees across to Spain, contemporary activists continue to facilitate those on the move in ways that reject a purely legal understanding of belonging. The Grimaldi pass, for example, is dotted with helpful signposts, deposits of food and rudimentary shelters that have been set up by locals. As documents of such acts of solidarity, both Fittko's memoir and *On the Bride's Side* offer an opportunity to reflect on how this kind of activism might be born of and in turn produce an aesthetic and imaginative engagement with the border that is collaborative and inclusive rather than exclusionary.

For Étienne Balibar, the geopolitical border begins with European colonisation: 'Europe is the point of the world whence border lines set forth to be drawn throughout the world, because it is the native land of the very representation of the border as this sensible and supersensible "thing" that should be or not be, be here or there [. . .]' (Balibar 1998: 216–17). For this reason, Balibar argues, the vacillation of borders is particularly connected with questions of European identity: with where it begins and ends and exactly what it comprises. Writing in the 1990s, Balibar was concerned with intensifying globalisation and the effects of the creation of the Schengen Zone, which made it easier for citizens of European Union countries to move between the 26 member states. Since then, ongoing forces of globalisation, the re-emergence of Russian imperial ambitions and the mass movement of people as a result of instability in Africa and the Middle East (most recently, the war in Syria) have further complicated the idea of the European border, one major effect of which has been its increased militarisation. Include Britain's 2016 vote to leave the EU and the question of European borders seems to be one of geopolitical magnitude deeply entangled with the continent's colonial history. Today European borders are especially tense. Perhaps because of this tumult, artists, writers and film-makers have begun to focus on European borders as sites where questions of national identity, displacement and globalisation intersect. The amount and diversity of arts projects taking place in and alongside European borders illustrates the extent to which 'border think-ing' (Mignolo 2000) remains a vital tool for understanding human precarity in the twenty-first century.[1] Moreover, like the wedding party en route from Italy to Sweden, 'exilic and émigré subjects' continue to use 'global media and entertainment industries to situate themselves historically, creating locally sit-uated syncretic communities of address and socially engaged historical and political agency' (Naficy 1999: 3). Given the current extent of mass move-ment and displacement, it may not be an exaggeration to say that the border experience is one of the defining experiences of the contemporary era.[2]

Borders have always been sites of both geopolitical tension and artistic and discursive negotiation. Examining how these aspects intersect, this chap-ter will set the context for border art concerning current refugee movement, focusing on documentary form in general and the film project *On the Bride's Side* in particular, a documentary that offers a distinctive aesthetics of the border. The project and the film emerged from a chance encounter at Milan's Porta Garibaldi station in October 2013, where the Italian journalist Gabriele Del Grande, the Palestinian-born writer and poet Khaled Soliman Al Nassiry and the poet and translator Tareg al Jabr were having coffee. Overhearing their Arabic conversation, the recently arrived Palestinian refugee Abdallah Sallam asked them where he might board the train to Sweden. He told them that he was a survivor of the 11 October shipwreck off the island of Lampe-dusa, and was keen to move further north to apply for asylum.[3] Though popular among newly arrived refugees, the move from southern to northern Europe is not an easy journey. The 1990 Dublin Regulation stipulates that refugees must claim asylum in the country in which they first arrive in the EU, which for the vast majority is southern European states such as Spain, Italy and Greece.[4] While EU citizens have freedom of movement across Europe's internal borders thanks to the Schengen agreement, non-EU migrants are forced into illegal and dangerous methods of travel if, as is common, they wish to move from the austerity-hit south to Europe's northern countries. In this context, the group hatched a plan to stage a wedding in order to get a small group of Syrian and Palestinian refugees out of Italy and into Sweden to claim asylum: as Del Grande notes on the project's website: 'What border policeman would ever stop a bride to check her documents?'[5] As conceived by the group, the journey overland from Italy to Sweden is an act of civil disobedience that rejects the reduction of human belonging to biometric data and documentation. In acting outside the law in the service of a higher law, the plan lays claim to an ancient lineage whose archetypal figure is Antigone, a woman who breaks the laws of the land so that she may attend to the sacred familial burial rites owed to her brother, Polynices. The group's counter-narrative to European restrictionism and border control is thus routed through a dual vision of the law that echoes Jacques Derrida's distinction between conditional and unconditional hospitality: while the former consti-tutes the multiple laws that surround the concept of hospitality such that any home – or nation – may remain sovereign, the latter, by contrast, considers the possibility of welcoming an 'absolute, unknown, anonymous other' (Derrida and Dufourmantelle 2000: 25) without asking them to account for themselves. With unconditionality as a guiding principle, such acts of welcome are played out repeatedly in *On the Bride's Side* as the wedding party is hosted in safe houses across Europe. Aesthetically as well as politically subversive, the film undermines prevalent assumptions about refugee movement. In place of clandestine, furtive border crossing, viewers are presented with the spectacle of a wedding, a bold and visible rite of passage at which the presence of cameras and the frank curiosity of strangers is nothing remarkable. Scenes depicting music and dancing in public spaces combine to provide an aesthetics of the border in which the encounter with difference engenders a space of convivial interaction and exchange.

Much border art coming out of the 'refugee crisis' (literature, film and theatre) has been in a creative non-fictional mode, which acknowledges refugee testimony as integral to the preservation of rights by balancing claims to truth with effective storytelling and metaphorical approaches. As both documentary and political act, *On the Bride's Side* generates a productive tension between its aesthetic and activist aims through the notion of performance. Drawing on narrative genres such as the thriller, the road movie and (in tone) the caper, the film's performative aspects reach beyond the symbolic fiction of the wedding to include formal considerations such as narrative plotting and character development. At times the film also documents the process of its production, as in an early scene where the group convenes to map the journey. Though effectively 'backstage', the bride wears her gown, suggesting the need to perform the role of bride not only for the European border police but also for the film's viewers. This meta-theatricality works to highlight the fact that performance is integral to both the political act of border crossing and the aesthetic act of making a film. But what are the ethical implications of filming vulnerable groups such as refugees? What kind of agency can these subjects have in the context of a documentary? And can such films intervene in the public perception and/or treatment of refugees in a meaningful way? These are questions that have long attached themselves to documentary film, whether or not the subject matter is as controversial or affecting as the movement of refugees across borders.

My discussion of *On the Bride's Side* sets it in the context of a flourishing of documentary over the last twenty years in which the genre has engaged in formal innovations that push at its own borders in ways that are both aesthetically exciting and actively engaged with the subjects they depict. My interest here is in what these formal innovations mean for refugee subjects: a context in which the artistic and ethical demand on aesthetic work is highly contested.[6] As a mode that exists at the intersection of fact and narrative fiction, documentary is well placed to deal with the complexities of the narrative environment of refugee movement and life on and at the border. Asking to whom, and how, people tell their stories, documentary negotiates the point at which representation meets reality; concerned both with revealing truth and examining how that truth is mediated through narrative forms. *On the Bride's Side* both conforms to and resists dramatic narratives of border crossing, navigating fact and fiction to offer a renewed aesthetics of the border.

Border art: disrupting the logic of the border

The focus of global attention to refugee issues in recent years has been on the rising numbers of refugees on and around European borders and the strategies that have been implemented to manage the movement of people at a national and EU level.[7] But much as European leaders might wish to draw a clear line between inside and outside when it comes to European belonging, such pronouncements are haunted by the continent's history of colonial and postcolonial intervention, which explains why conflicts such as that in Syria 'spark powerful resonances within the European nations, which will not be suppressed by security policies that reduce everything to the idea of "terrorism"' (Balibar 2016: 167). As Balibar argued in his 2004 book *We, the People of Europe*, the very idea of a hierarchy of belonging invoked by EU borders is a legacy of colonialism. Closer to Tunisia than it is to mainland Europe, the Italian island of Lampedusa, where large numbers of refugees arrive in the EU, has become a major frontier-battleground in Europe's confrontation with refugees, described by Joseph Pugliese as a 'fault line' between north and south (Pugliese 2010: 105). Having been used as a penal colony for rebellious southern Italians during unification in the nineteenth century, Lampedusa has now been mobilised by Fortress Europe as a frontline space that 'must thwart, through imprisonment and deportation the landfall of asylum seekers and the undocumented on their shores' (Pugliese 2010: 108). For Pugliese, this is a 'structural not coincidental' continuation of colonial practices: '[a]s a geophysical and conceptual border [. . .] Lampedusa has historically been a space in which to hide the worst excesses of neo-colonial relations' (Pugliese 2010: 108).[8] *On the Bride's Side*'s critique of contemporary European bordering processes is evident in much recent border art, some of which I will outline below. But for Del Grande, the project – both film and act – is specifically about disavowing the border that divides Europe from its past. Strategically invoking a 'pan-Mediterranean' affiliation, as opposed to the neoliberal political ideals embodied in the EU, Del Grande confronts and at times celebrates the 'single dramatic history' (Balibar 2016: 167) that entwines Europe and its Middle Eastern and African neighbours. If colonial ideas of European liberal democracy – the 'European sense of the world', as Simon Gikandi puts it (2001: 630) – are what attract many refugees and migrants to the continent, then *On the Bride's Side* aims to realise the promise of those Enlightenment ideals of hospitality and freedom, which have operated so unevenly.

Del Grande's temporally and spatially expansive sense of belonging opens up the border space in productive ways that echo the emergence of the concept of the 'borderscape'. Far from simply a line that orders and divides cultural or national groups, spheres of influence and the exercise of the law, the border space is 'a zone of resistance, agency, and rogue embodiment' (Rajaram and Grundy-Warr 2007: x). Rather than consolidating the reduction of people to abstractions such as 'the citizen' or 'the community', the border

> is a zone between states where the territorial resolutions of being and the laws that prop them up collapse. It is a zone where the multiplicity and chaos of the universal and the discomforts and possibilities of the body intrude. We use the term *borderscapes* to indicate the complexity and vitality of, and at, the border. (Rajaram and Grundy-Warr 2007: x)

This conception of the border zone redescribes the singular border as multivalent, encompassing the multiple levels on which the process of bordering operates: social, psychological, material, discursive, aesthetic and so on. It articulates both its precarities and its possibilities; a duality that emerges in *On the Bride's Side*'s at times jubilant vitality in the face of adversity and risk. The disruptive logic that characterises this conception of the border emerges in the film's convivial, heterogeneous and translatory image of the border, which disrupts its regulating and normalising force. Though not always explicitly rendered in the film's visual grammar, Del Grande's articulation of an expansive border space projects a broader conception of what it means to be European, one that accommodates and acknowledges commonalities and shared histories.

Such an expansive image of the border can be traced to the supposed birthplace of border art: the highly contested border between Mexico and the United States. Here, in 1984, a collective of Chicano-inspired artists set up the BAW–TAF (Border Art Workshop–Taller de Arte Fronterizo), which produces work on and of the border, most notably by the performance artist Guillermo Gómez-Peña. Gloria Anzaldúa's seminal work, *Borderlands/La Frontera: The New Mestiza* (1987), also emerged from this context; a book whose combination of autobiography, criticism and poetry gives voice to the complex positioning of the border artist. For Anzaldúa,

> Art and la frontera intersect in a liminal space where border people, especially artists, live in a state of 'nepantla.' Nepantla is the Náhuatl word for an in-between state, that uncertain terrain one crosses when moving from one place to another, when changing from one class, race, or sexual position to another, when traveling from the present identity into a new identity. (Anzaldúa 2009: 180)

Documentary is itself a liminal art form, which sits at the intersection of fact and fiction and has a compulsive interest in 'who tells the stories and what stories and histories are told' (Anzaldúa 2009: 183). Such reflexivity makes documentary adept at negotiating these tensions within the mobile context of border crossing. Anzaldúa's sense of the border as a multivalent space which 'contains all other places within it' prefigures the idea of the 'borderscape' (Anzaldúa 2009: 180) and describes liminality as a state of plenitude rather than privation, one that can encompass the often contradictory energies of Mestizaje existence. If borders are 'mobile, relational and contested sites' as subsequent theorists have suggested, they open up a space within which to configure new social relations (Brambilla, Laine and Bocchi 2015: 2).

With increasing numbers of people on the move, new border spaces have opened up in Europe – the 'Jungle' in Calais, makeshift camps on the borders of Hungary and Greece – which have fostered artistic interventions devoted to interpreting and documenting, but also shaping, life on the border. One of the most high-profile British border art projects is Good Chance Theatre, which based itself in the Calais 'Jungle' throughout 2015.[9] According to its website, Good Chance's mission is 'to convey the humanity that exists at the core of this international crisis' through a programme of events including writing and performance workshops, poetry slams and large communal evening events on site in the camp.[10] Bringing the border to the centre, Good Chance subsequently set up a residency on London's Southbank in the summer of 2016, and in 2017 co-produced a play – *The Jungle* – with the National Theatre and Young Vic, which opened in December 2017 and transferred to the West End in summer 2018. Also engaging with life on the UK–France border, *Breach* by Annie Holmes and Olumide Popoola was published in 2016. The book comprises a series of short stories derived from the narratives of refugees (and others) whom the authors talked to while in Calais; a frequently used tactic that gives voice to refugee experience by dramatising testimony.

Unsurprisingly, Europe's southern borders, where most refugees arrive, have become key sites of encounter and analysis for journalists, artists, volunteers and policy makers alike. Théâtre Senza, a pan-European theatre company, worked with refugees on the Italian island of Lampedusa to produce *Miraculi*, a devised, site-specific play on and about Lampedusa. Similarly, the Italian art collective Askavusa, whose most prominent figure is the artist Giacomo Sferlazzo, has been operating in the area for a number of years and runs the Lampedusa Festival, which takes place every summer. A key project of theirs is 'Porto M', an exhibition of objects found on the island pertaining to refugees. Sferlazzo and others worked with the salvaged objects by remodelling them in ways that work to expand, rather than simply conserve, memories of migration. The small museum was open on the island and the collection has travelled to other sites in Europe with the aim of countering dominant imaginaries of what happens along Europe's external borders and specifically on Lampedusa.

Commonly referred to as 'la porta di Europa', Lampedusa (and the Mediterranean as a whole) has become symbolically associated with a threshold or doorway between Africa and Europe, an image also evoked by Askavusa's use of the name, 'Porto M'. Perhaps inevitably, ideas of crossing figure in much contemporary European border art, but there is also a kind of border crossing implied in the undertaking and reception of the creative act. This may be to do with the idea of empathy – of crossing from self to other by putting oneself in another's shoes – or it may be a formal and even disciplinary crossing that generates new forms with which to engage with displacement and migration. In performing the act of solidarity it documents, *On the Bride's Side* grafts together an aesthetic work and a piece of activism, staging a utopian vision of the border while intervening actively within the border space by materially realising spaces of hospitality in Europe en route from Milan to Malmo.

For Elena dell'Agnese and Anne-Laure Amilhat Szary, 'cultural production and borders have developed a more-than-representational relationship that appears to reveal a lot of the political mechanisms at work in the spaces concerned by borders and border-crossings' (dell'Agnese and Amilhat Szary 2015: 4). Produced by the border, artistic intervention also disrupts it, revealing the ways in which the border works to delimit identities. According to Cristina Giudice and Chiara Giubilaro, the borderscape is a Foucauldian 'dispositive': 'a thoroughly heterogeneous ensemble consisting of discourses, institutions, architectural forms, regulatory decisions, laws, administrative measures, scientific statements, philosophical, moral and philanthropic propositions' (Foucault, cited in Giudice and Giubilaro 2015: 81). The border dispositive is secreted within the linear shape of the border, and its multiplicity emerges from within its reductive and homogenising tendencies. By 'chip[ping] away at the logic of the border', border art stages 'alternative visions and possibilities'. The border artist 'inverts the reduction process on which border is based, destabilising and perturbing the certainty and definiteness of its essentialist categories' (Giudice and Giubilaro 2015: 85).

Such 'more-than-representational' approaches to border art can intercede in the border's operation in productive ways. But how does documentary, as already often an interventionist form, engage with the border space in the way that recent understandings of border art suggest? And how do formal, dramatic and aesthetic choices reshape both the documentary form and the border space? Far from straightforwardly indexical, documentary always blurs the borders between fact and fiction, offering a particularly rich space within which to interrogate geophysical and discursive border zones. Further, as documentary theorist Stella Bruzzi points out, 'documentaries are performative acts, inherently fluid and unstable and informed by issues of performance and performativity' (Bruzzi 2013: 1). In line with much border art, they are 'more-than-representational'. Documentary is itself already a kind of border art that operates at the edges of formal categorisations and boundaries. It is this, perhaps, that makes it so responsive to those geophysical and discursive borders that impose a hierarchy of belonging.

Documenting the border: fact, fiction and reality

David Shields's 2010 manifesto, *Reality Hunger*, asserts that we have never had a greater desire for the real. We long for facts, albeit delivered via the recognisable formats of dramatic fiction. It's true to say that the twenty-first century has seen a fascination with testimonial forms in the West: with 'life writing' in literature and 'verbatim' in theatre. Feature films are routinely prefaced with the words 'based on true events', no matter how tenuous the relationship is between fact and fiction in the ensuing story. The theatre critic Lyn Gardner attributes this obsession to the notion that in a post-9/11 world preoccupied with the 'war on terror', there is a sense that only docudrama, which she terms 'the new journalism', is capable of tackling the seriousness of our times (Gardner 2004). As Shields points out, however, fact and fiction are historically entangled: 'the novel has always been a mixed form [. . .] from Defoe through Flaubert and Dickens' (Shields 2010: 14). In line with early photography, documentary film has conventionally been considered a window on to the world. Following the French film theorist André Bazin, the influential British-Canadian documentary maker John Grierson pioneered a vision of objectivity in early twentieth-century documentary film that has been pervasive, and was considered crucial to giving voice to those at the margins of society by revealing oppressive social conditions to bourgeois audiences. Yet the sharp distinction between indexical and figurative modes that has been the legacy of the Grierson school has never really been the case in practice. Instead, as Michael Renov points out: '"fictive" elements *in*sist in documentary as in all film forms' (Renov 1993: 10). Though the border between fiction and non-fiction is historically blurred, our renewed desire for the real in recent decades has seen a surge in creative non-fiction modes of storytelling. As Derek Paget notes, 'Docudrama on screen and stage has been an astonishingly burgeoning field for at least the past two decades' (Paget 2010: 191). This is especially prevalent in renderings of refugee narratives.

Perhaps paradoxically, the responses by documentary makers to the idea that our challenging times require a serious and sober engagement with 'reality' has been anything but the delivery of objective truth in a world obfuscated by mediatised forms. Where *On the Bride's Side* stages a performative intervention into refugee discourse and policy, other documentaries, such as Gianfranco Rosi's 2016 Berlinale hit *Fire at Sea*, offer highly aestheticised, metaphorical and figurative engagements with the same subject matter. While these approaches may seem poles apart, they form part of a multifaceted development in non-fiction film-making that has responded to Shields's 'reality hunger' in creative, challenging and stimulating ways. Each with their own nuances, forms of 'docudrama', 'docufiction', 'creative documentary', 'poetic documentary' and 'performative documentary' have come to dominate the non-fiction storytelling scene.[11] Techniques include re-enactments and dramatisations of real events, which, though used in much earlier films such as Robert J. Flaherty's *Nanook of the North* (1920), have taken a more avowedly self-reflexive turn in recent hybrid documentaries such as Clio Barnard's *The Arbor* (2010), Carole Morely's *Dreams of a Life* (2011) and Joshua Oppenheimer's *The Act of Killing* (2012). Other styles include setting testimony to music, as in *London Road* (dir. Rufus Norris), and 'slow cinema', defined as 'the type of contemplative, observational movie where image (and soundtrack) takes precedence over conventional narrative' (Sandhu 2012).

These experiments with the form respond not only to a general scepticism about the delivery of objective truth but also, as Bruzzi notes, to the changes inaugurated by an understanding of the ways in which the performative shapes our society and culture. At a time when the world seems to demand a confrontation with the facts, they become ever more elusive.[12] Given that the safety of refugees and asylum seekers often relies on the demand for both verifiable evidence of persecution and a convincing performance of the truth for border control officials, the dual narrative space of documentary is ideally placed to accommodate this paradox. As a form that is interested in revealing truth and the ways in which that truth is mediated, documentary storytelling coincides with the modes by which asylum seekers must present themselves as genuine or authentic refugees.[13] Creative non-fiction is especially well suited to the exploration of marginal lives that are vulnerable to (mis)appropriation precisely because its border-crossing form alerts audiences to questions of representation. My interest here is in how the idea of engaging with 'reality' as an act of political and ethical seriousness in the context of refugeeism and mass displacement acts in tension with anxieties over authenticity and the possibility of objective truth.

The tropic character of *On the Bride's Side*, and other recent and more highly aestheticised documentaries such as *Fire at Sea*, connects it to fictional forms through dramatic and narrative structuring, metaphor and imagery. For Renov, this is what permits documentary to move beyond its traditional conception as solely a 'a discourse of sobriety' (Bill Nichols, cited in Renov 2004: 23), and to encompass 'sometimes at the same time, a discourse of *jouissance* – of pleasure, desire, and of appeals to the Imaginary – even of delirium' (Renov 2004: 23). Renov's psychoanalytic approach to documentary draws it into the same critical tradition as fictional film and opens up the form's affective, as opposed to effective, aspects: the ways documentary works on our feelings as well as our knowledge. *On the Bride's Side* does both kinds of work by pausing the onward imperative of the narrative (and the journey itself) at strategic moments. En route through the Grimaldi pass, the bridal party comes across a derelict house, which evokes unmistakably the kinds of bombed-out buildings some of the group have escaped. The building bears the traces of many who have passed through in the form of discarded clothing and graffiti, asserting the transitory presence of these travellers: 'From Egypt – Libya – Malta – Italy – France'. Here, for the first time in the film, Abdallah recounts the devastating details of his journey to Italy by boat, describing how he was hauled out of the sea by Maltese officials along with several dead bodies. As he speaks the camera pans across the faces of the rest of the group standing in a circle around him, listening. He proceeds to name those he got to know on the journey who died en route, saying something about each before committing their names to the crumbling plaster in chalk. He also acknowledges the nameless 250 people still missing (presumed dead) from the wreck. Instead of the visual spectacle of the bodies themselves as corroboration of the events Abdallah describes, what is documented here – as well as the memory work involved in reciting the names of those who have been lost – is a relation of feeling among the speaker, the listeners and the film's viewers. This affective connection is 'more than representational' in the sense that it documents something that cannot be rendered visually within filmed documentary.

Affective moments such as these are part of the film's imaginative structure. *On the Bride's Side* appeals to the imaginary by foregrounding desire in a context (refugee movement and human displacement) that would seem to require only sober investigation. Its 'fairy-tale' wedding narrative is a case in point. As Emma Cox points out, it's not clear in the film that the wedding conceit is the deciding factor in the group's safe passage, with the result that the wedding 'manifests as an aesthetic and narrative device within the documentary as much as it does a necessity for illicit border crossings' (Cox 2016). Moreover, Cox notes, the visual semantics of the wedding, whose key image is the bride in the white dress, conform to heteronormative, patriarchal norms of marriage and social relations. However, as well as being 'slyly challenged' (Cox 2016) by the bride's decidedly un-bride-like comportment in the film, the heteronormative aspects of the wedding are also undermined by the project's clear rejection of Western understandings of kinship, which are built on the basis of 'relations of procreation and biology' (McKinnon and Cannell 2013: 13). Here, a Syrian activist 'marries' a Palestinian refugee in a performance that not only exposes the heteronormative wedding as a masquerade, but asserts alternative ties of kinship based on shared experience and solidarity. With others playing the roles of parents, in-laws and grandchildren, the project remakes family ties and asserts relatedness beyond blood and nation. Self-identified kinship ties are powerful acts of agency for refugees, who here assert a sociopolitical family that moves beyond the ties of blood and soil so potently symbolised in the semiotics of the wedding. The vision of borderlessness presented in *On the Bride's Side*, in which the group are welcomed warmly in each country they pass through, extends this self-identified 'family', shifting the ground on which notions of belonging are determined. It's important to note, however, that the film's most affirming scenes of hospitality and welcome are *real* and not performed. The group are received by citizen-hosts at each stopping point, where scenes of singing, drinking, dancing and storytelling document a genuine conviviality in the face of a generalised public hostility towards refugees. This blending of fantasy and reality mobilises 'the forces of desire' (Renov 2004: 14) as an alternative way of executing documentary's conventional aims of raising awareness of an issue and proposing solutions.

On the Bride's Side also has an underlying dramatic logic that allows it to lay claim to certain narrative traditions of fiction. Edited to reflect the high stakes inherent in the journey, the film incorporates elements of the road movie and the thriller. Road movies are inherently idealistic, tapping into North American ideas of freedom and autonomy from which most refugees are debarred. Yet they also tend to feature 'desperate characters lighting out for something better, someplace else' (Laderman 2002: 2). As David Laderman suggests, 'the road movie celebrates subversion as a literal venturing outside of society' (2002: 2). The utopian vision of *On the Bride's Side* takes the film beyond the borders of existing societal structures that delimit legitimate dwelling, and in this sense the film is less a document of existing circumstances than an idealised alternative. The drive for 'something better' shapes refugee journeys just as it does the narrative conventions of the road movie, and both operate in *On the Bride's Side* through Renov's sense of the forces of desire at play in documentary form. As characters in a road movie, refugees are no longer abject dependents, but co-conspirators in a rebellious act of autonomy. Though it appears to be an organic development, it is inside vehicles that some of the film's most compelling conversations take place. Just as in road movies, sitting side-by-side in a car rather than face-to-face seems to permit the expression of otherwise suppressed emotion. In *Claiming the Real* (1995) Brian Winston describes the convenience of the journey as a narrative device for solving the problem of closure in documentary film because there is an inbuilt narrative logic: 'a journey film ends with the end of the journey' (cited in Bruzzi 2013: 82). The journey trope has commonly been used as a means of creating what Winston calls 'chrono-logic' out of potentially shambolic or unrelated events. Journeys in documentaries thus provide narrative coherence to an otherwise fragmentary series of events and images. Given that the journeys that refugees make are almost always unpredictable, risky and fragmentary, with long periods of stasis, the imposition of a 'chrono-logic' on the journey in *On the Bride's Side* is another way of countering conventional understandings of refugee movement. It offers an alternative framework for the journey, which is meticulously planned and mapped out strategically using a network of support across several countries. The end of the journey in any documentary is an imposition, and this becomes starkly apparent in the film's coda, which informs viewers that several of the party were eventually deported back to Italy.[14]

On the Bride's Side is also a thriller with seriously high stakes. If caught, the refugees risk deportation back to Italy or Turkey, and the Italian citizens – including the Palestinian Khaled, who is shown receiving confirmation of his Italian citizenship during the journey – risk criminal prosecution for people trafficking. At times, the thriller mode is enhanced by editing and the use of music, which sets up audience expectations in ways that reveal our desire for narrative. At one key moment of high tension, the convoy is crossing the border between Germany and Denmark by car and are fearful that there will be a checkpoint at the border. A car full of Italian citizens goes ahead and the scene cuts back and forth between the cars as they grow increasingly tense at the possibility of being stopped. In fact, they cross the border without incident and, later, despite some anxiety that they will be stopped on the train crossing between Denmark and Sweden, they have no problem when tickets are checked. Indeed, despite the tension created by the formal construction of the film, the wedding party never has a confrontation with any national authorities and at every turn they are welcomed by open European citizen hosts. This runs counter to a conventional thriller, which requires the protagonists to pass through the narrative ups and downs of risk, danger and ultimate safety; to sense that all is lost before their ultimate triumph. In some ways, then, the film fails to provide viewers with the familiar plot points set up by the drama inherent in the scenario. Yet this subversion of expectation can actually be part of the film's intervention into the representational politics around refugees, because it subverts viewers' narrative expectations about the inherent drama of the refugee experience. Instead, what it reveals is an aesthetic of the border characterised by hospitality and intercultural encounter.

For Bruzzi, 'the pact between documentary, reality and the documentary spectator is far more straightforward than many theorists have made out: that a documentary will never be reality nor will it erase or invalidate that reality by being representational' (Bruzzi 2013: 6). So, documentary is a form that constructs and reconstructs reality without necessarily compromising on truth. As such, *On the Bride's Side* is faithful to the truth of its refugee characters, even as it constructs an elaborate fiction at the level of narrative (the wedding) and, more implicitly, at the level of form where editing and storyboarding have shaped the final film. To some extent, then, documentary is unavoidably *about* the encounter before the camera, because the camera will always make whatever is seen through its lens inauthentic. If 'the filmmaking process disrupts and intrudes upon the reality of the world it is documenting' (Bruzzi 2013: 78), then this is rendered an explicit process in *On the Bride's Side*. Here, the camera becomes part of the cover story for the journey: they purport to be documenting one thing (a wedding), while actually documenting another (border-crossing refugees). Far from being an objective observer, the camera participates in the fiction of the wedding. Its presence is integral to the project of the act and a contributing factor to the improvement of the material circumstances of the participants. In some ways, the presence of the camera makes the act *more* authentic given that weddings are routinely filmed for posterity. Elements of performance are therefore central to both the project and the film, and to the experience of the border itself. As Cox notes, the film's viewers 'come to recognize that getting through [the border] requires some kind of role-playing, or at least, sufficient preparedness for it' (Cox 2016).

Crossing the border as the participants in the film do is a physical engagement in space and time, but it is also a symbolic act of transgression and, when done collaboratively as here, an act of solidarity. It is both a practice of solidarity with those whose material circumstances and capacity for agency is compromised by physical borders, *and* an aesthetic work that crosses figurative borders between fact and the fiction of the wedding. The film documents an act that has tangible outcomes for the participants and shapes that act into the recognisable forms of dramatic narrative. This makes *On the Bride's Side* performative in the Butlerian sense that Bruzzi employs. The film functions as an utterance that simultaneously both describes and performs an action: it *is* the political act that it documents. Bruzzi calls performative documentary 'a mode which emphasises – and indeed constructs a film around – the often hidden aspects of performance, whether on the part of the documentary subjects or the filmmakers' (Bruzzi 2013: 185). The opening sequence of the film shows the bridal party being fitted for formal clothing and getting their hair styled, documenting the 'pre-performance' which is, of course, also the performance. Importantly, however, the film does not simply render visible the inevitable performativity that unfolds in front of a camera. Rather, the idea and indeed necessity of the performance at the point of border crossing is integral to the safety and security of the refugees. The participants are performing not only for the camera, which is itself a part of the fiction of the wedding, but for the authorities, whose assumptions about the kinds of movement refugees undertake become the enabling factor. The film-makers are also participants in the action. They play wedding guests, they facilitate the journey by setting up safe houses for the refugees in the various cities they stop at, and, importantly, they also share a portion of the risk as they are open to charges of people trafficking. This puts them 'on the side of' the refugee by sharing, in small part, their exposure to the law. The results are both affective and effective, intervening directly in the events being documented. Performance is central to *On the Bride's Side*'s political and aesthetic aims: to change the course of events for this particular group of refugees, but also to change the perception of refugees in general.

With its performative aspects in mind, *On the Bride's Side*'s dramatic intervention into the restrictive space of the border becomes 'more-than-representational'. In the film, the border is imaginatively reconceived as a convivial space and materially transgressed in a splicing together of art and activism. Dell'agnese and Amilhat Szary note the significance of place and space to much contemporary art, the political import of which they place in the context of the situationists:

> The spatial turn of visual and contemporary arts implies that the creators of artistic objects are making explicit use of the place in which they locate their work. Based on the situationist tradition that denounces the political spectacle by public intervention and on the claiming of public space through the power

of the aesthetical relation, many cultural creations can be analyzed through the
lenses of counter-politics and resistance to imperial geopolitics. (Dell'agnese
and Amilhat Szary 2015: 9)

On the Bride's Side's claim on public space is made through the power of
the aesthetic relation. In reconceiving the border space as de-privatised, de-
militarised and de-terrorised, the film offers a glimpse of the version of Europe
implied in its Enlightenment ideals, yet which is more often co-opted by the
neoliberal imperatives of mobile capital, goods and people. Jacques Rancière
calls this kind of artistic intervention 'relational', noting that '[s]ince the turn of
the century, there has been increasingly frequent talk of art's having "returned
to politics". A re-assertion of art's capacity to resist forms of economic, political and ideological domination' (Rancière 2010: 134). Rancière's conception
of the 'relational' artwork is a model of the efficacy of art he calls a pedagogy
of 'ethical immediacy' whereby the stake 'is not to improve behaviour through
representation' – that is, to elicit identification with a represented ethical act –
but to 'have all living bodies directly embody the sense of the common'
(Rancière 2010: 137). In this formulation, the community itself becomes the
artwork.[15] This kind of artistic work, which subscribes to the pervasive contemporary assumption that 'art has to leave the art world in order to be
effective in "real life"', operates by 'making the spectator active, by turning the art exhibition into a place of political activism or by sending artists
into the streets of derelict suburbs to invent new modes of social relations'
(Rancière 2010: 137).

On the Bride's Side fits neatly into this category of artistic intervention,
which seeks to map and transform social relations. Its approach to the grave
situation faced by displaced people is not to present the facts, but to create situations that engender new social relationships and envision alternatives. In fact, relationality – as opposed to other narrative strategies such as
empathy – is central to the film's political impetus. The film's Italian title,
which translates literally as 'I'm with the bride', connotes being part of,
belonging to, the wedding party and is an affirmation of that participation.
The journey itself also brings refugees, citizens and activists together as communities become the artwork in the way Rancière highlights. This suggests a
kind of borderlessness that is part of the film's utopian vision, and is found
not only in its particular conception of the convivial border space, but also
in the very fabric of the making of the film. The film's post-production was
crowdfunded by thousands of people who pledged money to get it made
and into cinemas. In so doing, funders were implicated (ideologically, if not
legally) in the film-makers' avowed act of 'trafficking', both extending the act
of civil disobedience exponentially and inoculating the film from legal challenges. The often overstated borderlessness of the digital sphere here realises
its best utopian aspirations of enabling forms of solidarity that are otherwise
unthinkable. These aspects highlight the relational importance of the film

above and beyond the more frequently deployed empathetic means through which audiences are encouraged to identify with refugees through narrative: we are 'with' the bride despite not having had her experience. Again, this is where documentary's inherent self-reflexivity offers an alternative to narrative forms that rely on empathetic engagement to generate change for those depicted; to use Alison Jeffers's terminology, viewers stand shoulder to shoulder with them. A consciousness of the dialogic interrelationship between film-makers, fact and subjects reasserts the agentive capacity of refugees in the face of institutional and bureaucratic erasure.

This notion of relational art, which takes us to a specific place and interpellates us into the artwork, has its limitations and, according to Rancière, is not the most effective form of political aesthetics. Drawing on the work of visual artists such as Chantal Ackerman and Sophie Ristelhueber, Rancière advocates instead a displacement from the stark political facts: 'setting aside all economic and social "explanations" [. . .] to identify a more specifically political element' (Rancière 2010: 150). Rancière's 'dissensual' art deliberately 'suspends the correlation between artforms and social function' (2010: 150). But *On the Bride's Side* insists on their indivisibility. While it wears its 'social function' on its sleeve, it also makes affective use of fiction and fantasy to generate an alternative vision of the border and those who cross it. It succeeds in setting aside 'economic and social "explanations"' in favour of something else altogether: genuine moments and spaces of unconditional hospitality as part of an ongoing utopian vision of borderlessness. The fantasy and the reality work together to produce an interventionist model of documentary that utilises its own borderline status as a means of transformation with and for refugees.

Notes

1. Mignolo attributes his notion of 'border thinking' to Gloria Anzaldúa's seminal 1987 book *Borderland/La Frontera: The New Mestiza*.
2. It is important to acknowledge the Eurocentric basis of this discussion, which takes the so-called refugee crisis as its starting point as a result of a proliferation of artistic engagements with what has been happening at European national borders. The border experience is a long-standing aspect of refugee movement in refugee-receiving countries in Africa and in newer border zones and extraterritorial detention centres on islands such as Nauru and Papua New Guinea.
3. Known as the 'Lampedusa Disaster', the shipwrecks of 3 and 11 October 2013 were deemed the deadliest in the Mediterranean, before other tragic events in the last few years set new records for fatalities. The shipwrecks seem to mark the beginning of what is now known as the 'refugee crisis' in and around Europe.
4. Germany temporarily suspended this rule in 2016 in response to rising numbers of Syrian refugees.
5. www.iostoconlasposa.com/en (accessed 17 May 2018).

6. For analyses of the representation of refugee and asylum-seeking subjects in creative work, see Cox (2014; 2015), Farrier (2011) and Woolley (2014).
7. In 2014 the European border agency, Frontex, implemented Operation Triton to patrol European seas after Italy cancelled its national operation known as 'Mare Nostrum' (Our Sea).
8. As historian Stephanie Malia Homhas notes, the colonial relations between Italy and Libya are an unacknowledged historical force underpinning both contemporary forced migration to Italy and Italy's neo-colonial treatment of the refugees. See http://www.stephaniemaliahom.com/current-projects (accessed 3 January 2017).
9. Worth noting is the political agreement that pushes back the UK border to French sovereign territory, a deal now under threat post-Brexit.
10. www.goodchance.org.uk/about (accessed 3 January 2017).
11. This last term has varying interpretations. See, for example, the differences between Bruzzi's Butlerian interpretation outlined below, and the more schematic definition provided by Bill Nichols in his 1994 book, *Blurred Boundaries: Questions of Meaning in Contemporary Culture*.
12. As well as adopting fictional narrative conventions, one aspect of these formal innovations has seen documentary coinciding with forms of activism and advocacy, even influencing outcomes for their subjects. This is especially true of long-form documentary such as *Making a Murderer* (2015) and *Serial* (2014), both of which have resulted in retrials/appeals for the protagonists.
13. For more on performance and authenticity in the asylum context, see Jeffers (2011) and Woolley (2017).
14. In an extra-filmic coda, the premiere of the film at the Venice film festival was attended by activists, supporters and refugees who were encouraged to attend dressed as brides. This celebratory reunion of sorts reiterates the aesthetic of the hyper-visible border engagement.
15. Drawing on Rousseau, Rancière uses as his example the Greek city festival in which a city enacts its own unity through hymns and dances.

Bibliography

Anzaldúa, Gloria (2009 [1987]), 'Border arte: Nepantla, el lugar de la frontera', in *The Gloria Anzaldúa Reader*, ed. AnaLouise Keating (Durham, NC: Duke University Press), 176–86.

Balibar, Étienne (1998), 'The borders of Europe', in Pheng Cheah and Bruce Robbins (eds), *Cosmopolitics: Thinking and Feeling Beyond the Nation* (Minneapolis: University of Minnesota Press), 216–29.

Balibar, Étienne (2004), *We, The People of Europe: Reflections on Transnational Citizenship*, trans. James Swenson (Princeton: Princeton University Press).

Balibar, Étienne (2016), 'Europe at the limits', *Interventions: International Journal of Postcolonial Studies*, 18.2: 165–71.

Brambilla, Chiara, Jussi Laine and Gianluca Bocchi (eds) (2015), *Borderscaping: Imaginations and Practices of Border Making* (London: Routledge).

Bruzzi, Stella (2013), *New Documentary* (Abingdon: Routledge).

Cox, Emma (2014), *Theatre and Migration* (Basingstoke: Palgrave).

Cox, Emma (2015), *Performing Noncitizenship* (London: Anthem).

Cox, Emma (2016), 'Concealment, revelation and masquerade in Europe's asylum apparatus: intimate life at the border', *Lateral: Journal of the Cultural Studies Association*, 5.2, special issue, 'Leveraging Justice', ed. Janelle Reinelt and María Estrada-Fuentes,http://csalateral.org/issue/5-2/concealment-revelation-masquerade-europe-asylum-cox/ (accessed 14 May 2019).

dell'Agnese, Elena, and Anne-Laure Amilhat Szary (2015), 'Borderscapes: from border landscapes to border aesthetics', *Geopolitics*, 20.1: 4–13.

Derrida, Jacques, and Anne Dufourmantelle (2000), *Of Hospitality: Anne Dufourmantelle Invites Jacques Derrida to Respond*, trans. Rachel Bowlby (Stanford: Stanford University Press).

Edwards, Adrian (2014), 'World Refugee Day: global forced displacement tops 50 million for first time in post-World War II era', 20 June, http://www.unhcr.org/53a155bc6.html (accessed 3 January 2017).

Farrier, David (2011), *Postcolonial Asylum: Seeking Sanctuary Before the Law* (Liverpool: Liverpool University Press).

Fittko, Lisa (2000 [1991]), *Escape Through the Pyrenees*, trans. David Koblick (Evanston: Northwestern University Press).

Gardner, Lyn (2004), 'Review: *Guantanamo*, New Ambassadors, London', *The Guardian*, 29 June, http://www.guardian.co.uk/stage/2004/jun/29/theatre (accessed 20 August 2016).

Gikandi, Simon (2001), 'Globalization and the claims of postcoloniality', *South Atlantic Quarterly*, 100.3: 627–58

Giudice, Cristina, and Chiara Giubilaro (2015), 'Re-imagining the border: border art as a space of critical imagination and creative resistance', *Geopolitics*, 20.1: 79–94.

Jeffers, Alison (2011), *Refugees, Theatre and Crisis: Performing Global Identities* (Basingstoke: Palgrave).

Laderman, David (2002), *Driving Visions: Exploring the Road Movie* (Austin: University of Texas Press).

McKinnon, Susie, and Fenella Cannell (2013), 'The difference kinship makes', in Susie McKinnon and Fenella Cannell (eds), *Vital Relations: Modernity and the Persistent Life of Kinship* (Santa Fe, NM: SAR Press), 3–38.

Mignolo, Walter (2000), *Local Histories/Global Designs: Coloniality, Subaltern Knowledges, and Border Thinking* (Princeton: Princeton University Press).

Naficy, Hamid (1999), *Home, Exile Homeland: Film, Media and the Politics of Place* (Abingdon: Routledge).

Nichols, Bill (1994), *Blurred Boundaries: Questions of Meaning in Contemporary Culture* (Bloomington: Indiana University Press).

Paget, Derek (2010), 'Editorial', *Studies in Documentary Film*, 4.3: 191–3.

Pugliese, Joseph (2010), 'Transnational carceral archipelagos: Lampedusa and Christmas Island', in Joseph Pugliese (ed.), *Transmediterranean: Diasporas, Histories, Geopolitical Spaces* (Brussels: P. I. E. Peter Lang), 105–24.

Rajaram, Prem Kumar, and Carl Grundy-Warr (2007), *Borderscapes: Hidden Geographies and Politics at Territory's Edge* (Minneapolis: University of Minnesota Press).

Rancière, Jacques (2010), *Dissensus: On Politics and Aesthetics* (London: Continuum).

Renov, Michael (1993), 'Introduction: the truth about non-fiction', in Michael Renov (ed.), *Theorizing Documentary* (London: Routledge/AFI), 1–11.

Renov, Michael (2004), *The Subject of Documentary* (Minneapolis: University of Minnesota Press).

Sandhu, Sukhdev (2012), 'Slow cinema fights back against Bourne's supremacy', *The Guardian*, 9 March, https://www.theguardian.com/film/2012/mar/09/slow-cinema-fights-bournes-supremacy (accessed 3 January 2017).

Shields, David (2010), *Reality Hunger: A Manifesto* (London: Hamish Hamilton).

Winston, Brian (1995), *Claiming the Real: The Documentary Film Revisited* (London: BFI Publishing).

Woolley, Agnes (2014), *Contemporary Asylum Narratives: Representing Refugees in the Twenty-First Century* (Basingstoke: Palgrave Macmillan).

Woolley, Agnes (2017), 'Narrating the "asylum story": between literary and legal storytelling', *Interventions*, 19.3: 376–94.

Chapter 9

Crossings, Bodies, Behaviours

Liam Connell

A good deal of the recent academic work on refugees approaches the topic as a matter of biopolitics.[1] The understanding of biopolitics most commonly employed here is that set out by Giorgio Agamben in his conception of *homo sacer*. According to Agamben, the state's capacity to create an exception, that is, to place some object beyond the law as a means of establishing its ability to govern, produces *'a biopolitical body'* as *'the original activity of sovereign power'* (Agamben 1998: 6, italics in original). In such terms, Agamben concludes that the concentration camps of the Second World War are the 'biopolitical paradigm of the modern' (1998: 119) because they totally transformed politics into biopolitics. From here, he argues that the refugee becomes the 'limit concept' that integrates bare life with the 'state order' and with the concept of human rights (1998: 134). Agamben's insights into the nature of state power have been readily used to account for contemporary refugeeness in influential work such as Peter Nyers's *Rethinking Refugees* (2006), Vicki Squires's *The Exclusionary Politics of Asylum* (2009) and Imogen Tyler's *Revolting Subjects* (2013). This has been matched in the area of literary and film studies where prominent work such as David Farrier's *Postcolonial Asylum* (2011), Agnes Woolley's *Contemporary Asylum Narratives* (2014) and Emma Cox's *Performing Noncitizenship* (2015) have all looked to Agamben to offer a theoretical frame for reading the textual representations of asylum or refugeeness. While Agamben's philosophical account of sovereignty is undoubtedly valuable as a means of opening up a discussion of the technologies of exclusion that frame refugees as apart from citizens, its emphasis on exception as the enduring component of sovereign power may limit its capacity to account for the embodied refugee as a subject of politics rather than merely as subject to the regimes of biopolitics. As Judith Butler has recently noted, Agamben's concept of bare life relies upon a particular, classical conception of the *polis* in which only certain kinds of action are allowed to count as political. The risk of Agamben's emphasis on the exception is that it suggests that, 'once excluded', refugees 'lack appearance or "reality" in political terms, that they have no social or political standing or are cast out and reduced to mere being' (Butler 2015: 78–80).[2]

This chapter takes its cue from Butler's assertion that verbalisation is not the only form of 'expressive political action' and that 'certain kinds of bodily enactments' can operate as a kind of speech act that is not precisely discursive (Butler 2015: 18). In response to this provocation, I offer readings of two films, Marc Forster's *World War Z* (2013) and Philippe Lioret's *Welcome* (2009), in order to explore what happens when the biopolitical body of the refugee is read through the depiction of the somatic body of refugees within the narrative text. In exploring the relation of these two forms of the body, it is useful to recall Sophie Nield's distinction between the natural body and the political body as a repository of citizenship and rights. For Nield, these two bodies are disaggregated by the founding of rights within the frame of citizenship and by the contemporary technologised border that demands the representation of the body, rather than the body itself, as the prerequisite of ingress (Nield 2008: 140–1). Nield argues that theatrical work can draw attention to the disparity between the body's material presence and its capacity to represent, and she suggests that the border constitutes a kind of theatrical space whereby bodies must act out a representation of themselves in a bid for rights (2008: 138–9). This resonates with Butler's assertion that the fact of assembly constitutes a performative act designed to claim an eligibility to rights (Butler 2015: 50). Building on these observations, I want to suggest a distinction between the representation of the body that speaks and the body that appears in order to think about the capacity of the refugee's body to bridge the representational gap between the natural and the political body. While the body of the refugee is framed by the technologies of the *polis* in a bid to constitute the sovereign authority of the state, and while this act aspires to separate the natural and the political body, the body that appears is also capable of a kind of testimony. As such, beyond the linguistic, the fact of appearance can open up a space for politics in the ways that Butler describes.

The distinction I am proposing serves to qualify some of the accepted versions of the refugee's mode of appearance within the representational forms through which refugeeness is constituted. If, as Liisa H. Malkki has suggested, refugees are frequently 'speechless emissaries' whose visual representation takes the place of a verbal record of their experience in order to accommodate their predicament within a 'mobile' discourse of humanitarianism (Malkki 1996), it is possible to counter that the refugee's body is also asked to perform an evidentiary role in legitimating or disproving the validity of the claim to asylum. The form of the refugee's body is commonly subject to scrutiny, such as in the recent cases of UK politicians advocating the use of dental X-rays as a means of determining the age of children claiming asylum (BBC News 2007; BBC News 2016). Likewise, evidence of injury can be used as the basis to grant asylum, allowing the body to testify to the veracity of claims of persecution. A well-documented instance of this in the UK is the case of the Iranian Kurd Abas Amini, who sewed together his lips and eyes when the Home Office appealed against the immigration court's granting of asylum (Farrier 2011: 14–15; Tyler 2013: 76–9). While Amini's body formed the stage upon and through which a somatic protest was articulated, it also comprised evidence that the UK Border Agency, the Appeal Judge and the Home Office used to determine proof of torture (BBC News 2003). Amini's body achieved a double significance, and alertness to this double signification can work as an important strategy for critics trying to analyse the representation of refugees in cultural texts. This is to extend the critical work that notes the significance of refugees' bodies for the performance of asylum aesthetics and as a component of refugees' protests against the authoritarian disciplining of asylum applicants (Borcliă, Maricniak and Tyler 2014; Farrier and Tuitt 2013; Jestrovic 2008). In light of the demonstrable capacity of the body to testify, it is possible to regard the body as constitutive of the refugee as a category. For instance, if the asylum claim is an inaugural speech act that brings the refugee into being (Farrier 2011: 6), it is important to recognise that the speech act is not purely an act of verbalisation. It requires a bodily presence that has performed some act of crossing in advance of the speech act itself. Moreover, speaking may rely upon 'bodily enactments' that are not purely discursive. In order to think about what this might offer to textual analysis I want to consider two simple fictional examples that will serve to illustrate the expressive potential of the refugee's body, in order to open up my more extensive readings of the films below.

The first of these occurs at the beginning of UK-based Tanzanian writer Abdulrazak Gurnah's novel *By the Sea* (2002), which describes the Tanzanian refugee Saleh Omar's arrival in Britain. Although Omar's first-person narration declares that he is 'a refugee, an asylum-seeker' (Gurnah 2002: 4) and while he voices the words 'refugee' and 'asylum' when being interviewed by an immigration officer at Gatwick Airport (2002: 9), he has been advised to pretend not to speak English. Consequently he must act out a role that involves gestures and looks, that involves 'suppressing a sigh of relief' or restraining his desire to lean forward and inspect the writing on an official's notepad (2002: 7). While Gurnah's narrative might signal the disparity between the citizen's body and the refugee's 'body without words' that is uncoupled from representation (Agamben 2004; Nield 2008: 141–2), Butler's notion of *appearance* offers a different reading of the scene in which Omar's embodied presence acts to confirm the vocalised claims to asylum. Butler's discussion of the idea of appearance plays with the homonymic status of this word as a way of linking individual performativity to 'forms of coordinated action' through which precarious or excluded groups enter 'the public sphere' in order to demand the right to rights (Butler 2015: 7–9). Accordingly, Butler deploys the term 'appearance' as a way of describing both a visible façade *and* the act of emergence as a form of politics (2015: 32). At the textual level, unpicking Butler's homonym involves an interpretative practice that reads the textual description of the body in writing, or its visual framing in film, as carrying political content. That is to say, the representation of the body's physicality orientates the body's capacity to enter the realms of the civic. The visual appearance of the body is not a neutral manifestation of the body but rather a performative response to the state's attempt to circumscribe the forms of political action.

By the Sea speaks to this double sense of appearance through its focus on the somatic qualities of the body, such as the circulation of the breath or the rotation of the eye, which Gurnah suggests are components in the claim to asylum. So, for instance, when Omar describes his passage through the airport and towards the passport desk he suggests that the airport's architecture funnels the arrived towards the securitised frontier and records his response to this as a kind of somatic dialogue with 'signs and instructions' that form the tokens of state authority. Omar explains that he 'walked slowly so that [he] would not miss a turning or misread a sign, so that [he] would not attract attention too early by getting into a flutter of confusion' (Gurnah 2002: 5). This dialogue is repeated in Omar's interrogation by the immigration official. For much of this Omar acts the part of the resigned object of the securitised state, 'shutting' his 'eyes now and then to suggest distress' (Gurnah 2002: 7), but at other times his gestures indicate a more subjective engagement with the structures of securitisation. For instance, he describes matching his breathing to his interrogator or returning his look as a way of pressing his claim to asylum (Gurnah 2002: 7, 9). A critical reading of this encounter that frames it only through the notion of exception would struggle to account for the obvious agency that sits alongside the structures of securitised objectification. By narrating his subjective experience of the border as a largely mute but somatic encounter, Omar stakes his 'right to have rights', which Butler identifies as an alternative model of the political to the one that she finds in Agamben (Butler 2015: 80).

The second example, from Bangladeshi-born British writer Monica Ali's novel *In the Kitchen* (2009), offers a slightly different sense of the body by underlining the expressive potential of the refugee's somatic appearance. Through a depiction of the protagonist's engagement with a Liberian refugee, *In the Kitchen* draws the reader's attention to the different testimonial value of the refugee's voice and body. Ali's novel is set mainly in a hotel kitchen and revolves around the exploitation of migrant labour in Britain's agricultural and catering economies. At its centre is a liberal British protagonist, Gabe, the kitchen's head chef, who negotiates his growing feelings of sympathy and obligation towards his 'United Nations' of kitchen staff (Ali 2009: 129). Gabe's curiosity is pricked by the 'jagged scar' running across the face of his *chef de partie*, Benny, and he considers asking Benny about his history of exclusion, wondering 'which country he had left behind' (Ali 2009: 78). Although the scar implies violence, which may relate to Benny's status as refugee, the questions that it prompts remain largely unanswered. However, this is not the result of the body's failure to articulate but rather of Benny's verbal reticence, which resembles Omar's mute encounter with immigration officials in *By the*

Sea. When Gabe invites Benny to join him for a drink, he coyly tries to find out where his chef is from by asking him about other workers in the kitchen. This tactic is matched by Benny himself so that, when Gabe asks him directly about where he calls 'home', Benny answers by sharing illustrative stories of his friends, other refugees whose histories he feels able to recount. Significantly, in telling stories Benny is clear that the measure of testimony is not whether it is 'true' but whether it is 'credible'. As he tells Gabe, 'if you worry that your own suffering is not enough to gain permission to stay in this country, you can buy a story and take it with you to this government office in Croydon' (Ali 2009: 151–4). Benny's account of verbal unreliability does not indicate that persecution has not taken place; it does not, for instance, equate falsity with fraudulence or with an unwarranted claim to asylum. Instead it stresses that verbal testimony is subject to interpretation and that the claim to asylum is not judged against the evidentiary proof of the applicant but against the affective response of the auditor. In light of this, the somatic testimony of Benny's scar takes on a different significance. The body appears and has an appearance that speaks of violence. While Benny's body cannot tell his story with any more certainty than his voice, it nevertheless stands as evidence that something has happened, if not evidence of precisely what. The body's appearance makes 'credible' whatever story Benny's voice chooses to tell.

Literary renderings of the body's materiality such as these can be interpreted as descriptions of a kind of speech act that is not immediately discursive but that nevertheless involves a non-verbalised dialogue with the institutional gatekeepers of the state. However, I want to turn my attention to the visual framing of the body in two contemporary examples of cinematic representations of refugees. The shift from literary fiction to film is prompted by the body's prominence in the visual aesthetics of narrative film, where bodily spectacle is typically apparent across a wide range of cinematic genre. Film theory has long recognised that cinema's form relies upon the framing and manipulation of the actor's body. For instance, in *The Photoplay* (1916), Hugo Münsterberg linked many of film's aesthetic properties to the form of the body, including silent acting's 'heightening of the gestures and of the facial play'; the use of close-up to enlarge the face, hand or feet to convey the impression of emotion; or the selection of 'ready-made' body types to credibly or naturally perform character (Langdale 2002: 100–3). More recently, in his account of the racial coding of film technologies, Richard Dyer has argued that 'to represent people is to represent bodies' and that the physical properties of the human body have led to 'innovation in the photographic media' which 'has generally taken the human face as its touchstone' (Dyer 1997: 14, 90). Perhaps the landmark work in this direction is Laura Mulvey's seminal account of the psychoanalysis of spectatorship. While her approach has undergone considerable refinement (Clover 1992; Doane 1988; Silverman 1988) and even a radical repudiation (Shaviro 1993), this has focused primarily upon her reading of the spectator's desire. However, for my purpose it is significant that Mulvey also identified aesthetic tendencies that follow from the role of spectatorship that place the body at the centre of film. Arguing that 'the conventions of mainstream film focus [the spectator's] attention on the human form', she noted that narrative cinema is composed of 'the human face, the human body, the relationship between the human form and its surroundings, [and] the visible presence of the person in the world' (Mulvey 1999: 807).

Mindful of this tradition, I want to set Butler's notion of appearance (in the double sense of a façade and of an emergence) in the context of these cinematic representations of the body. I propose that the representation of the body of the refugee is a political movement in so far as this representation constitutes a demand for rights. In both *World War Z* and *Welcome*, the figure of the refugee is caught in official structures of exclusion that are intended to render refugees the objects of state power. The forms of exclusion propel the narrative so that the visual capture of the body within film mirrors the securitised state border that serves the ends of a biopolitics. Nonetheless, in both films the represented bodies of refugees seem to appear as subjective eruptions into the narrative by way of a set of somatic demands for shelter, food, sanitation or burial. In line with Butler, I propose that the depiction of these demands constitutes a form of appearance (emergence) that speaks beyond the immediately somatic wants to form a demand for rights. Tentatively, I suggest that this subjective demand exceeds the diegetic articulations of the refugee on screen, especially where the somatic needs are enacted by, for example, eating rather than a request for food. To that end the representation of the somatic body stands as a political intervention that is not immediately or solely rooted in discourse and constitutes a non-verbal speech act of the kind that Butler theorises.

World War Z

World War Z is a recognisable zombie apocalypse movie, which narrates the travels of United Nations investigator Gerry Lane as he attempts to find a cure to a global zombie plague. Although on the surface its generic form might appear to distance the text from what is normally understood to be a refugee film, it contains a representation of refugeeness that exploits the conventions of its genre. Transplanting components of the post-Romero zombie film such as infection and fortification on to a global scale, *World War Z* encourages a geopolitical reading of the zombie phenomenon and permits an interpretation of the film's zombies as the spectral double of human refugees, who are made monstrous by the requirement of the state to constitute itself as an organic whole. Following Adriana Cavarero's analysis of the organic metaphor for the state in *Stately Bodies* (2002), I suggest that the demonisation of this outer threat is a necessary camouflage for the state's own monstrosity in defending its borders. In the film's world, state governments have largely collapsed and the UN now has executive authority. Due to the zombie threat, this world government must oversee a kind of global levelling in which populations from high-income and low-income nations alike are subject to comparable conditions of deprivation. The manner in which this global levelling manifests itself is through the forced migration of the human survivors who find themselves relocated to refugee camps, a language that the film uses explicitly and that originates in Max Brooks's source novel (Brooks 2013). The language of refugeeness marks out Forster's film from earlier cinematic depictions of a global zombie pandemic and invites a reading of the politics of migration and citizenship as the film's subtext.

The most important scenes for this element of *World War Z* comprise a pivotal section in Jerusalem. Although most national governments have disappeared in the world of the film, Israel has preserved its national integrity by acting on advance intelligence to complete a preventative barrier around the entire state. In Israel, Lane is taken to the 'Jerusalem Salvation Gates' and is surprised to see Israel 'letting people in' when the film shows a procession of refugees crossing the securitised border into the state. In keeping with the formulaic conventions of the zombie movie, *World War Z* depicts various forms of fortification throughout, but the scenes in Israel provide the only depiction of a securitised national boundary.[3] In retaining the national frame these scenes emphasise a connection between refugees and the idea of hospitality by depicting a process of asylum. The presentation of Israeli humanitarianism has obvious resonance with modern and contemporary politics and this episode has provoked commentary on its allegorical significance. Some Arab viewers argued that the film portrays 'Israel as a moral power that protects human beings', which 'justifies the [West Bank] wall' constructed between 2002 and 2012 (*The Malta Independent* 2013). Even the *Times of Israel* described the scenes as 'the greatest piece of cinematic propaganda for Israel since Otto Preminger's "Exodus"' (Hoffman 2013). Certainly, the film presents Israel as a compassionate state and, by panning out to contrast a zombie-occupied desert beyond its borders, portrays Israel as an oasis of peace in a hostile environment. At an allegorical level this implies Israel's exceptionalism in the Middle East, stressing its secular credentials as distinct from its monstrous neighbours. The Israel of the film appears to offer no preference to Arab or Jew, and both Muslim and Jewish refugees celebrate their survival in a crowd waving both Israeli and Palestinian flags. At the centre of this, two young women, one wearing a hijab and the other dressed secularly in a casual vest-top, lead an ecumenical choir in singing Mosh Ben Ari's 'Salaam', a peace song that mixes Hebrew and Arabic. However, these very celebrations serve as a lure to the walled-off zombie hordes who then breach fortified Israel so that it too falls to infection.

In reading these scenes, Mary Bloodsworth-Lugo and Carmen Lugo-Lugo have suggested that it appears as if the refugees 'bring Jerusalem down', and that the resulting zombie incursion challenges 'the original idea that saving humans was the right thing to do' (Bloodsworth-Lugo and Lugo-Lugo 2014: 172). Such a reading partly works by imagining some kind of correspondence between zombies and humans, and this is supported both by the textual presentation in *World War Z* and by the extra-textual conflation of refugees with other threatening kinds of migration. *World War Z*'s Israeli scenes intercut images of human refugees inside the wall with images of the zombies beyond the border. Notably, when the zombies are drawn to scale the wall, the figure of one particular female zombie is picked out turning towards the sound of celebrations and then running to join the insatiable host. Her clothing, in particular her vest-top, shows a visual echo of the secular refugee inside the wall and creates an uncanny resemblance that serves to connect the monstrous enemy with the living survivor.[4] Of course, as viewers of zombie movies well know, a survivor is always a potential zombie; as Steven Shaviro remarks, 'the high point of shock' in George Romero's *Night of the Living Dead* comes 'when the little girl, turned into a zombie cannibalistically consumes her parents' (Shaviro 1993: 90–1). What distinguishes the zombie movie from films about global epidemics such as Steven Soderbergh's *Contagion* (2011) is the manner in which the disease is embodied. In Soderbergh's film, other people are to be shunned as the source of infection and at times the disease is discussed in anthropomorphic terms, such as when a virologist describes the mutations of the virus as a thought process. However, when operatives from US Homeland Security visit the Centre for Disease Control, suspicious that the disease is a terrorist attack, they hypothesise a human agent who will 'weaponise the bird flu'. In contrast, in *World War Z*, the zombie represents the deceased transformed into the disease, which takes on an anthropomorphic shape in order to infect further victims. Accordingly, when the female zombie is drawn to the sound of survivors it is not only her clothes that resemble those of her human counterparts but also her appetites, which embody infection as a kind of somatic want. The tilt of her head and her pelt towards the wall are monstrous but also recognisably humanlike.

The film's representation of refugees and zombies as congruent marries with recent political discourse that has undermined the rights to asylum by linking refugees to threats to civic integrity and indeed health. For instance, the state's obligation to refugees is often cited as its own justification for refusing hospitality to so-called 'bogus' asylum seekers (Tyler 2013: 83–7). For Didier Bigo, the 'humanitarian discourse' is itself 'a by-product of the securitization process' since the desire to help 'genuine asylum seekers' emerges only because it allows the state to condemn 'illegal migrants' as a way of 'justifying border controls' (Bigo 2002: 79). Most relevantly, David Farrier interprets the refugee and the terrorist as competing but twinned tropes that link the refugee to a 'spectral double' and legitimise or mitigate acts of violence towards non-citizens (Farrier and Tuitt 2013: 262, 266). The most obvious and brutish recent example of this double representation has been the pronouncements of President Trump, whose repeated demand for a sectarian immigration policy has literalised his rhetorical conflation of migration, Islam and terrorism. During his election campaign this took the form of a refusal to respect the right of Syrian refugees to enter the United States because of the risk that they would represent a 'Trojan horse' for ISIS. It is easy to see this as a form of contagion narrative that resembles the zombie incursions of Forster's text. Images of disease suffused the political discussion of migration and terrorism during the 2015–16 primary campaign. In the edition of ABC's *This Week* in which the future president made his remarks, his challenger Ben Carson repeatedly raised the spectre of radicalisation and likened the vetting of refugees to protecting your family from a rabid dog. Likewise, when interviewed about President Obama's handling of the threat from ISIS, Republican Congresswoman Martha McSally described the group as a 'metastasized' form of 'militant Islam'. In the same vein, the Democratic challenger Martin O'Malley likened the fight against ISIS to 'an immune system' that requires coordination to defeat the 'bad germs of this world' (ABC News 2015).

If the idea of terrorists as a kind of disease that is capable of infecting the hospitable state is evocative of the zombie film, it is appropriate that the future president's justification for his fears turned on the somatic form of the refugee. Responding to George Stephanopoulos, he explained that 'when I look at the migration and the lines and I see all strong, very powerful looking men, they're men, and I see very few women, I see very few children' (ABC News 2015). While there is an implicit xenophobia in his fear of foreign men, the key to the future president's comments is his use of corporeality to identify adult masculinity as a threatening form of embodiment. There is, of course, an irony in the fact that Trump has compulsively reiterated the need for (masculine) strength as the main virtue required for politics. In the same interview he defended the use of torture for interrogation, saying 'we have to be strong', and questioned Hillary Clinton's suitability for the office of president, claiming that, 'we're dealing with very, very strong people. And you need strength and you need stamina' (ABC News 2015). Again, the comparison with *World War Z* is suggestive, since Brad Pitt, its star and producer, exemplifies the physically strong action hero who might be thought capable of defending the civic against this vicious external threat. Although in his escape from Jerusalem, Lane is escorted by a troop of Israeli soldiers that contains several women, it is only because of his physical decisiveness – including the abrupt amputation of an arm to prevent infection – that the group escapes. In this, it might be possible to find a further correspondence between the human survivors and the threatening zombies whose strength and ferocity is their chief advantage.

The history of contamination as a form of political metaphor is a long one and one that is clearly linked to a masculine conception of the state. As Adriana Cavararo records, the association between disease and political imbalance dates to the classical era in the work of Plato (Cavarero 2002). Where the concept of the body politic elaborates the healthy body as the hierarchical ordering of people, it becomes possible to imagine the exclusion of certain bodies from the bounds of the state as a way to maintain political health. The logic of the body politic as an organic metaphor for the healthy state is self-evidently useful as a way of justifying or normalising state power. The securitised border becomes the epidermis that ensures that the social space remains an 'unmarked' body by allowing only unmarked bodies ingress (Ahmed 2000: 46). However, as Cavarero's work records, the anxious desire of Greek culture to suppress the body in defence of 'logos, techne, and the polis' sees the 'expelled' body 'stubbornly return', so that the organic metaphor 'binds the body to politics' (Cavarero 2002: 34, viii). This 'return' seems particularly amenable for thinking about the zombie movie as a kind of political allegory, and it is telling that Cavarero's language takes on the vocabulary of horror when she accounts for the re-emergence of the body in classical Greek culture. Through a reading of Sophocles' *Antigone*, Cavarero explains that the effort of the *polis* to expel the body of Polynices ends with the corpse emerging victorious by initiating a 'dark vortex of death' and securing the 'desired burial' that Creon has denied it and that is the objective of Antigone's rebellion (Cavarero 2002: 16). This account of Polynices as a cadaverous combatant reads like a ghost story and is echoed in Cavarero's language when writing about the failure of Greek philosophy to elevate the psyche over the somatic. Here she sees the body become the 'disquieting and nocturnal matter' or 'the nightmare of nocturnal impulses' (2002: 57, 103). Most tellingly, perhaps, in detailing Aristotle's attempt to construct the body politic as 'a perfect, static, and adult male body', Cavarero argues that this body 'is more like the corpse lying on the dissecting table than a living thing that passes through the cycles of aging' (2002: 96–7).[5]

Beyond any generic similarity, it is this account of Aristotle that encourages me to read Cavarero's zombie-version of Greek political philosophy alongside *World War Z*'s double representation of refugees. If the film's zombies can be read as the spectral double of the refugee made monstrous, Cavarero's depiction of the state's body as equally monstrous usefully reveals the cost to the *polis* of defending its integrity. In the film's denouement, Lane finds a way of hiding from the zombie plague, devising a form of 'camouflage' by infecting the healthy human body with a fatal disease. This renders the human prey invisible to the zombies, presumably because the body has become, like the zombies themselves, the walking dead. Reading this solution back into the Israeli scenes, an episode that is crucial in helping Lane to this conclusion, it is possible to reimagine these scenes as a form of critique of the political discourses of asylum and the double representation that these employ. Rather than simply highlighting the folly of humanitarian hospitality, it becomes possible to see these scenes as an indictment of authoritarian politics. The logic of Lane's solution is that the only way to keep the threatening other at bay is to become, or to appear to be, the very thing that is debarred. Tellingly, the film ends with a montage of the human 'push back' against the zombie plague, involving scenes of carnal military brutality in which human soldiers display an appetite for violence that has marked the zombies throughout. To echo current political discourse, the fight against the zombies is to be fought by 'strong, very powerful looking men'. Lane's solution means that the body politic can only be protected by inflicting damage on the bodies of its citizen. Moreover, this becomes an instrument of violence, allowing the *polis* to inflict damage on the somatic bodies of the other. In so far as the term *sōma* originates as a description of the corpse rather than the living body (Agamben 1998: 66; Cavarero 2002: 203 n.3), Lane's inoculation, which leads the human survivor to resemble the zombie, may establish the zombie as the perfect instantiation of the somatic body. Consequently, although the zombies' appearance in the nominal sense distinguishes them from humans, their appearance as a vehicle for appetites establishes much clearer parallels between their violence and that of the state.

Welcome

If the different kinds of bodies that populate Forster's *World War Z* indict the technologies of exclusion that are used by the state to regulate refugees, a similar technique might be found in other films. While much of the force of Forster's film derives from the viewer's generic expectations of the zombie movie, Phillipe Lioret's politically engaged romance *Welcome* utilises the conventions of social realism to similar effect. In its political mode the plot pivots upon the conflict between refugees and liberal French citizens on the one hand, and the state as represented by magistrates and police officers on the other. It dramatises the enforcing of Article L622-1 of French law, which forbids direct or indirect assistance of illegal migrants (*séjour irréguliers*) in France, by recording the prosecution of Simon, a Calais resident and local swimming instructor who tries to offer shelter to Kurdish refugees attempting to cross the English Channel to reach the UK.[6] At the level of the script Lioret makes obvious allusions to the discriminatory biopolitics of the Nazi Party as well as to the collaboration of French citizens under German occupation during the Second World War. Through these devices he appears to suggest that the state's desire to exclude '*clandestins*' leads it to become increasingly draconian with regard to its own citizens. As with *World War Z*, the act of exclusion is shown to make the state resemble the monstrous states from which refugees might flee.

As a romance, the film is driven by the twin stories of Simon and Bilal, the Iraqi Kurd whom Simon tries to help. Simon initially offers Bilal help in a bid to win back his estranged wife, Marion, who runs a soup kitchen providing aid to the refugees in Calais's Jungle.[7] However, as he comes to know Bilal he responds to Bilal's own hope for reunion with his girlfriend, Mina, the sister of a friend from Iraq who now lives in London. Entranced by Bilal's story, Simon compares Bilal's 4,000 kilometre walk from Mosul to Calais with his own failure to fight for his marriage. Lioret has inferred a similar feeling among viewers, arguing that these love stories attracted viewers to the film, and Will Higbee argues that it is chiefly this which 'humanised' Bilal for French audiences (2014: 35). The sentimental presumption here is of a kind of universalism whereby the common experience of romantic love nudges audiences to imagine that refugees are 'just like us'. *Welcome* consistently exploits this notion, with both plot and visual presentation pointing to similarities between the men while drawing attention to material differences between the citizen and the refugees. At its conclusion, for instance, when Simon visits Mina in London after Bilal has drowned trying to swim across the Channel to England, he offers her Marion's engagement ring as a token of Bilal's love. Mina is immune to Simon's sentimentality, however, and refuses the ring on the grounds that she 'never could wear it'. Mina's refusal inserts a political reality into the romantic element, obliquely referencing her arranged marriage to her father's cousin and disrupting the implied equivalences between Simon/Marion and Bilal/Mina. What is more, the ease with which Simon is able to make the journey to London when this had been so fatally impossible for Bilal serves to highlight the fact that any universal aspirations must confront the incommensurability of the rights that attach to citizens and to refugees.

Arguably, the film's conclusion reminds the viewer that its real subject is the act of exception. Nevertheless, the sense of correspondence between Simon and Bilal cannot be fully undone, not least because Simon's movement is also curtailed by the French state: having been charged with aiding refugees he is confined to the department of Pas-de-Calais pending trial, and so his journey to London breaches the conditions of his bail. By tethering Simon to Calais, the state enacts a curtailment of rights that causes him to resemble the refugee whose journey to the United Kingdom is obstructed by the Anglo-French border. As in *World War Z*, the actions of the state transform the citizen into a replica of the excepted refugee, though in keeping with its genre this takes a less sensational form.

At the visual level this replication is supported by strong parallels in the presentation of the two characters throughout the film. For instance, many of the scenes that Bilal and Simon share occur in tight interior spaces such as Simon's flat or car. In the latter of these, especially, the conventional shot/counter-shot of conversational exchange produces an effect of visual mirroring between the two faces. More commonly, however, the use of visual resemblance points towards meaningful contrasts. The film includes many scenes in which either Bilal stares wistfully at the Calais coastline or Simon sits alone in sombre meditation staring into space. Although there are clear echoes in the presentation of the two characters here, the setting and filming indicates a substantial difference. Where Simon is routinely shown indoors, shot predominantly with a static camera in his flat or in the local bar eating and drinking, Bilal is more often filmed with a tracking shot, outside wandering the streets or beach. The contrast here has obvious symbolic purpose, and positioning Bilal outside has the implication that the refugee represents a form of excess that sits outside the civic with no visible function or purpose. Related scenes in which he queues with other refugees for the soup kitchen or huddles with other refugees in the Jungle's undergrowth seeking warmth from a small fire exaggerate this suggestion. The refugees, here, are outside the social infrastructure of civil society as an obvious metaphor for their exclusion from the economy of rights. In this way the filming suggests that the human bond between the men is undermined by the politics of exception, which operates through the variable bestowal of rights.

This pattern is repeated in numerous other scenes where certain kinds of visual similarity are used to underline radical differences between the two men. For example, late in the film when Bilal is detained in a refugee retention centre, a slow zoom and pan left shows him staring out of a barred window that fills a substantial portion of the shot. This then cuts to a similar shot of a barred window that continues the leftward movement of the camera to reveal Simon in a cell also staring outwards. However, while Bilal's stare continues throughout the whole shot, Simon's gaze is drawn back inside by the entrance of a police officer, who lists the conditions of his bail and orders him out of detention and back into the world of the civic. After he is charged, Simon appears to become deeply insular, uttering few lines of dialogue and continually staring ahead with a look of perplexed intensity. Although Simon has a depressed demeanour throughout the film, the intensification of his introspection suggests that once he is denied the opportunity to be hospitable he retreats from social interactions of any kind. It seems significant, then, that this sequence contains a final, striking instance of visual resemblance in a scene in which Simon dives into the local swimming pool and begins to swim lengths. This scene closely mirrors a number of earlier episodes where Bilal is shown shuttling back and forward in the swimming pool in preparation for his Channel crossing. In these scenes the film often uses long-takes to linger on Bilal's bodily effort, placing his semi-naked body at the centre of the visual field. This depiction of the body invites a reading that is attentive to the different significance of the body as a biopolitical and as a natural entity. Across the film Bilal appears to perfect his stroke, moving from a mixture of breaststroke and clumsy freestyle to an accomplished front-crawl. As such the film suggests that he acts out a somatic response to the authoritarian state by adapting his body to evade the structures of exclusion. Although Bilal's biopolitical body cannot become unmarked (indeed, one of these scenes draws attention to the refugee registration number written prominently on his hand), he may train his somatic body to find a route through the cracks of the securitised frontier. Because the viewer has become accustomed to seeing Bilal in this way, when

Simon dives into the pool it is initially unclear that it is Simon rather than Bilal, and the experience of watching the scene involves a jolt of disassociation once the viewer realises who it is. At the visual level, then, Simon has become or *appears to be* Bilal. Yet once again, the film insists that this resemblance is only partial because it immediately cuts to a parallel image of Bilal swimming the Channel as he makes his fatal attempt to cross.

Despite Bilal's unfortunate fate, I want to reassert the value of addressing the somatic quality of the body as a means of appearance in the sense of emergence. *Welcome* is extremely attentive to the needs of the body, and the need for food, shelter, hygiene and air dominates much of the early part of the film. In the opening scenes that depict Marion's charitable soup kitchen, the focus on the need for sustenance offered to refugees is aided by the cinematography that uses extreme close-ups of food and bottled water. A running trope in the film is the need for breath. As a counter-narrative to Bilal's swimming training, which includes learning to breathe properly while swimming front-crawl, Bilal tries to train himself to breathe inside a plastic bag so that he might evade the carbon-dioxide sensors used to police the border. In an early scene when he attempts to cross the border inside a lorry his failure to remain inside the plastic covering leads to his detection. This scene provides a dramatic enactment of the need to breathe since it involves a vivid struggle between Bilal and his friend Zoran, who tries to keep the plastic bag in place. When they are discovered by French border police their travelling companion Eyaz is found to have suffocated.[8] Eyaz's death demonstrates the consequence of Bilal's tussle with Zoran, since Zoran's victory might have been fatal to Bilal.

Reading back to *World War Z*, Bilal's desire to train his body to make it more efficient at illicit border crossings immediately seems to contrast with the image of the refugee as an infected body. Nevertheless, there is a degree of correspondence in that Bilal's desire to circumvent the structures of exclusion requires him to become the very form of strong masculinity that constitutes the fearful representation that is used to rationalise the state's inhospitality towards refugees. To this degree, the securitised border is shown to be self-justifying because it appears to produce the very threat that it is intended to repulse. Appropriately, while the demand for the basic needs of the body is a constant feature of Lioret's film, he also repeatedly depicts refugees being denied access to sustenance by the state. After his failed attempt to cross the Channel by truck, Bilal appears in a French court and is sentenced for trying to cross illegally. Although the law mandates that he is entitled to a bed in a hostel, the prosecuting judge denies him this right because his attempt to reach England is taken as evidence that he 'has no desire to go to a hostel'. This is one of many instances where refugees are shown being denied their corporeal needs. For instance, a group of refugees provokes a minor disturbance when they attempt to take a shower at the local swimming pool and are turned away by Simon because it is 'forbidden' for them to pay to shower there. Shortly afterwards Marion confronts a supermarket security guard who bars two refugees from shopping because it upsets other customers. Through the device of Simon's hospitality the trope of shelter is a constant motif, but his humanitarianism is repeatedly counterposed against images of the state's violent and authoritarian refusal of hospitality. At one point Simon remorsefully seeks out Bilal after an argument at the swimming pool. When he arrives at the port he finds that police with tear gas have cleared Marion's soup kitchen 'just to stop [refugees] eating'. After he finds Bilal in the Jungle and drives him home to his flat, they pass refugees running along the portside chased by gendarmerie wielding batons and kicks. The needs of the somatic body, then, provide Lioret with a structure of differentiation, which distinguishes not between the genuine and the illegal migrant but between the humanitarian citizen and the authoritarian state.

This feature of the film depends extensively upon the corporeal presence of the refugee and it seems plausible that this presence can be read as a form of Butler's appearance-as-politics. If the association of the refugee with basic human need seems to speak of life as *zoē*, which Agamben glosses as 'the simple fact of living', rather than the political life of *bios*, which Agamben defines as 'the form or way of living proper to an individual or a group' (Agamben 1998: 1), the demand that these needs should be met by the French state stands as the political claim to have rights. To that end, those episodes in *Welcome* where refugees present themselves to the eye in order to express this demand can be read as instances of appearance (in the sense of emergence). The scene at the swimming pool, in particular, when a group of refugees collectively request access to clean water ties the somatic need to a form of embodied appearance that contains a non-discursive articulation. As a result of the complicated multilingual character of the film this exceeds the strictly verbal content of the film's dialogue. *Welcome* includes dialogue in English, French and Kurdish, all of which are subtitled, and also speech in other languages that is part of the diegetic soundtrack but not subtitled.[9] The words used by refugee characters when they try to shower at the swimming pool are divided between untranslated hubbub and a few lines in English. Verbally the demand for basic needs is limited and much work is done by sheer weight of numbers and the physical performance of clamour, with men reaching over one another eager to offer their money to the pool's cashier.

The representation of Bilal's body might do similar work. Though his character is given ample dialogue and he can speak about his desire to reach the UK, the demands of the body are often acted physically through, for instance, shivering at the cold. This is perhaps best exemplified when, after he drowns in the Channel, his body is returned to France where, like Polynices, it demands burial. As Cavarero records, this demand drives Sophocles' *Antigone*. Burial is the final somatic gesture and the one that marks out the human difference from animals as proof of *techne*. The act of burial protects the human body from becoming the 'horrible meal' of some other animal predator, but the granting of burial also symbolises the founding of the *polis* as a mark of human superiority (Cavarero 2002: 36). The viewer does not see Bilal's body, only a coffin lowered into a grave and a wreath that bears his nickname Bazda (The Runner). Nevertheless, the viewer infers the somatic content of the coffin and, through the ritual of burial, allows Bilal to *appear* as human in a way that demands rights, or at the very least rites. The conclusion to the film marries with the growing recognition that Europe's borders have become necropolises that house the bodies of illegalised migrants who were unable to traverse the securitised borders. Attempts to memorialise these deaths have become sites of dissent for those wishing to oppose the policies of their governments that can be seen to have rendered the national border so perilous (Horsti and Neumann 2019; Musarò 2017). In line with such attempts, the presentation of Bilal as a somatic being, just as much as his presentation as a thinking subject, opens up a space for politics in the film. To that end, *Welcome* offers a model for critical practice that uses attention to the corporeal fact of the refugee as a way to critique the politics of exception that are used to govern asylum in the contemporary moment.

Notes

1. I am indebted to Emma Cox for her thoughtful editing of this chapter and to the participants at the 'Troubling Globalization' workshop at Nottingham Trent University, 22 April 2017.
2. For a further critique of Agamben's position, see Owens (2009).
3. While some of the boundaries in the film resemble the militarised fortification of the contemporary border, they seem closer to the concept of the stockade than the geopolitical boundary. There is, no doubt, a line of continuity between the fortified citadel and the contemporary nation, and in the present context it is worth noting the archaeology of fortification in W. G. Sebald's *Austerlitz* (2001) and Arne De Boever's attempt to link this to Agamben's state of exception (De Boever 2014).
4. In a sign that the film-makers were aware of the potential for controversy it is notable that when the zombies encroach into Israel, none conspicuously wears religious clothing. This is in contrast to the visible appearance of *kufi* hats or *kippah* on the heads of fleeing humans.
5. I have argued elsewhere that the visual technologies of border securitisation, which capture images of illegalised migrants secreted into the infrastructures of global logistics from which the embodied migrant is supposed to be debarred, leads the migrating body to appear as a form of revenant that demands recognition (Connell 2012). Reading across from that argument to this, there seems some scope for a further study on the hauntological aesthetics of refugees.
6. 'Code de l'entrée et du séjour des étrangers et du droit d'asile –Article L622-1 | Legifrance', https://www.legifrance.gouv.fr/affichCodeArticle.do?idArticle=LEGIARTI 000006335286&cidTexte=LEGITEXT000006070158&dateTexte=20111110&o ldAction=rechCodeArticle (accessed 20 July 2017). Laura Rascaroli explains the relevant history of the law (2013: 28) and Will Higbee records Lioret's ambivalent

cooperation with the French Socialist Party in its attempt to repeal L622-1 (2014: 33–4).

7. The 'Jungle' is the colloquial but semi-official name for the large migrant encampment in the vicinity of the Calais ferry port that developed when the Red Cross centre at nearby Sangatte was closed in 2002 (Martinetti 2016).

8. This is a common trope in refugee films, and both Michael Winterbottom's *In This World* (2002) and Gianfranco Rosi's documentary *Fire at Sea* (2016) depict death by suffocation as a consequence of illegalised crossings.

9. The French edition of the DVD subtitles Kurdish and English dialogue whereas the English edition subtitles French and Kurdish.

Bibliography

ABC News (2015), '"This Week" transcript: Donald Trump and Ben Carson', http://abcnews.go.com/Politics/week-transcript-donald-trump-ben-carson/story?id=35336008 (accessed 7 April 2017).

Agamben, Giorgio (1998), *Homo Sacer: Sovereign Power and Bare Life*, trans. D. Heller-Roazen (Stanford: Stanford University Press).

Agamben, Giorgio (2004), 'Bodies without words: against the biopolitical tattoo', *German Law Journal*, 5.2: 168–9.

Ahmed, Sara (2000), *Strange Encounters: Embodied Others in Post-Coloniality* (London: Routledge).

Ali, Monica (2009), *In the Kitchen* (London: Black Swan).

BBC News (2003), 'Protester's tortured past', http://news.bbc.co.uk/1/hi/england/nottinghamshire/2941780.stm (accessed 5 April 2017).

BBC News (2007), 'Asylum youths face X-ray checks', http://news.bbc.co.uk/go/pr/fr/-/1/hi/uk_politics/6382081.stm (accessed 6 April 2017).

BBC News (2016), 'Calais child migrants: "unethical" dental checks ruled out', http://www.bbc.co.uk/news/uk-37706862 (accessed 6 April 2017).

Bigo, Didier (2002), 'Security and immigration: toward a critique of the governmentality of unease', *Alternatives*, 27.1: 63–92.

Bloodsworth-Lugo, Mary K., and Carmen R. Lugo-Lugo (2014), *Projecting 9/11: Race, Gender, and Citizenship in Recent Hollywood Films* (Lanham, MD: Rowman and Littlefield).

Borcliă, Rozalind, Katarzyna Maricniak and Imogen Tyler (2014), 'The political aesthetics of immigrant protest', in K. Maricniak and I. Tyler (eds), *Immigrant Protest: Politics, Aesthetics, and Everyday Dissent* (Albany: SUNY Press), 45–63.

Brooks, Max (2013 [2006]), *World War Z: An Oral History of the Zombie War* (London: Duckworth Overlook).

Butler, Judith (2015), *Notes toward a Performative Theory of Assembly* (Cambridge, MA: Harvard University Press).

Cavarero, Adriana (2002), *Stately Bodies: Literature, Philosophy, and the Question of Gender*, trans. R. de Lucca and D. Shemek (Ann Arbor: University of Michigan Press).

Clover, Carol J. (1992), *Men Women and Chainsaws: Gender in the Modern Horror Film* (London: BFI).

Connell, Liam (2012), 'The worker as revenant: imagining embodied labor in contemporary visualizations of migration', *Social Text*, 111: 1–20.

Cox, Emma (2015), *Performing Noncitizenship: Asylum Seekers in Australian Theatre, Film and Activism* (London: Anthem Press).

De Boever, Arne (2014), *States of Exception in the Contemporary Novel: Martel, Eugenides, Coetzee, Sebald* (London: Bloomsbury).

Doane, Mary Ann (1988), *The Desire to Desire: The Woman's Film of the 1940s* (Basingstoke: Macmillan).

Dyer, Richard (1997), *White* (Abingdon: Routledge).

Farrier, David (2011), *Postcolonial Asylum: Seeking Sanctuary before the Law* (Liverpool: Liverpool University Press).

Farrier, David, and Patricia Tuitt (2013), 'Beyond biopolitics: Agamben, asylum, and postcolonial critique', in G. Huggan (ed.), *The Oxford Handbook of Postcolonial Studies* (Oxford: Oxford University Press), 253–70.

Gurnah, Abdulrazak (2002), *By the Sea* (London: Bloomsbury).

Higbee, Will (2014), 'Hope and indignation in Fortress Europe: immigration and neoliberal globalization in contemporary French cinema', *SubStance*, 43.1: 26–43.

Hoffman, Jordan (2013), 'In Turkey, "World War Z" is no World War Zion', *The Times of Israel*, http://www.timesofisrael.com/in-turkey-world-war-z-is-no-world-war-zion/ (accessed 4 April 2017).

Horsti, Karina, and Klaus Neumann (2017), 'Memorializing mass deaths at the border: two cases from Canberra (Australia) and Lampedusa (Italy)', *Ethnic and Racial Studies*, 42.2: 141–58, doi:10.1080/01419870.2017.1394477.

Jestrovic, Silvija (2008), 'Performing like an asylum seeker: paradoxes of hyper-authenticity', *Research in Drama Education: The Journal of Applied Theatre and Performance*, 13.2: 159–70.

Langdale, Allan (2002), *Hugo Münsterberg on Film: The Photoplay: A Psychological Study and Other Writings* (London: Routledge).

Malkki, Liisa H. (1996), 'Speechless emissaries: refugees, humanitarianism, and dehistoricization', *Cultural Anthropology*, 11.3: 377–404.

The Malta Independent (2013), 'World War Z's contentious wall scene shot in Malta', http://www.independent.com.mt/articles/2013-07-22/news/world-war-zs-contentious-wall-scene-shot-in-malta-2124152835/ (accessed 25 March 2017).

Martinetti, Isabelle (2016), 'A history of the Jungle in Calais 1999–2016 [in pictures]', RFI, http://en.rfi.fr/france/20161027-history-Jungle-Calais-1999-2016-pictures (accessed 20 December 2017).

Mulvey, Laura (1999 [1975]), 'Visual pleasure and narrative cinema', in L. Braudy and M. Cohen (eds), *Film Theory and Criticism: Introductory Readings* (Oxford: Oxford University Press), 833–44.

Musarò, Pierluigi (2017), 'Beyond the border spectacle: migration across the Mediterranean Sea', in F. Vecchio and A. Gerard (eds), *Entrapping Asylum Seekers: Social, Legal and Economic Precariousness* (London: Palgrave Macmillan), 57–82.

Nield, Sophie (2008), 'The Proteus cabinet, or "we are here but not here"', *Research in Drama Education: The Journal of Applied Theatre and Performance*, 13.2: 137–45.

Nyers, Peter (2006), *Rethinking Refugees: Beyond States of Emergency* (New York: Routledge).

Owens, Patricia (2009), 'Reclaiming "bare life"? Against Agamben on refugees', *International Relations*, 23.4: 567–82.
Rascaroli, Laura (2013), 'On the eve of the journey: Tangier, Tbilisi, Calais', in T. S. Michael Gott (ed.), *Open Roads, Closed Borders: The Contemporary French-Language Road Movie* (Bristol: Intellect), 19–38.
Sebald, W. G. (2002 [2001]), *Austerlitz*, trans. A. Bell (London: Penguin).
Shaviro, Steven (1993), *The Cinematic Body* (Minneapolis: University of Minnesota Press).
Silverman, Kaja (1988), *The Acoustic Mirror: The Female Voice in Psychoanalysis and Cinema* (Bloomington: Indiana University Press).
Squire, Vicki (2009), *The Exclusionary Politics of Asylum* (New York: Palgrave).
Tyler, Imogen (2013), *Revolting Subjects: Social Abjection and Resistance in Neoliberal Britain* (London: Zed Books).
Woolley, Agnes (2014), *Contemporary Asylum Narratives: Representing Refugees in the Twenty-First Century* (Basingstoke: Palgrave Macmillan).

Filmography

Contagion, dir. Steven Soderbergh, Warner Bros, 2011.
Fire at Sea, dir. Gianfranco Rosi, Curzon Artificial Eye, 2016.
In This World, dir. Michael Winterbottom, Optimum Releasing, 2002.
Night of the Living Dead, dir. George A. Romero, The Walter Reade Organisation, 1968.
Welcome, dir. Philippe Lioret, CineFile, 2009.
World War Z, dir. Marc Forster, Paramount Pictures, 2013.

Chapter 10

The Digital Border: The Media of Refugee Reception during the 2015 'Migration Crisis'

Lilie Chouliaraki and Myria Georgiou

Introduction: the Mediterranean 'migration crisis'[1]

More than one million people arrived at the Mediterranean shores of Greece and Italy throughout 2015 and until March 2016.[2] How has Europe responded to this unprecedented challenge? Early signs of benevolent reception, such as the ephemeral openness of Germany and Sweden, gradually turned into resolute hostility, with Eastern European states sealing their borders and others following suit. By March 2016 around 57,600 refugees were encamped in Greece, with those seeking asylum waiting for permission to reside and the rest facing deportation. This trajectory shows Europe's response to the 'crisis' to be a precarious combination of competing ethical claims, security and care; an ongoing 'search for the balance of humanitarian needs with concerns over sovereignty'.[3] The focus of this chapter is the communicative structure of this dual morality: to uphold the humanitarian imperative to care for vulnerable others and, simultaneously, to protect European citizens from potential threats from those same others.

Our starting point is the practical enactment of this requirement at one of Europe's outer borders, the Greek island of Chios.[4] Drawing on participant observation and interviews with key actors receiving migrants and refugees on the island, we explore the formation and implications of the communicative architecture of the border. By 'architecture of the border' we mean the dynamic networking of the communicative technologies, practices and discourses that hold together the island's structures of reception, as well as their implications both for those who arrive and for those who receive them. Our analysis proposes that at the heart of the care/protection duality lies a particular moral order, what we term *hospitability*: a contingent and contradictory system of communication practices that reproduces existing global orders of power and exclusion while also allowing for intersecting connections of local affect and solidarity that may challenge but never interrupt these orders of power.

Drawing upon the notion of 'hospitability maps' as military spaces with the capacity to both embrace and constrain a moving target's opportunity for manoeuvre within a particular territory (Kanchanavally, Ordonez and Layne 2004), hospitability captures Europe's outer border as an ambivalent moral order that reshapes both Europe's humanitarian ethics and its politics of security. Hospitability is here introduced as an alternative to the two discourses of reception that have so far dominated academic and public debates on human mobility in Europe: hospitality and securitisation. On the one hand, hospitability reformulates hospitality, a normative discourse of caring reception that defines the moral imagination of progressive Europe, for instance in Chancellor Merkel's summer 2015 invitation to migrant populations to apply for asylum in Germany or in the #refugeeswelcome hashtags. On the other hand, hospitability complicates securitisation, a conservative discourse that, under the threat of terrorism, financial crisis or cultural contamination, prioritises the indiscriminate closing of borders over care for victims of war. Rather than treating these two discourses as polar opposites associated with different institutional actors and ideological positions, we employ the concept of hospitability to demonstrate that they intersect in and through the communicative architecture of reception across actors and positions, shaping Europe's borders as sites of hospitability. The communicative architecture of the border, we argue, is not an optional add-on to hospitability but its very condition of possibility.

We first introduce the theoretical and empirical context of Chios as a site of humanitarian securitisation – characterised by the fusion of care for and regulation of mobile populations (Duffield 2011). We proceed with our conceptual framework, according to which the communicative architecture of Chios is analysed along two dimensions of humanitarian securitisation: 1) networks of mediation, referring to the technological connections between and across media platforms (and how these remediate, intermediate and transmediate information); and 2) networks of discourse, referring to the meaning formations or voices articulated through these multiple mediations (human rights, military/security procedures, practical management, solidarity). These two dimensions, mediation and discourses of the border, we subsequently demonstrate, cut across and reconstitute the three relatively distinct spheres of reception at the border: *military securitisation*, which involves the Greek navy and police forces, as well as the European border security service (Frontex); *caring securitisation*, which involves UNHCR agents and a number of NGOs active on Chios; and *compassionate solidarity*, which encompasses a small but significant number of activist and volunteer groups on the island, such as the Collective Kitchen and local resident groups. In conclusion, we discuss the inherent ambivalence of the emerging moral order of reception as hospitability and reflect on its implications for understanding the politics and ethics of Europe's border today.

Theoretical context: the humanitarian securitisation of European borders

The care/protection regime in Chios participates in the wider order of securitisation, dominant in the politics of reception in Europe. Defined as a practice of power through which 'a political community' is invited to 'treat something as an existential threat . . . and to enable a call for urgent and exceptional measures to deal with the threat' (Buzan and Wæver 2003: 491), securitisation is today established as the dominant paradigm of Western government. Even though it is regarded as a key element of inter-state regulation, securitisation is nonetheless more complex than straightforward military control. This is so because, rather than the use of armed force (though this happens too), securitisation relies on the performative capacity of communication to produce and circulate differential meanings about different populations. For instance, through 'neutral' practices of passport control or biometric profiling, migrant populations are positioned within particular 'biological epistemologies' (Ticktin and Feldman 2010) that define whether they are 'legitimate' or 'illegitimate' with regard to border crossing, in line with Western governments' security interests. Evidently, then, securitisation does not approach the border simply as a physical line separating territories, such as European from non-European lands, but as a symbolic practice of 'bordering' that 'seeks to rhetorically identify and control the (very) mobility of certain people, services and goods that operate around its jurisdiction' (Vaughan-Williams 2015: 6). On Chios, for instance, rhetorical identification occurs through the registration of new arrivals.[5] Here, institutional forces of protection, such as the Greek police and Frontex, name and classify the new arrivals according to nationality, thereby selectively granting them a set of limited rights: some could claim asylum and hope for admission to certain European destinations, while others are detained and subsequently expelled to non-European countries.

Humanitarian agencies are also crucially involved in this process: NGO staff fuse into the securitisation process by operating on and supporting the registration process through translation assistance and information sharing. Indeed, critical migration studies and securitisation literature have long been critical of the ways in which state-controlled bordering is entangled with humanitarian practices (Dalakoglou 2016; Dillon 2008). The articulation of protection with benevolence, the critique has it, subordinates the latter to the former, prioritising discipline over care. Theorised in terms of its biopolitical potential, the humanitarian aspect of bordering is here seen primarily as a technology of power that aims at the management of life, in the form of ensuring survival, but not fully engaging with the humanity of mobile populations. In the UNHCR camp, for instance, set up close to the original registration centre on Chios, care for such populations involves the use of number-based identification bracelets and the distribution of one nutrition bar a day per person. Such practices, the literature claims, may provide bare essentials but do not grant the dignity that people deserve as human beings, nor do they listen to their voices (Watson 2009). Reflecting Darling's analysis of the asylum seeker as a figure who carries 'paradigmatic status as the outsider par excellence' (2009: 649), humanitarian care on Chios seems to reproduce a process of biopolitical dehumanisation, where migrants' biological integrity is protected, but symbolic recognition is denied them (Ticktin 2006).

At the heart of the biopolitical theorisation of the border lie two epistemological assumptions of the migration and security studies literature. The first claims that 'the human' is not an *a priori* given but is itself a material effect of power embedded within the practice of humanitarian securitisation (Ticktin 2006; Millner 2011). Through regulative acts of institutional benevolence, such as the identification bracelet or the nutrition bar, the migrants are deprived of their human quality as individuals with biographical and emotional depth, and are constructed as 'bare life': ambivalent subjectivities, whose lives may be worthy of protection yet whose deaths are not a cause for prosecution and may go unpunished or ungrieved (Agamben 1998). The second epistemological assumption, following from this, is that bare life is the only and inevitable modality of the human in humanitarian securitisation, independently of the historical and political contexts in which bordering practices occur (Fassin 2005). Agents of humanitarian care, such as NGOs or activist groups, it follows, also participate in this regime of power and are, consequently, regarded as themselves benevolent perpetrators of dehumanisation.

Even though, in line with this literature, our analysis understands migrant subjectivities to be inherently linked to various forms of control, we nonetheless challenge the view that securitisation is a homogeneous regime of power singularly bearing the universal dehumanising effects of bare life. Rather than conflating a theoretical account of power as biopolitics with the empirical account of how historical practices of the border actually address the needs of human suffering, our approach aims at establishing the relative autonomy of the latter from the former and at keeping the two in a reflexive tension. Following this dialectical approach, which allows for a more open understanding of biopolitical effects, we next introduce our conceptual framework and analytical approach.

Conceptual framework: bordering practices as a communicative architecture

In order to avoid the determinism of bordering as biopolitical subjection, our approach conceptualises humanitarian securitisation as a configuration of incomplete and fragmented situational engagements that respond to an emergent situation of uncertainty in a variety of ways. Our assumption is that this mobilisation of agents, practices and discourses relies upon multiple networks of communication that, in different ways, may legitimise or challenge those actors, practices and discourses – thus constituting a communicative architecture inherently linked to regimes of power but bearing different effects of power. This is a move from a homogeneous conception of power as totalising towards what Barnett refers to as 'a more modest understanding of what state and non-state actors are capable of doing, for good or ill' (2015: 21). It implies that, while we do expect that, in line with the biopolitical account, the communicative networks of securitisation work to exclude certain refugees and migrants from the spaces of freedom and safety they aspire to inhabit, we are also open to the possibility that other modes of care and subjectivity may emerge – ones that overlap, complement or conflict with the biopolitical account.[6]

Our conceptual approach defines humanitarian securitisation as an unstable process of population government with its own range of institutional and non-institutional agents, which include the state and EU agencies; international NGO professionals, such as the UN; as well as local activists and volunteer groups; and not least refugees and migrants themselves. The former – state and EU staff, the police and army forces – *operate on the mandate of security* and their job is to identify and register the status of all arrivants with a view to protecting the Greek and European borders from illegal border crossings. The latter, essentially two distinct groups, operate on the *mandate of care*: international and Greek NGOs work on clearly delineated agendas, sharing the responsibilities of migrant accommodation, nutrition, information/translation and medical care; and local activists and volunteers contribute by offering dry clothes, drinks and food to refugees on arrival, pre-and post-registration at the registration centre and at the UN camp. While each of these agents operates independently, they inevitably communicate with one another so as to facilitate the swift management of arrivals. As mentioned, for instance, even though Chios's registration centre consists of army and police staff only (Greek special forces, intelligence and Frontex), there is collaboration between these and UN personnel, who also populate the registration centre offering advice to those waiting to be registered. At the same time, the camp for temporary accommodation is in close proximity to the registration centre, establishing direct links between the different care networks. It is these necessary, or, at least, inevitable, connectivities between and across the agents of human securitisation that we take as our analytical unit.

Our analysis focuses specifically on reconstructing the communicative networks of this architecture. It avoids a top-down framework which perceives institutions as the agents of securitisation, and populations – local or migrant – as mere subjects of institutional power. It works instead in a dialectical manner so as to map out networks of communication as we experienced them on the ground, yet inevitably also informed by our theoretical and conceptual approach. Depending on the agents involved, whether security or care-oriented ones, these communicative practices are linked through two kinds of networks: mediation and discourse. *Networks of mediation* refer to differential distributions of technological platforms and information flows across three media routes: *remediation*, which is about the vertical mobility of social media content shifting on to mass media platforms (for instance, from local Facebook posts to the local or national press); *intermediation*, which is about horizontal mobility across social media contexts and contents (for instance, when an activist Facebook message becomes a twitter hashtag or when an activist twitter message appears on local websites); and *transmediation*, which is about mobility from online to offline contexts (for instance, from online Facebook contact to offline cooking and food distribution by the Collective Kitchen; see Chouliaraki 2013 for this analytical vocabulary). *Networks of discourse* refer to the differential distribution of discourses of international law (rights), geopolitical interests (policy mandates), activism (solidarity) or practical management (information, coordination, etc.) that circulate via different agents. Here, the analytical task is to identify which discourses of reception shape which practices of care or security across the spaces of the border: registration centre, UN camp, volunteers' kitchen etc. We next proceed by mapping out the networks of media and discourse in the island's architecture of reception.

The communicative architecture of bordering in Chios

Our empirical material comes from ten days of fieldwork on Chios in December 2015; all analytical discussions below refer to that period and reflect reception arrangements that were consolidated throughout 2015. Our pre-existing connections with key actors on the island enabled us to establish immediate engagement with a range of agents in the field. We had access to all relevant locations and could witness and participate in the whole circuit of bordering, from the provision of local care on arrival to the process of formal registration (though aspects of this were naturally off-limits) and from UN/NGO management meetings to activists' work for food provision, baby-care and legal aid; we also had one meeting with the local authorities. As Greeks among Greeks accompanied by local informants, but also, perhaps, as women willing to participate in the care process, relationships of trust developed quickly and we were able to obtain significant insight into the everyday practices of those involved. Our data collection relied mainly on multi-sited observation (divided between us) and, where appropriate, participation, online communication (through our inclusion in local Facebook groups), document collection and interviews. In many cases, the latter took the form of informal conversations rather than protocol-driven events and, occasionally, took place in between hectic activity; for this reason, we chose to prioritise informality and mutual trust and kept notes instead of using tape-recorders.

What emerges out of our rich fieldwork material is a pattern of intersecting media and their meanings that can be categorised in terms of three core communicative spaces: military securitisation, securitised care and compassionate solidarity. Networks of mediation refers to the configuration of media platforms and their contexts through which agents connect and flow through one another or, in others words, through which they are remediated, intermediated and transmediated. In military securitisation, for instance, networks of mediation refer to the connection between EURODAC (digital fingerprint identification) technologies, situated in an old factory (the registration centre), and international crime registers, available through the intermediation of intelligence data, in the course of migrant identification. Networks of discourse refers to the formations of meaning that each network of mediation articulates and to the identities established through these meanings. In compassionate solidarity, for instance, intermediations of Facebook and twitter activist messages bring together discourses of compassion with critical discourses of 'Fortress Europe', thereby constructing activists as radical political subjects who go beyond benevolent humanitarianism and practise a form of counter-hegemonic resistance against neoliberal bordering practices in Europe. Let us now explore each dimension of this communicative architecture of the border in turn, keeping in mind that all descriptions refer back to December 2015.

Military securitisation

Military securitisation refers to the networks of mediation and discourse that render the border a practice of identification, classification and control for mobile populations. During the peak of arrivals on Chios, military securitisation took place exclusively at the registration centre. There was a conspicuous absence of the state at various other crucial locations, such as arrival bays, by the port, en route to the registration centre or at any other transit spots, and this absence was filled by NGOs and local volunteers. The registration centre was the space where refugees were subjected to the compulsory processes of passport control, debriefing (short interviews) and digital identification – a process that decided whether they could continue their journey towards northern Europe (if they were Syrian, Iraqis or Afghanis) or go to Greek detention camps (if they belonged to any other nationality). Military staff consisted of fourteen Greek army and police officers as well as seven Frontex (European Security Agency) agents. They were all hosted gratis in a derelict factory; a large, sheltered area with no proper flooring (uneven and semi-destroyed cement), a number of smashed windows and no proper heating or lighting. The area was powered by a temporary electrical generator and was divided into working areas: a medical area at the back, the queuing corridor and the interview and identification areas at the front, consisting of six passport control desks as well as four EURODAC PCs (the digital system of fingerprint identification); next to this was the translation desk, where the certified NGO Metadrasi offered translation services in Arabic and Farsi. Despite this inadequate working infrastructure, assembled piecemeal through the personal initiative of local officers, the pace and efficiency of the process rendered Chios an example of 'best practice in refugee management'. Given the combination of low resources and high arrival numbers (up to 1,800 people a day), this achievement was largely due to the working ethos of the registration team, with its relentless processing rates (working 24/7) and coordination abilities. The chief of the registration process justified this performance on multiple grounds, speaking of the team's sense of patriotic duty and professional commitment, but also their compassionate spirit: 'we can't let those poor people and their small children wait for days, as they do in Mytilene [Lesbos]'; one of the officers further mentioned that they did it because of their team spirit and professional devotion to their chief: 'we would never let our Chief or each other down'. What are the networks of mediation and discourse that organised these processes of securitisation?

Remediation

Even though the registration centre was a critical node in the mobility route of migrants, it was absent from the process of remediation – hardly ever republished or broadcast in mass or social media. This is for obvious reasons. Regarded as matters of national security and classified as highly confidential, debriefing and identification were kept resolutely outside the spotlight of publicity – we, as researchers, were allowed to take only a very limited number of selected shots. Media reports, in general, came primarily from refugee camps, rather than registration centres, and mostly involved ceremonial snapshots or statements by visiting state officials. Consequently, the networks of discourse available in mainstream media, throughout the 2015 period, involved the remediation of both securitisation claims (such as the Greek Minister of Humanitarian Aid requesting 'European partners to send more officials to help register and process refugees') and human rights claims (when the same minister pleaded for Europe to stop using racist criteria for reception: 'statements such as "we want 10 Christians", or "75 Muslims" . . . are insulting to the personality and freedom of refugees'; Tagaris 2015).

Intermediation

The efficiency of registration as a site of securitisation rests on the identification system of EURODAC. A digital technology that works across space in near real time, EURODAC offers confidential information on the biometric make-up of each migrant, enabling their insertion into global matrices of surveillance and their subsequent classification into categories of legality/illegality. Intermediation operates thus as biopolitical practice, separating 'authentic' from 'non-authentic' claims to entry on the basis of bodily attributes used as 'instruments in the politics of mobility' (Ticktin 2011: 319). Rather than a stand-alone technique of power, however, this digital biopolitics of intermediation was effectively used in parallel with the face-to-face cross-examination of suspect cases of entry. The most prominent example of combined securitisation was the arrest of two Chechen criminals posing as Afghani refugees, who, having come under suspicion because of their accents, were held in a provisional detention area. They were exposed as illegal arrivals only when the Chios officers brought into their detention cell a couple of Russian women who worked at a local bar. After 24 hours of waiting and chatting together, one of the suspects accidentally used the original name of his co-traveller in a clear Chechen accent – a detail that the women passed on to the border officers. A discourse of humanitarian care also informed practices of intermediation, in that digital speed and efficiency were appreciated by registration officers in reducing the waiting time of families with small children and sick arrivants. Yet the predominant understanding of the process was one of security. EURODAC helped protect Europe from what the chief officer termed an 'invasion' of foreigners and potential terrorists – particularly in light of information that one of the November 2015 Paris attack terrorists had entered Europe through Leros, an island in the vicinity of Chios.

Transmediation

Moving from online to offline contexts, transmediation was about corporeally grounded rather than digital encounters. The process, nonetheless, did foreground the role of the passport and of the migrants' habitus (linguistic, bodily) as themselves technologies of mediation that generated meanings regarding where people came from (passports), and how they related to registration officers (body language and verbal communication). Indeed, according to the officers, the arrivants' readiness to make eye contact, their posture, tone of voice and dress code predisposed them in particular ways – with the middle-class habitus of Syrian families perceived as respectable and dignified and thus regarded as 'like ours', while that of others (for instance, Pakistanis and Africans) was seen as a habitus of outsiders and potential 'cheaters'. Migrants were, in turn, acutely aware of the role of such technologies in border control and intentionally attempted calculated performances of 'the refugee': claiming to have lost their passports (piles of Pakistani or Algerian passports accumulated by the main road outside the town of Chios) and pretending to be Syrians in the hope of being granted asylum. Discourses of transmediation, much along the lines of intermediation albeit through different technologies, thus subordinated a discourse of humanisation and care for others to security and the protection of 'our own'. These same technologies and discourses, however, simultaneously offered resources for migrants to negotiate their identities in the hope of claiming entry and continuing their journey.

Military securitisation, in summary, relied on a network of mediations that combined 1) official practices of censored mainstream publicity, such as leaders visiting camps (remediation) with 2) digital practices of biometric governance that guaranteed the security prerogative (intermediation) and 3) local engagements, juridical and cultural, through the mediation of passports and habitus (transmediation). This network produced, in turn, the articulation of dominant discourses of threat, where migrants figure as potential terrorists, with ambiguous discourses of humanisation, reflected in the evocation of international law as well as the selective recognition of some migrants as 'people like us' and in the denial of such recognition to others. Military securitisation emerges here as a heterogeneous regime of meanings that is subject to the pressures of its specific historical and geopolitical context. On the one hand, security, rather than being purely a matter of digital surveillance, appears also to be a matter of co-presence and cultural sensibility; gazes and bodies appear to be as important to the biopolitical management of mobile populations as the long-distance operations of digital media. On the other hand, security discourses incorporate not only elements of professional duty and nationalist rhetoric but also self-criticism, hints of compassion and an implicit but intense distrust of authority. Similarly, migrants do not simply figure as passive 'bare life' but also as active and creative agents who seek to take their fates into their own hands. Far from a monolithic structure of biopolitical power, securitisation emerges here as an impure regime of meanings, which reveals its actors' heterogeneous range of reflections, desires and commitments and which, at least momentarily, may humanise the dehumanising practices of those who enact it.

Securitised care

Unlike security, which is about protecting European borders, the mandate of care is about protecting migrant lives, through the provision of humanitarian assistance and human rights advocacy by international and national agencies. Assistance and advocacy on Chios were geared towards emergency care, addressing the urgent needs of the continuous migrant flows and bringing agencies into collaboration with one other, as well as with the local authorities. The largest were UNHCR (accommodation and nutrition; rights), the Red Cross (missing persons; psychological help), Doctors of the World (medical aid) and the Norwegian Refugee Council (information), but there were also smaller agencies, such as WAHA and Drop in the Ocean (a group offering assistance at sea).

The two priorities of emergency care, to offer immediate aid and information on asylum applications and travelling options, were shaped by two prerogatives: first, the temporary character of the migrants' sojourn, since, unlike the long-term camps of Turkey or Lebanon, the duration of their stay on Chios in 2015 was seldom longer than two days; secondly, the significance of the migrants' border experience, which, brief as it may have been, was also the moment of decision: asylum or deportation. This double prerogative shaped care provision on the island in terms of what NGOs called 'proactive humanitarianism': care oriented towards 'transit', rather than 'resident' needs, including shelter, food and health, as well as towards the provision of information – from advice about registration to ferry itineraries and maps. In the process, the areas and practices of care were closely articulated with security ones, as for instance, Doctors of the World shared the securitised space of the registration centre and had a say on the registration protocol; sick migrants on Chios, in contrast to Lesbos, would be seen by doctors prior to, not after, registration. Similarly, in the rare cases of unrest at the camp, NGO staff would help ensure that order was re-established.

The transit character of securitised care rendered speed an important challenge for proactive humanitarianism (how to take equally good care of everyone in 48 hours), further impacting on the emotional dynamics of the site. Migrants, anxious and tired as they were, were also euphoric after having survived the sea crossing and hopeful about their next steps (their first question on arrival at the UN camp was often 'where is the port?'). NGO staff, however, felt that such a pace deprived them of deeper bonds with individual people. For some this meant minimising interaction with migrants and simply handing out leaflets to them, while others made a point of speaking to them; some would defend the nutrition bar or the ID bracelet as 'legitimate options' to manage the mass needs of the camp, but others would demonstrate a more profound sense of care: 'at nights, I cannot sleep for long. I need to visit the camp again and again to make sure they sleep well and have a good rest. They are in the middle of a long journey', confessed the head of the Norwegian Refugee Council. Within this complex structure, what are the networks of mediation and discourse that communicate the practices and affects of securitised care?

Remediation

There were two ways in which securitised care gained visibility in mainstream media: first, through mainstream news reports on what NGOs did on the ground and how they reacted to political developments that affected their practice, and secondly, through news reports on other actors' (e.g. politicians', celebrities' etc.) evaluations of the NGOs themselves. Remediation primarily relied on journalists' own reports from the island, registering the invaluable work of securitised care in the absence of state infrastructures, but also expressing concern about the implications of the minimal regulation of their operations. Journalistic criticism focused on a number of minor

NGOs plus volunteer groups and individuals, some of which did not even register with local authorities and acted without coordination with others, potentially creating 'more chaos on their small islands rather than a coordinated response' (Nianias 2016). Remediation was also about quoting NGO statements on various political actors, as, for instance, the UN's demand for 'stronger leadership' from Greece in the face of massive incoming flows (Tagaris 2015). By the same token, what was also remediated was the Greeks' mixed reactions to the UN (and other global actors) regarding such criticism, as local politicians both thanked UNHCR for its assistance and accused it of having unrealistic expectations from a country in deep economic crisis.

Remediation, consequently, established a contradictory network of discourses around securitised care. On the one hand, there was a positive discourse of gratitude towards the humanitarian sector, where media acknowledged its decisive significance in the management of migration flows; yet, on the other, there was a negative discourse of suspicion and critique towards them – either for voicing criticism of Greece (in the case of global players) or for their dubious intentions and their potential for damaging rather than assisting caring practices (in the case of minor aid groups).

Intermediation

If remediation is about the global visibility of securitised care, intermediation is the backbone of its horizontal communication on the ground. Two intermediation networks coordinated NGO activism in Chios: that between NGOs themselves and that between NGOs and external parties – notably refugees and migrants. The former relied on WhatsApp's instantaneous and multi-participant communication functionality that enabled major NGOs to be on a 24/7 alert and to keep contantly updated, rendering their mobile phones their most important work instrument. Even though it was geared towards collaborating with local authorities and minor agencies, however, this closed circuit did establish an internal hierarchy in the field, relegating minor humanitarian players to satellite status. The latter were involved in the circuit only through hashtag groups or twitter accounts (e.g. @wahaint) – as a local volunteer put it, 'they [international NGOs] are friendly with us, but they just want us to follow'.

Nonetheless, it is in the second intermediation network that the most significant hierarchy was established, that between NGOs and migrants. While intermediation was multi-platform, utilising a range of media to reach out, there were no social media links between NGOs and migrants – despite 80 per cent of the latter owning smartphones. Online communication was restricted to 'Nethope', a minimum-function WhatsApp circuit that simply forwarded pre-formulated messages, such as 'I'm OK', to a restricted number of contacts (migrants' families or friends). The bulk of intermediation occurred through pre-electronic and hence non-connective technologies: pamphlets, maps,

diagrams, posters or announcement boards or screens. Printed UN pamphlets, for instance, offered information on rights and asylum appeals at the
registration centre while announcement boards were used for information on
further travel. Pre-electronic forms of intermediation further encompassed
rumour or word-of-mouth, which NGOs regarded as an effective way to
spread news; 'the ripple effect' of these modes of communication was instrumental in 'raising awareness' and 'inspir[ing] trust' among local populations,
but also reaching those on the Turkish coast waiting to cross. While maximis-
ing communication efficiency was a priority among care structures, however,
NGOs were reluctant to contemplate using social media more inclusively –
with the exception of the Norwegian Refugee Council. Consequently, and
despite their smartphone ownership and literacy,[7] migrant populations were
kept outside the digital mediation and discourse networks of securitised care.

Transmediation

The transmediation of securitised care similarly took a dual form, first,
through the use of online platforms, notably WhatsApp, which updated and
coordinated NGOs' offline action. For instance, the nocturnal arrival of boats
(any time between 3:00 and 5:00 a.m.) would be signalled on mobile phones
to get everyone on their feet and on their way to their posts. Secondly, pre-
electronic technologies were used to coordinate the mobility of migrants on
the island; for instance, speaking trumpets were used on arrival at registration. Even though these transmediations did succeed in guiding large groups
through the often chaotic process of queueing, their effects were restricted to
contexts of physical proximity, inevitably having no impact across extended
and multiple space-times; nor did they offer options for interactivity, feedback and fine-tuning with the receivers. Migrants' smartphones remained,
again, largely unexploited as a communications resource and, as with intermediation, online-offline transmediations were also defined by a hierarchical
structure that excluded migrants from the networks of securitised care and
prevented them from having their voices heard.

The communicative structure of securitised care sustained, in turn, a
polyphonic but stratified discourse network. This consisted of two major
discourses: an operational discourse of emergency care that intermediated
and transmediated connections among major NGOs; and a mixed discourse
of practical guidance (where to buy boat tickets or eat) and advocacy (the
UN's advice on asylum application or the human rights of refugees) that
included migrant and refugee groups as well as local populations. These networks were organised around a differential distribution of media use: inter-
and transmediations among bigger NGOs occurred through digital media,
only selectively including satellite ('secondary') NGOs, but those between
NGOs and local or mobile populations occurred through pre-digital technologies; finally, inter-migrant digital communication was further restricted
to minimal, formulaic phrases. Consequently, even though this mediation

network allowed for a range of relevant voices to be heard, its structure was ultimately highly hierarchical. The major actors of securitised care not only perpetuated uni-directional, top-down channels of communications with all actors other than themselves, but, by being reluctant to explore interactive technologies, they also fully silenced the migrants.

Compassionate solidarity

Driven by a progressive politics of solidarity and operationalised through informal and emotionally charged acts of support towards newcomers, the network of compassionate solidarity was distinctly different to the previous ones. Despite its informality, this network was impressively effective: for example, the Collective Kitchen used to cook up to 1,600 portions of food a day; the volunteers of the fishing village Ayia Ermioni provided, on a daily basis, dry clothes to dozens and sometimes hundreds of migrants and refugees landing on their shores soaked; and the lawyer group 'Lathra' prided itself on exposing a case of torture by the port authorities on the island, a case the migrants won. Different in their constitution and values to security forces and NGOs, non-institutional local structures of care represented an organic element of the bordering architecture, as they themselves were a product of their unplanned but inescapable encounter with the arriving migrants.

Remediation

Despite their intense local presence, mainstream media only occasionally focused on the work of the compassionate solidarity groups: 'Chios does not attract much attention [in the media]. That can only be a good thing', said a volunteer, who explained that the media were always looking for negative stories, and the story of Chios was not one of those. The mass media had little interest in the acts of these networks and, correspondingly, activists did not seek their attention. On the contrary, they were very wary; in fact, their engagement with digital platforms was itself a contestation of mainstream media authority. The only case when these groups were systematically remediated, therefore, was in the course of the mass media driven campaign for a 'Nobel Prize for the Greek islanders' (December 2015–January 2016) – a nationalist campaign that depoliticised their solidarity, turning it into a manifestation of the 'Greek spirit' of benevolence and hospitality.

Intermediation

The effectiveness and accountability of activist groups on the ground relied on two digital sub-networks of intermediation: their inter-group platforms of coordination and action (SMS, Facebook, WhatsApp, Viber); and the public platforms that communicated narratives of solidarity to the local population.

Intermediation here was about empowering civic voices beyond those of institutional militarisation and securitised care. To this end, members of the volunteer and activist networks used the online newspaper *Aplotaria* – popular among Chios locals. Alongside their Facebook network, *Aplotaria* allowed activists to be vocal about their own experience of reception, by condemning both Europe's dehumanising security and major NGOs' managerial care provision. Thus, as a popular portal to the local society, *Aplotaria* became an interface between the wider population of Chios and the activists' alternative voices of resistance.

Transmediation

Most encounters among activists and between activists, refugees and migrants were face-to-face and enacted through collective action, such as meal distribution and the provision of dry clothes at the shore. Yet this physicality of care was both managed and regulated through a feedback loop that linked the digital to the physical, in three ways. First, it was through social media that calls for help were circulated beyond the core group of activists, appealing for collaboration; for instance, through invitations to bring donated goods to particular locations or participate in low-key fundraising activities. Secondly, transmediation through Facebook groups or WhatsApp facilitated social get-togethers among groups of volunteers and activists, which functioned as support mechanisms of 'decompression' after the intense emotional and physical strain of reception (many reported an inability to sleep and one reported recently developed heart problems). Thirdly, it enabled semi-public systems of accountability or feedback, as in the case of the volunteers at Ayia Ermioni; every time a dinghy arrived at the village port, locals mobilised to support arrivants and, at the end of their exhausting shifts, lasting up to twelve or even eighteen hours, one of them would regularly return to Facebook to report on the day. In this way, the transparency of their activity and its moral economy unfolded on the ground as much as online.

Compassionate solidarity's networks of mediation articulated a complex discourse of solidarity defined by a spirit of resistance to the power of the border and an acknowledgement of the humanity and vulnerability of arrivants that directly contested all structures of securitisation. This discourse was founded on the ethics of an unconditional commitment to help others in need without asking for anything back, and, indeed, the Chios activists and volunteers not only dedicated all their efforts to assisting the needy without reward but disliked any manifestation of public acknowledgement. This reluctance emanated from their politicised understanding of compassion as a radical act of resistance against established power structures rather than as impartial do-gooding inviting praise from the establishment – such as the Nobel Prize. Thus, compassionate solidarity, in practice, combined empathy towards the vulnerability of others with the imperative of sociopolitical critique. From this perspective, activists regularly criticised humanitarian NGOs as a neutral space of 'administering needs' that prioritised emergency care over struggle against the exclusionary policies of the European establishment: 'We are a movement, not a bureaucratic organisation', they said, and 'we need to be prepared to defend the refugees against the fascists'.

The treatment of refugees as 'people like us' highlights humanity as the third dominant discourse of compassionate solidarity. The key feature of this discourse is its explicit reference to the activists' affective identification with migrants: 'It is obvious why we help them. They could have been us', a member of the Collective Kitchen explained. 'The difference between those in solidarity movements and others is that the former are emotionally attached', added another. Such claims are important because they entail an explicit recognition of the humanity of arrivants, that is, 'a concern for the existential fate of other human beings, a concern that extends into the affective' (Honneth 2007: 123); and this differentiated compassionate solidarity from both securitisation, with its emphasis on policing, and securitised care, with its reliance on professionalised service provision.

However, the discourses of compassionate solidarity are neither pure nor unaffected by securitisation. Despite stark opposition to it, these discourses still functioned within the wider regime of bordering that contributes to the classification of newcomers and their needs from an uneven position of privilege and recognition (as citizens of Europe 'inside' the border). For example, some volunteers strongly criticised some arrivals' eating habits, manners or gender roles, mobilising mechanisms of othering that separate 'us' from 'them' and privilege a view of humanity as exclusively 'our own'. Such familiar narratives represented these people's attempts to make sense of these 'new strangers' from within familiar cultural frameworks and discourses, in a context where the briefness of their encounters, combined with pressures for timely care and severe linguistic constraints, resulted in significant ruptures in communication and an inevitable depersonalisation of solidarity relations – a fact that activists and volunteers were themselves painfully aware of: 'We . . . used to know them, now we don't any more. They have all become one. The voice of the people has been lost. And the political work in this direction is also lost, as we are just trying to meet needs.'

The communicative architecture of bordering: from humanitarian securitisation to hospitability

In this chapter, we have sought to identify the communicative architecture of Europe's outer border in the 'migration crisis' of 2015–16, and to reflect on its implications for those involved: reception agents and migrants/refugees. We saw that, rather than a matter of either strict military policing or open borders, reception was a complex structure of practices and discourses informed by diverse ethical values. Bordering, we have established, was not simply a geopolitical or legal order but, primarily, a moral one. By a moral order we mean the structured practices that recognise refugees' and migrants' right to cross borders as well as the hosts' right to accommodate them (or not), and the normative discourses that legitimise these practices through particular moral claims. While existing literature defines the contemporary moral order of reception in terms of humanitarian securitisation, the fusion of military border security with professional humanitarian benevolence, our attention to the communicative aspects of the border reveals a more nuanced understanding of this moral order.

Specifically, Chios's communicative architecture of reception complicates the anti-humanist determinism of bordering as a biopolitical order that produces undifferentiated power effects of exclusion and dehumanises arrivants as 'bare life'; at the same time, it also challenges the optimism of hospitality, which relies on the moral order of unconditional openness to strangers. Instead, the communicative architecture works through multiple and intersecting networks of connectivity and competing discourses, which establish the European border as a hybrid: both bearing biopolitical effects, in that it reaffirms the border as a site of biological and legal knowledge, and simultaneously producing new relationships of openness, solidarity and sociopolitical critique. It is this hybrid moral order that we attempted to capture through the concept of 'hospitability'.

Hospitability, let us recall, refers to a flexible regime of reception that contains and regulates mobile populations at the same time that it contains and protects them. Even though the term originally referred to the capacity of military techno-spaces to enclose moving targets, while offering them enough space to manoeuvre, hospitability, we argue, can also aptly capture the techno-discursive capacity of bordering to encompass refugees and migrants, allowing them various degrees of mobility in Europe. The moral order of hospitability resides in this hybrid capacity, suspended as it is between controlling enclosure and enabling mobility. Drawing on our analysis of its three communicative structures – military securitisation, securitised care and compassionate solidarity – we now conclude by reflecting on three key points of tension and contradiction that define the moral order of hospitability on the outer borders of Europe.

Military securitisation is defined by a dual tension: between digitality and corporeality (mediation), and between obedience and self-reflexivity (discourse). The first tension refers to the registration process, which, as we saw, uses the EURODAC platform to digitally access transnational data and establish migrant identities as genuine and safe. Simultaneously, however, it also relies on corporeal and cultural clues to 'read' authenticity and trust from migrants' posture, face and language. What this tension throws into relief is the intimate complicity of technology with the body in the power relations of the border. Digital technology may have produced what we earlier called new biometric epistemologies of the border, yet it appears that these epistemologies continue to be undercut by technologies of co-presence – bodies, gazes, spoken words.

Similarly, unlike accounts of biopolitical security as all-encompassing surveillance, the 'performances' of the refugee, for instance when migrants throw their passports away and turn to face-to-face communication in the hope of being granted asylum, point to minor but occasionally effective acts of agency that challenge the impenetrable bordering military securitisation.

The second tension refers to the competing discourses of the security agents. They spoke proudly about their national ('protecting "our" borders') and professional (the 'need to process them') commitments, while, at the same time, employing a range of self-reflexive discourses, including empathy for the arrivants ('we can't let them wait'), light-hearted self-criticism, strong camaraderie (doing it 'for each other') and critical commentary over their invisible labour (24/7 working; minimal pay), which rendered protection possible in the first place. This tension suggests that, its dehumanising potential granted, military securitisation does not simply operate as an impersonal, totalising technology of power, devoid of humanism. It is rather infused with contradictory judgements and emotions that place its actors in the fluid position of the 'perpetrator/benefactor/victim' and renders biopolitical judgement difficult to sustain.

The hospitability of military securitisation is, therefore, a contingent and fragile regime of reception: it inevitably contains, classifies and dehumanises migrants, yet simultaneously allows for individual performativities that may undermine its boundaries and turn a critical and reflexive gaze upon itself. Similarly, its agents are both policing experts who guard the border of Europe and simultaneously part of an invisible labour force that bears the consequence of this continent's policies.

Securitised care is organised around two related tensions: between facilitating and excluding voice (mediation) and between detachment and attachment (discourse). The first tension highlights the fact that the very media connections that maximise care for migrants and refugees simultaneously marginalise the voices of these populations. What this tension demonstrates is that, for all its celebrated horizontal connections, social networking ultimately entails its own hierarchical orders: who gets to speak and who is listened to is a matter of the power relations through which the network's enabling practices emerge in the first place. The second tension highlights the competing discourses of care in the border: service provision or affective attachment. Whereas this tension between minimal engagement with the vulnerable and emotional acknowledgement of their individuality has always been intrinsic to the professionalisation of compassion (Chouliaraki 2013), the size and transit character of mobile populations on the border has foregrounded this ambivalence, rendering it an object of intense problematisation for its practitioners.

Just like military securitisation, therefore, the hospitability of securitised care emerges as a contradictory regime of reception: it inevitably regulates and dehumanises migrants, yet is also informed by unspoken desires and minor acts of emotional attachment and personalised contact, while subjecting itself to a reflexive critique of its own tenuous ethos and effects.

Compassionate solidarity offers, finally, the clearest manifestation of networked mediation as a means of social activism that can establish the border as a space of hospitality and make a difference in the lives of arriving migrants. Going beyond the neutral do-gooding of securitised care, it combined a politics of resistance to Europe's practices of bordering with emotional identification with those who suffer; as a result, it came closest to any network of reception to the pure ideal of open borders. Its use of social media platforms, from Facebook and WhatsApp to blogging and online journalism, coordinated a considerable number of people to maximum effect, online and offline. Simultaneously, however, contact with the arrivants remained minimal and fragmentary and the latter were given no voice in the process; local activists, in this sense, formed part of the privileged European population that military securitisation seeks to protect and excluded the very subjects of their solidarity in the process of supporting them. As Millner puts it: 'how can activists protest against the racial and economic biases of contemporary border controls, without appealing to their own condition of citizenship as a basis for political speech?' (2011: 323). The same ambivalence was further evident in the discourses of compassionate solidarity, which often articulated with cultural stereotypes and moral judgements towards Europe's 'others', combining a sociopolitical critique of the West with Orientalism. This contradiction constitutes a major existential challenge for those involved in practices of compassionate solidarity, compelling them to engage in a constant negotiation of various and often opposing affective states: compassion and guilt; dedication and powerlessness; sadness and indignation; hope and despair.

Conclusion

Our empirical research into Europe's communicative architecture of the border during the 2015–16 'migration crisis' revealed the border as a hybrid network that produces its own moral order, hospitability. Hospitability, we demonstrated, relies on three overlapping networks of mediation and discourse that both reproduce transnational hierarchies of humanity and accomodate an ethics of hospitality and critique. Hospitability is also traversed by ironic or self-critical forms of reflexivity, as well as by competing affects, desires and judgements, which render it a tenuous, fluid and fragile moral order that, nonetheless, does not challenge the border's *raison d'être*: the classification of populations and the preservation of the global order. This dialectical micro-account of the border, we wish to emphasise, matters because it challenges the one-sided normativity of biopolitical accounts of security, and, at the same time, complicates the simplistic benignness of hospitality. It is by keeping this dialectic in sight that we can hope to deepen our understanding of the structures of power that continue to operate at Europe's border. And it is this dialectic that can help us better understand both how such structures of power dehumanise others in the name of humanity, but also how minor acts of humanity are still possible in the midst of such dehumanisation.

Notes

1. 'Migration crisis' is placed in quotation marks to challenge Eurocentric uses of the term, which point to the high number of 2015 arrivals as their main cause for concern and policy focus, while ignoring the ongoing conflict-related crises in the Middle East that led populations to flee in the first place (Vaughan-Williams 2015).
2. See http://frontex.europa.eu/news/frontex-publishes-risk-analysis-for-2016-NQuBFv (accessed 12 April 2016).
3. Report of the European Council on Foreign Relations, 22 December 2015, http://www.ecfr.eu (accessed 26 January 2016).
4. The securitisation of Europe starts earlier, during the migrants' sea-crossings which are regulated by Turkish, Greek, Italian and NATO marine forces. This dimension of securitisation, however, falls outside the scope of our fieldwork (but see Basaran 2014).
5. Arrivals from Turkey to the Greek islands between January and August 2015 increased by 886 per cent compared with 2014. Chios is the second biggest entry point to Europe in the eastern Mediterranean (Chios Marine Force PPP, EU Poseidon Report, 2015).
6. Our approach can be defined as 'critical fieldwork' along the lines of Madison's definition as a knowledge-producing practice that 'takes us beneath surface appearances . . . bringing to light underlying and obscure operations of power', thereby also moving 'from "what is" to "what could be"' (Madison 2011: 5).
7. See UNHCR, 'Connecting Refugees' report (2015), http://www.unhcr.org/5770d43c4.pdf (accessed 20 May 2019).

Bibliography

Agamben, G. (1998), *Homo Sacer: Sovereign Power and Bare Life*, trans. D. Heller-Roazen (Stanford: Stanford University Press).
Albahari, M. (2013), 'The birth of a border: policing by charity on the Italian maritime edge', in J. L. Bacas and W. Kavanagh (eds), *Border Encounters: Assymetry and Proximity at Europe's Frontiers* (New York: Berghahn Books), 232–53.
Barnett, C. (2015), 'On the milieu of security: situating the emergence of new spaces of public action', *Dialogues in Human Geography*, 5.3: 257–70.
Basaran, T. (2014), 'Saving lives at sea: security, control and adverse effects', *European Journal of Migration and Law*, 16: 365–87.
Buzan, B., and O. Wæver (2003), *Regions and Powers: The Structure of International Security* (Cambridge: Cambridge University Press).
Carter, D., and M. Heather (2007), 'Bordering humanism: life and death on the margins of Europe', *Geopolitics*, 12.2: 248–64.

Chouliaraki, L. (2013), 'Re-mediation, inter-mediation, trans-mediation: the cosmo-politan trajectories of convergent journalism', *Journalism Studies*, 14.2: 267–83.

Dalakoglou, D. (2016), *The Road: An Ethnography of (Im)mobility, Space and Cross-border Infrastructures in the Balkans* (Manchester: Manchester University Press).

Darling J. (2009), 'Becoming bare life: asylum, hospitality, and the politics of encamp-ment', *Environment and Planning D: Society and Space*, 27: 183–9.

Dillon, M. (2008), 'Underwriting security', *Security Dialogue*, 39.2–3: 309–32.

Duffield, M. (2011), 'Total war as environmental terror: linking liberalism, resilience and the bunker', *South Atlantic Quarterly*, 110: 770–9.

Fassin, D. (2005), 'Compassion and repression: the moral economy of immigration policies in France', *Cultural Anthropology*, 20.3: 362–87.

Honneth, A. (2007), *Disrespect: The Normative Foundations of Critical Theory* (Cambridge: Polity Press).

Kanchanavally, S., R. Ordonez and J. Layne (2004), 'Mobile target tracking by net-worked uninhabited autonomous vehicles via hospitability maps', in *Proceedings of the 2004 American Control Conference*, 6: 5570–5.

Madison, S. D. (2011), *Critical Ethnography: Methods, Ethics and Performance* (London: Sage).

Millner, N. R. (2011), 'From "refugee" to "migrant" in Calais solidarity activism: re-staging undocumented migration for a future politics of asylum', *Political Geog-raphy*, 30.6: 320–8.

Muller, B. (2013), 'The skeleton versus the little grey men: conflicting cultures of anti-nuclear protest at the Czech-Austrian border', in J. L. Bacas and W. Kavanagh (eds), *Border Encounters: Assymetry and Proximity at Europe's Frontiers* (New York: Berghahn Books), 68–89.

Nianias, H. (2016), 'Refugees in Lesbos: are there too many NGOs on the island?', *The Guardian*, 5 January, https://www.theguardian.com/global-development-professionals-network/2016/jan/05/refugees-in-lesbos-are-there-too-many-ngos-on-the-island (accessed 14 May 2019).

Squire, V. (2010), 'The contested politics of mobility: politicising mobility, mobilising politics', in V. Squire (ed.), *The Contested Politics of Mobility: Borderzones and Irregularity* (London: Routledge), 1–26.

Tagaris, K. (2015), 'EU must stop "racist criteria" in refugee relocation – Greece', Reuters, 11 October, http://uk.reuters.com/article/uk-europe-migrants-greece-minister-idUKKCN0S509920151011 (accessed 14 May 2019).

Ticktin, M. (2006), 'Where ethics and politics meet: the violence of humanitarianism in France', *American Ethnologist*, 33.1: 33–49.

Ticktin, M. (2011), *Casualties of Care: Immigration and the Politics of Humanitari-anism in France* (Berkeley: University of California Press).

Ticktin, M., and I. Feldman (2010), 'Government and humanity', in I. Feldman and M. Ticktin (eds), *In the Name of Humanity: The Government of Threat and Care* (Durham, NC: Duke University Press), 1–26.

Vaughan-Williams, N. (2015), '"We are not animals": humanitarian border security and zoopolitical spaces', *Political Geography*, 45: 1–10.

Watson, S. D. (2009), *The Securitization of Humanitarian Migration: Digging Moats and Sinking Boats* (London: Routledge).

Part IV

Intra/Extraterritorial Displacement

Intra/Extraterritorial Displacement: Introduction

Sam Durrant

According to UNHCR, a citizen becomes a refugee only through being forced to flee across a national border. However, states deploy a range of internal and external borders such that citizenship and sovereignty do not necessarily correlate with geographical borders: one may lose access to the rights of citizenship while remaining inside the nation-state, and the state may continue to exercise juridical control over territory beyond its geographical borders. This section explores forms of both intra and extraterritorial displacement that complicate UNHCR's conception of how a refugee comes into being.

Maureen Moynagh's chapter explores the fate of the internally displaced, now estimated by the UN to number over forty million people. Like the refugee, the IDP often seems to have lost the rights accorded not only to the citizen but also the human being. The UN's Guiding Principles on Internal Displacement (1998) seeks to affirm the rights of the internally displaced, but it does so by appealing to the very category of citizenship that has failed to afford protection against forcible displacement. As Moynagh points out 'this insistence on the figure of the citizen in IDP law should be taken as verging on catachresis, in so far as the citizen in this context strains to shore up the concept and its attendant rights against their effective loss'. Her chapter analyses novels by Mia Couto, Yvonne Vera and Ahmadou Kourouma featuring IDPs generated by civil conflict in Africa. These novels explore a 'negated version of citizenship' through the trope of the orphan, with the loss of familial protection standing in for the loss of state protection. But rather than constitute the IDP as the helpless object of humanitarian aid, the novels bear witness to the creative agency of the displaced, working to re-establish forms of 'sociality on the move' and providing new spatial and temporal frames of reference to replace those that have been blown apart by conflict. The road, in particular, while often a precarious space in times of conflict, nevertheless turns out to offer an imaginative space in which the rhythms of what Achille Mbembe describes as 'life-in-common' can be recovered.

The next chapter, by Norbert Bugeja, considers Hisham Matar's *The Return*, a memoir that offers an intimate account of Matar's return to (post-Qaddafi) Libya and his quest to discover the fate of his missing father, interned and probably executed by the security apparatus of the *ancien régime*. This chapter thus also looks at the fate of the internally displaced or disappeared, but from the perspective of the exile, the son whose return to the land of his father is perpetually deferred both by his father's absence and by the failure of post-Qaddafi Libya to cohere into an inhabitable state. The memoirist's response is to turn the memoir itself into a mode of 'psychic asylum', a 'writing of refuge' in the absence of justice. Denied the possibility either of mourning or of repatriation, Matar must find a way to live vicariously, within and through his own writing, in what Bugeja describes as the 'limited manoeuvre' of the 'fugitive'.

Douglas Robinson's chapter continues to explore this dialectic between the loss of agency involved in displacement and its potential recovery through acts of imagination. Focusing on poems by Arseny Tarkovsky, Richard Hoffman and Li-Young Lee, of Russian, US and Indonesian Chinese origin respectively, the chapter starts by offering a neuroscientific explanation of what it means to be displaced. We create a sense of home by affectively charging, or exosomatising, people and objects. In the absence of those people and objects, we feel psychically traumatised or 'blasted'. As in the previous chapters, literature has a crucial role to play for the displaced not only in articulating and working through psychic trauma but also in producing alternative somatisations. Hoffman's poem, from which the chapter takes its title, is particularly evocative here in its imagining of how the refugee carries his door with him as a 'metonym for home', an 'exosomatic mooring' that provides a kind of psychic resilience against the experience of homelessness. In line with Moynagh's analysis of storytelling on the move and Bugeja's analysis of the memoir form, we might say that Hoffman's door is also a metaphor for the imagination's capacity to provide alternative, albeit temporary, respite from the experience of displacement.

Byron Caminero-Santangelo's chapter differs from the previous chapters in so far as it positions literature not as refuge but as a mode of critique. Reading across Cole's literary and non-literary writing, it advocates for what Cole, following Walter Benjamin, describes as constellational thinking. Such thinking exposes the patterns of power behind isolated 'disasters' in ways that awaken us from the humanitarian fantasies of innocence and salvation that Cole dubs the White Saviour Industrial Complex. The narrator of Cole's novel *Open City* is alive to these patterns of power, but, and this is part of the novel's criticality, also 'deeply flawed' as a constellational thinker in so far as he is unable to turn his gaze inwards and critique his own privileged position as a voluntary migrant and trainee psychiatrist. While the literature explored in the previous three chapters is written from within an experience of forced displacement, *Open City* is written from a position of professional privilege that both imagines and shies away from the refugee's experience of destitution. This movement of engagement and distance also characterises the novel's oblique relation to climate change and environmental trauma. Caminero-Santangelo shows how the novel can be read as a critique of the discourses around climate change and the ways in which the desire for scientific objectivity can occlude the marginalised perspectives of climate refugees and elide complex questions of responsibility and agency.

Chapter 11

The 'Dead Road', Displacement and the Recovery of Life-in-Common: Narrating the African Conflict Zone

Maureen Moynagh

In situations of armed conflict, even the dead suffer displacement. Spiritually dislocated from ancestral lands, unburied for the living for whom they are 'never finishing to die', as Mia Couto puts it (cited in Hammar 2011: 135), the dead are also unsettled, suspended between worlds. It is hardly surprising that the dead road should serve so pervasively as a motif in literary representations of internal displacement, for even roads 'killed' by war, to paraphrase the narrator in Couto's novel of the Mozambican Civil War, *Sleepwalking Land*, serve the ends of narrative and its temporal investments. Associated with mobility and a social world, the chronotope of the road readily evokes the experience of 'masses in flight' and, through the deadly disruptions brought by war, the suspended temporality conventionally associated with being uprooted from 'places of habitual residence' (UNHCR 2001; African Union 2009). While it is resonant enough in these terms, in the three novels of displacement I will focus on here – Mia Couto's *Sleepwalking Land*, Yvonne Vera's *The Stone Virgins* and Ahmadou Kourouma's posthumously published *Quand on refuse on dit non* (When one refuses one says no)[1] – the road offers more than an evocative illustration of the phenomenology of wartime displacement. Alternately dead and revivified, it also offers a narrative trajectory through conflict that juxtaposes dislocation and death with sociality on the move.

It is tempting to understand the impact of such displacements on human attachments and subjectivity in the terms Achille Mbembe describes, following Giorgio Agamben, as the experience of entering a 'zone of indistinction', which is to say 'a space set outside of human jurisdiction' (2002: 267). Displacement is doubly internal in this sense: it occurs not only within the borders of a nation-state, but within the social order and the subjectivities that social order produces. The 'terror' of armed conflict, Mbembe suggests, lies in the way it 'fragments inhabited spaces, blows apart temporal frames of reference and diminishes the possibilities available to individuals to fulfill themselves as continuous subjects' (2002: 267). Yet diminishing such possibilities is not the same as eliminating them entirely. Addressing the straitened prospects imposed by war, the novelists whose works concern me here find ways both to represent the profound disruptions to human existence that displacement in armed conflict occasions and to insist on narrating these experiences in ways not entirely captured by a 'sovereignty of loss' (Mbembe 2002: 267, 268). These works are concerned with what it means to disrupt meaningful community by suspending or severing ties to place, with the ways that, in a 'state of war' (Mbembe 2002: 267), links between identity and territory can be mobilised in the service of a 'politics of enmity'.[2] The logic of the 'dead road' motif, then, has to do on the one hand with the way internal displacement functions as a mechanism of necropower that strives to impose a living death on sizeable populations.[3] On the other, the road signifies the writers' insistence on the possibilities for new forms of conviviality in the face of such technologies of power and thus on the possible routes through the deadly dislocations imposed by conflict. The 'dead road', that is to say, refuses to stay dead. In opposing the politics of enmity, these works offer narrative structures that inscribe a sense of community unfolding in time. If these literary works and the necropolitical formations they represent may be said to share in a particular 'distribution of the sensible' (Rancière 2005:14), the narratives are invested in a different economy, one opposed to the purely instrumental calculus responsible for the 'fabrication of disposable people' (Vergès 2001: 11).

Against the fabrication of disposable people, human rights discourse erects the figures of the human and the citizen. The troubling dissonance between these figures was long ago raised by Hannah Arendt in her consideration of the refugee who, in losing all civil and political rights by virtue of being stateless, seemed also to lose the human rights meant to be inalienable (1958: 267). This human–citizen dissonance haunts the internally displaced, too, although the 'perplexities of the rights of man' identified by Arendt work somewhat differently in this case. The fact of being within the borders of one's country – the key distinction between refugees and the internally displaced – is likewise not enough to guarantee access to human rights let alone civil rights. One of the difficulties that besets international law where IDPs are concerned is that 'displacement in and of itself may contradict basic human rights guarantees' (Cohen and Deng 1998: 73). Indeed, the very absence of 'an expressed right not to be unlawfully displaced' (Cohen and Deng 1998: 74) can be understood as a nullification of the 'rights and freedoms' of citizen-subjects.[4] If armed conflict generates 'space[s] set outside human jurisdiction' – Agamben's conception of the camp – then the human rights on which political rights are predicated are rendered void. As Jacques Rancière puts it, 'any kind of claim to rights or any struggle enacting rights is thus trapped from the outset in the mere polarity of bare life and the state of exception' (2004: 301). A way out of this trap is crucial.

Both the non-binding legal framework set out in the United Nations Guiding Principles on Internal Displacement (1998)[5] and the African Union Convention for the Protection and Assistance of Internally Displaced Persons in Africa (the Kampala Convention) (2009) attempt to bridge the gap that displacement introduces into human rights precisely by making explicit the right not to be displaced. Both legal instruments, moreover, seem intent on imagining the citizen, not merely the human, as the figure in need of protection from conditions that frequently have the effect, if not also the explicit purpose, of negating citizenship. According to the Guiding Principles, internally displaced persons are to 'enjoy, in full equality, the same rights and freedoms under international and domestic law as do other persons in their country'. Similarly, the Kampala Convention advises that states parties are to 'Take necessary measures to ensure that internally displaced persons who are citizens in their country of nationality can enjoy their civic and political rights, particularly public participation, the right to vote and to be elected to public office'. Displacement, in other words, is not grounds for an abrogation of the basis for incorporation as citizen-subject as conventionally understood in both legal and literary plots.[6] This insistence on the figure of the 'citizen' in IDP law should be taken as verging on catachresis, in so far as 'citizen' in this context strains to shore up the concept and its attendant rights against their effective loss. In this way, the 'citizen' in IDP law arguably has, in the terms Rancière proposes to counter both Arendt and Agamben, 'the rights of those who have not the rights that they have and have the rights that they have not' (Rancière 2004: 302). Faced with their loss or negation, one becomes a subject of rights through a 'process of subjectivization that bridges the interval between two forms of the existence of those rights', through a process, that is to say, of staging a 'dispute about what is given' (Rancière 2004: 302, 304). The novels of displacement I explore here put such disputes into narrative, imagining both subjection to necropolitical regimes and efforts to contest them.

While they tend to foreground either the slow erosion of, or outright assaults on, civil and human rights in times of war, the works of fiction I analyse also strive to keep a negated version of the citizen in view. The orphan is the most evocative figure for precarious citizen-subjectivity in literary representations of displacement, and armed conflict produces many of these literary orphans.[7] Christopher Mlalazi's depiction of the Gukurahundi killings in Zimbabwe's rural Matebeleland in the 1980s, *Running with Mother* (2012), is a rare exception to the pervasiveness of the orphan as protagonist, at least in those works centred on children and youth. An orphan's ties to community, to a past and therefore to a future, are symbolically suspended, her path to incorporation more difficult and strewn with obstacles, and as a consequence the plots of incorporation so central to human rights narrative and to what Agnes Woolley (2016: 3) calls the 'asylum story' are likewise in jeopardy. In Mia Couto's *Sleepwalking Land*, not only Muidinga, the child protagonist whose narrative we encounter in the opening chapter, but also Kindzu, the adult protagonist who wrote the notebooks that Muidinga finds and reads, are represented as orphans. The fate, even the identity of Muidinga's parents is a mystery that the novel refrains from solving; the possibility that he is the lost son of one of the characters he reads about in Kindzu's notebooks is only that, a possibility. It is Kindzu, however, who articulates the orphan's alienation from nation, family and conventional orders of temporality through wartime displacement. Kindzu is haunted by his father's ghost, who explains that Kindzu 'would never fulfil any of [his] dreams' and that 'the same thing was happening to our whole country, which had divorced itself from its ancestors' (Couto 2006: 40). The suspension of personal development runs parallel with that of the nation, disordering the linear trajectory of both *Bildung* and national development. Present dissension likewise invades the past, rendering the ancestors themselves 'orphans of the soil' (Couto 2006: 84), and these displacements of the dead prevent the living from seeing the future. If the figure of the orphan puts the citizen under erasure, however, the writers whose works I address attend not only to the difficult paths their protagonists tread, but to the ingenuity they exhibit in forging human ties anew. The capacity for civil engagement is apparent even as the conditions for its realisation are suspended.

Fragmented spaces in exploded times

The temporal suspension of citizenship seemingly effected by displacement is both registered thematically in the novels I explore and challenged by the narrative structures that the writers employ to foreground what was and what could be – and not necessarily with a view to any simple restoration of the past or a (re)turn to a developmental trajectory. While I will come back to the temporal investments of these narratives below, I want to begin with the spatial dislocations that are aligned with the suspended temporality of the war machine. The fictive treatment of roads, borders and camps – among the most emblematic sites of displacement – in the works by Couto, Vera and Kourouma is characterised as much by the writers' evident concern with narrating the possibility of 'life-in-common' as by their need to find ways of depicting the politics of enmity and death. The 'roads of the novel' have long been devices for exploring 'the range and limits of human agency' (Gumbrecht 2006: 614), questions posed with renewed urgency in the body of fiction concerned with displacement. The writers' insistence on agency, even under conditions most inimical to it, distinguishes their narratives not only from 'the discursive construction of the refugee as bare humanity' by humanitarian NGOs, international agencies and states alike (Malkki 1995: 11), but also from the figure of the displaced in international law. The necessarily normative and universalising approach of the latter, despite clear efforts in both the non-binding legal framework of the Guiding Principles and in the Kampala Convention to build in culturally specific protections and provisions for consultation and decision making on the part of the displaced, tends to rein-force the vision of the IDP as a 'generic, ideal-typical figure' (Malkki 1995: 8), even as the law attempts to preserve or reinstate individual rights and free-doms. The apparent preoccupation with the topos of the 'dead road' in works of fiction, which should be taken as an imperative recognition of the corrosive effects of necropolitical regimes, nonetheless cedes ground to acts of narration that insist on the agency and imaginative sociality of the displaced. Mbembe addresses this tension between abstract universalism, which for him offers 'inclusion in something already constituted', and an alternative approach to ending the contemporary politics of enmity. Mbembe proposes the 'in-common' as a foundation for peace and democracy, an approach that 'pre-supposes relations of mutual belonging and sharing' forged by a 'collective body of beneficiaries' (Mbembe 2016: 59).[8] The fictive treatment of sites of displacement in the novels I consider here is about imagining the possibilities of such relations in the face of efforts to destroy and divide populations.

In fact, the conviviality of the road as the 'space where strangers meet and are never entirely strangers', which Franco Moretti considers the 'great sym-bolic achievement of the picaresque' (1998: 51), is strangely evident even on the liminal, fractious and deadly avenues that roads become in these novels. Thus, while in *Sleepwalking Land* the 'dead road' is the site of a burned-out bus filled with charred corpses, it is also the setting in which Muidinga and Tuahir live out their invented father–son, uncle–nephew relationship; it is where they encounter both strangers and an old friend; and, crucially, it is the scene of their imaginative life, where they discover and read Kindzu's notebooks. The Bulawayo–Kezi road in Vera's *The Stone Virgins* both leads to rural community, symbolised by the Thandabantu [love people] Store at the Kezi-end of the bus route, and becomes a zone of roadblocks and danger once the Fifth Brigade massacres in Matabeleland begin. From the perspec-tive of Birahima, the *pícaro* who narrates Kourouma's *Quand on refuse on dit non*, the road between Daloa and Bouaké is 'black with refugees in the frantic hurry of those with diarrhoea' (Kourouma 2004: 37).[9] This satiric inversion of conviviality is also regularly interrupted by darker scenes of mass graves and menaced by the prospect that 'all of Côte d'Ivoire . . . was on the road like a platoon of legionnaire ants' about to be crushed (2004: 37–8).[10] Different as the narrative strategies in these works are, they all set in motion this dual preoccupation with life and death on the road.

The borders in these novels, as is fitting for works concerned with inter-nal displacement, are rarely those associated with the nation-state. In fact, the inadequacies or outright betrayals of nationalist projects come in for cri-tique in view of the enmity they generate. The fictive borders are instead the divisions between land and sea, friend and stranger, foreigner and national, migrant and native, civilian and soldier, city and village, past and present. The proliferation of such borders in these works draws attention not only to the condition of the IDP, defined in international law as 'persons or groups of per-sons who have been forced or obliged to flee or to leave their homes . . . and who have not crossed an internationally recognized state border' (UNHCR 2001; African Union 2009), but also to the ways even this distinction between the refugee and the IDP disguises the transnational dynamics of many conflicts (Mamdani 2001: xiii) and the traces of colonial space making (Quayson 2012: 364–5) that produce persistent divides within and across the borders of former colonial territories. These spatial dynamics are particularly evident in *The Stone Virgins* and *Quand on refuse on dit non*, but all of the novels find ways of grappling with the divisions endemic to armed conflict.

The politics of enmity are intimately bound to the erection of internal borders, as Mahmood Mamdani makes clear in his study of the colonial production of the categories of citizen and subject and the concomitant distinctions between race and tribe and urban- versus rural-dwellers (1996: 18). These dynamics have frequently played out in destructive ways since decolonisation, aggravated by the borders between states produced by the scramble for Africa and by the history of migration across and within those borders (Mamdani 2001; 2002: 495). More recently, Peter Geschiere has identified the re-emergence of a discourse of belonging across Europe and Africa that in several instances has provoked the eruption of conflict between so-called autochthons and those designated as 'strangers', despite the fact that both groups are frequently citizens of the same nation-state (2009: 2–3). While the novels differ in the degree to which they opt for a metaphorical approach to the idea of the border or cleave instead to a more evidently historical one – I hesitate to say 'realist', as none of these works operates in a conventionally realist mode, although even the most lyrical among them is historically grounded – all are preoccupied with what Geschiere styles the 'perils of belonging'. Once again, however, the narrative thrust of these works is towards a reimagining of a life-in-common rather than one variously divided.

Owing in part to this investment in conviviality, the camp is not as pervasive a topos as one might expect in literary depictions of conflict-driven displacement. Camps may figure among the sites of violence and conflict in some works, but they are rarely, if ever, represented as places of refuge. Certainly, when politics takes the form of war as it does in those 'figures of sovereignty whose central project is . . . *the generalized instrumentalization of human existence*' (Mbembe 2003: 14), internal displacement becomes one weapon among others and IDP camps are often enough part of the arsenal. While camps are ostensibly created to 'protect' the internally displaced – a legal obligation under international humanitarian law – they are all too frequently a biopolitical mechanism for regulating populations by 'letting die' a group defined as undesirable (Foucault 2003: 247). The inadequacy of facilities in the camps makes conditions ripe for malnutrition and disease and thus leads to elevated levels of mortality (see Finnström 2008; Branch 2011). More infamously, camps are also sites for the exercise of necropolitical power with its 'appeals to exception, emergency, and a fictionalized notion of the enemy' (Mbembe 2003: 16). Engaged in equally by state and non-state actors, this dynamic interplay of the biopolitical and the necropolitical vitiates the extent to which any camp can offer the 'protection and assistance' the displaced are owed under international law.

Unsurprisingly, the novels of displacement that do depict camps do so in resoundingly negative terms. In *Sleepwalking Land*, for instance, Kindzu's tenth notebook is baldly titled 'In Death's Camp'. Those in the camp, we learn, sleep in holes dug in the ground on the camp's edge to avoid bombs aimed at the huts built to shelter them. As one of the displaced wryly observes, 'those who suffer most in war are those not involved in the job of killing' (Couto 2006: 192). Muidinga, we also learn, nearly died of malnutrition and neglect in a camp; he was saved from being buried alive only by Tuahir's chance recognition that the boy was not quite dead, and the old man's efforts to nurse him back to life. This pattern of novelistic critique of the displaced persons camp dates back to one of the best-known novels of the Nigerian Civil War, Ken Saro-Wiwa's *Sozaboy* (1985). An old soldier with experience of the Burma campaign of the Second World War explains what a refugee camp is to the narrator: 'Zaza say that refugee is somebody that they just throwaway like rubbish . . . So the camp where plenty of them are staying is like compost pit' (1994: 147). It would be hard to find a starker metaphor for the figure of the displaced as 'bare humanity' (Malkki 1995: 11), not to say 'bare life' (Agamben 1998), but the novels' refusal of a merely biological existence means that the spectre of the camp is raised in these works – if it is raised at all – largely in order to reject its terms.

There is another reason the camp itself is displaced in favour of the road in these works. As a 'space set outside human jurisdiction' (Mbembe 2002: 267), the camp is a mechanism for producing regimes of subjectivity antithetical to rights and citizenship, for 'seiz[ing] power over life itself' (Mbembe 2002: 269); it is a dumping ground for the not-yet-dead sacrificial victims of war. The effort to found a self and a *polis* on the basis of such a sacrificial process is, as Mbembe puts it, 'doomed' (Mbembe 2002: 272). If citizenship can no longer take the form of *Bildung*, if the figures of the citizen and the human have fallen victim to the politics of enmity, these novels suggest, alternative forms of community and human attachment must be pursued on the move. In the place of *Bildung*'s developmental time or the sacrificial time of the camp, the road represents a narrative form that can capture a more fragmented temporality, a form better suited to mobile practices of the self, to social heterogeneity, to what Bakhtin characterises as 'the flow of historical time' (1987: 243–4). Narrative structure itself turns out to be a particularly fruitful means of elaborating such a social world.

Narrative strategies for a life-in-common

These concerns with self and *polis*, the writers propose, must be thought together with an often underplayed aspect of displacement: its temporality. The tendency to conceive displacement, whether in humanitarian discourse or in refugee policy work, as exceptional, temporary, and as giving rise to nothing more than an unthinking impulse to flee (Lindley 2013: 291; Hammar and Rodgers 2008: 362; Jahn and Wilhelm-Solomon 2013; Malkki 1995) neglects not only the long-term character of many of the conflicts that have given rise to displacement, but also the ways in which everyday 'social struggles, interpersonal negotiations and life projects' (Lubkemann 2008: 13) persist, however much they may undergo transformation. The widespread view that displacement imposes a temporality of waiting is contradicted by the novelists' concern with more complex temporalities. Without denying that conflict disrupts time, the novelists emphasise both the long history of necropolitics and the ways those inhabiting 'warscapes' are not wholly constituted by violence and continue to pursue both more mundane and more life-affirming projects. The novels, in other words, attend to the long and contested histories of citizen-subjectivity and the impact of enmity on time while making use of the temporal medium of narrative to offer 'meanings that are temporally unfolded and recovered, meanings that cannot otherwise be created or understood' (Brooks 1985: 21).

A life-in-common is also a life-in-time, and narrative is a particularly fruitful medium for exploring both what conflict does to the sensible experience of time and for recovering the meanings of the different timescales of displacement. The temporality of enmity, the time of violence and the pain it causes, is an impossible temporality, as the narrator of Yvonne Vera's *The Stone Virgins* observes: 'Even the smallest embrace of pain needs time longer than a pause; the greatest pause requires an eternity, the greatest hurt a lifetime.' Vera insists on measuring time in human terms and so, counter-intuitively but fittingly, her narrator also insists that 'a lifetime is longer than eternity: an eternity can exist without human presence' (2002: 36). All three novels, while they register the temporality of enmity in different ways, also reassert human presence by narrating community – and the violence frequently done to it – across lifetimes. In this way, the novelists reinstate the 'temporal frames of reference' that on Mbembe's account the 'state of war' 'blows apart', and they require of readers the kind of postcolonial hermeneutic that Ato Quayson proposes would allow us 'to understand history not merely as a sequence of past events, but as a cluster of temporalities whose implications were not exhausted by the passage of time' (2012: 360). Reading in this way, we see that the spatial motifs of displacement are also artefacts of both the apparently discrete 'events' of armed conflict and 'cluster[s] of temporalities' such as 'colonial encounter, neo-colonialism, nationalism . . . and globalization' (Quayson 2012: 363), and we learn from the novelists that the dehumanising space-time of necropolitics can be thought and felt alongside the lifetimes it threatens.

Of the three novelists I consider here, Kourouma brings 'effective history' (Gadamer 1975; see Quayson 2012: 362) closest to the surface of narrative discourse. The 'event' that precipitates the journey of the rogue narrator of this picaresque tale is an 'ethnic conflict' in Côte d'Ivoire in 2001 that the novel attempts to frame both historically and geopolitically, and it is this framing that proffers the understanding readers seek. The vehicle for Kourouma's grim satire is the former child-soldier Birahima, whose knowledge of armed conflict in Liberia and Sierra Leone equips him to serve as bodyguard in the present conflict, but significantly leaves him without the means to make sense of it. Conflict, we come to understand, blows apart temporal frames of reference in part by imposing ignorance on key portions of the population. Fortunately for Birahima (and for readers), his displacement from one part of the country to another is educational, a journey through historical time, by virtue of the lessons his companion imparts.

The narrative trajectory in the novel seems to follow a spatial map. Birahima and Fanta, who is the daughter of his slain Koranic teacher, make their way from Daloa – 'a city right in the middle of Bété territory' – to Bouaké, a city in the rebel-held north, on 'roads overloaded with refugees fleeing the city as though there were a plague' (Kourouma 2004: 15, 37).[11] The road in this novel, that is to say, lies between two ethnicised territories, 'liminal or mobile spaces' (Marshall-Fratani 2006: 12) that are the objects of a struggle for control over meaning, resources and power. Under the presidency of Laurent Gbagbo and that of his predecessor Henri Konan Bédié, northern ethnic groups were redefined as 'foreigners' lacking in what Bédié termed '*ivoirité*', despite having long tilled the soil in regions now held to belong to the 'autochthonous' Bété. The ensuing 'war of "who is who"' territorialises identity and makes autochthony-as-citizenship a weapon to use against particular national groups, newly (re) defined as 'foreign' (Marshall-Fratani 2006: 11, 23). This story of flight, however, with its fairly immediate historical referent and impetus – Kourouma was writing the novel as its real-world correlate unfolded – is but the scaffolding for a more temporally layered and multidirectional narrative.

The *longue durée* of the historical narrative that Fanta supplies not only runs counter to the speed of the journey she undertakes with Birahima, but her lessons contest the logic of the ethnicised map that their journey apparently obeys. Fanta traces the pre-colonial and colonial dis/placements that have a bearing on the twenty-first-century perils that she and Birahima flee. She begins with the long history of migration that brought several ethnic groups to the geographic space known as Côte d'Ivoire, including the groups currently contesting belonging, and points out that 'All of the ethnicities became Ivoirian the same date, in 1904, when . . . the European colonizer specified the borders of Côte d'Ivoire' (Kourouma 2004: 57).[12] In and of itself, pointing out the colonial origins of '*ivoirité*' subversively undermines the competing claims to autochthony of different ethnicities, as does the history of migration that Fanta offers. *Quand on refuse on dit non* thus offers more than a satirical encapsulation of the violent internal border wars of the early twenty-first-century Ivoirian crisis. It telescopes a longer history of colonial space making and its post-independence repercussions, thereby unfolding a long-standing narrative of life-in-common against the divisive politics of enmity that mark the crisis.

In Vera's *The Stone Virgins*, the telescope seems to be trained more firmly on the historically more immediate events that the novel depicts, the Matabeleland massacres in Zimbabwe in the early 1980s. The short opening section of the novel (1950–80) offers a longer *durée*, taking readers from the period of colonial rule and black migrant labour through the struggle for independence or second *chimurenga* to independence itself. The main narrative (1981–86), however, focuses readers' attention on two key acts of violence in the years following independence. Here, too, the first act appears to overwhelm the second. The first is the murder of one sister and the rape and mutilation of another by an ex-ZIPRA soldier called Sibaso.[13] This is the hurt that Thenjiwe, the murdered sister, will not have time to forget, and perhaps in narrative compensation readers dwell longest on this harm and, especially, on the harm to her surviving sister Nonceba. The second act of violence, the burning down of the communal meeting place, the Thandabantu Store, and the slow torturous murder of its owner by the notorious Fifth Brigades, although far more representative of the violence in Matabeleland than those acts carried out by so-called 'dissidents' such as Sibaso, takes up comparatively less narrative time. In forcing readers to dwell on the harm done to the sisters and on the harm done to and by Sibaso, Vera uses narrative temporality to instantiate the damage that armed conflict does to the experience of time. Yet the Gukurahundi campaign[14] and the narrative of historical transformation from the colonial period through to independence sketched out in the first part of the novel remain crucial to making sense, both historically and on the level of the narrative, of the central event and its repercussions. In fact, they are key also to Vera's feminist vision.

As Dorothy Driver and Meg Samuelson point out, Vera is particularly attentive to the gendered nature of post-independence violence (2007: 102) and in this respect her novel offers an important counterpoint to the more conventionally masculine perspectives in the works by Kourouma and Couto. Not only does the novel focus on the sexualised violence inflicted on two sisters by an ex-ZIPRA soldier traumatised by his own wartime experiences, *The Stone Virgins* puts this violence into narrative in a way that is manifestly distinct from the nationalist and masculinist mode of African self-writing that Terence Ranger has called 'patriotic history' (2005: 220) – the narrative of Zimbabwe's past promoted by Robert Mugabe's ZANU-PF.[15] The nationalist or 'patriotic' discourse effectively hijacks citizenship – the idea of the *polis* – so that 'citizen rights [have] been funnelled into rights for party loyalists; and the [individual] citizen . . . is deprived and traumatized' (Chan 2005: 369). Vera, on the other hand, puts those deprived of citizenship and traumatised by the enmity that has ruthlessly usurped national community at the heart of her narrative. The ZANU-PF narrative of 'yet-to-be liberation' (Chan 2005: 370) defers the notion of liberated statehood in order to justify a state that, since 1980, has redirected the *chimurenga* towards its 'enemies' within. Forging a narrative structure for her novel that can address the corrosive effects of this 'patriotic' plot and its appropriation of liberation-as-endpoint, Vera rejects 'a redeemed nationalist future' in favour of 'ambiguous traces of past events and alternative perspectives' (Driver and Samuelson 2007: 105). Through its indirect and fragmented narrative strategies, the novel enables readers to reconstruct a gendered genealogy from the pre-colonial sacrifice of young women – the stone virgins of the title – through the fleeting possibilities for women civilians and soldiers forged during the 'Bush War', to the urgent need for new and creative possibilities for both genders following the 'state of emergency' when 'independence ends' and the 'guns rise . . . anew' (Vera 2002: 65). The traces of historical harm that Vera exposes in the novel undermine the temporality of enmity from within.

Like both Kourouma and Vera, Couto's exploration of displacement in the context of armed conflict engages with competing post-independence projects to define nation and citizenship. The apparent fate of the nationalist project led by Frelimo after independence is aptly signalled, as Luís Madureira argues, in the metonymic relation that the dead road and the burned-out bus bear to the ideas of mobility and collective transport – among 'the more visible symbols of Frelimo's program of modernization and . . . [a] forward-moving national collective' (Madureira 2008: 212) that came under attack by Renamo forces.[16] If we can read the novel as a meditation on the possibilities of nation in the wake of civil war, as Madureira proposes (2008: 213), it is clear that Couto's effort to narrate the prospects for a life-in-common at a time when enmity had become profitable – 'everyone was sowing his own private war. Each made money out of other people's lives' (Couto 2006: 134) – involves attending to the ways war works 'to poison the womb of time, so that the present would give birth to monsters instead of hope' (2006: 210). Yet by putting the exploded times and fragmented spaces of wartime displacement into narrative form, Couto makes it possible to read across temporal frames and to locate the 'invented place[s]' (cited in Hammar 2011: 134) that his characters seek as alternatives to the dead(ly) ones they travel through.

These 'invented places' Couto refers to can, on his account, 'only be born in the border between the written and the oral world' (cited in Hammar 2011: 134), a border that runs through Mozambican communities variously joined and divided by literacy, the legacies of colonialism and degrees of rootedness in oral traditions. That these are temporal borders as much, if not more, than they are spatial ones is clear from the way one of the narrators characterises the internal displacements he and others have experienced as a consequence of necropolitical formations from colonial times through to the present conflict: 'Our memories were peopled by ghosts from our villages', Kindzu observes, and 'these ghosts spoke to us in our native languages. But by now we only knew how to dream in Portuguese. And there were no longer any villages in our future dreams' (Couto 2006: 93). Community, at least as traditionally conceived in the form of the village, is now merely a ghostly presence disrupted by colonial rule and seemingly no longer a future possibility either. That Kindzu himself is, from the perspective of the narrative present, a ghost and his words available to the novel's other key protagonist, Muidinga, only through the notebooks he finds in a suitcase next to Kindzu's corpse compounds the resonance of this passage. It speaks not only of the displacements depicted in the novel, but draws our attention as readers to the form of narration in *Sleepwalking Land*, which emphasises the borders between the oral and the written and between past, present and future, while insisting that it is precisely on the border that the invented places sought by the displaced must be born. The novel's narrative structure reinforces this idea of narration/creation on the border, as the story of Muidinga and Tuahir's civil war experiences opens with their encounter with Kindzu's narrative, which carries us in turn through the civil war back to the moment of independence and back further still to the colonial era. These interwoven narratives carry readers back and forth between past(s) and present through alternating chapters, tracing continuities and discontinuities across temporal frames and inhabited spaces, while on the border that war itself erects 'death and life become the exchangeable sides of one same line' (Couto 2006: 80).

Yet out of this crisis in truth precipitated by war, narrative emerges to enliven the road that 'war had killed': 'the road listens to the story as it unfolds', regaining the mobility it otherwise lacks – 'the road doesn't always move along', Muidinga observes; 'It only does so every time he reads Kindzu's notebooks' (Couto 2006: 1, 6, 100). Reading, it turns out, is also a remedy for the loss of community that Muidinga and Tuahir experience: 'If it weren't for reading, they would be condemned to solitude' (2006: 143). Acts of imagination repeatedly conjure conviviality out of an otherwise static landscape, and for Muidinga, 'it's as if the earth is waiting for villages, dwellings to nurture dreams of future happiness' (2006: 45). The 'spirit' in the stories he hears inspires Muidinga to utopian visions, as 'listening to Tuahir's dreams, with the noises of war in the background, he begins to think they should invent a gentle, more affable gunpowder, capable of exploding men without killing them'. Against the exploded times that are the setting for this vision, the 'inverse gunpowder' Muidinga dreams of 'would generate more life', rather than ending lives, 'and out of one exploded man, the infinity of men within him would be born' (2006: 65). Couto sees all of his stories and novels as insisting that 'identities that are singular and fixed in time do not exist'. There could hardly be a more urgent occasion for making this point than a novel about civil war. Countering the rifts and partitions imposed by violent conflict and the attendant loss of imagined community, Couto maintains that 'we are all made up of various crossings, various lives and cultures' (cited in Madureira 2008: 208). Couto's insistence that narrative and conviviality are bound to the road, which is to say to acts of imagination carried out on the move, is confirmed in the works by Vera and Kourouma.

The urgency of imagining the possibility of a new basis for a life-in-common is evident in Kourouma's novel despite its apparently more cynical take on the conflict it addresses. Gilles Carpentier, who prepared Kourouma's novel for posthumous publication, usefully characterises the 'internal rhythm' of the novel as fast and slow at once: 'a race against time in the historical long term' (Carpentier 2004: 145).[17] Capturing both the urgency of the task of writing and the predicament of the internally displaced, as well as the novel's focus on Fanta's history lessons, which train the reader's attention on the long-standing and complex processes that constitute a kind of absent cause for the present crisis, the fast–slow temporality that Carpentier adduces is not resolved by the end of the novel. However much the lack of resolution is an artefact of Kourouma's death, it is also a peculiarly fitting way of registering the different timescales of displacement in the narrative form itself. Neither the novel as published nor the action it imitates has an ending. In the very act of putting history, including actually unfolding history, into narrative, Kourouma promises to satisfy our desire for a kind of order and sense that the events themselves appear to vitiate. What happens, mostly, in *Quand on refuse* is narrative: Fanta narrates the history of Côte d'Ivoire and Birahima summarises and comments on that narrative. While the plot also follows their movement from Daloa to Bouaké, there is very little dwelling on this journey, and if we are to deduce intention from nothing else, surely we can say that even in this framing of the narrative core, Kourouma insists more on *durée* than on speed or flight and more on the messy contests that the narration puts in evidence than on the implied triumph of the ethnicised map in the destination Birahima and Fanta approach. Writing against the ostensible ending, in other words, and against the apparent direction of events, Kourouma's resolutely anti-heroic plot compels readers to anticipate a different politics than those of enmity, even if we cannot be certain about either the fictive or the historical endpoint.

Vera's approach to narrating community against the harms inflicted by colonial and national necropolitics is different from the strategies that either Couto or Kourouma adopts. Vera not only demands that readers dwell on the gendered violence of the post-independence nationalist project, but also narrates the slow and patient working towards trust and alternative intimacy in the life-in-common that Nonceba and her sister's former lover Cephas build together. Against the temporality of war, which holds 'the past a repast, the future a talisman' (Vera 2002: 84), Vera offers a re-past of the sort that Cephas, a historian, engages in: a careful and creative reconstruction of a beehive hut, traditionally a woman's dwelling, 'in which the tender branches bend, meet, and dry, the way grass folds smoothly over this frame and weaves a nest, the way it protects the cool, livable places within' (2002: 184). While the novel ends, quite literally, with this vision of 'deliverance' – its last word – the domestic space that Cephas shares with Nonceba is not located in a pre-colonial past but in the modern city of Bulawayo. Kezi, Nonceba's village, has become a 'naked cemetery' (2002: 159) in the wake of the ruthless massacres unleashed by the Fifth Brigades, and while the modern domestic space that Nonceba comes to share with Cephas is not unalloyed by traces of the violence and death she has lived in Kezi, it is significant that Nonceba's displacement from Kezi is one that is ultimately life-affirming. If Vera stops short of imagining citizenship in terms of the *polis* in the novel – the conviviality we end with is private – Stephen Chan is surely right to suggest that Cephas's work reconstructing King Lobengula's throne room may be read as a way of refashioning archaic community as a symbolic language, if not practicable solution, for modern times (2005: 379). It also matters for our reading of Vera's novel that the archaic basis for modern community be a beehive hut rather than a stone virgin.

Fiction for unsettled times

While social scientists acknowledge the power of fiction to present 'captivating illustrations' of displacement (Hammar and Rodgers 2008: 36; see also Chan 2005), 'illustration' is really too narrow an understanding of what fiction can do. In fitting narrative forms and strategies to the displacements of the war machine, novelists extricate the sensible phenomenon of displacement from its (extra)ordinary political work and subject it to the 'heterogeneous power' (Rancière 2005: 18) of narrative art that allows displacement to be thought and felt beyond the 'zones of indistinction' (Mbembe 2002: 267) between life and death. While the displaced themselves exhibit agency and creativity in the face of the ruthless instrumentality of necropolitical regimes, these novels create a space both apart from and linked to that lived creativity where agency and imagination can be apprehended alongside the lived experience of enmity and infrahumanity. One way of thinking about the 'distribution of the sensible' that I have been after in this chapter is in terms of the heteronomical contest between the politics of enmity and the politics of friendship waged both on the ground, as it were, and in the literary texts. On Derrida's account, the 'sort of originary sociality' of friendship entails an ethical response/responsibility *for* oneself, *before* the law (even before any particular law), and *to* the Other (Derrida 1998: 634, 638–40).[18] Arguably, it is precisely this sort of responsibility to the IDP to which the Guiding Principles aspire and which the Kampala Convention makes into positive law. Indeed, the latter sets out very explicitly what the states parties and non-state actors are responsible for, to whom they are responsible – the internally displaced themselves – and before whom – the African Union, its courts and tribunals. The literary works, by virtue of their preoccupation with the particular, their truck in the sensible, offer a different order of response. It is to take up the politics of enmity in all of its lived and felt detail, in its historically determined specificity, in its grim and deadening effects, and yet to make perceptible also – set apart from the present tense of the war machine – that 'undeniable future anterior which would be the very movement and time of friendship' (Derrida 1998: 638).

Notes

1. All translations from Kourouma's *Quand on refuse on dit non* are my own.
2. I borrow this phrase from Achille Mbembe's recent book, *Politiques de l'inimitié*, the aim of which is to offer an analysis and critique of the contemporary moment – 'le temps du repeuplement et de la planétarisation du monde sous l'égide du militarisme et du capital et, conséquence ultime, le temps de la sortie de la démocratie' (Mbembe 2016: 17; the era of the repeopling and planetarization of the world under the aegis of militarism and capital and, the ultimate consequence, the departure from democracy). All translations from this book are my own.
3. Mbembe defines necropolitics as the way that 'life, death and the human body' are 'inscribed in the order of power' when politics takes 'the form of war' (2003: 12). It is, in this sense, a technology of power that extends beyond biopolitics, 'which takes life both as its object and its objective' and which 'no longer recognizes death' as an object of power (Foucault 2003: 254, 248). In the 'death worlds' of necropolitics, in contrast, 'vast populations are subjected to conditions of life conferring upon them the status of *living dead*' (Mbembe 2003: 40).
4. There is some disagreement among legal scholars on this point. Elizabeth Ruddick argues, contra Deng, that the Universal Declaration of Human Rights already prohibits forcible displacement, citing the provisions of Articles 12, 13, 16 and 17 (Ruddick 1997: 437).
5. These principles were developed by a team of international lawyers under the direction of Francis M. Deng in his capacity as representative to the UN Secretary General on internal displacement.
6. Joseph Slaughter's work on human rights and the *Bildungsroman* has come to be foundational for thinking about the literary and legal forms of citizen-subjectivity; building on Slaughter's work, Agnes Woolley addresses the challenges that asylum seekers face in seeking incorporation in a nation-state that is not their country of origin.
7. The very title of Tierno Monénembo's novel of the Rwandan genocide signals the protagonist's parentless state: *L'aîné des orphelins* (2000); other novels of displacement in armed conflict that centre on orphans include Emmanuel Dongala's *Johnny Mad Dog*, Chris Abani's *Song for Night*, and the novels by Kourouma and Couto that I take up in this chapter.
8. 'L'universel implique l'inclusion à quelque chose ou quelque entité déjà constitué. L'en-commun présuppose un rapport de coappartenance et de partage . . . [et] doit être partagé par l'ensemble de ses ayants droits.'
9. 'La route . . . était noire de réfugiés pressés comme des diarrhéiques.'
10. 'C'était toute la Côte d'Ivoire qui était sur les routes comme une bande de magnans.'
11. 'Daloa est une ville en pleine terre Bété'; 'Toutes les routes étaient encombrées de réfugiés fuyant la ville comme s'il y avait la peste.'
12. 'Toutes les ethnies se sont trouvées ivoiriennes le même jour, en 1904, lorsque . . . le colonisateur européen a précisé les frontières de la Côte d'Ivoire.'
13. ZIPRA, the Zimbabwe People's Revolutionary Army, was one of the forces that engaged in the struggle for the liberation of Zimbabwe from Ian Smith's minority rule, alongside ZANLA, the Zimbabwe African National Liberation Army.

14. *Gukurahundi* is Shona for 'early rain that washes away the chaff' and was the name given to the campaign carried out by Robert Mugabe's specially constituted Fifth Brigades against the Ndebele peoples in Matabeleland north and south, beginning in 1981. Ostensibly targeting former ZIPRA soldiers regarded as dissidents, the Brigades massacred thousands, if not tens of thousands, of Ndebele civilians.
15. ZANU-PF, the Zimbabwe African National Union-Patriotic Front, is the political wing of ZANLA that came to form the government of an independent Zimbabwe under the leadership of Robert Mugabe in 1980.
16. Frelimo stands for the *Frente de libertação de Moçambique*, or the Liberation Front of Mozambique, which led the struggle for independence against Portugal and formed the first independent government in 1975. Renamo, *Resistência nacional moçambicana*, or the Mozambican National Resistance, was sponsored initially by Rhodesia and by the apartheid regime in South Africa.
17. 'une course contre la montre dans la longue durée historique'.
18. In proposing the politics of friendship as an alternative to the politics of enmity, I do not mean to imply an opposition between Mbembe and Derrida; in fact, the idea of response/responsibility at the core of Derrida's conception of the politics of friendship can be understood as a complement to the 'in-common' that Mbembe proposes as the foundation of 'démocratie planétaire' (planetary democracy).

Bibliography

Abani, Chris (2007), *Song for Night* (New York: Akashic Books).

African Union (2009), *Convention for the Protection and Assistance of Internally Displaced Persons in Africa (Kampala Convention)*, 23 October, au.int/en/treaties/african-union-convention-protection-and-assistance-internally-displaced-persons-africa (accessed 2 July 2019).

Agamben, Giorgio (1998), *Homo Sacer: Sovereign Power and Bare Life*, trans. Daniel Heller-Roazen (Stanford: Stanford University Press).

Arendt, Hannah (1958), *The Origins of Totalitarianism* (Cleveland, OH: Meridian).

Bakhtin, Mikhail (1987), 'Forms of time and of the chronotope in the novel', trans. Caryl Emerson and Michael Holquist, in *The Dialogic Imagination*, ed. Michael Holquist (Austin: University of Texas Press), 84–258.

Branch, Adam (2011), *Displacing Human Rights: War and Intervention in Northern Uganda* (Oxford: Oxford University Press).

Brooks, Peter (1985), *Reading for the Plot* (New York: Vintage).

Carpentier, Gilles (2004), 'Note sur la présente édition', in Ahmadou Kourouma, *Quand on refuse on dit non*, ed. Gilles Carpentier (Paris: Éditions du Seuil), 141–7.

Chan, Stephen (2005), 'The memory of violence: trauma in the writing of Alexander Kanengoni and Yvonne Vera and the idea of unreconciled citizenship in Zimbabwe', *Third World Quarterly*, 26.2: 369–82.

Cohen, Roberta, and Francis M. Deng (1998), *Masses in Flight: The Global Crisis in Internal Displacement* (Washington, DC: The Brookings Institute Press).

Couto, Mia (2006 [1992]), *Sleepwalking Lands*, trans. David Brookshaw (London: Serpent's Tail).

Derrida, Jacques (1998), 'The politics of friendship', trans. Gabriel Motzkin, *The Journal of Philosophy*, 85.11: 632–44.

Diop, Boubacar Boris (2006 [2000]), *Murambi, the Book of Bones*, trans. Fiona McLaughlin (Bloomington: Indiana University Press).

Dongala, Emmanuel (2005 [2002]), *Johnny Mad Dog*, trans. Marie Louise Ascher (New York: Farrar, Straus, and Giroux).

Driver, Dorothy, and Meg Samuelson (2007), 'History's intimate invasions: Yvonne Vera's *The Stone Virgins*', *English Studies in Africa*, 50.2: 101–20.

Finnström, Sverker (2008), *Living with Bad Surroundings: War, History, and Everyday Moments in Northern Uganda* (Durham, NC: Duke University Press).

Foucault, Michel (2003), '*Society Must Be Defended*': *Lectures from the Collège de France, 1975–1976*, trans. David Macey (New York: Picador).

Gadamer, Hans Georg (1975 [1960]), *Truth and Method* (New York: Continuum).

Geschiere, Peter (2009), *The Perils of Belonging: Autochthony, Citizenship, and Exclusion in Africa and Europe* (Chicago: University of Chicago Press).

Gumbrecht, Hans Ulrich (2006), 'The roads of the novel', in Franco Moretti (ed.), *The Novel, Volume 2: Forms and Themes* (Princeton: Princeton University Press), 611–46.

Hammar, Amanda (2011), 'Sleepwalking lands: literature and landscapes of transformation in encounters with Mia Couto', in Byron Caminero-Santangelo and Garth Myers (eds), *Environment at the Margins: Literary and Environmental Studies in Africa* (Athens: Ohio University Press), 121–40.

Hammar, Amanda, and Graeme Rodgers (2008), 'Notes on political economies of displacement in Southern Africa', *Journal of Contemporary African Studies*, 26.4: 355–70.

Jahn, Ina Rehema, and Matthew Wilhelm-Solomon (2013), '"Bones in the wrong soil": reburial, belonging and disinterred cosmologies in post-conflict Northern Uganda', *Critical African Studies*, 7.2: 182–201.

Kourouma, Ahmadou (2004), *Quand on refuse on dit non*, ed. Gilles Carpentier (Paris: Éditions du Seuil).

Lindley, Anna (2013), 'Displacement in contested places: governance, movement and settlement in the Somali Territories', *Journal of Eastern African Studies*, 7.2: 291–313.

Lubkemann, Stephen C. (2008), *Culture in Chaos: An Anthropology of the Social Condition in War* (Chicago: University of Chicago Press).

Madureira, Luís (2008), 'Nation, identity and loss of footing: Mia Couto's *O Outro Pé Da Sereia* and the question of Lusophone postcolonialism', *Novel*, 41.2–3: 200–28.

Malkki, Liisa (1995), *Purity and Exile: Violence, Memory, and National Cosmology among Hutu Refugees in Tanzania* (Chicago: University of Chicago Press).

Mamdani, Mahmood (1996), *Citizen and Subject: Contemporary Africa and the Legacy of Late Colonialism* (Princeton: Princeton University Press).

Mamdani, Mahmood (2001), *When Victims Become Killers: Colonialism, Nativism, and the Genocide in Rwanda* (Princeton: Princeton University Press).

Mamdani, Mahmood (2002), 'African states, citizenship and war: a case study', *International Affairs*, 78.3: 493–506.

Marshall-Fratani, Ruth (2006), 'The war of "who is who": autochthony, nationalism and citizenship in the Ivoirian crisis', *African Studies Review*, 49.2: 9–43.

Mbembe, Achille (2002), 'African modes of self-writing', *Public Culture*, 14.1: 239–73.

Mbembe, Achille (2003), 'Necropolitics', *Public Culture*, 15.1: 11–40.

Mbembe, Achille (2016), *Politiques de l'inimitié* (Paris: La Découverte).

Mlalazi, Christopher (2012), *Running with Mother* (Harare: Weaver Press).

Monénembo, Tierno (2000), *L'aîné des orphelins* (Paris: Éditions du Seuil).

Moretti, Franco (1998), *Atlas of the European Novel 1800–1900* (London: Verso).

Nuttall, Sarah (2005), 'Inside the city: reassembling the township in Yvonne Vera's fiction', in Robert Muponde and Ranka Primorac (eds), *Versions of Zimbabwe: New Approaches to Literature and Culture* (Harare: Weaver Press), 177–92.

Quayson, Ato (2012), 'The sighs of history: postcolonial debris and the question of (literary) history', *New Literary History*, 43: 359–70.

Rancière, Jacques (2004), 'Who is the subject of the rights of man?', *South Atlantic Quarterly*, 103.2–3: 297–310.

Rancière, Jacques (2005), *The Politics of Aesthetics*, trans. Gabriel Rockhill (London: Bloomsbury).

Ranger, Terence (2005), 'Rule by historiography: the struggle over the past in contemporary Zimbabwe', in Robert Muponde and Ranka Primorac (eds), *Versions of Zimbabwe: New Approaches to Literature and Culture* (Harare: Weaver Press), 217–43.

Ruddick, Elizabeth (1997), 'The continuing constraint of sovereignty: international law, international protection and the internally displaced', *Boston University Law Review*, 77.2: 429–82.

Saro-Wiwa, Ken (1994 [1985]), *Sozaboy, a Novel in Rotten English* (New York: Longman).

Slaughter, Joseph (2007), *Human Rights, Inc.: The World Novel, Narrative Form, and International Law* (New York: Fordham University Press).

UNHCR (2001), *Guiding Principles on Internal Displacement*, www.unhcr.org/protection/idps/43ce1cff2/guiding-principles-internal-displacement.html (accessed 2 July 2019).

Vera, Yvonne (2002), *The Stone Virgins* (New York: Farrar, Straus, and Giroux).

Vergès, Françoise (2001), 'The age of love', *Transformation*, 47: 1–17.

Woolley, Agnes (2016), 'Narrating the "asylum story": between legal and literary storytelling', *Interventions: International Journal of Postcolonial Studies*, http://www-tandfonline-com.doi/full/10.1080/1369801X.2016.1231585 (accessed 4 March 2017).

Chapter 12

'What do you do when you cannot leave and cannot return?': Memoir and the Aporia of Refuge in Hisham Matar's *The Return*

Norbert Bugeja

and the stray black dog stares into the river
as if it already knew everything we don't want to see. (Ritsos 1995: 22)

On 11 June 2017 the Abu Bakr al-Sadiq brigade, a militia made up of former rebels in control of the north-western city of Zintan in Libya, released its erstwhile prisoner Seif al-Islam Qaddafi, the politically prominent son and heir-apparent to former Libyan ruler Muammar Qaddafi, after five years in its custody (Stephen 2017). If anything, this move, motivated by interests that currently remain under wraps, goes a long way in showing to what extent prospects for national reconciliation, the question of transitional justice, infrastructural reconstruction, constitutional progress and economic recovery continue to be kept well out of reach for the people of post-Qaddafi Libya. Right now, Libya is a country internally riven by an insidious and complex power-grabbing factionalism, a country undermined from the outside by regional and broader-based financial interests that are fomenting its destabilisation by way of ripening the climate for a 'renewed, bolstered authoritarianism after the Arab Spring' (Aboueldahab 2017). In this perverse context, as Noha Aboueldahab has noted, 'the timing [of Seif Qaddafi's release] makes sense', and wheeling Seif – wanted at The Hague for war crimes – out into the open cannot but be understood as a ploy to test the waters, ahead of a more pointed drive at re-establishing some form of despotic order in Libya (Aboueldahab 2017).

The profile of Khalifa Haftar himself as a strongman on the make, and that of his self-professed Libyan National Army, are on the rise, with the General now being courted by Russia, France and most recently, Italy. Even as, at the time of writing, general elections in Libya are set to take place at some point in early 2019, political and state-institutional actors, both local and international, are in ongoing disagreement over Libya's way forward. Neither can the fact be ignored that Haftar had already told France24 Arabic that he '[does] not care about elections' but about 'the future of Libya as a stable and civil state' (R.M. 2017). If Haftar gets his way, his bid for power will in all likelihood be pitched under the pretext of a 'realistic' and 'implementable' prospect of bringing Libya together and, as Aboueldahab (2017) has observed, will inevitably be offered alongside an anti-Islamist, counter-terrorist, national security and counter-Daesh narrative. And as the tensions between Libya's eastern and western constituencies that have repeatedly led the country to the brink of fragmentation are being fanned and provoked, the subtext of a return to the 'one-stop-shop' model that Qaddafi was known for remains an acceptable scenario for many, including the various international stakeholders from different sectors currently awaiting change (and their chance) in the wings.

The spectre of a return to despotic rule for Libya has also been recently raised, however, in tones of concern, in a very different political space of activity than the one introduced above: a work of memoir in relation to post-2011 Libya that also pitches itself as an intimate space of political refuge in the process of telling a harrowing personal story. This essay will examine Hisham Matar's *The Return: Fathers, Sons and the Land in Between*, arguing that Matar's memoir offers up its resources as a space of asylum and political shelter while simultaneously affording the memoirist a dimension of surrogate agency by which to perpetuate his disappeared father's political voice. In his memoir, published in late 2016, Matar gives an account of his return to and a renewed relation with the land of his upbringing after the 2011 uprising that resulted in the ousting of Muammar Qaddafi. Matar embarks on an intense personal journey, a meandering quest for information about the exact circumstances surrounding the obscure fate of his father, Jaballa Matar – an eminent political dissident and successful entrepreneur who, in March 1990, was abducted in Cairo by Qaddafi agents assisted by Egyptian president Hosni Mubarak's secret services (Matar 2016: 41). The abduction of Matar's father was, of course, in the vein of the initiative launched by Qaddafi in 1980, noted by veteran diplomat Ethan Chorin as 'the infamous "stray dogs campaign", designed to neutralise and make an example of dissident expatriates' (2012: 45). Writing in the aftermath of Qaddafi's ousting, almost a quarter of a century after the event, Matar observes that

> Soon, in the absence of a strong army and police force, armed groups [across Libya] would rule the day, seeking only to advance their power. Political factions would become entrenched, and, amidst the squabble, foreign militias and governments would violently enter, seeking their opportunity. The dead would mount. Universities and schools would close. Hospitals would become only partially operative. The situation would get so grim that the unimaginable

would happen: people would come to long for the days of Qaddafi. It was of course impossible to imagine such a nightmare back in March 2012, yet in those night hours, lying there listening to the city in the dark, I could sense the possibility of horror. (Matar 2016: 123)

In a memoir devoted to a son's return in search of the father and of his fate, this passage offers the only apparent direct allusion to the prospect of a return to a Qaddafi-like era – and yet this 'possibility of horror' looms large over the entire memoir, and underpins many of its anxieties (Matar 2016: 123). Taken on its own merits, the sheer proximity in time that the memoir evinces between the return of the disappeared Jaballa's son to a newly liberated Libya and his having to contemplate the 'unimaginable' scenario of some *nostos* or return-by-default to a pre-2011 political state of play induces a sense of historic dizziness or vertigo, to say the least. Here is a moment of liberation from four decades of Qaddafi rule that had barely even understood or savoured its own significance before the country was being induced to contemplate its *revenants* up close. In this scenario, the notion itself of 'return' in Libya today would not suggest some condition of being in transit to greener pastures, but a reversal into a politically transitless condition – one that is captured in Matar's response early on in his account as he writes of his divided feelings from London in late August 2011, when Tripoli fell to the rebels and they took control of Abu Salim prison: '*I want to be there and I don't want to be there*' (2016: 11). This founding aporia, this afflictive liminality in the memoirist's post-Qaddafi outlook, is established early on in Matar's work, and it sets the scene for the *angst*-ridden narration that will follow from it and course through his account. 'What you have left behind has dissolved', he writes. 'Return and you will face the absence or the defacement of what you treasured [. . .] What do you do when you cannot leave and cannot return?' (2016: 4).

As I pored over Matar's words, they reminded me of the character of Khalil in Elias Khoury's great novel *Gate of the Sun* (Bab al-Shams), as Khalil recalls the comatose fighter Younes's words to his dispersed Palestinian comrades: 'We're not refugees. We're fugitives and nothing more' (Khoury 2007: 16). It seems to me that the delicate yet searing line that Khoury draws between the fugitive and the refugee has, despite the separate context it was conceived in, a strong bearing on the Libya that Matar is both writing *from* and writing *towards*. Libya's post-Qaddafi fortunes up until today show the country's political bid for true national reconciliation in flight without a horizon of refuge. The fact that the ex-Italian colony's efforts towards geographic and national unity have, in historical terms, been notoriously difficult and elusive, and its geopolitical fabric prone to splintering, is well documented.[1] After 2011, however, the political status quo that Libya has been striving to flee, and the one it seems to be hurtling towards, have become uncannily and worryingly akin to each other. Qaddafi's stranglehold over the narrative of Libya's post-colonial nationhood since 1969 has, of course, severely degraded the country's prospects of hammering out a working, nationwide political consensus in the immediate term.[2] Neither do the signs of a potential collusion of European governments with Khalifa Haftar and his forces bode well for the prospect of a compromise solution any time soon (see, for instance, Stephen and Wintour 2017).

Of stray dogs and spaces: the refuge of vicarious agency[3]

In what follows, and by looking more closely into the narrative dynamics at play in Matar's recent work, I want to propose the memoir form as that locus of political shelter and flight – in turns dialectical and fortuitous – that comes to be activated and accessed as a dimension of refuge precisely at those specific instances when the interests of both national (re-)formation and political justice seem to resolve only in an impassable aporia. Matar's memoir forges specific strategies by which the prospect of political foreclosure comes to be confronted, such that a certain ambivalent mode of relating both personal and national terms of (af)filiation comes to be redistributed through the lens of an exilic agency. This mode of self-narrating gains traction in the memoir as a credible and relational zone of apprehending post-2011 – in part because the terms of its narration emphatically continue to operate outside the hold of the entrenched backroom agendas that still have Libya in their grip. '*It was as if I was a stowaway being claimed back by the fatherland*', Matar notes in mid-memoir, as people come forward to give him stories about his absent father (2016: 137, my italics). At once psychic exile, erstwhile 'stowaway' and informed objector to Qaddafi, and one who is now witnessing the internecine strife that threatens to dissolve the country's brief window of liberation, Matar takes up the memoir form in an attempt to prise open the internal resources of the sentiment itself of 'being-torn-between'.

The Return, I argue, adopts and harnesses this equivocal sentiment as its own, idiosyncratic narrative terrain, elaborating the aporetic in the process as a delicate narrative counter to the political and humanitarian deadlock that currently prevails in the post-Qaddafi polity. In *The Return*, it is not only the nation-space that has undergone the 'being-torn-between'. On the contrary, this mode of living-in-two-minds, in an ambivalence towards the fatherland that Matar cannot (but) flee, is shown in the course of the memoir to evince a last instance dimension of political shelter – a safe haven wherein the assertion of the contingent presence of a hitherto deferred prospect of transitional justice in Libya comes to be afforded an *asylum-in-memoir*.[4] In *The Return*, therefore, that which is politically fugitive comes to be endowed with an agency of conscience as a consequence of its effort to seek refuge within the memoir-space itself, within the exilically self-conscious process held forth in its very construction. In other words, through the memoir form, Matar's sensation of 'being-torn-between' is also afforded a window of possibility to feel at home within the anxious unfolding of its self-narration. As he lays out his

father's story through his own, the memoirist's *angst* rallies together a semantic terrain of refuge across which his father's abducted, dissident political
conscience may unfold and come into focus. In this sense, Matar's memoir
seeks a moral sanctuary for the father's veiled fate through a negative memorial quest, one that is distinctly reminiscent of the answer that the Foreigner
(*Xenos*) gives Theaetetus in Plato's *Sophist*: to 'forcibly, establish that non-
being somehow is, and that being, in its turn, in a certain way is not' (Derrida
and Dufourmantelle 2000: 7).[5]

This effort to proffer a restored material presencing to Libya's hounded dis-
sident voices by absorbing, redimensioning and then resocialising the political
schemata of the regime itself is powerfully experienced in the work of Sadiq
Naihoum, the Benghazi-born journalist and dissident writer described by
Chorin as 'Libya's pre-eminent political philosopher of the 1970s and 1980s'
(Chorin 2012: 1). In Naihoum's thinly veiled parable of Qaddafi's rule, titled
'The Sultan's Flotilla' and translated by Chorin himself, the Xenos's haunting
missive to Theaetetus transpires in the manner in which Qaddafi's motif of the
'stray dog' – the epithet that Libya's erstwhile strongman used to describe his
opponents – is, in a feint of *détournement*, turned upon Qaddafi himself.

> [T]he Sultan was condemned to endure a bizarre sort of apocalypse, a living
> nightmare so awful, he couldn't bear to rest his head on his pillow or close his
> eyes at any time of day or night, for fear of dreaming of a certain black dog.
> The dog was a hideous sight, putrid, offensive, with gouged-out eyes. Invari-
> ably it appeared to the Sultan above the hills of dry sand which spread behind
> Jalu's ramparts. It reared its ugly head, howling in such a crazed state that
> the hills themselves appeared to drown in its odious inhalations. Upon some
> unknown cue, the black dog lunged at the bare heels of the Sultan, who then
> ran for his life [. . .] (Naihoum 2006)[6]

In hindsight, Naihoum's parable, written some three decades before Qaddafi's ousting, transports its reader straight to the scenes that played out
just outside Qaddafi's home town of Sirte, located on the south coast of the
Gulf of Sidra, on 20 October 2011, when a NATO airstrike hit the armed
convoy carrying the embattled leader who had by then spent forty-two years
at the country's helm. Qaddafi was found a few moments later by National
Transitional Council fighters sheltering inside a graffiti-scrawled drainage
pipe – a spot that, it must be said, happened to be quite liminally placed,
exactly half-way between his erstwhile headquarters in Tripoli and the iconic
rebel city of Benghazi to the east. In the vistas of desolate space as well as
the psychic and somatic atmospherics they evoked, the Sultan's vision of
the dog's 'hideous sight' and his flight in Naihoum's parable were uncannily reminiscent of the scenes of the dazed and bloodied Qaddafi minutes
or hours before his execution.[7] Not only did Naihoum's narrative 'break'
Qaddafi's cover early on during the latter's rule, it must also have served the

regime's opponents – many of them in exile – as a moral refuge-by-proxy, one that must have somehow truly mattered in the thick of Qaddafi's 'stray dogs' witch-hunt. Many have perceived Qaddafi's own gruesome end as a form of poetic justice.[8] Here, it would be more apt, perhaps, to keep in mind Marek Tamm's reminder, following Jan Assmann, that 'in the long term, *the way* events or other historical phenomena are remembered could be more influential than what [actually] happened' (Tamm 2015: 3, my italics). The retroactive impact of Naihoum's parable, in this sense, was its instancing of how the Sultan's nightmare could be both envisaged and forged in narrative as a hopeful – but equally real – space of consolation for the Libyan opposition ahead of the Sultan's actual demise.

Much of the tension that activates Naihoum's parable is also attributable to the manner in which, 'on the hill of dry sand' beneath the ramparts of the Sultan's nightmare, it manages to conceive of space as a psycho-political dimension – one that, above and beyond its allegorical bearing on the Sultan himself, remains broad and fathomless enough to be able to incubate and simmer in its folds the fragile imaginary of a political change away from a post-colonial despotism. Likewise, as it seeks its own forms of psychic shelter in new information about his father's fate, Hisham Matar's memoir also comes to be configured through spaces that become receptive of political meaning precisely by dint of their erstwhile obscurity or fathomlessness. *The Return* is overshadowed by a searing inner awareness that the father will never be located, or his fate known with total assurance or certainty. The account of the son's own quest derives an element of poignancy from its refusal to give too much contemplation to the latent intimation that the father may have been killed. Libya thus often becomes a space that withholds its meaning from the memoirist, while revealing just about enough in terms of reticent suggestions of the father's potential demise.

In so far as a space is expected to afford a reassurance of the embodiment of the love-object, various of the politically loaded sites in Libya that Matar reconstructs in the course of his inquiry take on the form of spaces devoid of spatial fabric: they seem to be bereft of, or unable to hold forth, an adequate potential for sentimental refuge in the face of the ongoing impossibility of closure. To quote a terse and haunting phrase from one of three letters that Jaballa Matar managed to smuggle out of Abu Salim close to the mid-1990s, some three or four years into his incarceration, 'The world here is empty' (Matar 2016: 10). These words are echoed in mid-memoir by Matar himself, when his request for information about his grandfather Hamed, a member of the Libyan resistance against the Italian coloniser, yields no tangible information either, and he discovers that not even the apposite archive of his grandfather's story exists: 'I was back in that familiar place', Matar writes, 'a place of shadows where the only way to engage with what happened is through the imagination, an activity that serves only to excite the past, multiplying its possibilities, like a house with endless rooms, inescapable and haunted' (2016: 161).

The place of self-narration that Matar speaks from is here constrained by reticence, and by the equivocal responses he is having to confront in his inquiry, but it is also a place that is familiar to him in his own inquiring solitude. The returned exile's relation to the childhood spaces that he hopes will shine a light on to his father's last years comes to be filtered through 'the recognition [that] something is only slightly different from the actual, like revisiting a place you once lived in but one that has changed without you by way of time, process, and orientation', as Nick Houde argues (2015: 22). The baggage that the native space carries at once profiles it as both the cause and the consequence of its mnemonic subject – a vertiginous convergence that comes to inflect him ontologically, such that his writing cannot find solace anywhere but within the 'only slightly different' relation to this 'land in between' afforded by the temporal lapse between the traumatic event and the present (Matar 2016: 161, title page). 'Something alien becomes both you and the place you knew so well', Houde notes (2015: 22). 'The space has become a condition of our own situation, compelling us to share in its alien strangeness. We are held within it as much as we have now become part of it' (Houde 2015: 22). In these terms, the memoir-as-process becomes important for Matar, in so far as it nativises the strangeness itself rather than the space. It is this acquaintedness, this intimacy with the performative dynamics of absence and incertitude that ensue from it, its attunement to and its sobriety within this anarchival void, that affords the memoir form its liminal grammar and its credentials as a site of affective refuge. Within a receding heuristic window of hope, the 'endless rooms' of possibility and the contrasting last sightings of his father that Matar receives, the narrative journey seems to find a degree of solace in the labour of grief – somewhere, that is, on the encrypted inside of the nervous dialectic of subjective affection and its formal quest for knowledge and justice. Matar writes that:

> Disbelief is the right instinct, for how can the dead really be dead? I think this because absence has never seemed empty or passive but rather a busy place, vocal and insistent. As Aristotle writes, 'The theory that the void exists involves the existence of place: for one would define void as place bereft of body.' [. . .] Only time can hope to fill the void. The body of my father is gone, but his place is here and occupied by something that cannot be just called memory. It is alive and current. How could the complexities of being, the mechanics of our anatomy, the intelligence of our biology, and the endless firmament of our interiority – the thoughts and questions and yearnings and hopes and hunger and desire and the thousand and one contradictions that inhabit us at any given moment – ever have an ending that could be marked by a date on a calendar? [. . .] Perhaps memorials and all the sacred and secular rituals of mourning across our human history are but failed gestures. The dead live with us. Grief is not a whodunnit story, or a puzzle to solve, but an active and vibrant enterprise. It is hard, honest work. It can break your back. (2016: 167)

In a context in which neither commemorative memory and its ritualisation of grief nor the labour of requital can create an adequate space of enunciation for either the missing father or the abducted dissident, the memoir form steps in as an ever-expansive *Jetztzeit* (Benjamin 1968: 253–64), the extra-juridical terrain wherein a conscience that has been bilaterally thwarted makes recourse to the 'endless firmament of our interiority' – an affectional recess the nuances of which can, perhaps, best be explored within the protean, sub-jective folds of the self-narrative form.[9] The labour of grief 'is hard, honest work. It can break your back', Matar writes (2016: 167). This is a crucial passage, because in *The Return* the burden of grief is not, *cannot be*, distrib-uted across the schemata of mourning. It must, instead, be subsumed within those of the vicarious. Matar's, it seems to me, is a quest for closure that negotiates its elusiveness by means of reaching out – not towards the elusive horizon, but beyond its facile exhortation – whether tacit or otherwise – to merely 'begin to mourn'. Instead, the memoir imbricates the elusive quest for the father – and its attendant terrors – within the son's own, rich and complex subjectivity. As a product of this relation, the memoir comes to be marked with a vicarious brief: to dynamise the forebear's activity in its ambient and its often taciturn signals, which Matar seeks to interpret from the surviving writings, recordings and testimonies of his father. The memoir seeks, there-fore, to attain a certain augmentation – to echo Paul Ricoeur – of the father's political and interpersonal lives, not least by deriving from his absent physi-cality, from his 'place bereft of body', the necessary mandate to reorganise the forebear's relations with and into the present (Matar 2016: 167).

The memoirist hence becomes both an affective and a lyrically effective surrogate to his father: the memoir lends itself as a unique locus wherein the noumenal tension within the subject between the vicarious mandate and its *being* after-the-event, its articulation of the political bequest, can materialise and function. The gravity of this responsibility transpires even in Matar's ear-lier work. In the novel *Anatomy of a Disappearance* (2012), for example, the teenage boy Nuri observes that 'The shock and anguish inflicted by the sud-den and yet ambiguous loss of my father felt like a weight on my chest. It had never felt heavier' (Matar 2012: 156). In *The Return*, however, the author's own solitude, with its often monologic voicings, strives to take ownership of that place 'occupied by something that cannot be just called memory' (Matar 2016: 167). Matar's own desire to nurture this presence as a non-memorial motivation to afterwardly life is palpable. What the memoirist begins to desire is the spawning of a contingent orbit wherein it becomes possible for the father's unrestorable corporeality to be reindexed as a motor of histori-cal agency, one that can reinstate faith in the political present. Exiled from its original agent, the father's political imagination hence comes to be trans-planted into the memoir as both its live interlocutor *and* the place wherein its past sentience, its ownership of the homeland through an organised dis-sidence, may – to quote Jaballa's repeated exhortation to his son – '*Work and survive, work and survive*' (Matar 2016: 124).

On the cusp of hope and exclusion: the enclave of the exformal[10]

In *The Return*, the ability to perpetuate the 'alive and current' agency of the forebear is, of course, affected by the apparent impossibility of a definite closure to Jaballa Matar's case. '[U]nlike Telemachus', Matar writes,

> I continue, after twenty-five years, to endure my father's 'unknown death and silence'. I envy the finality of funerals. I covet the certainty. How it must be to wrap one's hands around the bones, to choose how to place them, to be able to pat the patch of earth and sing a prayer. (2016: 135)

It is this self-same uncertainty that consigns the filial narrative to a definition of afterwardly life that, to quote Teofilo F. Ruiz, can be described as an 'unfolding, unpredictable and contentious' zone of historical activity (Ruiz 2011: 4). As Marek Tamm has observed, the question of *Nachleben*, or 'afterlife', 'does not refer to an afterlife in the sense of *another* life beyond this one, but should be understood as continued life, the past that becomes actual in the present [. . .]' (Tamm 2015: 9). Tamm's reading of Walter Benjamin's concept here is apt, in that Matar's quest after his father's story requires not the conditions of some post-factual inquiry as much as the space for a certain unravelling or unfolding, such that, as Hans-Georg Gadamer has pointed out, 'the history of the interpretations of an event constitutes a self-unfolding of the event itself' (Gadamer 2004: 300; Tamm 2015: 6). In this sense, *The Return* behaves as a two-pronged affectional harbour, at once allowing for the unfolding of the son's exilic predicament and via that, the perpetuity of the father's presencing-as-event, of its voicing both *in* and *through* the harrowing decoding of the fragments and silences that obscure it. 'I looked into the man's face as he told me this', Matar writes as he describes one particular meeting at a London café with a former Abu Salim prisoner who claimed he had seen Matar's father 'from a distance' (2016: 174). 'I felt the powerful urge not so much to know how Father had appeared to him but literally to possess his eyes, the eyes with which he had seen my father, to pluck them out of the man's skull and insert them into mine' (2016: 174).

The memoirist's yearning for the eyes that had allegedly seen the father is a desire for their surrogate value. At once, it embodies the extent to which self-narrative mediation – the faith, that is, in memoir-as-limit-text and as a final resort of historical relation – is expected to somehow fulfil the absence of a nexus. This is the suffering not only of a son exiled from the reality of his father, but also of an exile mediated by the ongoing damage to the polity his father had fought for and believed in. Hence, the labour of grief as an effort 'to build death' and to master the sensing of it, in Matar's case, becomes, in Michel de Montaigne's phrasing, 'the continuous work of our life' (de Beauvoir 2011: 1). The convulsive force of Matar's desire for this nexus becomes even more tangible as he contemplates his father's first letter from Abu Salim prison in 1993, in which he warns that no one should know about the letter itself except for his family, or else, the father writes, 'I will fall into a bottomless abyss' (Matar 2016: 175). Matar reacts by confessing that

> the description of the abyss as bottomless unnerved me even further. The word 'abyss' was bad enough; why add the adjective? That, for reasons I could not explain then, upset me more than any other detail in the letter. It shook a place in me that remains dislodged. (2016: 176)

Here, a fractured consciousness speaks through a doubly inscribed affectional space: the 'bottomless abyss' his father is threatening to fall into, and the place that was shaken and 'remains dislodged' within the memoirist himself as a result of reading the father's sinister allusion to the bottomless abyss (2016: 175). These two inscriptions forge a sentimental continuum between the imprisoned father's anxiety recorded in the letter, and Matar's own as the latter's mnemonic path unfolds. In disturbing Matar so forcefully, the 'bottomless abyss' also portends a question that underpins the *raison d'être* of the account itself. For, while it seeks access to a certain presencing of loss, Matar's anxiety is both occasioned *and* haunted by the problematic of what Paul Ricoeur identifies as the prefigurative or 'prenarrative quality of experience' itself (Ricoeur 1984: 74; Erll 2011: 153).[11] In Ricoeur's grasp of the literary text, its 'pre-understanding of the world of action, its meaningful structures, its symbolic sources, and its temporal character' are elements that come to be, in the fullness of the mnemonic work, 'connected syntagmatically and moulded into a specific story [. . .] arranged, or employed, in a certain temporal and causal order', as Astrid Erll incisively explains, *pace* Ricoeur (Erll 2011: 153).

This problematic lies right at the kernel of the affectional impasse out of which the memoir speaks: the painful fade-out of a significatory realm – Jaballa Matar's own life – out of which the existence of the quest(ion) itself comes to be replenished. What happens within the memorial task when the 'prenarrative quality of experience' that it seeks to harness fails to be positively constitutable as such, in terms, that is, of 'meaningful structures', of traceable 'symbolic sources' or even, for that matter, of a precise and identifiable framework of time for the mapping of the actual loss (Ricoeur 1984: 74; Erll 2011: 153)? What if, in other words, and beyond the sentimental chasm that has occasioned the memoir, the causal agent of that traumatic loss – the Qaddafi intelligence structure – is *also* itself ultimately only identifiable or construable within the devastating grammar of a 'bottomless abyss'? The bewilderingly nefarious methods used by the Qaddafi regime to contain or quell both internal and external threats and oppositions – real or perceived –

is flagged by various commentators, including the diplomat Chorin himself, who writes that

> Within a decade of taking power [that is, by 1979], Gaddafi had identified a fundamental set of behavioural strategies that served to keep him safely in power. A core strategy was to sow confusion – the idea that for every issue there needed to be multiple competing interests, none of which was absolute. This applied to associates, to relationships with other countries, to ministries, and even to his immediate family – whom he trusted no more than any other constituency not to dominate or attempt to harm his interests. A related successful strategy was to impute suspicion to others by selectively bestowing favors or taking away privileges. (Chorin 2012: 33)

Matar's firm, constant question to Seif al-Islam Qaddafi and his agents – 'what have you done with my father?' – is entrammelled precisely within such a game of shadows, an elusive and labyrinthine sphere that Matar describes in his account of his correspondence with Seif and his collaborators (Matar 2016: 212, 198–219). As he toils to find out whether or not his father was murdered in the infamous – and under-documented – Abu Salim massacre of 29 June 1996, in which over 1,200 political prisoners were extrajudicially executed, Matar therefore confronts an experience that is impossible to refigure 'syntagmatically', as it were, in narrative.

Instead, in attempting to capture this anxious journey through the terrain of deferrals and diversionary tactics laid out by Seif and his agents, *The Return* seeks to open up a field of narrative manoeuvre in between the foreclosed exercise of a factual representation of the originary event, and the soul-destroying world of hide-and-seek he must indulge in order to acquire information about it. Matar's work here resonates with Ricoeur's discussion of the *phantasma*, wherein the literary account seems to be making this ludic and cruel *modus operandi* appear within its own tonal, stylistic and sensory structures, with the perverse and ambiguous underworld the memoirist has had to wade through – its presencing and its 'inscription' – affecting the mood of the memoirist and his inquiring narrative (Ricoeur 2006: 11, 17).[12] In the process, its symptoms of ambivalence, ruse, circumvention and vagueness begin to lend themselves to a contingent ambit of affect, one that becomes politically relevant and even agenda-setting in terms of how self-narrative non-fiction today is beginning to memorially resocialise human rights breaches and broader manifestations of historical violence. Attesting, in this case, to the attempted process of erasure of a political prisoner's history and subjectivity, the memoir begins to remediate this politics of erasure by remapping or rethinking its secretive, arcane presence as what Ricoeur would term the *allou phantasma* within it – that liminal mode of inscription that contains at once 'itself and the representation of something else' (Ricoeur 2006: 17). At one and the same moment, the memoir begins to attest to the organised disappearance of Jaballa, to reinscribe its politics of erasure, and by dint of this act, to repurpose itself as a humane zone of sanctuary within a prevalent climate of indefinite deferral of factual truth.

But how does *The Return* actually wedge such an active zone of relation into the systematic politics of obscurantism? Writing, for instance, of the immediate aftermath of the Abu Salim massacre, in which the prison guards who routinely 'managed a clandestine economy of confiscated and stolen goods [. . .] went later from body to body, quickly unstrapping watches and pulling rings', Matar notes that 'The [prison] cook made a mental note of the number of watches. This is how his testimony, during those years when all news of the massacre was suppressed, gave campaigners and human rights organisations an early indication of the numbers killed that day' (Matar 2016: 175). In another passage, Matar makes reference to the lifting-anchor holes in the precast concrete walls of the Abu Salim prison cells, and how the prisoners discovered that through these,

> if they chipped away at the plaster, they could open a channel to the next cell, one big enough to pass a book through. I know these because Father describes these holes in his letter [. . .] Every time I dared to read Father's prison letters, my mind would search for signs of how he might have changed, been altered or reduced by his incarceration. Regardless of their quality, books passed through these openings, which were concealed by day and opened at night. (Matar 2016: 171)

These narrative 'wedges' through which the precast anchor-holes become a living – if last-ditch – conduit of psychic asylum, whereby the cook's mental note becomes an indispensable index for the survival of what happened at Abu Salim, point the reader to a certain substrate or enclave of apocryphal agency that Matar's account is bringing to the fore, and that can be perhaps described as 'meta-dimensional' (Eaglestone 2014: 15).[13] The meta-dimensional nature of Matar's work, as I see it, emanates from its commitment to a certain narrational organicity, to the task of forging a protean account that is both self-vigilant and capable of monitoring its own evolving sentimental map, of routinely examining the implications of its own situatedness as a doubly exilic subjectivity. 'There was something desperate about having those two impressions, steadfastness and despair, sit side by side', Matar writes as he reflects on the mental image of his father's emotional state in Abu Salim that he is trying to picture (2016: 273). 'I felt an abject confinement, as though I were lost in a tunnel' (2016: 273). The narrative strategy of *The Return* may be read as a meta-dimensional one, therefore, in the way it seeks to elicit and to gauge-to-itself the shifting affectional itinerary upon which the ambivalent subject's return to a fractured polity is predicated.

The choice of the memoir to harness the socialising of one's affectional processes as a language of exilic agency, therefore, the mandate to ponder one's own distressed *état de l'âme* in spatial terms, as a means of prising open within its 'fathomless' folds a liminal enclave of exilic refuge, is, in the last instance, premised on the 'perpetual instability' (Bourriaud 2016: 37) that marks the memoirist's justice-driven quest. The 'tunnel' of the regime's obscurantist tactics, and especially the 'abject confinement' it evinces in Matar (2016: 273), is also reminiscent of that specific site outlined by Bourriaud as the space of the *exformal*, which, like meta-dimensional spatiality itself, may be understood as 'the site where border negotiations unfold between what is rejected and what is admitted, products and waste. [This is] a point of contact [. . .] floating between dissidence and power' (Bourriaud 2016: x). This is surely a spatial coordinate that *The Return* finds itself in repeatedly. But Bourriaud qualifies this further: 'Gestures of expulsion and the waste it entails', he writes, 'constitute an authentically organic link between the aesthetic and the political' (Bourriaud 2016: x).

This 'organic link' between the aesthetic and the political features in the memoir as a salient relation through which the politically fugitive comes to reappropriate a withheld legitimacy through an unusual practice of the aesthetic. Writing from the exformal cusp of hope and exclusion, Matar grasps the potential of rallying an answer to his condition in the form of what Ruiz would term 'the aesthetic response to tragedy' (Ruiz 2011: xiv). Like the books and letters shuttling to and fro across the lifting-anchor holes, Matar's own choice points to a belief that, in Jonathan Flatley's words, 'Affect is the shuttle on which history makes its way into the aesthetic, and it is also what brings one back into the world' (Flatley 2008: 81). *The Return* is a work of memoir that is eminently conscious of the attunement of aesthetic form to psychic devastation and, therefore, of its ability, in such conditions, to '[induce] a state of active lucidity in the observer, which proves inseparable from political action' (Bourriaud 2016: 30). This realm, and Matar's lyrical mastery of it, promise the exilic imaginary a perceptional form of political asylum – one that begins to seek *through* the work of art a metaphysics of political refuge.

'In sharp broken fragments': aleatory readings[14]

In the fifteenth chapter of *The Return*, titled 'Maximilian', Matar writes about the way in which his affinity with art changed in the year he lost his father – and about the ensuing exercise of regular, long, contemplative vigils in front of paintings which he has kept going ever since (Matar 2016: 169). Writing that 'I find certain paintings mysterious', Matar homes in on two specific paintings that he has observed at length – Titian's *The Martyrdom of Saint Lawrence*, housed at the Chiesa di Santa Maria Assunta detta I Gesuiti in Venice, which Matar saw at a Titian exhibition in Rome, and Edouard Manet's *The Execution of Maximilian*, on permanent exhibition at the National Gallery in London. Both paintings are, of course, depictions of executions: the first represents the painful death of a foremost Christian martyr, the second is one of Manet's versions of the death by firing squad of

Maximilian I of Mexico, who took the crown after the French intervention in Mexico at the behest of Louis-Napoleon Bonaparte, Emperor Napoleon III.[15]

> The one [of Manet's paintings] at the National Gallery happens to be the most poignant, not least of all because, after the artist's death, the painting was cut up and sold in fragments. The impressionist artist Edgar Degas purchased the surviving pieces, and it was not until 1992, two years after my father's disappearance, that the National Gallery assembled them on a single canvas. (Matar 2016: 183)

One can immediately sense the appeal that the story of Manet's *The Execution of Maximilian* has to Matar's own imagination – the analogy between the fragmentary history of the painting and the scattered nature of Matar's own information about his father is as thinly veiled as it is implicit. Equally present is the echo of Jaballa Matar's physical absence in his son's observation that 'You cannot see Maximilian [in the painting] – only his hand, gripped tightly by one of his generals' (2016: 183). The more subjective affinity that Matar builds with Manet's painting, however, is that

> Most of all, what sent a shiver through me was the fact that, on the day 1,270 men were executed in the [Abu Salim] prison where my father was held, I chose to switch my vigil [of paintings at the National Gallery], which by then I had been keeping for six years, to Edouard Manet's *The Execution of Maximilian* [. . .] Learning of the fact that my unknowing 25-year-old self was guided, whether by reason or by instinct, to this picture on the same day as the massacre unnerved me and has since changed my relationship to all the works of this French artist [. . .] (2016: 183)

The fact itself that the world (and of course Matar) was unaware of what had happened at Abu Salim on 29 June 1996 as the events unfolded, the circumstances of which remained for a long time a secret closely guarded by the Qaddafi regime, lends Matar's disclosure of his own experience on that day a particular power and poignancy (2016: 247).[16] Here, the regime's tactic of convolution and silence is, by means of Matar's hindsight on that uncanny *déja vu*, being absorbed, and its impact distributed, through a disclosure reminiscent of the historical dynamic of 'aleatory materialism' that Louis Althusser theorises in *Philosophy of the Encounter* (Althusser 2006: 193). There, Althusser argues that

> Every encounter is aleatory, not only in its origins (nothing ever guarantees an encounter), but also in its effects. In other words, every encounter might not have taken place, although it did take place; but its possible non-existence sheds light on its aleatory being. And every encounter is aleatory in its effects, in that nothing in the elements of the encounter prefigures, before the actual encounter, the contours and determinations of the being that will emerge from it. (2006: 193)[17]

The improbable and coincidental nature of Manet's painting's 'encounter' with the Abu Salim horror in Matar's consciousness comes to be spliced with the intimation of the contingency he was unwittingly experiencing in real time with the executions. In its raw juxtaposition of an extreme and murderous violence with an unforeseeable aesthetic chance, this becomes perhaps one of the memoir's most powerful, albeit sober, communiqués to the Qaddafi regime: that no prevalent political or social formation or order is construable either as some precast *idée fixe* or a permanent arrangement, and that any such formation will always remain both interrogable *and* subvertible. It would always stay, that is, subject to the Xenos's missive to Theaetetus in Plato's *Sophist* quoted earlier: 'that non-being somehow is, and that being, in its turn, in a certain way is not' (Derrida and Dufourmantelle 2000: 7).

Matar's liminality, his meta-dimension of narrative, becomes in these terms an optimal host to the aleatory encounter – the painting's subjective grammar for Matar comes to be inscribed by the violent 'shuttling' of a discursively interred past event into the real-time materialism of the present, and its inquiring consciousness. As Bourriaud would put it, 'Art's historical function – and therefore its political function, too – has substance only on a stage open to purely contingent human history; at the very least, it requires the productive aporia of chance and necessity meeting in opposition' (Bourriaud 2016: 34). Matar's own contemplation of Manet's painting, itself a painful trope of the birth of a political modernity, attests to the strength of the idea that, in the last instance, 'History is aleatory' precisely because 'we discover meaning in it as it unfolds, or after the fact' (Bourriaud 2016: 40). In Matar's case, the bilateral bearing of the execution motif lends, perhaps, a fresh insight into the impact of an aesthetic contemporaneity on the reception of traumatic history. And this is because *The Return* projects the aleatory as a hospitable condition for a 'meaningful political action', one that accedes to the contingency of the violence by alternately drawing from and reading back into the painting '[t]he problem posed by the entanglement of memory and imagination' (Ricoeur 2006: 7). More importantly, perhaps, *The Return* situates its own value as a life narrative within the eminently human folds of that very 'entanglement'.

Finally, as he contemplates that other execution, Titian's *The Martyrdom of Saint Lawrence*, Matar recounts one of those rarefied moments when he comes close to an almost eidetic (to extend Ricoeur) experience of his father's last moments. 'And then, without noticing that I had surrendered to them', Matar writes, 'I was surrounded by sounds and images, coming at me in sharp broken fragments, of Father's final moments: what they might have told him, what his last words might have been, the past and how it seemed to him then' (Matar 2016: 170). This passage recalls Flatley's incisive discussion of Theodor Adorno's 'aesthetic shudder' in the latter's *Aesthetic Theory*, the sensation experienced at that precise point of return, of transit, when the beholder is 'exiting' the world of the painting and 'returning', as it were, into their own subjectivity (Flatley 2008: 82).[18] Flatley observes that

According to Adorno, such a shudder is generated not by the emotion evoked itself but by the transition from this emotion – experienced in [the painting . . .] – back to my subjectivity as I experience it in everyday life. At the moment of this return from the work, one has the sensation that one has just been temporarily dislocated from one's subjectivity. This is because one has, for a moment, had an affect in a space not defined by one's subjectivity, and then one is returned to that subjectivity [. . .] (Flatley 2008: 82)

Likewise, this extra-subjective 'shudder' that Matar experiences as he gazes at Titian's work, and returns to narrate it in the memoir, speaks to the effectiveness of the contemplated work of art as both a deputised and a deputising dimension: at once conducive to the ambience of the father's emotive sensorium during the ordeal itself, as well as to Matar's own vicarious enduring of it through the visual image. This, then, becomes a very particular 'aesthetic response to tragedy' (Ruiz 2011: 4). For that very same shudder of 'disjuncture' (Flatley 2008: 82) that displaces the memoirist from an intense *eidos* within the painting back into his investigative task is also, in a sense, registered as that shudder of temporal disjunction that permits Matar to channel the intimate sounding of his father almost symbiotically *in his own life*. '[W]e have nothing better than memory', Ricoeur has written, 'to guarantee that something has taken place before we call to mind a memory of it' (Ricoeur 2006: 8). In this sense, Titian's and Manet's aleatory rendezvous with the horror at Abu Salim has provided Matar with a productive memorial refuge, one that, in being retroactively endured, has worked as a catalyst to a trans-generational conscience that can now keep giving. Under these terms, it would perhaps be Matar's 'shudder of return' to the father's voice, to that 'soft howl' his son could hear 'as though from within me', that has the strongest claim to the title of this memoir (Matar 2016: 142).

 In the early pages of this essay, I flagged the moment in Khoury's *magnum opus* when the contrast – at once delicate and fraught – between the refugee and the fugitive is invoked. It seems to me that to speak of the 'fugitive' outside the positivist semantic of an 'escape from justice' constitutes an important transgression – one that would have fugitive subjectivity becoming deeply inscribed, even overdetermined, by an *absence* of justice. This thought, of running from an injustice of epistemic proportions, lies, I believe, at the kernel of Khoury's deployment of the term. Only a few months ago, credible reports emerged from just outside Libya's Tripoli involving open slave trading, with accompanying allegations of hundreds of migrants being bought and sold on the slave market (Al-Jazeera 2017). It is only one of those events of violence that will always catch writing ahead of its intervention. In this sense, at least, to summon the 'fugitive' in writing is to admit to the latter's limited manoeuvre in determining the terms of its beholdenness to the circumstances that call it into being. If there is a crucial wisdom, then, to be drawn from Matar's memoir, it is that writing may aspire to become a writing of refuge only in so far as it takes upon itself the onus not merely of *becoming*, but of ongoingly rendering itself susceptible to the effects and consequences of a justice withheld.

Notes

1. For a detailed historiography and analyses of the trajectory of the pre- to post-colonial geopolitical dynamics that have characterised the history of Libya, see Ahmida (2005; 2011), as well as Vandewalle (2012).
2. The post-2011 dynamic in Libya has been very different, not least because of Qaddafi's long reign, from that in neighbouring countries such as Tunisia – a country that has repeatedly sought political refuge, both under Habib Bourguiba and again today under Beji Essebsi, in a deep-seated political memory of its nineteenth-century social reformist and anti-colonial efforts, among other aspects.
3. The phrase 'vicarious agency' was deployed (in a different scholarly context than the present one) in relation to the question of 'authorship processing' and associated rubrics in psychology studies by Wegner, Sparrow and Winerman (2004).
4. For detailed expert analyses of questions of judicial process, transitional justice, politics, citizenship and migration in and concerning Libya, see Judge Marwan Tashani's contributions at *The Legal Agenda* (http://legal-agenda.com/en/makalat.php?katib=260; accessed 20 May 2019). Matar refers to Judge Tashani in *The Return* itself.
5. I have chosen to use here the version that Jacques Derrida gives of the Xenos's answer to Theaetetus, which speaks to me strongly in terms of the precision it lends to the reading of my primary text in this chapter. I find Christopher Rowe's translation, which I reproduce here, also to be pertinent: 'In order to defend ourselves we're going to need to cross-examine what our father Parmenides says and force the claim through both that what is not in a certain way *is*, and conversely that what is also in a way is not' (Plato 2015: 136 [d5]).
6. For a broader context, see also Chorin (2015).
7. See, for more information, Human Rights Watch (2012).
8. A cursory glance at the write-ups and cartoons published in newspapers and online international media portals following Qaddafi's demise would be enough to reinforce this notion. See, for instance, Gaynor and Zargoun (2011).
9. For a broader sense of Walter Benjamin's conception of the *Jetztzeit*, see his 'Theses on the Philosophy of History' (1968: 253–64).
10. 'Exformal' is Nicolas Bourriaud's term (Bourriaud 2016).
11. Astrid Erll provides an intriguing discussion of the Ricoeurian prefigurative and the context of 'Literature as a Medium of Cultural Memory' (2011: 144–61).
12. This dynamic is deeply reminiscent of one of Ricoeur's foundational arguments in *Time and Narrative*, namely that 'narrative [. . .] is meaningful to the extent that it portrays the features of temporal experience' (1984: 3). However, in the deeply sensitive rendering of political experience in Matar's memoir, this presencing is registered not so much as a Ricoeurian *tekhnē eikastikē* (or the 'making of likenesses'), as it is as a melancholy tone, a rarefied, slightly detached sense of Ricoeur's *phantasma*, or a strategic 'making of appearances' (Ricoeur 2006: 11).

In Matar's case, the *allou phantasma* is at once intended to inscribe, invoke and render alive to its reader the mood (*Stimmung*) of having to make contact with a dangerous, obscure and labyrinthine world. In her essay 'The Disappointed of the Earth', Caroline Rooney raises the notion of 'redemptive or compensatory counter-identifications' through which 'all those who would transform their chronic disappointments into cases of "specialness", "apartness" or "appointment" look less like special cases' (2009: 172). Matar's own Ricoeurian bringing-to-life of his experience of obscure political strategy as a tonal effect on the memoir is also readable as a 'redemptive' form of counter-identification in relation to it – one that, while not in this case necessarily directed towards achieving a form of 'appointment' or 'apartness' (Rooney 2009: 172), is placed in the service of a heightened visualisation of the ordeal – ultimately helping fulfil the memoirist's vicarious responsibility towards, and voicing of, his father's fate.

13. I first encountered the term 'meta-dimensional', which is used by the Holocaust historian Otto Dov Kulka in his *Landscapes of the Metropolis of Death*, in Robert Eaglestone's article 'Knowledge, "Afterwardsness" and the Future of Trauma Theory' (2014: 15).

14. The quote in this sub-heading refers to a phrase from Matar (2016: 170).

15. For more information on Maximilian I of Mexico and the Second French Empire, see McAllen (2014) as well as Ibsen (2010).

16. Matar notes that 'The first signs that something horrible had occurred inside the walls of Abu Salim did not surface until several years after the massacre' (2016: 247).

17. In *The Exform*, Bourriaud makes a profound revisitation of Althusser's aleatory materialism with an incisive commentary on its affinity with contemporary art and beyond (Bourriaud 2016: 34–45).

18. Flatley argues, in relation to this, that 'The affect that one has in the space of the artwork (which hovers alongside the cognitive experience as what Adorno calls a "Trans-aesthetic subject") links one back to the world like a rubber band or the bungee on a bungee jumper, pulling one back from the artwork into the world, but pulling one back through a strange parabola which has altered one's view of the world and unsettled one's relation to it' (Flatley 2008: 82).

Bibliography

Aboueldahab, Noha (2017), 'Why was Saif al-Islam Gaddafi released from prison?', *Aljazeera Inside Story*, 11 June, http://www.aljazeera.com/programmes/inside-story/2017/06/saif-al-islam-gaddafi-released-prison-170611213032233.html (accessed 30 July 2017).

Ahmida, Ali Abdullatif (2005), *Forgotten Voices: Power and Agency in Colonial and Postcolonial Libya* (New York: Routledge).

Ahmida, Ali Abdullatif (2011 [2009]), *The Making of Modern Libya – State Formation, Colonisation and Resistance* (Albany: SUNY Press).

Al-Jazeera (2017), 'Migrants for sale: slave trade in Libya', 26 November, http://www.aljazeera.com/programmes/countingthecost/2017/11/migrants-sale-slave-trade-libya-171126063748575.html (accessed 10 December 2017).

Althusser, Louis (2006 [1993]), *Philosophy of the Encounter – Later Writings 1978–87* (London: Verso).

Amnesty International (2010), '"Libya of Tomorrow": what hope for human rights', 23 June, Index: MDE 19/007/2010, https://www.amnesty.org/en/documents/MDE19/007/2010/en/ (accessed 14 July 2017).

Amnesty International (2014), 'Libya: end long wait for justice for victims of Abu Salim prison killing', public statement, 26 June, Index: MDE 19/006/2014, https://www.amnesty.org/en/documents/mde19/006/2014/en/ (accessed 14 July 2017).

Benjamin, Walter (1968 [1955]), *Illuminations* (New York: Schocken Books).

Bourriaud, Nicolas (2016), *The Exform*, trans. Erik Butler (London: Verso).

Chorin, Ethan (2012), *Exit Gaddafi – The Hidden History of the Libyan Revolution* (London: Saqi Books).

Chorin, Ethan (2015 [2008]), *Translating Libya – In Search of the Libyan Short Story* (London: Darf Publishers).

de Beauvoir, Simone (2011 [1948]), *The Ethics of Ambiguity* (New York: Philosophical Library/Open Road).

Derrida, Jacques, and Anne Dufourmantelle (2000), *Of Hospitality: Anne Dufourmantelle Invites Jacques Derrida to Respond*, trans. R. Bowlby (Stanford: Stanford University Press).

Eaglestone, Robert (2014), 'Knowledge, "afterwardsness" and the future of trauma theory', in Gert Buelens, Sam Durrant and Robert Eaglestone (eds), *The Future of Trauma Theory – Contemporary Literary and Cultural Criticism* (London: Routledge).

Erll, Astrid (2011), *Memory in Culture* (Basingstoke: Palgrave Macmillan).

Flatley, Jonathan (2008), *Affective Mapping – Melancholia and the Politics of Modernism* (Cambridge, MA: Harvard University Press).

Gadamer, Hans-Georg (2004 [1960]), *Truth and Method*, trans. Joel Weinsheimer and Donald G. Marshall (London: Continuum).

Gaynor, Tim, and Taha Zargoun (2011), 'Gaddafi caught like "rat" in a drain, humiliated and shot', *Reuters World News*, http://www.reuters.com/article/us-libya-gaddafi-finalhours-idUSTRE79K43S20111021 (accessed 31 July 2017).

Houde, Nick (2015), *Enclosure – Adventures in Acquiescence* (Dresden and New York: Atropos Press).

Human Rights Watch (2010), 'Libya: reveal fate of "disappeared" – use Arab League summit to resolve longstanding cases', 26 March, https://www.hrw.org/news/2010/03/26/libya-reveal-fate-disappeared (accessed 30 July 2017).

Human Rights Watch (2012), 'Death of a dictator – bloody vengeance in Sirte', 16 October, https://www.hrw.org/report/2012/10/16/death-dictator/bloody-vengeance-sirte (accessed 30 July 2017).

Ibsen, Kristine (2010), *Maximilian, Mexico and the Invention of Empire* (Nashville: Vanderbilt University Press).

Khoury, Elias (2007), *Gate of the Sun*, trans. Humphrey Davies (New York: Picador).

McAllen, M. M. (2014), *Maximilian and Carlota – Europe's Last Empire in Mexico* (San Antonio: Trinity University Press).

Matar, Hisham (2012), *Anatomy of a Disappearance* (New York: Dial Press).

Matar, Hisham (2016), *The Return – Fathers, Sons and the Land in Between* (London: Viking Penguin).

Naihoum, Sadiq (2006), 'The sultan's flotilla', trans. Ethan Chorin, in *Words without Borders – The Online Magazine for International Literature*, http://www.wordswithoutborders.org/article/the-sultans-flotilla (accessed 31 July 2017).

Plato (2015), *Theaetetus and Sophist*, ed. Christopher Rowe (Cambridge: Cambridge University Press).

Ricoeur, Paul (1984), *Time and Narrative, Volume 1* (Chicago: University of Chicago Press).

Ricoeur, Paul (2006 [2004]), *Memory, History, Forgetting*, trans. Kathleen Blamey and David Pellauer (Chicago: University of Chicago Press).

Ritsos, Yannis (1995), 'Back then', in *Late into the Night – The Last Poems of Yannis Ritsos*, trans. Martin McKinsey (Oberlin: Oberlin College Press).

R.M. (2017), 'Will the new peace deal end the conflict in Libya?', *The Economist*, 31 July, http://www.economist.com/blogs/economist-explains/2017/08/economist-explains (accessed 31 July 2017).

Rooney, Caroline (2009), 'The disappointed of the earth', *Psychoanalysis and History*, 11.2, special issue, 'Psychoanalysis, Fascism and Fundamentalism', ed. Julia Borossa and Ivan Ward, 159–74.

Ruiz, Teofilo F. (2011), *The Terror of History – On the Uncertainties of Life in Western Civilization* (Princeton: Princeton University Press).

Stephen, Chris (2017), 'Gaddafi son Saif al-Islam freed by Libyan militia', *The Guardian*, 11 June, https://www.theguardian.com/world/2017/jun/11/gaddafi-son-saif-al-islam-freed-by-libyan-militia (accessed 30 July 2017).

Stephen, Chris, and Patrick Wintour (2017), 'Libyan rival leaders agree to ceasefire after Macron-hosted talks', *The Guardian*, 25 July, https://www.theguardian.com/world/2017/jul/25/france-raises-hopes-of-deal-between-libyan-rival-factions (accessed 30 July 2017).

Tamm, Marek (2015), 'Introduction: afterlife of events: perspectives on mnemohistory', in Marek Tamm (ed.), *Afterlife of Events – Perspectives on Mnemohistory* (Basingstoke: Palgrave Macmillan).

Vandewalle, Dirk J. (2012 [2006]), *A History of Modern Libya* (New York: Cambridge University Press).

Wegner, Daniel M., Betsy Sparrow and Lea Winerman (2004), 'Vicarious agency: experiencing control over the movements of others', *Journal of Personality and Social Psychology*, 86.6: 838–48.

Chapter 13

'A man carries his door': Affective Displacement and Refugee Poetry

Douglas Robinson

It goes without saying that the refugee experience is severely traumatising. Not only do all the studies affirm it; common sense affirms it. It may, therefore, seem purely academic, in the worst possible sense of that word, to ask *why* it is traumatising; but I want to suggest that there is a payoff to that kind of questioning in enhanced empathy – especially if I am right that the reason is grounded in our ability to construct a coherent, meaningful and affectively *safe* world. A secondary payoff, I submit, is that answers to the *why* question may also help explain the importance of story, of words and images, of the imagination, in coping with refugee trauma.

In *Displacement and the Somatics of Postcolonial Culture* I raised the *why* question in the context of 'the dysregulatory and traumatizing effects of scattering either familiar *people* (the regulatory group) or familiar *places and things*', noting that there is a signal oddness to 'the parallel between people (who can feel) and places and things (which cannot)' (Robinson 2013: 36). Obviously we do grow attached to places and things as well as people, not necessarily in the same way, or with the same intensity, but it did and does seem to me that the loss of familiar people, places and things may be *equally* traumatising. I explained that possibility in *Displacement* with my notion of the somatic exchange:

> Since somatic response is a function of the mammalian nervous system, the somatic exchange is primarily a circulation of regulatory body language and body states through human groups – though it is also possible for humans to enter into a somatic exchange with other mammals, and people often do with their pets. It is also possible, however, for humans to exosomatize (put somatic roots down into) objects and spaces by circulating regulatory somatic responses to them through the human group: the way an object is touched or held or looked at, the way a space is walked through or paused in, the postural and gestural and other kinesic orientations to a thing or a place that a group circulates in the sense of picking them up from others mimetically and modeling them in turn for others' mimetic appropriation, all make it seem to

the group as if somatic response (the 'exosoma') were actually *growing out* of the objects and spaces in question. In the process, sense impressions – sights, sounds, smells, feels, tastes – are somatized as well, indeed often fetishized as the media through which exosomatic response is channeled between humans and objects and spaces. (Robinson 2013: 36–7)

Now, that model was speculative when I generated it in around 2009, but it seemed quite plausible to me then and continues to seem plausible to me now. Recently, however, I read Hirstein and Ramachandran's (1997: 442) account of the neurological disorder known as reduplicative paramnesia as the 'parent category' to which the Capgras delusion or Capgras syndrome (for which see also Ramachandran and Blakeslee 1998: ch. 8) belongs. While Capgras presents as the sufferer's delusional belief that a *person* has been killed or kidnapped or otherwise removed and replaced by an exact double, reduplicative paramnesia presents as the belief that an *object or location* has been removed and replaced with an exquisitely constructed fake. First diagnosed and named by Arnold Pick in 1903, reduplicative paramnesia offers what I take to be a more precise neuroscientific account of the affective 'making real' of places and things that I earlier dubbed exosomatisation, and thus a possible neural etiology of the traumatic depletion of 'reality'.

Brain scientists have determined that the recognition of familiar faces and places involves the interaction of two neural pathways: the analysis of visual features in the inferior temporal (IT) lobe and fusiform face area (FFA), and emotional response in the amygdala. Neuronormals use both: the FFA, for example, analyses appearances (not just faces but familiar objects, such as cars and houses) based on lines, contours and so on, and the amygdala sorts the results into greater and lesser degrees of familiarity, based on the presence or absence and relative intensity of an emotional 'glow' signalling the 'acceptance as familiar' of a person or place they/we care about. Lesions in the FFA cause 'face-blindness' (prosopagnosia): sufferers claim not to recognise the faces of friends and loved ones, but electrodermal activity tests indicate a somatic response to them. They recognise loved ones emotionally, but because they don't recognise them analytically, consciously, they are not aware of recognising them, and so claim not to.

Reduplicative paramnesia and the Capgras delusion are the opposite of face-blindness: they are caused by damage to the circuits that connect the IT/FFA to the amygdala. Capgras sufferers, for example, have fully functional FFA capabilities. They can analyse visual features perfectly, and recognise that the person sitting across from them at the dinner table 'is' their partner, or that the face in the mirror 'is' the self; but they feel no emotional 'glow' signalling familiarity, and so confabulate otherness. To them it is uncanny that that person can look *exactly* like a loved one but not *be* the loved one – which is to say, not be the *real* loved one. Or, in reduplicative paramnesia, the old familiar place looks exactly the same as before, but it is not (felt as) the same: it has been replaced, or moved to a different location, or doubled. A lesion in the relevant neural circuit creates a sense that reality has been sucked out of the 'recognised' face or place. As a result, the person or place is recognised but not 'real'. The 'simulation' theory – that the loved one (or the self, or a pet, or a whole house, or a whole neighbourhood) has been kidnapped or killed or destroyed and replaced with a double – is the mind's desperate confabulatory attempt to explain the discrepancy.

The upshot of this research is that the feeling of reality is generated by somatic response, measurable by an electrodermal activity (polygraph) test. As cognitive neuroscientists present this theory, the power to make things feel real tends to be localised in individual brains; but I suspect that the generation of that feeling in the amygdala of individual brains is at least partly social. I suspect, or perhaps I should say I hypothesise, that the 'exosomatisation' of faces, objects and places involves the *group circulation* of somatic responses to those things, including 'the postural and gestural and other kinesic orientations to a thing or a place', the collective process of 'picking them up from others mimetically and modeling them in turn for others' mimetic appropriation' (Robinson 2013: 36–7). This is, obviously, merely a hypothesis, based not only on an intuition about how we typically familiarise ourselves with things, but on increasing complaints from social neuroscientists over the last decade or two that hardcore neuroscientific determinists are still far too focused on individual brains (see, for example, Gazzaniga 2011: 117–42), too little interested in brain/mind 'emergence' as a social phenomenon. Confirmation of that hypothesis would lend added explanatory power to the devastating effects of the scattering of groups in the refugee experience: not only is the 'home' or the 'neighbourhood' destroyed or lost, but so is the community that made the house feel like a home and the streets and houses feel like a neighbourhood. It takes a long time to develop a 'replacement' community that feels enough like one's own to have the power to generate a 'home' and a 'neighbourhood' with a shared sense of reality. Unlike the sufferer from a misidentification syndrome, the refugee's brain is still functioning normally, but both the external environment to which that functioning was existentially tethered and the community that used to tether it there have been swept away, leaving no affective basis for new reality-construction. The old familiar reality has been destroyed or left behind, leaving the affective glow displaced – still looking for something to attach itself to, something to feel as real, some group of like-minded people to share its reality with, but finding nothing that it has that feeling for, and so feeling blasted instead. This is the affective displacement.

What we call 'home' is not just a physical shelter against the weather: it is an affective shelter against the big world that doesn't know us, doesn't care about us, has no inclination to cherish or protect us. 'Home' is the *safe* affective world that we and our community have created around us. (Even when it is a place that we were born into, and have lived in as long as we have been alive, we have nevertheless created it, and kept creating it, by living in it, by experiencing its reality affectively, and especially by sharing it with our friends and family.)[1]

One might schematise the affective trajectories of displacement for the refugee experience in terms of two vectors: from home to the road, and from the road to the destination, whether that be a camp or a relocation site in a new town or city. That second vector might, of course, be thought of as two separate vectors – from the road to the camp and from the camp to the relocation site – but let's keep things simple. The overall trajectory might also be thought of as from the old home through the unsettled middle to the new home, or from the idealised but lost past through the disorienting present to a frightening future. The affective displacements in those vectors would include at least the pain of traumatic loss, paralysing existential dread in an affectively depleted present, fear and anxiety for the future, agitation at not knowing the rules of a strange new cultural situation, frustration and panic in the face of expectations that seem overwhelming, and of course continuing grief at traumatic loss.

Let us explore a small imaginative sample of the combinatorial possibilities of such affective displacements in three refugee poems: by Arseny Tarkovsky (1907–89), in 'Беженец' (*Bezhenets*, 'Refugee', 1941); by Richard Hoffman (b. 1949), in 'Refugee' (2005); and by Li-Young Lee (b. 1957), in 'The City in Which I Love You' (2008). The three poems explore three different affective trajectories: the feeling of having been cast adrift into a hostile or indifferent world (Tarkovsky); the desperate clinging to the past and projection of a restored future as a replacement for an intolerable present (Hoffman); and the affective turbulence of adapting to the new host locale while still feeling a deep ache at the loss of old affiliations (Lee).

From home to the road: Arseny Tarkovsky, 'Беженец'/'Refugee'

Arseny Tarkovsky, who outlived his famous son Andrey Tarkovsky (1932–86, director of *Andrey Rublev* [1966] and *Solaris* [1972]) by three years, is considered one of the greatest twentieth-century Russian poets. He wrote the sonnet 'Беженец' or 'Refugee' while himself a refugee during the evacuation of Moscow, under threat of Nazi invasion and occupation.

The evacuation began in the summer of 1941, when Tarkovsky was 34; in August he escorted his first wife and their children (including Andrey, the future film-maker, then nine) out of Moscow to Yur'yevets in Ivanovo Industrial Oblast, and around the same time his second wife and her daughter set out for Chistopol' in the Tatar ASSR (now the Republic of Tatarstan), on the Kama River. Chistopol' was where members of the Union of Soviet Writers and their families were mostly relocated, including Boris Pasternak, Leonid Leonov and many others. Tarkovsky and his elderly mother followed on 16 October, the official date of the evacuation of Moscow – though in the end only about half of Moscow's four million inhabitants left the city. (Stalin stayed, but had Lenin's corpse shipped to safety in Chumen, in Siberia.) It was a few weeks later, on 13 November 1941 in Chistopol',[2] that Tarkovsky wrote 'Refugee': an actual refugee, but imagining his refugee status in intensified, and intensely individualised, form, as a lone traveller through the snow, with no food and no way to keep warm. The Kama River, on whose banks he and his family were now settled, cared for (at least in theory) by the Soviet state – preparations for the arrival of evacuees were notoriously bad – becomes a dark and almost malevolent force in the poem, coursing by in the blackness of night, part of the cold and indifferent natural environment that Tarkovsky personifies as a mother (Mother Earth, perhaps – but is it entirely wrong to hear echoes of Mother Russia as well?)

Here is Tarkovsky, along with my translation, maintaining Tarkovsky's classical sonnet form:

Не пожалела на дорогу соли,
Так насолила, что свела с ума.
Горишь, святая камская зима,
А я живу один, как ветер в поле.

Скупишься, мать, дала бы хлеба, что ли,
Полны ядреным снегом закрома,
Бери да ешь. Тяжка моя сума;
Полпуда горя и ломоть недоли.

Я ноги отморожу на ветру,
Я беженец, я никому не нужен,
Тебе-то все равно, а я умру.

Что делать мне среди твоих жемчужин
И кованного стужей серебра
На черной Каме, ночью, без костра?

'I'll send along some salt for the road', you said,
Then pelted me with it till outs were ins.
You burn, you blessed Kama winter wince,
But me, I live alone, like wind across a stead.

You couldn't, Mother, spare your son some bread?
Heaped high with sturdy snow are all your bins:
Eat that. My bag is weighted down with pins:
A half a pood of pain, a slab of dread.

The winter wind is freezing off my feet:
A refugee, I'm needed by nobody.
It's all the same to you if I deplete.

Beside the Kama's current, black and muddy,
What good to me are pearls, or all your cold-
Wrought silver, nights, without a fire's glow?

One line whose images I was unable to rescue from the formalist demands of the rhyme scheme was the second in the first stanza: 'Так насолила, что свела с ума' (*Tak nasolila, chto svela s uma*) is literally 'So (much) you salted (me) that you brought (me) away from reason', or, more loosely, 'You salted me till I went crazy.' What that literal translation misses is that 'насолить' means both 'to salt' and 'to annoy'; I tried to capture some of the annoyance in 'pelted me with it', which also suggests the sensation of sleet in a strong wind. The literal translation does suggest the difference between 'свести с ума' (*svesti s uma*) and 'drive someone crazy', though: while both are idioms indicating motion, the English phrase means driving someone *towards a bad thing* (into insanity, a kind of cognitive refugeeism), while the Russian phrase means driving someone *away from a good thing* (away from reason, sanity, a kind of cognitive home).

And this is the defining imagistic movement throughout Tarkovsky's poem: away from home. One reading of the poem's reigning conceit is that the son's mother has sent him out on a journey, with food – but not enough food to live on, and the wrong kind of food, salt but no bread. The mother is rich, loaded with pearls and silver, but those riches do the son no good, because she was generous only with her salt, and with pain and dread, not with anything he could use for nourishment or shelter.

The affective world evoked by the poem is one of resentment, the resentment of a victim who feels mistreated. 'Не пожалела'/'didn't begrudge (me)' (which again I've had to fade out of view in order to reproduce Tarkovsky's sonnet form) in the first line of the poem is bitter irony: the implication is that the mother should by rights (the son feels) have loved him enough to give him everything he needs, and did not; not only did she not *pity* him (жалела, *zhalela*), which would have been but a poor imitation of love, but the Russian negation of жалеть (*zhalet'*, 'to pity') is не жалеть (*ne zhalet'*, 'not to begrudge'): the only way this cruel or indifferent mother is going to give the son anything at all is grudgingly, and the only thing she *doesn't* begrudge him is salt, which is a metaphor for inedible snow. He should have bread in his bag, but his mother 'скупится' (*skupitsya*, 'stints, skimps, is cheap'), with the result that his bag is heavy with 'горя' (*gore*, 'woe') and 'недоля' (*nedolya*, 'calamity'). (A 'pood' is 40 pounds.)

Another reading would be that, since his bag is a сума (*suma*), a raggedy beggar's bag, which the beggar holds out to the poor peasants on his road for them to put bread in, the 'mother' in the vehicle of the conceit is not the speaker's biological mother but any peasant woman on whose door he knocks, begging. There is a saying in Russia: от тюрьмы и от сумы не зарекайся (*ot tyur'my i ot sumy ne zarekaysya*): 'never say never to jail or the beggar's bag', with the implication that things may go badly for you some day. Given the frequency and intensity with which the Russian people have suffered over the centuries, not only do they prepare themselves for it mentally, but they have historically had a great deal of respect for those who are suffering. The Orthodox religion sanctifies sufferers – hence perhaps the reference to sanctification in святая камская зима (*svyataya kamskaya zima*, 'holy Kama winter') – and beggars have traditionally been regarded as (potential) saints, to whom one gives bread even if one is slowly starving oneself. There is also a Russian mythology of Mother Earth as *Damp* Mother Earth – Мать сыра земля (*Mat' cyra zemlya*) – the wet earth to which we all go when we die.

The interesting fact, however, is that not one of the possible mothers in the poem – either the explicitly named one, winter, or the four conjectural implicit ones, the speaker's biological mother back home, the peasant woman from whom he begs bread, Mother Earth or Mother Russia – gives him bread. All the Orthodox myths of sanctification are breaking down. Nothing is working as it should. And the speaker resents that.

But why resentment? Where does that affective charge come from, in responding to the refugee experience? The affects normally (stereotypically?) associated with the home-to-the-road vector, as I noted above, are desolation and despair, a deep sense of grief, pain and disorientation at the loss of a safe reality. Tarkovsky's speaker mentions those affects in Полпуда горя и ломоть недоли/*Polpuda gorya i lomot' nedoli*/'A half a pood of pain, a slab of dread' – but he blames that on Mum. She *put* those things in his bag, along with the salt that she didn't begrudge him. What is going on there?

'Я беженец', he says, 'я никому не нужен': 'I'm a refugee, I'm needed by nobody.' In the reading of the conceit in which the mother sent the son out on to the road without proper nourishment, this rings with whiny, self-pitying affect; on the explicit surface of the conceit, where the mother is Mother Winter (мать зима, *mat' zima* – though that is not a concept in Russian), or more generally Mother Earth (мать земля, *mat' zemlya*), it is easier to feel a deep existential desolation in that line, the despair of simple factuality. Since Tarkovsky wrote the poem in his relocation quarters, with his family and colleagues around him, we must in part imagine him *projecting* that desolation on to refugees more forsaken and isolated than him. But could it also be that his ability to project that desolation on to others, and to channel it outward into resentment, comes from some affective place in himself, some deep inner hurt that cannot be assuaged by family, friends and position?

I am thinking especially of his traumatic experience exactly two decades before, in 1921, at the young age of 14; shortly after the Red forces had defeated the Whites in Ukraine (where he lived), Arseny and his friends published an anti-Lenin poem in the newspaper. It was an acrostic: the first letters of its lines painted an unflattering picture of Lenin's leadership. The boys were arrested and sentenced to death. Arseny alone among the boys escaped that fate, somehow managing to jump off the train; he spent the next few years on the run, a fugitive, a refugee of sorts, working odd jobs – until in 1924 he was able to move to Moscow, where he lived with his father's sister and attended the Literary Institute. Eventually he became a respected translator of verse from the Caucasus, on the basis of which he was admitted into the powerful Union of Soviet Writers, and later evacuated to Chistopol'; his career as an original poet began with poems like the one cited and translated here, written in the 1940s and published in the 1950s.

The backdrop to his traumatic death sentence and fugitive status was that by the time he went on the lam, civil war had devastated the Russias. Infrastructure in much of the territory was destroyed: roads, bridges, factories bombed; mines flooded; raw materials pilfered; cattle and other food sources mercilessly pillaged. Industrial production was down to one-fifth of its prewar levels; food production down to one-twentieth. In 1921–22, due not only to the ravages of civil war but famine in the Volga and Ural regions, exacerbated by a severe drought, an estimated six million died of starvation. Three million died of typhus in 1920 alone. Genocidal death strikes killed many more. Pogroms against Jews were rampant. It is estimated that by 1922 there were seven million street children in the Russias. One of them was Arseny Tarkovsky.

The civil war was, of course, the brutal aftermath of the Revolution, as competing forces vied for control of Russia's political future: the Reds (Bolsheviks), the Whites (a coalition of anti-Bolshevik monarchists, capitalists and socialists, supported by the Allied forces and pro-German interests) and the Greens (armed peasant groups fighting to protect their local communities against requisitions and reprisals, supported by Socialist Revolutionaries or Essers).

Tarkovsky's adolescence, in other words, was blasted by war; the death sentence that he narrowly escaped at 14 was only the tip of the iceberg. And then, twenty years later, his world was torn apart again, this time by a German invasion that the Soviet forces were powerless to stop. Hence my speculation that 'Mother' is Mother Earth only on the imagistic surface: deeper down, the resentment towards 'Mother' may be aimed at Mother Russia (Россия-Матушка, *Rossiya-Matushka*, or Мать-Россия, *Mat'-Rossiya*). The most nature can muster is an icy indifference; for sheer viciousness, nature cannot hold a candle to culture.

Standing in a broken present, clinging to the past as a guarantee of a restored future: Richard Hoffman, 'Refugee'

Considerably less 'emotional' on the surface than Tarkovsky's poem is a 2005 poem by Richard Hoffman entitled 'Refugee':

> A man carries his door,
> the door of his house,
> because when the war is over
> he is going home
>
> where he will hang it
> on its hinges
> and lock it, tight,
> while he tries to remember
> the word for welcome.
>
> If his house is gone
> when he returns,
> he will raise it from rubble
> around this door.

If he cannot return,
the door will remember
the rest of the house
so he can build it
again, elsewhere.

And if he cannot go on,
his door can be a palette
for his rest, a stretcher
to carry him, his shade
from sun, his shield.

The matter-of-fact speaker here would seem on the surface to make this a purely factual account, neutral, even in a sense abstract, logical, propositional – without the kind of affective charge that might make a reader empathise, or else put up defensive distance as a shield against the pain of empathy.

What Hoffman's poem gives us, however, is an explicitly imagined *door* – an image of a familiar object – and an implicitly posed *puzzle*, namely: how can a door possibly be this important to a person? And it is in our attempts to solve that puzzle, our necessarily empathic attempts, that affect is displaced.

I suggest that for the man carrying it the door is an exosomatic mooring for the data compression of that whole affective world of familiarity called 'home'. Hoffman's speaker calls the structure a 'house', and it is that, of course, or was; but for the man himself it was a home, an exosomatised dwelling, a structure that *felt* safe and familiar because it was his own. The door is a metonym of that home – a part that stands for the whole – but specifically a mnemonic metonym, and I suggest that the memory channelled by the metonym is saturated in affect.

There are, of course, other metonyms for homes, and most of them are easier to carry around than a door: a photograph, a pebble from the garden, a fork from the kitchen, etc. One might want to insist that a simple memory image would be the easiest of all to carry around – and that the man is therefore crazy, or just silly, to carry around something as big and bulky as a door.

But a memory fades. A photograph lacks the physicality of an object that used to be part of the house or its grounds. A pebble lacks definition, character: its metonymic power is diminished by its vagueness of form and function. A fork is in some sense *too* portable. Even while you're living in the house you may carry a fork to work, on trips, and so on, making it a weak metonym for home.

A door really is perfect. Despite its bulkiness, its heaviness, and therefore the difficulty one would have carrying it long distances, it is the ideal metonym of home. It is powerfully exosomatised by frequent touch, by frequent swinging open and shut, by the ingress and egress it facilitates, by the protection it gives the inhabitants of the house/home against the outside world. It shuts in and shuts out, lets in and lets out. It is charged affectively with safety, security, amity, peace. It is also, surely, affectively charged with welcome – with the affect for which the man has forgotten the word, but not, as long as he has the door with him, the feeling.

Another way of thinking about that door might draw positively on the term used in trauma studies for the negative kind of metonym: *trigger*. Unlike an object that triggers PTSD reactions, the man's door triggers *resilience* to PTSD: affectively warm memories of the past, affectively constructive plans for the future. 'The door will remember' is a trope for the tactile-becoming-affective trigger that enables the man himself to remember – to remember not just his house-as-home, and not just 'the word for welcome', but the affective reality of a safe, familiar world where he feels at home, and so also the possibility that he will one day have that kind of world around him once more.

Structurally Hoffman's poem is a series of fallback plans: Plan B if the house is gone, Plan C if he cannot return, Plan D if he becomes incapacitated. Tropically that makes the door not just a single metonym but a string of metonyms, each cueing the next, metaleptically: a metalepsis of affect-charged memory carrying him forward into an imagined/restored future. Whether he reaches that future is in an important sense secondary: *believing* in it keeps him sane and functional in the present.

The clash of the affectively present old home in the disturbing alienness of the new home: Li-Young Lee's 'The City in Which I Love You'

Perhaps the most affectively moving – indeed, wrenching – poem of the three is the 2008 long poem 'The City in Which I Love You' by Li-Young Lee (李立揚, b. 1957), in which all of the complexly and overlappingly displaced affects of the refugee experience crash in upon the speaker at every moment in his new home town, or what he calls 'this / storied, buttressed, scavenged, policed / city I call home, in which I am a guest' (Lee 2008: 162). A home in which he is a guest – and, he feels, not a particularly welcome one.

Lee is an ethnic Chinese with a pedigreed ancestry. On his mother's side, his great-grandfather was a famous and powerful general in the late Qing Dynasty, Yuan Shikai (袁世凱, 1859–1916), who helped bring the Xinhai Revolution of 1911 to a close by agreeing to a political compromise with Sun Yat-sen (孫逸仙, 1866–1925), the United League (*Tongmenghui* 同盟會) leader. As part of that compromise, Yuan also agreed with Edward Selby Little, as the representative of the six Western powers involved in the negotiations, to force the six-year-old Emperor Puyi (溥儀, 1906–67) to abdicate, on 12 February 1912. In return, Yuan would become the president of the Republic, and the abdicated/deposed emperor would be allowed to maintain a kind of imaginary shadow court in the New Summer Palace, as the ruler of an imaginary separate country. Unfortunately for the Republic, Yuan seized power, built a new dictatorship, and in 1915 had himself crowned emperor; Sun Yat-sen led a rebellion against him, calling on warlords to help defeat Yuan. The rebellion failed, but Yuan died in 1916, and what is now known as the Warlord Era (1916–28) in Chinese politics ensued.

On his father's side, Lee's ancestors were mostly businessmen and gangsters, but his father was a medical doctor. During the Chinese Civil War Dr Lee was physician to a nationalist general; when that general switched sides and joined the Communist Party of China, he briefly served as personal physician to Mao Zedong (毛泽东, 1893–1976). Later he moved the family to Indonesia, where he helped found Gamaliel University in Jakarta. His son Li-Young, the future poet, was born in Jakarta in 1957; while he was a toddler, violent anti-Chinese sentiment arose in Indonesia, and his father was arrested on political charges and thrown into jail (in Macao) for nineteen months. On his release his father moved them out of Indonesia, and they ended up in Hong Kong, where his father became a successful if hot-headed evangelical preacher and businessman. After one particularly heated argument, Dr Lee packed up the family and headed for the United States, through Japan, ending up in Pennsylvania in 1964, where he became the pastor of a small church. Li-Young was seven years old.

Like Tarkovsky's 'Беженец'/'Refugee', Lee's refugee poem is addressed to a female 'you', but clearly not the speaker's mother:

> As bone hugs the ache home, so
> I'm vexed to love you, your body
>
> the shape of returns, your hair a torso
> of light, your heat
> I must have, your opening
> I'd eat, each moment
> of that soft-finned fruit,
> inverted fountain in which I don't see me.
>
> My tongue remembers your wounded flavor. (Lee 2008: 163)

She's a lover, presumably, back in the old home, the one that was lost; Lee's speaker is now in the new home, where the woman he loves is not. His memory of her vagina is vivid, especially its 'wounded flavor', but he doesn't see himself in it, and the rest of her body in his memory has taken on the mystical form of his longing, the vortical 'shape of returns'. His own body, too, in this new place without her, unravels into the textures of the city:

> hulls clogged, I continue laden, translated
>
> by exhaustion and time's appetite, my sleep abandoned
> in bus stations and storefront stoops,

> my insomnia erected under a sky
> cross-hatched by wires, branches,
> and black flights of rain. Lewd body of wind
>
> jams me in the passageways, doors slam
> like guns going off, a gun goes off, a pie plate spins
> past, whizzing its thin tremolo,
> a plastic bag, fat with wind, barrels by and slaps
> a chain-link fence, wraps it like clung skin. (2008: 164)

This is the nightmarish chaos of unfamiliarity, the screaming of PTSD against which Hoffman's refugee's door triggered resilience; now the doors are alien noise-makers, neither passageways-in (of welcome) or passageways-out (of quest) but rifle reports, *crack*. Now the wind is not the cold passage over frozen fields with which Tarkovsky's speaker identifies – alone, sure, but free – but a 'lewd body' that prevents him from passing through those slamming doors. He is a ship laden with blockages, hindrances, snags, his 'hulls clogged', but also 'translated' – carried across from point A to point B – a hopeful trajectory, we think, translated to a better place, we hope, until we find that he has been translated 'by exhaustion and time's appetite' into the angles of the city, the stations and stoops, his 'insomnia erected under a sky / cross-hatched by wires, branches, / and black flights of rain'.

His memories of 'that other city', the one he escaped, the one where he had his lover, are no less horrific:

> During the daily assaults, I called to you,
>
> and my voice pursued you,
> even backward
> to that other city
> in which I saw a woman
> squat in the street
> beside a body,
> and fan with a handkerchief flies from its face.
> That woman
> was not me. And
> the corpse
>
> lying there, lying there
> so still it seemed with great effort, as though
> his whole being was concentrating on the hole
> in his forehead, so still
> I expected he'd sit up any minute and laugh out loud:
>
> that man was not me;
> his wound was his, his death not mine.

> and the soldier
> who fired the shot, then lit a cigarette:
> he was not me. (2008: 164–5)

He was, we surmise, driven out of that city by war: urban warfare, ordinary citizens lying dead in the street with bullet holes in their foreheads and flies on their faces, grieved over by loved ones. That dead body was not the speaker, which again seems like some small reason to rejoice – he survived! he's still alive! – until 'not me' is replicated endlessly, becomes a fractal litany of negation, and everything and everyone in every city becomes 'not me':

> The woman who is slapped, the man who is kicked,
> the ones who don't survive,
> whose names I do not know;
>
> they are not me forever,
> the ones who no longer live
> in the cities in which
> you are not,
> the cities in which I looked for you. (2008: 165)

There is an entropic proliferation of not-mes and cities-in-which-you-are-not that seems almost apocalyptic in tendency: an expanding black hole in which (felt) reality is increasingly engulfed in nothingness.

That felt nothingness is the true danger in all three of these poems, in fact. It is the danger against which Hoffman's man guards by carrying his door, which *feels real*, and by feeling real wards off the collapse of a safe, familiar world. It is the danger implied in Tarkovsky's speaker's negation in 'needed by nobody': if you're needed by nobody, you *are* nobody, and there is around you no-thing, an alien thinginess that feels vacuous. The *horror vacui* is at base a horror of the loss of an affective grounding in felt reality; and when the 'exosomatised' affective home base is displaced, lost, destroyed, what remains *feels* as if reality has been exsanguinated out of it:

> If I feel the night
> move to disclosures or crescendos,
> it's only because I'm famished
> for meaning; the night
> merely dissolves.
>
> And your otherness is perfect as my death.
> Your otherness exhausts me,
> like looking suddenly up from here
> to impossible stars fading.
> Everything is punished by your absence. (2008: 166)

The female 'you' whose absence punishes everything is increasingly no longer a woman, a lover, but an affective/cosmic construct, *das Ewig-Weibliche* that *zieht uns hinan* as Goethe put it in *Faust*, the Eternal-Feminine that draws us onward, the affective embodiment or enfleshment of reality troped as female. As that affective making-real is displaced, disembodied, it is othered, and its otherness 'exhausts' the speaker, empties him, drains his contents, sucks all meaning-as-nourishment out of life. 'The night merely dissolves.' In the same way, it's not that 'your absence' punishes everything; 'Everything is punished by your absence.' The passive voice displaces affective agency along with everything else.

And yet, despite rampant despair, an accommodation occurs. Even without a door to trigger resilience, resilience recurs:

> Straight from my father's wrath,
> and long from my mother's womb,
> late in this century and on a Wednesday morning,
> bearing the mark of one who's experienced
> neither heaven nor hell,
>
> my birthplace vanished, my citizenship earned,
> in league with stones of the earth, I
> enter, without retreat or help from history,
> the days of no day, my earth
> of no earth, I re-enter
>
> the city in which I love you.
> And I never believed that the multitude
> of dreams and many words were vain. (2008: 167)

Yes, his 'birthplace' may have 'vanished'; yes, his entrance into 'the city in which I love you' may still be shot through with negativity ('days of *no* day', 'earth / of *no* earth'). But life, it seems, may again be possible. Reality may again surge felt into flesh. The speaker has 'earned' his 'citizenship' – a tawdry, high-school civics class cliché, presumably used with some cautious irony here, some self-protective distance, but still *used*, and perhaps even exploratorily felt. No longer a citizen of his birthplace, which – whether it is Lee's Jakarta or some other impossibly distant place, now ruined to affect – is lost, he is a citizen of 'the city in which I love you'. He does not retreat from that citizenship, into nihilistic despair, into the nightmares of PTSD. He does not seek 'help from history', that intellectual regime that organises reality propositionally. He enters and re-enters 'the city in which I love you' by stepping carefully, feelingly, realisingly, on 'stones of the earth'.

'And I never believed', the speaker proclaims, 'that the multitude / of dreams and many words were vain.' This sounds like denial, in the twelve-step sense: I was never lost; I was never displaced; I was never caught up in a nightmare of non-existence. Or, perhaps, it sounds like a parody of normality, a normal 'positive attitude' built on the quaky bog of repression: once you acclimate, assimilate, once you become a citizen of your new homeland, you forget everything that went before, because you have got over it, you are past it, it can't hurt you now, it is safely buried in the past, and the past is just an abstraction. It doesn't exist.

But I suggest that there is another way of reading those last two lines that is neither so naively hopeful nor so bitterly sarcastic. After all, this is a long poem. It is made up of 'many words' – 1,110 of them, to be exact. Most of the words are saturated in the despair of displacement and dispossession, in loneliness, in the frustrations of failing to comprehend the complexities of the new host culture. The 'multitude / of dreams and many words' that constitutes the poem is largely negative, anxious, fear-driven – but not in vain. Those dreams and words are the poet's door. He carries them through the nightmare of affectively depleted reality, trusting them to serve some purpose, to achieve some kind of accommodation with an apparently meaningless existence that begins, against all odds, to generate new meaning – a new, or newly felt, affective reality.

And this brings us back to my second reason for asking why the refugee experience is so traumatising: if our sense of reality is an imaginative construct, a sense filled with the feeling of flesh and blood and mass and weight by *affect*, then it is not substantially different from poetry, from story. The old objectivist metaphysics made it seem as if 'reality' were one thing and 'literature' were another. 'Reality' was the destructive brutality of war, of genocide, of natural disasters that wipe out whole living environments and slaughter hundreds of thousands, displace millions; 'literature' was pure aesthetic decoration, stale sedentary fripperies, worse than useless. In a constructivist metaphysics such as the post-Kantian tradition has theorised and cognitive neuroscientists have affirmed, what is destructively brutal about war and genocide and natural disasters is that they disrupt and displace our affective creation of the meaningful, familiar and welcoming realities that we variously call 'home', 'community', 'neighbourhood', 'friendship' and so on – and whatever symbolic resources we can marshal to restore our ability to create those realities, whether they be an actual door or a literary door, are infinitely valuable to us.

Notes

1. And even when the family we share it with is horribly dysfunctional, and we are not particularly *happy* or emotionally safe in that home, to the extent that we voluntarily stay in it, do not move away, we still find it 'existentially' safe, in the sense of a familiar reality where we know the rules.
2. Note that the town name Chistopol' (Чистополь) literally means 'clean field', referring to the 'bare ground' that is left for the winter after the last harvest. Tarkovsky arguably alludes to the town's name in the fourth line of the first

stanza: А я живу один, как ветер в поле *(A ya zhivu odin, kak veter v pole)*, lit. 'But I live alone, like wind in a field.' Поле, *pole*, 'field' is the basis of the last syllable of the town's name – and since the fields would have been 'clean' (bare) under the November snow, Tarkovsky could very well have been hinting at his new place of residence, to which he was blown by the winds of war. Chistopol' is 140 km from Kazan' (Казань), the capital of Tatarstan, on the Volga.

Bibliography

Gazzaniga, Michael S. (2011), *Who's in Charge? Free Will and the Science of the Brain* (New York: Ecco).

Hirstein, William, and Vilayanur S. Ramachandran (1997), 'Capgras syndrome: a novel probe for understanding the neural representation of the identity and familiarity of persons', *Proceedings of the Royal Society of London B*, 264.1380: 437–44.

Hoffman, Richard (2005), 'Refugee', *Literary Review*, 48.4: 185.

Lee, Li-Young (2008), 'The city in which I love you', *New Labor Forum*, 17.1: 162–7.

Pick, Arnold (1903), 'Clinical studies. III. On reduplicative paramnesia', *Brain*, 26: 260–7.

Ramachandran, V. S., and Sandra Blakeslee (1998), *Phantoms in the Brain: Probing the Mysteries of the Human Mind* (New York: Morrow).

Robinson, Douglas (2013), *Displacement and the Somatics of Postcolonial Culture* (Columbus, OH: Ohio State University Press).

Tarkovsky, Arseny (1983 [1941]), Стихи разных лет (Poems from Various Years) (Moscow: Sovremennik).

Chapter 14

Reframing Climate Migration: A Case for Constellational Thinking in the Writing of Teju Cole

Byron Caminero-Santangelo

In the late 1980s and early 1990s, scholars began making the case that climate change would displace millions of people in the not-too-distant future (e.g. Milliman, Broadus and Gable 1989; Lewis 1990; Myers 1993). This work coincided with an IPCC report warning that millions would be uprooted by shoreline erosion, coastal flooding and agriculture disruption, and that 'migration and resettlement may be the most threatening short-term effect of climate change on human settlement' (Tegart, Sheldon and Griffiths 1990: 5–9). More recently, estimates of numbers of climate change migrants have grown to between 150 and 200 million (Stern 2007) and climate change migration has become an increasingly studied, politically charged field of inquiry.

This is often driven by the goal of addressing 'a normative gap in the international legal protection regime' (McAdam 2012: 1) and the lack of policy recognising 'the needs and rights of climate migrants' (Ross 2011: 245). Even though 'by 2010, according to a Red Cross estimate, they outnumbered the population of refugees from war and violence' (Ross 2011: 245), 'climate change refugees' do not have a legal designation and without it they have a much higher 'risk of interdiction, detention, and expulsion if they attempt to cross an international border' (McAdam 2012: 1). For those focused on drawing attention to the threat of climate change, making claims for huge numbers of people who will be forced from their homes helps paint a picture of a dire future. Alternatively, research on climate change migration by the Pentagon identifies it as a security problem that is linked with 'the politics of the armed lifeboat' based on 'exclusion, segregation, and repression' (Parenti 2011: 11) in order to keep (often faceless) '"blood dimmed" tides of climate refugees at bay' and protect resources (Ghosh 2016: 143). In addition, the projection of 'hordes' of climate change migrants has been used to bolster populist anti-immigrant rhetoric and greenwash white nationalism (Elliott 2010; Ross 2011).

Beyond the more obvious political implications of studying climate change migration, efforts to diagnose the scope and, indeed, the very nature of the problem can, whether intentionally or not, reinforce the representational economy of colonial discourse. For whatever purpose it is used, climate determinism all too easily suppresses the intertwining of climate change and socio-economic factors and elides complicated questions about responsibility and agency (Brown 2008: 9; Kelman et al. 2015: 165–6; McAdam 2012: 30; McLeman 2014: 8). While politically expedient, focusing on a single, environmental driver limits our ability to understand both the specific conditions delimiting decision making and the decision-making process itself – including the role of agency among migrants (Barnett and Campbell 2010: 171). In addition, the very idea of a climate change 'refugee' risks turning those who move into victims of natural disaster, and of persecution and discrimination in their countries of origin. In the process, it risks downplaying the significance of transnational processes and relationships (for example, those involving the historical inequities of CO_2 emissions). It can enable geographic and temporal delimitations of responsibility and reinforce problematic notions of innocence and distance in the places to which people try to move and which get positioned as sanctuaries. For all these reasons, many of those labelled climate refugees or potential refugees reject that categorisation (McAdam and Loughry 2009). They challenge the image of helplessness and lack of agency embedded in the term, question the focus on victims (as opposed to offenders), and point to the ways in which it makes consideration of causal responsibility across borders difficult (McAdam 2012: 41).

The potential colonial implications of climate change migration research is particularly striking when one considers its intersection with discourses of expertise and intervention. A focus on the '"scientisation" of environmental knowledge' all too easily 'serves to delegitimize the perceptions and perspectives of local laypeople, and may undermine local capacity to intervene' (McAdam 2012: 33), even as it reinforces the image of heroic, cosmopolitan experts. Underpinning this dynamic is the elevation of science over local, lay knowledge based on notions of the objectivity, transferability and universality of empirical knowledge production. Such an epistemological discourse has ties to colonial histories and can contribute to forms of imperial domination in the present, regardless of the sincere intentions of individual researchers. In this way, the study of human migration and climate change can become another site for 'planetary management' in which technocratically oriented environmental discourse is linked with the imposition of 'green agendas dominated by rich nations and Western NGOs' (Nixon 2011: 4–5).

As a result of such pitfalls, some of those in the social sciences who are studying the intersection of climate change and forced migration argue that we need transformed or new normative narratives based not only on better empirical evidence but also more expansive sources of knowledge (McLeman 2014: 9) – for example, from 'affected groups' about their 'needs and desires'

(McAdam 2012: 8). Such claims coincide with a call for the study of climate change adaptation and mitigation to be more 'holistic and methodologically variegated', including by bringing together empirical science and indigenous knowledge and by engaging with indigenous peoples as 'coproducers of knowledge' (Kelman et al. 2015: 162, 164).

Yet there remains the danger that even those trying to take into account the perspectives of 'affected groups' will perpetuate the primacy of expert, cosmopolitan knowledge and an underlying discourse of epistemological progress. Hastrup and Olwig argue that the social sciences are 'particularly well placed to investigate the multi-faceted relationship between climate change and migration', in part because they can account for how knowledge produced at one scale ('from below') impacts at another scale ('science') and, ultimately, 'address the interpenetration of local and global climatic issues and of different registers of knowledge at a more comprehensive theoretical and conceptual scale' (2012: 2–4). Such a view can reinforce an assumption that indigenous peoples lack a global perspective, bolster the authority of the outside expert, and undermine the notion of truly co-produced research (Kelman et al. 2015: 163, 176).

The possibility that seemingly enlightened and/or politically innocent projects might be entangled with illiberal relationships points to the role that the postcolonial and environmental humanities can play in the study of climate change and human migration. Together these forms of inquiry offer means to interrogate how knowledge production about environmental change and social crisis have been discursively mediated and to open space for alternative forms of knowledge and for silenced voices. The result of such work need not be the rejection of social and environmental scientific knowledge (which is manifestly problematic in the context of climate change), but it does necessitate interrogating valorising representations of this knowledge, and foregrounding, indeed privileging, marginalised epistemological perspectives.

Teju Cole's novel *Open City* (2011) and essays from his collection *Known and Strange Things* (2016) offer one possible strategy for decolonising the study of human migration and climate, as well as an opportunity to explore the relevance of the postcolonial and environmental humanities. Cole's writing frequently deals with themes of migration, and *Open City* repeatedly, if subtly, draws attention to climate change. Admittedly, he does not explicitly raise questions about connections between the two issues; however, his writing offers a potentially productive angle on narratives about those connections.

Cole advocates for a strategy that he calls 'constellational thinking' for understanding trauma and disaster (2016: 349). His use of the term points to the influence of Walter Benjamin, which is apparent both from his essays and in *Open City* (Foden 2011; Messud 2011; Wood 2011). In *Known and Strange Things*, Cole references the 'montage-like effects' in Benjamin's 'Arcades Project' associated with what the latter called 'dialectical images'

(Cole 2016: 191). Such images generate 'constellations' in which idealising, mythic images of progress are juxtaposed with representations of suppressed histories of barbarism and disaster. The result is a demystifying double focus that disrupts conventional histories of development without necessarily producing a new myth of progress. In Cole's own writing, his 'constellations' undermine myths of objectivity, freedom and, ultimately, human development (as measured by an ideal of the Western white male) by bringing together references to those myths with allusions that they cannot accommodate – for example, allusions to slavery and colonial violence – and that implicate them in the crises with which he is concerned. These myths, he suggests, are hard to shake and can all too easily continue to shape knowledge production about crises even when we think we are producing new or better narratives, and especially when we assume our own innocence and civilisational transcendence. The problem, Cole suggests, is not simply the need for more knowledge but also a rethinking of underlying approaches to knowledge about and interventions in phenomena such as human migration and climate change. In this regard, Cole also echoes Benjamin by emphasising how oppositional narratives cannot escape mediation by the conditions from which they emerge; there is no critique from 'outside', and we must be constantly vigilant regarding our own heroic myths.

In Cole's essay 'White Savior Industrial Complex' (WSIC), he defines 'constellational thinking' in terms of its potential disruption of the eponymous manifestation of colonial discourse (2016: 349). The 'complex' is a projection of 'white fantasies of conquest and heroism' in the Global South and especially in Africa, which 'has provided a space onto which white egos can conveniently be projected . . . Many have done it under the banner of "making a difference"' (2016: 345). In the WSIC, colonial formulations of race and place position the 'white savior' as having an objectivity and disinterestedness that bestow a right to speak and intervene, even as those formulations render invisible the role of transnational 'patterns of power' and 'networks of oppressive practices' in disaster and the 'savior's' own connections with them (2016: 344). Meanwhile, those who would make visible 'the larger disasters' behind the 'humanitarian disaster' – for example, 'educated Africans' – are positioned as inadequately disinterested and civil (2016: 343).

In contrast with the forms of representation associated with the WSIC, 'to think constellationally' entails an effort 'to connect the dots or see the patterns of power behind . . . isolated "disasters"' in ways that awaken us from sentimental projections of innocence and salvation (2016: 344). It necessitates turning the critical gaze inward as well as outward, striving towards emancipation precisely by recognising that one can never be free from entanglements with 'networks of oppressive practices' (2016: 344). Cole notes that if he writes as someone subject to the 'microaggressions of American racism', he also does so 'as an American, enjoying the many privileges that the American passport affords and that residence in this country makes possible'. His 'critique of privilege' must take into account that 'the coltan' in his 'phone can probably be traced to the conflict-riven Congo' and that his 'own privileges of class, gender, and sexuality are insufficiently examined' (2016: 344). Constellational thinking requires humility: not only a relinquishing of the politically transcendent knowing subject and of objective (universal) knowledge, but also a willingness to listen to the voices marginalised by the dream of colonial modernity and to consider their knowledge about and agency 'in their own lives' (2016: 346). Ultimately, Cole argues, without constellational thinking there is the perpetuation of the very trauma that the white saviour claims to address. For example, without bringing together 'the money-driven villainy at the heart of American foreign policy' with the illusion of innocent heroism, there cannot be a critical consideration of how the 'savior' and the WSIC continue to serve as 'a valve for releasing the unbearable pressures that build in a system developed on pillage' (2016: 348–9).

Cole's narrator in *Open City* (Julius) seems to be someone engaged in 'constellational thinking' in that he turns a critical gaze on the narrative underpinning his profession and takes into consideration sociopolitical causes for trauma. He is an immigrant from Nigeria, training as a psychologist in New York and pursuing 'a clinical study of affective disorders in the elderly' (Cole 2011: 7). He finds a 'reminder of freedom' from 'the tightly regulated mental environment of work' with its 'regimen of perfection and competence' in his aimless wanderings through the streets of the city (2011: 7). In these walks and his many conversations with friends and strangers, he continues to do the work of reading symptoms of trauma and crisis, but he does so more holistically, in ways not sanctioned by his discipline's knowledge regime. As he notes, 'our teachers favored the potent neurotransmitter, the analytic trick, the surgical intervention. Holism was looked down on by many professors' (2011: 207–8). In contrast with 'the best students', Julius's 'instinct was for doubts and questions', and for him 'what psychology really ought to be' is 'provisional, hesitant, and as kind as possible' (2011: 206). He questions, for example, the use of 'some imaginary statistical mean of normalcy' as a tool to differentiate between 'the tribe of the normal' and 'the mad, the crazy', and to plot the development of the latter (2011: 205). His interrogation of this dream of mastery, embodied by 'the statistical mean of normalcy', is spurred by a conversation in which a friend challenges the division of social injustice from conceptions of insanity embedded in scientific psychiatric practice: 'The racist structure of this country is crazy-making' (2011: 202–3). Neither Julius nor the novel necessarily rejects the potential value of the 'science and praxis' of psychiatry, or of academic and professional disciplines more generally, but they do challenge the underlying approach to knowledge and intervention embedded in those disciplines. Such a challenge is also applicable to the study of climate change migration in which '"experts" have squeezed out opportunities for local approaches' and which rely on models that 'homogenize people, see social life as the sum of rational individual action, assume "culture" is separable from other aspects of society, and assume that nature and society are independent "facts"' (McAdam 2012: 33).

Ultimately, however, Julius is deeply flawed as a constellational thinker in that he does not reflect on the links between his own ideals of knowledge and expertise, on which his idealised image of himself relies, and histories of exploitation and violence. He cannot or will not go so far as to bring into crisis those representations that separate him from others and that position him as outside the conditions he critiques. Chief among these representations is the image of the idealised cosmopolitan.

Much of the critical commentary on *Open City* reads Julius as embodying key elements of a cosmopolitan outlook (Messud 2011; Wood 2011; Vermeulen 2013; Oniwe 2016). He is detached from ways of seeing as determined by ethnic, cultural and national delimitation, even as he strives for connections beyond borders through curiosity, attentiveness and empathy. For those critics reading the novel as an endorsement of Julius's cosmopolitanism, his estrangement from a fixed sense of belonging and a striving for multiple attachment lead to a 'productive alienation' (Wood 2011); from 'a cosmopolite's detachment from his American experience' (Messud 2011) he is able to develop an epistemological vantage point that approaches 'multifarious realities, stories, and memories in a way that allows multiple resonances and interconnections to emerge' (Vermeulen 2013: 41). Such an outlook is often associated with a commitment to human rights as underpinned by the values of translatability, commonality and the importance of identifying with the suffering of others (Robbins 1998; Benhabib 2006; Levy and Sznaider 2011).

Yet to read the novel as endorsing Julius's cosmopolitanism is to ignore both how he turns back efforts by others to foster a sense of connection and responsibility, and his inability to make connections among the stories of difference with which he seems to engage (Vermeulen 2013; Oniwe 2016). Julius certainly embraces an image of himself as an empathetic cosmopolitan interested in the lives of others, one who listens well and tries to make connections across boundaries that delimit identity. He also believes that these qualities enable him to effectively diagnose trauma and disaster. However, the novel repeatedly undermines this image by entangling it with histories of violence and exploitation that it cannot accommodate. Ultimately, his cosmopolitanism masks its own complicity in such histories. The novel, in particular, brings into question Julius's assumptions about the human as a universal category and about an emancipatory, global outlook; these assumptions simultaneously suppress and perpetuate difference by positioning a certain kind of person and set of practices as the embodiment of human development. In this sense, Cole joins those critics of elite cosmopolitanism who note how it has worked in the service of empire and reinforced economic inequality (Brennan 1997; Dabiri 2017). Ultimately, Cole draws attention to the dangers of a privileged cosmopolitanism that does not take into account its own possible complicity in oppression and injustice.

Cole's essay 'A Piece of the Wall' brings together his notion of constellational thinking with the issue of immigration. It tells the story of his effort 'to find out more about the border and immigration' in Tucson and 'the Sonoran desert in Arizona' (Cole 2016: 363). Many of those with whom he speaks foreground the historical impact of neoliberalism and geopolitical relationships behind immigration and immigration policy. They are American but they turn their critical gaze on America and what it means to be American. In a conversation with two activists, one of them tells Cole that people 'don't want to deal with root cause. They don't want to deal with the six million jobs NAFTA took. They don't want to think about American intervention in Central America and all the refugees that caused' (2016: 371). In addition to the explicit transnational relationships at work, the very lack of constellational thinking – the fact that people 'don't want to deal with root cause', with a certain kind of disruptive history – is in itself an indirect but important factor shaping immigration and policy. Such wilful ignorance works in a mutually reinforcing way with the non-dialectical, reified images of the US as a space of rationality, freedom and opportunity, and immigrants as a source of danger coming from corrupt, violent and disordered places.

The essay foregrounds the need to engage critically with our stories of progress and of who we are. We must, in Benjaminian fashion, see the entanglement of civilisation and barbarity rather than frame the relationship between the two with a narrative of progressive separation and transcendence. Cole creates constellations that disrupt the association of America and whiteness with civilisational development, in part by foregrounding how that association enables the brutal treatment of migrants. Policies that are intended 'to discourage' immigrants from crossing the border by letting hundreds die 'out there' (Cole 2016: 367–8) are intertwined with myths of what it means to be American and what it means to be human. Cole describes men in a courtroom 'charged with illegal entry, reentry, or false claim to citizenship' as 'like animals in a pen, fastened to one another' and under the control of 'security officers' who are 'imposing, white, and impassive' (2016: 364). Cole asks the judge if he is 'from a Mexican family'; the judge responds, 'My father didn't fight for this country in World War Two so that people could call me Mexican.' Cole associates the judge's whitening sense of distance from the prisoners with the treatment of them as less than human. 'But the chains: these men are not dangerous. Why the chains?', Cole asks. 'It's more convenient', proclaims the judge (2016: 364).

In certain ways, Julius is like Cole himself in his use of constellational thinking for understanding immigration and discourses about it. By dialectically connecting past and present, he brings into question hegemonic narratives about the relationship between migration and the US as a haven offering freedom, refuge, opportunity and progress. His reflections about New York City point to how human movement has been tied to the violence of colonial exploitation, how the 'freedom' experienced by some people – the flowering of their 'humanity' – has relied on the instrumentalisation of others, and the ways that the association of the enlightened, Western subject with freedom and civility enables barbarity. He repeatedly considers how prominent myths embodied by the Statue of Liberty and Ellis Island serve to repress the history of slavery and its significance: 'Ellis Island, the focus of so many myths . . . was a symbol mostly for European refugees. Blacks, "we blacks," had known rougher ports of entry' (Cole 2011: 54–5). At one point in his wanderings, Julius looks from Battery Park 'right across to Brooklyn, to Staten Island, and the glimmering green figurine of the Statue of Liberty', and remembers that, while 'trading in slaves had become a capital offense in the United States in 1820 . . . New York long remained the most important port for the building, outfitting, insuring, and launching of slavers' ships' (2011: 162–3). In profiting from slavery, 'the City Bank of New York was not unlike the other companies founded by merchants and bankers in the same time period – the companies that later became AT&T and Con Edison emerged from the same milieu' (2011: 163). The intertwining of memories of the slave trade and the references to AT&T and Con Edison remind us of the ways in which the institutions representing spectacular technological human prowess have also been built on violence, even as the visibility of that prowess and the promise of freedom it offers serve to put unimaginable suffering further into shadow.

Again and again, Julius returns to this theme of how the supposed symbols of civilisation embedded in the predominant history of immigration turn people into waste and enable the horrors of their annihilation to be rendered invisible. One of the narrator's patient's, V, is 'an assistant professor of history at NYU, a member of the Delaware tribe', who has written a book entitled *The Monster of Amsterdam* about the slaughter of Canarsie Indians and members of the Hackensack tribe by Cornelius Van Tienhoven in seventeenth-century New Amsterdam: 'the relevant seventeenth-century records . . . were written in calm and pious language that presented mass murder as little more than the regrettable side effect of colonizing land' (2011: 26). The book makes visible how the opportunities for some immigrants in the past entailed genocide, even as the seventeenth century records, put in this context, suggest how their 'civility' (their 'calm and pious language') enabled a suppression of such crimes. Ironically, V's training in the distancing discourse of her discipline makes possible this visibility: 'pitched though it was to a general readership', the book 'came with all the scholarly apparatus and with much of the emotional distance typical of an academic study' (2011: 27). At the same time, Julius constructs a critical constellation by bringing together V's 'book' with his perception of her trauma. Her 'depression was partly due to the emotional toll of [her] studies', and 'the horrors Native Americans had had to endure at the hands of white settlers, the horrors . . . they continued to suffer, affected her on a profound personal level' (2011: 26–7). In this situation, the cosmopolitan tools of historical discourse that supposedly help generate a more enlightened vision sensitive to difference are also the means by which trauma is perpetuated in the present.

Yet despite Julius's challenges to hegemonic myths, he does not go so far as to question the cosmopolitan ideals on which his image of himself depends. This failure is especially apparent in his interaction with a young Liberian refugee, Saidu, with whom he talks in a detention facility for undocumented immigrants. Saidu has been detained 'for more than two years' (2011: 64). He lost his family in the Liberian civil wars, was made to work as a slave on a plantation, and 'knew he had no choice' but to leave when he saw the 'stump' of a friend whose 'right hand had been severed at the wrist' (2011: 65). When he arrives in the US, he is detained and processed in ways that make clear that he is viewed as a body to be managed – deprived of dignity, freedom of movement and control over his own fate. And from his misery, others profit; the facility, positioned to be invisible, 'had been contracted out to Wackenhut, a private firm' (2011: 62). In other words, the US continues the process of persecution and exploitation that he experienced in Liberia, and this process is tied to a hope of salvation that only ended up perpetuating his devaluation.

Julius's behaviour throughout this episode seems to reflect his cosmopolitan values. He listens to Saidu sympathetically and openly: 'I encouraged him, asked him to clarify details, gave, as best I could, a sympathetic ear to a story that, for too long, he had been forced to keep to himself' (2011: 64). Yet this stance masks Julius's distancing of himself from Saidu, the role that his cosmopolitanism plays in the distance he maintains, and the way he ends up only furthering Saidu's exploitation as a result. Julius listens to Saidu's story but he does not engage with it. He does not think about the implications of that story for his own relative privilege. Instead, he uses Saidu as a means to reinforce his own image as heroic cosmopolitan immigrant – including by telling the story to a woman he pursues: 'Perhaps she fell in love with the idea of myself that I presented . . . I was the listener, the compassionate African who paid attention to the details of someone's life and struggle. I had fallen in love with that idea myself' (2011: 70). If Julius seems to question that 'idea' of himself, this questioning does not go far. He does not interrogate it by, for example, considering how he does not develop a sense of responsibility towards Saidu and, in fact, contributes to Saidu's devaluation: 'When I got up to leave, he remained seated, and said, Come back and visit me, if I am not deported. I said that I would, but never did' (2011: 70). Julius's interaction with Saidu suggests that his cosmopolitanism serves as means to legitimise his own status, by suppressing his links with the processes that devalue and entrap Saidu and by revealing his ethical and epistemic 'development'. The result is a further instrumentalisation of Saidu. Failing to interrogate his image of himself, Julius is part of the problem – just like the white saviour. He is by no means free from a form of cosmopolitanism that can all too easily become a 'mask for hegemonic neoliberal practices of class domination and financial and militaristic imperialism' (Harvey 2009: 84).

Both 'A Piece of the Wall' and *Open City* point to some precautions for the study of forced migration. For example, Cole suggests the need for and dangers in categorising immigrants, including in terms of a forced/voluntary divide; we must always be attuned to the rhetorical significance of those categories in specific circumstances. In the essay, an activist refers to the migrants coming across the border as 'refugees'; by doing so, she positions them as having been forced to flee – which challenges prominent notions in the US about who those immigrants are and has significant implications given that she emphasises the causal responsibilities of neoliberalism and US political policy. This use of the term also challenges dominant notions of what constitutes the category of 'the refugee', since, for example, most of these immigrants would be classified as 'economic', and they often flee towards the place that supposedly represents refuge but that also bears significant responsibility for the conditions they seek to escape. This latter point about the US as refuge is made apparent through *Open City*'s treatment of the history of slavery, genocide and immigration in the US. The novel alludes to the implications of hegemonic definitions of a 'refugee' in terms of separating brutal economic and political processes from understandings of immigration and, concomitantly, for suppressing responsibility.

Open City also suggests that the problem is not the pursuit of knowledge about migration per se but how knowledge production and the possibilities for intervention are framed. For example, we need to ask if that framing traffics in notions of enlightened global perspectives and human development that themselves suppress or instrumentalise the voices of those who are supposedly being represented, and if it is linked with processes that circumscribe their agency. Julius's projection of a heroic cosmopolitanism finds a corollary in celebratory claims about social science investigation into climate change migration based on an ability to transcend 'the idea of bounded and easily identifiable units', and, in turn, to 'address the interpenetration of local and global climatic issues and of different registers of knowledge at a more comprehensive theoretical and conceptual scale' (Hastrup and Olwig 2012: 3–4). Through its skewering of Julius's ideas about himself, *Open City* points to the potential pitfalls of such claims regarding expert cosmopolitan knowledge production. It suggests that those studying phenomena such as climate change migration need to be cautious about the unavoidable discursive mediation of the knowledge they produce, the epistemic limitations that this mediation imposes, the challenges posed by marginalised knowledge, and, ultimately, the possibility of unwitting complicity in exploitative colonial dynamics.

Finally, Cole alludes to the need to interrogate how images that frame academic and activist work as heroic can contribute in subtle ways to exploitation and disempowerment. Such interrogation is a form of constellational thinking relevant to representations used to project the threat of forced migration

due to climate change: 'the vulnerability of [small Pacific islands] is a symbol used by researchers who need problems to investigate, journalists who
need problems to sell, and NGOs who need problems to solve' (Barnett and
Campbell 2010: 177); and, 'while they may be well intentioned, the effect is
frequently to deprive affected communities of agency' and 'capacity to make
their own decisions' (McAdam 2012: 33–4). As the 'symbol' of 'vulnerability'
is brought together with representations of those who benefit and those who
suffer from its use, the way (neo-)colonial relationships can be enabled by
that symbol is brought to light, and its naturalising function is disrupted.

In many ways, the perspectives created by Cole's writing on climate change
and on migration are similar. He suggests that ecological crisis in general has
been shaped by concepts of the human and emancipation embedded in the
history of modernity – that is, the dream that we can transcend our entanglement with the non-human world and master it through reason and technology.
The climate crisis, as Naomi Klein notes, is a particularly salient example of
the ultimate price we pay for the notions of freedom and mastery at the heart
of the Enlightenment, 'the civilizational narratives about endless growth and
progress within which we are all, in one way or another, still trapped' (2014:
170). Thinking climate change constellationally entails disrupting myths of
what we can do and know – and how we know. Yet to a degree greater than
many of the other crises in *Open City*, climate change requires the perspectives offered by science and expert forms of cosmopolitanism for diagnosis.
The novel points to this need, even as it alludes to the necessity of recognising
that restricting a framing of climate change to scientific and 'global' expertise
can reproduce ideas about knowledge and intervention that have helped generate the problem and that hamper addressing it – for example, by discount-
ing other forms and scales of knowledge.

Dipesh Chakrabarty offers particularly astute insights into the challenges to knowledge production posed by climate change and has done so
in what might be considered constellational terms. He argues that Enlightenment themes of freedom have led us to 'unintended consequences', and
that any 'optimism about the role of reason' must account for 'the most
common shape that freedom takes in human societies: politics'. At the same
time, 'any thought of the way out of our current predicament cannot but
refer to the idea of deploying reason in global, collective life' (Chakrabarty
2009: 210–11). Furthermore, climate change necessitates both reliance on
the scalar category of the global and universal, since 'scientists' discovery
of the fact that human beings have . . . become a geological agent points to
a shared catastrophe that we have all fallen into', and a Marxist and postcolonial 'suspicion of the universal' resulting from the relationship between
climate change and 'the unfolding of capitalism in the West and the imperial . . . domination by the West of the rest of the world' (Chakrabarty
2009: 216). In that 'the crisis of climate change calls for thinking simultaneously in both registers', it 'stretches, in quite fundamental ways, the very

idea of historical understanding' (Chakrabarty 2009: 220). Yet as much as Chakrabarty draws out the epistemological tensions associated with climate change, ultimately he prioritises challenging politically based critiques of scientific knowledge and embraces the global nature (based on the category of a 'species') of such knowledge. In contrast, Cole offers us a story that always returns to the social positioning of knowledge and resists more fully notions of the natural and the universal used to separate science and politics.

Open City frequently evokes the spectre of climate change. These evocations come from a pattern of references to changes in weather patterns and extreme weather events that create a sense of the uncanny. Julius notes again and again that the autumn and winter in New York have been disturbingly mild; 'it was to be a year without a real winter . . . I was unnerved by that mildness . . . The impression of unseasonal, somewhat uncanny warmth persisted in my mind, keeping the world, as I experienced it, on edge' (Cole 2011: 149–50). When he is in Belgium for a short holiday, a woman, looking at a news report about an extreme storm and flooding across Europe, proclaims 'this is the strangest winter we've had in years' (2011: 140).

Yet Julius himself only brings up climate change twice, and only once, early on in the narrative, does he raise the possibility that the unseasonable weather could result from it. Despite the patterns he observes, he does not think again about the possible linkages, and he never reflects seriously on their causes or the threat they pose. In the context of the novel as a whole, the two moments when he does discuss climate change suggest the danger of an epistemological discourse that suppresses the political inflection and deployment of scientific knowledge production.

In Julius's first reflection, he notes his 'recurrent worry about how warm it had been all season long' and his 'discomfort' about the 'absence of cold when it ought to be cold', even as he claims there 'there was no evidence that this warm fall in particular wasn't due to a perfectly normal variation in patterns that stretched across centuries'. Although he 'was no longer the global-warming skeptic that [he] had been some years before', he 'still couldn't tolerate the tendency some had of jumping to conclusions based on anecdotal evidence . . . It was careless thinking to draw the link too easily, an invasion of fashionable politics into what should be the ironclad precincts of science' (Cole 2011: 28).

In a sense, Julius is right; climate activists misstep when they make 'snap judgements' to assert the connection between local weather and climate change, and this is also a danger for claim making about the relationship between climate and human migration. His observation coincides with the novel's more general emphasis on the inadequacies of focusing only on everyday parochial experience to read the symptoms of trauma and crisis. One needs the scalar perspectives offered by history and science, including the history of human impacts on the non-human world. This need is especially relevant for making visible climate change, which requires drawing connections between events at vastly different geographic and temporal scales.

Yet *Open City* also points to the limitations of expert and disciplinary knowledge and to the dangers posed by assumptions about objective, dispassionate knowledge production. For example, it suggests that a belief in one's ability to read the world accurately through a transcendence of social (and ecological) entanglement and a corresponding assertion of one's own heroic mission can be tied to the invisibility and exacerbation of violence. Julius himself believes that, as a psychiatrist, he understands and is able to read the symptoms of trauma in his patients. Yet the novel foregrounds his failure to read those signs in his personal life, how that failure maintains his own sense of innocence, and the dangers that it poses. Having suppressed memories of raping the sister of a friend (Moji) in Nigeria when they were younger, he continues to add to her anguish through his failure to read the symptoms of that violence and through his evasion of responsibility when he meets her again in New York.

In this context, Julius's equation of a grounded (non-'fashionable') perspective with 'the ironclad precincts of science' becomes suspicious. This suspiciousness is substantially deepened by the other moment in the novel when climate change is explicitly raised. Describing a conversation with Moji on the topic, he notes that she is further along than he is; she tells him that 'she was more worried than ever about the environment'. When he responds flippantly 'that I supposed we all were', she corrects him: 'What I mean is that I actively worry about it . . . I don't think that's generally true of other people . . . My awareness of it has intensified in the past couple of months.' Rather than reflect more deeply about the threat and its relationship with his own lifestyle, the narrator strikes out by asking her 'if she worried about things like air travel . . . Wasn't she worried about the environmental effect of jet fuel.' He later acknowledges to himself that while he knows 'how earnest a priority it was for some people', he 'did not, as yet, feel it seriously in [his bones]. [He] had not experienced a fervor over it' (Cole 2011: 198). This distance is also reflected in his lack of consideration, after the initial comment about the unusual autumn, of the possible meaning of the weather conditions he repeatedly notes. As the novel progresses, Julius's appeal to 'the ironclad precincts of science' in that initial comment begins to look like a strategy to suppress a pressing sense of climate change's threat, political aspects of that threat, and his particular role in them. When he flies to Brussels, he does not give a thought to 'the environmental effect of jet fuel'.

More generally, *Open City* brings into question Enlightenment ideas about human knowledge of and relationships with the natural world precisely by foregrounding how such ideas have led to ecological crises and by pointing to their ties to colonialism. In a discussion about 'the mass death of bees', Julius notes that 'scientists don't know why' bees are dying, and he and others reflect on the possibility that the deaths stem from uninformed uses of 'pesticides' and the instrumentalisation of non-humans: 'For so long, they have been used as machines for making honey, their obsession was turned to human advantage' (Cole 2011: 199). In another discussion, Julius and a friend discuss a 'tree of heaven', which 'botanists call an invasive species' and 'which was first brought over from China a long time ago, in the 1700s'; over time, it 'grew freely and wildly in almost every state, often displacing native species' (2011: 178–9). Growing 'anywhere', casting 'shade over other plants, cutting off their sunlight', the tree 'reduces local biodiversity' and has come to be 'thought of as a pest, no good for timber or wildlife, and not even all that great for firewood'. As the friend notes, this story of how our manipulation of the non-human world far exceeds human intentionality points to 'what force is about, how it motivates action and loses control of what it has motivated' (2011: 180). It is also a colonial story; as Aldo Leopold argued, 'the conqueror role is eventually self-defeating' because 'it is implicit in such a role that the conqueror knows . . . just what makes the community clock tick, and just what and who is valuable, and what and who is worthless, in community life. It always turns out that he knows neither' (1949: 204).

The connections between colonialism, modern scientific disciplines, planetary ecological transformations and environmental crises – including climate change – have been traced by many scholars and writer activists. Mary Louise Pratt and Nancy Stepan argue that Linnaean classification both developed through the collection of unknown species by imperial explorers and encouraged imperial expansion. Creating 'a new planetary consciousness' underpinning 'modern Eurocentrism', science instrumentalised the natural world in ways that grounded colonial development (Pratt 1992: 15). Naomi Klein emphasises the connection between these dynamics, Enlightenment dreams of transcendence and hydrocarbon use. Colonial science and colonialism were tied up with the pursuit of liberation from 'the constraints of living on a planet bound by geography and governed by the elements'; fossil fuels seemed to offer a crucial means towards these ends (Klein 2014: 172–3). At the same time, a narrative of progress based on distance from the restraints of the physical world through reason and technology continues to fuel climate change, undermines solutions that require a recognition of ecological limits, and renders disposable the peoples and places that are destroyed in the extraction of fossil fuels and that are most immediately at risk.

Cole's writing does not necessarily endorse a rejection of scientific knowledge. However, he does encourage a consideration of the relationship between, on the one hand, the meaning ascribed to scientific knowledge and, on the other, coloniality and ecological crisis. In *Open City*, the problems lie in a narrative representing the sciences and scientific method as offering the only proper way of understanding threats such as climate change and, more generally, as enabling knowledge production that is objective and politically free. Such a myth, he suggests, is tied to images of salvation and intervention

that have deeply problematic consequences and that all too easily shape supposedly new practices meant to address those consequences.

The ending of *Open City* potentially brings together Cole's call for constellational thinking and the themes of knowledge production, human migration and
climate change. The narrator reflects on the death of large numbers of birds in
the nineteenth century that 'somehow lost their bearings when faced with [the]
single monumental flame' of the Statue of Liberty (Cole 2011: 258). Throughout the novel, the statue has been an image associated, on the one hand, with
problematic myths about salvation and immigration and, on the other, with
possibilities for the disruption of such myths when the image is treated dialectically. Meanwhile, Julius's mythic perspective on birds turns them into images
of the possibility for transcendent knowledge – including about migration –
grounded in nature. He watches 'bird migration' like 'someone taking auspices,
hoping to see the miracle of natural immigration' and wondering 'how our life
below might look from their perspective' (2011: 4). The novel does not deny
the possible value of trying to imagine a non-human 'perspective', but it does
undermine the hope of knowledge through mastery of such a perspective and,
more generally, through capture of nature's secrets – for example, the 'miracle
of natural immigration'.

A Colonel Tassin ruled that the bodies of the birds 'be retained in the
service of science'. He undertook 'a system of records' that enabled him to
'deliver detailed reports on each death, including the species of bird, date, hour
of striking, direction and force of the wind, [and] character of the weather'.
From these reports, he concluded that 'the weather and the direction of the
wind had a great deal to do' with the number of birds killed. However, 'the
sense persisted that something more troubling was at work'. One morning,
175 wrens were 'gathered in, all dead of the impact, although the night just
past hadn't been particularly windy or dark' (2011: 259). Julius's reflections
suggest that 'the monumental flame' of the statue has something to do with the
deaths, but he does not formulate a conclusive causal explanation. In fact, the
novel's ending emphasises the difficulties and even impossibility of complete
causal explanations – especially deterministic ones. 'The weather' cannot be
the only or even necessarily the primary factor, just as climatic determinism
is a necessarily reductive explanation for climate-change-induced migration.
In addition, the novel as a whole points to the importance of the perspective
of those impacted, in this case the birds themselves, knowledge of which will
always be limited and shaped by positioned (human) experience and desire.
Even if we try to accommodate the perspectives of those who move and those
who are most under threat, any explanatory narrative and set of categories
we develop will still be partial in both senses of the word – not complete and
not objective.

In juxtaposing images of expert knowledge production with allusions to
what remains unexplained and unaccommodated, the conclusion of *Open
City* offers us the kind of dialectical constellations that Cole endorses in his

essays. In turn, however, constellational thinking encourages consideration of what Cole's own image making might leave out. For example, the essay 'A Piece of the Wall' does not include in its picture of immigration at the US/Mexico border any allusions to climate change or other possible environmental drivers. Yet migration patterns have been deeply impacted by soil erosion, resulting not only 'from the NAFTA-driven abandonment of traditional sustainable agriculture' but also from

> an overall decline in precipitation from climate change . . . As early as 1994, a report for the U.S. Commission on Immigration Reform estimated that environmental migrants accounted for a substantial portion of the 900,000 annually who moved away from arid or semiarid regions of Mexico, and that the aridity was clearly on the increase. (Ross 2011: 245)

In this sense, any just immigration policy would entail a consideration of climate debt, of what is owed by those who have most benefited by high carbon emissions to those least responsible but most impacted: 'Indeed, climate refugees may have their own carbon-conscious version of the retort offered by postcolonials when they settled in cities like London and Paris: "We are here because you were there"' (Ross 2011: 265). The responsibilities incurred by climate change need to be taken into account, even as we must avoid turning migrants into 'caravans' of victims whose lives (and deaths) can be explained and perspectives captured by 'experts'.

Bibliography

Barnett, Jon, and John Campbell (2010), *Climate Change and Small Island States* (Washington, DC: Earthscan).

Benhabib, Seyla (2006), 'The philosophical foundations of cosmopolitan norms', in Seyla Benhabib (ed.), *Another Cosmopolitanism* (New York: Oxford University Press), 13–44.

Brennan, Timothy (1997), *At Home in the World: Cosmopolitanism Now* (Cambridge, MA: Harvard University Press).

Brown, Oli (2008), *Migration and Climate Change* (Geneva: International Organization for Migration).

Chakrabarty, Dipesh (2009), 'The climate of history: four theses', *Critical Inquiry*, 35.2: 197–222.

Cole, Teju (2011), *Open City* (New York: Random House).

Cole, Teju (2016), *Known and Strange Things* (New York: Random House).

Dabiri, Emma (2017), 'The pitfalls and promises of Afropolitanism', in Bruce Robbins and Paulo Lemos Horta (eds), *Cosmopolitanisms* (New York: New York University Press), 201–11.

Elliott, Lorraine (2010), 'Climate migration and climate migrants: what threat, whose security?', in Jane McAdam (ed.), *Climate Change and Displacement: Multidisciplinary Perspectives* (Portland, OR: Hart Publishing), 175–90.

Foden, Giles (2011), 'Review of *Open City*, by Teju Cole', *The Guardian*, 17 August, https://www.theguardian.com/books/2011/aug/17/open-city-teju-cole-review (accessed 2 July 2019).

Ghosh, Amitav (2016), *The Great Derangement: Climate Change and the Unthinkable* (Chicago: University of Chicago Press).

Harvey, David (2009), *Cosmopolitanism and the Geographies of Freedom* (New York: Columbia University Press).

Hastrup, Kirsten, and Karen Fog Olwig (2012), *Climate Change and Human Mobility: Global Challenges to the Social Sciences* (New York: Cambridge University Press).

Kelman, Ilan, J. C. Gaillard, Jessica Mercer, James Lewis and Anthony Carrigan (2015), 'Island vulnerability and resilience: combining knowledges for disaster reduction, including climate change', in Elizabeth DeLoughrey, Jill Didur and Anthony Carrigan (eds), *Global Ecologies and the Environmental Humanities* (New York: Routledge), 162–85.

Klein, Naomi (2014), *This Changes Everything: Capitalism and the Climate* (New York: Simon and Schuster).

Leopold, Aldo (1949), *A Sand County Almanac and Sketches Here and There* (New York: Oxford University Press).

Levy, Daniel, and Natan Sznaider (2011), 'Cosmopolitan memory and human rights', in Maria Rovisco and Magdalena Nowicka (eds), *The Ashgate Research Companion to Cosmopolitanism* (Aldershot: Ashgate), 195–209.

Lewis, James (1990), 'The vulnerability of small island states to sea level rise: the need for holistic strategies', *Disasters*, 14.3: 241–9.

McAdam, Jane (2012), *Climate Change, Forced Migration, and International Law* (Oxford: Oxford University Press).

McAdam, Jane, and Maryanne Loughry (2009), 'We aren't refugees', *Inside Story*, 30 June, https://insidestory.org.au/we-arent-refugees/ (accessed 2 July 2019).

McLeman, Robert A. (2014), *Climate and Human Migration* (New York: Cambridge University Press).

Messud, Claire (2011), 'The secret sharer', review of *Open City*, by Teju Cole, *New York Review of Books*, 14 July, https://www.nybooks.com/articles/2011/07/14/secret-sharer/ (accessed 2 July 2019).

Milliman, John D., James M. Broadus and Frank Gable (1989), 'Environmental and economic implications of rising sea level and subsiding deltas: the Nile and Bengal examples', *Ambio*, 18.6: 340–5.

Myers, Norman (1993), 'Environmental refugees in a globally warmed world', *BioScience*, 43.11: 752–61.

Nixon, Rob (2011), *Slow Violence and the Environmentalism of the Poor* (Cambridge, MA: Harvard University Press).

Oniwe, Bernard Ayo (2016), 'Cosmopolitan conversation and challenge in Teju Cole's *Open City*', *Ufahamu: Journal of the African Activist Association*, 39.1: 43–65.

Parenti, Christian (2011), *Tropic of Chaos: Climate Change and the New Geography of Violence* (New York: Nation Books).

Pratt, Mary Louise (1992), *Imperial Eyes: Travel Writing and Transculturation* (New York: Routledge).

Robbins, Bruce (1998), 'Introduction I: actually existing cosmopolitanism', in Pheng Cheah and Bruce Robbins (eds), *Cosmopolitics: Thinking and Feeling Beyond the Nation* (Minneapolis: University of Minnesota Press), 1–19.

Robbins, Bruce, and Paulo Lemos Horta (2017), 'Introduction', in Bruce Robbins and Paulo Lemos Horta (eds), *Cosmopolitanisms* (New York: New York University Press), 1–20.

Ross, Andrew (2011), *Bird on Fire: Lessons from the World's Least Sustainable City* (New York: Oxford University Press).

Stepan, Nancy Leys (2001), *Picturing Tropical Nature* (Ithaca: Cornell University Press).

Stern, Nicholas (2007), *The Economics of Climate Change: The Stern Review* (Cambridge: Cambridge University Press).

Tegart, W. J. M., Gordon Sheldon and D. C. Griffiths (1990), *Climate Change: The IPCC Impacts Assessment* (Canberra: Australian Government Publishing Service).

Vermeulen, Pieter (2013), 'Flights of memory: Teju Cole's *Open City* and the limits of aesthetic cosmopolitanism', *Journal of Modern Literature*, 37.1: 40–57.

Wood, James (2011), 'The arrival of enigmas: Teju Cole's prismatic début novel, *Open City*', *New Yorker*, 28 February, https://www.newyorker.com/magazine/2011/02/28/the-arrival-of-enigmas (accessed 15 May 2019).

Part V

The Camp

The Camp: Introduction

Emma Cox

In an era of totalising surveillant technologies, the privatisation of space, the yoking of rights to transit with governmentality and the militarisation of borders, a frequently repeated claim that the refugee camp is the paradigmatic spatio-temporal site of modernity has surely acquired the status of a truism. Most famously, of course, for political philosopher Giorgio Agamben, the administrative contours of state sovereignty, wherein capacities to enact exceptional suspensions of law and due process rapidly take on 'a permanent spatial arrangement that [. . .] remains constantly outside the normal state of law' (2000: 39), are not just characteristic but definitional.

Agamben's theorisation of the camp as a space of exception – paradoxically 'included by virtue of its very exclusion' (2000: 40) – looms large in humanities scholarship. But it is perhaps precisely the topics and techniques of enquiry that distinguish the humanities – that is, a concern with the aesthetics and politics of representation; a recognition of the importance of thick description for engaging with history and memory; a critical contextualisation of narrative strategies; and a creative engagement with word, image, performance and place – that foster an impetus to think deeply about the limits of Agamben's structural explication of camp biopolitics. Although profoundly instructive, Agamben's work raises as many questions as it answers when it comes to instrumentality. Tellingly, all three contributors to this section of the book – not to mention other authors throughout the volume – cite Agamben, but do so in order to propel a critical questioning of the conceptual limits of the biopolitical, effectively pursuing, as Adam Ramadan phrases it in an essay on 'Spatialising the Refugee Camp':

> a critical take on Agamben's 'space of exception' that accounts for the complex, multiple and hybrid sovereignties of the camp; an analysis of the camp as an assemblage of people, institutions, organisations, the built environment and the relations between them that produce particular values and practices; and an analysis of the constrained temporality of the camp, its enduring liminality and the particular time-space from which it draws meaning. (2013: 65)

Certainly, in a time of proliferative and (in some cases) increasingly visible forms of refugee encampment – whether the ad hoc destitution of Calais or Dunkirk, the simmering uncertainty of Idomeni on the Greece–Macedonia border, the urbanised sprawl of Zaatari camp in Jordan, the ceaseless encampment of Gaza, or the degradations of Australia's outsourced, high-security detention centres at Manus Island (Papua New Guinea), Nauru and Christmas Island – it may seem perverse to excavate what is *meaningful*, or *liminal*, in these spaces, given that such concepts seem to imply creative potentialities, or worse, ends that justify means. It is in the context of the camp's variegated entrenchment globally that the case for an Agambenian insistence on ontologies of *bare life* retains ethical force.

And yet the three chapters in this section of the volume demonstrate that a careful interrogation of what camps mean/do/are/may become can perform the intellectual, creative and practical work of recuperating minority, marginalised and indeed empowering perspectives on these brutal, contradictory spaces. The section's first two chapters set out ethnographic, autobiographical and artistic approaches – via analyses that are valuably intertwined – on prolonged encampment (primarily) in the context of Israel's decades-long occupation of Palestinian territories and the expulsion of Palestinian refugees to camps beyond their homelands. Drawing on extensive fieldwork undertaken over several years, Elena Fiddian-Qasmiyeh's and Yousif M. Qasmiyeh's chapters concern, respectively, the Sahrawi refugee camps in Algeria and Palestinian refugee camps in Lebanon and in Syria, and the Palestinian camps in Lebanon, in particular Baddawi (Qasmiyeh's place of birth). Fiddian-Qasmiyeh's chapter emphasises that 'far from being quintessential "spaces of exception" [. . .] refugee camps are simultaneously "reservoirs of memory" of the homeland and are themselves spaces of belonging and longing, both as "lived" home-camps and potent "symbolic" spaces'. Applying Deleuze and Guattari's metaphor of the rhizome (a subterranean network of horizontal interconnection), Fiddian-Qasmiyeh undertakes a 'rhizoanalysis' of the camp, which 'entails recognising the multiple relationships that exist between and produce different time-spaces, by acknowledging that these connections amount to more-than-a-network'. Fiddian-Qasmiyeh's nuanced analysis illuminates her claim – one that classical vocabularies of the 'camp' risk obscuring – that camps are not 'isolated spatial zones' but dynamic spaces, forged by their beginnings and endings, and importantly, bound by material, remembered and symbolic links.

In a chapter in which fieldwork and lived experience are productively entangled, Qasmiyeh combines ethnographic thick description with philosophy, autobiographical meditation and excerpts of his own poetry, offering a layered historicisation of life, death and burial at Baddawi camp. In so doing, his chapter demonstrates both politically and affectively what *writing the camp* can entail, from the perspective of one whose life oscillates between camp and non-camp spaces. When, as in the case of Baddawi, encampment dilates temporally to encompass the arc of a life and its natural death, it is necessary to ask whether concepts of the temporary or the exception make any sense in such spaces. Qasmiyeh identifies death as critical to such a questioning, tracing sites and practices connected to the cemetery at Baddawi, and dialoguing with Derridean notions of cinders in order to posit that '[t]here is nothing that is fixed in the camp except the cemetery', that in the face of arrivals and departures, 'death in the camp has become the sole marker of existence'.

Beyond their value as illuminations of too often ignored regional realities, Fiddian-Qasmiyeh's and Qasmiyeh's chapters implicitly insist on a contrast with the discursive (and dominant) construction of refugee 'crisis' in other contexts – most prominently, in recent years, the European, wherein encampment has become a spectacularised marker of en masse arrival, and accompanying notions of political extremity. In the latter construction, refugee encampment is often coterminous with bordering practices, with people coalescing along territories that hug coastlines (as in Calais or Dunkirk), or pressing up against political borderlines (as in the Idomeni encampment), or dwelling on that most precarious of topographies: small islands proximate to maritime traumas (Lampedusa, Lesvos). That these contexts of encampment have been subject to media thrall is suggestive of a link between visibility and briefer temporality. The camps that concern Fiddian-Qasmiyeh and Qasmiyeh are spaces of precarity *and* of duration – to the extent that they have developed effective-permanent cultural practices around arrival, departure, birth and death. These practices confound notions of camp stasis, but they may also mitigate narratives of urgency. A different permutation of the encampment–temporality–crisis nexus emerges in Gillian Whitlock and Rosanne Kennedy's chapter in this volume's 'Digital Territories' section, on testimonial narratives emerging from Australia's secretive Manus Island and Nauru camps. Whereas for Qasmiyeh, transnational arrival and departure are mapped out over a lifetime, and now intergenerationally, Manus and Nauru give rise to compressed temporality whose priority is to circumvent governmental prohibitions on communication between detainees and the media (a cornerstone of those camps' purpose of geo-social isolation). These and other contrasts between modes, sites and durations of encampment highlight the extent to which the notions of crisis or urgency are disarticulated from the intolerability and injustice of life in a camp zone; indeed, they show that, sometimes, the idea of 'crisis' is inversely proportional to how long the intolerable has continued.

The section's third chapter, by Madelaine Hron, takes a wider view, tracing the prevalence of the camp in a range of narrative and documentary films concerning refugee experiences over the second half of the twentieth and the twenty-first centuries. Setting out a contrasting critical-aesthetic methodology to Fiddian-Qasmiyeh's and Qasmiyeh's geo-culturally specific analyses, Hron's chapter identifies patterns as well as discontinuities over several decades of cinematic representation in order to present a 'broadened perspective' on how this most epoch-shaping of forms entrenches certain narratives, images and ways of recognising refugeehood for (primarily) non-refugee audiences. Paying close attention to the continuities between the photographic still of journalism and cinematic work, Hron picks up on complexities – if not contradictions – inherent in the moving image as an aesthetic mode for comprehending the ostensible camp-as-stasis. As she notes, '[t]he camp, a space typically defined by its hopeless lack of action, its unproductive inertia and, most importantly, its waiting and deferral, is notoriously difficult to film'; moreover, as her discussion highlights, the camp is a challenging spatial proposition for establishing images and narratives that transcend short-lived forms of empathetic identification. Hron reminds us, crucially, that the semiotics of the camp can work against a classical understanding of the refugee as a persecuted civilian. When images of detained refugees are counterposed with prevailing discursive associations between the appearance of a refugee and the security of a sovereign state, migrant encampment 'increasingly correlates refugees with crime'.

This section of the book presents unique insights into what encampment means in the contemporary era, how it is represented, and how it might be reimagined. While it cannot offer a comprehensive account of the refugee camp – such an endeavour would easily fill a volume on its own – it does underscore a key notion applicable in some sense to all manifestations of the camp, and one productive for future analyses: that, as Fiddian-Qasmiyeh eloquently maintains, 'camps are always-already "more-than-camps", being connected to and through other spaces (diverse camp and non-camp spaces), and other times (including diverse pasts, presents and futures)'.

Bibliography

Agamben, Giorgio (2000), *Means Without End: Notes on Politics*, trans. Vincenzo Binetti and Cesare Casarino (Minneapolis: University of Minnesota Press, 2000).

Ramadan, Adam (2013), 'Spatialising the refugee camp', *Transactions of the Institute of British Geographers*, 38: 65–77.

Chapter 15

Memories and Meanings of Refugee Camps (and more-than-camps)

Elena Fiddian-Qasmiyeh

This chapter presents a counter-analysis of the widespread depiction of refugee camps as quintessential 'spaces of exception' (Agamben 1998; 2005), as 'non-places' or 'spaces of indistinction' which 'do not integrate other places, meanings, traditions and sacrificial, ritual moments but remain, due to a lack of characterization, non-symbolized and abstract spaces' (Diken 2004: 91, referring to Augé). While this depiction is in many ways canonical, it has nonetheless been extensively critiqued, including for discursively reproducing – rather than resisting – the depiction of refugees as 'bare life' (Agamben 1998), as non-agentic bodies that are the subject of diverse forms of governmentality, and for dismissing, *a priori*, the multiple meanings and senses of (be)longing(s) that may be developed, negotiated, resisted and contested by the inhabitants of protracted refugee camps (see, for example, Puggioni 2006; Le Cour Grandmaison, Lhuilier and Valluy 2007; Huysmans 2008; Ramadan 2012; Qasmiyeh and Fiddian-Qasmiyeh 2013; Fiddian-Qasmiyeh 2016a; 2016b; Gabiam and Fiddian-Qasmiyeh 2017). Building on these critiques, this chapter examines the ways in which refugee camps become (and/or remain) spaces of memories, meaning and belonging for refugees that endure across time and space in spite of, or precisely because of, being spaces of temporary-permanence created through violence and precariousness. In addition to situating the importance of camps in the lives of displaced people, I also argue that camps must be conceptualised as being deeply connected with, and constituted by, diverse spatialities and temporalities: in essence, I posit that camps are always-already 'more-than-camps', being connected to and through other spaces (diverse camp and non-camp spaces), and other times (including diverse pasts, presents and futures).

The chapter is based on my long-standing research into three intersecting case studies – the Sahrawi refugee camps in Algeria, and Palestinian refugee camps in Lebanon and in Syria. In particular, I bring together research that I have conducted in refugee camps and refugee-hosting cities since 2005 as part of a series of projects in the Middle East, the Caribbean and Europe. This includes my multi-sited ethnographic research with over 100 Sahrawi refugees (originally from the non-self-governing territory known as the Western Sahara) in the Sahrawi refugee camps in Algeria and during Sahrawi refugee youth's primary, secondary and tertiary level studies abroad in Cuba, Libya and Syria (see Fiddian-Qasmiyeh 2013; 2014; 2015);[1] and with 50 Sahrawi refugee children participating in a Holidays in Peace programme in Spain (Crivello and Fiddian-Qasmiyeh 2010). I also draw on my ongoing research with more than 100 Palestinian refugees from Lebanon and Syria living in Palestinian camps in Lebanon (Fiddian-Qasmiyeh 2015; 2019a); and with Palestinians living, studying and/or working in Cuba, France, Libya, Sweden and the UK (Fiddian-Qasmiyeh 2016a; 2016b; 2016c; 2016d; 2018; 2019b; Qasmiyeh and Fiddian-Qasmiyeh 2013; Fiddian-Qasmiyeh and Qasmiyeh 2016; 2017; and Gabiam and Fiddian-Qasmiyeh 2017).[2] These projects have thus included research in, about and through Sahrawi and Palestinian refugees' home-camps on the one hand (in Algeria, and in Lebanon and Syria), and in a range of 'hosting' spaces (France, Spain, Sweden and the UK), including spaces that have been 'shared' by both Sahrawi and Palestinian refugees (Cuba and Libya).

While studies have examined the ways in which camps become memorials of past traumatic events[3] and of the homeland (Khalili 2005), the first part of this chapter traces the extent to which memories not only of the homeland but also of home-camps travel with refugees across time and space.[4] It does so, in the first instance, through reference to my research with Sahrawi refugees studying in Cuba and Syria and visiting Spain, and is guided by a framework of 'travelling memories' (following Said 1983; see Fiddian-Qasmiyeh 2012); subsequently, it draws on my research into Palestinian refugees in the Middle East and in Europe, by tracing the connections and affinities that people may have with violent and hostile places, which researchers have in the past often argued are *not* (or indeed cannot be) spaces of belonging or longing precisely due to those exclusionary and violent characteristics. It is my aim here to demonstrate the need to transcend a long-standing binary academic focus on the significance of the past/homeland and the present/host-state, by highlighting that people hold multiple and simultaneous spatialities of belonging, including to home-camps and spaces characterised by, and created through, overlapping forms of precariousness.

In the second part of the chapter I further examine the multiplicity and simultaneity of Palestinian and Sahrawi camps as spaces of departure, origin, return and (non-)arrival. This entails acknowledging camps as complex spaces of refuge that are concurrently characterised and *constituted* by death, dying and destruction. In particular, I examine a range of processes surrounding and being created through what I conceptualise as 'the death and after-life of the camp'. Where Ramadan (2009) has examined the destruction of Nahr el-Bared camp in North Lebanon as a process of 'urbicide', I focus on the 'deaths' (or perhaps 'campicide') of Yarmouk camp (Syria) and Nahr el-Bared and Tel el-Zataar camps (Lebanon), through two main lenses.

Through an expansion of the lens of travelling meanings, I argue that camps that have been destroyed – such as Yarmouk, Nahr el-Bared and Tel el-Zataar – have taken on great emotional, symbolic and political significance at an individual and collective level both among former residents and *also* among those who have never resided in those camps and who are currently situated within and outside of the Middle East and North Africa (MENA) region. In turn, I examine what I refer to as 'the remains' or 'the after-life' of the camp, by continuing to experiment – building on Deleuze and Guattari (2013) – with developing a *rhizoanalysis* of refugee camps (Fiddian-Qasmiyeh 2019a).

Explored in more detail below, a rhizoanalysis effectively entails 'redirect[ing] analysis away from identifying stable meanings of interactions to mapping possibilities produced through interactions' (Lowry 2013: 26). In this context, it includes particular attention to the multiple interactions and relationalities that are *produced* in and through camps in relation to overlapping and ongoing processes of displacement and violence. It entails recognising the multiple relationships that exist between and produce different time-spaces, by acknowledging that these connections amount to more-than-a-network. That is to say, it is not simply that camps and their inhabitants are *connected* to other camps, to the homeland, and to other host-states through, for instance, physical visits and journeys, emotional connections, symbolic mobilisation, political affiliations and/or financial remittance. In order to shape this idea, I experiment with applying the metaphor of 'the rhizome' as proposed by Deleuze and Guattari (2013: 1–27) to reconceptualise meanings of camps. In biological terms, the rhizome is the opposite of the vertical model of the root: unlike a tree or rooted plant – which dies when it is uprooted or its roots are broken – a rhizome is a network of subterranean stems that extend horizontally, sporadically erupting to the surface to create new shoots while the stems continue both to expand and interconnect. It is through conceptualising protracted camps through the metaphor of the rhizome and by tracing rhizomatic dynamics that I argue that a camp is always more-than-a-camp and that camps are always-in-becoming, even when, or precisely because, they have been 'killed' and razed to the ground.

On the one hand, this part of the chapter includes an empirical reflection on the significance of life and death in the camp through an analysis of people's memories and ongoing visits to camp cemeteries in both 'living' and 'killed' camps (see Qasmiyeh, this volume; Qasmiyeh and Fiddian-Qasmiyeh 2013; Fiddian-Qasmiyeh and Qasmiyeh 2017). On the other hand, since a rhizome by definition has 'no beginning or end; it is always in the middle' (Deleuze and Guattari 2013: 26), I argue that it is essential to trace the ways in which camps are constituted precisely by the process of always being 'in the middle' of displacement. It is through an application of a rhizomatic lens that I argue that refugees and camps are always-already-in-the-middle (of displacement, and of being), and are intimately connected to other (camp and non-camp) spaces and times in such a way that even the 'erasure' or 'closure' of a camp at a particular time does not mark their end, as these remain as traces, or even as camps *in potentia*.

Concretely, I pinpoint and examine four modalities of 'shoots'[5] that have erupted to the surface of these always-already-interrupted-territories, with these physical and more-than-physical shoots indexing, or offering topographical testament to, refugees' and camps' simultaneous absence and presence: these shoots correspond to the Al-Awda/Salloum camp(s) on the Libyan–Egyptian border; Nahr el-Bared and Tel el-Zaatar camps in Lebanon, and Yarmouk camp in/from Syria; in addition to the cemeteries and tombstones of Nahr el-Bared and Baddawi camps in Lebanon; and Al-Mazaar school, displaced from and for Nahr el-Bared and Baddawi camps.

The chapter argues that these reflections have broader implications for conceptualisations of camps in relation to different processes, times and spaces of refugees' journeys (and, indeed, processes of immobility) at personal, familial and communal levels alike. Recognising that camps are spaces of longing and belonging, of meaning and memory, and of production and reproduction, is not to romanticise camps – which in the Palestinian context in particular, as Sayigh has noted (2000), are 'islands of insecurity' – but to centralise the extent to which camps themselves – whether physically intact or demolished – travel across time and space, being reconfigured, recreated and re-membered in complex and often paradoxical ways. In turn, by starting from the premise that camps are not isolated spatial zones inhabited by (and providing a space to bury) refugees, the urgency of focusing more intently on what I refer to as 'refugee–refugee relationality' (Fiddian-Qasmiyeh 2016b) prompts us to go beyond tracing, for example, 'the Sahrawi rhizome' or 'the Palestinian rhizome' as separate entities, and instead to focus on the productive and constitutive nature of the intersections arising between and across *diverse* refugees' lines of movement across time and space; for instance, through the Sahrawi-Palestinian-Syrian rhizome(s) implicitly mapped out below.

Travelling memories and meanings of home-camps

There has long been an overarching tendency in diaspora studies to explore migrants' and refugees' commitment to their and their ancestors' place of origin – the homeland – to the detriment of exploring the emotional and existential commitments that people may hold, develop and resist vis-à-vis multiple geographies and temporalities (Fiddian-Qasmiyeh 2012). Indeed, the definitive (normative/archetypal) features of 'a diaspora' include the members' commitment to ensuring the survival and strengthening of a common and collective memory about the homeland, including their commitment to transmitting this memory of the past/homeland to their descendants, and to other members of the diaspora located in other present/host-states (Safran 1991; Cohen 2008). While implicitly centralising *intergenerational* memory and identity with regard to this time-place, however, the diverse ways in which refugees, including children and youth, inherit, contest, negotiate, transmit and mobilise memories of different times and spaces have been examined only infrequently (Fiddian-Qasmiyeh 2012).

In order to address this gap, and complementing insights from the broader field of transnational studies, I developed (in Fiddian-Qasmiyeh 2012) a multi-sited case study of Sahrawi refugee youth to explore the ways in which different types of memories are transmitted both across time (from the older to the younger generation of Sahrawi refugees) and across space (from the Algerian-based refugee camps, to educational/hosting contexts such as Cuba, Libya, Spain and Syria, and to international arenas such as the UN). Following Said's notion of 'travelling theory' (1983: 226–47), I explored these dynamics as embodying a process of 'travelling memories'. Given that the educational trajectories of Sahrawi children and youth have required their short- and medium-term absence from their refugee camp homes, with the expectation of returning to work in the camps upon graduation, I examined the extent to which the transmission of a collective Sahrawi memory can be considered to take place *in spite of* children's separation from their families and home-camps, or *because of* this distance. More precisely, throughout my research the transmission of official memories of the *homeland* (the contested territory of the Western Sahara), under the 'guidance' of Sahrawi 'memory supervisors' who accompany refugee-students during their time away from the camps, emerged as being complemented and at times superseded by the development of and longing for memories of the youth's *home-camps* (Fiddian-Qasmiyeh 2012).

In this regard, my interviews with Sahrawi children, youth and adults in, through and beyond their home-camps in Algeria and their 'hosting' spaces of Cuba, Libya, Spain and Syria have demonstrated the existence of multiple spheres and locations of both memory making and memory projecting, revealing the Sahrawi refugee camps to be both a location from which to remember the homeland, but also a space to be remembered (and constructed) by Sahrawi children and youth from a distance. In this context I have argued that the transmission and negotiation of individual and collective memories of the refugee camps are arguably as significant to attempts to promote overall political change as memories of the history of the struggle to regain the Western Saharan homeland per se. One of the implications of this is that multiple processes of memory making and memory recuperating underpin diverse political commitments to a plurality of home-spaces, including both the homeland and the home-camp.

In the context of protracted encampment – such as that experienced by Sahrawi refugees since the 1970s and by Palestinian refugees since the

1940s – refugee camps are therefore not only spaces from which refugees may solidify and transmit particular memories of the homeland in order to develop political campaigns, for instance to secure the establishment of an independent state (for example, the Western Sahara and Palestine). Rather, and precisely by virtue of the protracted nature of the camps' existence and the diverse mechanisms developed to ensure their survival and that of their refugee inhabitants, refugee camps themselves may become spaces to be remembered, and equally spaces for political intervention and action in their own right. Even if refugee camps are themselves not conceptualised as permanent spaces by academics, international stakeholders (such as representatives of the UN or international organisations) or by many refugees themselves, refugees living in (and born into) protracted encampment situations may nonetheless – among other things – feel a sense of belonging to and longing for 'their' home-camp (Peteet 2005); the politicisation of memories of the homeland may correspond to only one dimension of their means of ensuring the survival of the refugee community, in the present and future.

In essence, while prioritising the commitment to the Palestinian homeland is, of course, pivotal on multiple levels for Palestinian refugees,[6] my ongoing research has aimed to show the urgency of going beyond the commonplace binary – which is essentially a spatio-temporal one – between the past/ sending/homeland and the present/receiving/host-state (Gabiam and Fiddian-Qasmiyeh 2017: 735).[7] Brun – building on Olwig's work – has argued that 'though many refugees and migrants *feel that they live*, or want to live, their lives elsewhere [i.e. in the homeland], they have a present life, where they need to survive' (Brun 2001: 19, emphasis added). This highlights not only that people hold and develop 'multiple spatialities of belonging' (Gabiam and Fiddian-Qasmiyeh 2017: 735), but also that these are characterised by *simultaneity*. Brun introduces this as a 'contradiction' – by noting 'the contradictions of being physically present in specific localities, but at the same time being part of translocal communities "rooted" in distant places' (2001: 19) – and yet this simultaneity directly 'disrupts the notion of the homeland being a place inhabited in the past, longed for in the present and desired for the future, by recognising that migrants may feel that their lives are *currently* lived in the homeland, even if this is from a physical distance' (Gabiam and Fiddian-Qasmiyeh 2017: 735).

Such examples demonstrate the extent to which studies undertaken through diasporic and transnational lenses have typically reproduced – rather than interrogated or situated – a focus on migrants' and refugees' connections with their past/homeland and the place in which they are currently present (Vertovec 2001; Mason 2007). On the one hand, the homeland and the '"home" of the lived reality' (Mason 2007: 275) are clearly of great significance on individual and collective levels; however, on the other hand, nuanced analyses have yet to carefully examine 'the complexities of being simultaneously affected by, attached to, and mobilising for, not only the homeland and the current place of residence, but also other places which may or may not be physically inhabited by family or community members' (Gabiam and Fiddian-Qasmiyeh 2017: 736). Importantly, such home-places and places of 'affinity' include hostile and precarious places – including violent home-camps – which researchers have in the past often argued are *not* spaces of belonging or longing (or indeed, are 'non-places' and 'spaces of indistinction'; Gabiam and Fiddian-Qasmiyeh 2017: 736) precisely due to those exclusionary and violent characteristics.[8]

By complementing a focus on the affective and political connections of refugee children, youth and adults to their and their families' 'home-camps' with attention to the significance of camps (and indeed other spaces) which have *not* been personally inhabited, it is possible (and urgent) to transcend a focus on the long-standing homeland/host-state dichotomy and to acknowledge the significance that diverse in-between spaces (and spaces-in-becoming) hold for different people in situations of displacement; as noted above, these include, precisely, diverse refugee camps characterised by violence and erasure.

Camps as spaces of origin, return and arrival

During my ongoing research in Baddawi refugee camp in North Lebanon – as part of a multi-sited analysis of local experiences of and responses to displacement from Syria in nine refugee-hosting and refugee-host communities in Lebanon, Jordan and Turkey – Palestinians formerly based in besieged (and often destroyed) Syrian camps and cities such as Yarmouk camp in Damascus have repeatedly indicated that when they fled Syria to Lebanon 'we arrived in the camp' and just 'passed through Lebanon' (Fiddian-Qasmiyeh 2016b). Having crossed the Syrian–Lebanese border, my interlocutors (including both Palestinians from Syria and Syrians displaced by the conflict) explained that they had travelled directly to, and arrived in, Baddawi camp, where established refugee-residents offered them shelter, food and clothes. Baddawi refugee camp was identified as their intended destination point from the very onset of their journeys, as they fled their 'original' home-camps in Syria to seek refuge in other Palestinians' home-camps precisely by retracing not (only) their own or their families' past steps, but rather the collective lines of movement and segmentation that constitute what I conceptualise as part of 'the Palestinian refugee camp rhizome'.

Refugees' home-camps have often been conceptualised and positioned as Palestinian and Sahrawi refugees' spaces of origin/departure/destination *in* which, or *from* which, safety can be sought in the context of diverse conflict situations. In this regard, Baddawi camp is currently both the 'origin(al)' home-camp for its circa 50,000 'permanent residents' and is also the camp-of-destination for Palestinian refugees (and indeed Syrian nationals) displaced by the conflict in Syria; equally, in previous processes, it has been the point of destination for tens of thousands of Palestinians displaced by recurrent conflicts, including elsewhere in Lebanon and in Iraq, Kuwait and, just prior to the Syria conflict, Libya (Fiddian-Qasmiyeh 2012; 2015).

The case of Baddawi highlights the extent to which 'non-Baddawi' Palestinians from Syria and Syrian refugees alike sought out the camp through their own means – often physically walking from Syria to Baddawi – while in the context of the 2011 Libyan conflict about 900 Sahrawi children who were studying in Libya were formally 'repatriated' to the Algeria-based refugee camps by the Algerian state (Fiddian-Qasmiyeh 2012). Among other things, this reasserts that the Sahrawi refugee camps are not merely points of *departure* (from which young people leave to seek an education, employment or indeed asylum), or places from which durable solutions must be sought. Rather, the Sahrawi camps in Algeria have been positioned as the Sahrawis' 'home' and (a) point of origin. 'Return' from Libya to the refugee camp origin in 2011 may well have been 'a solution' for these Sahrawi refugee adolescents, and may indeed have been longed for by young people who hold affective and political links to their home-camps; and yet it was certainly far from a *durable solution* as traditionally understood within the context of the formal international refugee regime (which denotes durable solutions as local integration into a host-state, repatriation to *the country of origin*, or resettlement to a third state).

Nonetheless, in the context of Sahrawi refugees' inability to return to the original *patria* (the Western Saharan 'homeland'), Sahrawi refugees' return to this refugee camp origin demonstrates that far from following a linear process (displacement–protraction–solution), Sahrawi refugees, like so many other protracted refugees including Palestinians, are always-already in the middle of displacement, where the camp is simultaneously the space of refuge, space of danger, point of origin, point of departure, point of return, and everything in between and in becoming. Indeed, well before 2011, both Sahrawi and Palestinian refugees had endured multiple experiences of displacement from Libya since at least the 1970s. These experiences of living in and being displaced in/from Libya constitute the nature of 'the Sahrawi rhizome' and 'the Palestinian rhizome' respectively, but also delineate traces of what we can refer to as the Libyan dimension of 'the Sahrawi-Palestinian rhizome'. Likewise, the encounter and relationality between Palestinians *and* Syrians displaced by the Syrian conflict and currently living in Baddawi camp highlights the extent to which 'the Palestinian camp rhizome' is always and already 'more-than-Palestinian', intersecting as it does with the 'Syrian rhizome' to constitute part of the 'Palestinian-Syrian rhizome'.[9]

Perhaps the most relevant case for the proposition of a rhizomatic approach to the study of camps derives from the expulsion of an estimated 30,000 Palestinian refugees from Libya in 1995, through which Gaddafi protested against the PLO's signing of the Oslo Accords. This mass expulsion was accompanied by the construction of a 'great camp' on the Salloum border between Libya and Egypt, ostensibly, according to Gaddafi, to secure Palestinians' 'return to Gaza and Jericho'. In Gaddafi's words:

> And as I care about the Palestinian cause, and in order to achieve the best interest of Palestinians, I will expel the thirty thousand Palestinians who currently live in my land, and *try to secure their return to Gaza and Jericho*. If Israel would not let them in, while Egypt does not allow them to pass through its territories, then *I shall set a great camp for them on the Egyptian–Libyan borders*. (Gaddafi, quoted by Sarhan in Al-Majdal 2010: 46, emphasis added)

It is notable – among other remarkable things – that Gaddafi's choice of name for the 'great camp' clearly centralised the Palestinian Right of Return, as enshrined in UN Resolutions 194 and 3236: *Mukhayyam Al-Awda* – the Return Camp.

In this dramatic example, Palestinian individuals, families and communities were simultaneously forcibly displaced and rendered immobile as a sacrifice for the greater good: to force 'the' durable solution of Palestinians' right to return to Palestine. We can indeed conceptualise the erection of the Return Camp precisely as a 'forced shoot' (in the sense of a bulb that is forced to bloom out of season), which Gaddafi drove to the surface, thereby topographically indexing both the existence of Palestinian refugees and, precisely, their inability to 'return'.

While Palestinian refugees were evidently not able to return to Gaza and Jericho at this time, and the Return Camp disappeared through diverse means (including the fraught relocation of Palestinians to various camps and cities that they had or had not previously inhabited across the Middle East, and the 'return' of Palestinians to different cities and towns across Libya), the closure of the camp was far from its end. At the outbreak of the 2011 Libyan war – which affected 50,000–70,000 Palestinians who were working and studying in Libya at the time (Fiddian-Qasmiyeh 2015) – several thousand Palestinians were once again left stranded on the Libyan–Egyptian border, including at the Salloum crossing where Gaddafi had, in 1995, created the Return Camp.

The closure of Al-Awda camp in the late 1990s may have temporarily suppressed the Palestinian camp/shoot that Gaddafi had forced to the surface on the Libyan–Egyptian border in 1995; however, a new line of flight in 2011 led to *a* camp's physical re-eruption in the same place at another time. This re-eruption reconnected both the new camp and the *remains* of Al-Awda camp to an ever-evolving Palestinian rhizome that is constituted through a multiplication of (current, past, future) places and spaces. In 2011 the camp for Palestinian refugees on the Salloum border – a camp that *returned*, even if it was not the Return Camp – demonstrates that the erasure or closure of a camp at a particular time does not mark the camp's end, as it remains as a trace, or, as this case study suggests, a camp *in potentia*. Here, the inhabitants, name and purpose of the camps have formally changed over time, and yet both camps are intimately related and intrinsically connected.

Where the construction, disappearance and return of Al-Awda camp remains an under-explored trace of Palestinian experiences of expulsion and encampment, the extreme violence and destruction that characterised the siege of Yarmouk camp (referred to in the vignette from Baddawi above) has meant that this camp in many regards became – and remains – a key symbol of the ongoing vulnerability of Palestinians in Syria, and also of the brutality of the Syrian conflict as a whole (Steele 2015). However, as argued in more detail in Gabiam and Fiddian-Qasmiyeh (2017), Yarmouk camp acquired a visceral centrality precisely as a symbol of the ongoing Palestinian catastrophe (Sa'di and Abu-Lughod 2007): 'the hermetic siege [of Yarmouk] will be remembered by historians along such infamous memories like that of Deir Yassin, Sabra and Shatila, Jenin and Gaza' (Baroud 2014).

Camps, death and campicide

To these 'remembered' besieged camps and territories I add Nahr el-Bared and Tel el-Zaatar camps in Lebanon, as being among the innumerable destroyed spaces for which both former residents and those who have never resided there (including Palestinians who currently live inside or beyond the MENA region) have strong emotional and political affinities, and as spaces that have taken on great symbolic and political significance at an individual and collective level across time and space. In addition to this, I argue that they are camps with important 'afterlives', beyond the dimension of remaining through memories and affinities, even in the context of total erasure and destruction.

Qasmiyeh's account – as a Palestinian who was born and raised in Baddawi camp in North Lebanon and who has long researched and 'written' the Palestinian camps from a 'middling' vantage point as a British citizen in the UK since the mid-2000s (see Qasmiyeh, this volume) – is particularly poignant vis-à-vis the multidimensional significance of Nahr el-Bared camp in North Lebanon and its destruction by the Lebanese army:

> We used to visit my mother's family in Nahr el-Bared . . . [T]hroughout my life, the journey itself to Nahr el-Bared has embodied an unbreakable link between one camp and another through a non-camp space. However, the unbreakable nature of this link was both amputated and transmuted due to the Lebanese military's destruction of Nahr el-Bared in 2007, which entailed the physical erasure of the camp and the relocation of the entire camp population, including my relatives, to my own home camp – Baddawi – and other camps across Lebanon. Despite the physical destruction of the camp infrastructure, or what Ramadan [2009] refers to as an instance of 'urbicide', this space, this land, still bears the traces of both the living and the deceased, and my mother has continued to visit the cemetery where my grandparents and relatives are buried in Nahr el-Bared. If the destruction

of Nahr el-Bared in and of itself embodied a *Nakba* within the *Nakba*, the determination to return, visit and revisit the cemetery there has become a central form of solidarity with memory and history. (Qasmiyeh, cited in Qasmiyeh and Fiddian-Qasmiyeh 2013: 132–3)

Even in the case of the 'urbicide' (or 'campicide') of Nahr el-Bared and Yarmouk camps, the 'death of the camp' through physical erasure and forced depopulation is far from an absolute process. The 'e/razed', flattened camp retains people's emotional and political affinity through their memories and longings, but also through the subterranean trace of Palestine within the camp cemetery's remains.

In the same context, Baddawi camp has come to witness the enduring trace of refugees whose overlapping experiences of displacement have led to their (temporary or permanent) relocation to live in Baddawi – including the arrival of refugees displaced from Yarmouk and Nahr el-Bared – and also to their burial in one of Baddawi's cemeteries. The tombstones in Figures 15.1 and 15.2 respectively mark the multiple processes of displacement and violence experienced by internally displaced refugees from Nahr el-Bared to Baddawi, and by Palestinian refugees displaced from Yarmouk camp in Syria, whose remains now lie, and are inscribed through their tombstones, in Baddawi camp.

As Qasmiyeh and I argue with regard to the tombstones and that which they continue to protect in Nahr el-Bared (in spite of the camp's destruction), the camp cemetery

> ironically represents a form of physical permanence which is sadly embodied by the dead while the living continue simultaneously to seek transience in the camps and permanence through a desired return to Palestine. As such, while the living 'desire' transience and refuse their permanent situatedness in the camps – wanting to move, migrate or return to the Palestinian home-land – the inevitability of leaving physical and spiritual traces through both bodies and shrines continues to force a never-ending bond with this transience. (Qasmiyeh and Fiddian-Qasmiyeh 2013: 133)

The multiple places of origin – born in Haifa, displaced from Yarmouk, died in Baddawi – marked on the tombstone depicted in figure 15.2 point to this simultaneity of transience and permanence, of multiple origins and belongings in contexts of overlapping displacements. The tombstones – and indeed the graves marked, in poverty, by stones, earth and wild flowers (Fig. 15.3) – are branching shoots nurtured to rise above the camp's surface, offering topographical testament to refugees' simultaneous presence and absence, here and there.

In addition to highlighting the extent to which 'ex-camps' continue to have an afterlife through traces and never-ending bonds with these times and spaces, Qasmiyeh's invocation of the destruction of Nahr el-Bared as 'a *Nakba* within the *Nakba*' not only refers to an additional catastrophe (such as the destruction of the camp and subsequent displacement from Nahr el-Bared) within the overarching national catastrophe (the loss of Palestine

Figure 15.1 The tombstone of a young woman killed during the war on Nahr el-Bared in 2007 (photograph: Elena Fiddian-Qasmiyeh)

Figure 15.2 A tombstone marking the longest of journeys: 'Born in Haifa in 1945 . . . died in Baddawi in July 2016 . . . Palestinian from Syria . . .' (photograph: Elena Fiddian-Qasmiyeh)

Figure 15.3 The unmarked grave of a child in Baddawi camp's fifth cemetery (photograph: Elena Fiddian-Qasmiyeh)

and the displacement of Palestinians from their territory); it also offers a tempo-spatial conceptualisation which can be tied to the rhizomatic notion of a never-ending eruption of memories, traces and physical structures emerging within always-already-interrupted territories.

A topographical conceptualisation within this context can be indexed to both the rebirth of Al-Awda/Salloum camp on the Libyan–Egyptian border and the birth of the tombstones in Baddawi – as individual 'shoots' erupting from subterranean remains to the surface of the earth, with the cemetery performing its dual role as a gatherer and gathering of markers of presence, absence and potentiality (Fiddian-Qasmiyeh and Qasmiyeh 2017). Hence, while the notion of the destruction of Nahr el-Bared as 'a *Nakba* within the *Nakba*' can clearly be extended to the siege of Yarmouk, and also more broadly to the violence experienced by Palestinians across Syria throughout the uprisings in that country, we can also reconfigure this to argue that we must conceptualise 'the camp' itself as both embracing and embodying other camps, becoming more-than-a-camp and also more than a-camp-within-the-camp. The latter is reflected not only through the arrival and enduring presence of Yarmouk in Baddawi camp, but also through the 're-emergence' of Tel el-Zaatar camp, which was destroyed in 1976, during the Lebanese Civil War, *in* Baddawi itself – Tel el-Zaatar was erased, and yet continues to exist, physically as well as metaphorically, in Baddawi (see Fig. 15.4).

Here, it is not merely memories and meanings of camps that travel across time and space, nor merely the inhabitants of camps who travel physically throughout and across the camp rhizome: camps themselves travel over time – as exemplified in the case of the return of the trace of the Return Camp through the eruption of a new camp on the Salloum border – and over space – through the 're-emergence' of Tel el-Zaatar within and *as* Baddawi camp and, some could argue, the more recent arrival of Yarmouk camp in Baddawi.

Within the broader refugee-camp rhizome, where the eruption of tombstones and ex-camps marks the presence/absence of reconfigured camps, it is equally the case that concrete components of an ex-camp may re-emerge in, and even migrate to and from, a different camp, produced by and producing new encounters. One such 'migratory' shoot is Al-Mazaar school, which in 2018 hosted the largest number of Palestinian children from Syria currently living in Baddawi:

> Al-Mazaar school [in addition to Majiddo and Amqa schools] *travelled* with the people from Nahr el-Bared . . . It used to be in Nahr el-Bared camp but when the camp was destroyed, and the people arrived here, schools were built for the children of Nahr el-Bared and they were *given the same names*. When the war in Nahr el-Bared ended, Amqa school *returned* to Nahr el-Bared while Majiddo and Al-Mazaar *stayed* in Baddawi, both for the children from Nahr el-Bared who remain here. and also for the children from Syria who have more recently arrived.[10]

Figure 15.4 The entrance to Tel el-Zaatar neighbourhood in Baddawi refugee camp (photograph: Elena Fiddian-Qasmiyeh)

A new structure was erected in Baddawi under the same signifier 'Al-Mazaar', to educate the same displaced children absent/present in both spaces – the collective departure (from Nahr el-Bared) and arrival (in Baddawi) of the children and their families was accompanied by the 'migration' of their school. This school bears the same name and, initially, taught the same students, but is now (in) a different-same place. While both Al-Mazaar and Majiddo schools migrated to and have 'stayed' in Baddawi, with their physical presence and names now marking the continued absence/presence both of the children of Nahr el-Bared and of Palestinian children from Syria, the secondary level Amqa school 'returned' to Nahr el-Bared as the camp's reconstruction progressed. Amqa school is both a rekindled shoot in/of Nahr el-Bared and a withered shoot in Baddawi, marking the place where the displaced children once were, are no longer, but may, potentially, be again.

Towards a rhizoanalysis of 'more-than-camps'[11]

As highlighted by Qasmiyeh (Qasmiyeh and Fiddian-Qasmiyeh 2013: 132–3), journeys between camps (whether 'regular', to visit family or cemeteries, or in the context of conflict and mass violence), and the afterlives of camp residents, camps and camp-components alike, simultaneously mark *spatial* connections between different types of space ('an unbreakable link between one camp and another through a non-camp space'), *temporalities* (a simultaneous desire for 'transience' and 'permanence' and an imposed 'never-ending bond with this transience'), *directionalities* and *im/mobilities* (visits, relocation, situatedness, remains and return).

The presence, absence and trace of people and camps within, under, through and *as* a camp such as Baddawi mark the overlapping histories and spatialities of displacement that both define Palestinian-ness and also 'make' the camp – through their symbolic and physical resonance, Yarmouk, Nahr el-Bared and Tel el-Zaatar camps are more than physically 'within' Baddawi camp, they *are* the history, present and potential future of Baddawi. Baddawi cannot be visited, seen, heard, photographed or written (Qasmiyeh 2016; 2017a; 2017b; 2017c; this volume) as a camp, even a home-camp, in isolation – it is, by definition more than 'a' camp, not only because of the movements of people for whom the camp is an origin, a point of departure, a destination and place of refuge, but also because of both the mobility and immobility of different camps and camp-elements in and out of and emerging through the camp. It is always a camp-in-relation, always a camp-in-becoming and both a 'home-camp' and an 'ex-camp' *in potentia*.

Here I am continuing to re-member camps through a rhizoanalysis. In my analysis of Baddawi camp's position in relation to other camps such as Yarmouk, Nahr el-Bared and Tel el-Zaatar, I have aimed to draw the figure/metaphor of the rhizome, which Deleuze and Guattari conceptualise (or, as some decry, overly romanticise) as characterised by a seemingly limitless adaptability and multiplicity. In line with Deleuze and Guattari's conceptualisation of the rhizome, I have argued that 'sporadic eruptions' – including, in this case, the interconnected eruptions of people, tombstones, schools and camps themselves – change the camp-rhizome's very 'nature as it expands its connections' (Deleuze and Guattari 2013: 7): these productive eruptions themselves mean that, although a camp-rhizome 'may be broken, shattered at a given spot . . . it will start up again on one of its old lines, or on new lines' (Deleuze and Guattari 2013: 8). In this way, a camp-rhizome is always in a process of *becoming*: it is 'a model that is perpetually in construction or collapsing' and which is characterised by 'a process that is perpetually prolonging itself, breaking off and starting up again' (Deleuze and Guattari 2013: 21).

As I have argued elsewhere (Fiddian-Qasmiyeh 2019a), what is essential in developing a rhizoanalysis of camps is to 'examine how power works through the organization and conceptualization of space and movement' (Stepputat 1999: 416), and to 'simultaneously challenge and redefine locatedness', rather than deny its significance (Gedalof 2000). As my research demonstrates (in line with Turton's assertion with regard to the Mursi people of Ethiopia, 1999: 421), being displaced should not (only) be defined in terms of having been forcibly removed from a nurturing homeland which one longs for, but as the perpetual risk of being displaced from a broader terrain across which one has multiple, and yet at times paradoxical, attachments and affinities.

Deleuze and Guattari remind us of the coexistence – rather than duality – and mutually constitutive relationship between territorialisation and deterritorialisation, of locatedness and the permanent risk of expulsion:

> Every rhizome contains lines of segmentarity according to which is it stratified, territorialized, organized, signified, attributed, etc., as well as lines of deterritorialization *down which it constantly flees*. There is a rupture in the rhizome whenever segmentary lines *explode into a line of flight*, but *the line of flight is part of the rhizome*. These lines always tie back to one another. (Deleuze and Guattari 2013: 8–9, emphasis added)

The conceptualisation of territorialised, segmentary lines of a rhizome 'constantly flee[ing]' and 'explod[ing]' into deterritorialised lines of flight that are essential *constitutive* parts of the rhizome is of particular relevance to my reflection on the nature of camps as more-than-camps: the erasure of Yarmouk, or Nahr el-Bared, or Tel el-Zaatar has not led to the death of the camp per se, not only because Nahr el-Bared is being physically 'reconstructed' (on a different scale) as I write, but also because of the flight, eruption and re-emergence *of* these camps *into* another space (in this case, Baddawi camp) which itself is *constituted* by the immanence of such ruptures, explosions and eruptions.

The multiple processes of erasure, displacement and dispossession that refugees have directly experienced, observed and anticipated from afar lead me to recognise the significance of Deleuze and Guattari's conceptualisation of the rhizome as having 'no beginning or end; it is always in the middle, between things, interbeing, *intermezzo*' (Deleuze and Guattari 2013: 26). It is this 'middle' 'from which it grows and which it overspills', with the rhizome – and the camp – composed 'not of units but of dimensions, or rather directions in motion' (Deleuze and Guattari 2013: 22). When viewed through this analytical lens, refugee camps and their residents are always-already in the middle of displacement, never at the beginning or at the end. Recognising that there is no end to 'the refugee cycle' (Black and Koser 1999) is not to refute the significance of developing lines both of segmentarity and of deterritorialisation to continue life and living. Rather it encourages us to examine displacement and camps by 'proceeding from the middle, through the middle, coming and going rather than starting and finishing' (Deleuze and Guattari 2013: 27). To do so is to challenge, rather than reify, a sense of liminality by recognising that there are multiple attachments to multiple 'plateaux' and that with each eruption into a line of flight, the camp-rhizome itself changes and continues its process of *becoming*, rather than reaching a (re)solution.

In effect, as I have argued above, refugees, including Sahrawis and Palestinians, develop strong attachments to certain places and territories, including but not limited to the historic homelands and home-camps, but also to diverse camp and non-camp environments that may or may not have been personally inhabited; this is the case even if such forms of attachment are ambivalent in nature, simultaneously attractive and yet repulsive, spaces of refuge and of persecution (Fiddian-Qasmiyeh 2013; Qasmiyeh and Fiddian-Qasmiyeh 2013; Gabiam and Fiddian-Qasmiyeh 2017). These multiple forms and directionalities of attachment, and the recognition that refugee camps and their residents, like rhizomes, 'can act at a distance, come or return a long time after, but always under conditions of discontinuity, rupture, and multiplicity' (Deleuze and Guattari 2013: 16), require us to continue developing alternative conceptualisations of displacement and camps alike.

Refugee camp-rhizomes – which are constantly changing in light of local, national and geopolitical shifts – encompass infinite spatialities and temporalities, including homelands, home-camps, host-states and past, present and future other-same-camps (Gabiam and Fiddian-Qasmiyeh 2017). Camps are always more-than-camps, characterised by multiple origins, presents and futures (see also Maalouf 2009), and both connected to and constituted by other camp and non-camp spaces and times. As I have argued elsewhere (Fiddian-Qasmiyeh 2013; Qasmiyeh and Fiddian-Qasmiyeh 2013; Gabiam and Fiddian-Qasmiyeh 2017), far from being quintessential 'spaces of exception' (Agamben 1998; 2005) or 'non-places' (Diken 2004: 91, referring to Augé), refugee camps are simultaneously 'reservoirs of memory' of the homeland and are themselves spaces of belonging and longing, both as 'lived' home-camps and as potent 'symbolic' spaces; they are a symptom of displacement and are also 'original' spaces, spaces of origin, of destination, of return, and spaces-in-becoming that intersect, connect with and are constituted by the eruption of 'other' and 'other-same' refugees' lines of flight. Furthermore, rather than camp-rhizomes developing in isolation (i.e. assuming the existence of 'the Sahrawi rhizome' or 'the Palestinian rhizome'), it is essential to continue to be attentive to the productive and constitutive processes through which diverse refugees' lines of movement intersect and connect with other refugees' lines of movement (i.e. the Sahrawi-Palestinian rhizome and the Palestinian-Syrian rhizome implicitly traced above and in Fiddian-Qasmiyeh 2019a); and indeed how these intersecting and multiplying lines of flight tie back to one another to constitute the very nature and directionality of these and other rhizome(s).

Notes

1. This multi-sited research formed the foundation of my ESRC-funded doctoral research vis-à-vis the protracted Sahrawi refugee situation (Fiddian-Qasmiyeh 2014).
2. Research with a dozen Palestinians undertaking their studies in Cuban universities formed part of my ESRC-funded doctoral research; interviews with 49 Palestinians based in France, Sweden and the United Kingdom at the time (between 2012 and 2014) formed part of the broader 'Stateless Diasporas in the EU' project funded by the Leverhulme Trust that I led at the University of Oxford (as part of the university-wide Oxford Diaspora Programme) and which examined how Kurds and Palestinians in Europe conceptualise statelessness and diasporic belonging; interviews with Palestinians based in seven camps across Lebanon were funded by a grant from the Henry Luce Foundation; and my ongoing research with Palestinian refugees from Syria and with Palestinians based in Lebanon is part of a broader project examining local community responses to displacement from Syria across nine communities in Lebanon, Jordan and Turkey, funded by a large AHRC-ESRC research grant (see www.refugeehosts.org, grant reference AH/P005438/1).
3. In relation to the Palestinian camps, these include memorials for past/ongoing events such as the *Nakba* and the Right to Return (Gabiam and Fiddian-Qasmiyeh 2017).
4. This part of the chapter draws upon sections from Fiddian-Qasmiyeh (2013).
5. Acknowledging that these are different 'modalities' and 'directionalities' of shoots, I have not labelled these different shoots, given my concerns around typologies and categorisation, other than referring to Al-Mazaar as a 'travelling' or 'migratory' shoot. I anticipate dwelling further on the modalities and directionalities of these and other shoots within/across/as the Palestinian-Syrian rhizome in future.
6. See Fiddian-Qasmiyeh (2016a; 2019a) and Gabiam and Fiddian-Qasmiyeh (2017). Indeed, it is worth stressing that 'forms of attachment and belongings to places other than Palestine do not necessarily come at the expense of refugees' sense of connection with the Palestinian homeland or their political activism in relation to the homeland. Not only do affective links to the camp and the homeland often co-exist (see Fiddian-Qasmiyeh 2015; 2016) but they can also feed off each other' (Gabiam and Fiddian-Qasmiyeh 2017: 740).

7. The following sections are based on arguments I have made in Gabiam and Fiddian-Qasmiyeh (2017).
8. See Mason (2007) on a reported lack of (be)longing to Kuwait among ex-Kuwaiti Palestinians based in Australia; cf. Fiddian-Qasmiyeh's research with Palestinians displaced in/from Libya in the 1970s, 1990s and 2000s, who yet report 'missing' and 'longing for' the country (2015: 131).
9. On the Sahrawi-Cuban-Palestinian rhizome, see Fiddian-Qasmiyeh (2019a).
10. This extract is taken from an interview by the author and Yousif M. Qasmiyeh with a female Palestinian teacher from and in Baddawi refugee camp, Lebanon in April 2017. Translated by Qasmiyeh from Arabic into English; emphasis added by the author.
11. This section builds on my experimentation with rhizoanalysis in relation to reconceptualising 'durable solutions' for Sahrawi and Palestinian refugees (Fiddian-Qasmiyeh 2019a).

Bibliography

Agamben, G. (1998), *Homo Sacer: Sovereign Power and Bare Life*, trans. Daniel Heller-Roazen (Stanford: Stanford University Press).

Agamben, G. (2005), *State of Exception* (Chicago: University of Chicago Press).

Al-Majdal (2010), 'The Palestinian crisis in Libya 1994–1996: interview with Professor Bassem Sirhan', *Al-Majdal*, 45: 44–9.

Baroud, R. (2014), 'Tears of Yarmouk: the Palestinian lesson that every Syrian should know', *The Palestine Chronicle*, 5 March, http://www.palestinechronicle.com/tears-of-yarmouk-the-palestinian-lesson-that-every-syrian-should-know/#.VK2WqmTF-Kc (accessed 15 February 2015).

Black, R., and K. Koser (eds) (1999), *The End of the Refugee Cycle? Refugee Repatriation and Reconstruction* (Oxford: Berghahn Books).

Brun, C. (2001), 'Reterritorializing the relationship between people and place in refugee studies', *Geografiska Annaler*, 831: 15–25.

Cohen, R. (2008), *Global Diasporas: An Introduction*, 2nd edn (London: Routledge).

Crivello, G., and E. Fiddian-Qasmiyeh (2010), 'The ties that bind: Sahrawi children and the mediation of aid in exile', in D. Chatty (ed.), *Deterritorialized Youth: Sahrawi and Afghan Refugees at the Margins of the Middle East* (Oxford: Berghahn Books), 85–118.

Deleuze, G., and F. Guattari (2013), *A Thousand Plateaus* (London: Bloomsbury).

Diken, B. (2004), 'From refugee camps to gated communities', *Citizenship Studies*, 8.1: 83–106.

Fiddian-Qasmiyeh, E. (2012), 'Invisible refugees and/or overlapping refugeedom? Protecting Sahrawis and Palestinians displaced by the 2011 Libyan uprising', *International Journal of Refugee Law*, 24.2: 263–93.

Fiddian-Qasmiyeh, E. (2013), 'The inter-generational politics of "travelling memories": Sahrawi refugee youth remembering home-land and home-camp', *Journal of Intercultural Studies*, 34.6: 631–49.

Fiddian-Qasmiyeh, E. (2014), *The Ideal Refugees: Gender, Islam and the Sahrawi Politics of Survival* (Syracuse: Syracuse University Press).

Fiddian-Qasmiyeh, E. (2015), *South-South Educational Migration, Humanitarian-ism and Development: Views from the Caribbean, North Africa and the Middle East* (Abingdon: Routledge).

Fiddian-Qasmiyeh, E. (2016a), 'On the threshold of statelessness: Palestinian narratives of loss and erasure', *Journal of Ethnic and Racial Studies*, 39.2: 301–21.

Fiddian-Qasmiyeh, E. (2016b), 'Refugees hosting refugees', *Forced Migration Review*, 53: 25–7.

Fiddian-Qasmiyeh, E. (2016c), 'Refugee–refugee relations in contexts of overlapping displacement', *International Journal of Urban and Regional Research*, http://www.ijurr.org/spotlight-on-overview/spotlight-urban-refugee-crisis/refugee-refugee-relations-contexts-overlapping-displacement/ (accessed 16 July 2019).

Fiddian-Qasmiyeh, E. (2016d), '*Repress*entations of displacement in the Middle East', *Public Culture*, 28.3: 457–73, doi:10.1215/08992363-3511586.

Fiddian-Qasmiyeh, E. (2018), 'UNRWA financial crisis: the impact on Palestinian employees', *MERIP*, 48.286: 33–6.

Fiddian-Qasmiyeh, E. (2019a), 'From roots to rhizomes: mapping rhizomatic strategies in the Sahrawi and Palestinian refugee situations', in M. Bradley, J. Milner and B. Peruniak (eds), *Shaping the Struggles of their Times: Refugees, Peace-building and Resolving Displacement* (Washington, DC: Georgetown University Press).

Fiddian-Qasmiyeh, E. (2019b), 'The changing faces of UNRWA: from the global to the local', *Journal of Humanitarian Affairs*, 1.1: 28–41.

Fiddian-Qasmiyeh, E., and Y. M. Qasmiyeh (2016), 'Refugee neighbours and hostipitality: exploring the complexities of refugee–refugee humanitarianism', *The Critique*, 5 January, https://refugeehosts.org/2018/03/20/refugee-neighbours-hostipitality/ (accessed 12 July 2019).

Fiddian-Qasmiyeh, E., and Y. M. Qasmiyeh (2017), 'Refugee–refugee solidarity in death and dying' (multi-media piece), invited contribution to *The Absence of Paths*, Tunisian Pavillion, Venice Biennale, May.

Gabiam, N., and E. Fiddian-Qasmiyeh (2017), 'Palestinians and the Arab uprisings: political activism and narratives of home, homeland and home-camp', *Journal of Ethnic and Migration Studies*, 43.5: 731–48, doi: 10.1080/1369183X.2016.1202750.

Gedalof, I. (2000), 'Identity in transit nomads, cyborgs and women', *The European Journal of Women's Studies*, 7: 337–54.

Huysmans, J. (2008), 'The jargon of exception – on Schmitt, Agamben and the absence of political society', *International Political Sociology*, 2: 165–83.

Khalili, L. (2005), 'Palestinian commemoration in the refugee camps of Lebanon', *Comparative Studies of South Asia, Africa and the Middle East*, 25.1: 30–45.

Le Cour Grandmaison, O., G. Lhuilier and J. Valluy (eds) (2007), *Le Retour des Camps? Sangatte, Lampedusa, Guantanamo* (Paris: Autrement).

Lowry, C. S. (2013), 'Lines of flight: a rhizomatic exploration of transparency in three international humanitarian sites', *Kaleidoscope*, 12: 19–33.

Maalouf, A. (2009), *Origins: A Memoir* (New York: Farrar, Straus, and Giroux).

Mason, V. (2007), 'Children of the "idea of Palestine": negotiating identity, belonging and home in the Palestinian diaspora', *Journal of Intercultural Studies*, 28.3: 271–85.

Middle East Monitor (2014), 'Children in Gaza demand protection for the starving children in Yarmouk refugee camp', *Middle East Monitor*, 15 January, https://www.middleeastmonitor.com/news/middle-east/9245-children-in-gaza-demand-protection-for-the-starving-children-in-yarmouk-refugee-camp (accessed 17 February 2015).

Peteet, J. (2005), *Landscape of Hope and Despair: Palestinian Refugee Camps* (Philadelphia: University of Pennsylvania Press).

Puggioni, R (2006), 'Resisting sovereign power: camps in-between exception and dissent', in J. Huysmans, A. Dobson and R. Prokhovnik (eds), *The Politics of Protection. Sites of Insecurity and Political Agency* (London: Routledge), 68–83.

Qasmiyeh, Y. M. (2016), 'Writing the camp', *Refugee Hosts*, 30 September, https://refugeehosts.org/2016/09/30/writing-the-camp/ (accessed 16 July 2019).

Qasmiyeh, Y. M. (2017a), 'Refugees are dialectical beings', *Refugee Hosts*, 5 September, https://refugeehosts.org/2017/09/05/refugees-are-dialectical-beings-part-two/ (accessed 16 July 2019).

Qasmiyeh, Y. M. (2017b), 'Writing the camp-archive', *Refugee Hosts*, 1 September, https://refugeehosts.org/2017/09/01/refugees-are-dialectical-beings-part-one/ (accessed 16 July 2019).

Qasmiyeh, Y. M. (2017c), 'A sudden utterance is the stranger', *Refugee Hosts*, 15 April, https://refugeehosts.org/2017/04/25/a-sudden-utterance-is-the-stranger/ (accessed 16 July 2019).

Qasmiyeh, Y. M. (2017d), 'The camp is time', *Refugee Hosts*, 15 January, https://refugeehosts.org/2017/01/15/the-camp-is-time/ (accessed 16 July 2019).

Qasmiyeh, Y. M., and E. Fiddian-Qasmiyeh (2013), 'Refugee camps and cities in conversation', in Jane Garnett and Alana Harris (eds), *Migration and Religious Identity in the Modern Metropolis* (Farnham: Ashgate), 131–43.

Ramadan, A. (2009), 'Destroying Nahr el-Bared: sovereignty and urbicide in the space of exception', *Political Geography*, 28.3: 153–63.

Ramadan, A. (2012), 'Spatialising the refugee camp', *Transactions*, 38.1: 65–77.

Sa'di, A. H., and L. Abu-Lughod (2007), 'Introduction', in Ahmad H. Sa'di and Lila Abu-Lughod (eds), *Nakba: Palestine, 1948, and the Claims of Memory* (New York: Columbia University Press), 1–24.

Safran, W. (1991), 'Diaspora in modern societies: myths of homeland and return', *Diaspora*, 1.1: 83–99.

Said, E. W. (1983), *The World, the Text, and the Critic* (London: Vintage).

Sayigh, R. (2000), 'Greater insecurity for refugees in Lebanon', Middle East Research and Information Project, 1 March, www.merip.org/mero/mero030100 (accessed 14 May 2019).

Steele, J. (2015), 'How Yarmouk became the worst place in Syria', *The Guardian*, 5 March, http://www.theguardian.com/news/2015/mar/05/how-yarmouk-refugee-camp-became-worst-place-syria (accessed 6 July 2015).

Stepputat, F. (1999), 'Responses to Kibreab, "dead horses?"', *Journal of Refugee Studies*, 12.4: 416–19.

Turton, D. (1999), 'Response to Kibreab', *Journal of Refugee Studies*, 12.4: 419–21.

UNESCO (2011), *The Hidden Crisis: Armed Conflict and Education*, EFA Global Monitoring Report.

Vertovec, S. (2001), 'Transnationalism and identity', *Journal of Ethnic and Migration Studies*, 27.4: 573–82.

Chapter 16

Writing the Camp: Death, Dying and Dialects

Yousif M. Qasmiyeh

This chapter assesses the ways in which refugees *write* the camp into their own multiple narratives vis-à-vis markers (and embodiments) of temporality, permanence and liminality. It sets the scene by situating the Palestinian camps in Lebanon, in particular Baddawi (the author's place of birth), both spatially (i.e. in conjunction with neighbouring places in Lebanon and beyond) and as places that embody the ultimate capacity to welcome as well as repel old and new refugees. The second part of the chapter sheds light on how traversing, deserting and eventually revisiting the camp clash and collaborate to give the refugee the necessary time and space to ponder the act of writing from within and without. The third part enters into conversation with Derrida's concepts (and/or clusters) of 'cinders', 'the shibboleth' and the figure (and the manifestations) of 'the arrivant'. As such, it speaks to the notion of cinders as the material elements that constitute viable traces in and of the camp. Such an interrogation will in particular trace the geographical and practical history of the first cemetery in Baddawi camp and how its *middleness* both encapsulates and truncates the journey (back) to the camp. The discussion then moves to what is deemed the shibboleth in the camp amid the influx of other refugee groups into that space. It briefly explores how dialects (Palestinian or otherwise) in the camp have become signifiers of inclusion and exclusion and how new arrivants negotiate (in)visibility in this medium of precariousness. The chapter concludes by returning to the subjective in writing, interrogating how personal accounts of leaving the camp and (re)turning to it are a clear manifestation of the impossibility of arrival.

Space-time in Baddawi camp

The Palestinian refugee camps in Lebanon have never been places devoid of politics. Nor have they been places that have been in charge of their own destinies in the ways that independent places can form and reform histories and memories. In other words, their very presence has become contingent on the interpretation and reinterpretation of the politics therein. This is, first, through what became known as the *Nakba* ('the catastrophe' – see Zureik 1948), which led to the establishment of Israel and, as a result, to the expulsion of hundreds of thousands of Palestinians into neighbouring Arab countries, in particular Lebanon, Syria and Jordan; and secondly, through the dynamics that have come to govern these refugees' relationships with their hosting people/countries and the wider region.

The Palestinian camps in Lebanon have been run and managed for over six decades under the auspices of the United Nations Relief and Works Agency (UNRWA). For such management to take shape, different UNRWA-run institutions and facilities have been built, such as schools (mainly primary and intermediate), distribution centres and clinics in and/or around the camps. For many Palestinians, UNRWA has become synonymous with the term 'Palestinian refugee' and, as such, a complex relationship of gratitude (mainly in the early years) and repulsion has come to constitute the camp–UNRWA nexus. Being unable to provide for all Palestinians in the camps, and at times being identified as a bystander more than an active participant on issues pertaining to unemployment, education and medication, some Palestinians have increasingly started to view UNRWA as an institution whose agendas have continuously shifted; first, as the main helper and provider for the Palestinians and, secondly, as the institution that has more recently been trying to monitor as well as censor certain practices and events of remembrance (and at times resistance) in the camps.

The latter is in line with what UNRWA claims to be the protection of 'neutrality' in environments that are highly precarious both politically and socially. Such tensions have not only punctuated the relationship between Palestinian refugees and UNRWA, but have also shed a special light on the ever-changing nature and conditions of hospitality in insecure contexts. The relationship that used to be linear (giver vs recipient) in the early years of the *Nakba* has now become multifarious, complex and most certainly antagonistic. Indeed, in determining to voice concerns about the continual reduction of rations and, in particular, the censorship that UNRWA has imposed on certain inaugural events in schools, people in the camps have not only enacted the role of the protectors of themselves, but have equally ensured the emergence of other forms of resistance in the camps.

Far from the refugee camps in Lebanon having achieved a state of security, they have always been seen as its antithesis (Sayigh 2000). The large number of refugee camps and gatherings in a small country such as Lebanon, which has itself lived through wars, civil wars and sectarian tensions for as long as one can remember, must have contributed to, and at times aggravated, in one way or another, the question of stability there. Palestinians in Lebanon have historically held the roles of refugees, members of militias and various factions, active participants in, and at times configurers of, the Lebanese sociopolitical fabric due to their military and ideological might, especially in the early 1970s, and because of the extensive solidarity they have attracted in Lebanon and beyond. In other words, both the camps and the refugees in Lebanon have responded to changes, be they political or social, and, to a certain degree, they have generated changes to constitute histories whose aim is to vocally declare their presence in light of the absence of any political solutions on the horizon. Baddawi camp, for instance, is no longer the same camp that was established in the 1950s, but is a site through which various transformations can take place without it losing its camp-like nature (Qasmiyeh and Fiddian-Qasmiyeh 2013; Fiddian-Qasmiyeh 2019; and this volume).

Baddawi camp is located on the outskirts of Lebanon's second largest city, Tripoli, in the north of the country; along with Nahr El-Bared camp, it has ensured Palestinians' presence in northern Lebanon for almost seven decades. It is a small camp compared with other camps, which are considered big, 'more insecure' and overpopulated. Its location is seen as both significant and strategic in the history of the Palestinian military resistance, and with regard to its involvement in the Camps War in the 1980s and in other military clashes in Tripoli.[1] Baddawi camp, generally, has never been neutral in its handling of political events in the camp itself, in Lebanon or further afield.[2] This historical lack of neutrality has always been seen as a form of active involvement for the sake of protecting the camp and its inhabitants.

Death and dying in Baddawi[3]

Although the camp itself constitutes as well as evaluates our relationship with other places, its position as a place/time in our lives has always been that of an independent place whose survival rests solely on the camp itself. In other words, it is through living and dying in the camp that we come to terms with who we are, as refugees, never in the infinite sense but as a means of querying the dynamics therein. One of many questions is who are we to maintain geographical coexistence between life and death? How is it possible always to desire to be buried in the camp when 'legally' it is a place that it is impossible to 'own'? Nor is it a place in which the 'existential invariables', such as graves, memorials and murals, can be transferred to other more 'permanent' spaces (Fiddian-Qasmiyeh and Qasmiyeh 2017; Khalili 2005). In order to approach these questions, it is important to situate the cemetery in relation to Baddawi camp, and vice versa.

Cemeteries are never built: they simply exist in the camps. When the peripheries of the space that is Baddawi were occupied by Palestinian refugees, this occupation marked the unintentional erection of what I refer to as *quasi-borders*. Those Palestinians who used to live in stables in a north Tripoli neighbourhood called Khan Al-'Askar descended into Baddawi as soon

Figure 16.1 Masjid al-Quds, Baddawi camp (photograph: Elena Fiddian-Qasmiyeh)

as UNRWA secured a lease on the land in the 1950s. Barracks were quickly erected on the edges of this space, and families who mainly originated from the Palestinian cities of Haifa, Jaffa and Acre and were then based in Khan Al-'Askar and other neighbouring places started to cluster there.[4] Masjid Al-Quds, which was seen by many as the first praying space in Baddawi, was built soon after.[5] Masjid Al-Quds is now a mosque and is completely managed by the Committee of Mosques, a congregation of Palestinian elders and religious figures inside Baddawi whose funding comes mainly from weekly collections – normally collected after Friday prayers – and donations from within the camp, including from small businesses, and from Palestinians who live abroad in Scandinavia, Germany and Britain (Qasmiyeh and Fiddian-Qasmiyeh 2013).

The presence of the mosque in Baddawi has meant that in order for the camp's residents to bury their dead, a cemetery should exist:

From [Baddawi's] very birth, the cemetery has hosted the living and the dead. The arrival of the living to the camp was traced by the arrival of the dead. From that core, the camp has grown, and so too have its residents. (Fiddian-Qasmiyeh and Qasmiyeh 2017)

Figure 16.2 Baddawi camp's 'original' cemetery (photograph: Elena Fiddian-Qasmiyeh)

This main and oldest cemetery lies in close proximity to Masjid al-Quds, almost equidistant from the lower and upper parts of the camp, and is situated in a depression that acts as the juncture between these. To welcome the dead, the cemetery spreads across a rectangular piece of land, with slightly elongated corners, where alleyways acting as paths to different corners in the camps go either through or around it. Thus, as is the case in Baddawi, '[d]etermining a place consists in determining the death of its people at the same time' (Fiddian-Qasmiyeh and Qasmiyeh 2017). The cemetery in a sense is the core of the camp, its dead and beating heart, *a* place upon which ties are established and negotiated with *the* place that is never ours, and yet it is what we have been assigned to contain and memorialise our dead and their remains in one place.

As the population in Baddawi continues to increase exponentially – especially given the ongoing arrival of refugees from Syria – so does the cemetery, not size-wise but capacity-wise, where the new dead share the same graves with the old dead, representing another mode of intergenerational refugeeness.[6] This mode is precisely what gives the camp itself a transcendental potentiality – a potential to regather what is deemed ungatherable and scattered in static places such as cemeteries.

In the case of Palestinians who manage to leave the camp only to die abroad, it is common practice for their families and relatives (and, at times, the wider community in Baddawi) to ensure the repatriation of the deceased to the camp. It is as if this kind of return were the only return that they are capable of, in contrast with their strandedness and stasis in Baddawi and beyond:

> Those refugees who left the camp in life return in death: a sense of belonging to that land, 'a' land that is 'theirs' even if 'their' land remains elsewhere. Those who live on the borders of the camp – whose citizenship does not afford them the riches to be buried in a citizen-grave – arrive in a space that is not theirs. Now, the shared spaces have become denser, with the camp and its cemeteries welcoming the living, dying, and the dead who originated elsewhere (at some time, always-already in the middle of time). (Fiddian-Qasmiyeh and Qasmiyeh 2017)

Thus, the cemetery resembles a state of being within another state of being, which is that of the camp itself, and as such, the cemetery is neither entirely dependent on nor independent of the camp. In essence, the cemetery in Baddawi is where refugees barter the dissolution of their lives with the solidity of the cemetery – as a medium that can neither be carried (away) nor transferred to another place. In this way, the cemetery, as both a symptom and a product of the camp, becomes the only remnant of 'the community' when refugees, *as communities*, are dispersed and are therefore no more.

So long as the cemetery exists, there must always be a gravedigger (Fiddian-Qasmiyeh and Qasmiyeh 2017). As I write (in spring 2018), there are five cemeteries in Baddawi and although at times family members are involved in the digging of the grave, it is mainly the gravedigger's responsibility to identify an available spot in (primarily) cemeteries four or five, since they are the only ones that still have available spots, and to dig a new grave for the next deceased person. This process of allocation is to a large extent determined by the camp's gravedigger himself, Abu Diab, with requests from the deceased's family pertaining to the location and accessibility of the grave at times being addressed jointly by the gravedigger and a representative from the camp's Committee of Mosques. Such deliberations about the logistics of digging and burying show once again a people striving to be in charge of their dead, given that it has historically proven impossible to be in charge of their lives.

As burials, alongside weddings, are the most communal practices in the camp, their perception as rites of presence not only becomes interwoven into the everyday life of the refugees, but also leads us to the unavoidable collision between the 'age' of the camp and that of the cemetery: 'Which is older: the camp or the cemetery?' (Fiddian-Qasmiyeh and Qasmiyeh 2017). In interrogating the historicity of this dialectic, we may be able to come to terms with the coupling of death and dying (in the camp) – thereby 'promoting' the death, any death, of the new arrivals in the camp – as a new act of hospitality.[7] Perceiving death, its representations and mechanics, as both a space within a space and a notion, shared by all refugees in Baddawi, old and new, regardless of their nationalities and affiliations, makes the cemetery 'the only cinders, the traces that remain, a "becoming-space of time" of which life and death are only traces' (Wolfe 2014: xv). Such a perception finds its basis in the cemetery's 'solidity' and continual presence, in contrast with the camp, which is often viewed as a place governed by precariousness, destruction and at times total erasure (see Fiddian-Qasmiyeh, this volume).

There is nothing fixed in the camp except the cemetery. Since their inception, cemeteries have represented the cinder, 'that which preserves in order no longer to preserve, dooming the remnant to dissolution' (Derrida 2014: 17), and, since 'cinder [is] more trace than trace' (Wolfe 2014: ix), death in the camp has become the sole marker of existence. However contrary this proposition is, the old and new refugees' insistence on inscribing, and thereby preserving, their names, dates of birth and death, and their multiple places of reference and origin, alongside four generic (and yet stable) Qur'anic verses calling for the return of the soul to its creator on the tombstone,[8] centralises the 'cinder as the house of being' (Derrida 2014: 23). In this sense, 'cinder is the best paradigm of the trace' (Wolfe 2014: xii) and it is never the camp's life that matters, but the cinders of those who come, go, and eventually return to it.

Figure 16.3 The tombstone of a young man who died in Baddawi camp bears dual points of origin – Al-Yarmouk camp, Damascus, Syria and Acre, Palestine (photograph: Elena Fiddian-Qasmiyeh)

Unlike the mosque in the camp (which is only the gatherer of worshippers),[9] the cemetery, in all its manifestations, is the gatherer, the gathered and the gathering (Qasmiyeh, in Kwek 2017; Fiddian-Qasmiyeh and Qasmiyeh 2017). Such a representation asserts once again how '[death] inscribes itself in the name' (Derrida 2001: 34). The cemetery in and with its name, clear or otherwise, will always '[make] possible the plurality of deaths' (Derrida 2001: 46) of those who come to the camp seeking life and death at the same time:

> In Baddawi, reaching the camp only occurs through the cemetery.
> Is the cemetery not another home, host and God? (Qasmiyeh 2017a)

Such an approximation in death and dying is conspicuously juxtaposed with and opposed by the 'rhetorical device of distantiation' (Ahmed 2000: 12), embodied in dialects of Arabic and their epistemic potential to identify as well as calumniate the Other.[10]

In such a dialectal apparatus, one that expands and contracts some dialects at the expense of others, dialects become the objective correlative of skin in their absolute exteriority and audibility (Ahmed 2000: 39, 185 n3). In Baddawi, as different refugees come together to negotiate their presence in these insatiable precariousnesses, the dialect departs from its own language, Arabic, and yet it instantly usurps the latter's prototypical characteristics: the Other is *only* judged by the dialect (and not the language). As the dialect starts to permeate other dialects and bodies, it gains a new capacity to reconfigure the terms and conditions of hospitality in the camp in reinstating its own law – that which is premised solely on its purity (Derrida 2000).

(Non)-arrival and dialects in Baddawi

Baddawi's close proximity to overpopulated Lebanese neighbourhoods such as Al-Mankubeen, Wadi Al-Nahleh and most recently the ever-expanding area of Jabal Al-Baddawi has meant that the borders of these places, with their blurry and fluid nature, continually overlap and traverse; in so doing they facilitate the movement of mainly poor Lebanese families into the camp. It is, in fact, a rarity for Palestinians to settle in areas deemed entirely Lebanese for a variety of reasons, including the unaffordability of rents (in contrast with cheaper places inside the camp) and the difficulty (often impossibility) of accessing Lebanese state schools and medical services. To be exposed to such internal movements of people, albeit limited, has positioned the camp as a *host* within its *hosting* country, that is, Lebanon. The other journeys towards the camp are those of Palestinians who live abroad, in particular in Scandinavia, Germany and Britain, and who continuously set their sights on the camp: they do so to visit their families, to marry, to attend weddings and funerals, and to observe and be observed in and by the camp. These Palestinians – and I am one of them – return to the camp, on the one hand, in order to return to their places, without knowing what and whose places these are (Qasmiyeh and Fiddian-Qasmiyeh 2013). On the other hand, they return because it is the holy element therein that pulls them to the camp. When those returnees insist on burying their dead in the camp and not where their futures lie, they insist on the permanence of the cemetery (without the camp) and on being part of a continuum of remembrance whose validity is solely contingent on the 'community of the dead' now scattered across five cemeteries (Qasmiyeh and Fiddian-Qasmiyeh 2013).[11]

Baddawi is no longer a camp for Palestinian refugees (only), but also a place – at times an only place – for those who have arrived in the camp as 'new' refugees seeking safety and anonymity while waiting for a resolution to the upheavals that have engulfed their homes and countries, including Syrians, Kurds and Iraqis.[12] While it is the camp that has borne the different dialects of such different groups, it is also the eyes and ears of those who have always lived in Baddawi who can see, hear as well as observe such apparent dialectal shifts. As Derrida poignantly reminds us, 'one must pronounce *shibboleth* properly in order to be granted the right to pass, indeed, the right to live' (Derrida 2005: 1). These new arrivants, like their Palestinian counterparts in Baddawi, never arrive completely. Such a (non-)state, a product of the (anthropological) machine, according to Agamben, is 'a zone of indeterminacy in which the outside is nothing but the exclusion of an inside and the inside is in turn only the inclusion of an outside' (Agamben 2004: 37). Thus, for the new refugees, arriving in the camp hardly connotes an unconditional bond with the human; it is, however, a realisation of a presence that is shared with other refugees and displaced people that is not necessarily a co-presence but a signification of solitude 'not only [as] a despair and an abandonment, but also a virility, a pride and a sovereignty' (Levinas 1987: 55).

In addition to Islam, whether personally practised or otherwise, the vast majority of the newcomers share Arabic as their only language, with one another and/or with the 'old' Palestinian refugees. In its formal register (*fusHa*), Arabic appears entirely monolithic, homogeneous and unifying, but in its dialectal multiplicities it separates from this fragile monolingualism. In other words, the *dialect* in Baddawi, without knowing precisely what a dialect is, has transformed itself to an ineffability, which neither remains in its place (i.e. the place of origin) nor traverses it – it simply occupies a middleness of sounds and utterances that tend to outlive their speakers. As such, the dialect – the marker of Othering *par excellence* in a temporal setting – has become the shibboleth. It is the shibboleth, both the constructor of dialectal borders and that which gives 'ciphered access to this collocation, to this secret configuration of places for memory' (Derrida 2005: 24). In effect, '[in] a language [. . .] there is nothing but *shibboleth*' (Derrida 2005: 33).

In Baddawi, for instance, the dialect is now more detectable than the arrivant: it travels across the camp, and as it travels it exposes itself and us. This
double exposure transforms the encounter between 'old' and 'new' refugees
into new borders – borders whose main task is to guard the othering nature
and significance of dialects in a place whose very premise is based on being
an other-place:[13]

> In entering the camp, time becomes suspended between dialects.
> The dialect that survives is never a dialect.
> The dialectal subtleties in the camp are also called silence.
> For the dialect to become an archive, no utterance should be uttered.
> Who is the creator of dialects? Whose tongue is the shibboleth?
> The dialect is a spear of noises.
> Ontologically, the dialect is a being in the shape of a knife.
> Only dialects can spot the silent Other. (Qasmiyeh 2017a)[14]

Inter alia, this direct collision between dialects inside the camp engenders
crucial questions as to the suppression (and at times inflation) of the dialect and its connotative facets as it takes over from the entire body. On our
home's threshold in Baddawi, as I was standing with my eldest sister observing the camp at night, a group of women, dressed mainly in black, walked
past us almost silently; and yet within seconds my sister was able to situate
them, on the basis of a few words and sounds uttered by them in passing, as
new arrivals from northern Syria. As we continued the conversation indoors,
it became apparent to me that my sister based her identification of these
women's dialect, and as a result their point of origin, both on the length of
their attire and a small number of barely audible utterances. As such, the
dialectal at times merges and magnifies physical identifiers, or vice versa. In
this example, the face of the *arrivant* has been absented or at least is not
entirely 'there' to be recognised or to invoke a presence that goes beyond the
dialectal question; and yet, simultaneously, it is the appearance of the Other,
embodied in the attire that is supposed to cover and veil, through which the
'dialect' is exposed and recognised most – as though the outer garment were
nothing but an extra limb of the dialect. To put it simply, the perception and
detection of the dialect as a signifier of foreignness, whether this is happening premeditatedly or not, has relegated the face of the 'new' refugee to total
absence, since '[without] the face, the represented is not present by means of
his sheer presence, but to a large extent is there(in) at the expense of his presence' (Qasmiyeh and Ammann 2017); in so doing, the new refugee essentially
dwells on the utterances that not only constitute alterity but also transform
the entirety of their dialect into a shibboleth.[15] In such a dialectal discourse,
the refugee is metamorphosed into a series of sounds that either correspond
to what is there, or simply forge a road towards the 'irregular' as the prototypical sign of Otherness.[16]

Writing the camp-archive

In light of these multi-dialectal precepts – competing, collisional as well as coexistent – who writes the camp? Who traces the camp's evolution into (a) space? Who demarcates its limbs as they retreat internally in order to accommodate more refugees? The camp has never been entirely a place, but a multiplicity of entwined histories and times (see Fiddian-Qasmiyeh, this volume). These times bear witness to the construction as well as dissolution of these refugee communities. In Baddawi, in particular, it has become exceedingly urgent to document the lives of these individuals in both life and death through processes that would privilege the ordinary and the daily at the expense of the extraordinary and the unique (Fiddian-Qasmiyeh 2017), which rarely belong to the community itself but to those who claim its representation.

This entails maintaining a healthy distance between 'writing' as a determination to exist despite all the renewed adversities in such places, and as an act of continuous archiving whereby refugees themselves (consciously) narrate the camp in their daily presence in ways that instate their solitude, but also in order to remember who they are. Such a practice poignantly resonates with Derrida's conceptualisation of the archive as a creation towards the future and as a domain in which people are its mere agents. One might say that such are the only processes that remind the camp's inhabitants that it is their right to write what is deemed theirs in the spatial and territorial sense, even though such markers are never conspicuous, nor are they markers of permanence as such.

In 'Writing the Camp', a series of responses and engagements with and around the camp, its battles with itself, its people and its surroundings, that have appeared periodically on the website for the AHRC-ESRC funded 'Refugee Hosts' research project (www.refugeehosts.org), I have attempted to turn my focus on the camp in two way (Qasmiyeh 2016a; 2016b; 2017a; 2017b; 2017c; 2017d):[17] first, as a site where the holy and the profane amalgamate, for it is their marriage, forced or otherwise, that keeps inviting as well as shunning people; secondly, it is through documenting the camp's innards that we witness what will never be witnessed again, through transforming the relationship between the writer of the camp and the camp itself into a form of unbreakable bond, not in the tribal sense, but as a memory that is there simply to keep both the camp and its inhabitants alive. To return to Derrida's notion of the archive (1996: 20–1), it is the body, the body of the refugee, her skin, which becomes the parchment, the very piece of paper that holds the specificities of being a refugee, of being an outcast in a space that will never go away (n)or stay. As such, the refugee's existence becomes solely contingent on an archive that is 'an impression associated with a word' (Derrida 1996: 29) that is in the process of being written by the refugee herself.

Derrida's engagement with bodily markers as essential components of the archive, those that incise as well as circumcise,[18] appears to presuppose difference on behalf of those who intend to write the archive or those whose 'writing' ought to play a role in reclaiming the age(ing) of the camp by tracing the event therein. Writing in this context becomes an act of bearing witness,[19] a testimony to/for the individual and the camp simultaneously. While it is essential for me to write what is worthy of writing, without delving deeply into the personal but hovering above it, writing emerges as a memory hunting down more memories. So who is the witness in a refugee camp? Who is the owner of the testimony? Is it the refugee herself or those who (are able to) come and go? As it is the camp itself that validates and corroborates what is going to be narrated, the writer becomes a witness-agent, a gatherer of details, details that continuously refer the refugee to the camp through cumulative memories and sounds.[20] In the camp, we bear witness to ourselves first and foremost, to our multiple lives and deaths in this space of containment. As if it were our 'duty' to leave something behind us, a palpable thing upon which our names are inscribed – the names that tie us to those who have borne us while also giving the latter the opportunity to bear witness to creating more refugees as time passes. The trace that we normally leave intentionally or otherwise in spaces and through journeys that we, at times, attempt by force to normalise is what keeps us attached to this state of tentativeness: we are neither fully en route, in an actual place, nor are we promised an arrival.[21] As I have argued elsewhere (Qasmiyeh 2016c), in documenting the trace, in bearing witness to its presence in the shape of the static, animate or otherwise, we forge a link between all the tenses at work. In other words, remembering the camp becomes the prerequisite for remembering ourselves in/outside the camp.

This is after all how '[the archive] opens out of the future' (Derrida 1996: 68) and the way in which its engagement with the past and the present defines and reconfigures its nature – be it that of the individual or that of the collective. In the same vein, it is the unity between witnessing and archiving in the refugee camp that maintains the momentum of writing, as an overarching means through which details are captured as soon as they leave their source. Such an immediacy is that of the future,[22] the future that is yet to be defined as an upcoming event, and yet it is its promise that keeps the camp afloat.

Since it is the archive of the refugee that will (might) be gathered, it is worth pausing briefly at the question of performativity. The refugee has never assigned herself the role of the initiator of the archive. It is a role that has been bestowed upon her by a series of instants: these are the instants of the camp. One might argue that sensing that there should be an archive of/for the camp is what keeps the camp alive for the time being, as it transfers both the person and the place towards the future. Thus, the 'camp-archive' ties the refugee, the camp and time together in an insoluble chain in which, in order for the archive to survive its own destiny, it should survive its writing:

The camp is a passing human, a book, a manuscript, an archive . . . Bury it; smother it with its own dust, so it might return as a holy text devoid of intentions. (Qasmiyeh 2017a)

The same question, however elliptical it is, keeps returning: Who writes the archive?

Only refugees can forever write the archive.
The camp owns the archive, not God.
For the archive not to fall apart, it weds the camp unceremoniously.
The question of a camp-archive is also the question of the camp's survival beyond speech.
Circumcising the body can indicate the survival of the place.
Blessed are the pending places that are called camps. (Qasmiyeh 2017a)

Although it is the writing that reminds us of the value of what we write, it seems that a clear distinction between the divine and the human in writing is urgently needed. Such a distinction would not only equate the status of the camp with that of the 'owner' of the archive, but it would also delineate a total synergy between the 'pending' in the camp and the 'pending' in the archive.

The lack of clarity vis-à-vis what the archive *really* is, and realising that 'nothing is less reliable, nothing is less clear today than the word "archive"' (Derrida 1996: 90), should undoubtedly not diminish the archive's capacity to privilege the written at the expense of what is already there. In the end, 'the structure of the archive is *spectral*. It is spectral *a priori*: neither present nor absent "in the flesh", neither visible nor invisible, a trace always referring to another. . .' (Derrida 1996: 84). For it is what can be archived that is worthy of the name 'archive'; it is thus essential to consider the language that is employed in such records. More importantly, as we are seeking to write 'the then', transcending the rhetoric of empathy towards refugees becomes some sort of a 'minor' language – a language that is 'the instrument *par excellence* of that destratification' (Deleuze and Guattari 2012: xvi; Stonebridge 2015; 2018). In 'writing the camp', this 'destratification' manifests itself in two different (and yet entwined) ways: in writing the camp and in order to write with the intention of continuity, the means, the language in this context recoils into itself, not to disappear or shrink, but to reinstate its conditions from within. Finally, inviting an act of writing from within does not necessarily imply a *uni*-writing that is based upon one 'narrative' or on a language that claims absolute entitlement to the future by virtue of having been born in/to the camp. On the contrary, it is in fact the direct opposite of such an archival monopoly. To put it simply, the writing that we are putting forward is that which 'deals with the acknowledged doubt of an explicit division [. . .] of the impossibility of one's own place' (De Certeau, cited in Bensmaïa 2012: ix).

This 'division' or fragmentariness, inherent within these narratives, is exactly what enables us to 'regather' from different sites (whether the camp or its (de) placement) and 'write' at the same time as we write the camp.

Conclusion

From within Baddawi we can see a camp and nothing else. Such a proposition is not intended to reject the different lives therein or its ever-expanding selves; it is in fact a stance that is proposed in order to delve deeply into the specifics of the camp as a *naked name*, a proper name, as the sole constituent of the epitaph/archive (Derrida 1989: 27). When people return to the camp as its decentralised (diaspora-ed) offspring (Qasmiyeh and Fiddian-Qasmiyeh 2013; Gabiam and Fiddian-Qasmiyeh 2017), some still arrive in it for the first time, escaping their fractured lives or building new ones – but will the camp ever offer refuge? Will it ever be the host when it is itself hosted as an other? From the Baddawi of the past to the Baddawi of the present (and the future), the camp has overgrown its original space from within – multi-storey buildings have been erected, always in haste and with minimum attention to safety, to accommodate the newcomers, be they returning Palestinians from abroad during their seasonal visits or new refugees seeking refuge in the camp. Throughout, the alleged singularity of the dialect has been disrupted or made to hear other dialects that have come from various places to settle in the camp.[23] Thus, the dialect has become the shibboleth *par excellence*. Further, more cemeteries in Baddawi have forged more space in an already overcrowded and spaceless place, to honour the trace of those who are no longer alive and can never leave or be made to leave (see Fiddian-Qasmiyeh, this volume).

In the end, as we write Baddawi, we write its histories of diverse subjectivities: parasitic and self-impregnating they might be, but never self-imposed. It is the camp's subjectivity that '[engenders] duration as the illusion of a continuity' (Derrida 1989: 83) and grows and ages within its means and corpus. In the past, in Baddawi, artificial borders and markers may have been erected to protect the camp from the place and the place from the camp. Now, such barriers are no longer visible. They may be detectable, graspable and above all existent, and yet they are never ours. Refugees will continue to 'write' what they see with their 'naked' eyes and in their 'naked names' (Derrida 1989: 27), bearing witness to what will take place. Writing the camp 'neither lives nor dies; it lives on' (Derrida, cited in Donato 1988: 128).

Notes

1. This refers to the period between 1985 and 1989 (although some would say it endured to the 1990s), during which time the Palestinian camps were under siege by different Syrian and pro-Syrian militias (Al-Jazeera 2009).

2. The recent events and the internecine fighting in Syria might count as one of the few exceptions in this regard. Palestinians in Baddawi and beyond, in addition to the vast majority of camp-based Palestinian factions, offered popular support for the 2011 Syrian uprising in its early stages, and yet the Popular Front-General Command was the only faction actually to be present on the ground and to fight alongside the Syrian army (especially in Al-Yarmouk camp in Damascus and in other sites on the outskirts of the city).

3. This section builds on an earlier multi-media piece by Fiddian-Qasmiyeh and Qasmiyeh, commissioned by the Tunisian Pavilion for the 2017 Venice Biennale (Fiddian-Qasmiyeh and Qasmiyeh 2017).

4. Within Baddawi, terms pertaining to claims of origin and *nativeness* among some Palestinian families are still in use. For instance, it is common knowledge in Baddawi that certain Palestinian families who arrived mainly in the 1970s and 1980s, in particular after the destruction of other camps such as Al-Nabatiyyeh and Tel Al-Zaatar, continue to be viewed by other Palestinians as 'displaced' people (compared to the 'natives' of the camp who have been there since its establishment in 1954). One might say that this hierarchy and its discriminatory undertones have to a large extent contributed to the creation of two very specific 'clusters' of 'displaced' people in what is commonly known as the upper part of Baddawi camp. Further, it is worth noting that with the arrival of new refugee groups including Palestinians from Nahr Al-Bared camp in north Lebanon, Iraqi Arabs and Kurds from Syria, and Palestinians, Kurds and Syrian Arabs from Syria, the hierarchical paradigms have shifted and the question of Othering has become far more splintered (see Fiddian-Qasmiyeh and Qasmiyeh 2017; Fiddian-Qasmiyeh 2016b and this volume).

5. Although the archiving of places, in this context praying spaces, has never been undertaken systematically, some people claim that Masjid Omar Bin Al-Khattaab in the upper part of Baddawi, where the main market and UNRWA distribution centre and main schools are located, was the first praying space to be recognised as the first mosque. This claim appears particularly credible given the extent to which small businesses in the camp have always contributed to the sustainability of mosques.

6. On the question of dying, death and burial in Baddawi, see Fiddian-Qasmiyeh and Qasmiyeh (2017). The centrality of the deceased's origin or multiple origins has become a new signifier in the presentation of tombstones on some of the graves, especially of those who have recently arrived in the camp. Although it has been common in the camp to write/engrave the date and place of birth of the deceased on the tombstone, the inclusion of *multiple* points of reference and origin marks an entirely new approach to lineage and death in Baddawi (see also Fiddian-Qasmiyeh, this volume).

7. With Derrida's notion of 'hostipitality' in mind, hospitality within the Arabic tradition, in particular, is never entirely benign (Fiddian-Qasmiyeh and Qasmiyeh 2016). In fact, its propensity to be impregnated by its alliterative opposite, hostility, is what makes practices such as 'hosting', 'sharing' and 'belonging' in Baddawi inherently conflictual.

8. These are verses 27, 28, 29 and 30 of Chapter 89: 'O reassured soul, return to your Lord, well-pleased and pleasing, and enter among My servants and enter My Paradise.'

9. In Arabic, one of the words for 'mosque' is the equivalent of the word 'gatherer' in English.
10. Since Baddawi is identified as a camp for Palestinian refugees in Lebanon, the question of dialectal 'autochthony' and 'purity' there becomes a matter that is primarily managed through the lens of the Palestinian dialect as the litmus paper by which other groups' dialects are ascertained. Although it is impossible to control and contain these dialectal shifts, it is important to view such influences in light of the camp's proximity to Lebanese rural/urban places.
11. The 'sacred' in the camp transcends the sacred in the religious sense, since it is the camp in its entirety that has become 'holy' in its potential to continuously reproduce followers/refugees, securing both the (relative) survival of the camp/ the worshipped and the refugee/the worshipper (see Qasmiyeh and Fiddian-Qasmiyeh 2013). When we were children, my mother used to state on a regular basis: 'It is because of God and UNRWA that we are surviving.' In this statement, my mother placed God and UNRWA on the same scale, despite the seniority of God in popular discourse and in how it is placed 'first' followed by UNRWA in the statement.
12. As I was conducting research in Baddawi in the summer of 2017, one of the Palestinian interviewees described Baddawi 'as a multinational camp'. Although it was a statement made in response to the ever-changing 'nature' of what a (Palestinian) camp is, such a description still bears opposing interpretations: on the one hand, the camp has successfully, to a certain degree, accommodated other groups. On the other hand, it is the preconceived homogeneity of Baddawi as a place for the Palestinians that has come under the spotlight due to the presence of these different groups. The vast majority of the Syrians, Iraqis and Kurds who have arrived in Baddawi in the last five years or so pursue small jobs either inside the camp or in other areas within the city, and at times it is the 'competition' over very limited resources in and beyond the camp that creates friction between these different groups.
13. In tracing the meaning of shibboleth, Derrida ponders its other meaning: river (2005: 22–3), in an attempt to take us from the vocal (mispronunciation or mis-articulation of the secret) to the physical (river).
14. Ammann's reading of the act of writing as a two-way sign is of relevance here: '[Writing] is the lips of the silent' (unpublished work on file with the author). It is the correspondence between reading and writing that (re)produces the body.
15. Cf. Derrida on the encapsulation of promise through speech and vice versa: 'the essence of speech is the promise, that there is no speaking that does not promise, which at the same time means a commitment toward the future' (1989: 97). Since it is the dialect that *promises* in the camp, the notion of alterity in all its manifestations (citizens, 'old' and 'new' refugees) seems to be reduced to sound without its body proper.
16. The word 'dialect' in the camp context can be perceived as the first 'cut' in the body of the refugee – 'a circumcised lip' (Qasmiyeh 2017c) whose imitability is impossible.
17. Writing (in) the camp is not assigned a specific outcome as such, as much as it is a response to the very presence of the camp itself. In other words, 'writing: doing, when nothing is to be done, when nothing is being done. . .', it is 'madness against madness' (Blanchot 1995: xiii, 43).

18. Using the term 'circumcision' in this context is intended to shed light on how marking the body, the refugee body, can be both segregational in nature as well as a sign of attesting to the legal and existential limbo that refugees commonly experience. It is precisely in the 'archival strata' (Derrida 1996: 22) that the skin is centralised; this is the case both memorially and as a layer that exposes as well as conceals the writing that is taking place in the camp.

19. It is worth noting that as in Greek (Agamben 2012: 26), the Arabic root 'SH-H-D' is shared by both the words 'martyrdom' (dying for) and 'bearing witness' (seeing/surviving to tell or renarrate). Such a clash between 'dying' and 'surviving' offers a poignant insight into the different ways of reading the word 'testimony' and 'post-testimony' in a place as fluid and static as the refugee camp.

20. To hear 'soundscapes' from Baddawi camp recorded by Fiddian-Qasmiyeh, visit Refugee Hosts' Creative Archive (www.refugeehosts.org).

21. For a rhizoanalysis of refugee camps, and the extent to which refugees are 'always-already-in-the-middle', see Fiddian-Qasmiyeh (this volume and 2019).

22. According to Derrida, 'the question of the archive is not [. . .] a question of the past. It is not the question of a concept dealing with the past that might *already* be at our disposal or not at our disposal, *an archivable concept of the archive*. It is a question of the future, the question of the future itself, the question of a response, of a promise and of a responsibility of tomorrow. The archive: if we want to know in times to come. Perhaps. Not tomorrow but in times to come, later on or perhaps never' (1996: 36, emphasis in the original).

23. Derrida's astute reading of the word 'soil' apropos language itself and its actual *soil*, especially in Levinas's case with reference to the French language, is of relevance to our discussion here (Derrida 1998: 91–2). In this abstract-concrete soil, Derrida problematises the question of belonging to a language, a feature that finds a home and resonance in the notion 'dialect'. One might ask: where is the soil (of dialects) in Baddawi, when the soil is never owned by the refugee?

Bibliography

Agamben, G. (2004), *The Open: Man and Animal* (Stanford: Stanford University Press).

Agamben, G. (2012), *Remnants of Auschwitz: The Witness and the Archive* (New York: Zone Books).

Ahmed, S. (2000), *Strange Encounters: Embodied Others in Post-Coloniality* (London: Routledge).

Al-Jazeera (2009), 'Lebanon's Palestinian refugees', Al-Jazeera, 4 June, http://www.aljazeera.com/focus/2009/05/2009527115531294628.html (accessed 12 February 2018).

Bensmaïa, R. (2012), 'Foreword: the Kafka effect', in G. Deleuze and F. Guattari, *Kafka: Toward a Minor Literature* (Minneapolis: University of Minnesota Press), ix–xxi.

Blanchot, M. (1995), *The Writing of the Disaster* (Lincoln: University of Nebraska Press).

Deleuze, G., and F. Guattari (2012), *Kafka: Toward a Minor Literature* (Minneapolis: University of Minnesota Press).

Derrida, J. (1989), *Memoires for Paul de Man*, rev. edn (New York: Columbia University Press).

Derrida, J. (1996), *Archive Fever: A Freudian Impression* (Chicago: University of Chicago Press).

Derrida, J. (1998), *Monolingualism of the Other OR the Prothesis of Origin* (Stanford: Stanford University Press).

Derrida, J. (2000), *Of Hospitality: Anne Dufourmantelle invites Jacques Derrida to Respond*, trans. R. Bowlby (Stanford: Stanford University Press).

Derrida, J. (2001), *The Work of Mourning*, ed. P.-A. Brault and M. Naas (Chicago: University of Chicago Press).

Derrida, J. (2005), *Sovereignties in Question: The Poetics of Paul Celan*, ed. T. Dutoit and O. Pasanen (New York: Fordham University Press).

Derrida, J. (2014), *Cinders* (Minneapolis: University of Minnesota Press).

Donato, E. (1988), 'Spectacular translation', in C. McDonald (ed.), *The Ear of the Other: Texts and Discussions with Jacques Derrida* (Lincoln: University of Nebraska Press), 126–9.

Fiddian-Qasmiyeh, E. (2016a), 'Refugees hosting refugees', *Forced Migration Review*, 53: 25–7.

Fiddian-Qasmiyeh, E. (2016b), 'Palestinian and Syrian refugees in Lebanon: sharing space, electricity and the sky', *Refugee History*, 21 December, http://refugeehistory.org/blog/2016/12/22/palestinian-and-syrian-refugees-in-lebanon-sharing-space-electricity-and-the-sky (accessed 16 July 2019).

Fiddian-Qasmiyeh, E. (2017), 'Representations of displacement: introducing the series', *Refugee Hosts*, 1 September, https://refugeehosts.org/representations-of-displacement-series/ (accessed 16 July 2019).

Fiddian-Qasmiyeh, E. (2019), 'From roots to rhizomes: mapping rhizomatic strategies in the Sahrawi and Palestinian refugee situations', in M. Bradley, J. Milner and B. Peruniak (eds), *Shaping the Struggles of their Times: Refugees, Peacebuilding and Resolving Displacement* (Washington, DC: Georgetown University Press).

Fiddian-Qasmiyeh, E., and Y. M. Qasmiyeh (2016), 'Refugee neighbours and hostipitality: exploring the complexities of refugee–refugee humanitarianism', *The Critique*, 5 January, https://refugeehosts.org/2018/03/20/refugee-neighbours-hostipitality/ (accessed 12 July 2019).

Fiddian-Qasmiyeh, E., and Y. M. Qasmiyeh (2017), 'Refugee–refugee solidarity in death and dying' (multi-media piece), invited contribution to *The Absence of Paths*, Tunisian Pavilion, Venice Biennale, May.

Gabiam, N., and E. Fiddian-Qasmiyeh (2017), 'Palestinians and the Arab uprisings: political activism and narratives of home, homeland, and home-camp', *Journal of Ethnic and Migration Studies*, 43.5: 731–48, doi: 10.1080/1369183X.2016.1202750.

Khalili, L. (2005), 'Palestinian commemoration in the refugee camps of Lebanon', *Comparative Studies of South Asia, Africa and the Middle East*, 25.1: 30–45.

Kwek, T. (2017), 'In conversation: Yousif M. Qasmiyeh on language and liminality', *Asymptote*, 15 February, https://www.asymptotejournal.com/blog/2017/02/15/in-conversation-yousif-m-qasmiyeh-on-language-and-liminality/ (accessed 12 July 2019).

Levinas, E. (1987), *Time and the Other* (Pittsburgh, PA: Duquesne University Press).

Qasmiyeh, Y. M. (2016a), 'Writing the camp', *Refugee Hosts*, 30 September, https://refugeehosts.org/2016/09/30/writing-the-camp/ (accessed 12 July 2019).

Qasmiyeh, Y. M. (2016b), 'My mother's heels', in Y. Suleiman (ed.), *Being Palestinian: Personal Reflections on Palestinian Identity in the Diaspora* (Edinburgh: Edinburgh University Press), 303–5.

Qasmiyeh, Y. M. (2016c), 'If this is my face, so be it', *Modern Poetry in Translation*, 1: 119–23.

Qasmiyeh, Y. M. (2017a), 'Refugees are dialectical beings', *Refugee Hosts*, 5 September, https://refugeehosts.org/2017/09/05/refugees-are-dialectical-beings-part-two/ (accessed 12 July 2019).

Qasmiyeh, Y. M. (2017b), 'Writing the camp-archive', *Refugee Hosts*, 1 September, https://refugeehosts.org/2017/09/01/refugees-are-dialectical-beings-part-one/ (accessed 12 July 2019).

Qasmiyeh, Y. M. (2017c), 'A sudden utterance is the stranger', *Refugee Hosts*, 15 April, https://refugeehosts.org/2017/04/25/a-sudden-utterance-is-the-stranger/ (accessed 12 July 2019).

Qasmiyeh, Y. M. (2017d), 'The camp is time', *Refugee Hosts*, 15 January, https://refugeehosts.org/2017/01/15/the-camp-is-time/ (accessed 12 July 2019).

Qasmiyeh, Y. M., and O. Ammann (2017), 'The multiple faces of representation', *Refugee Hosts*, 14 September, https://refugeehosts.org/2017/09/15/the-multiple-faces-of-representation/ (accessed 12 July 2019).

Qasmiyeh, Y. M., and E. Fiddian-Qasmiyeh (2013), 'Refugee camps and cities in conversation', in Jane Garnett and Alana Harris (eds), *Migration and Religious Identity in the Modern Metropolis* (Farnham: Ashgate), 131–43.

Sayigh, R. (2000), 'Greater insecurity for refugees in Lebanon', Middle East Research and Information Project, 1 March, www.merip.org/mero/mero030100 (accessed 14 May 2019).

Stonebridge, L. J. (2015), '"To be borderline": poetic statelessness, Auden and Qasmiyeh', *Textual Practice*, 29.7: 1331–54.

Stonebridge, L. J. (2018), *Placeless People, Writing, Rights and Refugees* (Oxford: Oxford University Press).

Stonebridge, L. J., and Y. M. Qasmiyeh (2018), 'The camp as archive', *Politics/Letters Live*, February, http://politicsslashletters.org/features/the_camp_as_archive/ (accessed 12 July 2019).

Wolfe, C. (2014), 'Introduction: *Cinders* after biopolitics', in J. Derrida, *Cinders* (Minneapolis: University of Minnesota Press), vii–xxx.

Zureik, C. (1948), *Ma'na al-Nakba* (The meaning of [the Palestinian] catastrophe) (Beirut: Dar al'ilm lil malayiin).

Chapter 17

Reel Refugees: Inside and Outside the Camp

Madelaine Hron

In his epic documentary *Human Flow* (2017), the Chinese artist and activist Ai Weiwei offers a global range of images that call attention to the many stereotypes associated with refugee representation in contemporary media, be these camps of white tents, huddled masses on rickety boats, or traumatised children with pleading eyes. In spectacular, sweeping aerial shots filmed by drones, we soar high above the turquoise sea as a boat with escapees slowly moves into the frame; through a wide-angle lens, we survey verdant landscapes scarred by barbed-wire borders, or we hurry along dusty roads with thousands of travellers, as Ai stretches out his smartphone. However, some of *Human Flow*'s most memorable scenes are arguably the brief glimpses it offers of the abject spaces of refugee camps: among the forty camps featured, we witness the makeshift roadside camp at Idomeni, Greece; the gridlocked sterility of Turkey's Nizip camp; Germany's organised, yet improvised camp at Tempelhof Airport; Kenya's massive Dabaab camp shrouded in sand and trash; or the merciless incineration of the transit camp in Calais, France. In contrast to the perpetual mobility propelling the rest of the film, the spaces inside the camp connote stasis and stagnation. Indeed, the film fitfully reminds us that the average refugee is displaced for twenty-six years, and that only 1 per cent of encamped refugees will be able to gain asylum in Western countries. The film concludes that 'becoming immune to [refugees'] suffering is very, very dangerous. It's critical for us to maintain this humanity.'

Much like *Human Flow*, which spans 23 countries in order to offer a broadened perspective on forced migration in the current era, this chapter surveys dozens of films that depict refugees, both feature narrative films and lesser-known documentaries, so as to outline some of the key trends, cinematic conventions and established narrative arcs in refugee films. In so doing, this chapter aims to expose some of the generic patterns that can, inadvertently, render viewers 'immune to refugees' suffering', and to reveal some of the strategies that film-makers deploy to transcend these generic trends, in order to help viewers understand refugees' humanity or grapple with the sufferings they experience. Just as *Human Flow* travels inside and outside refugee camps, this chapter features films that take place both inside and outside the camp. The camp, a space typically defined by its hopeless lack of action, its unproductive inertia and, most importantly, its waiting and deferral, is notoriously difficult to film and is often superseded in artistic representation by spaces outside the camp that grant refugees greater mobility and agency. Nonetheless, encampment continues to haunt refugees on screen, both inside and outside the camp.

Theorising the camp: off and on screen

Though only half of the world's 65 million displaced people live in official refugee camps, the camp has become the synecdochal image for the refugee experience of persecution, marginalisation, confinement, powerlessness, stasis and victimhood. Though camps are supposed to be humanitarian sanctuaries or zones of safety aimed at protecting fragile populations on an ad hoc basis, in our global economy camps have increasingly become the de facto solution to political inertia concerning complex problems ranging from climate change to civil war. For instance, a constellation of camps – from Lampedusa in Italy to Calais in France – has become Europe's unofficial answer to the Mediterranean migration crisis. Though by definition refugees are innocent civilians fleeing persecution or insecurity, because of their growing numbers the language of threat and danger now dominates refugee discourse, and fleeing victims have been reframed as 'security threats', associated with 'insecurity', 'militarisation' and 'terrorism' (Mogire 2011). Enhanced border securitisation, detention, or incarceration of undocumented migrants increasingly correlates refugees with crime, so much so that scholars and activists refer to this nexus as 'crimmigration' (Stumpf 2006).

Encampment has been studied in various ways in academic discourse. Geography scholars such as Nick Gill (2013) have analysed refugee camps as 'carceral spaces', in line with prison, labour, POW and concentration camps, so as to reveal the incarcerating, confining and punitive praxes in which migration is managed. Anthropologists such as Michel Agier and Carmen Bernand have developed Mary Douglas's notions of purity and danger to argue that camps represent a 'form of bio-segregation', which deploy 'prophylactic rhetoric' (Agier 2008: 33) to place the unwanted elements of society 'at the confines of society' (Bernand 1994: 78). Conflating refugee camps with Nazi death-camps, the political theorist Giorgio Agamben has famously argued that the camp is a 'state of exception' (1998: 167) existing outside ordinary law (*nomos*). Rather than living a political life (*bios*), camp inmates are reduced to the epitome of bare life (*zoe*), a 'life devoid of value' or 'unworthy of being' (1998: 139, 142), as perpetually absent-but-included outsiders, who are subject to the law of the state, but lack any rights or recourse within the state themselves. For the literary critic Achille Mbembe, camps may be even

considered 'necropolitical spaces', wherein refugees are 'subjected to conditions of life conferring upon them the status of *living dead*' (2003: 40, italics
in original). Some of these overarching frameworks, especially Agamben's
conceptualisation of the camp, have been criticised by refugee scholars as failing to provide useful analytical tools to grasp the complexity of social relations in refugee camps, and especially as devaluing the tactics and strategies
of resistance that camp inhabitants adopt in their everyday lives.

In film, one of the key challenges is how to represent the confining space
of the camp cinematically, without depriving refugees of their agency or
dismissing their subjectivity. Michel Agier attempts to define the camp's
ambiguous essence in words, deploying the terminology of 'bio-segregation',
'a state of liminal floating', or an 'empty [desert-like] space', but concedes
that 'durable life is not supposed to exist in a space outside of place, a
moment outside of time, an identity without community' (2008: 33, 30, 40,
49). Cinematically, it is equally difficult to capture the camp's 'lasting space-
time of anomie' (Agier 2008: 30), especially its suspended temporality, or
the limbo of refugeedom. The refugee advocate Ezat Mossallanejed even
compares the prolonged limbo of the asylum determination process to practices of torture, wherein victims are 'stretched across the poles of absolute
hope and despair by prolonged waiting' until they break (2005: 199). Film
audiences who are not themselves refugees only have passing experience of
the torture of limbo, or of the paralysis, stasis or exclusion, or the 'frozen
otherness' (Agier 2008: viii), that refugeedom entails, and would rather
avoid it. For these reasons, refugee films often eschew or escape the space of
the camp altogether, and privilege refugees' mobility and progress outside
the camp. However, only a small percentage of camp refugees will be able
to gain asylum in foreign countries, or be able to leave the camps to return
to their homelands. Rather, most of them will acquire 'campzenship', a
'situated form of political membership produced in and by the camp' (Sigona
2014: 1) and will form identities and communities within these microcosms
of local globalisation. Countering stereotypes of destitution and inactivity,
these camp-towns bustle with shops, activities and volunteer groups, and
eventually, in this social space, refugee subjects have the potential to shed
their identities as victims.

However, in critical theory and in film, it is all too easy to reify both
the camp and the refugee as the inaccessible 'other', and thus deny refugees'
agency or even subjectivity. For instance, the sociologist Zygmunt Bauman
has famously argued that many aspects of refugeedom are beyond representation: that refugees signify the 'un*touch*ables', 'un*think*ables' and '*unimagi-
nables*' of contemporary globalisation, 'the very embodiment of "human
waste" with no useful function to play' (2007: 41, 45). Even Agier describes
refugees as 'no longer being in the world', as 'the powerless, the un-free' or as
having a 'collective identity as the simple undesirable residue of war: shame-
ful, clandestine or hunted' (2008: 62, 22, 29). Similarly, in film, the refugee

has long been subject to visual stereotypes, most notably that of the nameless, pure victim, associated with humanitarian aid.

Screening refugees: diverging trends

In film, stereotypical images of refugees are inextricably linked with those disseminated by humanitarian media coverage, as evinced in the late 1970s with Biafra or the Nigerian Civil War (1967–70). In this grisly war, the Igbo people tried to secede from the Republic of Nigeria, but through an aid blockade the Nigerian government left women and children to starve in refugee camps. Biafra signalled a watershed moment in media coverage: along with Vietnam, it was the first war covered extensively on television, and because of the mass starvation that ensued, the first televised famine in history. Biafra established the basic visual vocabulary of humanitarian media coverage, which was repeated on a celebrity-studded scale during the Ethiopian famine (1983–85), and in numerous humanitarian campaigns since. Pervasive in these humanitarian campaigns is affective sentimentalism. Biafra first put on display skeletal African children with bloated, kwashiorkor-affected stomachs, with the hope of eliciting pity and charity from Western viewers. Such imagery has in many ways become more exploitative or 'pornographic' since (Lissner 1981), compounded by the mass circulation and pervasiveness of images on social media. For instance, fifty years after Biafra, it took graphic images of a dead toddler – the corpse of Alan Kurdi, as photographed by photojournalist Nilüfer Demir – to finally inspire international concern for Syrian refugees, four years into the crisis; and then only relatively fleetingly.

The digital revolution in the 1990s signalled another landmark in the representation of refugees in film. The rise of digital media made it much easier for professional and amateur film-makers alike to create videos, just as in the 2000s the rise of the internet and platforms such as YouTube made them much easier to distribute. In *Human Flow* for instance, Ai Weiwei initially captured footage of migrants landing on Lesbos with his smartphone, and throughout the film, despite their dire circumstances, refugees continue to communicate with loved ones via mobile phones. That being said, most films are not filmed or directed by refugees themselves. Most refugees do not have the time, means or desire to relive their traumatic pasts or to compile their experiences via the medium of film. Thus, despite much greater access to technology, refugees rarely direct or produce films about their own experiences; in most widely available films about refugees, refugee experiences are mediated, ever more realistically, by well-meaning others. Most of the films produced since the 1990s about refugees have been documentaries, often low-budget documentaries, rather than narrative films.

Documentaries about refugees conventionally privilege realism as a form of testimony. Drawing on various realist ethnographic techniques, such as the use of direct sound, natural lighting, hand-held cameras and non-professional agents (including, of course, refugees themselves), such documentaries aim to expose refugeedom with more factuality and immediacy than narrative fiction films. As the visual anthropologist Steffen Köhn argues, migrants are largely shrouded by 'visual clichés and stereotypes' in Western media that render them largely 'illegal'; realist documentary praxes help 'expose their truths' in a legitimising forum (2016: 30). Moreover, as the film scholar Isolina Ballesteros points out, such documentary techniques lend a sense of 'urgency and actuality' to the problems faced by refugees, and work 'to eliminate the simple reduction of Western/non-Western characters to binary oppositions' by encouraging viewers to become familiar and intimate with refugees' daily lives (2015: 20). By seeking to screen refugees' real-life experiences, documentary film-makers such as Ai Weiwei, Christian Petzhold or Karen Cho hope that knowing the 'truth' about the refugee condition will urge viewers to sympathise with and intervene in their plight.

As film scholars have pointed out, films about refugees – both documentary and narrative – oscillate between the polarities of sentimentalism and realism to represent the refugee experience, but both tendencies are problematic if excessive. On one hand, the 'affective expectation' (Berlant 2008) that refugee stories be dystopic, tragic or melancholic reduces refugees to objects of pity, whose only subjectivity is victimhood. As the film scholar Ipek Celik elucidates, it creates a situation of 'inescapable victimhood' (2015: 131) wherein 'suffering and victimization . . . perpetuates a liberal sense of European self that validates itself through humanitarian concerns' (2015: 27). Sentimentalism thus reinforces the binaries of self/other, and also largely disallows the potential for ideological critique. However, realist regimes of truth and authenticity are also questionable, as they risk rendering refugees into objects of ethnographic interest, and privileging 'truth' at the expense of experience. As the literary scholar Agnes Woolley explains, relying too much on 'epistemological verities' risks reducing all refugee stories to 'single linear, verifiable narratives' similar to asylum claims (2014: 20). The viewer then is placed in the position of judging the authenticity and legitimacy of refugee stories, and disallowing experiences – such as those shaped by trauma, emotion or memory lapses – that do not fit generic patterns. Let us now consider some of these generic trends in films featuring refugees, extending the discussion to include narrative fiction film as well as documentary film.

From Hollywood to sci-fi: the camp in narrative film

Refugees and refugee camps were not adequately represented in mainstream feature films for much of the twentieth century. In Hollywood, although some directors and stars, such as Milos Forman, Marlene Dietrich and Billy Wilder, were political refugees from Nazi or Soviet regimes, refugees on screen were largely formulaic and oversimplified. In action films, refugees were often pigeonholed as victims of smuggling or human trafficking, such as in *Lazy River* (1934), *Daughter of Shanghai* (1938) or *Soldier of Fortune* (1955) about Chinese smuggling. Male refugees, often from the Soviet Bloc, were typically cast as scientists or dissidents in possession of secret knowledge, such as in *The Prize* (1963) or *City of Fear* (1963), or Lazlo in *Casablanca* (1943). Female refugees were typecast as exotic, mysterious, spirited damsels in distress, such as in *Dark of the Sun* (1968), *A Lady without a Passport* (1950) or Ilsa in *Casablanca*.

Casablanca, directed by Michael Curtiz, perhaps best epitomises the cursory treatment of the refugee camp in mid-century Hollywood film. The film is set in a 'way station' for refugees escaping Nazi-occupied Europe, and many of the patrons at Rick's *Café Americain* are desperate refugees trying to secure 'exit visas' to America. However, Rick's glamorous café, where patrons drink cocktails in dinner jackets and evening gowns, bears little resemblance to a refugee camp. Similarly, the stylish Laszlo hardly resembles a traumatised concentration camp survivor. However, despite its glamorised representation of the refugee camp and of refugee subjects, *Casablanca* does grasp some key aspects of refugeedom. In its opening sequence, the film alludes to the limbo that asylum seekers face: the 'waiting, waiting, waiting'. It also points to the risks that asylum seekers take by entrusting their lives to smugglers who view 'human life as cheap' or who describe refugees as Casablanca's 'leading commodity'. But ultimately, seventy-five minutes later, most viewers still find themselves in Rick's position at the outset of the film: that of isolationist bystanders unwilling to take an active role in the plight of refugees.

Beyond Borders (2003), directed by Martin Campbell, illustrates some of Hollywood's continuing failures in representing the refugee camp, sixty years after *Casablanca*. Humanitarian in scope, this romantic drama takes as something of a backdrop refugee camps and war zones as it charts the tumultuous love story of a benevolent rich socialite Sarah (Angelina Jolie) and a jaded relief-worker Nick (Clive Owens). Beginning with the 1984 Ethiopian famine, shifting to Khmer Cambodia and then to Chechnya, the film hops from horror to horror, conflating refugees with famine and genocide; seemingly, there was not enough drama in Ethiopia to warrant a full-length film – just 'waiting, starvation and hopelessness', to cite one of the film's aid workers. Though the film deploys yellow and blue filters to mimic news documentaries, it offers no explanation of specific political situations: instead, corrupt militias everywhere need only be bribed to quell violence; as Nick puts it, all the world's problems are simply due to 'closed minds and funding shortfalls'. Throughout the film, close or medium shots spotlight the White Western Saviours and reaffirm Western superiority; the only agency adult refugees seem to have is driving trucks or burying corpses. Even the sounds of the camp are erased by the film's epic soundtrack or Sarah's piano-playing in a relief tent. Most obviously, the film sentimentally exploits, to quote an un-ironic Nick, 'the weirdest, purest thing: suffering'. For instance, in a re-enactment of photojournalist Kevin Carter's iconic 1993 photograph, Sarah snatches up a baby about to be devoured by a vulture. In Cambodia, a toddler is given a hand-grenade to demonstrate a guerrilla leader's ruthlessness. And in the opening sequence, Nick brings an emaciated boy to a glitzy charity ball to plead for relief aid, shaming the audience by making the boy perform being a monkey – ironically also shaming and dehumanising the unwilling boy in the process. Though Nick attempts to satirise humanitarian fundraising techniques, the film fails to move beyond these modes itself; for instance, the audience never learn more about this forever emaciated refugee boy (who was saved years ago and is supposedly like Nick's 'son'), just as we never learn anything about the other refugees in the film, who basically serve as setting or as pathos. In all, *Beyond Borders* patronisingly and sentimentally exploits refugees' pain, especially the pain of refugee children, so as to add drama to an insipid love affair between two Western saviour figures.

Mainstream narrative films that fail to adequately represent refugee encampment usually do so because of the simplification, sentimentalism or infantilisation outlined above. There are, however, fiction films that manage to represent the refugee camp in creative and complex ways – notable examples include the science-fiction thrillers *Children of Men* (2009) and *District 9* (2006). Both of these films comment obliquely – but unmistakably – on the situation of contemporary asylum seekers, and imaginatively engage audiences who might be unwilling to endure a serious documentary on the subject. In Alfonso Cuarón's *Children of Men*, set in 2027, the UK, on the brink of societal collapse during a global plague of infertility, is deluged by asylum seekers fleeing war, and places brutal restrictions on refugees. In Neill Blomkamp's *District 9*, which alludes to the continued segregation of space and culture in post-apartheid South Africa, insect-like aliens are segregated in refugee slums. Despite their dystopic alternative futures, the films reflect real-world locales, including Auschwitz, Guantanamo Bay, the Maze and Cape Town's District Six, and both deploy a documentary, newsreel style, featuring fictional interviews, news footage and video from surveillance cameras to underscore the realism of events. The carceral space of the refugee camp is particularly well represented in both films; for instance, *District 9* clearly defines the camp as a 'form of bio-segregation' (Agier 2008: 33) with aliens set apart in policed ghettos, just as *Children of Men* underscores practices of surveillance, policing and 'crimmigration' (Stumpf 2006) in harrowing scenes where refugees are monitored in outdoor cages. In both films, viewers are encouraged to sympathise with – but not to sentimentalise – marginalised 'others' fleeing persecution, and even, via immersive sci-fi realism, to experience their complex subjectivities, which include, but are not limited to, flight, fear and loss.

Outside the camp: the immigrant narrative

Many films about refugees eschew camp life altogether, and instead conflate refugee stories with immigrant narratives. In marketing terms, films about camps or war zones risk being too 'depressing' or 'complicated' in comparison to the immigrant narrative, which usually follows predictable patterns of progress: the rags-to-riches genre, the pursuit of the American Dream (and its variants) and assimilation or acculturation. Also prevalent in immigrant films is the 'myth of success', associated with the specious belief that everyone can succeed, if only they try hard enough (Weiss 1969). While there clearly are successful immigrants, all too often the immigrant story is condensed to a triumphant struggle over all obstacles, be they language barriers, ethnic discrimination or past trauma. As I have shown elsewhere (Hron 2009), the standard immigrant narrative naturalises and neutralises the suffering of immigrants and refugees. The trauma, violence or hardship that migrants experience is generally glossed over as a necessary 'series of trials' (Boelhower 1982: 5) that need to be endured until a happy ending appears. Ultimately, the immigrant success story reflects the narrative of the successful host nation – as economically thriving, socially classless and pluralistically hospitable – proudly embracing racial, ethnic and gender differences.

Docudramas about the 'Lost Boys of Sudan' epitomise the subsuming of the refugee experience with narratives of immigrant assimilation. 'The Lost Boys' refers to some 20,000 Sudanese children who fled to Kenya during the second Sudanese Civil War (1983–2003) and spent more than ten years in Kenya's Kakuma refugee camp; in the early 2000s, some 3,800 of them were granted asylum in the United States. Docudramas such as *The Lost Boys of Sudan* (2003), *God Grew Tired of Us* (2007) and *The Good Lie* (2014) condense these children's decades-long refugee experience to a few sequences, focusing instead on their acculturation in the welcoming United States. The hardships of immigration – involving cultural alienation, the loss of family, isolation or the trauma they may still be suffering – are glossed over or erased. Instead, instances of 'culture shock' are emphasised – such as the boys' first time eating at McDonalds, encountering snow, or using a toothbrush. In such cases, the immigrant narrative as *Bildungsroman* often serves a pernicious purpose: to educate or 'civilise' non-Western others, and thus to reaffirm Western superiority. As Rey Chow has argued (1995), it engenders an 'epistemological hierarchy' in which the foreign other is the pre-modern 'primitive', as opposed to the civilised Westerner. There are many such films, including *Moving to Mars* (2009) about the Karen refugees from Burma, or recent films about Syrian refugees, such as *The Resettled* (2016) or *Children of Syria* (2016). Just as the Lost Boys do not know how to use a toothbrush, the Karen refugees do not know how electricity or gas stoves work – for them, Western civilisation is as alien as moving to Mars, as the title implies. In these films, refugee culture is usually depicted as quaintly charming but sorely antiquated; refugees must adapt to modern society and leave their culture and their encamped pasts behind them.

In contrast to such assimilationist films, there are films that resist this immigrant narrative of success and the facile binaries it engenders, and which instead question the easy integration of migrants by exposing the hardships they endure. Examples range from documentaries about undocumented workers in the US, such as *This (Illegal) American Life* (2011) or *La Cosecha/The Harvest* (2011), to feature films about illegal migrants in Europe such as *Welcome* (2009), *The Good Postman* (2016) or *The Other Side of Hope* (2017). These European fiction films all revolve around the encounter between the refugee and the citizen; in this common story arc, conservative citizens learn about the culture and humanity of the non-Western 'other' by engaging with refugee individuals directly. Cross-cultural encounters and misunderstandings are often fleshed out with dry humour or irony so as to engage audiences, but also to insert critical distance between them and their xenophobic peers. Indeed, there has been an upswelling of comedies about refugees, such as *One Hundred Foot Journey* (2014), *Willkommen bei den Hartmanns* (2016) or *Welcome to Norway* (2016). Instead of affirming Western superiority, these comedies draw on humour to self-reflexively criticise Western ways, or to spotlight misunderstandings, myths and hostilities towards refugees. Unfortunately, though, these comedies tend to privilege the perspective of Westerners; refugees in these films are often caricatured, and their experiences of refugeedom drolly simplified.

While the experience of encampment is often glossed over in immigrant assimilation films, some occasionally reflect encampment in scenes of confinement, limbo or stasis, such as being locked in the bathroom to fool the police in *The Other Side of Hope* or being stuck in Calais camp in *Welcome*. *Hotel Problemski* (2016), directed by Manu Riche, offers a particularly thought-provoking portrait of encampment experienced by a group of hotel-bound asylum seekers in Belgium. Plot-wise, the film recalls the classic *Dirty Pretty Things* (2002), directed by Stephen Frears, which follows a familial trio of undocumented hotel employees who together face such hardships as sexual exploitation or organ trafficking. In *Hotel Problemski*, a disparate group of refugees is similarly confined to a hotel while their asylum claims are being processed, and they also create a community with its own codes. All of these claimants have experienced horrible sufferings as refugees, but often have to deal with the sequelae alone; for instance, a seven-year-old refugee, traumatised because he was the sole survivor of a school bombing, daily faces an unsympathetic schoolteacher who insists that he 'get over' drawing pictures of mutilated bodies because they unnerve his classmates. Much like a refugee camp, the hotel's atmosphere is one of boredom and impatient nervousness as the inmates await news of their claims, and suicidal desperation when their claim is denied. The camera repeatedly pans long, drab corridors or empty boardrooms to reflect these refugees' abandonment and imprisonment in this soulless building. In a metaphor of the refugee condition, the group can find no place in the building to erect a Christmas tree – scene after scene shows the refugees moving the tree up and down stairs to various locales, cutting the tree down ever more. Finally, *Hotel Problemski* suggests that gaining entry into Belgium is a quixotic quest; the only chimeric possibility is escape, often at great personal cost. At the film's climax, a teen mother gives birth to a baby and then murders it so that she can gain passage in a container ship.

Outside the camp: the road movie

The refugee's journey to freedom – by land or by sea – is a recurrent mode of both narrative fiction films and documentaries. Numerous films explore refugees' arduous journeys from their broken homelands to promised lands in the West, and address the anxieties related to 'invading' or 'illegal' others, be they Hispanics into the US or Syrians into Europe. For instance, the treacherous desert crossing to the US is depicted in feature films such as *El Norte* (1983) and *Sin Nombre* (2009) and documentaries such as *Crossing Arizona* (2006) and *El Imigrante* (2007). Similarly, many docudramas, including *La Pirogue* (2012), *Terraferma* (2011) and *Mediterranea* (2015), show the death-defying sea voyage across the Mediterranean. Although thematically the refugee journey harks back to foundational cultural narratives and the epic journeys of such heroes as Gilgamesh, Odysseus or Sundiata, these films do not depict refugees as heroic adventurers, but rather as escaping war victims, who are hunted and vilified as they try to seek a better life. Most journey films try to dispel prevailing misconceptions about refugees – such as the threat of alien 'invasion' or the 'crimmigration' erroneously associated with undocumented migrants – by humanising refugees as individuals and showcasing the extreme risks they endure to achieve freedom. Cinematically, these films reflect and sometimes mimic the road-movie genre, albeit in dystopic form, while also drawing on elements from survival films, disaster movies, and gangster and Western genres.

Michael Winterbottom's *In This World* (2002), which follows the journey of Afghan teens Jamal and Enayat from a Pakistani refugee camp to London, showcases key elements of the dystopic refugee road-movie genre, as outlined by Terrence Wright (2000). For instance, the boys' trip is first blessed by the slaughter of a sheep, signalling a ceremonial rupture from their previous life. Their journey then consists of a series of 'encounters' – with human smugglers, border guards and ordinary people – as well as episodic 'setbacks', which become increasingly more dramatic, from flat tyres to fleeing gunfire at border crossings (Wright 2000). This last scene, filmed in infrared, pits the boys' body heat against shell blasts and exemplifies the turn to 'forensic surveillance measures' described by Steffen Köhn (2016: 49–52). The worst calamity of the boys' journey occurs when, with another family, they travel in a sealed freight container: apart from Jamal and a toddler, everyone slowly suffocates to death. Viewers are forced to imagine, albeit for only a few minutes, the horror of the passengers' gradual asphyxiation in darkness. Unlike more conventional road movies, Jamal experiences little personal growth or liberation on his journey. Although his destination is London, after Enayat's death this endpoint seems arbitrary. Rather the film, bookended by refugee camps, Shamshatoo in Peshwar and Sangatte in Calais, suggests that he will never escape the scars of camp life.

Though refugee road movies privilege movement and mobility, many of their characters, like those of *In This World*, cannot ever fully escape the confines of encampment or achieve full-fledged freedom. On the contrary, journeying refugees often find themselves trapped in a state of 'permanent transience' or 'liminal drift' (Bauman 2007: 38) which reflects conditions of encampment. Rather than rendering escape and liberty, these films reveal the mechanisms of hunting and surveillance that define the refugee experience, notably the binaries of 'in/visibility', 'il/legality' and 'concealment/exposure' (Köhn 2016). Finally, in many of these road movies, refugees find themselves, much like Jamal, trapped in the vehicles that transport them. Film scholars have noted the 'claustrophobic emphasis' (Bennett 2014: 190) or 'claustrophobic proximity' (Ballesteros 2015: 189) that characterises the vehicular entrapment in many of these films. Moreover, this sense of confinement is often furthered by camera techniques, such as Winterbottom's restrictive close-ups. Films about sea voyages, set on rickety or crowded ships, showcase even more of such suffocating claustrophobia, helpless immobility and death.

Inside the camp: from Darfur to Zataari

Compared to the many films about assimilation experiences or the refugee journey, there are very few films set in refugee camps that focus on camp life itself. Aside from the sci-fi films outlined earlier in this chapter, other noteworthy examples include documentaries about Darfur, such as *Darfur Diaries*, *Darfur Now*, *Darfur: On Our Watch*, *Sand and Sorrow*, as well as recent documentaries about Syrian refugees in Zataari camp in Jordan, including *Jordan: Home Away from Home*, *After Spring*, *Salam Neighbor* and *Clouds over Sidra*. As intimated above, films focusing on refugee camps face several crucial impediments: that of granting viewers some form of engaging narrative, while also capturing the protracted waiting or 'limbo' that camp life entails, and that of depicting refugees as subjects with agency, while also pointing to the dehumanisation that encampment engenders.

Film-makers seeking to document camp life are thus faced with the difficulties of capturing lives defined by loss, lack and limbo – be it a loss of one's home, one's identity as citizen, or the lack of movement and progress – but of not further stripping away refugees' humanity in the process. As

Zygmunt Bauman argues, the identity of camp refugees is defined by lack: 'state-less, placeless, functionless, and paper-less', camp refugees 'are pulped into a faceless mass, having been denied access to the elementary amenities from which identities are drawn' (2007: 40). Much of this indeterminacy is due to the 'temporary permanence' of the camp: refugees 'are suspended in a spatial void where time has ground to a halt . . . neither settled nor on the move . . . neither sedentary nor nomadic' (Bauman 2007: 45). Narratively, the indefiniteness, deferral and inertia of encamped limbo limit the conventions of action, plot progression or character development. Instead, artistic representation must find ways to render the psychological structures of PTSD and related disorders, marked as they are by intrusive, relentless repetition, wherein sufferers re-enact or relive scenes or actions from their past trauma (Herman 1992: 41–2). For the torture survivor and policy analyst Ezat Mossallanejed, the limbo of encampment also recalls the limbo of torture. Under torture, limbo includes being forgotten, being given false news, waiting for torture, waiting for sentencing or being placed on death row; many of these torture techniques reflect praxes engaged in camps or during the asylum process. As Mossallanejed summarises, limbo 'causes tremendous psychological tension, depression and re-traumatisation for thousands of refugees especially those who were survivors of war and torture' (2005: 231). Documentaries about camp life must therefore somehow representationally capture or depict this torturous limbo; however, it is challenging since contemporary audiences lack both the experience of prolonged waiting or of being survivors of war and torture, retraumatised by such limbo.

Documentaries about Darfur showcase how difficult it is to convey the interminable waiting, the lack of basic services such as schools or hospitals, and the declining mental state of a traumatised population living in limbo for years on end. For the past fifteen years, some 300,000 Darfurians have been living in Chadian camps, unable to return home. Documentaries about Darfur often portray these massive camps, but rarely explore the conditions of camp life. Rather, in order to give evidence of genocide, documentaries such as PBS's *Darfur: On Our Watch* (2007) elaborate on historical events and re-enact the three-pronged attacks in Darfur: government-led aerial bombings, followed by the looting and burning of villages by the Janjaweed Arab militias on horseback, who concomitantly killed and raped fleeing civilians. Other documentaries, such as Ted Braun's *Darfur Now* (2007), aim to inspire viewers to activism by interweaving stories of refugee escape with those of resistance fighters, Western activists and UN prosecutors. Only *Darfur Diaries* (2006), by the amateur film-makers Aisha Bain and Jen Marlowe, foregrounds daily life in Chadian camps and effectively compels viewers to share in refugees' lives. In this collection of interviews, viewers observe these survivors' lingering trauma by their physical manifestations, such as silent pauses, or close-ups on their shaking hands and trembling lips. In other sequences, the camera silently lingers on survivors sitting immobile in front of their tents, zooms in on their intense blank gazes, or slowly sweeps across the barren desert – thus prompting viewers to pause, to be immobile and to contemplate, albeit for a minute, the limbo that survivors bear on a daily basis.

Ten years later, a number of documentaries similarly struggle to represent encamped life in Zaatari, a refugee camp in Jordan that shelters more than 80,000 Syrians who have fled the ongoing Syrian civil war. Films such as *Jordan: Home Away from Home, After Spring, Salam Neighbor* and *Clouds Over Sidra* reveal a similar dilemma: how to compel viewers' compassion for the suffering of Syrian refugees, while at the same time showcasing Zataari's vibrant camp life, which points to refugees' resilience and community building. *After Spring* (2015), directed by Ellen Martinez and Steph Ching, exemplifies this quandary. Using a multi-dimensional perspective akin to that of *Darfur Now*, the film follows two refugee families transitioning to life in Zataari camp, as well as aid workers managing the camp, and thus oscillates between emotions ranging from despair, loss and fear, to optimism, courage and solidarity. Like documentaries about Darfur, the film flashes back to the past in various snippets and reminiscences to reveal the horrors of the Assad regime and to remind viewers of these refugees' many losses. It also success-fully captures encamped limbo by the use of repetition; various sequences – such as that of refugees constantly watching television newscasts or reminisc-ing about the same memories– emphasise the repetitious monotony of refugee existence. Finally, some of the documentary's most powerful scenes reveal the precarious mental state of these encamped refugees: it shows that there are no facilities for physically and mentally disabled refugees and no treatment options for refugees suffering from depression, anxiety and PTSD, and sug-gests that, as a result, domestic abuse, elder abuse and sexual abuse are rife in the camps.

However, *After Spring* also undercuts notions of refugees' perpetual suf-fering and limbo with its narrative of progress and community building. Zataari is depicted as a model camp, with caravans instead of tents, electric-ity, a Twitter account, stalls selling delicious food, and opportunities such as Taekwondo for camp children. When viewers observe refugees loading up grocery carts, preparing mouth-watering pizza or repeatedly sitting around watching television, their sympathy for refugees' plights might somewhat sub-side. However, the many scenes revolving around the market emphasise refu-gees' resilience, entrepreneurship and potential. Instead of reifying encamped life as one 'devoid of value' or 'unworthy of being' (Agamben 1998: 139, 142), films such as *After Spring* reveal that many refugees are 'campcitizens' living in a bustling 'anti-city' of their own making (Dalal 2015: 276).

Increasingly, humanitarian agencies are turning to more creative and opti-mistic representations of vibrant encamped life to engage viewers and poten-tial donors. *Clouds Over Sidra* (2015), an eight-minute virtual reality film produced by UNHCR, described as 'the ultimate empathy machine' by sup-porters, and an important weapon in the 'empathy arms race' by UN creative director Gabo Arora, works to curb compassion fatigue about refugees by 'immersing' viewers into camp life from the perspective of a twelve-year-old girl living in Zataari camp (Robertson 2016). Instead of being a passive victim, Sidra comes across as a curious, capable and knowledgeable informant about camp culture. Again, the camp is not depicted as a space of abjection or exclusion, but rather as a lively community, albeit one that is severely lacking resources. It is questionable, however, whether viewers can fully appreciate the sufferings of refugees when presented with such an optimistic, if not infantilised, perspective on camp life and whether it is constructive, from the perspective of awareness raising if not of aesthetics, to present encampment as a space of potential growth and development.

Inside/outside the camp: *Human Flow*

Ai Weiwei's formidable *Human Flow* (2017) draws on the contrasts between inside and outside the camp to reveal the sufferings of refugees, as well as their humanity, agency and heroism. *Human Flow* represents the most comprehensive, big-budget documentary about refugees discussed in this chapter; its 2,000-member crew travelled to 23 countries and 40 refugee camps, shot 900 hours of footage and conducted 600 interviews to create this two-hour-and-twenty-minute documentary. Unlike refugee films which appeal to viewers' sense of pity or compassion, *Human Flow* appeals to viewers' aesthetic sensibilities in its depiction of both migration and encampment. Shot from a variety of different perspectives, from hand-held smartphones to unmanned aerial vehicles, the film's cinematography impresses and recalls Ai's wider oeuvre. Particularly stunning are aerial sequences shot by drones which conceptually illustrate the sheer scale of refugee migration, but which also emphasise the fragility of the human condition on a planetary scale. In one scene, the camera seemingly hovers over ants scurrying on a mound of red earth; as it zooms in, the drone shot reveals children playing amid container housing in Turkey's Nizip refugee camp. This scene resembles Ai's *Sunflower Seeds* installation, which featured 150 tons of porcelain seeds, individually hand-painted by Chinese artisans, so as to prompt contemplation of the individual within the collective and the mass produced. Similarly, the film's closing shot zooms out on millions and millions of lifejackets to once again show the sheer scale of the refugee crisis and the vulnerability of its victims. This scene evokes abandoned suitcases at concentration camps, and their display at many camp memorial sites, as well as Ai's various installations about litter, scale and mobility, most prominently his lifejacket installations, for which he transported thousands of life vests from Lesbos to be wrapped around the columns of Konzerthaus Berlin.

Human Flow's cinematography emphasises refugees' freedom and mobility, movements that are always threatened by authorities or completely curtailed by closed borders or in refugee camps. The whole documentary may be considered a road movie, in which Ai, along with his viewers, gains greater knowledge and self-awareness on the journey. Various scenes feature Ai as ethnographer-protagonist: we see him cutting refugees' hair, exchanging passports with a Syrian or bundling a lifeboat survivor in a blanket. However, some of the film's most poignant scenes offer us glimpses into the lives of the refugees themselves: for instance, in one camp scene, a woman turned away from the camera facing a wall sobbingly testifies that 'I cannot live like this', and then completely breaks down and throws up. The camera speeds up to show Ai comforting her. Disturbed, viewers are left unsure why exactly her situation is untenable; all that is clear is that she is encamped and profoundly in pain.

Despite its perpetual movement, *Human Flow* offers brief yet powerful glimpses into the encamped life of refugees. Some of the film's most striking scenes concern the creation of the makeshift camp at the railway station in Idomeni, Greece, and its 'relocation' in March 2016. For a few sequences, viewers share in refugees' entrapment at the Greek–Macedonian border, and the horrible, muddy, squalid conditions that they must endure. The destitution, confinement and rejection that these refugees experience is later echoed in temporary camps in Turkey, or the long-established camp in Daabab, Kenya, which is depicted as abandoned to sand and trash. The entrapment and policing they experience, emphasised by numerous scenes of barbed wire fences and guard dogs, is later reiterated in scenes of Palestinian camps in Gaza which demarcate the apogee of the refugee camp as a prison-like police state. Viewers are then witness to the destruction of the Idomeni camp by armed police and tear gas; even children are not spared. This destruction parallels the merciless razing of the Calais camp in northern France. In all, some of *Human Flow*'s most harrowing scenes of violence, cruelty and suffering concern refugee encampment. However, the film emphasises that the hardships of encampment do not solely comprise the visible violence of tear gas and bulldozed tents. Near the end of the film, a young girl living in Germany's Tempelhof Airport camp sums up her encampment as 'the most difficult time in my life', explaining that 'everything is forbidden' and life is 'so very boring'. This young girl's experience is contrasted throughout the film with more lighthearted, sentimental shots of children playing or being silly, underscoring that despite this playfulness, encamped children are receiving little education, and are indeed susceptible to militarisation. *Human Flow* signals, in no uncertain terms, that the cycle of violence will continue for future generations of refugee children unless some radical change occurs as far as the concept of encampment itself is concerned.

Encamped children: *Turtles Can Fly*

In closing, it is necessary to pause on the cinematic representation of the encamped child. As we have seen, children figure in many refugee films, from *Beyond Borders* to *Human Flow*, and are even more prominent in humanitarian or awareness-raising campaigns, from UNHCR's *Clouds Over Sidra* to Save the Children's video marketing campaign, *Most Shocking Second a Day*

(2014). Various narrative films also feature child protagonists, including *In This World* (2002), *Turtles Can Fly* (2004), *Live and Become* (2005), *Welcome* (2009) and, most recently, *Sea Sorrow* (2017), Vanessa Redgrave's directorial debut about Alan Kurdi. It is perhaps not surprising that children figure so prominently in refugee representations: according to UNICEF, more than half of the world's refugees are children, numbering more than 50 million in 2016. Narratively, the figure of an innocent child fleeing war invites explanation or redemptive storytelling. Moreover, child heroes render the hardships of refugeedom more palatable and engaging to non-refugee audiences, thus helping to battle compassion fatigue and indifference. Most importantly, the power of children to enact social change cannot be underestimated, especially in terms of visual representation. For instance, in 1972, the photograph of Kim Phuc, a girl fleeing a napalm bombing, changed public opinion about the Vietnam War. Similarly, in 2015 Nilüfer Demir's photographs of Alan Kurdi, a toddler washed up on a beach in Bodrum, Turkey, prompted international outcry over the Syrian refugee crisis. Notably, once the initial outcry had subsided, Ai Weiwei provocatively re-enacted the shot of Kurdi by posing as the corpse himself, so as to prompt people to continue to keep Syrian refugees in mind; moreover, Ai's haunting image also poignantly draws attention to the difference between child and adult victims on display.

Children perform several important functions in refugee films. First, they personalise the 'faceless refugee mob' through an engaging, memorable example, be it the 'monkey boy' in *Beyond Borders* or the Afghani teen Jamal in *In this World*. More abstractly, children also serve as 'national avatars' or 'metonyms' for specific ethnic groups (Donald, Wilson and Wright 2017: 2), as well as being 'stand-ins' for many deaths (Lury 2010: 107). Sentimental pathos is maximised when children are involved, as they are fragile, vulnerable and innocent of any wrongdoing. To cite Karen Lury, children are 'perfect victims', 'blameless', who make 'wrong seem more wrong' (2010: 105). Unlike adults who may or may not be perceived to be responsible for their predicament, children wholly circumvent notions of guilt and innocence, and instead maximise compassion for their plight. Emotional impact and identification are sharpened when children are involved: 'looking at childhood . . . the human mind loses an element of distance or at least, its span of judgement shifts' (Donald, Wilson and Wright 2017: 3). When viewing a child fleeing war, viewers typically curtail more complex reactions such as callousness, jadedness or indifference that may be elicited by adult victims; annoyance, irony and sarcasm are inappropriate when children are involved. Children bearing arms, playing with guns or running amid landmines also forcefully showcase the incongruity of war and other human rights violations that often become normalised in mainstream media. Finally, because of children's fragility and the brevity of childhood, children invoke a sense of urgency and emergency: the sense that action must be taken immediately to 'save the children'.

However, screening encamped children can also present various representational challenges. Just as it is easy to stereotype refugees or the experience of encampment, it is all too easy to draw on children as shorthand for the refugee experience, as in the case of Alan Kurdi, or as pathos-laden tokens of miserabilism, as in Hollywood's *Beyond Borders*. Moreover, deploying children can serve to normalise the conditions of encampment: some viewers watching children gambolling among refugee containers may be misled into believing that the refugee situation cannot be as dire as otherwise depicted. Furthermore, utilising children can elide thorny political problems or the 'moral complexity inherent in any conflict' (Lury 2010: 107). All too often, complex political issues underpinning the refugee experience are simplified to the point of being reductionist or generalising, just as the solutions to the refugee condition appear facile or unsustainable. Lastly, all too easily child refugees risk being infantilised as naïve half-beings, and their stories reduced to sentimentalist melodramas.

The Iranian narrative feature film *Turtles Can Fly* (2004), directed by Bahman Ghobadi, poignantly portrays encamped life from the perspective of children, without sentimentalising or infantilising its child heroes. Set on the eve of the US invasion of Iraq in 2003, this gritty neo-realist film explores the daily life of Kurdish children living at the Turkish–Iraqi border. Set amid military wreckage and abandoned weapons, the film starkly reveals the aftermath of war, and explores life in unofficial, makeshift refugee camps in border zones. Notably, Ghobadi employed local camp children, adding further degrees of authenticity and representational complexity to the film. Though sprinkled with humour and playfulness, the film broaches serious themes – most basically how this community of children, bereft of responsible adults, manages to survive the harsh conditions of encampment.

The children's main occupation in these border camps is defusing landmines for resale. As implied in the film's title, the children resemble turtles because they carry backpacks of defused mines on their backs; if they set off a landmine, they will become 'turtles that fly'. There are an estimated 25 million landmines in Iraq, going back to the Second World War, the Iran–Iraq war, the 1991 Gulf War and the 2003 US invasion. The children pick up landmines from all of these different eras, but the most valuable ones are the undetectable American plastic ones. Some of the film's most harrowing scenes feature a young teen, Hengov, defusing landmines with his teeth, since he no longer has any arms as a result of previous accidents. There is no soundtrack, as with bated breath, viewers watch Hengov deftly but awkwardly remove the pin with his mouth. In another scene, a blind toddler, Riga, climbs on to a landmine and forces the teen leader, Satellite, to try to defuse it. Again, diegetic sound increases tension, but in this case Satellite maims his foot. Until then, Satellite had been directing the children to dangers he did not experience first-hand.

The plot of *Turtles Can Fly* revolves around three new arrivals to the camp: the armless but clairvoyant Hengov, the blind toddler Riga and his sister Agrin, all Kurdish refugees from Halabja, site of the infamous 1988 chemical attack by 'Chemical Ali', Saddam Hussein's cousin. The teen leader Satellite courts pretty Agrin; for instance, in a gesture of affection perverted by war, he procures her a gas mask to keep her safe. Throughout the film, Agrin acts strangely; ultimately, we learn that she was brutally raped during an attack, and that her toddler brother Riga is in fact the product of this rape. Her trauma is overwhelming and she repeatedly tries to rid herself of Riga or expose him to dangerous situations. The film ends with Riga's drowning and Agrin's suicidal jump from a cliff. In an interview, Ghobadi explained that Hengov, Riga and Agrin can be seen as symbolising the Kurdish people: the prophetic future, the blind present and the traumatic past (Vehmeyer 2005). As in many films, these child refugees become 'national avatars', 'metonyms for national affiliation', oscillating between 'agency and allegory' (Donald, Wilson and Wright 2017: 2).

Although it would be easy to sentimentalise these maimed children with editing, close-up shots and a pathos-laden soundtrack, *Turtles Can Fly* exposes the children's hardships matter-of-factly, with sober realism. As Fran Hassencahl explains (2012), these children's lives reflect 'pooch' or 'hüzün', a form of sadness or pessimism about the future that is untranslatable from Persian/Turkish into English, but that affects many war survivors. In a world with increasing numbers of child refugees, there will be more children experiencing complex forms of trauma as a result of war, itinerancy, statelessness and experiences of encampment. In all, instead of deploying child protagonists as naïve half-beings, *Turtles Can Fly* effectively grants child protagonists as much agency, subjectivity and knowledge as adult refugees. In many ways, especially in their knowledge of satellite technology or landmines, and their entrepreneurial trading of these goods, these children know better how to operate and navigate within spaces of encampment than do their adult peers.

Concluding beyond the 'reel'

One of the most powerful statements in Ai Weiwei's *Human Flow* is Hanan Ashrawi's contention that 'being a refugee is the most pervasive kind of cruelty that can be exercised against a human being. You are forcibly robbing this human being of all aspects that would make human life not just tolerable, but meaningful.' In its survey of refugee films, this chapter has identified some pervasive generic, cinematic and narrative conventions that can rob refugees of meaningful representation, reducing them to victimised stereotypes or furthering their dehumanisation. Concomitantly, this chapter has also explored various tactics that film-makers deploy to blur, resist or subvert these generic models, often by showcasing refugees' sense of agency, mobility or community building – as well as ways in which refugees themselves make their lives more tolerable and meaningful. Finally, this discussion reveals how the pervasive cruelties of encampment are represented in films both inside and outside the camp. It shows that some of the defining characteristics of encampment – whether of limbo, confinement or 'campzenship' – may also be discerned in films outside the camp. As Michel Agier sums up, 'each displaced person, each refugee, carries within them the [encampment] experience of being undesirable and placeless. A lived experience of the original act of violent persecution' (2008: 28).

Ultimately, however, the real-life effects of these reel representations remain questionable. Does screening these films simply recapitulate the failures of refugee policies? Or does it enable viewers to imagine alternatives to refugee encampment? How many more films need to be produced about refugee suffering so as to change cruel and pervasive policies? Can screening a documentary such as *Human Flow* have positive real-life effects, even among the xenophobes or border police it portrays? Or will the narrative of refugee encampment continue to be, as *Casablanca* intoned some seventy-five years ago, 'the same old story . . . as time goes by?'

Bibliography

Agamben, G. (1998), *Homo Sacer: Sovereign Power and Bare Life*, trans. D. Heller-Roazen (Stanford: Stanford University Press).
Agier, M. (2008), *On the Margins of the World: The Refugee Experience Today* (Cambridge: Polity Press).
Ballesteros, I. (2015), *Immigration Cinema in the New Europe* (Bristol: Intellect).
Bauman, Z. (2007), *Liquid Times: Living in an Age of Uncertainty* (Cambridge: Polity Press).
Bennett, B. (2014), *The Cinema of Michael Winterbottom: Borders, Intimacy, Terror* (New York: Columbia University Press).
Berlant, L. G. (2008), *The Female Complaint: The Unfinished Business of Sentimentality in American Culture* (Durham, NC: Duke University Press).
Bernand, C. (1994), 'Ségrégation et anthropologie, anthropologie de la ségrégation', in J. Brun and C. Rhein (eds), *La Ségrégation dans la ville* (Paris: L'Harmattan), 73–84.
Boelhower, W. (1981), 'The immigrant novel as genre', *Melus*, 8.1: 3–13.
Celik, I. A. (2015), *In Permanent Crisis: Ethnicity in Contemporary European Media and Cinema* (Ann Arbor: University of Michigan Press).
Chow, R. (1995), *Primitive Passions: Visuality, Sexuality, Ethnography, and Contemporary Chinese Cinema* (New York: Columbia University Press).
Dalal, A. (2015), 'A socio-economic perspective on the urbanisation of Zataari camp in Jordan', *Migration Letters*, 12: 263–78.
Donald, S., E. Wilson and S. Wright (2017), *Childhood and Nation in Contemporary World Cinema: Borders and Encounters* (London: Bloomsbury).
Gill, N. (2013), *Carceral Spaces: Mobility and Agency in Imprisonment and Migrant Detention* (Farnham: Ashgate).
Hassencahl, F. (2012), 'Experiencing Hüzün through the loss of life, limbs, and love in *Turtles Can Fly*', in D. Olson and A. Scahill (eds), *Lost and Othered Children in Contemporary Cinema* (Lanham, MD: Lexington Books), 307–26.

Herman, J. L. (1992), *Trauma and Recovery* (New York: Basic Books).

Hron, M. (2009), *Translating Pain: Immigrant Suffering in Literature and Culture* (Toronto: University of Toronto Press).

Köhn, S. (2016), *Mediating Mobility: Visual Anthropology in the Age of Migration* (London: Wallflower Press).

Lissner, J. (1981), 'Merchants of misery', *New Internationalist*, 100: 23–5.

Lury, K. (2010), *The Child in Film: Tears, Fears and Fairytales* (London, I. B. Tauris).

Mbembe, A. (2003), 'Necropolitics', *Public Culture*, 15.1: 11–20.

Mogire, E. O. (2011), *Victims as Security Threats: Refugee Impact on Host State Security in Africa* (Burlington, VT: Ashgate).

Mossallanejed, E. (2005), *Torture in the Age of Fear* (Hamilton, ON: Seraphim Editions).

Robertson, A. (2016), 'The UN wants to see how far VR empathy will go', *The Verge*, 19 September, https://www.theverge.com/2016/9/19/12933874/unvr-clouds-over-sidra-film-app-launch (accessed 14 May 2019).

Sigona, N. (2014), 'Campzenship: reimagining the camp as a social and political space', *Citizenship Studies*, 19.1: 1–15.

Stumpf, J. (2006), 'The crimmigration crisis: immigrants, crime, and sovereign power', *American University Law Review*, 56.2: 367–419.

Vehmeyer, B. (2005), 'IFFR: turtles can fly', http://www.brnrd.net/blog/archive/2005/01/31/iffr-turtles-can-fly (accessed 23 April 2017).

Weiss, R. (1969), *The American Myth of Success: From Horatio Alger to Norman Vincent Peale* (New York: Basic Books).

Woolley, A. (2014), *Contemporary Asylum Narratives: Representing Refugees in the Twenty-First Century* (Basingstoke: Palgrave Macmillan).

Wright, T. (2000), 'Refugees on screen', working paper, Toronto Refugee Studies Center.

Part VI

Sea Crossings

Sea Crossings: Introduction

David Farrier

In 2014 the artist Nicolaj Larsen submerged 48 concrete-canvas and wire mesh sculptures, suspended from a specially constructed platform off the coast of Calabria. Each sculpture was made to resemble a shrouded body – a body bag that, when immersed, would develop a layer of sea organisms. Larsen's plan was then to retrieve and exhibit all 48 sculptures to memorialise the thousands of people who die crossing the Mediterranean. However, a violent storm, which destroyed the platform and scattered the sculptures across the seabed, drastically intervened. Larsen employed a local diver to 'rescue' the sculptures, and to film the process. In all, 13 sculptures were recovered, and subsequently exhibited in 2015 along with footage from the search in an exhibition Larsen called *End of Dreams*.

End of Dreams protests against the dehistoricisation of those who risk perilous sea crossings in search of a better life. The Tyrrhenian Sea where Larsen immersed his sculptures is mostly used by people crossing to Europe from Iran and Afghanistan, and concrete-canvas is frequently used in emergency zones as a temporary building material. While this doesn't allow Larsen to suggest the distinctiveness of individual histories, it nonetheless insists that these journeys *do have* stories that precede entry into the water and that these stories are, moreover, multifaceted, with political, economic and geographical dimensions. The coating of barnacles and other marine organisms, by contrast, highlights how these stories are subsumed by other, more powerful narratives – forms of discursive violence, which reduce refugees to mere 'bodies of water', in concert with forms of structural violence, such as the EU's Bossi-Fini prohibitions against helping migrants in distress.

The four chapters in this section expose and explore the way refugees must not only negotiate some of the most hazardous environments, but also navigate a sea of stories – a set of discursive currents that threaten to pull them in particular directions, or even submerge them entirely. According to the Missing Migrants Project, 11,221 people drowned trying to cross the Mediterranean between 2014 and 2018. Joseph Pugliese's chapter situates these fatalities in a biopolitical framework; more specifically, in the context of what he calls 'zoopolitics' – a biopolitics of race that transmutes the refugee into a non-human animal, a being outside the application of rights or legal protection. As Pugliese has written elsewhere, bodies that wash up on beaches or are brought out of the water in fishermen's nets are reduced to transparent 'bodies of water', signifying nothing beyond their relationship with their environment (Pugliese 2006). In this chapter he takes this further, arguing that recursive fears that consuming Mediterranean fish might also imply consuming migrants' flesh rely for their intelligibility on a much older history of colonial othering (the indigenous subject as cannibal) and on the absorption of the refugee into a zoopolitical dialectic of the sovereign and the beast that legitimises their dehumanising treatment.

Hakim Abderrezak's chapter also addresses the calamity of migrant deaths in the Mediterranean. Deploying what he calls a 'south-of-the-sea terminology', Abderrezak examines both what the Mediterranean has become and what it could become, as well as what it means for those who cross – the *harragas*, a term whose etymology is in the Arabic *hrig/harga* (burning). Linguistically playful but deadly serious, via a series of tropes he explores how the sea of stories is also a space of rich (and often lethal) imaginings: as a sieve, it is a porous body, defined by how effectively it controls who gets through (literally embodied by SIVE, or *Sistema Integrado de Vigilencia Exterior*, the EU's electronic monitoring system); as a spring, Abderrezak delineates the relationship between the refugee 'crisis' and the Arab Spring that preceded it, and anxieties about particularly racialised bodies passing through the sieve; finally, as 'seametery', he addresses the irony that a place of flows can also become the world's largest marine cemetery, where even death is not the end of injustice.

While Pugliese and Abderrezak's chapters remain out at sea, Mariangela Palladino's contribution makes landfall. Via a reading of Erri De Luca's long poem *Solo Andata* (2005), Palladino explores the concept of *islandment*: a state of being, with an accompanying rhetoric of (in)hospitality, where to reach the shore does not constitute arrival. As with Abderrezak's emphasis on 'south-of-the-sea terminology', 'islandment', she suggests, specifically invokes the complexities of migrants' own experiences of making landfall. It signifies a liminal space materialised by the apparatus of the detention estate; those caught up in it inhabit a state of double incarceration through the fences of the camp and the sea. Her paradigmatic example is Lampedusa, one of the EU's pre-emptive frontiers; as well as possessing a long history as a carceral archipelago, in Palladino's reading Lampedusa also becomes a place of harvest – a 'sea harvest' of lost lives that also brings to mind the labour dynamics that undergird the politics of Mediterranean migration.

Parvati Nair's chapter closes the section by asking what keeps refugees and migrants perpetually 'at sea' – that is, captured in a state (both affective and structural) that is defined by despair and exposure. The visual grammar of most images of refugees undertaking sea crossings is conditioned by a stark binary – citizen/other, land/sea, protection/precarity – that reinforces associations between the sea and mortality. But such crossings, while highly dangerous, are not possible, Nair says, without an essential element of hope. To consider refugees at sea as only elements in a humanitarian crisis is not only to work within a narrow critical framework; it also contributes to the disempowering of refugees. To misread images only for the despair they convey rather than the hope is to reinforce the imperilling of the most vulnerable. Yet while it may not be as visibly encoded in images of sea crossings, hope is nonetheless present. Nair argues that we must learn to read 'this extreme form of dislocation' as also 'the most extreme act of hope'. Hope in this context entails tenacity and imagination, resilience and agency. It signifies that the bleak narratives imposed on those who cross the sea are not the whole story, and do not tell the future for all. Building on the work of Adrienne M. Martin, Nair calls for a 'pragmatics of hope', a hope that makes survival and sustenance possible. In a situation where refugees are reduced to 'bodies of water' in the Mediterranean 'seametery' and exposed to the discipline of 'islandment', Nair's emphasis on hope provides an important revisioning of the sea of stories.

Bibliography

Pugliese, Joseph (2006), 'Bodies of water', *Heat: Literary International*, 12: 13–20.

Chapter 18

Zoopolitics of Asylum Seeker Marine Deaths and Cultures of Anthropophagy

Joseph Pugliese

On raising their nets from the depths of the Mediterranean, Italian fishermen have often brought to the surface the bodies of drowned asylum seekers. Some fishermen, fearful of the protracted bureaucratic processes that would ensue if they brought the bodies to shore, turf the corpses back into the sea as though they were simply an unpalatable part of their catch. On the shores of the Mediterranean countries that face North Africa and the Middle East, the bodies of those who have drowned in the course of their asylum journeys wash up on the beaches, where often they remain in full view of European holidaymakers who blithely disregard their presence – as though they were merely part of the ecology of beach detritus.

In this chapter, I situate these maritime deaths in a biopolitical framework. In my use of the Foucauldian term 'biopolitics', I refer to the state's political power 'to *foster* life or *disallow* it to the point of death' (Foucault 1990: 138). The statist (and EU supra-state) regimes of letting asylum seekers die at sea or at the border pivot, I contend, on a biopolitical matrix of power, bodies, life and death. In his *Lectures at the Collège de France*, Michel Foucault examines the category of race in an in-depth manner that is strikingly absent from his previously published corpus. Race, indeed, assumes a fundamental role in his theorising of biopolitics. In his analysis of early nineteenth-century European culture, Foucault identifies a decisive break with the past in relation to the uses and abuses of race and the 'discourse of race struggle':

> It [the discourse of race struggle] will become the discourse of a centered, centralized, and centralizing power. It will become the discourse of battle that has to be waged not between races, but by a race that is portrayed as the one true race, the race that holds power and is entitled to define the norm, and against those who deviate from that norm, against those who pose a threat to the biological heritage. At this point, we have all those biological-racist discourses of degeneracy, but also all those institutions within the social body which make the discourse of race struggle function as a principle of exclusion and segregation and, ultimately, as a way of normalizing society. (Foucault 2003: 61)

Foucault identifies the resultant 'race wars' that this discourse of race struggle enables as what is 'articulated with European policies of colonization' (Foucault 2003: 61). The biopolitics of race in the context of colonialism as theorised by Foucault is, in fact, underpinned by a governing biopolitical category that remains at once unspoken and untheorised: speciesism – understood in all of its anthropocentric dimensions. The entire apparatus of the biopolitics of race, its colonial and imperial dimensions, its discriminatory, exclusionary and necropolitical effects, are, I propose, all rendered culturally intelligible and biopolitically enabled by the category of the absolute non-human other: *the* animal – and I deploy the problematic definite article here precisely in order to underscore the violent operations of homogenisation, totalisation and genericity that are operative in the binary logic of anthropocentrism. Biopolitical arguments of race and 'the norm', 'the biological heritage' and threats of 'degeneracy' are all premised, in the first instance, on the unspoken assumption of an anthropocentrism that has assiduously laboured to construct and consolidate species hierarchies and their attendant knowledge/power effects in terms of the valuation, fungibility and governance of diverse life forms. If, as Foucault suggests, biopolitics was principally 'focused on the species body', then what remains unsaid in his work is the critical relation between the human species and its animal others.

In what follows, I address the otherwise untheorised speciesism that insistently inscribes the biopolitics of race, and its power to foster life or to let die, by drawing on Jacques Derrida's concept of 'zoopolitics' in order to materialise the link between two inextricably tied forms of knowledge/ power. Operative in the relations of power that at once produce and inscribe these deaths is a specific form of biopolitics: *zoopolitics*. Zoopolitics draws its violent metaphysics and operational logics from biopolitics, with its focus on the management of the life and death of its subjects. I deploy the concept of zoopolitics as, at its very etymological level, it enunciates the question of the *zōon* or the animal. In the course of this chapter, I examine how what is operative in the waters of the Mediterranean, and on its shores, is a zoopolitics that transmutes asylum seekers fleeing the harrowed lands of the Global South into non-human animals. Categorised zoopolitically as non-human animals, they effectively possess, regardless of international protocols and conventions, no jural standing; they thus live and die outside the purview of the category of the human and the attendant rights and protections afforded by this legal category. Zoopolitics, in the context of asylum seeker marine deaths, evidences the lethal effects of that combinatory form that I have elsewhere termed 'racio-speciesism', which binds targeted human subjects to the possibility of being killed or being allowed to die with impunity, precisely as though they were non-human animals (Pugliese 2013: 41–2). I deploy the term 'racio-speciesism' as the subjects of the Global South who have died in their thousands in the Mediterranean are people of colour from Africa, Asia and the Middle East branded with the racio-speciesist imprimatur of being less than human. As such, the EU players in the biopolitical drama of unending asylum seekers' deaths in the Mediterranean mobilise, through their deployment of racio-speciesist descriptors, arguments that they pose threats to the biological and racial heritage of Europe and that, in Foucauldian terms, they need to be 'excluded', 'segregated' and, if necessary, allowed to die.

Bodies of water

Over the last two decades, thousands of asylum seekers have drowned in the waters of the Mediterranean. In one maritime incident alone, 'as many as 700 . . . are feared to have drowned just outside Libyan waters' (Kingsley, Bonomolo and Kirchgaessner 2015). The Missing Migrants Project keeps daily tallies of the asylum seeker dead on its website. The project tabulates the deaths in a type of bookkeeping exercise that organises the deaths by region, year and month (Missing Migrants Project 2016). Even as it is an essential record of these deaths, this project also reproduces a number of disturbing unintended effects. The Missing Migrants Project emerges as a type of electronic morgue that, precisely as a digitised repository, has an infinite capacity to absorb the asylum seeker dead. As digital morgue, the project transmutes flesh and blood bodies into anonymous numbers. The numerical scale and weighting of these thousands of deaths suggests that we are dealing with a type of death that can be calculated in terms of human tonnage and transmuted into decorporealised infographics. News reports, indeed, further evidence this conversion of the human into the non-human by referring to asylum seekers as so much 'human cargo' and as 'ballast' (Agence France-Presse 2016).

The discursive forces that are at work in the transmutation of the human into the non-human operate along a number of biopolitical axes. The bodies of the asylum seeker dead that wash up on the shores of the Mediterranean are often are viewed as little more than beach detritus. The asylum seeker, the undocumented and the *clandestino* live and die the onto-tautology of their clandestine status, literally remaining invisible to Western subjects *despite being directly in the line of sight* of the European holidaymakers enjoying their day out on the beach. On one occasion, in the wake of an asylum seeker shipwreck, the bodies of two Roma girls washed up on the southern Italian beach of Torregaveta. Marked by their pariah status, these two dead Roma girls signified as nothing more than mere beach litter in the eyes of the European beachgoers. Images of the two dead Roma children show the bodies covered with beach towels. In the background, only a few metres away, sit holidaymakers basking in the sun, with the bodies of the dead girls in their line of sight (Pugliese 2009: 662). Inscribed by a combination of racial and biopolitical vectors, they are assigned their rightful place amid the beach detritus, as they cannot be seen as possessing any proper claim to the category of the human subject. The corpses of these two young Roma girls delineate border zones of the dead. In their death, they stake out littoral death zones that mark the line of division between the human and the non-human, between the dead worthy of commemoration and mourning and the dead who are, rather, a nuisance or a form of pollution that needs to be dealt with. The assignation of such outlaw bodies as nothing more than environmental pollution contaminating the ecology of the tourist beach has been spelled out by the former mayor of Lampedusa, Bruno Siragusa, angry at the unsolicited arrival of dead refugee bodies on the holiday beaches of his coast: 'he has complained about the number of bodies being washed ashore. He says Lampedusa needs additional boats from Sicily to help clean up the waters, because the corpses are spoiling the tourist trade' (Waugh 2005: 11).

On the night of 25 December 1996, a rusting boat carrying 450 South Asian asylum seekers collided with a ferry in the Strait of Sicily; 283 asylum seekers died. For four and a half years, the survivors 'struggled to convince the Italian authorities that 283 of their companions had been killed in a collision off the coast of Sicily' (Kennedy 2001), despite the fact that Sicilian fisherman, soon after the shipwreck, began to catch in their fishing nets whole corpses and body parts of the victims of this maritime disaster:

> A fisherman in the village of Portopalo has told the Rome daily newspaper *la Repubblica* that he pulled a corpse out of his nets in early January 1997. The man said he had felt compassion but then remembered another fisherman who had once lost days of work after handing in a body. 'I picked it up and heard a thump, the head had fallen off the neck', he recalled. 'I closed my eyes and heaved it overboard, then I gathered up the head and threw it back too.' A local politician, priest and historian confirmed that many fishermen had had similar experiences. (Kennedy 2001)

In the course of the fisherman's work, the drowned corpse of an asylum seeker hauled up in his nets amounts to little more than dead human cargo that temporarily supplements his catch of the day, only to be unceremoniously discarded as it is not worth the cost of bureaucratic red tape and lost wages. As such, these bodies are rendered void of the category of the human-rights-bearing subject and they thus become coextensive with their marine environment, dissolving into 'bodies of water' (Pugliese 2006: 18). As bodies of water, they fail to signify. Despite the testimonies of the survivors of this shipwreck, and the literal bodies of evidence brought to light by the fishermen's nets, the Italian authorities continued cynically to describe this disaster as a 'phantom shipwreck' ('*naufragio fantasma*') and a 'presumed shipwreck' ('*presunto naufragio*') until a fisherman, in June 2001, years after the event, hauled up in his fishing net the laminated identity card of a 17-year-old Tamil victim, Medialagan Ganeshu, whose brother had also drowned (Bellu 2002). In the eyes of the Italian authorities, the oral testimonies of the survivors had failed to carry any evidentiary status. It was only the existence of Ganeshu's identity card that led to the commencement of an official investigation into this tragedy. These bodies of water literally signified nothing:

invisibilised, transparent, they were mere phantoms that could neither represent themselves nor be represented. Their death was not death; rather, it was a presumed death, a phantom death, or only the untrustworthy testimony of would-be 'immigrants' who had tried to breach the law of the border. It was only the survival of Ganeshu's identity card that could provide the proof of his death and the confirmation of the reality of the larger suppressed and effaced disaster.

The rendering of asylum seekers into little more than transparent bodies of water that fail to signify as human-rights-bearing subjects is perhaps most graphically evidenced in the infamous 'left-to-die boat' case (Pugliese 2014). The 'left-to-die boat' was detected by a number of European surveillance agencies and operatives drifting in the Mediterranean with 72 asylum seekers on board who were fleeing the upheaval in Libya. The boat was left to drift for two weeks across the Mediterranean – a sea assiduously surveilled and patrolled by an ensemble of EU and NATO forces and busily criss-crossed by scores of commercial boats and ships. Despite 'an alert from the Italian Coastguard', no rescue mission was ever mounted (Hayes and Vermeulen 2012: 16). This resulted in the death by starvation and dehydration of 63 people. The death of asylum seekers by neglect to offer assistance has been, in turn, augmented by lethal interventions that have been termed 'death by rescue' (Spinelli 2016).

The Mediterranean is awash with the bodies of drowned refugees and asylum seekers.[1] Across this body of water, rubber dinghies and boats overloaded with asylum seekers float, drift and often break apart and sink. Historical repetitions, they trace the itinerary of journeys destined to achieve no landfall. On the sinking of their flimsy craft, bodies are set adrift on currents and tides before being drawn to the bottom. Here they rest, in the deep ocean sleep of the drowned. The trawl of the fishing nets will awake them: exilic bodies returning to the light, the drag of the lines sloughing away waterlogged flesh, bodies cradled in nets, unloaded with the catch of the day – glazed unblinking eyes that have looked into the abyss, mute traumatism of the dead enlivened by the frantic flapping and gasping of fish out of water. Cradled in fishing nets, the asylum seeker dead become interchangeable with their piscatorial kin. Consanguineous relations of exchange bind one to the other: 'In the net you had hands, heads, feet coming out . . . There were dolphins jumping in the waves, as well as bodies in the water' (cited in Kingsley 2016). In such moments, as I discuss below, complex forces are operative that perturb species boundaries and materialise zoopolitical relations of power.

European cultures of anthropophagy

In the instance in which asylum seeker maritime dead are hauled up in fishing nets with their piscatorial kin, a blurring of the categories of prey and predator transpires – with the consequent unsettling of the tautological category of the European civilised subject who now fears that she or he may be accused of being a cannibal for eating fish. 'The next time you eat a fish from the Mediterranean', warns one journalist, 'just remember that it may well have eaten a corpse' (Farrell 2016). Aldo Busi, an Italian writer, spells out his fear: 'I don't buy fish from the Mediterranean any more for fear of eating Libyans, Somalis, Syrians and Iraqis. I'm not a cannibal and so now I stick with farmed fish, or else Atlantic cod' (cited in Farrell 2016). For Busi, a tenuous thread of connection still works to maintain the valency of the concept of the human in this scene marked by the troubling equivocation of species boundaries; he signals as much in naming the ingestion of Mediterranean fish as tantamount to an act of cannibalism. The seemingly ethical declaration, 'I'm not a cannibal', comes with its own disavowed history of Eurocentrism, colonialism and racio-speciesism. The very figure of the cannibal achieves its purchase and conceptual intelligibility within the racio-speciesist parameters of a European history that could only maintain its hold on the privileged category of the human by dispatching the Indigenous subjects of Europe's colonies to the realm of the non-human animal/cannibal – as the bestial figure that consumed its own kind. The framing of the colonised Indigene as cannibal licensed the genocidal campaigns that were crucial in securing Europe's colonial territories (Barker, Hulme and Iversen 1998).

The eruption of the term 'cannibal' in these accounts of fish that have ingested the asylum seeker dead unintentionally serves to bring to light everything that would otherwise remain occluded: the colonial, racio-speciesist and geopolitical histories that continue to inform the journeys of asylum seekers and irregular migrants fleeing the harrowed lands of the Global South.[2] The invocation by Busi of the place names Libya, Somalia, Syria and Iraq, from whence Europe's asylum seekers journey forward, works to materialise embedded and stratified histories of European cannibalisation of the resources and the people of these once-subject colonial states. In the context of this at once effaced and yet still material colonial history, the gesture of ethical refusal that Busi articulates undermines itself. Busi here exposes the untenability of a European position predicated on the purity of a prelapsarian space not contaminated and virulently inscribed by European genealogies of race, colonialism and empire. What appeared to be an ethical gesture of refusal instantiates, rather, a self-righteous arrogation of ethicality that, always already, has been undone by its own disavowal of past and contemporary relations of colonial and racialised violence. In the past, the European subject cannibalised its colonial other – through expropriative practices of pillage, exploitation and consumption of people and resources – precisely from such former colonies as Libya, Somalia, Syria and Iraq. In the present, the EU continues to cannibalise its racialised other through technologies of neocolonial extraterritorialisation that push the boundaries of Europe down and into the lands of North Africa and the Middle East, and through the maintenance of exploitative economic regimes that ensure that the flourishing of Europe comes at the cost of cannibalising the subjects of the Global South.

The insistent return of the colonial past is embodied in the trans-animal-human served up for the nourishment of the European subject. What had been confined to the remote depths of the ocean returns through a mediated proximity that refuses to sanction gestures of either disavowal or repressive forgetting.

On yet two more levels the convoluted scene of the non-cannibal European that Busi self-represents cuts against the grain of its avowed intentionality in order to signify otherwise. Busi's preference for Atlantic cod, as a way of avoiding cannibalism, unintentionally reiterates another history of European mass killing and consumption of the other. As embodied metonym, the Atlantic cod breaches the smooth surface of a body of water that, for Busi, represents an elsewhere space not contaminated by the corpses of the human dead. This moment of unintended historico-discursive rupture exposes another oceanic grave, specifically, a mass grave that holds the remains of the two million African slaves who died in the course of their enforced transport across the Middle Passage. The Atlantic, like the Mediterranean, is no pristine body of water that transcends histories of European colonialism and cannibalism. Rather, in the context of the Middle Passage, the Atlantic is also a graveyard for the African dead. In the very instant that a pure figure untrammelled by European colonial history had apparently been secured, the naming of the Atlantic cod stirs up the phantoms of the African slave dead from the depths of their oceanic graves. They materialise, through the charged signifier 'Atlantic', what had been invisibilised. In the very moment when the African slave dead had seemingly been consigned to oblivion, the inexpungable history of European colonialism once more reasserts itself. The freighted indexicality of Atlantic cod signs and countersigns this violent history. And it evokes, in turn, the dense and stratified history of the Mediterranean slave trade and the necropolitical transport of slaves across this body of water. The trade in slaves across the Mediterranean predates the establishment of the transatlantic slave trade by centuries and it did not end 'until several decades after the latter was halted' (Hunwick 1992: 5). Even as there are significant differences between the Mediterranean and transatlantic slave trades, 'These differences should not overshadow the trauma and suffering of Mediterranean slavery' (O'Connell and Dursteler 2016: 243). Both bodies of water, through this shared and differential history of slavery, work to constitute a type of topological fold that I have elsewhere termed the 'Mediterranean-Atlantic' (Pugliese 2008: 8).

This slave history redoubles itself on the mainland and islands of contemporary Europe. I refer here to the contemporary conditions of enslavement that so many African migrants – including Senegalese, Gambians, Nigerians and Malians – are compelled to endure on many of the EU's farms. Yoro, a 17-year-old boy from Senegal, barely surviving his conditions of enslavement on a farm in Sicily, says: 'Look around . . . That's what we are: 1,200 slaves. Look at us. Look at our hands. Look at our faces. They are the hands and faces of slavery' (cited in Tondo 2016). The reality of contemporary European cultures of anthropophagy is perhaps best exemplified by this testimony from Salvatore Vella, a Sicilian prosecutor investigating the systemic exploitation of African migrant labour: 'The exploited immigrants in the countryside are treated as dead meat. They are considered objects, the property of business-men, slaves' (cited in Tondo 2016; see also Pugliese 2008). The African slave-labourers work in Sicilian olive groves and fields of tomatoes and aubergines – vegetarian produce that is shipped and consumed across Europe. This veg-etarian produce, however, as what has been enabled by the labour of 'dead meat', is in fact inscribed by European economies of symbolic cannibalism. Europe's culture of disavowed cannibalism embraces both the fruits of the land and sea. A structural topology folds one into the other, generating, in the process, a general economy of disavowed anthropophagism.

In a profound reflection on the complex and entrenched lines of co-implication and simultaneous denegation that insistently inform ethico-political postures that claim to transcend their absolute other, Jacques Derrida writes: 'The so-called non-anthropophagic cultures practice sym-bolic anthropology and even construct their most elevated socius, indeed the sublimity of their morality, their politics, and their right, on this anthropophagy. Vegetarians, too, partake of animals, even of men' (1995: 282). The sublimity of European morality that, for example, refuses to eat fish caught in the Mediterranean or the dead meat of non-human animals fails, on both counts, to escape its rooted implication in European cultures of anthropophagy. It is only through the process of sublimating all of the human 'dead meat' – *qua* drowned asylum seekers and enslaved migrant labourers – that European culture can lay claim to its elevated socius and the sublimity of its morality, to its enlightened politics and its charters of rights. European physico-symbolic cultures of anthropophagy inscribe the continent's cycle of consumption and waste.

Even as Europeans consume the 'dead flesh' of either migrant slave labour or the fish that have ingested the asylum seeker maritime dead, they also reduce those seeking asylum in Europe to so much disposable waste that can be warehoused in such places as a disused toilet paper factory:

> At the Softex refugee camp in northern Greece, it is lighter by night than it is by day. Inside this windowless former warehouse, the lamps only work in the evenings. That is partly because the place was not designed to house people. It is part of what was a toilet paper factory. (Kingsley 2016)

The significance of their dispatch to a disused toilet paper warehouse does not escape the asylum seekers quartered there: '"It's insulting", says Hendiya Asseni, a 62-year-old Syrian, 'being housed in a one-time loo-roll store. But then everything here is insulting – the life, the food, the fact we have a toilet in front of our tent"' (cited in Kingsley 2016). Reflecting on the political message that this gives to the asylum seekers warehoused in the former Softex factory, Nico Stevens, head of projects for Help Refugees, says: 'How symbolic is it that of all the empty buildings, of all the places for a refugee camp, one of the biggest and most permanent has been set up in a disused toilet paper factory? . . . It's very emblematic of the situation as a whole' (cited in Kingsley 2016).

Through his disavowal of these violent histories of European cannibalism, Busi consoles himself with the illusion that it is only by eating farmed fish or Atlantic cod that he can continue to maintain his otherwise at-risk ethico-human status. It is at this juncture, in which a clear division between the human and non-human animal is clearly delineated, that the fault line of zoopolitics opens. It is to this biopolitical concept that I now turn in my attempt to illuminate the discursive lines of force that inscribe and constitute the embodied figure of the asylum seeker maritime dead.

Zoopolitics

The fault line that establishes the decisive cut between the figure of the human and the non-human animal marks the operations of the biopolitical caesura. The lines of forces that inform and charge the biopolitical caesura compel the articulation of this foundational question: What are the onto-epistemological conditions of possibility that work to render flesh and blood subjects into either the figure of the human-rights-bearing subject or, in absolute contradistinction, into the figure of the non-human animal that can be killed and consumed with impunity or dispatched in watery graves as just so much necropolitical tonnage and disposable waste? I want to answer this question by situating it within the conceptual ground of zoopolitics. Zoopolitics is not separate from biopolitics. On the contrary, it draws its violent metaphysics and operational logics from biopolitics and its attendant concerns with the management of the life and death of its subjects. I deploy the concept of zoopolitics as, at its very etymological level, it visibly marks the question of the *zōon* or the animal, while, philosophically, it 'binds together . . . the beast, power, knowledge, seeing, and having' (Derrida 2009: 283). In what follows, I discuss how the concept of the beast is, in Derrida's schema, inscribed by a double valency: it is at once the savage animal and the rogue sovereign; and this charged figure, in the context of the concerns of this chapter, proceeds to deploy regimes of power, knowledge, seeing and having in relation to its target subjects: asylum seekers coming to Europe from the countries of the Global South.

In his theorisation of the link between sovereignty and the animal, Derrida fleshes out the specific inflections that distinguish the concept of zoopolitics. He identifies the crucial interlinking of economy and sovereignty in the exercise of zoopolitics: '*oikonomia*', he notes, is the 'general condition of this *ipseity* as

sovereign mastery over the beast' (Derrida 2009: 283). The zoopolitical relation between economy and sovereignty in the context of asylum seekers and
irregular migrants from the Global South was evidenced in my discussion of the
'dead meat' of Europe reproducing, through economic regimes of contemporary
enslavement, sovereign mastery over the 'beast'. Europe's zoopolitical transmutation of asylum seekers and refugees into non-human animals is evident in the
language used to describe them. Katie Hopkins, then a British tabloid columnist,
wrote 'that she was resolutely unmoved by the plight of those risking their lives
by crossing the Mediterranean': 'No, I don't care. Show me pictures of coffins,
show me bodies floating in water, play violins and show me skinny people looking sad. I still don't care' (cited in Jones 2015). Hopkins need not care as she
views the bodies floating in water as little more than lower forms of life that
can be left, in biopolitical terms, to die, precisely because, zoopolitically, they
are non-human vermin: 'Make no mistake, these migrants are like cockroaches.
They might look a bit "Bob Geldof's Ethiopia circa 1984", but they are built to
survive a nuclear bomb' (cited in Jones 2015). The crossing of the signs 'Ethiopia'
and 'cockroaches' underscores the operations of a racio-speciesism that, once
again, finds its conceptual locus in the colonial language of the West.

Instantiated in Hopkins's African 'cockroach' is that hierarchised bina-
rism identified by Fanon as crucial to the operations of the (neo-)colonial
racial state:

> Sometimes this Manicheanism reaches its logical conclusion and dehumanizes
> the colonized subject. In plain talk, he is reduced to the state of an animal.
> And consequently, when the colonist speaks of the colonized he uses zoologi-
> cal terms . . . In his endeavours at description and finding the right word, the
> colonist refers constantly to the bestiary. (Fanon 2004: 7)

Europe's zoological rendition of asylum seekers, refugees and irregular migrants
as non-human animals, and their quartering in its quarantined 'bestiaries' and
'holding pens', works to legitimate practices of punitive containment and systemic humiliation. As asylum seekers fled the catastrophic conditions unleashed
by the civil war in Syria, their arrival in Hungary mobilised a series of zoopolitical operations that ensured that they were duly quartered in cages where they
were fed like non-human animals imprisoned in the squalor and overcrowding
of factory farms, with the guards throwing loaves of bread – 'like animals in [a]
pen' (Kenya 2015).

The zoopolitics of the asylum seeker bestiary is perhaps nowhere more
concretely realised than in the naming of the camp on the outskirts of Calais,
France, as the 'Jungle', as zoopolitical site of savage animal life in contradistinction to the civilised culture of Calais city. The master metaphor of the 'Jungle'
derives its signifying force from the colonial imaginary of Africa as the savage
heart of darkness and all of the attendant relations of violence and subjugation
that this licensed. Located on the outskirts of Calais, the 'Jungle' represented

a contemporary embodiment of Fanon's 'bestiary' that was characterised by 'the odors from the "native" quarters, to the hordes, the stink, the swarming, the seething, and the gesticulations' (2004: 7). Fanon here identifies the racio-speciesist locus that animates Hopkins's zoopolitical figure of the 'cockroach' and the squalor and the swarming that is represented as threatening the civil order of Europe, and that compelled the violent demolition and erasure of the 'Jungle' – despite protests from its residents, who had managed to establish a community of precarious coexistence in the face of displacement, loss and trauma. The general economy of European anthropophagism that I outlined above can be seen to encompass the 'Jungle'. Media agencies reported on the fact that local hotels and Airbnb apartment renters were 'cashing in' on the 'Jungle': 'The hotel industry has benefitted enormously, with a spike in bookings since Thursday and the weekend already looking strong. This isn't just Calais – it includes Saint-Omer, Dunkerque, Boulogne-sur-Mer. Restaurants too' (Chazan, Mulholland and Alexander 2016). 'White racism, imperialism, and sexist domination prevail', bell hooks sardonically underscores, 'by courageous consumption. It is by eating the Other . . . that one asserts power and privilege' (1992: 36). The racio-speciesist topos of the 'Jungle' exemplifies the zoopolitical binding together of the non-human beast, the white sovereign, the onto-epistemic violence of neocolonial practices and the very seeing, in Derridean terms, of the asylum seeker subject as 'beast'.

Critically, in his deconstruction of zoopolitics, Derrida refuses to stop at the human/animal divide that informs the exercise of this particular modality of biopolitical power. His deconstructive move entails the disclosure of the lines of inextricable connection between the sovereign and the animal, of the ways, indeed, in which the sovereign/human is indissociably animal/beast. At every turn, he insists on interrogating the anthropocentrism that continues to animate the operational logics of zoopolitics:

> We should never be content to say, in spite of temptations, something like: the social, the political, and in them the value or exercise of sovereignty are merely disguised manifestations of animal force, or conflicts of pure force, the truth of which is given to us by zoology, that is to say at bottom bestiality or barbarity or inhuman cruelty. (Derrida 2009: 14)

As though the figure of the beast were somehow outside the structuring purview of political figuration and its charged tropologies; as though it were thus capable of self-evidently inhabiting the pure and unmediated locus of its own naturally inherent savagery – in which the animal's 'natural' savagery would be guaranteed by the scientific truths of zoology. Refusing this anthropocentric schema, Derrida insists on acknowledging,

> on the contrary, not that political man is still animal but that the animal is already political, and exhibit, as is easy to do, in many examples of what are called animal societies, the appearance of refined, complicated organizations,

with hierarchical structures, attributes of authority and power, phenomena of symbolic credit, so many things that are so often attributed to and so naïvely reserved for so-called human *culture*, in opposition to *nature*. (Derrida 2009: 14–15)

In contradistinction to the work of Giorgio Agamben (1998: 7–9), who argues for the separation of *bios* from *zoé* in his theorisation of biopolitics, Derrida articulates the conceptual impossibility of this division. By returning to the Aristotelian text that Agamben cites as the originary source of this division, Derrida notes that 'this distinction is never so clear and secure, and that Agamben himself has to admit that there are exceptions'. It is thus impossible to determine and maintain a historical periodisation and indivisible conceptual categorisation on the basis of '[s]uch an insecure semantic distinction' (Derrida 2009: 316).

Derrida deconstructs the lines of force that inscribe the beast/sovereign binary. The 'relations between the beast and sovereign', he writes, 'are also relations between an animal, a *zōon* supposed to be without reason, and a *zōon* supposed to be rational, the sovereign being posited human' (Derrida 2009: 339). What is of critical significance in this theorisation of the sovereign as also constitutively *beast*, as animal, is that it brings to light the disavowed bestiality that animates the exercise of zoopolitical sovereignty by a supra-state such as the EU, which self-referentially presents itself as the paragon of enlightenment, culture and law. Rather than doxically reproducing the seeming line of absolute difference that separates one, the human sovereign, from the other, the animal, Derrida materialises the parallel qualities that inscribe and conjoin both categories. In the first instance,

> sovereign and beast seem to have in common their being-outside-the-law. It is as though both of them were situated by definition at a distance from or above the laws, in nonrespect for the absolute law, the absolute law that they make or that they are but that they do not have to respect. (Derrida 2009: 17)

Even as a number of EU spokespersons frame and indict asylum seekers and irregular migrants as outlaw subjects, as wild beasts of the 'Jungle' and as rogue animals that respect no civilised laws, their own actions squarely situate them in the bestial space of a rogue supra-state that violates and overrides an ensemble of human rights laws and conventions.

The epistemological configuration that makes the asylum seeker intelligible within the spaces and texts of the EU must be seen as constituted by a structural contradiction. This contradiction is generated by a bipolar system of conceptuality that is endemic to the production of racial stereotypes. On the one hand, asylum seekers, refugees and irregular migrants are inscribed by zoopolitical forces that mark them as non-human animals and that thus render them into forms of disposable consumption and waste; on the other hand, and cutting across the grain of these zoopolitical forces, they continue to evidence their irrefutably human status (think of the consternation and soul searching that the image of the dead toddler, Alan Kurdi, washed up on a beach caused in Europe); this, in turn, sets in train moves of displacement and sublimation ('I will only eat farmed fish or Atlantic cod').

Zoopolitics of border fencing

The EU's moral panic over the flow of asylum seekers into its territories has led to the large-scale construction of fences across the national borders of a number of EU countries in order to block this flow. In the process, these border security fences have also worked to stop the free movement of non-human animals such as wolves, deer, lynx and bears – with often devastating results (Linnel et al. 2016: 3). Entire habitats are 'now being fragmented by fences between Macedonia and Greece, and Bulgaria and Greece, as well as those around Hungary and in Slovenia and Croatia' (Coghlan and Tatović 2015). These moves exemplify the topological enfolding of different subjects within zoopolitical regimes of subjugation and entrapment. Non-human animals, in the context of this EU border fencing expansion, are being imprisoned in the equivalent of carceral regimes of indefinite detention. Non-human animals thus become refugees in their own lands, effectively displaced, entrapped and exposed to lethal regimes of zoopoliticality. The lethality of this regime is graphically captured by the image of a deer trapped in the vortices of a border fence's razor wire. Encoiled and lacerated by the barbed concertina, the deer died a slow death from her wounds, blood loss and exhaustion (Neslen 2016). Zoopolitical lines of relationality connect this image to that of a refugee who plunged into the coils of razor wire of a detention centre fence and was lacerated with every move he attempted to make (Pugliese 2004: 23–5). These two traumatised bodies supply the *corpus delicti* of the border fence and they enflesh the sovereign logics of its brutal geometry. The border security fencing that is being rolled out across Europe exposes the manner in which the borderless zones of the Schengen Area, which enable the free movement of EU subjects across national borders, are in fact underpinned by a zoopolitics of a bestial EU sovereign and its violent governance of the non-human animal. The hyperbolic vortices of razor wire that augment these border fences are the material indices of absolute excess and overkill: they emblematise the EU's sovereign exercise of zoopolitical violence.

The asylum seekers fleeing war, famine and persecution who survive the perilous journeys across the Mediterranean and manage to make landfall on Europe's shores instantiate a breach of the EU's self-referential interiority. Exterior to its interiority, they are what can only be interiorised through zoopolitical practices of quartering in holding pens and attendant cultures of anthropophagy that ensure that they are rendered within economies of consumption and waste. These economies are predicated on the disavowal of their constitutive violence. Either in the water or on land, the 'dead meat' of Europe supplies the onto-epistemological substratum to the continent's cultures of anthropophagy: it is what can only be consumed through recursive practices of thwarted arrival, death by neglect or refoulement,[3] punitive detention and exploitative enslavement. It is upon this disavowed 'dead meat' that Europe constructs the sublimity of its morality, even as the ethical force and weight of this dead flesh both interrogates and hollows out its claims to an elevated socius.

Notes

1. On the drowning of asylum seekers off the Australian coast that parallel the Mediterranean drownings, see Perera (2006).
2. On the histories of European colonialism that inscribe the itineraries of asylum seekers seeking refuge in Europe, see, for example, Pugliese (2007; 2008; 2009; 2014), Cresti and Melfi (2006), Melfi (2008) and Ahmida (2009).
3. 'Refoulement' refers to the forcible return of asylum seekers or refugees to their country of origin where they are at risk of persecution. The practice of refoulement violates one of the fundamental principles of international law and refugee conventions.

Bibliography

Agamben, Giorgio (1998), *Homo Sacer: Sovereign Power and Bare Life*, trans. D. Heller-Roazen (Stanford: Stanford University Press).

Agence France-Presse (2016), 'Italian navy recovers 45 bodies after refugee boat sinks', *The Guardian*, 28 May, https://www.theguardian.com/world/2016/may/28/italian-navy-recovers-45-bodies-after-refugee-boat-sinks (accessed 29 May 2016).

Ahmida, Ali Abdullatif (2009), *The Making of Modern Libya: State Formation, Colonization, and Resistance* (Albany: SUNY Press).

Barker, Francis, Peter Hulme and Margaret Iversen (eds) (1998), *Cannibalism and the Colonial World* (Cambridge: Cambridge University Press).

Bellu, Giovanni Maria (2002), 'Portopalo, fiori e preghiere tamil per i morti del naufragio fantasma', *la Repubblica*, 4 August, http://ricerca.repubblica.it/repubblica/archivio/repubblica/2002/04/08/portopalo-fiori-preghiere-tamil-per-morti-del.html?refresh_ce (accessed 29 November 2016).

Chazan, David, Rory Mulholland and Harriet Alexander (2016), 'Calais "jungle" demolition', *The Telegraph*, 24 October, http://www.telegraph.co.uk/news/2016/10/24/calais-jungle-demolition-riots-and-chaos-as-police-warn-that-bri/ (accessed 25 October 2016).

Coghlan, Andy, and Mićo Tatović (2015), 'Fences put up to stop refugees in Europe are killing animals', *New Scientist*, 17 December, https://www.newscientist.com/article/dn28685-fences-put-up-to-stop-refugees-in-europe-are-killing-animals/ (accessed 22 November 2016).

Cresti, Federico, and Daniela Melfi (2006), *Da maestrale e da scirocco: Le migrazioni attraverso il Mediterraneo* (Milan: Dott. A Giuffrè Editore).

Derrida, Jacques (1995), *Points. . . Interviews, 1974–1994* (Stanford: Stanford University Press).

Derrida, Jacques (2009), *The Beast and the Sovereign, Volume 1* (Chicago: University of Chicago Press).

Fanon, Frantz (2004 [1961]), *The Wretched of the Earth* (New York: Grove Press).

Farrell, Nicholas (2014), 'Italy is killing refugees with kindness', *Spectator*, 6 September, https://www.spectator.co.uk/2014/09/italys-decriminalising-of-illegal-immigration-has-acted-as-a-green-light-to-boat-people/ (accessed 30 November 2016).

Foucault, Michel (1990), *The History of Sexuality, Vol. 1: An Introduction* (London: Penguin).

Foucault, Michel (2003), *'Society Must Be Defended': Lectures at the Collège de France, 1975–1976* (New York: Picador).

Hayes, Ben, and Mathias Vermeulen (2012), 'Borderline: the EU's new border surveillance initiatives', *Heinrich Böll Stiftung*, June, http://www.statewatch.org/news/2012/jun/borderline.pdf (accessed 23 November 2016).

hooks, bell (1992), *Black Looks: Race and Representation* (Boston: South End Press).

Hunwick, J. O. (1992), 'Black slaves in the Mediterranean world: introduction to a neglected aspect of the African diaspora', *Slavery and Abolition*, 13.1: 5–38.

Jones, Sam (2015), 'UN human rights chief denounces *Sun* over Katie Hopkins "cockroach" column', *The Guardian*, 24 April, https://www.theguardian.com/global-development/2015/apr/24/katie-hopkins-cockroach-migrants-denounced-united-nations-human-rights-commissioner (accessed 30 November 2016).

Kennedy, Frances (2001), 'Fishermen hauled up corpses from "phantom wreck"', *The Independent*, 7 June, http://www.independent.co.uk/news/world/europe/fishermen-hauled-up-corpses-from-phantom-wreck-5364463.html (accessed 3 December 2016).

Kenya, Capital FM (2015), 'Video shows refugees fed "like animals in pen" in Hungary camp', YouTube, https://www.youtube.com/watch?v=4IKRQPsGxus (accessed 23 November 2016).

Kingsley, Patrick (2016), 'Prisoners of Europe', *The Guardian*, 6 September, https://www.theguardian.com/world/2016/sep/06/prisoners-of-europe-the-everyday-humiliation-of-refugees-stuck-in-greece-migration (accessed 7 September 2016).

Kingsley, Patrick, Alessandra Bonomolo and Stephanie Kirchgaessner (2015), '700 migrants feared dead in Mediterranean shipwreck', *The Guardian*, 19 April, https://www.theguardian.com/world/2015/apr/19/700-migrants-feared-dead-mediterranean-shipwreck-worst-yet (accessed 22 November 2016).

Linnel, J. D. C., Arie Touborst, Luigi Boitaini, Petra Kaczensky, Dura Huber, Slaven Rljic et al. (2016), 'Border security fencing and wildlife', *Plos*, 14.6: 1–8.

Melfi, Daniela (2008), *Migrando a sud: Coloni italiani in Tunisia (1881–1939)* (Rome: Aracne).

Missing Migrants Project (2016), 'Latest global figures', *Missing Migrants: Tracking Deaths Along Migratory Routes*, https://missingmigrants.iom.int/latest-global-figures (accessed 3 December 2016).

Neslen, Arthur (2016), 'Balkan wildlife faces extinction threat from border fence to control migrants', *The Guardian*, 16 August, https://www.theguardian.com/

environment/2016/aug/11/balkan-wildlife-faces-extinction-threat-from-border-fence-to-control-migrants (accessed 17 August).

O'Connell, Monique, and Eric R. Dursteler (2016), *The Mediterranean World: From the Fall of Rome to the Rise of Napoleon* (Baltimore: Johns Hopkins University Press).

Perera, Suvendrini (2006), '"They give evidence": bodies, borders and the disappeared', *Social Identities*, 12.6: 637–56.

Pugliese, Joseph (2004), 'Subcutaneous law', *Australian Feminist Law Journal*, 21: 23–34.

Pugliese, Joseph (2006), 'Bodies of water', *Heat*, 12: 11–20.

Pugliese, Joseph (2007), 'White historicide and the returns of the souths of the South', *Australian Humanities Review*, 42, http://www.lib.latrobe.edu.au/AHR/archive/Issue-August-2007/Pugliese.html (accessed 21 November 2016).

Pugliese, Joseph (2008), 'Whiteness and the blackening of Italy', *Portal*, 5.2: 1–35.

Pugliese, Joseph (2009), 'Crisis heterotopias and border zones of the dead', *Continuum*, 23.5: 663–79.

Pugliese, Joseph (2013), *State Violence and the Execution of Law: Biopolitical Caesurae of Torture, Black Sites, Drones* (Abingdon: Routledge).

Pugliese, Joseph (2014), 'Technologies of extraterritorialisation, statist visuality and irregular migrants and refugees', *Griffith Law Review*, 22.3: 571–97.

Spinelli, Barbara (2016), 'Death by (failure to) rescue', *Death by Rescue*, https://deathbyrescue.org/foreword/ (accessed 3 December 2016).

Tondo, Lorenzo (2016), '"Ours are the hands and faces of slavery": the exploitation of migrants in Sicily', *The Guardian*, 24 November, https://www.theguardian.com/global-development/2016/nov/24/hands-faces-slavery-exploitation-sicily-migrant-community (accessed 25 November 2016).

Waugh, Louisa (2005), '"Resort" as both noun and verb', *Sydney Morning Herald*, 22 June, 11.

Chapter 19

The Mediterranean Sieve, Spring and Seametery

Hakim Abderrezak

Twenty-eight shipwreck survivors, including two smugglers, arrived in Sicily on 21 April 2015. The recounting of the terrifying conditions of their journey revealed that hundreds of people had died on the night of 18/19 April, trapped in the hull of the ship where they had been locked during the crossing. The previous week, other shipwrecks had claimed the lives of over 450 individuals. That month, the rescues of a few and the deaths of hundreds of others in the Mediterranean Sea shocked the world. Two years earlier, a chain of tragedies had taken place in the Mediterranean. The first one occurred on 3 October and caused 366 deaths. It was followed shortly thereafter by another media announcement that on 11 October, 27 people perished and at least 206 were rescued in the Maltese waters by Lampedusa. Similar scenarios have taken place more recently. Reports of capsizing incidents, until not long ago limited to local and regional news coverage, have appeared in international media, and outlets such as *The New York Times* have devoted articles to these events. The recent tragedies put clandestine Mediterranean crossings in the world's news, and thus a 'local' phenomenon has become a global 'problem'.

Yet for decades maritime deaths occurring in the Strait of Gibraltar have been covered by Spanish media, which, according to Ana Corbalán, have desensitised the public to the drownings off the Spanish coast. While the current extreme coverage leads one to wonder whether global concern might yield to an habituation to the spectacle of death, its handling in Western news outlets has affected how it has been perceived by the public and appropriated by world leaders and decision makers. Similarly, the continuation of a phenomenon well known to residents of North African seaside cities, villages and beyond has influenced the vernacular to the south and impacted Western languages as well.

This chapter looks at the contemporary Mediterranean Sea. It argues that these ongoing tragic events, their treatment by the media, the political discourse and the subsequent policies proposed and passed – both temporary and more permanent – are tools that help us to gauge how we are directed to view the Mediterranean as a geopolitical entity. It is also a reflection of what it has come to mean for those who have crossed this body of water, have perished in the attempt, are considering taking the journey or preparing to set off to sea. This piece proposes that a double standard – if not a multi-standard – modus operandi has presided over some key European responses to trans-Mediterranean clandestine crossings originating in North- and sub-Saharan Africa, the Levant and the Middle East. In the first section, I explore the trope of the Mediterranean as a sieve. In doing so, I suggest that policies have been put in place to implement a tight net that acts as a selective screening process to choose what types of migrants and refugees are allowed in. In the second part, which relates to sea crossings associated with the Arab Spring, I expand this notion by showing that it is precisely the ethnic, racial and religious identities of these individuals that dictates the nature of the anti-immigration policies that are responsible for the deaths we continue to witness. Finally, in the last section I examine the 'Mediterranean seametery', a neologism meant to capture the oxymoronic nature of the sea in which liquidity has become synonymous with immobility precipitated by preposterous and rigid policies that have transformed a sea into a cemetery.[1] I will show how racist policies have caused this body of water to fill with bodies.

Surveys have shown that a large majority of individuals residing in the Global South continue to seriously consider the prospect of emigrating clandestinely. *Leavism*, as I call it, is the burning desire to leave one's country. It is a neologism whose suffix connotes a philosophy or even an ideological movement, in this case one that advocates for free movement of humans across borders. Leavism can, but does not necessarily, result in a maritime crossing undertaken at all costs; and it may also involve the contestation of the political measures fighting it. *Burning*, from the Arabic *hrig/harga*, is another term in circulation in the Maghreb to signify unauthorised migration. 'Burning the sea' is a linguistic collage that I borrow from the Arabic 'to burn' (the road). It evokes the vivid image of desperate individuals attempting to dry the Mediterranean with their burning desire to make it to the other shore. Their attempts are at the core of Gianfranco Rosi's 2016 award-winning documentary *Fire at Sea*. Burning leads to the status of 'undocumented migrant', in that prior to the departure, would-be trans-Mediterranean hopefuls destroy or burn their identification documents in order to avoid repatriation should they be caught. Ironically, the act of burning documentation renders the migrant 'illegal' in the terms and languages of those countries whose anti-immigration policies criminalise illegality, while encouraging it by not providing legal routes and inciting illicit rites of (non)-passage. From *hrig* comes *harragas* (those who burn) – a term that is now in use in various languages, which refers to individuals who cross borders clandestinely. While this term has been used for decades to refer to those who cross the Mediterranean from North African shores, it could also be applied to individuals crossing the sea from the Middle

East and the Levant, fleeing geopolitical catastrophes and war, leaving behind burned borders and bodies, their cities and countries consumed by disaster and destruction. In effect, both groups cross the same sea, are headed to the same continent and use similar modes of transportation. Most of them are Arab or/and Muslim and all undertake the passage clandestinely. The burning desire of *harragas* is fired in spite of a range of policies fired at them that turn the Mediterranean into a powder keg. A growing number of fictional works, such as *Fire at Sea*, have condemned the increasingly homicidal approach to the *harragas* at the threshold of Europe, while also attempting to honour the memories of those who have been tossed into today's largest maritime mass grave. In this chapter I will employ *harrag* (sing.) and *harragas* (pl.) to mean both migrants and refugees. Although the distinction between 'refugee' and 'migrant' is crucial in the legal realm, *harrag* and *harragas* allow us to step outside the dichotomisation to address the phenomenon from a humanistic, pragmatic and empirical perspective. Put differently, I employ south-of-the-sea terminology, which is often self-assigned, to express the simple fact of desperate fleeing humans who do not see themselves and their actions in categories.[2] Privileging non-Western logos helps prevent essentialisation and the rendering of burning and the plight of *harragas* in obsolete or inadequate terms. The use of terminology rooted in the language of the individuals in question helps us (better) understand the phenomenon from a southern perspective and/or lived experience.[3]

The common notion is that refugees flee wars, terrorism and persecutions. In other words, their lives are in danger, whereas clandestine migrants, also qualified as 'economic migrants', leave home on a voluntary basis in search of better opportunities elsewhere. But material and economic considerations are not the only explanations for why clandestine migrants leave their countries. Isolation and humiliation back home are two of the most frequently invoked reasons for forced migration by nationals of a country at peace. These are forms of violence in their own right. Theoretically, a migrant is a potential refugee – by definition, someone seeking refuge from coercion, but in this instance one who cannot legally make a case for himself/herself. Both confinement and humiliation have been cited by locals and portrayed in literary and artistic productions as push factors. In Mohamed Hmoudane's novel *French Dream* (2005), the systematic refusal of visas is a setback that sets the narrative in motion. As for the Moroccan writer Salim Jay, he contends in *Tu ne traverseras pas le détroit* (Thou shalt not cross the strait) (2001) that frustration with the impossibility of travelling freely is a major component of people's 'obsession' with leaving; he writes that the Moroccan passport is known locally as 'Haddou Tanja' ('Its limit is Tangier'). This tongue-in-cheek statement indicates that the document is restricted to internal use, where obviously it is not needed, and does not permit its holder to, so to speak, 'pass ports'. As the sociologist and philosopher Zygmunt Bauman declares, '[t]he prime technique of power is now escape, slippage, elision and avoidance, the effective rejection of any territorial confinement with its cumbersome corollaries of order-building, order-maintenance and the responsibility for the consequences of it all as well as of the necessity to bear their costs' (Bauman 2000: 11). This point can be applied to most citizens of the Global South. The Algerian author Boualem Sansal is in agreement, for he contends that walls – both physical and invisible – that build up confinement reinforce individuals' conviction that to emigrate clandestinely is the only way forward (Abderrezak 2010).

The Mediterranean sieve

The 'refugee crisis' is a good illustration of the dangers of misnomers. A crisis constitutes a situation usually conceived as temporary. It is also viewed as negative – and it certainly is for those who sacrifice their lives in their attempt to make it across to Europe. However, the expression has been used in mass media and politics to convey the impression that it is Europe that has been the victim of this tragedy. Indeed, the now-accepted statement, which has become a consecrated expression, is that this phenomenon is 'Europe's biggest humanitarian crisis since the Second World War'. The Eurocentric emphasis bluntly discounts the well-known fact that the most affected countries are in the Middle East.[4] Additionally, the 'refugee crisis' has often been named the 'migrant crisis' by the very same sources – a conflation that is problematic in that their equivalence minimises what sociologist Helen Fein calls the 'universe of obligation', which reinforces Europe's duty to welcome refugees as laid out in the United Nations' 1951 Refugee Convention and its 1967 Protocol. In this chapter, I employ the expression with the idea that it is the refugees' crisis, which confirms the morbid nature of anti-migration politics, and not Europe's crisis caused by the arrival of refugees. To remind us of this fundamental nuance, I will use 'refugees' crisis' instead of the commonly employed 'refugee crisis'.

Well before the advent of this crisis, with the closing of Europe's external borders and the desperate departures prompted by recent wars, the Mediterranean had grown into a cemetery for those who failed the passage. This should invite us to think about which aspect of the term 'crisis' is dominant. Crisis usually implies a recent flaring up. Is it therefore meant to designate an emergency? If so, then such tragedies have occurred for several decades and, thus, the state of emergency has existed for much longer than one might insinuate. Or does the word suggest that the phenomenon has reached its highest point? But how can we be sure, for we do not have the necessary hindsight to determine whether this may or may not be the case? Or does 'crisis' simply indicate that Europe is facing a serious situation? At any rate, one is forced to probe, as with the term 'crisis' in the political and media arenas, the current significance of such notions as 'borders' and 'liquidity'.

Sandra Ponzanesi remarks that recent studies have turned away from traditional borders delineated by power relations as boundaries to focus instead on 'the idea of borders as *liquid figurations*' (Ponzanesi 2011: 67). Because the Mediterranean is a liquid body and yet bars access to that which lies on the other side of it, it must be conceived as a 'sieve' rather than a simple sea. This perspective permits me to approach the Mediterranean as a netted entity that allows a select few through while preventing most others from making it to the other side. Similarly, this vision permits me to examine new maritime borders and the experience from the South – related directly by those who encounter these borders first-hand. Many academic studies have focused on the experiences of migrants and refugees after reaching the mainland. In order to complete the picture of the journey and the ordeals of those who are slowed down or stopped by an ever-growing sieve-like sea, this chapter will focus exclusively on the act of the maritime crossing.

A widespread political discourse has depicted the Mediterranean as a porous border and has called for a tighter net over the sea. This net is not only that which fishermen cast into the sea – these days pulling up more dead bodies than fish, as the population of one increases and the other decreases.[5] In the western Mediterranean, the net in question is a sieve embodied quite literally by SIVE (Sistema Integrado de Vigilencia Exterior, Integrated System of External Vigilance), an electronic set of monitoring measures and units put in place by agencies deployed by the EU, such as Frontex. In the eastern Mediterranean, bilateral agreements have been signed recently, such as the one between Turkey and the EU, to sieve refugees away from the sea. Ponzanesi aptly notes that '[b]orrowing from "liquid" theories, recent discourses on transnationalism and globalisation have revised the notion of frontiers and borders as being connected to "solid" geographical barriers, invoking the notion of "liquidity" instead in order to pay attention to back-and-forth movements of goods and people' (Ponzanesi 2011: 67). Clandestine passages offer an important counterpoint to the notion of the sea as a site of circulation, in that they highlight the fact that human movements originating in the Global South are a privilege – and any attempt to trespass over a sea-turned-border entails the risk of passing away. This contradicts a universal right granted by international law whereby citizens may leave a country, including their own. Given that the Mediterranean has become a sieve of surveillance equipment and military ships, and that the act of seafaring from the southern rim has been identified as a criminal offence, I propose to address the Mediterranean through the lens of clandestinity.

While, on the one hand, public opinion is swayed by ethnic fears and increasingly populist rhetoric from European politicians such as Viktor Orbán, Norbert Hofer and Geert Wilders among others, there is also a vocal portion of the population advocating for a resistance to isolationist and xenophobic attitudes. When governments reject highly conservative, racist and protectionist agendas, they feel the need to justify themselves, as was the case when the newly elected French president, Emmanuel Macron, declared that his country would continue to welcome refugees because this attitude reflects the fundamental values of France. To appeal to the liberal contingent of the population while not endorsing humanitarian aid, officials have attempted to promulgate the idea that Europe must choose a closed-door policy – an approach not construed as egotistic, harmful or pernicious, but as protective of 'victims' of exploitative networks, such as those of smugglers, who are often depicted as modern slavers. Countless headlines covering the Mediterranean Spring have contained the word 'saved', such as these French, Italian and Spanish articles: 'Réfugiés: 13 991 migrants ont été sauvés par SOS Méditerranée en 2016' [Refugees: 13,991 migrants were rescued [saved] by SOS Méditerranée in 2016]; 'Méditerranée: "Que va-t-on faire pour sauver des vies"' [The Mediterranean: 'What are we going to do to save lives?']; 'Italie: 3700 migrants sauvés en trois jours' [Italy: 3,700 migrants saved in three days]; 'Méditerranée: 5000 migrants sauvés en 48 heures' [Mediterranean: 5,000 migrants saved in 48 hours]; 'Mediterraneo, ecco i piloti salva-migranti: il perché di una scelta' [The Mediterranean, here are the migrant-saving pilots: the reasons behind such a choice]; 'Villacampa se embarca en *Open Arms* para salvar refugiados en el Mediterráneo' [Villacampa embarks on *Open Arms* to save refugees in Mediterranean]; and 'Salvan vidas y se les juzga por tráfico de personas: los bomberos sevillanos de Lesbos' [They save lives and they are prosecuted for human trafficking: the firefighters from Seville in Lesbos]. The Spanish 'rescatar' (to rescue) is more commonly used than 'salvar' (save), as is exemplified in a plethora of headlines such as the following: 'Llegan a Galicia los primeros refugiados rescatados por el "Aquarius"' [First rescued refugees of the *Aquarius* arrive in Galicia], but it is noteworthy that 'salvar' is the preferred term in other news articles. The fact that individuals and NGOs from Christian-majority countries are portrayed as saving *harragas* by fishing them out of water cannot but recall the spiritual imagery of baptism and salvation. Does this image register with religious individuals, and if so, to what extent does it account for their positionality in the ongoing debate about saving vs. sieving? De facto, this image presents the viewer with his religious duty, as suggested by Pope Francis who urged help for refugees – a gesture that has, according to some interviewed 'saviours', prompted them to answer the call.

As for the title of Virginie Lydie's book *Traversée interdite!* (*No Crossing!*) (2010), it aptly summarises Europe's official position whereby those attempting undocumented crossings are guilty of an offence that must be stopped. A (pseudo?) moralising discourse has put forward the idea that Europe's injunction for *leavists* to remain at home is propelled by good intentions, in that its aim is to deter innocent individuals from undertaking a highly perilous passage. Additionally, the criminalisation of human trafficking networks that contribute to the increasing number of refugees crossing the sea helps present the illegalisation of clandestine crossings as an expression of a humanistic outlook – one that aims to protect against the inhumane actions of smugglers.

Fortress-Europe-turned-Saviour-Europe has thus become a feel-good self-congratulatory trope that too few commentators have questioned. Initially, many pointed to Europe's culpability in the death of *harragas*, but the terminology used to discuss Europe's role has shifted, and its actions are now presented as acts of generosity and humanity. Yet on the ground, or rather at sea, we are witnessing a different development, where to 'save' and to 'sieve' cohabit. This shift or slip in commentary has become part of the refugees' crisis lingua franca. I contend that the notion of national, governmental, federal and institutional hospitality has been adapted to promote the view that to save is to sieve. Likewise, I argue that official discourses have given the federated EU the licence to turn the sea into an unethical, illegal and lethal sieve that murders those it purports to save.

The ancient Roman designation of the Mediterranean Sea, 'Mare Nostrum', serves as the name for a European Commission operation implemented after the shipwreck of 3 October 2013, in order to help save lives at sea. Is the notion of a shared sea at the core of the operation's name? This designation suggests that the mission of the EU-mandated commission is to come to the rescue of *harragas* in distress. 'Mare Nostrum' did save many lives, but it is worth taking a closer look at its naming, which betrays a vision of the refugees' crisis that might be called paternalistic or simply awkward and by the same token revealing of the tensions experienced by the EU and the Italian navy which operated this mission. The Latin name denotes a binary (Europe vs. its periphery). What's more, 'Nostrum' inevitably suggests that the sea is Europe's and nobody else's. This appellation performs a post-Reconquista or post-Crusade enterprise whereby the Middle East is kept at bay via a neocolonial reappropriation of sites that were once disputed or belonged to non-European powers (Arab, Moorish, Byzantine, etc.). This practice implements a strict divide between a Christian Europe and its Other conceived historically as Sarasin, Mohammedan, Moorish, Ottoman, Arab, Muslim, an invading migrant, a burdensome refugee or a potential terrorist. 'Mare Nostrum' is a European initiative and its meaning ('Our Sea') is a reminder of who oversees Mediterranean affairs. North and sub-Saharan African nations have little to no say in the creation and execution of these supranational projects. Though it might have been meant to include the two shores of the Mediterranean, in light of unilateral decisions the name of the operation cannot but suggest that the fate and future of this entity is the ultimate responsibility of those who assume the right to claim the sea as their own, as Rome did centuries ago.

While the mission of saving those drowning at sea is a worthy one, and necessary, the operation is complicated by issues of national sovereignty at sea. Migration regulations – whether via humanitarian aid or monitoring of coasts – are the sole prerogative of the North. Any extension of these initiatives to North African or Middle Eastern shores risks further neocolonial meddling by Europe in the laws, policies and borders of the South. As a case in point, under the growing pressure of public opinion, Italian authorities have taken measures that make the rescue of refugees more difficult by, for example, imposing on NGOs a code of conduct whereby, for instance, they would not enter Libyan waters and transfer rescued individuals to other ships but would, instead, take them to shore, thus potentially leaving many others to die in the meantime.[6] This code of conduct was backed by the EU, as the European Commission spokesperson, Natasha Bertaud, made clear in the summer of 2017 by indicating that the interior ministers of the 28 member states had unanimously supported it. Italy's interior minister Matteo Salvini's statements and actions have exemplified another type of saving/sieving logic. His orders not to assist refugees in distress are steeped in the populist principles of far-right parties, such as his own, which claim that a 'sieving' of outsiders is necessary for the sake of 'saving' an alleged monolithic cultural identity on the verge of extinction. In this context, *Aquarius*, a ship carrying 360 passengers in the summer of 2018, was denied permission to dock at an Italian port but was welcomed by Spanish authorities. During the several days during which the ship was in limbo, some voices argued that Valencia was the closest port, thus absolving France of its duty to welcome the passengers of a rescue vessel jointly operated by SOS Méditerranée and Médecins Sans Frontières simply by temporarily erasing metropolitan France and its Mediterranean island, Corsica, from the map.

The Mediterranean Spring

Traditionally, international conventions pertaining to human rights are inspired by universal humanistic principles and are not adjusted based on the identity of those to whom they are applied. The refugees' crisis has been an opportunity for European powers to meet and greet the newcomer – regardless of his face, in Lévinas's words – in urgent need of a humane welcome. Yet with a few exceptions, including German Chancellor Angela Merkel's notable welcoming response despite a backlash against it, Europe has averted its gaze and withdrawn the helping hand from those who have knocked on the Fortress's door. Indeed, in spite of having signed the Geneva Convention, several European states have undertaken the illegal deportation of asylum seekers. I contend that a determining factor in further digging the moat that surrounds Europe's island of sorts and in undermining the laws of Derrida's unconditional hospitality with hostility is the racial and religious identity embodied by the 'face' of the other, who must be respected 'beyond grasp and contact' (Derrida 1978: 99). Politics have transformed the Mediterranean into a wider and circumvallated European property. Since the refugees' crisis has much to do with the Arab Spring, and the stiffening of borders has resulted in the debarring, deportation and drowning of Arabs and Muslims, it is fair to say that European anti-immigration policies betray a religious, ethnic and racial bias, which raises vital ethical issues. Additionally, as I mentioned earlier, the reframing of European borders to include the Mediterranean have made this sea a European property. The outcome of this self-attributed ownership creates a selective process of the survival of the fittest and the arrival of the fewest to European coasts.[7]

Selection, stopping and/or sieving processes highlight an incongruity in that quotas and initiatives to keep refugees from leaving their countries imprison individuals in places of chaos and war. In so doing, they not only fail to honour the rights of asylum seekers but also run counter to the very principle of refugee protection. Several arguments have been put forward to justify such questionable methods. Though the economic growth factor is one of them, the identitarian thesis has been the most audible. Contentions have been made that the arrival of Syrians, Afghans, Iraqis and Black African refugees (read, 'non-integratable'/'non-integrationable') represents a threat to an alleged homogeneous European cultural identity. Bauman remarks that

> *territorial* separation, the right to a separate 'defensible space' which needs defence and is worth defending precisely because of its being separate – that is because it has been surrounded by guarded border posts which let in only people of 'the same' identity and bar access to anyone else. The purpose of territorial separation being aimed at the homogeneity of neighbourhood, 'ethnicity' suits it better than any other imagined 'identity'. (Bauman 2000: 107)

Bauman's argument, which he develops mainly in reference to society and cities, is also applicable to the sea and bordering countries. These sites are subject to the same type of assessment in that the ethnic factor is used in propaganda to justify the exclusion of refugees who, by definition and for ethical and legal reasons, ought not be selected, screened, stopped, or worse . . . slaughtered. The sexual assaults that took place on 31 December 2015 in Cologne, Germany, regarding which the number of refugees involved remains to be determined, led to the rapid stigmatisation of migrants and refugees. A popularisation of a dangerous discourse unfolded, as the following excerpts make clear: 'Frauke Petry [the leader of the far-right AfD party] once said German police should "if necessary" shoot at migrants seeking to enter the country illegally' (BBC 2017) and 'Tatjana Festerling claimed that Muslim migrants entering Europe are waging "sex jihad" against Western women and urged people to "grab our pitchforks and fight the Islamisation of Europe"' (*Express* 2016). This event was quickly used to serve a pre-existing motive and highlighted the racist handling of alleged rapists.

In order to force this agenda, instil fear and further divide already divided public opinion, a connection is commonly made between terrorism and clandestine migration. The contention that ISIL recruits embarked on ships alongside refugees allowed many to press for intervention.[8] For instance, the maritime tragedies of spring 2015 were systematically linked to the chaos reigning in Libya, where vigilantes, mafiosi and smugglers had taken control of the country. This facile equation of a majority of peaceful *harragas* and a possible minority of ISIL followers partakes in the branding of migrants and refugees as not only criminals, but, with greater condemnation, terrorists as well.

During the Arab Spring that started in 2010, when ISIL had not yet taken centre stage in mainstream media, voices in Europe joined forces to present a horrific scenario of an impending incursion by the Muslim conqueror.[9] This discourse made its comeback in the context of another swell of human crossings, the spring 2015 clandestine calamities, even though the deaths of prospective migrants (or rather, refugees, since they were fleeing uprisings and the risk of civil war) were emphasised in the media.[10] In both situations, the prospect of imminent invasion provoked a call to action to stop migration at its origin, namely, at the points of departure. Thus it was proposed that European coastguards be sent to monitor North African shores. For instance, such a proposal was made for Tunisia in early 2011 and spring 2015. Opponents of such actions argued that this would constitute a case of intervention in the affairs of sovereign states. With regard to Libya, one of the solutions envisaged was to ask the country to grant Europe the authority to act on its soil, and in the event of a refusal, to seek permission from the EU to move forward using military action.

Given that most of the refugees' crisis is a direct consequence of the Arab Spring, I will refer to the post-Arab Spring migratory phenomenon as the Mediterranean Spring. Alongside the common narrative that the Arab Spring was a rebellion against non-democratic regimes, it can also be explained as a rebellion against seclusion within national boundaries and the need to flee nascent revolts. Both perspectives are sustained by the idea of hope – hope first expressed by Western governments that these regimes would achieve democracy and improve human rights, and hope that anti-immigration policies would soften to allow refugees to seek shelter on the other shore. After all, the 'Spring' in the 'Arab Spring' – an expression coined by Western media – suggests a hope for a better future and a new beginning. But what hope can there be when clandestine migration is commonly (and incorrectly) qualified as 'illegal' and elicits ever more stringent anti-immigration policies? What hope is there when the natural consequence of a revolution – human mass exodus – turns hope into fearmongering? In the first five days of the Jasmine Revolution, which sparked the Arab Spring, it was argued that more than 5,000 Tunisians took advantage of a more lax watchfulness over borders to flee a police state. Newspaper articles covering subsequent sea crossings have used this figure – and several others – as an established fact, despite numbers attributed to clandestine crossings being by definition estimates and fluctuating depending on ideological programmes. Indeed, it is impossible to tabulate the death toll from sea crossings precisely because this is a phenomenon that takes place in secret, and those who perish are only factored in when and if their bodies resurface or wash ashore. Besides, the news articles did not specify that their figures were based on the number of people apprehended. Thus, the round numbers that are often cited are simply practical ones. The coverage of the Mediterranean Spring is revealing as to how various agendas are served, how discourses are created and how opinions are shaped.

One should not conceptualise 'Arab Spring' in the way commentators did at the very beginning, in other words in relation to political expectations centring upon *coups d'état* in Tunisia, Egypt and Libya that would pave the way for democracy in these countries, with hopes that it could spread throughout the region in a domino effect. Rather, one should interpret the Arab Spring as the Europeans' hope that their own values would spread southward. This instance of wishful thinking would have produced a Mediterranean Spring in that the hopeful idea of a fresh beginning would have made for an effective, transcontinental, joint effort to initiate a trans-Mediterranean shared vision of a democratic modus operandi. Such an initiative would have given the region a geopolitical unity and force, as was supposedly sought by the creation in 2008 of the intergovernmental Euro-Mediterranean organisation called Union for the Mediterranean. In Europe, hope was expressed through several alternative names, including 'Democracy Spring', 'Arab Uprisings' and 'Arab Awakening'. With time, hope turned into a fear that southerners would reach the northern shore, bringing their values and customs along. Hope was appropriated in Tunisia where it was construed as *al-Nahda*, meaning 'Renaissance', which happens to be the name of the Islamist party, inspired by the Iranian Revolution and Egypt's Muslim Brotherhood, that saw its revival in the wake of the Jasmine Revolution (although it had existed since 1981). Just as for the Arab Spring, the appellation 'Mediterranean Spring' indicates that the phenomenon (in this case the refugees' crisis) was just beginning and was likely to seriously influence the fate of the region in the months and years to come. In this regard, the Arab Spring is a Mediterranean Spring because it is an unprecedented human migratory movement around, in and across the southern Mediterranean, one that has been driven by *harragas*. Conversely, while 'Arab Spring' contains the incorrect assumption that the revolts involved only Arabs, and while 'Europe's refugee crisis' implies that the migratory movements have only affected the North, 'Mediterranean Spring' turns the focus away both from Arabness, in that 'refugees' have also included non-Arabs, and from Europe, in that North Africa and the Levant, too, have experienced the crisis.

There have been other 'springs' before – one need only think of, for instance, Eastern Europe in the 1960s, 1970s and 1980s. These springs were European, and therefore familiar, whereas the Arab Spring elicits pause due to the ethnic qualifier 'Arab' which makes it stand apart. But analysts have insisted that the Arab Spring has had the most significant impact on Europe since the Second World War. Although the fate of sub-Saharan Africans is indelibly connected to this crisis, we are dealing with a specific region, as news outlets have made clear – North Africa, the Arab world and mostly Muslim countries. In addition, the Arab Spring covers a wide region, yet is most often associated in mainstream media and political discourse with select North African countries (Tunisia, Libya and Egypt). This factual distortion is troubling, since nations such as Bahrain that underwent first-time revolutions are patently excluded from major official historical accounts. Even the civil war in Syria is commonly dissociated from its roots in the Arab Spring. These omissions reveal hidden motivations. With regard to Syria, to remind the public that the civil war is an instance of a failed Arab Spring – one that was meant to implement democracy and human rights – risks prompting Westerners to pressure their governments into helping Syrians achieve these ideals and their freedom, and to save their lives. Bahrain is a small, oil-rich Gulf country that does not share borders with Europe and does not border the Mediterranean, and therefore is conceived of as less of a threat to the geopolitical stability, cultural identity and ideological unity of Europe.

The Mediterranean seametery

A cemetery is a human construction. Due to increasingly stringent and deadly anti-immigration policies being put in place, the EU is actively participating in the construction of a cemetery at its margins. Is a cemetery not traditionally built at one's borders? Do cities, towns and villages not build cemeteries on their outskirts? The geographic margin of the federated entity known as the EU happens to be the Mediterranean Sea. The site of death and the sight of the dead must be kept at bay. As is to be expected of a fortress, and Fortress Europe is no exception, it is surrounded by a moat that acts as a safeguard against the unwelcome Other. Coincidentally, in Arabic, موت, pronounced *moat* or *mawt*, means death.

Because a large number of the *harragas* are Muslims, it is important not to understand the seametery as a general cemetery, but rather to probe the implications it has for those who die in it as well as those who are to memorialise them as a specifically Muslim cemetery. The Mediterranean is a mass grave and a maritime cemetery, or 'seametery', in that migration politics related to the Mediterranean rely on a set of contradictions and illogicalities that provoke desperate acts and untimely ends. How does a sea associated with flow and fluidity become the world's largest maritime cemetery? Given that migration is a right granted by international law, why is lawful mobility met with forced immobility? Why does migration trigger criminalisation, deportation and detention? A mass grave has political and ideological implications. It is a place where the victims of a war are buried. As I have argued, *harragas* fit this profile. At the same time, the Mediterranean is a *seametery*, for as I have just explained, they are buried in a site that European authorities have conveniently set up and allowed to expand beyond the physical borders of their continent. Just like the expression 'burning the sea', seametery is purposefully oxymoronic in that it contains a contradiction in migration politics for Muslim countries. Indeed, Islam's original historical moment around which a whole set of understandings has evolved was the Prophet Muhammed's migration from Mecca, which he fled due to persecution in order to seek refuge in Yathrib in 622. This moment that started the Muslim calendar and gave a city the name of the first refugee of the Muslim community (Yathrib was later renamed Medina, which is short for *Madīnat an-Nabī* – the City of the Prophet) is a crucial element in understanding migration and refugeeism in Muslim societies. The Prophet is seen as an exemplar for Muslims, and his actions and sayings are recorded as such. The Prophet's city is not the one he was born in but the one he settled in after hardships back in Mecca. With this historical background in mind, migration is not perceived as a negative undertaking, but rather quite the opposite – as a path to follow. According to a *ḥadīth* (a saying attributed to the Prophet), the Ummah, or Community of Believers, was ordered to 'Seek knowledge even if all the way to China!' Although this phrase can be read as a call to make every effort to educate oneself, it could also be interpreted as a religious call to travel. If Muslims apply this *ḥadīth* by migrating to Europe instead of China it is because at the time of the Revelation, China was considered the centre of knowledge. Today, it is the West that is seen in this light. It should be noted that this *ḥadīth* is framed as a command. Consequently, in the context of stiffening borders, a long, trying and perilous journey is the only gateway, or way to a gated Europe, for many Muslims to fulfil this religious obligation.

Even death does not end the injustices of anti-immigration policies. A cemetery is a place that invites commemoration, yet visiting rights are not granted. Because of their national identity, families are not permitted to visit the Mediterranean (read, European) gravesite to mourn the deceased. A cemetery is traditionally an open and public space, whereas the seametery is selective – the Global South 'visitor' can only be admitted if dead. If alive he may only visit the dead at its margins when they wash ashore, as if the seametery were a detention camp or prison where the migrant and refugee were being held *ad aeternam*. Those left behind are confined in 'pays-camps' ('country-camps') as per Jerôme Valluy's term, or in 'the cementery'.[11] The refugees' crisis has set a new precedent in that it has imposed changes upon the religious practices of Muslims. According to historical Muslim burial practices, a body must be interred in a codified space and attended by specific rites and rituals. In addition to not being wrapped in shrouds and lacking steles displaying excerpts from the Qur'an carved or painted in the Arabic language, Muslim bodies are intermingling with non-Muslim ones. Whereas a Muslim body should be buried in dirt among others of his own faith, instead it is drowned in a sea that is increasingly branded as European and of strict Judaeo-Christian heritage. This uncovers an additional facet of the appellation 'Mare Nostrum' in that not only is the sea 'ours', but so is the seametery – the death toll, the modes of burial, and the ownership of the gravesite are all determined by the policies of the Global North. In dissolving and becoming an integral part of the unhallowed liquid element of the seametery (vs. the sacred nature of the sanctified Muslim cemetery), the wholeness of the Muslim *harrag* is compromised along with his holiness, which is believed to impede his ability to enter the sought-after heaven.

'Seametery' contains other meanings that beg to be unpacked. First, this neologism refers back to 'seme', which means 'meaning', and it suggests that the Mediterranean is becoming the death of meaning. It is the place where bodies no longer mean anything. In the seametery, bodies do not matter for more and more decision makers and for a certain portion of the world's population. Similarly, to employ Judith Butler's expression which gave the title to her seminal 1993 book, bodies do not matter, for they are left to become liquid and to feed the creatures of the sea. In other words, they are made to dissolve and in so doing to shed their threatening potential for those who fear them; hidden from sight, they cease to spark outrage from those who pressure their governments to make the dead matter and the matter no longer a dead-end issue.

Additionally, the maritime cemetery is a seametery in that it is a sea of seams. There is much at stake in this site where two Mediterraneans collide. Instead of two fabrics being joined by the act of sewing, it is a single substance ripped apart by divisive laws and racist policies. The two fabricated types of unmatched Mediterraneans bump against each other, and the seam is disjointed and dialogical, with one side of the sea being associated with certain idea(l)s such as peace and wealth while the other is associated with war and death. The recurring crossings honour the sea's function as a site of passages and exchanges, a crossroads for ongoing migration and circulation. Conversely, deterrent measures meant to slow and stop south-to-north travel normalise a double standard by reinforcing a racially motivated divide. The contemporary militarisation of the Mediterranean does not leave room for a middle ground. For the Global North, it is a sea to patrol and control. For the Global South, it is a sea where stiffening anti-immigration policies stifle *harragas* to death. For the northern seafarers, the Mediterranean is smooth sailing, and the seam is a wall ensuring their security and safety. This same seam is a fissure engulfing travellers from the Global South, who, by their northward journeys, are enacting a symbolic (but rejected) attempt at stitching. The two parts of the Mediterranean are in no way equal. The chasm in the sea is pulled ever wider as policing ships draw its split in their wake and the ongoing deaths of unwelcome refugees defy the romantic vision of the Mediterranean. Not a seam that stitches together to unite, this seam is a scar, a wound that continues to open rather than heal.

The crossing of the Strait of Gibraltar has often been gauged by prospective *harragas* by way of the 14 kilometres that separate the Moroccan from the Spanish shores, which are mentioned in literary or filmic narratives (often on the very first page of a novel or give the title to the production).[12] The distance is often minimised, especially because prospective *harragas* can see the Spanish coast from Morocco. The few kilometres of water are equated to a river that those who do not know how to swim will not hesitate to cross. But each *metre* of this part of the world can turn into a sea-meter-y. The first scene, preceding the opening credits in Chus Gutiérrez's 2008 film *Retorno a Hansala*, powerfully illustrates this deceiving aspect. It shows an anonymous character gasping for breath a short few metres away from the shore before he eventually drowns.

While some *harragas* are rescued, others are left to die, depending on the policy of the moment. Regardless of differing instructions as to what to do when encountering a *harrag* at sea, the Mediterranean presents itself as a *mouroir*, a place where death is a possible outcome and repeatedly the intended one. Smugglers share responsibility for the expansion of the seametery, as they have been witnessed throwing their clients overboard to escape detection or to lighten the load in times of peril. Indeed, *harragas* are more often than not left to fend for their lives, whether because a European stranger has left them to die or because a North African smuggler has thrown passengers into the sea. Among its various responses to the refugees' crisis, the EU proposed to host migrants and spread the 'burden' among countries on the basis of quotas. But was this proposal made because it was deemed necessary to allow all refugees to find a place to live or was it made to restore the image of a Europe weary of its characterisation as a Fortress? The trouble is that the Fortress that 'protects' its citizens and 'saves' *harragas* has also been denounced as an accomplice in mass murder. Assorted European anti-immigration policies, which include orders not to rescue *harragas* at sea – an offence in some cases severely punishable by law – have caused the sea to transform into a kind of abyss. For those who are deported, a powerful message is sent: next time, if they try to cross, rescue may not be forthcoming. This echoes similar scenarios, such as the fatal journey reconstructed by Forensic Architecture in 2011 that

> revealed how the 'Left-to-Die Boat' was not rescued despite the presence of many military vessels, aircraft and other actors in the Central Mediterranean as part of NATO-led intervention in Libya, and despite the distress signals sent by migrants on board.[13] Using surveillance technology, Forensic Architecture's video report, *Liquid Traces*, as well as their written report, maps how state actors evaded their legal responsibilities to rescue at sea and contributed to the deaths of sixty-three people on board the boat. (Mainwaring and Brigden 2016: 248)

Thus, despite its illegality, authorities are eager to impress the idea that once 'compassion fatigue' settles in, as per Susan D. Moeller's use of the expression, the sea crossing is doomed to be a dead end for the repeating transient, victim of a serial killer whose murderous weapon is its borders endowed with mounting artificial intelligence at the service of a sinister system of screens and sieves.[14]

Alongside individuals, institutions and organisations saving lives on a daily basis is a *necropolice*, one that assures that those who dare trespass on to their side of the sea perish as far away as possible from national waters, beaches, ports and cities. The absence of a systematic condemnation of these attitudes from the federated union renders the EU an accomplice to the necropolice that patrol the maritime necropolis. Whatever its name, the Mediterranean boils down to a *maris mortiferum*,[15] or necromaris. Traditionally viewed as the most frequented sea in the region, the Mediterranean could well be nick-named the Deadly Sea. From the vantage point of the *harrag*, the sea holds the deceased captive in the middle of a hostile environment; not in the pro-verbial war of religions that this region has experienced throughout history, but on the basis of overt and covert racism and rampant Islamophobia. This type of hatred emboldens policies allegedly passed to address threats but that in fact reduce the *harrag* to 'a bare life stripped of every right by virtue of the fact that anyone can kill him without committing homicide; he can save himself only in perpetual flight or a foreign land' (Agamben 1998: 183). The *sans part* (those of 'no account' or 'an indistinct mass of people of no posi-tion', as Rancière has it) embody what Lyotard called a *différend* in that they are deprived of the adequate means to make a case that they have been the victims of concerted, inter-, intra- and supra-national wrongdoing.

A wake for a conclusion

The Mediterranean has become an experimental laboratory in which new techniques are tested to reinvent the border. The implementation of supra-national policies and national practices have created additional boundaries inland, on the beach, in the sea and far into the Maghreb and the Levant, turning a liquid body of water into a solid body of walls. To burn the sea boils down to burning liquid borders or to being buried under water. The Mediter-ranean is a *maris funebris* for the prisoners of phantom sepulchres. Today's Mediterranean is synonymous with boundaries, boats, bodies and burning. In order to prevent one side of the divided entity from encroaching upon the other, the northern rim patrols with military ships that draw massive fur-rows, marking the disjuncture at sea and sending a signal to rickety dinghies. As they criss-cross the sea they draw a set of seams in the sea-sieve and risk capsizing the rowing boats full of migrant hopefuls.

The furrows that these boats create are one meaning that can be derived from the term 'wake' used in the subsection title above. However, this term has other implications for the Mediterranean Sea, sieve, spring and seam-etery. A wake refers to keeping vigil, as the Fortress does with its Frontex, its SIVE and other methods. But the verb 'to wake' also means to alert.

Literature and cinema – fiction as well as documentaries – have attempted to bring about a state of awareness of a war-ness as well, so to speak. So have various other sources, including journalists. Some of them have bet that a few years from today Europe might regret and be condemned for turning its back on *harragas*, leaving hundreds to die under the eyes of rescue crews and their equipment. At a wake the mourners are left to watch over a dead body, but who can watch those who have perished in the seametery?

The recent tragedies have shown that from a simple sea to a complex SIVE, the geophysical maritime border is used as a sieve by Fortress Europe. Presenting itself as saving the lives of the weakest, the EU also plays by the rule of the survival of the fittest. It faces multiple challenges and dilemmas, namely, to sieve or save *harragas*, to chase smugglers and to chastise rescuers. With its operational system that reaches the shores of Africa and beyond like a net cast on to the sea and bordering cities, the big 'fish' it catches have little hope of welcome or salvation. Needless to say, to discuss these deaths dispassionately is a difficult task. It is even more daunting when one attempts to bring into the discussion the terminology used south of the Mediterranean, which is often endowed with strong imagery meant to convey the lived experiences of *harragas*. This set of terms denounces racist discourses concocted by the media and in the political arena that suggest that surges of migration are a threat to the myth of a homogeneous European identity, as if migration were a new phenomenon rather than one that has benefited European societies throughout the centuries.

This essay has explored these tensions and how the situation is viewed from both the North and the South through the unpacking of various word interplays. From 'Mare Nostrum' to 'the European refugee crisis', we have seen how language frames a Eurocentric perspective regarding who has the right to manage and control the Mediterranean and maritime crossings. Additionally, word linkages convey and shape certain experiences and (non-)responses to those experiences. As Europe thickens its walls on land and at sea, making regular migration a luxury, a growing sense of confinement is experienced by those hoping to flee countries plagued by war and poverty, perpetuating the need for unauthorised migration, which is ever more strictly restricted and criminalised. And so the cycle continues, with no end in sight except for clandestine life and status in Europe at best, or death at sea at worst.

Notes

1. For other examinations of this concept, see Abderrezak (2016; 2018a).
2. For a thorough explanation of these terms that originate in the Arabic language, see Abderrezak (2018a).
3. Although *harragas* is not a common word in the Mashreq, an Arabic-language concept seems most appropriate in that Arabic is a language that the Maghreb and Mashreq share.

4. As the Pew Research Center stated in 2018, only about 1 million Syrian refugees are in various European countries, whereas estimates such as those published the same year on UNHCR's official website indicate that Turkey 'hosts the largest number of registered refugees – currently 3.3 million'. UNHCR also states that 6.6 million were displaced within Syria itself, that over 1 million were in Lebanon (a fifth of the country's population), and that Jordan, Egypt and even Iraq had a growing population of Syrian refugees (over 655,000, more than 126,000 and over 246,000 respectively).

5. Bodies caught instead of fish can be seen in such filmic productions as Mohsen Melliti's *Io, l'altro* (2006) where the too-heavy-to-handle colonial past reappears in the form of a deceased migrant resurfacing in the Italian national waters. For a discussion of this parallel, see O'Healy (2009).

6. See Ariane Debernardi's 2017 newspaper article 'Migrants: tensions entre les ONG et l'Italie'. (Of note is the subtitle of the article, which reads, 'Sauver mais pas trop' ('to rescue but not too much').)

7. Selective immigration policies have traditionally favoured the fittest for practical reasons, mostly for their potential as a labour force. They have also favoured, or at least claim to have favoured, the lowest possible numbers in order to assuage fears expressed by local populations about so-called sudden invasions, reversal of demographics and alteration of national identities.

8. The acronym ISIL is more accurate than ISIS in that it covers the Levant, a wider area targeted by the terrorist group, whereas the former applies exclusively to Iraq and Syria.

9. This trope automatically surfaces in European discourse when North African migration is discussed. For example, the expression Second *Reconquista* has commonly been used in Spain, well before 'refugees' came into the picture. For more information on this aspect, see Flesler (2008).

10. Mohamed Bouazizi was technically the first refugee of the refugees' crisis, but in his case he was not able to burn the sea. Instead, this Tunisian individual immolated himself and set the region on fire.

11. For an explanation of the cementery, see Abderrezak (2018b).

12. Examples include Tahar Ben Jelloun's *Leaving Tangier*, Laila Lalami's *Hope and Other Dangerous Pursuits* and Gerardo Olivares' *14 kilómetros*.

13. Rosi's *Fire at Sea* (2016) includes a scene featuring a similar scenario.

14. Numerous sources have qualified European borders as 'murderous'. Others have placed the blame on the Mediterranean border. As I have attempted to demonstrate, this comes to the same thing, since Europe's power has expanded well into the liquid element and much beyond.

15. This and other coined Latin-sounding appellations are not meant to follow common grammatical rules; case endings, for instance, were selected primarily for sound effect.

Bibliography

ABC (2018), 'Llegan a Galicia los primeros refugiados rescatados por el "Aquarius"', 26 June, https://www.abc.es/espana/galicia/abci-llegan-galicia-primeros-refugiados-abordo-aquarius-201806261953_noticia.html (accessed 19 July 2018).

Abderrezak, Hakim (2010), 'Entretien avec Boualem Sansal', *Contemporary French and Francophone Studies: Sites*, 14.4: 339–47.

Abderrezak, Hakim (2016), *Ex-Centric Migrations: Europe and the Maghreb in Mediterranean Cinema, Literature, and Music* (Bloomington: Indiana University Press).

Abderrezak, Hakim (2018a), 'Harragas in Mediterranean illiterature and cinema', in Véronique Machelidon and Patrick Saveau (eds), *Reimagining North African Immigration* (Manchester: Manchester University Press), 232–52.

Abderrezak, Hakim (2018b), 'The Mediterranean *seametery* and *cementery* in Leïla Kilani's and Tariq Teguia's filmic works', in yasser elhariry and Edwige Tamalet Talbayev (eds), *Critically Mediterranean: Temporalities, Aesthetics, and Deployments of a Sea in Crisis* (Basingstoke: Palgrave Macmillan), 147–61.

Agamben, Giorgio (1998), *Homo Sacer: Sovereign Power and Bare Life*, trans. D. Heller-Roazen (Stanford: Stanford University Press).

Bauman, Zygmunt (2000), *Liquid Modernity* (Malden, MA: Polity Press).

BBC (2017), 'German election: how right-wing is nationalist AfD?', 13 October, https://www.bbc.com/news/world-europe-37274201 (accessed 30 October 2017).

Ben Jelloun, Tahar (2009), *Leaving Tangier*, trans. Linda Coverdale (New York: Penguin).

Butler, Judith (1993), *Bodies that Matter: On the Discursive Limits of 'Sex'* (New York: Routledge).

Corbalán, Ana (2015), 'Searching for justice in *Return to Hansala* by Chus Gutiérrez: cultural encounters between Africa and Europe', in Debra Faszer-McMahon and Victoria L. Ketz (eds), *African Immigrants in Contemporary Spanish Texts: Crossing the Strait* (New York: Routledge).

Debernardi, Ariane (2017), 'Migrants: tensions entre les ONG et l'Italie', *Libération*, 2 August, https://www.liberation.fr/planete/2017/08/02/migrants-tensions-entre-les-ong-et-l-italie_1587758 (accessed 3 August 2017).

Derrida, Jacques (1978), 'Violence and metaphysics: an essay on the thought of Emmanuel Levinas', in *Writing and Difference*, trans. Alan Bass (Chicago: University of Chicago Press), 79–153.

elconfidencial.com (2018), 'Salvan vidas y se les juzga por tráfico de personas: los bomberos sevillanos de Lesbos', 31 March, https://www.elconfidencial.com/espana/andalucia/2018-03-31/salvan-vidas-y-se-les-juzga-por-trafico-de-personas-los-bomberos-sevillanos-de-lesbos_1542782/ (accessed 3 May 2018).

Express (2016), 'Cologne rapists WERE refugees: prosecutor slams reports exonerating migrants as "nonsense"', 19 February, https://www.express.co.uk/news/world/644379/Cologne-attacks-German-prosector-New-Years-Eve-rapists-migrants-refugees (accessed 27 October 2017).

Fein, Helen (1984), *Accounting for Genocide: National Responses and Jewish Victimization during the Holocaust* (Chicago: University of Chicago Press).

Le Figaro (2016), 'Italie: 3700 migrants sauvés en trois jours', 30 March, http://www.lefigaro.fr/flash-actu/2016/03/30/97001-20160330FILWWW00392-italie-3700-migrants-sauves-en-trois-jours.php (accessed 25 October 2017).

Flesler, Daniela (2008), *The Return of the Moor: Spanish Responses to Contemporary Moroccan Immigration* (West Lafayette, IN: Purdue University Press).

francetvinfo.fr (2017a), 'Méditerranée: 5 000 migrants sauvés en 48 heures', 21 May, https://www.francetvinfo.fr/monde/europe/naufrage-a-lampedusa/mediterranee-5-000-migrants-sauves-en-48-heures_2201388.html (accessed 25 October 2017).

francetvinfo.fr (2017b), 'Réfugiés: 13 991 migrants ont été sauvés par SOS Méditerranée en 2016', 7 March, https://www.francetvinfo.fr/monde/europe/naufrage-a-lampedusa/refugies-13-991-migrants-ont-ete-sauves-par-sos-mediterranee-en-2016_2085539.html (accessed 27 October 2017).

Hmoudane, Mohamed (2005), *French Dream* (Paris: Editions de la Différence).

it.euronews.com (2018), 'Mediterraneo, ecco i piloti salva-migranti: il perché di una scelta', 21 May, https://it.euronews.com/2018/05/21/mediterraneo-ecco-i-piloti-salva-migranti-il-perche-di-una-scelta (accessed 19 July 2018).

Jay, Salim (2001), *Tu ne traverseras pas le détroit* (Paris: Editions Mille et Une Nuits).

Lalami, Laila (2005), *Hope and Other Dangerous Pursuits* (Chapel Hill, NC: Algonquin Books).

Lévinas, Emmanuel (1960), *Totality and Infinity: An Essay on Exeriority*, trans. A. Lingis (Pittsburgh: Duquesne University Press).

Libération (2015), 'Méditerranée: "Que va-t-on faire pour sauver des vies"', 22 April, https://www.liberation.fr/planete/2015/04/22/mediterranee-que-va-t-on-faire-pour-sauver-des-vies_1258494 (accessed 15 July 2017).

Lydie, Virginie (2010), *Traversée interdite! Les Harragas face à l'Europe forteresse* (Paris: Le Passager Clandestin).

Lyotard, Jean-François (1983), *Le Différend* (Paris: Editions de Minuit).

Mainwaring, Ċetta, and Noelle Brigden (2016), 'Beyond the border: clandestine migration journeys', *Geopolitics*, 21.2: 243–62.

Moeller, Susan D. (1999), *Compassion Fatigue: How the Media Sell Disease, Famine, War and Death* (New York: Routledge).

O'Healy, Áine (2009), '"[Non] è una Somala": deconstructing African femininity in Italian film', *The Italianist*, 29.2: 175–98.

Ponzanesi, Sandra (2011), 'Europe adrift: rethinking borders, bodies, and citizenship from the Mediterranean', *Moving Worlds*, 11.2: 67–76.

Rancière, Jacques (1995), *La Mésentente: politique et philosophie* (Paris: Editions Galilée).

UNHCR (2018), 'Syria emergency', https://www.unhcr.org/en-us/syria-emergency.html?query=hosts%20the%20largest%20number%20of%20registered%20refugees%20–%20currently%203.3%20million (accessed 19 July 2018).

Valluy, Jérôme (2009), 'Aux marches de l'Europe: des "pays-camps" – la transformation des pays de transit en pays d'immigration forcée (observations à partir de l'exemple marocain)', in Ali Bensaâd (ed.), *Le Maghreb à l'épreuve des migrations subsahariennes – immigration sur émigration* (Paris: Karthala), 325–42.

Filmography

14 kilómetros, dir. Gerardo Olivares, Explora Films, Wanda Visión S.A., 2007.

Fuocoammare (Fire at Sea), dir. Gianfranco Rosi, Stemal Entertainment, 21 Unofilm, Istituto Luce Cinecittà, Rai Cinema, Les Films d'Ici, Arte France Cinéma, 2016.

Retorno a Hansala, dir. Chus Gutiérrez, Maestranza Films, Muac Films, 2008.

Chapter 20

'Island is no arrival': Migrants' 'Islandment' at the Borders of Europe

Mariangela Palladino

No one leaves home unless home is the mouth of a shark.
I have been carrying the old anthem in my mouth for so long that there's
  no space
for another song, another tongue, another language . . .
I tore up and ate my own passport in an airport hotel . . .
Look at all these borders, foaming at the mouth with bodies broken and
  desperate. (Shire 2011: 24–5)

'Today the mythical Mediterranean is brutally vernacularised in the fraught journeys of anonymous men, women, and children migrating across its waters: Caliban returns as an illegal immigrant, and Prospero's island, midway between Naples and Tunis in the sixteenth-century drama, becomes modern-day Lampedusa' (Chambers 2010: 680). Caliban in Chambers's words makes his return through the *wretched of the earth*, today's migrants[1] who cross the Mediterranean in search of safety and arrive in Lampedusa, a small island off the Italian southern coast. As Bernardie-Tahir and Schmoll observe, Lampedusa has been 'turned into a resonance chamber for many issues, including the management of maritime migrants, deportation and detention, hospitality and solidarity, and the intertwined interventions of local, national, and supra-national institutions' (2014: 94). Closer to Africa than it is to the European mainland, the island of Lampedusa (and its surrounding waters) is associated with some of the deadliest modern shipwrecks.[2] This small island is a 'place where the ordering of bordering' (Bernardie-Tahir and Schmoll 2014: 94) has become a spectacle (Cuttitta 2012). The spectacle of migration management unravels in Lampedusa most dramatically through amplified media accounts; as Jerome Phelps points out, '[t]his may be the most photographed humani-tarian crisis in history' (Phelps 2017). Migration today is over-reported in the news – either with a negative scapegoating spin to it, or shrouded by the veil of pity and victimisation. The dominant language, rhetoric and meta-phors surrounding forced displacement are inadequate and fail to account for migrants' emotional and geographical journeys.

This chapter offers a sustained reading of Erri De Luca's long poem 'Solo Andata' [One Way] from the eponymous collection (2005) to foreground the notion of 'islandment' – a term that obliquely emerges from the poem. Drawing on scholarship on carceral archipelagos, and using the development and management of migration hotspots at the borders of Europe as a backdrop, I propose a shift of emphasis in scholarship away from the journey to reflect on the complex ontological, emotional and social dimensions surrounding border crossing. What does it mean to reach the shores of Europe? I develop the concept of 'islandment' as a framework to interrogate and problematise the rhetoric of hospitality applied to the management of migration today on islands as sites of detention. In the first two sections of this chapter, I take De Luca's writing about arrival as a starting point to reflect on what arrival might mean to border crossers today. The notion of islandment functions as a new metaphor to illuminate and make sense of migrants' arrival and reception at the shores of Europe. In the final section, I turn back to the journey; islandment is mobilised as a counterpoint to deconstruct and defamiliarise geographies of the sea and to revisit narratives of crossing.

De Luca's 'Solo Andata' offers an allegorical narrative of trans-Mediterranean migration. Structured in nine distinct, yet interconnected sections, this epic poem is a lyrical account of tragic and perilous journeys across the Mediterranean aboard unseaworthy vessels to beach on the shores of an island in Italy (it most likely refers to Lampedusa, though that island is never named in the text). The journey by sea and the arrival are told by several narrators in a polyphonic narrative: the short opening section, 'Six voices', is followed by 'Six more voices', 'Two voices', 'One's tale' (twice), and four sections titled 'Chorus'. The poem features hybridity in its form, combining all three of Aristotle's influential division of poetry as a genre – narrative, lyric and drama. This form allows for multiple narrative perspectives, further enhanced by the use of the chorus. As in the ancient Greek tradition, the collective voices of the chorus comment on the dramatic action; they regularly punctuate the narrative and pass moral judgement. However, in 'Solo Andata' the chorus is not passively commenting on the dramatic action and tragic predicaments of one or two individual protagonists – the chorus here is the protagonist. The application of this classical rhetorical strategy reveals a specific narrative logic: there is a shift and revision in the use and significance of the chorus to narrativise a collective tragedy, rather than that of one hero. In doing so, De Luca's work illuminates the representational landscape of 'clandestine' sea crossings – the end-product of complex political and historical dynamics in a globalised, deeply divided and increasingly unequal world – and draws attention to sea crossings as a universal (rather than individual) human tragedy. De Luca's poem offers powerful accounts of the experiences at sea of the so-called 'boat people'. Rejecting the ubiquitous representations of an indistinct mass of asylum seekers as potential terrorists, 'Solo Andata' articulates counter-narratives of migratory experiences. Thus, the poem's multiple sections and formal strategies read as several attempts (and perhaps failures) to produce a sustained narrative of islandment and its manifestations – departures, crossings and arrivals, traumas, memories, and life and death at sea. The dominant rhetoric of the media, which portrays migration in terms of 'floods' and 'flows', is replaced by other liquid metaphors: the 'waves' in De Luca's poetry are not those of mass migration crashing against the inhospitable shores of Europe, but those that 'imprison' the island – a land bound by the sea and a site of entrapment for migrants themselves.

No arrival and islandment

The section 'Racconto di Uno' [One's tale] takes readers towards the end of the voyage, as hunger, thirst and exhaustion give way to delirium. The voice recalls home, a place to return to and die, as memory wanders off in search of familiar landscapes. While imagining himself/herself to be walking along the road leading to his/her village, the speaker sees 'dogs waiting on the doorsteps, not angels, / those dogs who loved our hands' (De Luca 2005: 29).[3] This image, which echoes the return of Odysseus to Ithaca and to his faithful dog Argos, articulates another voyage, another journey, one of imagination, which takes place during the last hours of the sea crossing. The second line of the couplet, referring to the hands, signifies familiarity, care and loyalty. This poignant hand imagery is brutally reversed in the following lines in which a reference to other hands effectively thrusts readers from the soothing vision of homecoming to the brutality of border policing and arrival at the borders of Europe.

> Hands grabbed me, Northern Customs,
> plastic gloves and surgical mask. (De Luca 2005: 30)

This couplet is a description of arrival; it is terse and effective in narrativising violence. This is far removed from the romanticised embrace celebrated by the Italian authorities in 2014 with a commemorative plaque depicting a white hand holding a black hand in a fraternal clasp.[4] The language of care and encounter, which typifies descriptions of the sea earlier on in the text, is replaced by a new register, one that does not contemplate emotions. The action of hand grabbing is followed by a list of things: authorities, gloves and a mask. We are faced here with a portrayal of border policing and sanitised humanitarianism; the arrival and the encounter are filtered through a barrier of latex and protective garments. This image conjures up fears of contamination from the new arrivals, fears inescapably connected with the discourses of race proclaimed in colonial times when blackness entailed impurity. Rejoicing over the long-awaited arrival in Italy, the speaker is soon told by a fellow migrant that they have beached on one of its islands.

I don't know what an island is, I ask and he replies:
'It is land planted in the middle of the sea'.

And does it not move? 'No, it is land imprisoned by waves,
like us by the fence'. Island is no arrival. (De Luca 2005: 30)

To those who have never seen the sea the concept of the island is an abstract one. These lines mobilise a naturalist semantic to connote incarceration and encampment: so, the metaphor of imprisonment – alongside references to planting – is adopted to describe the island of Lampedusa bound by waves, 'like us' by a fence. The simile equates the speakers to the natural world, and the syntax confines the migrants to a peripheral place in the sentence. The poem's speakers draw on the language of incarceration and on that of nature to make sense of the experience – to translate the unknown, the abstract idea of an island, into something familiar and comprehensible.[5]

The image of captivity in De Luca's text goes beyond the metaphor – it is not just a means to lyricise the geographical isolation experienced on an island. The last line, 'Island is no arrival', subtly yet powerfully gestures towards the complex dynamics of sovereign power, the politics of exclusion and the bureaucracies of confinement and reception. *Isola non è arrivo* is a harsh realisation that after a long and dangerous journey, landing on the island is not arriving. It draws attention to the idea of arriving, its significances and its implications. Arrival is the end of a journey, but it also entails a beginning in a new place; this is no arrival, the journey is not over. The fence obliterates any expectation of acceptance and welcome.

'Island is no arrival' is the suggestive foundation for the concept of islandment that this chapter foregrounds. The term is a syncretic neologism that brings together the words island and encampment, though islandment goes beyond the idea of 'encampment on an island' – its signification exceeds the portmanteau. I argue that the term islandment offers a more complex and more nuanced signification for migrants' experiences of reaching Europe in search of sanctuary than merely arrival and reception. De Luca's line, 'island is no arrival', illuminates received understandings of migrants' detention on islands today (such as Lampedusa, the Christmas Islands, Nauru, and others) and experiences of reaching and beaching on the southern borders of Europe, what Chambers calls the southern shores of Occidental modernity (2011: 252).

Islandment is a lived situation; it is arrival without an end to the journey; it signifies detention, and the double incarceration on the island by both the fences of the camp and the sea; islandment is inhabiting a liminal space in Europe but not quite so, neither geographically nor legally; it is a discursive category to defamiliarise the sea and reconfigure it as a destination. I place the notion of islandment amid a body of scholarship – especially in cultural theory and social studies – on islands as carceral spaces, on encampment, and the rhetoric of reception and hospitality surrounding immigration today.

As detention facilities on European islands have proliferated in the last few years (Bernardie-Tahir and Schmoll 2014: 99), recent debates about islands as sites of enforcement and detention focus on the ways islands have been constructed as sentinels and enforcers of the current EU bordering regime. Island detention signifies a more complex process of imprisonment as it both represents a detention facility and a geographical confinement in the sea. Nethery argues that

> islands have always played a powerful and evocative role in the governance and imagination of nation states. They are at once part of a state's territory under law, yet geographically separate from it. National rules apply, but islands seem curiously free of the gaze of the authorities. (Nethery 2012: 85)

McCulloch reminds us that islands have been 'used to exclude, isolate and imprison the ill, the insane and those reproduced as criminals in society' (McCulloch 2007: 3–4). In the words of Lemaire, islands have been deployed as

> a technology of government . . . to create carceral environments and divide populations. Over time, island detention has been reiterated, readapted, and reshaped to separate categories of people who have been identified as a threat to society. Small islands have been central in the construction of the image of other and the curtailment of their rights in Western societies. (Lemaire 2014: 158)

In this context, Lampedusa is a paradigmatic example of the use of islands for incarceration. Interestingly, Lampedusa itself has a history as a carceral archipelago: after Italian unification, it was used as a site of confinement for insurgent southerners. Today it has morphed into what Pugliese calls 'another form of island gulag with a contemporary immigration detention prison' (2010: 110). Referring to Lampedusa and the Christmas Islands, Pugliese notes that 'these island gulags arrest the deviant life forms of the Global South that wash up on their respective shores and imprison them within the crisis heterotopia of the immigration jail' (2010: 118). As Mountz points out, nation-states exploit islands as carceral sites not only because of the geographical isolation of the space of land in the middle of the sea, but also because islands are often surrounded by legal ambiguity. For instance, in the case of detention on Lampedusa, Mountz notes that 'not only was access to asylum inhibited for asylum seekers, but advocates and human rights monitors were restricted or removed from the centre, compounding the isolation of migrants inside' (2011: 126).

Lampedusa is one of the EU hotspots proposed and developed by the European Commission in 2015 to combat the migration crisis and support member states' border policing.[6] As Garelli and Tazzioli observe, the hotspot works as a *preemptive frontier* with the double goal of blocking migrants at the southern borders of Europe and, at the same time, impeding the highest number of refugees possible from claiming asylum . . . At Lampedusa this logic has so far worked to prevent high numbers of people who have made it to Europe from claiming asylum. (2016)[7]

As the European Database of Asylum Law confirms, the hotspot approach has no legal basis and significantly compromises the fundamental rights of 45,000–60,000 migrants every year (EDAL 2017). 'On Lampedusa we can see all the functions of the Italian and EU border concentrated in one place' (Cuttitta 2014: 199). The island, geographically – and in the eyes of the law – for matters of 'reception of migrants' is not like the mainland; hence, sovereign power exploits this geographical and legal liminality to segregate and isolate the unwanted and uninvited 'guests' from the south.

In this context, islandment functions both as a metaphor and a framework to signify and understand migrants' arrival and the subsequent mechanism of island detention – an integral stage in the heavily policed and bureaucratised system of migration management. It aims to propose a fresh approach that departs from conceptualising migration in terms of hosts and guests. Rosello observes that 'hospitality has become the privileged metaphor for immigration . . . it blurs the distinction between a discourse of rights and a discourse of generosity' (2002: 175–6). Hospitality entails a 'constant negotiation between competing demands'; it is based on the assumption that one 'has the right to both welcome a stranger and, conversely, to reject such a stranger' (Darling 2014: 163). The metaphor of hospitality applied to the context of migration is highly problematic (Fassin et al. 1997; Darling 2010; 2014; Squire 2011) and it has become increasingly inadequate with the shift from local spontaneous hospitality to a professional and institutionalised version. Friese reminds us that when the first migrants arrived in Lampedusa, the fishermen's ethos of hospitality was the rule: the 'boat people' were rescued by local volunteers, hosted and cared for. Compassion and solidarity were the governing terms of this host and guest relationship. Over time, an apparatus of humanitarian intervention and institutionalised management of arrivals has supplanted informal reception. While recognising the importance of technology at sea (e.g. radar-equipped vessels, relief and intervention systems, etc.) to save more lives, Friese draws attention to the implications brought about by this shift in intervention:

> whereas boatpeople had been visible as individuals for locals, they have been turned into invisibles in a doubled sense of the term: they are *clandestini* who have a fantastic presence and are assigned – as 'extraterritorial' – to a segregated place, a 'heterotopic' space of transition and a space of 'inclusive exclusion'. (2012: 73)

This institutionalisation of rescue, reception and allegedly welcome has radically transformed the experience of arrival for those who come to the shore. The professionalisation of reception and sovereign intervention – where humanitarianism and policing are 'intimately linked' (Ticktin 2005: 359) – has brutally impacted on the lives of those who seek sanctuary. Moreover, it further complicates relations between hosts and guests, rendering the metaphor of hospitality not only inadequate but wholly fallacious. As Pugliese writes,

> [w]hat must be relentlessly evaded is hospitality: don't expect refuge, only shelter; don't expect nourishment, only food; don't expect comfort, only harassment . . . Any ethical gesture of hospitality has to be extirpated . . . for fear that the parasitical refugee might actually become comfortable in their new home. (Pugliese 2002: par. 21)

The mechanisms of rescue and reception today have been stripped of hospitality; new terms of reference, frameworks and metaphors are needed to interpret and make sense of these processes. The notion of islandment – emerging from De Luca's text – translates the economy and dynamics of contemporary asylum practices played out on carceral archipelagos and offers the possibility of a new, more nuanced, alternative discursive category.

Island encampment, labour and sea harvest

The term 'islandment' needs to be placed among these interpretations about islands as spaces of incarceration and encampment. What I suggest here is a term that more specifically signifies the idiosyncrasies and complexities of migrants' own experiences of reaching the southern shores of Europe today. Beaching on Lampedusa does not fulfil the terms of the voyage, and the island fails to be a site of arrival; its geographical and legal liminality denies those in search of sanctuary actual access to sanctuary. It provides shelter without giving a home, it detains and incarcerates according to the ethics of encampment by transforming those who are enclosed into subjects other than themselves. Thus, islandment conjures up ideas of enclosure, it belongs to an equation made up of subtractions and negations – being on the island, but not arriving, not being. This idea of denial, of something missing, is reinforced by the last lines of De Luca's poem.

> Surveilled by the guards, us guilty of the journey . . .
>
> They want to send us back, they ask where I was before,
> the place I left behind.
>
> I turn around, this is all I have left behind,
> they take offence . . . (De Luca 2005: 31–4)

'Clandestine' sea crossings in the Mediterranean today negate and invalidate the concept of journey (which should also include return) and firmly establish new paradigms to tell of human displacement. In Lampedusa, in the south of the north, the survivors of war, famine, persecution, droughts, ecological disasters and the perils of sea crossings are offered no welcome that fulfils the sense of the word, both in the law of the voyage or in that of hospitality. Instead, encampment and imprisonment are part of the EU's immigration apparatus; hospitality provided for the unwanted guest is the embrace of the fence that obliterates expectations of reception, acceptance and welcome; it is islandment. De Luca's poetry lyricises the process of searching for sanctuary and asylum, the difficulties of making sense of the spaces, the gap between expectations of sanctuary and the reality of an institutionalised reception, the experiences of enclosure and detention. Migrants' long journeys still vibrate in their bodies, but the island proffers a denied arrival, an actual end to the journey itself. 'Thus, as the case of Lampedusa shows, detention centres represent neither the endpoint in one's migrational projects nor the place where migrants are "abandoned in the [juridical] void" [Papastergiadis 2006]' (Andrijasevic 2010: 158).

The island offers reception without hospitality, and the camp is the quintessential example of hosting without hospitality. One of the speakers in 'Solo Andata' questions fellow arrivants about the camp to try to make sense of it; asking what this yard is in which they are all enclosed, he wonders whether it is 'communism' (De Luca 2005: 31). To attempt both to comprehend and accept encampment, the text mobilises the idea of communism. What is referred to as the 'encampment turn' (Bakewell 2014) in contemporary scholarship – the significant increase in the use of camps for migrants and refugees – is now an established part of the state response to crisis. The camp plays a crucial role today in managing situations of emergency – even if such emergencies may be indefinite. Contemporary literature on encampment reminds us that 'the logic of the camp is thus one in which the ethical demands of hospitality and responsibility are transferred elsewhere, literally placed outside the nation' (Darling 2009: 656). The camp has become a legitimate tool, producing spaces to exercise sovereign power and exclusion. On the other hand, scholars have become increasingly preoccupied with the dynamics, politics and technologies of those camps (Agamben 1997; Harrell-Bond 1998; Kaiser 2006; Le Cour Grandmaison, Lhuilier and Valluy 2007; Bernardot 2008; Darling 2009; McConnachie 2014). The camp is demarcated as a space of exception in Agamben's terms: the inhabitant of this space is at once disenfranchised of her/his human rights and precluded from accessing the law. Darling reminds us of the political liminality of the camp as a site of inclusive exclusion where 'sovereign power does not produce political subjects, as in Foucauldian power relations, but, rather, produces exclusions as bare life' (Darling 2009: 651). Similarly, the carceral island transforms subjects into something else; in 'One's tale' the poem points to the transformative power of detention and draws on the metaphor of material resources:

> It is not communism, but a pen and us livestock.
> Even less than this, says one among the thousands.
>
> We are neither for milk, nor for meat.
> But labour. They just don't want us. (De Luca 2005: 31)

To make sense of the experience of incarceration, and the dehumanisation created by the politics of the encampment, the voice values migrants' lower than livestock. These lines quickly and effectively translate the experience of detention – from human to less than animal – according to the economy of migrant labour today. References to migrants as a labour force and as resources punctuate the whole text; while still at sea, 'The Chorus' antici-pates how migrants' lives will be 'valued' once they have reached the shore of Europe. Addressing a collective you – which could signify Europe or more broadly the West – it says:

> help yourself with us, a field of lives to exploit, / plant, metal, hands, more than just workforce . . . We will be servants, the sons and daughters you fail to be . . . We will shovel snow, smoothen lawns, beat rugs. (De Luca 2005: 25–36)

Once again, hand imagery recurs in the poem, in this case as a synecdochal transposition for labourers and hired hands. These lines make overt refer-ences to migrants' work in Europe and expose the irregular migrant labour market on which Western economy relies. Besides domestic and manual labour, the reference to care work for the elderly is particularly striking, yet understated. Scholarship suggests that figures for irregular migrant care workers are rising in relation to an increasingly ageing population in Europe (Anderson 2000; Ehrenreich and Hochschild 2003; Gallo and Scrinzi 2016). The often invisible (and gendered) role of care workers is here conjured up as a surrogate filial relation which implies complex moral obligations blurring the line between employment and dutiful care. The poem at once condemns the shortcomings of social care in the neoliberal age, and exposes the fragility of a labour force that contributes to the European economy (in domestic and care work, among other sectors) and is enmeshed with changing social and family dynamics.

De Luca utilises the language of labour and resources throughout the text. When the long sea journey has finally ended, there is no sense of closure to the crossing; no verb or noun is employed in the text to signify arrival. Instead, the reader infers that the boat has reached Europe, or that it has been intercepted close to European coasts:

> They sort the dead from the living ones, here the sea harvest,
> a thousand of us locked in a place for a hundred. (De Luca 2005: 30)

The sea harvest of lives is a striking and fitting image to sum up the dynamics of reception and rescue at the southern borders of Europe. In Italian the verb *raccogliere*, to harvest, contains another verb *accogliere*, to receive. For De Luca, harvest comes before reception, before welcome. Writing about migrants' rescue in the Mediterranean, he describes

> a harvest of lives which we have not sown, which we have not raised, educated. They come to us free, these lives . . . for some these are resources . . . I cannot share this view. These are lives willing to sacrifice for a brief stay . . . these lives are so low that we must use for them the verb harvest . . . the Mediterranean today is a field for lost sowing. (De Luca 2016: 1)[8]

The verb 'to harvest' compels us to think critically about what Malkki calls a 'human uniformity' (1996: 387); the insertion of this verb in the discourse about mass displacement alerts us to the inadequacies of our contemporary times. If harvesting – as for crops, plants or fish for consumption – offers a suitable signifier for receiving migrants at sea, this signals that humanity has failed to be humane; that the north's moral compass must be recalibrated.[9] Harvesting – *raccogliere* – substitutes for welcome – *accogliere* – and migrants' experience of reaching Lampedusa is islandment, the end of a journey without arrival. Islandment is landing in an interstitial space surrounded by the sea where states of exceptions – in the form of encampment – are easily established and far removed from sight. In 'Solo Andata', an exchange between two migrants captures the striking contradictions occurring at the borders of Europe.

> Italìa, Italìa is this Italìa?
> They have a good word for their country, vowels full of *aria*.
>
> 'It is Itàlia and this is one of its islands
> for capers, for fishing and for the rest of us locked up.' (De Luca 2005: 30)

The reference to Italy and the vowels in the word (full of *aria*) is a metaphor for the newcomer's expectations of what *Italia* would be like: the openness in the word itself faintly alluding to Italy's democratic values and its ratification of human rights and the refugee charter. Yet the speakers are surrounded by a fence, locked up and penned in like animals. The explanation about Lampedusa's geography provided by the interlocutor goes beyond spatiality: the island's attributes here allude to frugality, material resources, capers, fishing and 'the rest of us'. The reference to 'us' is syntactically delayed, drawing attention to the migrants' marginality, their subalternity, in a sequence that places them at the end of a chain of beings on the island, after capers and fishing. This is their islandment.

Reimagining the sea and refiguring the journey

In this final section, I explore the ways in which islandment as a discursive category encapsulates representations of sea journeys. The poetic counter-narratives articulated in 'Solo Andata' not only interrogate and subvert pernicious dichotomies such as going/returning, arrival/departure, they also problematise dominant accounts of migratory sea crossings which both defamiliarise and refigure the sea.

In 'Solo Andata' the sea is portrayed in multiple, complex and nuanced ways: far from being just a border, or a menacing body of water, De Luca's depictions of the Mediterranean bring to bear uncommon significances. *Il Mare* – the sea – appears in the very first line of the poem: 'it wasn't the sea to welcome us / we welcomed the sea with open arms' (De Luca 2005: 11). The importance of the Italian verb *accogliere* (to welcome, to pick up) is emphasised in these lines with all its nuances which echo harvesting. In this image, the sea is indeed a welcome presence: 'when in sight' it was 'the finishing line, waves embrace the feet' (De Luca 2005: 11). This first encounter almost celebrates the sea; it is greeted, it greets with open arms and it embraces. The narrating voices of the poem's first section entitled 'Six voices' tell of this one-way journey starting from the sea – the sea here is not the beginning, but the finishing line. This representation of the sea as arrival remaps the Mediterranean in the sequence of migrants' routes and reconfigures it as a destination, rather than a leg on the journey. Islandment here is uncannily prefigured in this reinvention of the sea as a finishing line – it is here that migrants' journeys end, because 'island is no arrival'. The poem describes, explores, invokes and names the sea through spatial and bodily metaphors which conjure up caring images and gestures: 'A strip put across to caress feet, / the most gentle of borders' (De Luca 2005: 12). Islandment here is pre-empted and prefigured, as the caring nature of the sea ominously announces the shores of Europe. In the poem, the sea functions as a device to emphasise the lack of welcoming and hospitality. Offering a much more definite arrival, the Mediterranean embraces border crossers; the sea is home to many who have been swallowed by its waves, while Europe's southern shores (and its hotspots)[10] fail to offer adequate reception and to signify arrival. Moreover, the poem's reconceptualisation of the journey reframes departures and arrivals and effectively narrates (by negation) the horrors of the routes preceding the sea – the desert. When the Mediterranean – a graveyard for thousands of unclaimed bodies of those who also left to reach Europe but never made it – is received with open arms, the readers' imaginations are left to wonder about what comes before the sea, what these journeys might entail.

The section 'One's tale' also opens with the sea, more specifically imagining the sea. Many migrants taking the Mediterranean sea route come from landlocked parts of Africa; some of them have never seen the sea; and very often their first encounter happens when boarding smugglers' vessels to cross to Europe. The sea is thus a repository of hopes and dreams, fears and uncertainty before reaching the shore; hence, it is imagined and reimagined. Before seeing it, the

> sea was a smell,
> salty sweat, everyone imagined a different shape.
> Will it be like waning moon, like a prayer rug,
> will it be like my mother's hair. (De Luca 2005: 14)

These speculations about the shape and forms of the sea – something uncanny – are articulated through associations with familiar smells, objects, people. Migrants' fear and excitement about encountering the sea are tamed through images that tell of home, safety and comfort: the moon, prayer (God), the mother. Once the sea is reached, it appears like a

> hem rolled at the edge of Africa,
> its eyes stolen from (hand) mirrors, tears of welcoming. (De Luca 2005: 14)

The uncanny that lurks behind the sight and idea of the sea is once again exorcised through familiar images. Here the hem brings the language of home dressmaking, of kitchen tables and women's hands into the picture. My translation of hand mirror from *specchietto* in the original text only partially conveys the nuances behind the term, which refers to an ordinary, familiar, personal object such as a compact mirror. To make sense of the sea, its immensity, its materiality, the poem translates such experience into a series of images taken from ordinary, domestic life. The associations of the sea as caring, loving and embracing – which characterise the opening of 'Solo Andata' – return in this section with 'tears of welcoming'. The dominant demonisation of the Mediterranean and its perilous waters is dissipated and contrasted by another anthropomorphic image which drapes over these waters a benevolent appearance and nurturing behaviour. In this section, there is no mention of borders and frontiers in relation to the sea, but only of welcome. Welcome is not usually a concept that figures in the context of migration from the Global South to the Global North. The poem articulates a displacement of common references conferring on the sea the role of *accogliere* which is denied at the shore; in this sense, islandment encapsulates the defamiliarisation of the sea. The speaker feels welcomed by the sea, which moves like a camel, *movimento di cammello*, while the boat is 'a piece of land bashed by a spade' (De Luca 2005: 21).

De Luca's text is firmly rooted in earthly and domestic images, yet it narrates sea journeys. 'Solo Andata' also revisits the ubiquitous image of overloaded boats and portrays agency, resilience and social relations at sea. Departing from dominant views, much influenced by bird's-eye images of vessels at sea bearing an indistinct mass awaiting to be saved,[11] De Luca's poetry presents more complex and nuanced accounts of social relations

aboard migrants' boats. While at the mercy of the sea, smugglers and puta-
tive rescuers (Palladino and Woolley 2018), migrants organise their social
space and employ complex strategies to resist, and in doing so illustrate how
they retain agency. Concepts such as communism, equality, freedom and
alliance can be (and are) fostered in impossible (abject) conditions among
migrants on the boat. Once food and water are no longer available to them,
migrants on the boat share drops of mist to quench their thirst: 'we are
equal, the tightest equality, / until the last drop of mist' (De Luca 2005: 26).
Discussing social relations with reference to migrants' camps around Calais,
Rygiel argues that it is important to 'take the camp itself as a social and
political space created through social relations that are developed in and as a
result of movement' (Rygiel 2011: 4). Like the camp, the boat is a social and
political space not only regulated by the sea and weather conditions, but also
by human power relations that govern the few square metres on vessels.[12]
Equality and communism find a place in this text to narrativise migrants'
experiences of sharing, resisting and surviving while crossing the sea to reach
the coasts of Europe.

Defamiliarisation as a polemical strategy and the narrativisation of agency
and resistance are continued in De Luca's text through a process of revision
and disruption of set references. The poem foregrounds a contestation of the
terms north and south, problematic and much-debated concepts in contemporary scholarship (Rigg 2007; Boată 2015; Sparke 2007; Méndez 2017).
The section 'Due Voci' [Two voices] opens with an invocation of a collective
you (as we have seen above), addressed to those on the other side of the border, those in the north, those in the west:

> they say: you are south. No, we come from the large parallel,
> from the equator, centre of the earth. (De Luca 2005: 13)

These two lines invoke long-lasting debates about mapping and its imbrication with imperial visions of the world (Said 1993; Howard 2010; Harley
1988; Jacobs 1993; Piper 2002; Gregory 2004). The 'multiple and mutable
Mediterranean', as Chambers calls it (2010: 9), 'proposes a multiplicity
that simultaneously interrupts and interrogates the facile evaluations of a
simple mapping disciplined by the landlocked desires of a narrow-minded
progress and a homogeneous modernity' (Chambers 2010: 25). Moreover,
the 'No' juxtaposed as a direct and unequivocal answer to what 'they say'
concisely echoes arguments explored in the seminal work *The Empire
Writes Back* (Ashcroft et al. 1989). It does so not only by contesting the
centre but by reappropriating it: 'we are the centre'. The following couplet
reiterates the idea:

> our skin blackened by straight light,
> we stick out from the middle of the world, not from the south. (De Luca
> 2005: 13)

This categorical repudiation of the south and its attached significances of subalternity and under-development effectively deconstructs the north/south dichotomy and brings to the table geography as proof of its fallacy.

'One's tale' reiterates this contestation of the north when migrants are inspected at the frontier by border guards, asked to go back to their home country and challenged regarding their journey and their very presence: 'We are not baggage to post and you north are not worthy of yourself' (De Luca 2005: 34). Reifying migrants through the metaphor of material resources and harvest, this line denounces the status quo: the north here is unquestionably scrutinised, yet the text plays with dominant and received associations attached to the north to contest them. If the north is developed, civilised, democratic, equal and a fair world, then this north does not live up to its name. This deconstruction (and defamiliarisation) of the north and its self-attributed significances and values completes the dismantling of the north–south divide initiated earlier in the text, and poses a challenge to Eurocentric views of the world and its current order.

The final pages of 'Solo Andata' compellingly locate migrant narratives in a broader postcolonial context and firmly insert human displacement within a global framework of interlinked cultural, geographical and political realities. Addressing the north, the chorus on the boat says 'our lives will be your adventure books' (De Luca 2005: 35); unequal distribution of mobility is taken even further when the hardships of the *wretched of the earth* can be consumed and diminished by the privileged few as entertainment. This line also situates contemporary migration in relation to colonial legacies and subtly strikes at the politics of cultural appropriation and (mis-)representation which typify centuries of Western literature narrativising otherness.

Notes

1. In this chapter I use the word 'migrant' as a general term; the word is used non-specifically in order to include a large population with diverse circumstances, such as asylum seekers, refugees, regular and irregular migrants. The term is purposefully inclusive and it also seeks not to reproduce legal categories (e.g. refugee) which differentiate people according to their status.
2. The infamous 3 October 2013 shipwreck – which allegedly signalled the beginning of what we know as the current 'refugee crisis' – brought this tiny island to international attention; the April 2015 shipwreck alone had an estimated death toll of 800.
3. All translations from De Luca's original Italian text are my own.
4. See Palladino and Woolley's (2018) discussion of humanitarianism and colonial legacies in relation to the 2014 Lampedusa commemorative plaque.
5. These lines resonate with many texts in the history of literature where experiences of isolation and imprisonment on an island are narrativised; Defoe's Crusoe

comes to mind: 'I was a Prisoner lock'd up with the Eternal Bars and Bolts of the Ocean' (Defoe 1998: 113).

6. See European Commission papers: 'As part of the immediate action to assist frontline Member States which are facing disproportionate migratory pressures at the EU's external borders, in the European Agenda on Migration presented in May, the European Commission proposed to develop a new Hotspot approach': https://ec.europa.eu/home-affairs/sites/homeaffairs/files/what-we-do/policies/european-agenda-migration/background-information/docs/2_hotspots_en.pdf (accessed 14 May 2019).

7. Garelli and Tazzioli explain as follows: 'as part of the identification process, migrants receive an Italian Home Office questionnaire bearing the question, "What is the reason for your being in Italy?" with four options to choose from: "poverty", "family reunification", "work", or "other reasons". War and persecution are not explicitly listed options and have to fall under the rubric "other", an odd bureaucratic choice for a form meant to discern refugees from economic migrants. Migrants we interviewed in Lampedusa in December 2015 and February 2016 and migrant rights associations report that the Italian police ordinarily filled in the document in their place. After the questionnaire step, migrants are held in the hotspot for a variable period of time, usually far beyond the 72 hours established by law, before being transferred to Sicily' (2016).

8. Harvest is a recurring idea in De Luca's writing in relation to the contemporary migratory phenomenon. This quotation is from an editorial entitled 'Harvesting' that De Luca wrote for the magazine *Emergency* (June 2016) of the NGO EMERGENCY, which provides medical care to victims of war, and rescue and relief for migrants in the Mediterranean. In this editorial he recalls the famous painting *Liberty Leading the People* by Eugene Delacroix, which glorifies the failed 1830 Revolution. At the time, Delacroix was concerned with 'the modern subject'. For him, it was the barricade – also a symbol of the revolution. De Luca, for whom the modern subject is a boat adrift at sea, draws on Delacroix's reflections. As depicted in Massimo Sestini's famous photograph, the drifting boat is a barricade at sea. This image echoes Malkki's discussion about photographs of mass displacement of refugees: '[b]lack bodies are pressed together impossibly close in a confusing, frantic mass. An utter human uniformity is hammered into the viewer's retina. This is a spectacle of "raw", "bare" humanity' (Malkki 1996: 387). The presence of this 'bare' humanity interrogates viewers and poses challenging questions about our contemporaneity.

9. See my discussion about morality in relation to treatment of refugees in Palladino (2017).

10. Hotspots are symptomatic of policies and practices enacted well before 2015, when they were officially instated.

11. Such as the award-winning Italian photographer Massimo Sestini's famous 2015 image of a boat packed with migrants off the Libyan coast taken from a helicopter.

12. The presence of smugglers often marks a clear separation between those who are in control, being armed and fewer in number but occupying more space, and all the others, the passengers, whose lives are at their mercy.

Bibliography

Agamben, G. (1997), 'The camp as the nomos of the modern', in H. de Vries and S. Weber (eds), *Violence, Identity, and Self-Determination* (Stanford: Stanford University Press), 106–18.

Anderson, B. (2000), *Doing the Dirty Work: The Global Politics of Domestic Labour* (London: Zed Books).

Andrijasevic, R. (2010), 'From exception to excess: detention and deportations across the Mediterranean space', in Nicholas De Genova and Nathalie Peutz (eds), *The Deportation Regime: Sovereignty, Space, and the Freedom of Movement* (Durham, NC: Duke University Press), 147–65.

Ashcroft, B., G. Griffiths and H. Tiffin (1989), *The Empire Writes Back: Theory and Practice in Post-Colonial Literatures* (London: Routledge).

Bakewell, O. (2014), 'Encampment and self-settlement', in E. Fiddian-Qasmiyeh, G. Loescher K. Long and N. Sigona (eds), *The Oxford Handbook of Refugee and Forced Migration Studies* (Oxford: Oxford University Press), 127–38.

Bernardie-Tahir, N., and C. Schmoll (2014), 'Islands and undesirables: introduction to the special issue on irregular migration in southern European islands', *Journal of Immigrant and Refugee Studies*, 12.2: 87–102.

Bernardot, M. (2008), *Camps d'étrangers* (Paris: Éditions du Croquant).

Boatcă, M. (2015), *Global Inequalities Beyond Occidentalism* (Farnham: Ashgate).

Chambers, I. (2008), *Mediterranean Crossings* (Durham, NC: Duke University Press).

Chambers, I. (2010), 'Maritime criticism and theoretical shipwrecks', *PMLA*, 125.3: 678–84.

Chambers, I. (2011), 'Race, modernity and the challenge of democracy', *Third Text*, 25:3: 251–6.

Chambers, I. (2013), 'Borders and beyond: reading in the margins of Ash Amin's *Land of Strangers*', *Identities*, 20.1: 9–17.

Cuttitta, P. (2012), *Lo spettacolo del confine. Lampedusa tra produzione e messa in scena della frontiera* (Milan: Mimesis).

Cuttitta, P. (2014), '"Borderizing" the island setting and narratives of the Lampedusa "border play"', *ACME: An International E-Journal for Critical Geographies*, 13.2: 196–219.

Darling, J. (2009), 'Becoming bare life: asylum, hospitality, and the politics of encampment', *Environment and Planning D: Society and Space*, 27.4: 649–65.

Darling, J. (2010), 'A city of sanctuary: the relational re-imagining of Sheffield's asylum politics', *Transactions of the Institute of British Geographers*, 35.1: 125–40.

Darling, J. (2014), 'From hospitality to presence', *Peace Review*, 26.2: 162–9.

De Luca, E. (2005), *Solo Andata* (Milan: Feltrinelli).

De Luca, E. (2016), 'Raccogliere', *Emergency*, 79: 1.

Defoe, D. (1998 [1719]) *Robinson Crusoe* (Oxford: Oxford University Press).

Ehrenreich, B., and A. Hochschild (eds) (2003), *Global Woman: Nannies, Maids, and Sex Workers in the New Economy* (New York: Metropolitan Books).

European Database of Asylum Law (EDAL) (2017), 'Hotspots under a spotlight: the legality of the hotspot approach in Italy', 26 June, http://www.asylumlaw-database.eu/en/journal/hotspots-under-spotlight-legality-hotspot-approach-italy (accessed 14 May 2019).

Fassin, D., et al. (1997), *Les lois de l'inhospitalité: les politiques de l'immigration à l'épreuve des sans-papiers* (Paris: la Découverte).

Friese, H. (2012), 'Border economies: Lampedusa and the nascent migration industry', *Shima: The International Journal of Research into Island Cultures*, 6.2: 66–84.

Gallo, E., and F. Scrinzi (2016), *Migration, Masculinities and Reproductive Labour: Men of the Home* (Basingstoke: Palgrave Macmillan).

Garelli, G., and M. Tazzioli (2016), 'The EU hotspot approach at Lampedusa', *openDemocracy*, 26 February, https://www.opendemocracy.net/can-europe-make-it/glenda-garelli-martina-tazzioli/eu-hotspot-approach-at-lampedusa (accessed 14 May 2019).

Gregory, D. (2004), *The Colonial Present: Afghanistan, Palestine, Iraq* (Oxford: Blackwell).

Harley, J. B. (1988), 'Maps, knowledge and power', in D. E. Cosgrove and S. Daniels (eds), *The Iconography of Landscape: Essays on the Symbolic Representation, Design, and Use of Past Environments* (Cambridge: Cambridge University Press), 277–312.

Harrell-Bond, B. (1998), 'Camps: literature review', *Forced Migration Review*, 6: 22–3.

Howard, D. (2010), 'Cartographies and visualization', in S. Chew et al. (eds), *A Concise Companion to Postcolonial Literature* (Oxford: Wiley-Blackwell), 141–61.

Isin, E., and K. Rygiel (2007), 'Abject spaces: frontiers, zones, camps', in E. Dauphinee and C. Masters (eds), *The Logics of Biopower and the War on Terror: Living, Dying, Surviving* (New York: Palgrave Macmillan), 181–204.

Jacobs, J. M. (1993), '"Shake 'im this country": the mapping of the Aboriginal sacred in Australia – the case of Coronation Hill', in Peter Jackson and Jan Penrose (eds), *Constructions of Race, Place and Nation* (London: University College of London Press), 100–18.

Kaiser, T. (2006), 'Between a camp and a hard place: rights, livelihood and experiences of the local settlement system for long-term refugees in Uganda', *Journal of Modern African Studies*, 44.4: 597–621.

Le Cour Grandmaison, O., G. Lhuilier and J. Valluy (eds) (2007), *Le Retour des Camps? Sangatte, Lampedusa, Guantanamo* (Paris: Autrement).

Lemaire, L. (2014), 'Islands and a carceral environment: Maltese policy in terms of irregular migration', *Journal of Immigrant and Refugee Studies*, 12.2: 143–60.

McConnachie, K. (2014), *Governing Refugees: Justice, Order and Legal Pluralism* (Abingdon: Routledge).

McConnachie, K. (2016), 'Camps of containment: a genealogy of the refugee camp', *Humanity: an international journal of human rights, humanitarianism and development*, 7.3: 397–412.

McCulloch, J. (2007), 'Christmas Island detention centre', paper presented at the sixth 'Sisters Inside Conference', Sydney, 30 June, www.sistersinside.com.au/media/conference2007/JudeMccullock.doc (accessed 31 October 2017).

Malkki, L. H. (1996), 'Speechless emissaries: refugees, humanitarianism, and dehistoricization', *Cultural Anthropology*, 11.3: 377–404.

Méndez, Á. (2017), 'Global governance in foreign policy', in C. Thies (ed.), *Oxford Research Encyclopedia of Foreign Policy Analysis* (Oxford: Oxford University Press), DOI:10.1093/acrefore/9780190228637.013.369.

Morrison, T. (1989), 'Unspeakable things unspoken: the Afro-American presence in American literature', *Michigan Quarterly Review*, 28.1: 1–34.

Mountz, A. (2011), 'The enforcement archipelago: detention, haunting, and asylum on islands', *Political Geography*, 30.3: 118–28.

Mountz, A., and L. Briskman (2012), 'Introducing island detentions: the placement of asylum seekers and migrants on islands', *Shima: The International Journal of Research into Island Cultures*, 6.2: 21–6.

Nethery, A. (2012), 'Separate and invisible: a carceral history of Australian islands', *Shima: The International Journal of Research into Island Cultures*, 6.2: 85–98.

Palladino, M. (2017), 'Violent evictions of refugees in Rome reveal inhumanity of modern democracy', *The Conversation*, 30 August, https://theconversation.com/violent-evictions-of-refugees-in-rome-reveal-inhumanity-of-modern-democracy-83062 (accessed 23 May 2019).

Palladino, M., and A. Woolley (2018), 'Migration, humanitarianism, and the politics of salvation', *Lit: Literature Interpretation Theory*, 29.2: 129–44.

Phelps, J. (2017), 'Why is so much art about the "refugee crisis" so bad?', *Open-Democracy*, 11 May, https://www.opendemocracy.net/5050/jerome-phelps/refugee-crisis-art-weiwei (accessed 31 October 2017).

Piper, K. L. (2002), *Cartographic Fictions: Maps, Race, and Identity* (New Brunswick, NJ: Rutgers University Press).

Pugliese J. (2002), 'Penal asylum: refugees, ethics, hospitality', *Borderlands*, 1.1: 1–8.

Pugliese J. (2010), *Transmediterranean: Diasporas, Histories, Geopolitical Spaces* (Brussels: Peter Lang).

Rigg, J. (2007), *An Everyday Geography of the Global South* (London: Routledge).

Rosello, M. (2002), 'European hospitality without a home', *Studies in 20th Century Literature*, 26.1: 172–93.

Rygiel, K. (2011), 'Bordering solidarities: migrant activism and the politics of movement and camps at Calais', *Citizenship Studies*, 15.1: 1–19.

Said, E. (1993), *Culture and Imperialism* (New York: Vintage).

Shire, W. (2011), *Teaching My Mother How To Give Birth* (London: MouthMark).

Sparke, M. (2007), 'Everywhere but always somewhere: critical geographies of the Global South', *The Global South*, 1.1: 117–26.

Squire, V. (2011), 'From community cohesion to mobile solidarities: the City of Sanctuary network and the Strangers into Citizens campaign', *Political Studies*, 59.2: 290–307.

Ticktin, M. (2005), 'Policing and humanitarianism in France: immigration and the turn to law as state of exception', *Interventions*, 7.3: 346–68.

Chapter 21

At Sea: Hope as Survival and Sustenance for Refugees

Parvati Nair

'I am in the middle of the sea. . .' (Galarraga Gortázar 2018)[1]

Late one night in the early summer of 2001, Samir[2] stepped into a small wooden boat off the northern coast of Morocco, his heart in his mouth, and surrendered his life to destiny. The twenty or so others who joined him on his voyage could barely fit inside. An Algerian by birth, he had left for reasons that were political as much as economic and was now seeking a route to France via Spain. He had spent over twenty months in Morocco, working as a day labourer in fields, often sleeping in the open, waiting for this moment of crossing over into Europe. As the smuggler's employee started up the noisy petrol engine and the boat set sail, he looked down at the water lashing the sides of the boat and spraying him, and then up at the night sky above. 'Kismet', he said to me, as he recounted his experience of being at sea, using the Arabic word for fate.

> Everywhere, everything was dark. The water was dark and furious. The sky was dark and furious too. I swallowed sea water. That is all I remember. Nothing else. Just the taste of the salt. And the shouts of people who were scared. Maybe I was shouting too. I cannot remember how long it took. Just the salt. That is all.

The mass movements of displaced persons in the Mediterranean region, sharply exacerbated in recent years by conflict in Syria, and fraught with the risks entailed in undertaking undocumented migration, have led to frequently repeated and dramatic media coverage of flimsy, unprotected boats carrying numerous persons. This reiterated image of refugees at sea has, in recent years, become entrenched in the global imaginary as synonymous with displacement at large. In turn, this trope extends and reinforces historically constructed perceptions of the problematic of human displacement, with the image of humans at sea being symbolic of humanitarian crisis more widely.

Throughout the twentieth and twenty-first centuries, there have been many examples of such refugees: Vietnamese boat people in the late 1960s who were fleeing conflict; migrants from Africa and elsewhere in the Global South who attempt crossings of the Mediterranean; the situation of Sri Lankans and others who are on boats off the coast of Australia before being sent to Nauru Island; Cubans who have sought exile in the United States via illicit crossings on flimsy boats; and many more.

In all such instances, the representation of refugees at sea is dramatic, its force deriving from the clash of dire human insecurity with the political priority afforded to border controls and sovereignty. Inevitably, the people concerned are portrayed as victims, trapped in crisis and facing grave risks. For example, June 2018 will remain in collective memory as the month when 629 people, rescued from boats that had left Libya in the hope of reaching Italy, remained aboard the *Aquarius* as it floated for several days in European waters in the Mediterranean, in search of a European state willing to offer moorings. While a new right-wing government in Italy and the existing government in France closed borders, a new socialist government in Spain offered 'sanctuary' by way of a political statement. As the drama unfolded, images abounded of the 629 people, some very ill, some pregnant, some bearing serious burns from the petroleum in the dinghies that they had been rescued from, all without doubt exhausted, thirsty and undernourished, waiting. Their predicament spoke of humanitarian crisis, reflecting back on a dire lack of regional and global responsibility.

The story of the *Aquarius* shed light on a range of interconnected issues and dynamics relating to debates on refugees. First, regardless of the triggers that had driven the 629 people on board to set sail, or indeed to have been in Libya in the first place, their plight at sea confirmed that the legal and political distinctions that frame 'refugees' as a collective apart from 'migrants' (or even, to use the increasingly common phrase, 'economic migrants') have become seriously blurred. Once at sea in such dangerous conditions, people, whatever their migratory motivations or contexts, are in need of refuge. Quite simply, they are at sea and caught on the border between life and death. Until they are on shore, they remain 'refugees' – boat people, with all the attendant dangers, hardships and uncertainties that remaining indefinitely at sea entails (Cargill and Quang Huynh 2000). Secondly, the political reverberations set off by the *Aquarius* and its passengers were numerous and divergent, confirming the fact that the topic of 'people at sea' detonates major political fault lines across the European spectrum, raising the fundamental question of the stability of the EU and highlighting the lack of cooperation between states.

Furthermore, life and death stories of rescue at sea, as witnessed aboard the *Aquarius*, with attendant images of large numbers of people on boats, often wearing bright-coloured life jackets, often sitting in cramped conditions with no shelter from the elements, if not floating desperately in the water after having capsized, have become the norm for how displacement is relayed by both social and mainstream media. The displaced at sea are 'others', physically and socially removed. Adrift, they are also passive. These images and their frequent repetition in the press shape how this mass phenomenon of displacement is imagined and perceived by the mainstream. The images repeat such displacement as that of 'others'.

Beyond doubt, to embark on an illicit crossing without documentation and often in the hands of smugglers is an extreme step, one that is taken only by those with no safer, more dignified alternative. The reasons are many: global inequalities between Africa and Europe, conflict as in Syria, political oppression as in Eritrea, or climate change as in so many regions of the world. To take to the sea is almost always to seek a way forward when other paths are closed. To quote the Somali-British poet Warsan Shire, 'No one puts their children in a boat unless the water is safer than the land' (Shire 2015). This is surely true. What we find, then, is that the act of despair involved in being at sea is also one final act of hope, that of risking all in the attempt to attain a better life on the other shore. This act is inevitably undertaken only by those to whom the borders of Europe and other hegemonic parts of the world would otherwise be closed. Many border policies have of late become so stringent that travel supported by due documentation has become a privilege for the global élite. As such, and within what is a very clear frame of displacement, disempowerment and despair, the image of refuge at sea offers, fundamentally, a narrative of hope.

This chapter focuses on the idea of hope that underlies the migratory act and that orients refugees and migrants alike, assisting them in negotiating very uncertain and risky political and socio-economic terrains. Assessing this representation of refugees at sea from diverse causal angles – that of the cultural history of images of people, boats and voyages at sea, as well as the drivers that propel people to cross international borders in this way – I shall engage with the persistence of hope as the bedrock from which courage, tenacity and determination arise. My aim is to contest the rhetoric of passivity inherent to conventional readings of this visual trope of refugees. My claim in this chapter is that this human struggle for a better life would not be possible without a basic fundament of hope. I argue that mainstream perceptions of refugees at sea as elements of humanitarian crisis are only partially apt, coloured as they are by a long history of narratives that associate the sea with danger and mortality. In turn, this predominant discourse leads to refugees at sea being perceived as victims in need of rescue. In this chapter, I would like to deepen this reading, so as to unpack the visual rhetoric of refugees at sea more fully and reveal the mixed nature of crisis at sea (and on land), whereby hope becomes inextricable from its opposite – despair – in the same paradoxical way in which life and death become entangled at sea. Despite the extreme despair that accompanies the 'crisis' of migration, and also because of it, hope functions as a vital strategy of survival, orientation and empowerment for those with little else left. Hope acts as the source of agency in contexts that overwhelmingly disempower and displace individuals and communities.

A visual rhetoric is well established, one that repeats images of boatloads of anonymous people – the now familiar trope of illicit and risky crossings, of thousands upon thousands of people, quite literally, at sea. The causes are numerous and diverse: conflict, poverty, political oppression or the simple, but compelling, dream of a better life elsewhere. These images therefore confirm a reality that is strangely paradoxical, because it is one that conflates crisis and hope. I shall probe beyond the stereotype of refugees as merely victims, caught in a deadly struggle for survival, to seek out the engagement with risk and the practice of resilience involved in such efforts, both sustained by hope. As such, my argument is that precarious conditions of life force individuals and collectives into uncertainties, invisibility and dangers, within which acts of hope abound as everyday strategies of empowerment against oblivion and obliteration. I further claim that the recognition of this hope is a vital step in dignifying migrants and refugees alike and in ensuring their inclusion in the places and societies that they go to.

This proposed analysis of hope as a key aspect of the refugee experience is based on an interdisciplinary analysis. I draw on the cultural history of the discourse of people at sea and the perceptions that frame this idea, because the refugee at sea is, in very obvious ways, the one whose life is on the line, that is, the refugee most in need of refuge. As such, I argue that this extreme form of dislocation is also, in less visible ways, the most extreme act of hope – that of a better life on the other shore. I refer as well as to studies of hope, most especially the work of Adrienne Martin on the psychology of hope (Martin 2015). Through this conceptual nexus, I shall highlight the ways in which hope emerges most forcefully in critical contexts of individual and collective precarity, so as to highlight the inherent agency of life that becomes most apparent when faced with possible death.

Displacement and visualising the refugee

Displacement has long featured in visual documentary. Early photography was concerned with the idea of bearing witness to reality. As a result, many images focused on life at the margins, thus helping to shape perspectives of the displaced. As with all representations, visual means sought, and still seek, to persuade as much as to inform, so that the visual narrative emerging from images of refugees at sea is, inevitably, weighted historically with ideology. Any readings of this framing must therefore balance the historical connotations of such images with the contextual ones that lend meaning and contingency to each one.

To cite Hill and Helmers (2004), the visual is anchored upon both a psychology and a politics, which must be borne in mind when images are studied. Every new image of refugees at sea forms part of a global archive of such images, one that has proliferated in recent years with the 'crisis' of the displaced in and around the Mediterranean. The invisible filter of the archive that we mentally associate with images can foreground some aspects of an image or some readings of it to the detriment of others. In the case of images of refugees at sea, I argue that too often the images are 'read' through the lens of the nation-state, whereby the priorities of citizenship, nationhood and belonging marginalise refugees as 'others'. These images are viewed through the lens of a political stability made possible by citizenship and belonging. Refugees appear politically driven, yet politically passive, because their conditions, contexts and contingencies are those determined by the very centrality of the viewer. This contrast is all the more stark for the implicit opposition of land and sea, mapped territory and fluid waters, collective self and collective other. Binary oppositions lead to limited perspectives, which remain blind to the contested, complex and inevitably connected nature of refugee contexts. Such a reading fails to take into account the fuller context of those who take to sea or their aspirations. It also neglects the extremely complex ways in which despair and hope are entangled in human endeavour at the margins of legality and political rights, rendering the idea of the refugee two-dimensional as one in need of shelter, rather than acknowledging the rounder personhood of the refugee that is as powerful and as valid as that of any legally acknowledged citizen. The connotations of sea versus land help to reinforce this idea of instability, risk and despair that ultimately colours the ways in which the displaced often become regarded in societies of relocation. One wonders, then, at what point a refugee may cease to be seen as such and can find inclusion in terms of citizenship predicated on commonality rather than difference?

At sea

The sea has long been associated in the collective imaginary of the West with voyages, forced or otherwise, questions of finding moorings and the experience of uncertainty. Water, as waves, surges, floods and currents, is a long-standing metaphor for life's greater fluidities, often viewed in contrast to land, which is stable, sure and mapped. The Mediterranean, for example, was often perceived as dangerous, despite the great natural beauty of this region. As Ruiz states in his book *The Western Mediterranean and the World: 400 CE to the Present* (2017), Scylla and Charybdis, two sea monsters that guarded the Straits of Gibraltar where Africa and Europe are at their physically closest points, were metaphors for the dangers of crossing. As such, the image of those in boats mid-ocean inevitably speaks of risk and potential loss of life.

The metaphoric power of the sea abounds in many languages. 'At sea. . .' the phrase, often used unthinkingly in the English language, conjures up several ideas: those of being lost, or in danger of getting lost, of water and flooding, and of nautical or other types of disorientation. To be at sea is to be not on land. The contrast is implicit, but stark: fluid, fraught with risk, and engulfing as opposed to solid, stable and charted. A nautical phrase, its first literary use refers metaphorically to confusion, both real and metaphorical, as experienced by the traveller transiting unknown terrain (Selous 1893).[3]

The Judaeo-Christian imaginary has also been shaped by biblical narratives, such as those of Noah's Ark, constructed around the ideas of inundation, boats and survival (Finkel 2014). Of course, while Noah was seeking survival, he was also chosen to be a survivor, with the divinely bestowed power to include in his ark the male and female of all selected species, so as to ensure procreation after the flood. As such, the narrative of Noah's Ark is, fundamentally, one of hope and projection towards the future as much as it is of fear, crisis, loss and rescue.

The collective Western imaginary is also marked by narratives from the Classical period, such as Homer's *Odyssey*, whereby sea voyages become quests for home, symbolic of longing and struggle. The condition of being at sea is perceived as arduous, fraught with risk. This idea of 'odyssey' persists in the contemporary global imaginary not as a process, but as the framing condition of the refugee. Take, for example, the title of Patrick Kingsley's book, *The New Odyssey: The Story of Europe's Refugee Crisis* (2016), which tracks the journey of a Syrian from Egypt to Sweden. Both the use of the word 'odyssey' and the idea of 'Europe's refugee crisis' are media-friendly terms that do not fully inform. The Syrians' struggles could have been ameliorated had European countries actually engaged better and in a more coordinated fashion with crisis in Syria and its humanitarian repercussions. Nevertheless, the term 'odyssey' triggers in readers an expectation of prolonged drama, as in the classic stories of quest. There is thus an interminability associated with the idea of refugees at sea, because it is as if they were suspended in a spatio-temporal interstice between life and death. Such a reading frames refugees at sea in terms of suspension in a hiatus between shores. Indeed, the sea, in contrast to the land, is a liminal space, so that the repeated image of refugees at sea is one of both border crossing – in this case, that from shore to shore, with the sea as a border to the land – and that of liminal existence, the lives, experience and circumstances of those who seek to move from dislocation to location and who, while at sea, remain on the fine line that separates the certain from the uncertain.

Voyages of hope

My informant Samir never made it to Paris, the destination he had in mind when he set sail. Instead, he found a new life in Barcelona, after having spent over a year at an immigrant reception centre. Speaking of his crossing of the Mediterranean on the boat, he said, 'it was a night of darkness, a night of hope. Hope for the new life I make here in this country.'[4]

Hope, mixed up as it is with fear, dread and anxiety, can be hard to discern. In 2017 the MS Amlin World Art Vote Prize, a national art competition in the United Kingdom, was awarded to Stephen Burgess for his painting entitled *Refugee Rescue*, based on an image taken from an Italian navy helicopter.

When asked about his painting, the artist stated that it 'signifies the small degree of hope that hopefully exists in us all'.[5] Burgess's statement is notable for identifying that glimmer that sustains the risk-filled voyage of so many. Indeed, the image captures that moment of hope as it breaks out collectively from despair: the group of people at sea look up at the helicopter from within which they are being photographed, realising that they have been spotted and that rescue is at hand. The crowded boat is full of an anonymous collective, but the image is singularly one of all heads raised, eyes expectant with the hope of rescue. The image may or may not be one of asylum seekers (the political blur in which people at sea are denoted extends to a discursive blur that conflates migrants, refugees and asylum seekers in common parlance), but it is certainly one of people framed at a hopeful moment. Most importantly, this spark of hope must be acknowledged because it is what connect us, as viewers of the artwork and/or of the image taken by the Italian navy, or as those who are settled with rights and papers, safely 'on land' in our citizenship, who form members of 'host' communities that receive migrants and refugees, with the subjects of the image: as fellow humans, we share hope as a life-sustaining force. This commonality is the ground from which relation, dignity, recognition and respect, as opposed to otherness, hostility and xenophobia, can emerge to ensure justice (Nair 2012).

The photograph by the Italian navy tallies closely to Burgess's painting. Nevertheless, what makes the artwork distinct and important is the identification of hope as the heartbeat that lifts the heads of all those in the boat as they see the helicopter overhead. The moment of rescue has arrived, and with it, the flash of hope. Burgess foregrounds this sentiment over the despair that led the many people in the boat to where they are now. In so doing, this artwork exemplifies the crucial distinction between mainstream and repeated media representations of refugees, on the one hand, and exceptional, if occasional, artistic engagement on the other. By highlighting the idea of hope, Burgess successfully aligns the aesthetic with the affective. In turn, this alignment leads to a revised ethics of vision, whereby the figure of the refugee is framed in terms of hope, that is, a positive narrative that connects her or him to the viewer. The limitations of media representations, prone to repeated sensationalism in refugee contexts, often mean that hope, indeed humanity, is too often stripped away. Instead, artwork, as seen here, brings to light the fact of hope as a connecting vector between opposites: refugee and citizen, subject and viewer.

Established readings of images of refugees at sea fail to include this narrative of hope that accompanies the refugee quest for social and political inclusion, framing them solely in terms of victimhood. Mainstream media repeatedly disseminate news of either rescues at sea or else lives lost. At best, such news is responded to by minutes of silence from politicians or the construction of graves and mortuaries for bodies found at sea.[6] Too often, it has become a matter of everyday news, sidelined and ignored, even if tragic. When images relay the arrival on shore of refugees, there is little beyond the drama of landing. The media often fails to follow up on the long story of those who make the crossings, thus making it difficult to dislodge the image of refugees at sea from their disconnection from land, nations, states and cities. This representation leaves little room for recognising the agency of the human or the potential that refugees and migrants can bring with them. As Cynthia Cockburn reveals in the course of her book *Looking to London* (2017), London is a city whose social and economic fabric is maintained and developed by layers upon layers of new arrivals from around the world. If London is a global city, then this is so because of the many diverse communities whose home it is. Refugees, migrants and asylum seekers make significant contributions to the social, cultural and political fabric of many urban neighbourhoods and centres. Yet the mainstream view of refugees is that they are, somehow, perpetually 'at sea'.

This limited perspective embeds the very idea of refuge at best in terms of charity, philanthropy or gift, that is, the granting of welcome to 'others' based on choice by the host country and society, not on justice or responsibility. This slant puts the receiver of charity into a passive position, one that repeats in and through the visual rhetoric of boatloads of migrants and refugees. Philanthropy may be admirable and even necessary in several contexts, but it confirms a power dynamic in favour of those who bestow philanthropic acts on those who are in need of them (Moody and Breeze 2016). As Moody and Breeze state, 'the word "philanthropy" means different things to different people . . . Etymologically, it means "love of humankind", but in practice it is often used to refer to significant donations of money to charitable causes' (2016: xiii). This is an instrumental perspective that conflates love with economics, obscuring questions of ethics, rights, responsibility and justice. In turn, this imbalance frames refugees as victims, in need of charity or philanthropy, thereby reinforcing the dynamics of inequality that both spurs, and is fed by, charity. Furthermore, this material perspective places the human in the dark, reinforcing thereby the anonymity assigned to the refugee subjects of charity, a trend confirmed by the repeated visual trope of large numbers of anonymous people whose life stories, motivations and contexts are never exposed. The givers of charity become celebrities of good causes: the receivers of charity remain nameless and faceless, lost in a collective of the displaced. This imbalance further drives the displaced into more displacement, disempowerment or marginality.

The recognition of hope as a shared human dynamic is important in the effort to address this imbalance and in the struggle to ensure inclusion for the displaced. Rarely does the question of hope feature in the many discourses and narratives on migration. While it is true that many migrants find themselves in circumstances of extreme vulnerability, nevertheless migration often requires a steadfastness of human spirit that can brook no weakness. Regardless of the triggers for their journeys and voyages, a single connecting thread that underpins almost every migratory experience is the question of hope. It is both a vital response and a key factor in sustaining the determination to change circumstance, in mapping the ways forward, in taking up risk and in negotiating conditions that are often unspeakably difficult. Hope, I argue, is much more than mere wish or desire. It is a vital feature of human well-being that remains unrecognised by states and policies. Hope is harnessed to the vision of a better future and, as such, is intrinsically connected to questions of dignity, recognition and human rights. While connected to, and inevitably shaped by, the ideological framework that drives migration and displacement – such as the hope of rescue, in the instance cited above – hope is also the politically charged bedrock from which humanistic priorities challenge the status quo in hegemonic discourses on migration in which humanitarian concerns often become sidelined in favour of data, economic concerns and political priorities of states. Almost without exception, when people either choose or are forced to migrate, they go in search of a better life elsewhere. This search, the quintessential migrant desire for empowerment and betterment, can only be directed and maintained by this dream of a better life – in other words, by hope (Davis 2011).

Hope as agency

Hope must be considered as a central modality of agency in contexts of migrancy. Beyond the stereotype of crisis and victimhood that accompanies the image of the refugee at sea, we must acknowledge that hope is most vital in contexts of humanitarian crisis and displacement. As such, there is a direct correlation between disaster, conflict, crisis and risk, on the one hand, and hope as a means, not solely of survival, but also as a means beyond such contexts, on the other. Hope sustains the displaced as they navigate fragile or uncertain terrain. This is amply in evidence across the globe, but can best be analysed in terms of a wide and inextricably interwoven diversity of triggers, contexts and aspirations at the all-too-often deadly border zone of Global South and North, where migration, as lived experience and as policy or border practice, reaches an unparalleled pitch. Refugees at sea exemplify this liminal experience of being neither here nor there. Recognising the centrality of hope to migrant endeavours is fundamental, precisely because this brings into focus the frequently sidelined issue of human rights for the displaced. As such, the recognition of hope is a key humanitarian step in working towards the implementation of human rights in the legal and political frames accorded to refugees and migrants.

Surprisingly, hope is vastly understudied. In actual fact, however, and despite it not being a major area of academic study in and of itself, hope repeatedly appears across geographical and historical periods as a base condition of the living. Too often, hope becomes subsumed in other, related areas of study, such as ideas of utopia or optimism. The literature on hope goes back in time, and can be found across cultures and religions, from ancient Hindu texts to Greek philosophy. In Greek mythology, Elpis, personification of hope, was the last to remain in Pandora's box. To quote Hesiod from his poem 'Works and Days', 'only hope was left within her unbreakable house' (Verdenius 1971: 66). The metaphorical significance for those who are displaced of hope remaining secure within an 'unbreakable house' remains stronger than ever today, as the numbers of those leaving home mounts in and around the Mediterranean and elsewhere. For those who have left home and now seek home in a new place, and especially for those without documentation, hope is the unbreakable 'home' or source of determination that allows them to orient and navigate the risks that threaten to otherwise engulf them.

The religions of the Book have, of course, focused in sustained ways on the idea of hope. In the Christian theological canvas, it has been framed as one of a trilogy of virtues: faith, hope and charity. Described as an anchor of the soul in the New Testament, it has been traditionally linked to faith in Christ and in redemption. This relegation of hope to theological or religious discourse is confirmed also by the casual ways in which hope is spoken about in the everyday, as a given, loosely attached to anything that one desires, irrespective of the intensity, or lack thereof, of that desire or aspiration. Devoid of gradation or nuance, decontextualised through the abstraction of theology that assigns to it a timelessness, and beclouded by the unthought iteration of proverbs such as 'hope springs eternal in the human breast' (drawn, as it happens, from Alexander Pope's poem *An Essay on Man* of 1733–34), hope remains largely ignored or, at best, taken for granted. Ironically, Pope's poem was in fact crucial in disengaging hope from timelessness. In keeping with the early modern focus on rationality in place of faith, *An Essay on Man* confirms humankind's place at the centre of the universe and, within this scheme, hope as a centrifugal force at the heart of humankind.

Surprisingly, this recognition of the centrality of hope to the modern quest, one that resonated with Voltaire's exploration of optimism in *Candide* (1759), lagged well behind the development of other philosophical concepts over the centuries to come. It took the humanitarian crisis of the Second World War for hope to regain critical attention against such a backdrop. Ernst Bloch's three-volume work, *The Principle of Hope* (1954–59), remains today the major inquiry into hope, not as a religious virtue, but as fundamental to the utopian dream that guides modernity. By centring hope in his analysis of how Marxism orients itself to the construction of a better future, Bloch also disengages hope from the abstraction of timelessness and firmly embeds it in history. While Bloch writes extensively on the Marxist idea of utopia, hope is seen as a guiding principle that provides a pathway to a humanistic future. Bloch wrote against the backdrop of his own experience of negotiating the ideological and social impact of the rise of Nazism, migration across the Atlantic and back and relocation in East and then West Germany. With displacement (both personal and more widely experienced) – that 'maelstrom' of modernity that Marshall Berman wrote about in his seminal text on the modern condition *All That is Solid Melts into Air* (1982) – as the backdrop to his exploration of hope, a clear link emerges between migrancy and hope. Several writings on the Holocaust have also since foregrounded the role of hope, leading to a body of scholarship on hope as the sustaining force of life in dire conditions (Frankl 2004). While hope is no doubt a subjective process, and as such a fundamental aspect of the human psyche, I posit the idea here that it also plays a key social function, especially in light of the collective displacements that form a central feature of contemporary global socio-economic and political ideologies and practices.

To cite Martha Nussbaum, 'hope is an important, yet recently neglected, philosophical topic' (endorsement to Martin 2015). Martin asks in her introduction 'How could hope seem to one person an unrealistic vagary and to another a solid anchor in a storm?' (Martin 2015: 3). In her book, Martin argues for a pragmatics of hope. By using what she calls a 'syndrome analysis', Martin teases out the rich gamut of elements, such as thought and imagination, as well as the fact that hope can sometimes be only a partial aspect of a larger whole, whereby it goes unrecognised, in order to construct the idea of 'contingent sustenance' (Martin 2015: 3). By this, she means that hope functions within contexts, but it is also that which allows certain contexts to be sustained and navigated. As such, hope girdles all human endeavour. Interestingly, Martin suggests that hope is lived, that is, the living body is tied to it, for without it the body would cease through suicide.

In this context, I would like to refer to the idea of corporeality. For refugees and migrants who are living life, literally and metaphorically, on the border, trauma, risk and the very real prospect of death or survival are experienced bodily (Nair 2018). In such borderline situations, as in the experience of being at sea, hope is a life force, and thus a performative practice of survival and orientation. As such, hope sustains life when life is most at risk. To consider a representation of refugees at sea and not see the fundament of hope that is at the heart of this image is to only partially see it – and hence to misread it.

Hope and inclusion

Samir, my informant, spent several months at a centre for immigrants without papers before being released due to overcrowding. He then spent over three years as a street vendor, surviving on the scant funds left over after paying off his dues to the network that supplied him with the goods that he sold.

> Everywhere you go, there are people selling things, but nobody asks why they are there. Nobody cares. But we are all the same. We all want the same things. To be safe, to have enough money, to have a home. This is what we all want . . . what we all need. But every day I asked myself. Is this why I crossed the sea? Is this why I kissed death? To live a life where nobody sees me? It is like . . . all that darkness in the sea. It never went away. It stayed with me for many years when I was selling on the street. Even the salt. I could taste it for so long. Sometimes even now. . .[7]

Samir is one of many people who blur the boundaries between refugee and migrant. The streets of many urban centres around the world are populated by vendors, who, as he did, remain unrecognised, politically, economically and socially marginalised. Conventional readings of the image of refugees at sea play an iconic role in furthering the alienation of the displaced and create obstacles to inclusion. If the image were to be read in terms of aspiring humans and the gift of human potential to new places, the idea of the refugee as other would be reshaped. The binary polarities of land and sea, self and other, citizen and refugee all support the legal and financial systems that demarcate citizenship and create political hierarchies of belonging, themselves predicated on the idea of the migrant or a refugee as 'other'.

How the mainstream public views refugees is very much shaped by preexisting, and often unthought, preconceptions, themselves shaped from collective memories and visual histories. Images and artwork are powerful because, in the same way that they can perpetuate stereotypes, they can also subvert them. If Burgess's artwork is notable, then it is because, like the photograph on which it is based, it acknowledges the shared humanity of the subjects and viewers through the idea of hope. In addressing human suffering, inequality and injustice, the recognition of hope, in however despairing a context, is a vital political pathway for welcome and inclusion.

Notes

1. The quote is part of the title of an article written by the journalist Naiara Galarraga Gortázar while aboard the *Aquarius*.
2. Aged 32, resident in Barcelona, interviewed on 9 October 2014. The informant's name has been changed to protect his privacy.
3. https://www.phrases.org.uk/meanings/all-at-sea.html (accessed 23 May 2019).
4. Interview with Samir, 9 October 2014.
5. https://www.standard.co.uk/go/london/arts/refugees-at-sea-painting-showing-small-degree-of-hope-wins-world-art-prize-a3643071.html (accessed 23 May 2019).
6. The 2013 High Level Dialogue on international migration held at the United Nations coincided with more loss of life at Lampedusa; see Longhi (2013).
7. Interview with Samir, 9 October 2014.

Bibliography

Berman, Marshall (1988 [1982]), *All That is Solid Melts into Air* (Harmondsworth: Penguin).
Bloch, Ernst (1995 [1954–59]), *The Principle of Hope*, 3 vols (Cambridge, MA: MIT Press).
Cargill, Mary Terrell, and Jade Quang Huynh (2000), *Voices of Vietnamese Boat People: 19 Narratives of Escape and Survival* (Jefferson, NC: McFarland).

Cockburn, Cynthia (2017), *Looking to London: Stories of War, Escape and Asylum* (London: Pluto Press).

Davis, Graham (2011), *In Search of a Better Life: British and Irish Migration* (Stroud: The History Press).

Finkel, Irving (2014), *The Ark before Noah: Decoding the Story of the Flood* (London: Hodder).

Frankl, Viktor (2004), *Man's Search for Meaning: The Classic Tribute to Hope from the Holocaust* (Sutton: Rider Press).

Galarraga Gortázar, Naiara (2018), 'What am I going to do? I am in the middle of the sea. Could this go on for a month?', *El País*, 12 June, https://elpais.com/elpais/2018/06/12/inenglish/1528789649_594782.html?rel=mas (accessed 8 July 2018).

Hill, Charles, and Marguerite Helmers (2004), *Defining Visual Rhetorics* (London: Routledge).

Homer (2003), *Odyssey*, ed. Dominic Rieu (Harmondsworth: Penguin).

Kingsley, Patrick (2016), *The New Odyssey: The Story of Europe's Refugee Crisis* (London: Guardian Faber Publishing).

Longhi, Vittorio (2013), 'The Lampedusa boat sinking was no accident', *The Guardian*, 4 October, https://www.theguardian.com/commentisfree/2013/oct/04/lampedusa-boat-sinking-no-accident-eu-migrants (accessed 23 May 2019).

Martin, Adrienne M. (2015), *How We Hope: A Moral Psychology* (Princeton: Princeton University Press).

Moody, Michael, and Beth Breeze (eds) (2016), *The Philanthropy Reader* (London: Routledge).

Nair, Parvati (2012), *A Different Light: The Photography of Sebastião Salgado* (Durham, NC: Duke University Press).

Nair, Parvati (2018), 'The razor's edge: image and corporeality at Europe's borders', in Tanya Sheehan (ed.), *Photography and Migration* (London: Routledge), 83–99.

Pope, Alexander (1733–34), 'Essay on Man', https://www.gutenberg.org/files/2428/2428-h/2428-h.htm (accessed 14 May 2019).

Ruiz, Teófilo (2017), *The Western Mediterranean and the World: 400 CE to the Present* (Oxford: John Wiley).

Selous, Frederic Courteney (1893), *Travel and Adventure in South East Africa* (London: Rowland).

Shire, Warsan (2015), 'No one puts their children in a boat unless the water is safer than the land', *Global Citizen*, 7 September, https://www.globalcitizen.org/en/content/no-one-puts-their-children-in-a-boat-unless-the-wa/ (accessed 8 July 2017).

Verdenius, W. J. (1971), 'A hopeless line in Hesiod: Works and Days: 96', *Mnemosyne*, 4th series, 24.3: 225–31.

Voltaire (2006 [1759]), *Candide, or Optimism*, ed. Michael Wood (Harmondsworth: Penguin).

Part VII

Digital Territories

Digital Territories: Introduction

Agnes Woolley

Film artist Richard Mosse's installation *Incoming* – first shown at London's Barbican in 2017 – uses a military-grade thermal-imaging camera to document the journeys of refugees from Syria, Afghanistan, Mali and Senegal. Presented on a series of multi-channel screens, the images narrate their content through the contrast between heat and cold. Now-familiar scenes of boat arrivals, crowded camps and border sites are rendered in shifting monochrome tones, evoking surveillance aesthetics made even more troubling by the subjects' unwitting participation in the project. In its deployment of cutting-edge digital cameras (they can detect humans from a distance of over 30 km), *Incoming* lays bare both the dehumanising and humanising aspects of such technologies. Allowing viewers to see *as* a missile sees, the project displaces the routine use of this technology on to a human viewing subject who is confronted with bodies that, while remaining anonymised, depersonalised and alien, are also made visible through their warm bodily tissue; a reminder that these are living, breathing human beings.

This duality speaks to the contradictory tensions at the heart of developments in digital technology, which pull in multiple directions for refugees and those on the move. The increasing use of data-driven techniques for migration management by both nation-states and humanitarian organisations has resulted in what Btihaj Ajana describes in this volume as the 'datafication of the body'. Tracking apps, smart ID cards and biometric technologies mean that enormous databases are generated from border crossers and put to use in initiatives such as the European Commission's 'hotspot' approach, which channels data into particular locations for the speedy sorting of migrants into legal categories. Yet, as a number of the essays in this section show, many of these same technologies have given refugees an unprecedented ability to connect with others and share information about access to support, quixotic entry policies and safe border-crossing sites. Like Mosse's project, then, this technology is often used against itself to humanise interactions. Digital platforms for social media have also provided new and affirmative opportunities for self-expression and the dissemination of testimony. As Arjun Appadurai (2006) has argued, this means that conventional 'minorities' might increasingly be able to see themselves as part of powerful global majorities.

While offering up distinct refugee imaginaries, these technological developments raise important questions that this section seeks to tackle: what are the varying uses to which biometric data is put? How does refugee-generated digital content inform both activist movements and cultural memory? And what is the lifespan of, and audience for, digitally produced testimony from refugees? As Mary Mitchell discusses in her chapter, one significant use of social media is to communicate with others *in the same position or group*; that is, to affirm affiliative links with shared experiences despite geographic displacement, rather than reaching out to those who may be able to use their cultural and political capital to make a change. The democratic potential of this kind of 'digital storytelling' is undermined, however, by the power dynamics inherent in social media platforms such as Facebook, a far from neutral space. Mitchell notes that '[t]he mediators of the stories are no longer individual storytellers, but the policies and algorithms of social networks that dictate the way in which the story is expressed and communicated'. This means that refugee testimonies are 'both owned and shaped by the platforms on which they exist'.

Also looking at the ways in which digital media might reach out to global constituencies, Dima Saber and Paul Long focus on how refugee imaginaries generated by citizen journalism might be conserved and maintained. Saber and Long take as their examples two projects that collate and archive visual records of the war in Syria and its effects: *Qisetna: Talking Syria* and *SyriaUntold*. Digital technologies enable the production and preservation of these records, but also 'signal their refugee status by virtue of their location in the dislocated geography of online space'. The affective, individual, citizen-led reflections found on *Qisetna* and *SyriaUntold* are contrasted with UNHCR's 'heritage' site, Refugees Media, which offers images and videos of refugees aimed at journalists and researchers. Like Mitchell, Saber and Long offer an important critique of the ways in which images and narratives of refugees circulate in the digital sphere; drawing out the effects of 'vernacular' and interactive modes while analysing the power dynamics inherent in corporate and institutional involvement.

Btihaj Ajana examines a different kind of digitally produced refugee imaginary, one that feeds into the critique of profit-making security and social media corporations offered by other contributors to the section. Pointing to the collusion between humanitarian and national security approaches to refugees' bodies and the data now increasingly being used to track and compile information about them, Ajana argues that all too often both systems reduce the refugee to an object of what F. J. Colman calls 'digital biopolitics'. What appears here, and throughout the section, is the ways in which refugees cross digital territories both as objects to be tracked and traced, and as deeply individualised and autonomous figures who, in making use of new technologies, are empowered not only to cross borders but also to share their stories.

Gillian Whitlock's and Rosanne Kennedy's contribution to the section focuses on the nature of – and audiences for – those stories. Eminent scholars of life narrative, they turn their focus to the ways in which refugees mobilise 'testimonial networks' through technologies that allow them to document, film, record and transmit their experiences, as well as the search for 'adequate witness' to those stories so that they may be heard on their own terms. Their focus is on *The Messenger*, a podcast that documents the testimony of Abdul Aziz Muhamat, indefinitely detained on Manus Island in Papua New Guinea. The title of the podcast refers not only to transmission, but to the mode by which Muhamat's testimony is transmitted: through Messenger apps on his (contraband) phone, which record ambient audio of the camp as well as Muhamat's own commentary. For Whitlock and Kennedy, such portable technological systems 'reformulate the self's relations with affect, time and space', demonstrating how these new 'technologies of the self' offer distinctive modes of testimony.

Through a series of case studies, these essays provide a richly detailed analysis of the ways in which refugee imaginaries are produced within and by digital technologies, exploring the extent to which refugee narratives are determined by the forms and platforms that make them possible. As Mosse's installation shows, we are still grappling with the ambivalent effects of digital territories, which both facilitate and complicate the embodied experience of border crossing.

Bibliography

Appadurai, Arjun (2006), *Fear of Small Numbers: An Essay on the Geography of Anger* (Durham, NC: Duke University Press).

Chapter 22

Networked Narratives: Online Self-Expression from a Palestinian Refugee Camp in Lebanon

Mary Mitchell

The power of expression and self-representation is a basic human function that has largely been denied to the displaced. For the philosopher Hannah Arendt, being deprived of the possibility of 'appearance' before others is to be deprived of reality itself, as 'Nothing could appear, the word "appearance" would make no sense, if recipients of appearances did not exist . . . Nothing and nobody exists in this world whose very being does not presuppose a *spectator*' (Arendt 1981: 19). Presenting oneself to others though narrating one's experience is a vital aspect of identity formation. While there has been a recent shift towards recognising, valuing and providing spaces for refugee voices in academia, journalism and the aid and development sector through first-hand testimonies and storytelling projects,[1] these voices still speak largely within boundaries that are set by the needs and concerns of external actors. An inequality of global resources has hitherto resulted in few opportunities for the displaced to represent themselves in their own words to audiences that transcend geographic, linguistic and cultural borders. Disempowerment and disenfranchisement have eclipsed those at the bottom of the ladder entirely, representing a crisis of voice inherently linked to the reinforcing of neoliberal values (Couldry 2010).

For the displaced, engaging with multiple identities and locations is an everyday experience evolving in a context with few avenues for self-representation and opportunities to intervene in prevailing narratives. Digital storytelling offers a means to address the injustices of misrepresentation and loss of self-representation by enabling refugees – alongside others who suffer from the 'hidden injuries of media power' (Couldry 2001) – to access the tools and distribution networks to share their narratives. This chapter analyses self-representation on Facebook by Palestinian refugees in Lebanon, and chooses a wide definition of digital storytelling as 'the whole range of personal stories now being told in potentially public form using digital media resources' (Couldry 2008: 42). In understanding digital storytelling broadly the discussion moves beyond textual analysis to consider the social effects of these stories and the ways in which they are told.

This chapter draws on my research conducted in the Palestinian refugee camp of Rashidieh in Lebanon. The creation of Israel in 1948 created almost 750,000 Palestinian refugees who lost their homes and livelihoods, and were expelled or fled to the West Bank and Gaza Strip as well as the neighbouring countries of Egypt, Jordan, Syria and Lebanon. The descendants of the 104,000 who crossed into Lebanon in 1947–49 (Sayigh 2013: 100) now number over 450,000, living in informal settlements and refugee camps managed by the United Nations Relief and Works Agency (UNRWA), the UN body established in the wake of the Palestinian refugee crisis. Rashidieh camp is one of twelve in Lebanon, hosting around 30,000 refugees ten miles from the border with Israel. The starting point for my research was a desire to understand how individuals were narrating their lives online and how different processes of media collaboration could result in different modes of listening and engagement. My offline research included developing media projects through a process of action-led research with those physically inhabiting the camp. My online research investigates the acts of self-representation and shared meaning making carried out by the wider online network using digital ethnography. My focus here is on the work of the poet Mohammed Al Assad who I first met ten years ago, and who became my collaborator for the *Humans of Al Rashidiya* (2014) project referenced here. Much of my research about digital self-expression and storytelling in this chapter has been conducted with him, focused on his work. This has enabled a collaborative research process that has given Al Assad control over the representation of his voice throughout.

In the context of one specific refugee community and through the prism of one storyteller and his experiences, my aim here is to elucidate wider debates around the issue of self-representation and social media for refugees. First, the chapter contributes to existing scholarship that shows the ways in which social media have created opportunities for self-expression for refugees that challenge mainstream representations of refugee voices. Second, it explores the co-construction of online narratives by analysing how localised network engagement with content reveals new layers of the refugee experience, with shared acts of remembrance and protest on social media connecting Palestinians in Lebanon with a wider community. This allows them to ground themselves in a national identity that is based in virtual territory. Finally, the chapter turns to the power dynamics of social media platforms such as Facebook, arguing that despite their democratic potential, they are embedded within power structures that are established and enhanced by hegemonic economic and political ideologies designed to include and exclude, and are therefore limited. If the power of 'voice', defined as the effective opportunity for people to speak and be heard on the issues that impact their lives, is the only force that can challenge neoliberalism (Couldry 2010), then the questions this chapter raises are all the more urgent.

Facebook and the potential for self-representation

> Before, Mohammed used to write poems but no one knew about them, now he can publish them online and become famous. (Hussein, 23, Rashidieh camp)

Refugees have consistently been denied the opportunity to speak their own truths and narrate their experiences to wider audiences (Malkki 1996; Turton 2003). Rather than nuanced individual narratives, dominant mainstream media portrayals of the displaced have dismissed refugees' historical, cultural and political circumstances (Wright 2002) and presented them as mass movements, swarms, or floods (Malkki 1996). While alternative narratives about refugees have become more available in liberal and progressive media outlets, the trend of negative or oversimplified depiction remains the norm. In a content analysis of two prominent Australian newspapers from August to December 2001 and October 2009 and September 2011, Bleiker et al. (2013) found that 66 per cent of all images portrayed asylum seekers as medium or large groups and only 2 per cent depicted them with clearly recognisable facial features. In this context, aid and development organisations, individual journalists and public media outlets such as the BBC and Canada's National Film Board have all developed pioneering projects that sit on the periphery of mainstream media and set out to rectify this by facilitating spaces for personal narratives to be told.[2] Projects such as Save the Children's *Inside Za'atari*, which facilitates Syrian teenagers in Za'atari refugee camp in Jordan to take photographs of their experiences and share them on a dedicated Tumblr account, create spaces for refugees to contribute their voices to wider debates about their lives (Save the Children 2014). Through empowering individuals and capturing nuanced stories, such projects have sought to repoliticise and contextualise the refugee experience and to equip grassroots actors constantly subject to outsiders' depictions of their lives to speak their own truths. However, the stories told by individuals through these initiatives are still created within frameworks established and managed by outside agents. Within these projects there are expectations about the type of story that will be told or the outcome that will result, the means by which the story will be told, and the timeframe in which it will take place. For example, if a project is run by an advocacy organisation, the expectation is that the content will lead to a specific advocacy outcome, and participants might not be enabled to create content about their daily life but directed towards topics that lead to the end goal of the project.

Mobile accessibility and connectivity have proven vital as motivators and facilitators of migration as well as enablers of the continuation of relationships within the diaspora. What has been less researched is the impact of mobile technology on self-expression and storytelling. Smartphones and social media have facilitated the taking and sharing of snapshots and videos, making possible a daily reflection on life within a wider network through which new connections can be created. These user-led, often spontaneous representations can be understood as distinct from project-led narratives mediated and owned by the journalists, humanitarian organisations, or film-makers who ideate and initiate them.

Al Assad is a 23-year-old business management and accounting graduate, and third-generation Palestinian refugee living in Rashidieh camp in Lebanon. From March 2015 to 2018 he shared 95 posts on Facebook using the hashtag #Inthecamp (#المخيم في), documenting his reality in Lebanon, and his hopes and dreams of a return to his homeland or escape from his immobility. He posts his poems alongside images he has taken on his iPhone or images or videos he has downloaded from Facebook, finding and creating meaning through the recirculation and distribution of content created and shared previously by others. Writing in *Index on Citizenship* magazine, Al Assad notes that:

> It's difficult to be a child here because there are so few opportunities. You are told to work hard in school, but then you graduate and realise that there are no jobs. We want to bring out the voices of these children and the frustrations of the youth. Although our families have been exiled from our country for nearly 70 years, we will never forget the right to return, and it is our job to communicate our existence to the outside world. (Mitchell and Al Assad 2015: 33)

Al Assad posts to reflect his reality of the camp in the face of stereotypes imposed upon him and his community by both their Lebanese hosts and the wider global community. In an interview I conducted with him in March 2018, Al Assad emphasised this, noting that 'Lebanese people are scared of the camps and call it a *time bomb* (قنبلة موقوتة). These poems challenge them to see the real image, to see that we are outside the image that they have of us and that we real people with dreams and hopes, good people, and not terrorists.'[3] Though his reflections are both personal and political, he is cognisant of his wider audience, and writing under a hashtag is a deliberate act of ensuring that his poems can be found by others: 'I saw some people using it before, once or twice, someone from Gaza used it. When you search using the hashtag you find poems that reflect the suffering. When my friends share my poems they use the hashtag too. Many others have shared it including the website Ya Sour.'[4]

The two most dominant themes in Al Assad's poems are political protest and a sense of confinement as he articulates both the day-to-day monotony and the beauty of camp life. On 13 October 2015 Al Assad uploaded a video he had seen in his Facebook newsfeed alongside a poem commenting on the irony and comedy of war. The origin of the video is unclear. Shot in the Occupied Palestinian Territories and seven seconds long, it shows a protestor mocking security forces with laughter in the background. To caption it he wrote:

> Also in our war there is peace . . .
> In our war there is laughter . . .
> In our war there is fun . . .

In our war there is pleasure . . .
Imagine that we are the caresses of death.
Imagine playing with missiles.
Imagine and imagine and imagine . . .
Imagine you're imagining people like them.
Don't imagine people like me because I've already fallen asleep.
In our war peace does not know peace . . .
In our war peace is drawn with debris . . .
Youth like the prophets have gone
Volcanoes have been left behind
The youth and the angels have celebrated
The Lord loves them and loves their trembling eyes
A child then a prophet and then a martyr . . .
This is how . . .
Thus the Canaanites grow . . .
This is how . . .
The smile keeps our war . . .
We smile for the shells as for life
#uprising
#in the camp
#martyr
#Al Aqsa
#Al Quds
#Mohammed Al Assad (Al Assad 2015a)

Al Assad's post adds his own meaning to a widely circulated video and connects the experience of a Palestinian in Lebanon with the violence faced by
Palestinians in the Occupied Territories. Both staking a claim in their experiences – 'our war' – and identifying from afar – 'imagine playing with missiles' –
this reflection shows the extent to which his identity is bound up with his
homeland and those who reside in it. The social network he is part of enables
him not only to understand and identify more fully with the experiences of
Palestinians in the Occupied Territories, but to integrate his own experiences
into a new product which can in turn be repurposed and shared by others.

Other poems focus more explicitly on the camp experience, displaying
both the pain and mundanity of exile and the joy he experiences in everyday
moments:

When calm prevails over my camp
It's ugly
It is beautiful with the laughter of children and their voices
It is beautiful with the sound of the vegetable seller calling in the morning
It is lovely to talk to women whose coffee cups touch together
The volcano of a volcano does not seem to be as calm as the bird who
doesn't set his limits to the tones of his voice and chirps whenever he wants
#morning success in the camp
#in the camp (Al Assad 2015b)

In creating these narratives and publishing them online where his friends, family and wider online community can interact with them, Al Assad is becoming visible on his own terms and inviting others to participate in these acts of self-expression, reflection and protest. The medium through which this immediate and intimate telling of his daily reality exists enables others not only to act as an audience and see his content, but to engage actively through commenting, liking and sharing. The audience participates in the co-construction of meaning of his narratives as they circumnavigate the cultural boundaries and physical borders that separate the author from those outside the camp.

From Al Assad's example, it is clear that acts of digital storytelling in social media have shifted the production of narratives away from those who report *from* refugee camps to those who live *in* refugee camps. Through activating previously unheard voices online the stories, poems or even mundane thoughts of individuals are made visible without requiring the mediation of outside storytellers in the form of journalists, aid workers or Western acquaintances. When sought out and engaged with, these stories have the potential to challenge top-down narratives about refugees, to contextualise, politicise and humanise those so often presented as the 'Other'. However, as the final part of this chapter explores, these new platforms continue to operate within a global system that is fundamentally imbalanced, thus raising questions about their emancipatory potential.

Networked narratives, virtual territories

Many people shared these images, especially Palestinian refugees in Lebanon because they . . . don't have any human rights . . . In Israel they have a phrase 'the old will die and the young will forget'. When we share these photos we are saying that we won't forget. (Hussein, Rashidieh, 2015)

For refugee and diaspora communities, social networking can allow them to continue to shape meaning and build relationships from afar (Aouragh 2011; Godin and Doná 2016; Halilovich 2013; Walton 2016). Social media enhance the potential for migrants to maintain strong ties with families and friends, to provide a means of communication with weaker ties that are useful when organising the process of migration and settlement, and to establish a new infrastructure consisting of latent ties (Dekker and Engbersen 2012). Facebook and other social media platforms offer a chance to build a community that transcends restrictions on movement and the borders that separate friends and family. Through wider community participation, however peripheral, narratives are mediated and shaped into a site of meaning for a group rather than solely for an individual publisher, as an understanding of the content takes us beyond reception and production towards its circulation within networks (Jenkins, Ford and Green 2013). Page, Harper and Frobenius term this co-construction of storyworlds by multiple narrators 'networked narrative' (2013). Networked communities play a role 'not as simply consumers of pre-constructed messages but as people who are shaping, sharing, reframing, and remixing media content in ways which might not have been previously imagined' (Jenkins 2008: 2). Furthermore, online communities are able to produce content collaboratively, creating, correcting and filtering each other's narratives for the first time *outside* of institutions or markets, as a result of the organisation of groups through the social web (Shirky 2009).

For refugee communities and those in the diaspora, this mediation of identities, places and memories is of particular significance. In the context of loss and dislocation, co-creating, co-remembering and mediating each other's experiences contributes to a collective memory and identity. The study of refugee narratives within networked media is therefore a rich area for exploration, posing questions about memory making, the interplay between physical and online geographies, and the virtual permeability of borders. These questions cut across divisions within migration categories, and have been addressed by scholars working with diaspora, transnational, migrant and refugee communities in ways that often intersect. In her study of photoblogging among the Iranian diaspora, Walton (2016) finds that perceptions of place, identity and community are negotiated online through digital photography, while Halilovich (2013) discusses the ways in which Bosnian refugees in Austria reconstruct, reimagine and sustain identities and memories online while making new homes in the diaspora. In their research with Congolese activists Godin and Doná (2016) find young people around the world participating in politics through the creation of new online territories in which the local, national, transnational, diasporic and virtual intersect and overlap.

In September 2014 I initiated a storytelling project in Rashidieh refugee camp in Lebanon working as both project facilitator and researcher. Working alongside Mohammed Al Assad, a total of 68 photo stories and one video story were created based on the successful viral concept 'Humans of New York'. These stories were uploaded to a Facebook page *Humans of Al Rashidiya* (2014), which gained 2,587 page 'likes' during the first stage of project implementation. Each story featured an individual in the camp, and was written by them based on a short interview. In sharing content online within a pre-existing community and online network, the narratives became 'networked narratives', taking on new meaning to those who were part of this community, rather than being shared solely with outsiders as in most participatory storytelling projects. While there have been several notable participatory media projects with refugees, equipping them with the skills to express themselves and their opinions through text, film and image, very few of these have been created in the context of a networked culture. Sharing content in a network enables participation through sharing, remixing and co-creating involving both the media creators and the wider community. The global extent of this audience engagement points to the wide-reaching relationships in this small refugee camp in Lebanon, with page likes in August 2016 from 45 different countries, with the largest audiences in the USA (666), Lebanon (404), the UK (309) and Canada (141).

In the project and Facebook page *Humans of Al Rashidiya* the community mediates memories and engages in the formation of identities through the content that the project creates. Individuals living in the camp and in the diaspora use 'tagging', 'commenting' and 'liking' to engage with narratives that speak of their experiences and family history. When an elderly man shared his experience of fleeing Safed when he was 11 years old and coming to Lebanon, three relatives commented below the post. 'Think [*sic*] you for sharing your story. You are a courageous, kind and compassionate man. May Allah bless you and your family. Inshallah!' wrote one user. 'Thank you all. Ms Sandia, I appreciate your really emotions', replied a relative of the man who is quoted in the story. Underneath another post, a man living in London wrote, 'so proud of my Dad'. One family member of an older man who featured in a story saved and uploaded the photo from the post as his header picture on Facebook. Many of the posts featured stories about the *Naqba* and memories of Palestine, engaging with the physical land lost and their right to return, supporting Miriam Aouragh's assertion that in the case of Palestine, a mediated national consciousness does not depend on possessing sovereign territory (Aouragh 2011). Comments also echoed the right to return: 'If God wants you will come back and we will all go back, we are the owners of the earth with the right'; 'We will go back to our homeland inshallah.' For those viewing the page from the diaspora rather than within the camp, the page also facilitated a recollection of the camp itself as the 'land lost'. In response to a post about a barber who opened his salon in the camp in 1990, a user from London said, 'huh nice Ayman. I remember when my dad he was take me to Ayman salon when I was young I was 4 years or 5 years.' The 'home' around which memories and belonging can be centred is twofold; land in Palestine lost by exile and the camp itself lost through emigration.

On the *Humans of Al Rashidiya* Facebook page, Palestinians from Rashidieh and the diaspora are both the audience and active participants in the storytelling, engaging with their representation online just as outsiders can. They are co-contributors to a shared sense of space and belonging facilitated by a virtual platform. Much of this active participation can also be characterised by the lending of support, particularly when stories feature dreams and aspirations. Beneath a post about a Syrian girl who had never been to school is the comment,

> Dear beautiful young lady, please do not give up. Your dream of going to school will come true. Your life now is very hard, and for all of the brave courageous Syrians. We pray for you, to have a happy future filled with peace, and the opportunity to go to school. Inshallah!

Elsewhere, other comments included, 'I hope your dream becomes true' and 'May God prolong your age and your wish come true to return to beloved Palestine.' In some cases, the individual in the story engaged directly with those who commented encouragingly, facilitating a direct two-way conversation between the 'subject' and the 'audience'.

As well as engendering interactions among Palestinians all over the world, these kinds of networked narratives can also work to strengthen attachments to a homeland. With findings from multi-sited ethnographic research conducted in Lebanon and the Occupied Territories between 2001 and 2005, and internet-based ethnography, Aouragh analyses Palestinian web production and consumption and illustrates the phenomenon of virtual mobility. She recounts how those in the camps in Lebanon were, for the first time, able to access the land lost, with virtual space enabling a sense of physical attachment. Interactive chatrooms, forums and an emerging blogosphere against the background of the Al Aqsa intifada in 2000 were mediating spaces through which the nation of Palestine was conceptualised, with Palestinians living in Israel and the Occupied Territories and Palestinians in exile contributing to this process (Aouragh 2011).

This kind of virtual mobility is further enabled by the immediacy and personal nature of social media platforms and messaging apps over websites and chat forums, which generate a sense of shared connections to place. In 2015 images began circulating on Facebook of places in Palestine with a handwritten note featuring a name and sometimes a message (Fig. 22.1). Initiated by the Jerusalem-based journalist Fatima Bakri, these photos provide a link between the diaspora community and the physical land from which they are separated. Those replicating the meme would take a photo at the request of an individual unable to visit Palestine, typically Palestinians in the diaspora, with their handwritten name on paper displayed prominently alongside landmarks from the territory that the subject is unable to visit. Occasionally the two participating in the meme had a pre-existing relationship, but in the majority of cases they were strangers who had connected via Facebook and were joined solely by their shared national identity. Bakri's Facebook page alone contains hundreds of these images, tagging people from the Palestinian diaspora and beyond, including Germany and the UK as well as Jordan and Lebanon. The virtual territory of the internet thus allows diasporic users both to lay claim to a grounded sense of identity and attachment to geophysical space, and to 'travel' to locations they cannot access physically.

The invitation Bakri extends to Palestinians in the diaspora via Facebook echoes the work of the Palestinian artist Emily Jacir in *Where we come from* (2001–3).[5] In a pre-Facebook era, Jacir asked the question 'If I could do something for you, anywhere in Palestine, what would it be?' to Palestinians living either inside or outside Israel, or in the Occupied Palestinian Territories, who face travel restrictions. Answers included, 'Go to my mother's grave in Jerusalem on her birthday and put flowers and pray', and 'do something on a

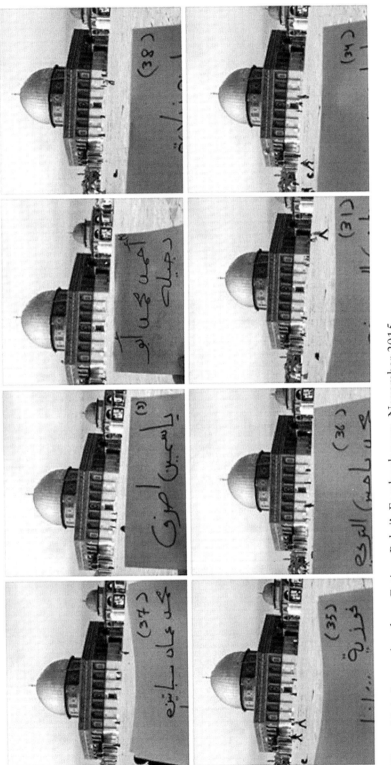

Figure 22.1 Screenshot from Fatima Bakri's Facebook page, November 2015

normal day in Haifa' (Demos 2013: 104). Able to travel due to her American passport, Jacir fulfilled these wishes and documented them in photographic form. However, rather than making visible those who responded to her question in the final exhibition, she made their *absence* the primary feature of the art, pointing to their erasure from the land and confronting the 'oppressive apparatus of spatial control in which these Palestinian subjects are enmeshed' (Demos 2013: 104).

Bakri's work confronts the same injustice, but in the networked collaborative context of Facebook she adopts *presence* rather than absence as the focus of her photographs. She fulfils the desire of those in the diaspora to be physically present in Palestine through the act of naming and creating an artefact that they can own and share online. The images become personal identifiers that individuals can use to represent themselves before others online, with Palestinians from Lebanon able to be connected to the land from which their ancestors were exiled. Bakri's photos are almost all taken at the Temple Mount/al-Haram al-Sharif, a site holy to Muslims, Christians and Jews and a vital pillar of Palestinian identity (Khalidi 2010). The online act of being named is to be present, albeit virtually, and thus to lay claim to the land lost. These photographs act both as a document of belonging and a virtual presence transcending the lack of physical presence that displacement entails.

The project *Humans of Al Rashidiya* and the meme initiated by Bakri are instances of content creation and sharing that can also be characterised as acts of political resistance, bringing dispossessed and immobile Palestinians from camps in Lebanon into online communities built on a shared sense of national identity. While virtual space is a reminder of the absence of shared territorial space, it offers displaced Palestinians with no right to the land, and no land of their own, an opportunity to stake their claim through the sharing and repurposing of narratives in online communities.

Digital storytelling, censorship and control of the public sphere

Technology has changed, but our situation is the same. (Fadhi, al Buss camp, 2013)

Spaces for voice are inherently spaces of power (Couldry 2010). Any act of digital storytelling or self-expression by refugees positions these individual narratives within the context of highly contested political debates about the validity of refugee experiences, immigration policy and the right to asylum. Indeed, 'our practices of recognition, and so our practices of voice, are limited by the histories of the spaces in which we find ourselves: the histories of others' struggles for recognition before us, the history of our own struggle to be recognised in contrast to the struggles of particular others' (Couldry 2010: 130).

Alongside the politicised context of refugee experiences and voices, any attempt to understand the wider spaces and contexts in which voice is used must therefore interrogate the social platforms themselves as the mechanisms for narrative dissemination.

A growing body of work exists that points to the power imbalances born of the neoliberalism that social networks operate from, which serves to perpetuate old colonialist structures (Aouragh and Chakravartty 2016; Tufekci 2017). Despite the important role that Facebook plays for refugee and diaspora communities in sharing memories and negotiating identity, the corporation's control over its content undermines the emancipatory potential of this online space. In publishing stories directly to Facebook, refugees are bypassing those who have traditionally been the owners or mediators of their stories in the form of journalists, aid workers or others crafting the frameworks for storytelling projects in which refugees participate. Yet in doing so they are not exercising this agency in a neutral space free from influence and outside control. The mediators of the stories are no longer individual storytellers, but the policies and algorithms of social networks that dictate the way in which the story is expressed and communicated. These moments of self-expression are therefore both owned and shaped by the platforms on which they exist. As research such as that of the techno-sociologist and activist Zeynep Tufekci has shown, real tensions exist between the possibilities that such social media platforms offer for activism, connection and self-expression leading to political change, on the one hand, and, on the other, the realities of censorship, failed uprisings and the limitation of audience by algorithms (Tufekci 2017).

The dominance of certain social media companies provides them with a degree of power that impacts minorities and those who have previously been denied their right to speak. While social media have been heralded by some as a new era for democratic storytelling, it is important to recognise that the continued dominance of neoliberalism has ensured that the identities, practices and representations that circulate in the old media system have not been lost and in fact still structure the new media system (Carpentier 2007). Indeed, Tufekci (2017) argues that the structuring of the new media system can result in an environment for minorities that is *less* inclusive and participatory than when public debate and representation was more evenly spread between different media and publishers. Through a system that she terms 'gatekeeping', those who already have power and are easily understood are privileged over those whose stories have existed on the margins. While gatekeeping used to be broad, now the digital communications gatekeeping ecosystem is reduced to a very few powerful chokepoints. From the availability of languages and fonts, to translation and direct acts of censorship, Tufekci describes how power is both top-down and tightening around a small, uniform demographic in Silicon Valley. Self-expression, public debate and activism has shifted from individual blogs and web pages to centralised platforms with algorithms controlled by corporations. The networked public sphere has largely shifted to commercial spaces, where conversations are dictated by commercial priorities through the rendering of opinions and narratives as unreliable (through censorship) or irrelevant (through algorithms) (Tufekci 2017).

The power dynamics of this architecture are such that questions must be raised about whether Facebook can be a platform for minorities and those who have traditionally had fewer opportunities to speak and be heard. Tufekci's analysis of how human censorship and algorithms have played out in situations of conflict is a useful starting point for answering this question. Describing Facebook's censorship of the Kurdistan Workers' Party, she argues that 'in almost any country with deep internal conflict, the types of people who are most likely to be employed by Facebook are often from one side of the conflict – the side with more power and privileges' (Tufekci 2017: 151). This privileging of one side of the conflict over the other can also be seen in the Palestinian case, mediated by software rather than the direct actions of individuals. In October 2017, *The Verge* and others reported that a Palestinian man had been arrested by Israeli police when his Facebook post saying 'good morning' was translated as 'attack them' in Hebrew and 'hurt them' in English. The mistake was not the result of a decision made by an individual but rather due to Facebook's AI-powered translation service not being programmed for Palestinian-accented Arabic (Ong 2017). Nonetheless, this occurrence demonstrates that all content shared online is at the mercy of dynamics of centralisation, inclusion and exclusion. A 21-year-old prolific Facebook user in Rashidieh camp identified this lack of neutrality as a factor that commonly interfered in his online activity:

> Sometimes Facebook closes our pages because people report us but we don't know why . . . I made a page for Hassan Nasrollah, I was just adding photos of him because I like him but Facebook closed it because they think he is a terrorist.. Facebook can be racist. People must respect other's opinions, and as long as the owner of Facebook is American they will not understand our interests or our religion. (Hussein, 12 October 2015)

My research and practice suggest that while there are ways of operating within the commercially driven and majority-led spaces offered by social media, the very fabric of how they are structured makes circumventing these priorities impossible. The hidden means through which social media networks prioritise profit over privacy and a commercial operating model over democracy are in many ways more dangerous than the erasure of first-hand narratives from newspaper articles or the humanitarian storytelling projects that define the boundaries for self-expression. Activists, and indeed personal narratives, trying to reach broader publics find themselves in new battles, trying to 'cut through' to have their voices heard, thus minimising the impact that these networked narratives can have on shaping public consciousness

(Couldry 2010; Jenkins 2008; Tufekci 2017). Before we celebrate the self-expression afforded by social media to communities who have previously been unheard, a fuller understanding of the ways in which these stories are mediated and shared needs to be gained, lest we find ourselves unwittingly celebrating their demise.

Conclusion

Social networks offer unique spaces for self-expression, particularly for refugees living in low-resource environments without access to professional storytelling technology. These networks have enabled digital storytelling to take place at the behest of individuals rather than as part of storytelling projects created and sustained by external actors. Social networks, in particular Facebook, have also enabled narratives to be shaped by a wider network where communities can engage with, share and repurpose content – becoming both the subjects of, and the audiences for, stories. In doing so, refugees have appropriated social media as a tool for virtual mobility and created online territories that defy the occupation and exile they face. However, the dominance of Facebook and the commercial structures in which it is situated is often at odds with transnational agendas that give value to voice irrespective of the position of the speaker in the global marketplace and nation-state. This poses important and concerning questions regarding the full extent to which these voices are audible and able to contribute to the public sphere.

Notes

1. Within academia this shift can be marked by the first publication of the *Journal of Refugee Studies* in 1998, with the inclusion of a section entitled 'Refugee Voices'. Within the aid and development sector this shift has been more recent, shaped largely by collaborations between large agencies and participatory storytelling organisations.
2. See BBC Wales, *Capture Wales*, http://www.bbc.co.uk/wales/audiovideo/sites/galleries/pages/capturewales.shtml; NFB Canada, *Challenge for Change*, https://www.nfb.ca/playlist/challenge-for-change/; and the work of Film Aid, https://www.filmaid.org/, and Photo Voice, https://photovoice.org/ (all accessed 2 July 2019).
3. Personal communication, 23 March 2018.
4. Personal communication, 23 March 2018. Ya Sour is a website sharing news and events from Sour, where Rashidieh is located.
5. *Where we come from* was first exhibited in New York and was later acquired by the San Francisco Museum of Modern Art, https://www.sfmoma.org/artist/Emily_Jacir (accessed 31 March 2018).

Bibliography

Al Assad, Mohammed (2015a), https://www.facebook.com/mohamed.elassad23/ videos/445111569011339/ (accessed 23 July 2018).

Al Assad, Mohammed (2015b), https://www.facebook.com/photo.php?fbid=36622 7840233046&set=a.112410222281477.1073741825.100005374994505&type =3&theater (accessed 23 July 2018).

Aouragh, Miriyam (2011), *Palestine Online: Transnationalism, the Internet and Construction of Identity* (London: I. B. Tauris).

Aouragh, Miriyam, and Paula Chakravartty (2016), 'Infrastructures of empire: towards a critical geopolitics of media and information studies', *Media Culture and Society*, 38: 559–75.

Arendt, Hannah (1981), *The Life of the Mind: The Groundbreaking Investigation on How We Think* (New York: Harcourt).

Bleiker, Roland, David Campbell, Emma Hutchinson and Xzarina Nicholson (2013), 'The visual dehumanisation of refugees', *Australian Journal of Political Science*, 48: 398–416.

Carpentier, Nico (2007), 'Theoretical frameworks for participatory media', in Nico Carpentier, Pille Pruulmann-Vengerfeldt, Kaarle Nordenstreng, Maren Hartmann, Peeter Vihalemm, Bart Cammaerts and Hannu Nieminen (eds), *Media Technologies and Democracy in an Enlarged Europe: The Intellectual Work of the 2007 European Media and Communication Doctoral Summer School* (Tartu: Tartu University Press), 105–23.

Couldry, Nick (2001), 'The hidden injuries of media power', *Journal of Consumer Culture*, 1: 155–77.

Couldry, Nick (2008), 'Digital storytelling, media research and democracy: conceptual choices and alternative futures', in K. Lundby (ed.), *Digital Storytelling, Mediatized Stories: Self-Representations in New Media* (New York: Peter Lang), 41–60.

Couldry, Nick (2010), *Why Voice Matters: Culture and Politics after Neoliberalism* (London: Sage).

Dekker, Rianne, and Godfried Engbersen (2012), 'How social media transform migrant networks and facilitate migration', *University of Oxford International Migration Institute Working Papers*, 64, 30 November, https://www.imi-n.org/ publications/wp-64-12 (accessed 2 July 2019).

Demos, T. J. (2013), *The Migrant Image: The Art and Politics of Documentary During Global Crisis* (Durham, NC: Duke University Press).

Godin, Marie, and Giorga Doná (2016), 'Refugee voices, new social media and politics of representation: young Congolese in the diaspora and beyond', *Refuge: Canada's Journal on Refugees*, 32: 60–71.

Halilovich, Hariz (2013), 'Bosnian Austrians: accidental migrants in trans-local and cyber spaces', *Journal of Refugee Studies*, 26: 524–40.

Humans of Al Rashidiya (2014), https://www.facebook.com/humansofalrashidiya/ (accessed 13 June 2018).

Jenkins, Henry (2008), *Convergence Culture: Where Old and New Media Collide* (New York: NYU Press).

Jenkins, Henry, Samuel Ford and Joshua Green (2013), *Spreadable Media: Creating Value and Meaning in a Networked Culture* (New York: NYU Press).

Khalidi, Rashid (2010), *Palestinian Identity: The Construction of Modern National Consciousness* (New York: Columbia University Press).

Malkki, Liisa (1996), 'Speechless emissaries: refugees, humanitarianism, and dehistoricization', *Cultural Anthropology*, 11: 377–404.

Mitchell, Mary, and Mohammed Al Assad (2015), 'Who tells the stories?', *Index on Citizenship*, 44: 31–3.

Ong, T. (2017), 'Facebook apologizes after wrong translation sees Palestinian man arrested for posting "good morning"', *The Verge*, https://www.theverge.com/us-world/2017/10/24/16533496/facebook-apology-wrong-translation-palestinian-arrested-post-good-morning (accessed 6 October 2018).

Page, Ruth, Richard Harper and Maximiliane Frobenius (2013), 'From small stories to networked narrative: the evolution of personal narratives in Facebook status updates', *Narrative Inquiry*, 23: 192–213.

Save the Children (2014), http://insidezaatari.tumblr.com/ (accessed 22 July 2018).

Sayigh, Rosemary (2013), *The Palestinians: From Peasants to Revolutionaries* (London: Zed Books).

Shirky, Clay (2009), *Here Comes Everybody: How Change Happens when People Come Together* (Harmondsworth: Penguin).

Tufekci, Zeynep (2017), *Twitter and Tear Gas* (New Haven, CT: Yale University Press).

Turton, David (2003), 'Refugees and "other forced migrants"', *RSC Working Paper Series*, 13, https://www.rsc.ox.ac.uk/publications/refugees-and-other-forced-migrants (accessed 2 July 2019).

Walton, Shireen (2016), 'Photographic truth in motion: the case of Iranian photoblogs', *Anthropology and Photography*, 4, https://www.therai.org.uk/publications/anthropology-and-photography (accessed 2 July 2019).

Wright, Terence (2002), 'Moving images: the media representation of refugees', *Visual Studies*, 17: 53–66.

Chapter 23

Refugee Writing, Refugee History: Locating the Refugee Archive in the Making of a History of the Syrian War

Dima Saber and Paul Long

Only refugees can forever write the archive.
The camp owns the archive, not God.
For the archive not to fall apart, it weds the camp unceremoniously.
The question of a camp-archive is the question of the camp's survival
beyond speech.
Circumcising the body can indicate the survival of the place.
Blessed are the pending places that are called camps. (Qasmiyeh 2017)

In 2011 five young men from Daraa, the birthplace of the Syrian uprising, took to the streets with hundreds of other protesters to march for freedom and social justice. Yadan Drajy, Uday al-Talab, and three cousins Masalmeh – Muhammad-Hourani, Hammoudeh-Shoukri and Rani – quickly realised the value of documenting their revolution for the world to see and hear. Initially, they had faith that a similar scenario would play out to that which had occurred in Tunis and Egypt. They imagined that Al-Jazeera and other mainstream channels would pick up their fight for social and political reform, that the Syrian revolution would garner worldwide support while the ruling regime would be put under pressure, and that President Bashar al-Assad would eventually step down, paving the way for the first democratic elections in decades. Over a period of eighteen months, the group of men filmed the peaceful protests in Daraa, which gave way to killing and then fighting. They managed to compile a collection comprising thousands of videos and images that attest to the transformation of the Syrian revolution from a peaceful movement to an Islamised and militarised conflict that quickly became a large-scale civil war.

A year and a half after their filming commenced, Muhammad-Hourani and Hammoudeh-Shoukri Masalmeh were killed by snipers in Daraa. Al-Talab was shot in the knee and fled to the UK for treatment. Rani Masalmeh took up arms and started fighting alongside Islamic factions, while Drajy crossed the

Jordanian border on foot. With him was a hard-drive containing the digital footage that he and his four fellow activists had shot in Daraa. The material is a raw digital record of a country's travails in a particular moment, attesting to the effort of those who were there and who recorded everyday life in crisis as they and those they recorded experienced it. As we have documented elsewhere (Saber and Long 2017), this footage currently sits in limbo, awaiting recognition, purposeful engagement and a permanent and sustained location – on or offline. Its precarious and refugee status thus echoes the fate of those who assembled it. At the time of writing, Drajy remains in Jordan and al-Talab is in London. The surviving Masalmeh managed to get to Turkey on a refugee boat, from where he travelled on to France and then to Germany, where he has applied for refugee status.

What is the fate of this representative group, the material they collected and the histories that might be made from it? This question resonates with Philip Marfleet's (2007; 2013; 2016) work on the relations between history, memory and population displacement. He notes that many major episodes of mass displacement are absent from official histories. As we discuss below, if the building of the nation-state is anchored to the establishment of the archive proper, its collapse leaves refugees not only stateless but without the historical record that affirms their origins and rights. In light of this absence, this chapter explores how records of refugees themselves are important sources for acts of retrieval – of individual and collective experience and perspectives on political and cultural disruptions. Informing our discussion, the Daraa material prompts a number of questions concerning the status and value of an assemblage of refugee accounts. In its case, for instance, should we defer to the claim of its creator-curators that their material constitutes an archive? What is at stake in applying the term to this material, and who determines whether this citizen-produced documentation of the early days of the uprising can be so called? Is this material a legitimate source for understanding the beginnings of the Syrian revolution in Daraa in 2011? Finally, its indeterminate status as an archive prompts the question of how such material is to be preserved so as to enable its use.

In the light of these questions, this chapter proceeds with a consideration of how the Daraa material emerged as a form of citizen-journalism, a witness to the Syrian uprising, and developed into historical record. Touching on the way in which displaced people have been dealt with in the historical record in the context of the relationship between the archive and the nation-state, we turn then to consider how the refugee figures in one supranational archive: that of the United Nations High Commissioner for Refugees (UNHCR). Here, we discuss the issues of representation and agency that UNHCR raises with regard to displaced peoples, before turning once more to the kinds of practices represented by the Daraa material and two further initiatives: *Qisetna: Talking Syria* and *SyriaUntold*. These records were enabled by digital technologies that have aided their collation but also signal their refugee status by virtue of their location in the dislocated geography of online space. Nonetheless, digital platforms and online cultures allow for the creation of what we describe as vernacular histories and archives. As we suggest, such documents of displacement continue to foreground questions around the preservation and durability of the materials of the archive; their uncertain status a reflection of that of refugees themselves.

From news to archive: on the making of a refugee history of the Syrian war

In spite of – or perhaps because of – its origins in a moment of conflict, its fraught journey in the hands of refugees and its precarious status, the Daraa material offers a tangibly affective and partisan resource when measured against more conventional journalistic accounts from Syria. In this context, and as Alessandria Masi (2017) notes on the website of the Committee to Protect Journalists: 'obtaining your own eyewitness account can mean jail or a death sentence'. As a result, journalists reporting on the Syrian conflict censor themselves by omission, whether protecting sources by changing names, or avoiding images of the dead on ethical grounds. She writes: 'We walk on eggshells for the sake of balance and because the majority of us cannot go to Syria to see things for ourselves, we are forced to report only what we are told.' This scenario and reports from within Syria affirm the oft-cited aphorism that the first casualty of war is truth. While this may be a condition of the confusion and propagandist manipulation that surrounds conflict, it nonetheless matters that records are maintained, that witnesses exist to inform the accounts and interpretations that follow and to affirm evidence, even as truth struggles to emerge. As Masi's insight suggests, a reliance on the press to provide the 'first draft of history' may prove problematic when the authority of the journalist as witness is undermined by a lack of access to events as they happen (on this idea, see Bingham 2012).

While Masi is suspicious of information provided by the Assad regime, Russia or the US, whatever form mainstream media witness takes it is often reliant upon, and perforce expresses the perspective of, authority. Within war zones for instance, the cameras, microphones and reporters operating for global organisations such as Reuters, CNN or the BBC either see events from behind police lines or are 'embedded' among infantry (Fahmy and Johnson 2005). As such, claims to objectivity appear to be underwritten by the representatives of the rule of law, anchored to a show of strength and power. Resulting reports often disregard accounts of those identified as 'insurgents', 'protestors' and 'citizens'. Perspectives offered from such positions of power – and the practicalities of access and witness – are challenged by the availability of new information and personal communication technologies. These allow for the production and distribution of 'crowd-sourced' reportage from crisis zones from a diverse range of perspectives. As a result, citizen-journalists can be as compelled as mainstream media to bear witness, and may even exceed that brief in the face of conflict, especially when war is taking place at home, and when walking away from events is not possible.

One such figure is Drajy who was conscious of the weight upon him and others, and who felt compelled to bear witness by recording events in Daraa: 'at the beginning, yes . . . I needed to record exactly what was happening'.[1] Recalling how he took to the streets in March 2011, Drajy says he very quickly comprehended that he was part of 'a very important and historic moment', and so sought to 'document this moment in the history' of his country and people in 'striving for freedom and social justice'. This was a form of citizen journalism; stepping into the breach of a situation in a highly censorious culture where international observers were not present from the outset. Thus, from the moment when Drajy and others began documenting the Syrian uprising, their activity was not pursued with the intention of creating material for posterity. As the situation escalated, however, a greater sense of mission emerged. As peaceful protests were punished by the regime, prompting the outbreak of civil war, Drajy and other activists began to reconceive of their documentary intent and its potential role beyond speaking of and to the present in appealing to the world for attention and aid. Consequently, footage shot on mobile phones or hand-held video was not merely a live mediation of the current moment as 'news' in which journalists were absent, but also acted as a mode of commemoration of the places shattered by bombardment and of the men, women and children killed in this war of the regime with its own people. As Drajy recalls: 'when the shelling started, I realised that some people will die, and some places will no longer exist, so I found myself in between two moments, the present and the future. I started shooting for history.' Reflecting further, Drajy noted that 'I was documenting so that a few years from now, we would be able to say this is how it all started, this is what happened in Daraa.'

The material captured by Drajy and his activist friends attests to the life-threatening conditions under which it was gathered; it is a document of suffering and a documentation of crimes committed by and against human beings. It is a testament to the impulse to share events as they are happening in the hope that someone would see, hear and *listen*, if not act and intervene in this situation. But the material also has a life and purpose beyond the moment in which it was captured. The preservation of this footage allows it to form part of the historical account of what happened: of Syrians left to their fate. For instance, the material would be invaluable to those gathering evidence of human rights violations or as part of post-war reconstruction and reconciliation efforts. Preserving past events captured in Daraa would thus serve as a means of imagining a future built on what was lost and addressing the cost of the conflict.

In an interview with Drajy in 2016, we asked him which one of the 12,756 videos that comprised his Daraa archive he thought was the most important then, five years into the uprising, after he had fled and become a refugee in

Jordan. His answer was 'Daraa el-Balad' – a tour of Daraa's streets, shot from his car with a secret camera hidden in a napkin box: 'it attests to the places that are no longer there, to the shops that were destroyed, to everyday life that was lost. And I often go back to it when I miss Daraa, the town, its shops and everyday life in it.' The distressing nature of this material and anxieties over what might befall it given that its creator-curators are now displaced draw attention to the status of the refugee in the archive and historical record of war. Peter Gatrell asks, 'What, then, should history and historians have to say about, and to, refugees?' (Gatrell 2016: 184). In his reflection on the major migrations and displacements of 2015 and how such events might be represented in the future, he notes the lack of attention afforded to the figure and experience of the refugee by historians. This analysis is amplified by the work of Marfleet, who complains that 'Many major episodes of mass displacement have [. . .] "disappeared" from official history – from accounts that constitute what the Indian historian Gyanendra Pandey calls "national memory"' (Marfleet 2016: 8). Michelle Caswell's description of the 'symbolic annihilation' of particular groups from the historical record resonates here too (Caswell, Cifor and Ramirez 2016), while Marfleet also references Tony Kushner's expression 'collective amnesia' as characteristic of the denial in national histories of all experiences of refugees (Kushner 2006: 234; Marfleet 2016). Marfleet explains, for example, how records of the First World War have silenced the refugees, expressing an absence and evaluation in which 'neither their experiences, nor those of millions of people with whom they came into contact had been judged worthy of interest by professional historians' (Marfleet 2016: 8).

Mike Featherstone summarises some of the reasons for this failure of historiography to deal adequately with the refugee, a failure that lies in the nature of archival practice. As he recounts, the great archives of the European powers are a feature of an emergent modernity, established in the eighteenth century as a means of underwriting the power of the nation-state. As a consequence, in the nineteenth century 'the archive became seen as the repository of the national history and national memory' (Featherstone 2006: 592). Here, then, we can understand the challenge posed by refugees to conceptions of history anchored in this way: by definition the refugee is a stateless person; stateless persons have either abandoned, or been abandoned by, their state and, as Marfleet and others show, by the archives of their national history. As is evidenced by the Daraa material and the other Syria-related initiatives we discuss below, conflict leaves many people in possession of little more than their lives and stories. It becomes a matter of urgency to account for and record the experience of being a refugee. Furthermore, and as the status of refugee is a label that no one inhabits intentionally, the expression of a desire for home or the establishment of new settlements need to be anchored to the collation of materials that attest to this experience, to narratives of origin, identity and explanation: of history. As Gatrell suggests: 'The past is a resource for refugees seeking to locate themselves not just spatially but also temporally' (2016: 184).

Marfleet argues that modern social-political landscapes are marked by episodes of displacement. As a consequence, an indelible adjunct to understanding contemporary realities, and indeed histories, 'are the experiences and memories of refugees and those who empathize and solidarize with them' (Marfleet 2016: 15). Recognising the struggles over historical claims alongside other issues faced by displaced persons for recognition, respect and settlement, he suggests that a conversation is needed between historians and refugees. In this, the latter might contribute to debates about their self-representation and role in shaping their own destiny. Such an approach would set to rights historical accounts of the refugee experience; as Gatrell argues, 'Where refugees do make an appearance in the pages of history books, there is still a tendency to portray them [. . .] as inescapable "victims" of war or revolution, not as agents of change' (Gatrell 2016: 175). It is therefore important to recognise the experiences of refugees, which in turn have significance for expanding historical comprehension. Where, then, are the accounts, histories and archives of the refugee? What is at stake here in the rootlessness and precariousness of collections such as the Daraa archive? In the following section we examine an example of an institutional archive that does recognise the refugee before moving on to a discussion of the grassroots/crowd-sourced archives *Qisetna* and *SyriaUntold*.

Refugee-on-demand: UNHCR's archive and the dominant narrative of the refugee experience

UNHCR is a highly visible resource that does recognise refugees and has the potential to generate an 'official account' (Marfleet 2016) of displacement in the evolving historical record. UNHCR Archives and Records was established in 1996, although it contains material predating 1950, the year in which UNHCR was founded. Its main purpose is to archive UNHCR's administrative record as well as a history of field operations from around the world. As its website attests, archival material is contained in a Geneva basement and comprises over 10 million documents stored on around 10 kilometres of shelving space on two basement floors. This is material that documents a vital global organisation, which rivals some nation-states in scope and impact if not in its affective status in the hearts of those it serves and whose histories it records. As such, the nature of the 'globally and historically unique' archive authorises a self-reflexive sense of the role of UNHCR: 'They contain a trove of detail about important historical events, including, for example, records from the 1956 Hungarian uprising, the first major emergency in which [UNHCR] became operational, as well as emergencies in Chile and Argentina in the 1970s, and in the former Yugoslavia in the 1990s'.[2]

Refugees Media is an archive service of UNHCR aimed at researchers and journalists, providing photos and videos of its operations and of refugees it has aided. At the time of writing, the front page of the Refugees Media site offered a number of highlighted features and resources, focusing, among other things, on Bangladesh, Nigeria, South Sudan, Yemen and Syria.[3] Along-side its laudable humanitarian purpose, Refugees Media nonetheless exhibits aspects of the political economy of the archive and the intellectual property determining its use and usefulness.

Registration is required to access the content of the online archive. By registering, one tacitly agrees to the 'Terms and Conditions' set out by UNHCR: 'images, moving footage, sound, graphics and other content on this website are copyright protected'.[4] On this site, guidelines for the use of photographs, graphics and videos are described at great length, and items may only be reproduced with permission: 'Use in a commercial or promotional context is not allowed. A credit is always required in the format "© UNHCR/Photographer" for photo images and "© UNHCR" for video, audio and multimedia unless stated otherwise'.[5] Entering a portal on 'Syria: Hope Amid the Destruction', one is presented with 33 virtual folders containing multimedia content, 562 videos and 23,439 images. Images are organised and thus searchable by country of origin (where the images were shot – from Syria itself to Lebanon, Greece, Germany, etc.), by status of those depicted (refugee, migrant, asylum seekers or 'unknown'), and by their gender, age and the number of people in the photos. For example, there are only two pictures of 'pre-teen boys' on Refugees Media, while one can find eight pictures of 'mid-adult women' and a sole picture of 'one teenage boy only'.

Images are also organised according to orientation (i.e. landscape or portrait), and by composition: where there is 'copy space' or where the individual is 'Looking at Camera', caught 'Full length' or offering an 'Over the Shoulder View'. Another filter is 'UNHCR visibility', whereby images with UNHCR tents, logos, food boxes and blankets could be found in 'refined searches'. Each selected picture is then presented with its own set of metadata: reference number, title, background information, photographer name, size and type. Users can add it to their 'cart' while continuing a 'shopping tour' of refugees' images. Once done, one is invited to 'place the order', requesting the right to use the images of Syrian refugees.

This arrangement suggests an audience for UNHCR's Refugees Media as consumable resource. The mediation and purposeful presentation of this archive is similar to that of a photo agency, and in both its form and content is quite dissimilar from the rawness and largely absent aesthetic *intent* of citizen-generated archives such as the Daraa material and other online sources discussed below. In all likelihood, Refugees Media is predominantly targeted at other UN agencies, at mainstream media outlets, and at NGOs and international organisations that make use of similar pictures in their fundraising and awareness-raising campaigns. The images of Syrian refugees, and by extension

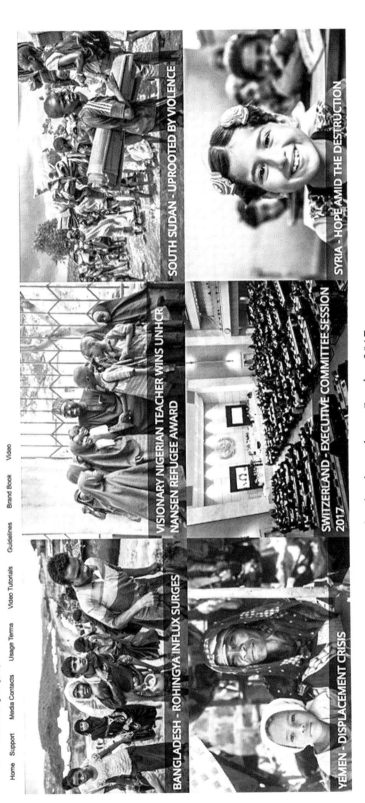

Figure 23.1 UNHCR Refugees Media, screenshot by the authors, October 2017

Figure 23.2 UNHCR Refugees Media, screenshot by the authors, October 2017

the refugee experience, become aestheticised as tradable promotional items for the work of UNHCR or the organisations and individuals that reuse their images. These materials attest to UNHCR operations but also serve as promotional material for the agency's value. However, the history of the unfolding Syrian conflict as represented through Refugees Media becomes limited to narratives of food distribution in camps, of children playing barefoot in the snow and of entire families cramped in UNHCR tents. Every once in a while there is a moment of exception; Syrian refugees cheering, for example, during a football match (REF 2126267 Brazil. Sao Paulo hosts Refugees World Cup), or an interview with a Syrian refugee who 'despite living in a camp', is pursuing a degree-level history course (REF 2122402 Jordan. Syrian refugee pursues higher education dreams). In spite of such examples, much of this material serves to underline Gatrell's point that representations of refugees afford them little agency. Perhaps, as Yousif M. Qasmiyeh, the poet cited at the head of this chapter, writes, 'Only refugees can forever write the archive' (2017).

In addition to all the concerns that Refugees Media raises in terms of the possibility of representations *of* and *by* refugees themselves, this archive obviously prompts questions about ethical issues pertaining to the representation of vulnerable people in conflict situations, notably in terms of consent, protection of identity, avoidance of objectification and attendance to security. When asked whether permission had been requested from the people represented in Refugees Media images and videos, UNHCR confirmed the use of rights release forms and of 'different agreements signed with people who appear through the visual material. Those forms vary depending on the relationship to UNHCR, the language and the region.'[6] UNHCR also confirmed that its 'Protection Teams' give guidance and clearance on the use of images showing minors or people in vulnerable situations. Although beyond the remit of this discussion, the ethical issues that this archive raises in terms of image capture, consent, representation, security and, indeed, cultural translation merit further investigation.

While dealing with many of the tragedies of the modern era, and in particular contexts in which the status of refugee is forced upon populations, Refugees Media tends towards the dispassionate in its presentation of images of refugees. This is after all the acme of the *official* archive, organised along familiar principles and practices of access policy, cataloguing, regulations, request forms and citation rules. As Marika Cifor (2016) suggests in a summary of issues concerning the lack of attention afforded to affect in archive discourse, archiving is still largely constructed in terms of modernity as a 'science'. The aim of 'objectivity' and 'neutrality' elides the power dynamics of knowledge production. Furthermore, this has a gendered inflection in validating a masculinised sense of reason at the expense of affective engagement and passion. Certainly, what UNHCR lacks in the presentation and organisation of its records is the affective intent of citizen-generated archival material, which in turn echoes the character of interactions and outputs generated in online social media.

Figure 23.3 UNHCR Refugees Media, screenshot by the authors, October 2017

RF2126267

SHOOT DATE:
16 September, 2017

LOCATION:
Sao Paulo
CERET - Centro Esportivo, Recreativo e Educativo do Trabalhador

COUNTRY:
Brazil

Brazil. Sao Paulo hosts Refugees World Cup

Syrian players celebrate their victory on penalties over Mali at the Refugees
World Cup in CERET Park, Sao Paulo, Brazil.

BACKGROUND INFORMATION:

The fourth edition of the Refugees World Cup, one of the largest sports events
for the refugee community in Brazil, kicked off in São Paulo in mid-September.
Refugee teams from 16 countries – Angola, Benin, Cameroon, Colombia,
Gambia, Ghana, Guinea, Guinea-Bissau, Iraq, Mali, Morocco, Nigeria,
Democratic Republic of the Congo, Syria, Tanzania and Togo – are competing
for the trophy. A partnership between UNHCR, África do Coração, Cáritas São
Paulo and SESC-SP, the Refugees World Cup unites the 9,552 refugees living in
Brazil and helps them integrate into their new country's society.

PHOTOGRAPHER
Gabo Morales

CREDIT LINE:
© UNHCR/Gabo Morales

SIZE: 5202px × 3468px (~51 MB)

KEYWORDS:
Arms Raised - Celebration - Cheering - Competition - Day - Football -
Football Player - Happiness - Male (Human Gender) - Man - Outdoors -
Refugee Football Cup - Running - Six People - Soccer - Soccer Field -
Soccer Team - Sports Team - Sports Uniform - Syrian Ethnicity - Winning
Expand keywords (Admin)

Direct link to image   Item 28 of 23469

Conceptually similar

RF2126263
Shot on 16 September, 2017

RF2126259
Shot on 16 September, 2017

RF2126261
Shot on 16 September, 2017

Figure 23.4 UNHCR Refugees Media, screenshot by the authors, October 2017

'Vernacular' practices: histories, space, mobility and memory

As a potential remedy for the official history's 'sanitisation and ignoring' of the testimonies of refugees, Marfleet suggests that special attention to oral histories could lead to a 'cultural retrieval' (2016: 13) and a better engagement with history and memory. As such, some historians, archivists and academics have already engaged refugees in ways that challenge mainstream approaches – 'addressing them as social actors whose life stories, aspirations, and ambitions are of intrinsic value in understanding forced migration and wider aspects of modern society' (Marfleet 2016: 13). Marfleet illustrates his argument with reference to the important advances in oral history that have taken place in relation to survivors of the Holocaust. As awareness developed of fascist atrocities in Europe during the 1930s and 1940s, he writes, 'there were sustained efforts to collect testimony, with projects focussed on "giving voice" to survivors' (Marfleet 2016: 13). This was achieved through the compilation of oral records, written memoirs as well as novels and poems. Such material created important historical records and served as constituents of collective memory-building efforts (Zelizer and Tenenboim-Weinblatt 2014). This plural approach to generating memory and historical resources can be usefully extended to encompass the practices that have emerged with digital cultures and that characterise individual, community and crowd-sourced activity.

The availability of digital tools on smartphones in tandem with social media platforms such as Twitter, Facebook and Pinterest has contributed to a democratisation of cultural production and dissemination. This availability has allowed for the capturing of sounds and images of places and events – as in the Daraa material. Likewise, it has enabled their circulation across online spaces. This activity contributes to the proliferation of what Wolfgang Ernst labels the *An-archive* (Ernst 2013). The prefix evokes the apparent anarchy of online spaces like those mentioned or platforms such as YouTube or Facebook, where digitised materials and records are deposited with no necessary anchors for their organisation or continued identification and access. Furthermore, blogs, Facebook groups and pages generate communities of interest and describe their activity by deploying terms such as 'memory', 'heritage', 'history' and indeed 'archive'. In comparison with the resources and professional conventions of the repositories of nation-states or international ventures such as UNHCR, online community sites produce archives and histories formed from the vernacular cultures of the online world.

We would suggest that online interactions are archival in nature in the manner in which communities are convened where materials are shared and dialogue exchanged, thus building cultures and leaving material traces. Whether or not such sites would be recognised or approved of by archivists and historians proper is another matter (for a discussion, see Long et al. 2017). For instance, Ernst's term highlights the challenge to the security, accessibility and authority of the material from which the online archive is made: after all, who assesses its utility or ensures its sustainability? Furthermore, the anarchy of the online world and its accretion of materials, relative to the formalities of the archive proper, is apparent in the manner in which vernacular practices evince a myriad of cultural codes and conventions in their expression and organisation. This is apparent when faced with the fact that among the online 'noise' are fragments, artefacts and extended articulations of refugee experiences, of accounts and records of conflict in locations to which, as described above, mainstream media institutions still have little access.

Two online initiatives illustrate the potential of these practices in generating and organising the record of contemporary conflicts, focused on the unfolding Syrian war. While *Qisetna: Talking Syria* and *SyriaUntold* are certainly not the only two initiatives of their kind, they allow us to develop insights into relations between refugee witness, issues of displacement and belonging and the making of a history of the continuing war and its legacy. Each pursues accounts from those based in Syria and abroad, shedding light on several elements of this struggle and reality that are ignored and overlooked by the mainstream media. Here, it is useful to label their work in terms of the practices described above for how they echo and extend existing practices. What is important is the value that these sites give to individual testimony and the informal, vernacular contribution of ordinary people. To overcome the potentially doubled dislocation of the online world identified by Ernst – the prodigiousness of information, its ephemeral, contingent nature – these sites create an anchor and order through the form of a durable space for eliciting and sustaining testimony. As Donatella Della Ratta, co-founder of *SyriaUntold*, explains, in the few months following the Syrian uprising in March 2011 the site's creators found themselves 'overwhelmed with a treasure trove of user-generated content produced by Syrian citizens trying to give their account of what was happening in Syria' (Della Ratta 2014). Information, data, videos, stories and pictures were being shared on the internet, she writes, 'mostly by anonymous users; a truly unprecedented phenomenon for a country where independent news reporting had always been a critical issue' (Della Ratta 2014). This demonstrates how for those with access and the requisite literacy, the affordances of digital culture have offered a voicing, recording and potential archive of experience and testimony.

Co-founded in 2014 by Syrian Dima Mekdad, Spaniard Juan del Gado and Scot Julia Rampen, *Qisetna* (Arabic for 'our story') is funded by the Arabic British Centre and is edited by a team of five Syrians. It announces to site visitors that it 'is a non-political social and cultural project aiming to engage Syrians and people with a connection to the country to share their stories. It provides a reminder of the humanity of ordinary Syrians through their relationship with arts, culture, sport and places.'[7] This enterprise has been described elsewhere as offering an inclusive space for narratives building upon a tradition of storytelling 'profoundly rooted within the Arab Culture', aiming 'to preserve the Oral Heritage of Syrians displaced inside their country, on the move crossing borders, and resettling across Europe'.[8] *Qisetna* is an open-access platform, and with no requirement for prior registration, it asks potential contributors to share their stories on Syria. It asks: 'Is there something you love about Syria? A place you remember? A favourite food?'[9] Published in Arabic and English, it offers a wide array of stories: from old tales of Aleppo nightlife to accounts of music festivals in the city of Homs and personal narratives of first-time cycling experiences in Damascene streets. The site presents reflections on current affairs coupled with memories of home and is indicative of the affective dimensions of so much online interaction. For instance, a typical post is 'Morning Meditation' by Nazdar Youssef, in which a now disrupted habitual experience is recalled around the site of Bab Sharqi, Damascus's eastern gate. The author writes of the repeated experience of passing through the alleyways of Bab Sharqi en route to a shift in a hospital, a trajectory that 'contained some of the most precious and calm moments of my life'.[10] He recalls the detail from each day – passing smoking bank workers: 'I always felt I would run into someone I knew coming the other way. The feeling continued until I stepped through the gate out of Old Damascus, and woke up from my brief daydream.' The account is layered with nostalgia in which there is difficulty in describing the longing for this place, 'so rich with history, soul and heritage'. It is also an important account of a space that has been definitively altered by the war and social turmoil. As such, it is a loving memory of the old Damascus, made possible by the recounting of native longing for his home town.

Unlike *Qisetna* – which predominantly features stories and memories of past experiences about Syria – *SyriaUntold* also documents the current situation. According to the site's editor-in-chief Mohammad Dibo, inspiration for the platform came with the peaceful protests of 2011 when its main aim 'was to document the cultural and civic activities of the Syrian uprising which were disappearing from social media a few weeks after they happened, and are ignored by the mainstream media' (Alhayek 2016). The site is 'an independent digital media project exploring the storytelling of the Syrian struggle and the diverse forms of resistance'.[11] With contributions from Syrians predominantly in exile, and from others with connections to the country, *SyriaUntold* focuses on the daily struggles of men, women and children in conditions of ongoing violence. It also documents the work done by Syrian civil society organisations, artists, activists, citizen journalists and 'creative resistants' – as the website calls them – to advance a positive narrative of the country and its uprising:

> With mainstream media focusing increasingly on geostrategic and military aspects and less on internal dynamics developing on the ground, we believe there are many aspects of the Syrian struggle that remain uncovered, many stories that we would not like to see forgotten. Welcome to the stories of daily resistance and creativity. Welcome to SyriaUntold.[12]

In addition, *SyriaUntold* is building an archive that documents the 'Syrian revolution' in six different cities: Zabadani, Deir ez-Zor, Salamiyah, Baniyas, Daraa and Qamishli. The project is funded by the European Union and CFJ (Training Centre for Journalists – France) and offers users the opportunity to read, watch and listen to stories in both English and Arabic. Reports are mainly developed and curated by exiled Syrian researchers, writers, journalists and artists. Its objective is to 'fill the gap' in mainstream media coverage, offering an account of events as they happen '[t]hrough the use of innovative forms of storytelling mixing research-based written content, infographics and documentary videos'.[13]

Under the headline 'Looking inside the uprising', *SyriaUntold* features a further initiative called *Collective Memory*. It is based on a collaboration with the global media platform *openDemocracy* that brings together a multiplicity of voices with the aim of reflecting on various cultural, social and political issues related to the Syrian movement: 'the re-building of a collective memory; the creativity at the base of daily practices of resistance; the state and role of the media; the issue of sectarianism and its consequences, just to name a few main themes and discussions this initiative aims to promote'.[14] Indicative features are articles on the fight for past and current political prisoners in Syria, Baathist indoctrination in school textbooks, and the thirtieth anniversary of the 1982 Hama massacre entitled: 'The uprising and Syria's reconstituted collective memory'.[15]

These two initiatives act as a direct counter to the forgetting or symbolic annihilation of Syrian displacement from the record. Likewise, they create space for a generation of vernacular accounts, affording agency to the displaced. In the case of *SyriaUntold*, Mohammad Dibo sees the platform and its different initiatives as an 'invaluable archive and historic record of the cultural and creative uprising against tyranny in Syria' (Alhayek 2016). The main motivation for it was prompted by a moment of illumination, that '[u]nless we did something, we realised that ten years from now, the memory of the Syrian uprising, and the day-to-day struggles of Syrian citizens, activists and artists would just disappear' (Alhayek 2016).

Qisetna's contribution was recognised in summer 2017 when the Community Archive and Heritage Group (CAHG) awarded it 'Overall 2017 Winner' and 'Most Innovative' initiative of the year at its annual conference in London. In the words of the group's judges: 'Talking Syria is an extra-ordinary example of an archive both preserving the voices of displaced and fractured communities for the future and acting as an engine of community resilience in the present.'[16] They praised the archive for offering 'raw emotion', and capturing real lives and the impact of events on individuals, their communities and organisations. The judges appreciated how the archive offers a 'focus on tomorrow', with the website offering a valuable resource for engagement and as support for the refugee cause. As they commented: 'This archive will become an outstanding research tool for the future. But it is also – evidently – succeeding in its principal short-term goal of community building.'

When compared to these initiatives, the Daraa material raises questions about its status as an archive or as a disparate collection of audio and video files (Saber and Long 2017). While digital spaces may not be as durable as they appear (Chun 2011), *SyriaUntold* and *Qisetna* at least offer a location and ordering for the material they collate. It might be productive therefore to think of the Daraa material as a representative 'refugee archive'. It is a collection of records in the process of becoming something more fixed, official and usable. It is an archive 'in the making', an idea that alludes to its status as well as to the experience of those who compiled its materials and who transported it. In this, the makers and their materials share a condition with those it depicts, 'and who were forced to migrate, not in search of a better life, but simply in order to stay alive' (Saber and Long 2017: 96). The status of this refugee archive reminds us that there are untold records yet to account for from those displaced, or whose testimonials may lie somewhere in the online 'An-archive'.

Conclusion

As we have argued, *Qisetna*, *SyriaUntold* and the Daraa material prompt reflections on the status, authority and economy of the archive and the place therein of the refugee. While specifically concerned with the Syrian context, these examples illuminate issues around the status of the displaced in the official record and thus the writing of history. In each case, they have collated evidence of refugees speaking about their experiences, recognising their agency in so doing and in the actions of those who seek to form the archive. Each attests also to the affordances of the digital and how its vernacular cultures contribute to the generation of affect in accounts, and the archives and histories that might be produced from them. As the material collated by each of these enterprises moves from the status of contemporary reportage to historical record, questions arise regarding preservation and durability, especially when compared to the archives of the nation-state. Likewise, such records are properly subject to interrogation about the claims to truth of their material and on what grounds we might frame their legitimacy. However, it is important to recognise the democratic nature of vernacular practice and its capacity to address continued elisions of refugee experience in the historical record. Amid the contemporary attention economy of the online world and plural media sphere, these vernacular 'refugee archives' offer an implicit challenge. Each bears witness to tragedy as it happened and reminds us therefore of a general lack of will across the world to respond. Once this material becomes the archival record therefore – *if* it does – what kinds of response will the histories written from it demand?

Notes

1. This and subsequent quotations are derived from an interview with the authors in 2016.
2. unhcr.org/uk/archives-and-records.html (accessed 24 May 2019).
3. media.unhcr.org/C.aspx?VP3=CMS3&VF=Home (accessed 24 May 2019).
4. media.unhcr.org/C.aspx?VP3=CMS3&VF=Home (accessed 24 May 2019).
5. media.unhcr.org/terms (accessed 24 May 2019).
6. UNHCR Head of Video Unit, email to the authors, 3 October 2017.
7. Since the time of writing, the site has relaunched as https://www.qisetna.com. This founding statement is archived at https://talkingsyria.wordpress.com/about/ (accessed 18 June 2019).
8. https://whoareweproject.com/2017-programme/learning-labs-seminars-talks/talking-syria-storytelling-platform (accessed 18 June 2019).
9. Archived at https://talkingsyria.wordpress.com/contact-us-3/ (accessed 18 June 2019).
10. https://www.qisetna.com/morning-meditation/ (accessed 18 June 2019).
11. http://www.syriauntold.com/en/about-syria-untold/ (accessed 24 May 2019).
12. http://www.syriauntold.com/en/about-syria-untold/ (accessed 24 May 2019).
13. http://www.syriauntold.com/en/2016/07/cities-in-revolution/ (accessed 24 May 2019).
14. http://www.syriauntold.com/en/category/looking-inside-the-uprising/ (accessed 24 May 2019).
15. http://www.syriauntold.com/en/2014/09/the-uprising-and-syrias-reconstituted-collective-memory/ (accessed 24 May 2019).
16. Quoted at www.archives.org.uk/news/678-talking-syria-wins-national-award.html (accessed 24 May 2019).

Bibliography

Alhayek, K. (2016), 'Interview with Mohammad Dibo', *Status*, 3.2, 27 January, http://www.statushour.com/en/Interview/181 (accessed 5 October 2017).

Anonymous (2017), 'Community Archive and Heritage Award 2017 – winners announced', Community and Archives Heritage Group, 11 October, http://www.communityarchives.org.uk/content/awards/community-archive-heritage-award-2017 (accessed 5 October 2017).

Bingham, A. (2012), 'Ignoring the first draft of history? Searching for the popular press in studies of twentieth-century Britain', *Media History*, 18.3–4: 311–26.

Caswell, M., M. Cifor and M. H. Ramirez (2016), '"To suddenly discover yourself existing": uncovering the affective impact of community archives', *The American Archivist*, 79.1: 56–81.

Chun, W. H. K. (2011), *Programmed Visions: Software and Memory* (Cambridge, MA: MIT Press).

Cifor, M. (2016), 'Affecting relations: introducing affect theory to archival discourse', *Archival Science*, 16.1: 7–31.

Della Ratta, D. (2014), 'The importance of telling Syrian stories as they should be told', *SyriaUntold*, 22 September, http://www.syriauntold.com/en/2014/09/40867/ (accessed 2 October 2017).

Ernst, W. (2013), 'Aura and temporality: the insistence of the archive', keynote lecture given at the conference 'The Anarchival Impulse in the Uses of the Image in Contemporary Art', University of Barcelona, http://www.macba.cat/en/quaderns-portatils-wolfgang-ernst (accessed 1 July 2016).

Fahmy, S., and T. J. Johnson (2005), '"How we performed": embedded journalists' attitudes and perceptions towards covering the Iraq War', *Journalism and Mass Communication Quarterly*, 82.2: 301–17.

Featherstone, M. (2006), 'Archive', *Theory, Culture and Society*, 23.2–3: 591–6.

Gatrell, P. (2016), 'Refugees – what's wrong with history?', *Journal of Refugee Studies*, 30.2: 170–89.

Kushner, T. (2006), *Remembering Refugees: Then and Now* (Manchester: Manchester University Press).

Long, P., S. Baker, L. Istvandity and J. Collins (2017), 'A labour of love: the affective archives of popular music culture', *Archives and Records*, 38.1: 61–79.

Marfleet, P. (2007), 'Refugees and history: why we must address the past', *Refugee Survey Quarterly*, 26.3: 136–48.

Marfleet, P. (2013), 'Explorations in a foreign land: states, refugees, and the problem of history', *Refugee Survey Quarterly*, 32.2: 14–34.

Marfleet, P. (2016), 'Displacements of memory', *Refuge: Canada's Journal on Refugees*, 32.1: 7–17.

Masi, A. (2017), 'Barred from Syria, a journalist must make sense of what she's told', *The Committee to Protect Journalists*, 25 April, https://cpj.org/2017/04/where-ive-never-set-foot.php (accessed 26 September 2017).

Qasmiyeh, Y. M. (2017), 'Refugees are dialectical beings: part one', 1 September, https://refugeehosts.org/2017/09/01/refugees-are-dialectical-beings-part-one/ (accessed 2 October 2017).

Saber, D., and P. Long (2017), '"I will not leave, my freedom is more precious than my blood": from affect to precarity: crowd-sourced citizen archives as memories of the Syrian war', *Archives and Records*, 1.38: 80–99.

Zelizer, B., and K. Tenenboim-Weinblatt (eds) (2014), *Journalism and Memory* (Basingstoke: Palgrave Macmillan).

Chapter 24

Digital Biopolitics, Humanitarianism and the Datafication of Refugees

Btihaj Ajana

Refugees and their bodies are increasingly becoming a contested site of struggle, control and resistance. With the recent refugee crisis that has seen hundreds of thousands of people fleeing their war-torn countries to seek shelter in Europe and elsewhere, various measures are being adopted by governments across European borders and beyond so as to manage the flow of forced migrants and administer support to asylum seekers. Such measures include the use of tracking apps, biometric technologies and smart ID cards. What these measures have in common is their reliance on two elements: data and the body. Every day, thousands of people crossing borders have their fingerprints, eye scans, photographs, names and nationality recorded and verified on various databases. Border officials, governments and security contractors use these data to monitor and track individuals crossing borders, while refugee agencies and aid workers can use the data to provide vital services to refugees. The 'datafication of the body' is therefore emerging as a major trend in both the security and the humanitarian responses to the current refugee situation.

In this chapter, I consider some recent examples of the data-driven techniques deployed by both governments and aid agencies to manage the mobility of refugees and securitise borders. These include the European Border Surveillance System, EUROSUR, and a series of European-wide databases such as the Schengen Information System, as well as the United Nations' refugee registration system, ProGres, and the recently launched project, ID2020, supported by the United Nations. I approach these examples through the lens of 'digital biopolitics' (Colman 2016), a concept describing the increasing convergence of body and digital technology in governmental practices and their life-management strategies. By critically reflecting on the digital ontology of the refugee body, this chapter also raises some ethical questions vis-à-vis issues of power and agency, and the interplay between care and control that underlies contemporary humanitarian approaches to the refugee crisis. One important question is to do with the issue of identification and how the identity of the refugee is increasingly becoming at once the target of surveillance and control as well as the basis of arguments for the refugee's rights. By juxtaposing analyses of governmental and humanitarian technologies of identification, the chapter reveals how in both contexts, refugees are often reduced to an object of digital biopolitics through the various biometric identification processes imposed upon them. I begin the discussion with a brief explanation of what digital biopolitics entails.

Digital biopolitics

Over the last decade the concept of biopolitics has become widely used in various academic fields, including refugee studies. Often associated with Michel Foucault, the term biopolitics indicates a form of politics that takes biological aspects as its primary site of intervention, manipulation and governance. In his later work, Foucault (1976) describes a shift in the ways in which power was enacted upon the body; both the individual body and the body of the population. He argues that from the eighteenth century, a form of power began to permeate the social order, taking the vitality of the body and the biological existence of the population as its main preoccupation. He calls this 'biopower'. Biopolitics is the name he gives to the mechanisms, techniques, technologies and rationalities that are put to work for the purpose of managing life and the living, and governing their everyday affairs. And what differentiates biopower and biopolitics from older forms of sovereign power and politics, according to Foucault, is that they are not so much about repressive discipline and coercion but normalisation and control. They are about the maximisation of productivity and the forces of economy. As Lemke further explains, 'while sovereignty seized hold of life in order to suppress it, the new life-administering power is dedicated to inciting, reinforcing, monitoring, and optimizing the forces under its control' (2016: 57). This does not mean, however, that the absolute sovereign power has completely disappeared from modern forms of power and politics; rather, it is now carefully concealed behind the calculated control over biological life and the administration of bodies.

So, whereas sovereign politics is about the power to kill and to let live, biopolitics is about the power to make live and to let die, according to Foucault. And as Baele (2016) succinctly points out, the more a state focuses on the life and well-being of its own population, the more it creates the conditions of possibility for others to die. Inherent within this notion of biopolitics is, therefore, a paradox whereby the same techniques that are designed to enhance life can also lead to exposing some people to death, 'or, quite simply, political death, expulsion, rejection, and so on' (Foucault 2003: 256). This paradox is indeed most apparent in the refugee crisis and in the way governments are heavily investing in keeping refugees at bay in the name of protecting the welfare and security of their own populations.

Crucial to the overall functioning of biopolitics is the mobilisation of diverse technologies 'in the hope of producing certain desired effects and averting certain undesired events' (Rose 1999: 52). With the advent of digital technologies, biopolitical capacities have been expanded, enhancing the methods by which the body and life itself are visualised, examined and governed. In her analysis of what constitutes 'digital biopolitics', Colman (2016) identifies key features that characterise contemporary forms of bio-politics and their interplay with the digital. Technologies and techniques of measurement (e.g. biometrics), identification (e.g. smart ID cards), biocoding (rendering the body as information and algorithm) and imaging (e.g. X-ray and airport scans) are all important aspects of digital biopolitics through which many areas of everyday life, such as health, work, migratory patterns, reproduction and so one, are being categorised, controlled and managed. In what follows I shall examine some of these aspects as they unfold in the context of the refugee crisis and the security and humanitarian responses towards it.

Smart control: the refugee–technology nexus

> Even though policymakers often claim that technology merely does the same job faster and better, technology also changes both the substance and the nature of policy. For one thing, it brings new actors to the scene. (Broeders and Dijstelbloem 2016: 242)

Over the years, technology has increasingly occupied a central place in the discussions, strategies and policies concerning the management of borders and migration issues. From human detector sensors to satellite tracking systems, from surveillance drones to interoperable databases, the smart control of borders through technology is currently on the rise. In 2016 and in response to the growing flows of refugees from the Middle East and Africa, the European border protection agency, Frontex, invited major tech companies, such as Securiport LLC, 3M, Thales and Crossmatch, to pitch refugee-tracking solutions in order to control the movement of migrants attempting to reach Europe and monitor those who are already there (Taylor and Harrison 2016). Ideas put forward included the use of big data, smartphone apps, biometrics and smart ID cards. Unisys, one of the pitching firms, proposed a 'refugee management suite' which could provide a registration system for asylum seekers. The proposal included the moni-toring of refugees before they reach Europe using phone apps and biomet-ric data gathering; tracking people once they are inside Europe using smart ID cards; and the implementation of a system of data analytics and red flags to highlight those with backgrounds considered as warranting further investigation.

Such proposals, although not entirely new in essence, are part of a growing trend towards the smartification of border security and surveillance in which Europe has been investing heavily in recent years. Increasingly, refugee issues are being framed in terms of technological solutions, highlighting the importance of already initiated mechanisms of control such as biometric identification, data mining and risk analysis systems, while also calling for the development of new techniques and mechanisms. Digitisation and datafication are emerging as prominent means of reshaping, enhancing and intensifying the methods by which cross-border mobility and migration flows are managed and policed. As Broeders and Dijstelbloem argue, '[m]onitoring mobility and migration have changed drastically in the digital age [. . .] Data from various different sources are broken down into bits and bytes and reassembled in databases that have become a cornerstone of modern migration policy' (2016: 244). Borders, as such, are no longer simply material frontiers that separate states. But they are now *everywhere* and go beyond physical spatiality. This quantitative as well as qualitative transformation in the nature, ontology and function of borders has been undoubtedly made possible through the continuous evolution of monitoring techniques and surveillance technologies. These developments have enabled border control 'at a distance' through visa systems, e-border schemes, biometric identification, visualisation and data-driven techniques. They have turned physical borders into portable, omnipresent and virtual borders through a panoply of techniques and technologies, including electronic passports, identity cards and networked databases (Guiraudon and Lahav 2000; Ajana 2013; van der Ploeg and Pridmore 2016).

Frontex's call is also indicative of how border control in Europe is being privatised and outsourced, a process that has been going on for some time.[1] Increasingly, the management of borders, migration and refugee issues is becoming a distributed task that is carried out not only by governments but by a plethora of private and professional entities, subcontracted companies and start-ups, technical experts and data scientists, independent software developers and so on. This has a profound impact on border policy itself, as the state's perception of reality as a whole becomes more technologically mediated, statistically informed and highly datafied (Broeders and Dijstelbloem 2016: 242). In fact, developments in border management and surveillance are increasingly driven by private actors and the lucrative security industry. These actors thus play a role in defining the refugee and migration experience in Europe and elsewhere and shaping the ideologies, imaginaries, rationales and responses adopted vis-à-vis these issues. This trend, which Ben Hayes (2009) refers to as the 'security-industrial complex', raises fundamental questions about accountability and the blurring of tasks between private companies and public authorities, as well as the expanding 'marketisation' of border control. As Antony Loewenstein argues, following the refugee crisis in Europe, a growing number of corporations have seen financial opportunity in the most vulnerable people:

'[r]efugees become numbers to be processed; the profit motive is paramount in the minds of many multinationals' (Loewenstein 2015). Examples of how the refugee crisis has been turned into a profitable business abound:

> In Germany, Air Berlin PLC was paid some $350,000 [in 2014] operating charter flights to deport rejected asylum seekers on behalf of the government. In Sweden, the government paid a language-analysis firm $900,000 [in 2014] to verify asylum-seekers' claims of where they were from. In Athens, a Western Union branch has been disbursing €20,000 a day (about $22,600) to migrants, reaping fees on each transaction. (Troianovski, Mesco and Clark 2015)

Fortress Europe, the term often used to refer to the ensemble of policies, strategies and mechanisms deployed to keep refugees and 'irregular' migrants from entering Europe, has been highly influenced by defence firms and arms companies. Military technology such as drones, sensors, satellites and patrolling robots are being repurposed in response to rising demands for border surveillance. As part of the move towards outsourcing asylum and immigration operations, private defence contractors such as Airbus, Thales, Safran and Finmeccanica have received much of the estimated $244 million invested by the EU's Research and Development fund for fortifying borders (Proctor 2015; Kane 2016). As Cetti argues, recent years have seen the consolidation of security companies into 'a powerful oligarchy of transnational corporations'. Not only are these companies being awarded 'a seemingly endless flow of public funds and guaranteed access to overseas markets [. . .] but also with a prime laboratory in which to develop new technological "security solutions"' (Cetti 2015). As a result, private security contractors and defence companies are increasingly being incorporated into the core operations of the EU's border management systems and policies, enabling them to set much of the border security agenda and define its activities.

Since the establishment of Schengen[2] for the purpose of abolishing internal borders between participating EU member states, a host of surveillance mechanisms and automated control systems have been unleashed to support the identification and monitoring of non-EU travellers, migrants and refugees. A series of European-wide databases have been implemented including the Schengen Information System (SIS I and SIS II), EURODAC and the Visa Information System (VIS). These databases are all cross-referenced by border authorities and rely on the registration of biometric details. The Schengen Information System is a large-scale information system that supports the management of external border control in Europe and law enforcement cooperation in the Schengen states. Through this system, participating states provide entries (also called 'alerts') on to the SIS database on travel bans, wanted and missing persons, and lost and stolen property. The information is directly accessible to all authorised police officers and other law enforcement authorities. EURODAC is an EU-wide database containing the biometric fingerprints of all asylum applicants in the EU. The aim of this database is to detect multiple asylum claims made by the same applicant and chart the distribution of asylum seekers across Europe. The VIS database is a system containing information, including biometrics, on visa applications by third-country nationals requiring a visa to enter the Schengen area. It globally connects the immigration authorities of the EU member states with their consular posts, providing aggregate information on trends in visa applications and mobility from certain regions.

In addition, the European Border Surveillance System, EUROSUR, deploys drones, satellites and reconnaissance aircraft to track so-called irregular migration and monitor Europe's external borders. It also works as an information-exchange mechanism, allowing Frontex and European member states to exchange data and information effortlessly in order to prevent the 'illegal' crossing of European borders. As such, these systems act as a 'digital border' primarily targeted at asylum seekers, irregular migrants and visitors on short-term visas. As Broeders and Dijstelbloem (2016: 252) point out, the EU's investment in such systems is considerable: a budget of €822 million has been dedicated to existing large-scale border IT programmes for the 2014–20 period.

What all these systems have in common, in terms of technicality and purpose, is their interest in identity and identification, and the management of these through data analytics and biometric technologies. Together they represent a sophisticated platform for 'abstracting' information from circulating bodies and fitting it into 'neat categories and definitions' (Adey 2004: 502), while enabling the distribution of collected data across a multitude of searchable database records. These systems have the technical ability to create various profiling mechanisms and deductive classifications in order to systematically 'sort among the elements to formulate what and who must be surveyed' (Bigo 2006: 39).

In fact, one of the primary biopolitical functions of these systems is to codify, categorise and profile in order to manage the (perceived and constructed) risks associated with global mobility, including the mobility of refugees. This way, the identity of the person attempting to cross an international border is established, encoded and profiled prior to reaching the physical border itself through the digital traces of applying for a visa, purchasing an air ticket, using a bank card, conducting a Google search, and so on. As I argue elsewhere (Ajana 2015: 73), the person's data and digital identity travel 'in advance' through the various information networks, circuits and databases, and wait for the physical referent (the body) to arrive. On arrival, and sometimes even before, the person's identity is matched with her body through biometric techniques, and screened against other profiling data associated with behavioural patterns and levels of risk. Border access is then either granted or denied.

Data-driven techniques of monitoring provide endless possibilities for control and surveillance. Not only do they institute and manage the conditions of access to borders and services, but they intensify the culture of sorting, pre-diction and pre-emption that has become the norm in border security policies and practices. Through these techniques, governments are increasingly able to target 'undocumented migrants with an unheard of ease, prevent refugee flows from entering their countries, and track remittances and travel in ways that put migrants at new risks' (Lee 2013). Moreover, the surveillance of human mobility is now not only conducted through the sophisticated data-base systems and the various border monitoring technologies put in place for this very purpose, but also through the everyday use of mobile smartphones by refugees and migrants themselves. As Linnet Taylor (2014) puts it, 'mobile phones are now the new passports. They identify, allow for real-time tracking and geolocation, and are unlikely to be discarded by undocumented migrants in the interests of anonymity.' As such, mobile phones become like an identity document that can transmit the refugee's whereabouts. The real-time geo-spatial tracking affordances of mobile phones makes it possible to 'identify groups on the move, their speed and trajectories, and (through their service providers) their places of origin' (Taylor 2014). Recently, Germany's interior minister announced a draft law that would allow German authorities to seize data from the smartphones, laptops and tablets of people seeking asylum in the country in order to determine their identities and nationalities (Toor 2017): 'Collecting mobile phone data would help us to determine the identity and origin of asylum applicants who don't have a passport', said Jutta Cordt, the head of Germany's Ministry of Immigration and Refugees (quoted in Jefferson and Wolfgang 2017). Merkel's cabinet is soon expected to endorse this controversial measure (Kirchsbaum 2017). Already in Denmark, Swe-den, Norway and Holland, immigration officials are allowed to confiscate and analyse mobile phones and other electronic devices belonging to asylum seekers to help establish their identities if they have no formal identity docu-ments when they enter these countries (Oltermann and Henley 2016).

In a way, then, the very technologies that have the capacity to help refu-gees throughout their arduous and dangerous journeys across borders can equally make them susceptible to detection by border authorities. For while smartphones have played a crucial role in helping refugees to stay in contact with their families and friends, reduce their social isolation, and gather poten-tially life-saving information, they are also turning into surveillance tools that enable governments and other entities to strengthen and intensify their con-trol of refugees' movement and identities. The confiscation and analysis of refugees' mobile phones is a forceful and imbalanced act of power that strips refugees of their privacy and leaves them with no alternative but to accept these intrusive measures if they want to access aid and receive help. As one refugee puts it, 'You don't feel that you have the right to say no. You're really in a bad situation and you think, Okay, I'm going to give you whatever you want, just help me' (quoted in Toor 2017). By tapping into the surveillance capacities of mobile phones, these measures risk deterring refugees from using their phones altogether and thereby depriving them of connectedness and information.

What all the above-mentioned examples indicate is the hybridity, heterogeneity and complex character of the mechanisms involved in the surveillance of refugees and the digital biopolitics of mobility. From advanced tools such as drones, satellite imagery, interoperable identification systems and big data analytics to everyday technologies of communication such as mobile phones and social media, the tracking and monitoring of refugees and their mobility have become more intensive than ever and highly technology-driven. What is also interesting about these developments is that governments, military agents and private security contractors are not the only actors using technology and data collection to monitor and control the movement of refugees – humanitarian organisations are also making use of a host of sophisticated techniques to administer aid and manage the identities of refugees. Ultimately humanitarianism becomes implicated in forms of control that often end up stripping refugees of their agency and subjecting them to biopolitical techniques of identification. In the next section, I shall expand further on these issues by examining some of the examples of 'humanitarian technologies' and the way they are being deployed to respond to the refugee issue.

Smart aid: the care–control continuum

Recently, aid agencies have started to deploy similar techniques to those deployed by border agencies in order to register refugees and provide them with the necessary support. As Favell (2015) puts it, in the context of Syrian refugees, '[f]orget the stereotype of the aid worker with the clipboard, the Syrian aid effort is digital – registration with biometric verification, smart-card-based aid, smart device data collection, mobile communications and telemedicine'.

Favell goes on to explain that without registration on the United Nations High Commissioner for Refugees (UNHCR) ProGres database, a Syrian in a host country is not officially recognised as a refugee and thus not entitled to protection and aid from UN agencies and other NGOs. ProGres was launched in 2004 to improve the collection, sharing and use of information on refugees and other individuals of concern. It is now in use in more than 70 countries. Commenting on the ProGres system, Dona Tarpey from UNHCR states that '[b]efore, we had dozens of databases that were not necessarily compatible [. . .] with ProGres, we now have one unified database that caters for a wide range of UNHCR operations and situations, from camp-based to urban refugees, from repatriation to resettlement' (quoted in Goldstein-Rodriguez and Tan 2004).

Designed to capture and store an extensive range of bio-data, ProGres creates a digital global record for every refugee, containing their personal details, contact information, place of origin, time of arrival, education, occupation, family members and other details. In addition, iris scans are performed on refugees during the registration process in which a digital capture of the individual's iris is taken and stored on the database to be later used as a method of identity verification. According to IrisGuard Inc., the provider of this biometric system, there are now more than 1.6 million Syrian refugees in the region who have been registered in this way (IrisGuard 2015). The iris database is used to deliver a variety of vital services to refugees including food, financial aid and health assistance.

Increasingly, the traditional approach of delivering aid in physical form (tents, blankets, food, household goods, etc.) is being replaced by digital financial aid in which beneficiaries can use biometrically enabled systems, such as smart cards, to access their allocated cash-based assistance and purchase products at designated retailers. But as Favell (2015) points out, digital aid programmes vary considerably between different host countries and aid agencies, depending on the local conditions and regulations. At the moment, Lebanon has the largest implementation of digital aid in which more than one million refugees are using either World Food Programme's smartcard to buy goods at participating supermarkets, and/or UNHCR-backed ATM cards to withdraw money instead of receiving physical goods. Jordan has reportedly the most sophisticated aid delivery methods. At designated ATM machines in Jordan, refugees are able to withdraw their cash entitlement from UNHCR by placing their eye against an IrisGuard scanner without the need of a card. The World Food Programme has also been piloting the use of a similar biometric system to allow refugees to purchase food in participating supermarkets using their irises. There are now more than 633,000 refugees in Jordan who are using this method to receive support (O'Donovan 2015).

Promoting its technical abilities, IrisGuard Inc. argues that as a testament to the accuracy and speed of its biometric technology, 'refugees are currently able to walk up to an IrisGuard enabled ATM on the street, present one eye only (no card or pin) and effortlessly withdraw their cash allocated financial subsidy immediately' (IrisGuard 2015). This biometric method is therefore promoted as a faster, simpler and more 'dignified' way of delivering aid to displaced refugees than the more traditional methods of 'in-kind aid' or even smart cards. It is also promoted as a way of combating fraud. The UN reported that since implementing this scanning system, the number of Syrians requesting aid has reduced by 30 per cent (O'Donovan 2015). IrisGuard Inc. elaborated on this aspect in the following way:

> Cards and pins can be traded on the black market where unauthorized persons continue to receive aid fraudulently. Only by implementing IrisGuard technology at the time the service or cash delivery is given, can any aid agency be 100% confident that the beneficiary is indeed the rightful recipient. IrisGuard pioneered 'Your Eye is your Card' concept, every individual has them, the card that cannot be stolen, lost or given to someone else. (IrisGuard 2015)

But despite the seemingly convenient features of biometric-based aid delivery solutions such as IrisGuard, these systems raise many issues that are at once ontological and political. The fact that access to refugee aid is made contingent on the imperative of submitting one's biometric information and registering on the ProGres database again strips refugees of any sense of agency and places them at the mercy of these systems and the administrating agencies. Refugees are thus left with no other choice but to enrol one of their most intimate aspects: their bodies. Here, the refugee body becomes a forensic stabiliser of identity, functioning more and more as a passcode, as a lie detector that can either condemn or exonerate the person. Through these biometric procedures, the refugee body becomes abstracted and broken down into a series of data which then define the person's legitimacy and right to access vital services.

Giorgio Agamben describes such processes as 'biopolitical tattooing', which amounts to 'the progressive animalization of man' (2008: 202) enabled through the sophisticated techniques of biometric surveillance, such as iris scanning. The term itself is reminiscent of the process by which inmates of Nazi concentration camps were identified and coordinated through tattooed serial numbers. Through this metaphor of biopolitical tattooing, Agamben is drawing a parallel between the paradigm of the concentration camp and contemporary biopolitical techniques of governance, to the extent that these are marked by a similar interest in the abstraction, organisation and filing away of 'the most private and incommunicable aspect of subjectivity: the body's biological life' (2008: 202). What Agamben is taking issue with here is precisely the ways in which biological life itself is becoming the object and target of mechanisms of control, including humanitarian interventions.

Elsewhere, Agamben argues that humanitarian organisations, despite themselves, 'maintain a secret solidarity with the very powers they ought to fight' in so far as they can only grasp human life in the figure of 'bare life' (1998: 133), a naked form of life that has been stripped of its political rights and reduced to its purely biological existence. Only as such, according to Agamben, does the human life of refugees become the object of aid and protection. Similarly, Slavoj Žižek contends that 'the privileged object of the humanitarian biopolitics [. . .] is deprived of his full humanity through the very patronising way of being taken care of' (2002: 91). He adds that refugee camps and the delivery of humanitarian aid 'are the two faces, "human" and "inhuman", of the same socio-logical formal matrix' (2002: 91). Fassin uses the term 'compassionate repression' to refer to the dual and paradoxical practices whereby force and humanitarianism dialectically go hand in hand, oscillating between 'a politics of pity and policies of control' (Fassin 2005: 366) in which care and repression are profoundly linked. In this sense, the compulsory registration of refugees on ProGres and their biometric enrolment and scanning create a form of humanitarian governance which, in the words of Schram, exchanges 'aid for discipline' (2006: 175) by forcing refugees, at their moment of vulnerability and need, to submit their bio-data and subscribe to the imposed biometric processes. This way, humanitarian organisations become the 'perfect supplement' (Schram 2006: 175) to the sovereign power of modern biopolitical states and a complicit agent in the surveillance of vulnerable groups, such as refugees and irregular migrants.

In this biopolitical order, refugees and their bodies are caught in the middle of what David Lyon refers to as the 'continuum between *care* and *control*' (2007: 3) in which they have to endure various forms of surveillance in the name of support and rescue. In this continuum, contested and problematic technologies of control, such as biometrics, become 'humanitarianised' and couched within a rhetoric of care that in turn imbues them with a humane value and gives them normative and scientific validation. In fact, refugees and their bodies have long acted as the testing ground for various technologies and interventions, be it in terms of compulsory biometric surveillance, experimental vaccine testing or the provision of food considered unsafe by Western standards. As Chandler rightly contends, 'humanitarian subjects can easily be seen as less valued as their lives and liberties are placed in jeopardy while humanitarian practices test and develop new technologies. The distinction between humanitarian aid and the new exploitation of humanitarian subjects seems to be a fine one' (2016: x).

Chandler's statement brings to mind a project recently launched under the name ID2020. The project is described as a 'call for action' which seeks to provide identity solutions for the estimated 1.1 billion people, including refugees, who are living without a legally recognised identity in order to help them access basic services such as healthcare and education. As a UN-supported public–private partnership, ID2020 brings together government representatives, humanitarian agencies, NGOs, charities, technology businesses and various experts on digital and legal identity. The inaugural ID2020 summit held at the UN headquarters in New York in May 2016[3] responded to one of the aims of the 2030 Sustainable Development Goals, adopted by world leaders at the United Nations on 25 September 2015: to provide legal identity for all, including birth registration by 2030 (United Nations 2015). Drawing on various emotive case studies, the summit started by highlighting some of the tragic consequences that can befall those lacking a legally recognised identity, including issues of human trafficking, forced labour, sexual exploitation, slavery, and exclusion from education, healthcare, social and financial programmes. As such, the overarching question driving the agenda of ID2020 is how to create an officially recognisable identity *for all*, starting with refugees and other vulnerable groups in society.

Technology featured prominently in the discussions, particularly with regard to the potential of 'Blockchain' technology[4] and biometrics to provide identity solutions. The summit was indeed a marketing opportunity for the tech industry to promote some of the most recent developments in digital technologies and discuss their relevance to the question of identity. The absence of refugees themselves from the ID2020 summit and its debates was jarring and raises questions about the agency of refugees and the true agenda of the project itself. While the aims of the ID2020 project are couched primarily in 'humanitarian' terms, this is also a project about 'security'. This is evident in the level of interest it has received from the banking sector (anti-money laundering) and the various security-related actors who attended the summit with the aim of exploring new ways of securitising everyday activities (movement, financial transactions, access to social services, etc.) through identity itself and the paraphernalia of technologies used to manage it, including biometrics. Discussions during the summit quickly shifted from the narrative of helping refugees and the 'unidentified' to narratives of security and monitoring in the banking sector and the like. In this sense, ID2020 is another clear example of where the discourse of care and the will to control converge. It is also an example of how the misery of vulnerable groups, such as refugees and the poor, is often used to advance an agenda that is (or at least has the potential to become) essentially about surveillance and control at a larger scale – if only as an unintended consequence of the development of mass global identity systems.

As Agamben has extensively argued, refugees and the mechanisms of control they are subjected to can be seen as precursors to how the whole of humanity itself will be treated in the future. The UN's goal of establishing a legal identity 'for all' is a case in point and raises the question as to whether a universal biometric identity card will eventually be required for everyone to access vital services, and whether those who refuse to submit their biometrics might risk becoming outcasts from society and being disqualified from receiving healthcare or education, holding a job, opening a bank account, etc. In countries such as Denmark, it is already impossible to function fully in society and conduct everyday activities without having a CPR number, a national registration mechanism that assigns a unique identity number to each Danish citizen and resident and without which one cannot access any services. A 'cashless' society is also being designed in which all economic activity will have to go through banks where transactions can be tracked, watched and monitored. As Snyder warns, '[w]hat the elite want to do is to make sure that everyone is "in the system". And it is a system that they control and that they manipulate for their own purposes' (2015). In terms of biometrics, we can already see its function creep through the example of biometric passport and ID cards, which some countries have adopted not only for foreign nationals but also for their own citizens.

Historically, many identity technologies and scientific methods have been initially tested on colonised subjects. In the nineteenth century, colonies were used as experimental sites for the development of identification technologies (this being particularly true of fingerprinting). In India, for instance, the bodies of local people were used to try out and master identification techniques before they were exported to the metropoles, just as the current biometric systems were initially trialled on people with the 'fewest rights' (such as asylum seekers, refugees and prisoners) before starting to spill over to the rest of the population (Ajana 2013; Fuller 2003).

Another issue has to do with the very essence of the question driving the UN's 2030 Sustainable Development Goals and the ID2020 project as a whole, namely *how* to provide a legal identity for *all*. This question seems to be undergirded by the defective assumption that *everyone* on the planet wants and needs an identity in the form prescribed by the authorities, and that all that is required is a system to provide it. This assumption ignores the fact that some populations, such as nomadic groups and remote tribes, might not wish to subscribe to this ideology of legal identity, and that, in fact, the lack of official identity might be convenient in certain circumstances and for some individuals and groups whose identifiability might cause them more harm than good.[5] This assumption also ends up rationalising the very bureaucratic and technocratic machinery that reduces people to numbers on a database or a piece of ID, without which the person becomes a 'nobody'. And this is precisely the core of the problem.

Makhtar Diop, the World Bank Vice President for Africa, argues that 'identification provides a foundation for other rights and gives a voice to the voiceless' (Diop 2016). But this increasing emphasis on legal identity and its casting as a *prerequisite* for exercising basic rights could very well result in strengthening or even creating further forms of exclusion. The 'humanitarian question' must therefore be reframed in a way that challenges the supremacy of legal identity rather than affirms it. Instead of asking how to provide a legal identity to all, the question that needs to be raised is how to *disassociate* access and entitlement to relevant services and programmes from the tyranny of legal identity, so that access to basic rights, such as education and healthcare, is not made contingent on birth registration and identity documentation, but on the mere fact of existing. In other words, *everyone should enjoy rights regardless of the lack of legal identity and documents of identification*. Undermining the validity, authority and importance of legal identity and identification technologies is a necessary step towards freeing the human from the juridico-political shackles of identity and legality. For after all, identity and its technologies have long been a powerful tool of state control.

Conclusion

In this chapter, I have examined the growing techniques and technologies that are being deployed to control the mobility of refugees, on the one hand, and to provide them with humanitarian aid, on the other. From biometrics to big data, from geo-tracking to smart ID cards, there is now a vast array of mechanisms whose *raison d'être* is to ensure the robust protection of borders from 'unwanted' others and to administer help to those fleeing war and other disasters. At the heart of such mechanisms is the increasing convergence of body and data whereby control of mobility occurs through and on the bodies of refugees and migrants themselves through the scanning, digitisation and filing away of biometric data on various interoperable and networked databases, such as EURODAC and the Visa Information System.

Looking at these developments through the lens of digital biopolitics has enabled me to unpack some of the complexities and paradoxes inherent in what has been referred to as the control–care continuum, and identify forms of power and surveillance that are concealed behind humanitarian and security claims, as well as the role of digital technologies in actualising these. Examples such as the ID2020 project and ProGres are clear cases of how techniques of control and monitoring are becoming humanitarianised and couched in the language of care. But if humanitarianism is to be truly humanitarian, it has to start comprehending its own complicity in the biopolitical machine of border management and exploring ways of disrupting the continuum between control and care. For without this, humanitarian effort is at risk of becoming part of the problem rather than the solution.

Notes

1. See, for instance, the research conducted by CoESS: http://www.coess.org/newsroom.php?page=white-papers (accessed 24 May 2019).
2. For more information about Schengen, see http://ec.europa.eu/home-affairs/what-we-do/policies/borders-and-visas/schengen_en (accessed 24 May 2019).
3. I was invited to attend the event as a participant.
4. Blockchain is the technology underlying cryptocurrency. It consists of a series of data blocks that are cryptographically linked together. It is often defined as a decentralised and distributed database or ledger that provides uneditable public record of digital transactions. Recently Blockchain technology emerged in discussions around online identity management. It is being looked to as a secure solution for identity authentication in real time. For more information on the relationship between Blockchain technology and identity, see Jacobovitz (2016).
5. In instances where someone is fleeing persecution, for example.

Bibliography

Adey, P. (2004), 'Secured and sorted motilities: examples from the airport', *Surveillance and Society*, 1.4: 500–19.
Agamben, G. (1998), *Homo Sacer: Sovereign Power and Bare Life*, trans. D. Heller-Roazen (Stanford: Stanford University Press).
Agamben, G. (2008), 'No to biopolitical tattooing', https://modernrhetoric.files.wordpress.com/2010/11/agamben.pdf (accessed 15 May 2019).
Ajana, B. (2013), *Governing through Biometrics: The Biopolitics of Identity* (Basingstoke: Palgrave Macmillan).

Ajana, B. (2015), 'Augmented borders: Big Data and the ethics of immigration control', *Journal of Information, Communication and Ethics in Society*, 13.1: 58–78.

Baele, S. J. (2016), 'Live and let die: did Michel Foucault predict Europe's refugee crisis?', http://theconversation.com/live-and-let-die-did-michel-foucault-predict-europes-refugee-crisis-55286 (accessed 15 May 2019).

Bigo, D. (2006), 'Globalized (in)security: the field and the ban-opticon', in D. Bigo and A. Tsoukala (eds), *Illiberal Practices of Liberal Regimes – The (In)security Games* (Paris: L'Harmattan).

Broeders, D., and H. Dijstelbloem (2016), 'The datafication of mobility and migration management: the mediating state and its consequences', in Irma van der Ploeg and Jason Pridmore (eds), *Digitizing Identities: Doing Identity in a Networked World* (London: Routledge), 242–60, https://www.researchgate.net/publication/290194722_The_Datafication_of_Mobility_and_Migration_Management_the_Mediating_State_and_its_Consequences (accessed 15 May 2019).

Cetti, F. (2015), 'Fortress Europe: the war against migrants', *International Socialism*, 148, http://isj.org.uk/fortress-europe-the-war-against-migrants/#footnote-263-48-backlink (accessed 15 May 2019).

Chandler, D. (2016), 'Foreword', in K. L. Jacobsen (ed.), *The Politics of Humanitarian Technology* (London: Routledge).

Colman, F. (2016), 'Digital biopolitics', in S. Wilmer and A. Zukauskaite (eds), *Resisting Biopolitics: Philosophical, Political, and Performative Strategies* (London: Routledge).

Diop, M. (2016), 'African partners, World Bank commit to provide identification to millions', http://www.worldbank.org/en/news/press-release/2016/04/14/african-partners-world-bank-commit-to-provide-identification-to-millions (accessed 15 May 2019).

Fassin, D. (2005), 'Compassion and repression: the moral economy of immigration policies in France', *Cultural Anthropology*, 20.3: 362–87.

Favell, A. (2015), 'How technology is helping deliver aid to Syrian refugees in the Middle East', http://www.computerweekly.com/feature/How-technology-is-helping-deliver-aid-to-Syrian-refugees-in-the-Middle-East (accessed 15 May 2019).

Foucault, M. (1976), *The History of Sexuality Volume 1: An Introduction* (New York: Random House).

Foucault, M. (2003 [1976]), 'Society must be defended', in *'Society Must Be Defended': Lectures at the Collège de France 1975–1976*, ed. M. Bertani and A. Fotana, trans. D. Macey (New York: Picador).

Fuller, G. (2003), 'Perfect match: biometrics and body patterning in a networked world', *Fibre Culture*, 1, http://one.fibreculturejournal.org/fcj002 (accessed 15 May 2019).

Goldstein-Rodriguez, R., and V. Tan (2004), 'UNHCR seeks ProGres in refugee registration', http://www.unhcr.org/news/latest/2004/9/4135e9aa4/unhcr-seeks-progres-refugee-registration.html (accessed 15 May 2019).

Guiraudon, V., and G. Lahav (2000), 'A reappraisal of the state sovereignty debate: the case of migration control', *Comparative Political Studies*, 33.1: 136–95.

Hayes, B. (2009), 'NeoConopticon: the EU "security-industrial complex"', http://www.statewatch.org/analyses/neoconopticon-report.pdf (accessed 15 May 2019).

IrisGuard (2015), 'IrisGuard – EyeBank® cash payment – serving Syrian refugees daily', https://www.prlog.org/12461828-irisguard-eyebank-cash-payment-serving-syrian-refugees-daily.html (accessed 24 May 2015).

Jacobovitz, O. (2016), 'Blockchain for identity management', https://www.cs.bgu.ac.il/~frankel/TechnicalReports/2016/16-02.pdf (accessed 15 May 2019).

Jefferson, C., and D. Wolfgang (2017), 'Questions surround German government's refugee phone surveillance law', http://www.dw.com/en/questions-surround-german-governments-refugee-phone-surveillance-law/a-38236850 (accessed 15 May 2019).

Kane, A. (2016), 'Meet the European corporations profiting from the misery of refugees', http://www.alternet.org/grayzone-project/meet-european-corporations-profiting-misery-refugees (accessed 15 May 2019).

Kirschbaum, E. (2017), 'In election year, Germany to tap asylum-seekers' phones for ID checks', http://www.reuters.com/article/us-europe-migrants-germany-asylum-idUSKBN15Z1Y1?feedType=RSS&feedName=worldNews&utm_source=Twitter&utm_medium=Social&utm_campaign=Feed%3A+Reuters%2FworldNews+%28Reuters+World+News%29 (accessed 15 May 2019).

Lee, C. (2013), 'Big Data and migration – what's in store?', http://noncitizensoftheworld.blogspot.co.uk/ (accessed 15 May 2019).

Lemke, T. (2016), 'Rethinking biopolitics', in S. Wilmer and A. Zukauskaite (eds), *Resisting Biopolitics: Philosophical, Political, and Performative Strategies* (London: Routledge).

Loewenstein, A. (2015), 'How private companies are exploiting the refugee crisis for profit', *The Independent*, 23 October, http://www.independent.co.uk/voices/how-companies-have-been-exploiting-the-refugee-crisis-for-profit-a6706587.html (accessed 15 May 2019).

Lyon, D. (2007), *Surveillance Studies: An Overview* (Cambridge: Polity Press).

O'Donovan, C. (2015), 'Tracking refugees puts a vulnerable population at risk', https://www.buzzfeed.com/carolineodonovan/tracking-refugees-puts-a-vulnerable-population-at-risk?utm_term=.jrGP4beVx#.gfmMNY7lb (accessed 15 May 2019).

Oltermann, P., and J. Henley (2016), 'German proposals could see refugees' phones searched by police', *The Guardian*, 11 August, https://www.theguardian.com/world/2016/aug/11/germany-security-proposals-refugees-phones-searched-suspicious-posts-social-media (accessed 15 May 2019).

Proctor, K. (2015), 'Europe's migrant crisis: defense contractors are poised to win big', http://fortune.com/2015/09/10/europe-migrant-crisis-defense-contractors/ (accessed 15 May 2019).

Rose, N. (1999), *Powers of Freedom: Reframing Political Thought* (Cambridge: Cambridge University Press).

Schram, S. F. (2006), *Welfare Discipline: Discourse, Governance and Globalization* (Philadelphia: Temple University Press).

Snyder, M. (2015), 'The UN plans to implement universal biometric identification for all of humanity by 2030', http://www.activistpost.com/2015/11/the-un-plans-to-implement-universal-biometric-identification-for-all-of-humanity-by-2030.html (accessed 15 May 2019).

Taylor, L. (2014), 'No place to hide? The ethics and analytics of tracking mobility using mobile phone data', https://www.law.ox.ac.uk/research-subject-groups/centre-criminology/centreborder-criminologies/blog/2014/07/no-place-hide (accessed 15 May 2019).

Taylor, D., and E. M. Harrison (2016), 'EU asks tech firms to pitch refugee-tracking systems', *The Guardian*, 18 February, https://www.theguardian.com/world/2016/feb/18/eu-asks-tech-firms-to-pitch-refugee-tracking-systems (accessed 15 May 2019).

Toor, A. (2017), 'Germany moves to seize phone and laptop data from people seeking asylum', https://www.theverge.com/2017/3/3/14803852/germany-refugee-phone-data-law-privacy (accessed 15 May 2019).

Troianovski, A., M. Mesco and S. Clark (2015), 'The growth of Refugee Inc.', *Wall Street Journal*, 14 September, http://www.wsj.com/articles/in-european-refugee-crisis-an-industry-evolves-1442252165 (accessed 15 May 2019).

United Nations (2015), 'Transforming our world: the 2030 Agenda for Sustainable Development', http://www.un.org/ga/search/view_doc.asp?symbol=A/RES/70/1&Lang=E (accessed 15 May 2019).

van der Ploeg, I., and J. Pridmore (2016), *Digitizing Identities: Doing Identity in a Networked World* (London: Routledge).

Žižek, S. (2002), *Welcome to the Desert of the Real* (London: Verso).

Chapter 25

The Messenger: Refugee Testimony and the Search for Adequate Witness

Gillian Whitlock and Rosanne Kennedy

The prison (or prison camp) is the house of witness, a maker of moral authority. . . (Durham Peters 2009: 31)

As scholars of life narrative, we constantly question under what conditions camps become 'the house of witness' that enables refugees to testify to their experiences as makers of 'moral authority'. It is now a given that refugee journeys are also mediated journeys. Refugees carry with them devices that document, film, record, photograph and transmit their experiences, mobilising testimonial networks that are carriers of their life story, and creating new archives, texts, records and histories. As their testimony moves in search of witnessing publics (Kennedy 2014), it is by no means assured that it will find 'adequate' witness – those who will receive testimony without deforming it by doubt, or substituting different terms of value than the ones offered by the witness themselves (Gilmore 2017: 5). We know that refugee life narratives can be urgent, and compelling, and they play a vital role in campaigns for human rights. As they migrate online and in print, however, they are constantly called into question across the different jurisdictions where they engage a witnessing public. The acceleration of forced migration in the recent past has produced a surge of life narratives by and about refugees, and in this chapter we focus on the transits of one specific example: *The Messenger*, a prize-winning podcast that broadcast the testimony of Abdul Aziz Muhamat, a refugee in indefinite detention at the remote Pacific processing centre on Manus Island, in Papua New Guinea (PNG), and the response of his addressee, Michael Green, the journalist who bears 'adequate' witness.[1]

The Messenger is one of a number of testimonial narratives from the detention centre on Manus, as the camp hosts a proliferation of content and producers that facilitate new forms of storytelling and challenge traditional notions of source, journalist and audience (Downman and Ubayasiri 2017: 56). The detention centre on Manus Island is one of two offshore processing centres serviced by private providers (G4S, Broadspectrum and Wilson Security) on behalf of the Australian government. The Australian policy of processing asylum seekers offshore in other nation-states is (to date) unique. At the time of *The Messenger* podcast, Aziz was one of nearly 700 men in detention – Australian Border Force statistics recorded 690 men in detention on Manus, and 345 men, women and children on Nauru.[2] Their options were limited, whether their claims to refugee status were recognised or not: to resettle or repatriate to their countries of origin. After the passing of new legislation in July 2013, those who arrived seeking asylum by boat were permanently ineligible for visas to enter Australia, and resettlement – in PNG or Nauru or a third country – was their only option. Aziz is one of the detainees who arrived by boat within a few months of the implementation of this new policy. A small window of opportunity opened in November 2016: a one-off bilateral agreement with the USA to resettle some refugees in offshore detention, prioritising the women, children and families on Nauru, with the single men on Manus a second priority. *The Messenger* podcast traverses this volatile period in the history of the Manus Regional Processing Centre (RPC) as it was experienced by Aziz: the new legislation proscribing access to Australia, the possibility of resettlement in the USA, the withdrawal of Broadspectrum from the business of managing the camps on Nauru and Manus, and the decision of the PNG Supreme Court in May 2016 that the Manus RPC breached the PNG Constitution, mandating the closure of the camp at the end of October 2017. Originally planned as a ten-episode podcast, *The Messenger* was interrupted in September 2017 when the risk of violence during the closure of the Manus camp and the forced relocation of detainees on the island silenced Aziz. The story of the resistance of the men and their final militant occupation of the camp and relocation to alternative facilities on the island was told in a series of thirteen brief exchanges with Aziz's interlocutor (*The Messenger*, 21 October–18 December 2017) and a new episode (7 February 2019). In addition, Aziz was one of the artists featured in the *Eavesdropping* exhibition at the Ian Potter Museum of Art in Melbourne, an open artwork where the men were asked to 'share the sounds of your life on Manus Island' (Dao 2018: n.p.).

How we come to recognise Aziz, and recognise the 'acoustic agency' (Rae et al. 2019: 1039) of his story, raises questions about the affordances of social media and opportunities for autobiographical representation, as new genres and digital platforms for self-representation become available to refugees. In their writing on human rights and narrated lives, Kay Schaffer and Sidonie Smith suggest that digital environments raise provocative questions about how to approach emergent acts and instances of witness. How, they ask, do forms of e-witnessing conjoin user, story, interface and device (2014: 224)? These assemblages of human and non-human elements create testimonial networks, and the mobilisation of first-person testimony from the remote Australian camps on Manus and Nauru uses social media to appeal to a witnessing public. Given that these refugees and asylum seekers are denied citizenship, recognition and the rights of habeas corpus in indefinite detention, what enables them to become agents in the creation of their own autobiographical accounts? Autobiography studies has a long history of concern for the life narratives of 'those who do not write' (Lejeune 1989). Now they tweet, post and email, and an array of rapidly changing discourses, technologies and practices have become available to host their life narratives. As a result, research on human rights and narrated lives now engages with 'technologies of the self': the production of online selves, and the access to power and knowledge that become available through online identities (Rak and Poletti 2014: 6). Equally, the multidisciplinary field of refugee and forced migration studies is opening to lived experiences, memories and representations of forced migration, and the politics of refugee voices in the production and consumption of emic narratives of forced migration and displacement (that is, narratives produced by forced migrants themselves) (Sigona 2014: 369).

Taking a case study approach, we focus on a single refugee, Aziz, and the podcast that features his story, *The Messenger*, during a volatile period that concluded with the evacuation of the Manus RPC. Through our analysis, we argue for and demonstrate an approach to refugee life narratives that is attentive to the specific negotiations, practices and devices that enable refugee voices and experiences to become audible, and how these shift – for example when Aziz turns to texting rather than voice recording as conditions at the camp deteriorate and the risk of violence intensifies. The timespan of *The Messenger*, which covers the period from Aziz's arrival in October 2013 to the closure of the Manus RPC in late 2017, coincided with a dramatic increase in forced migration in the North, as a rise in numbers of undocumented migrants became a global phenomenon. The editing of *The Messenger* podcast reminds us of this global context by incorporating news from the North as relayed in soundbites from nightly bulletins. As Aziz remains detained at the Australian-run immigration detention centre on Manus in April 2016, despite being recognised as a refugee in 2015, we hear that rescuers from a Spanish aid organisation have 'plucked' over 200 migrants from their dinghies in the Mediterranean; another train carrying refugees pulls into Munich central station, many escaping from the civil war in Syria; and the body of a small boy from Kobani in Syria has been washed up on the beach in Turkey (*The Messenger* #4). *The Messenger* splices these different yet contemporaneous sites together, and demands that we do likewise.

Indefinite detention

In her writing on indefinite detention in *Precarious Life*, Judith Butler speculates about effective sites of intervention in the dehumanising effects of the 'new war prison' (2004: 99). Her specific focus is the suspension of national and international law in the new regulations for the indefinite detention of detainees at Guantanamo in March 2002, and the extension of state sovereignty that this implies. Under what conditions, she asks, do some human lives cease to be eligible for basic, if not universal, human rights? To what extent is there a racial and ethnic frame through which these imprisoned lives are viewed and judged such that they are deemed to be outside the recognisable human community (Butler 2004: 57)? A few months earlier, in September and October 2001, the Australian government had introduced extraordinary offshore processing of people who had arrived in the Australian migration zone by boat. In a series of policies first introduced under the auspices of 'the Pacific Solution', offshore processing occurred in camps on Manus and Nauru between 2001 and 2008, and again since 2012. Mandatory detention of unauthorised arrivals was originally introduced by the Migration Amendment Act of 1992, and has been sustained in various forms by governments since, with bipartisan support. Despite ongoing protests at the island camps and reports of abuse and suffering documented by Human Rights Watch, Amnesty International and the Australian Human Rights Commission, for example, and evidence that these policies are inconsistent with Australia's obligations under international law, surveys consistently show public support for mandatory offshore detention from Australian citizens (Higgins 2017), and Australian citizenship is, ostensibly, secured by this rigorous offshore policing of the Australian migration zone.

Dehumanising stereotypes of asylum seekers as economic migrants recur in mainstream media representations in the Australian press. In 2014 the Australian government changed the guidelines on reporting on asylum seekers in government-controlled detention centres by restricting the media's ability to name or publish photographs of asylum seekers in Australia (Downman and Ubayasiri 2017: 45). In 2015 federal government legislation, the Australian Border Force Act, made it a criminal offence for whistleblowers working in the offshore camps to report on asylum seekers, further barring humanising representations of detainees (Barnes and Newhouse 2015). In August 2017 the Minister for Immigration and Border Protection, Peter Dutton, declared that lawyers representing refugees were 'unAustralian', emphasising the exclusion of refugees and their advocates from the community of the nation (Hall 2017). A Migration Amendment (Prohibiting Items in Immigration Detention Facilities) Bill 2017 circulated by the minister introduced amendments to the Migration Act 1958 for consideration when parliament resumed in 2018 'to allow the Minister to determine a thing as prohibited. Such a thing will be a prohibited thing in relation to immigration detention centres and detainees. These things may include narcotic drugs, mobile phones, Subscriber Identity Module (SIM) cards, child pornography and other things of concern.'[3] *The Messenger* was broadcast during a period when discourses of national security and integrity appealed for ever-increasing restrictions on asylum seekers.

The first iteration of the Pacific camps on Nauru and Manus was contemporaneous with the establishment of the notorious 'Black Site' at Guantanamo late in 2001, and the first asylum seekers sent to these camps were quick to make the association between their fate and that of the alleged terrorists held at Guantanamo Bay detention centre. Locating the Pacific camps in relation to the geopolitics of the war on terror, and drawing on Noam Chomsky's classic 1967 essay on 'The Responsibilities of Intellectuals', the Researchers Against Pacific Black Sites (RAPBS) collective argues for an activist and committed academic scholarship in refugee studies.[4] Their identification of Australia's offshore detention network on Nauru and Manus as a 'Black Site' is undoubtedly polemical. The term is associated with the war on terror, the new 'war prisons', and the distinctive architectures of enmity that have prevailed in the wake of 9/11. In making the case for identifying Australia's offshore detention centres under this rubric, the founders of RAPBS, Suvendrini Perera and Joseph Pugliese, identify characteristics that these camps share with the black sites of confinement, abuse and torture: they are characterised by and managed in secret with a lack of accountability; they are commercial operations in which government policy is implemented by private contractors; they are located in racialised and/or formerly colonised territories; and they continue practices of abuse and torture perpetrated in these locations against colonised peoples (Perera and Pugliese 2015). On Manus, despite the rigorous policing of private security contractors, smartphones enable testimonial narratives that document experiences of indefinite detention. Aziz's interlocutor Michael Green explains the microeconomics of the camp that trades these essential devices in *The Messenger*: 'Here's how it works in the detention centre. Detainees earn points when they go to activities like English classes or the gym. Then, they can spend these points at the canteen, where they buy cigarettes. They get local guards to swap those cigarettes on the outside for other stuff, like money or a phone. And of course, none of this is allowed. It all happens on the sly' (*The Messenger* #1).

Following Butler, we might think of *The Messenger* as a 'shard' of testimony, drawing on her reading of the poems inscribed on Styrofoam cups and written in toothpaste by detainees at Guantanamo Bay. In *Frames of War: When is Life Grievable?* Butler reads these poems as appeals and efforts to re-establish a social connection to the world by those rendered less than human and consigned to the 'socially dead' – a term originally coined by Orlando Patterson to describe the status of the slave. 'Shards' of testimony are broken and sharp, they testify to experiences of being rendered less than human by taking and transforming objects of all kinds, breaking and reassembling inherited genres and forms to create a carceral art and text. They also make some response to the question that Butler poses: how and where might we recognise sites of intervention in the dehumanising effects of mandatory detention? Can the camp become a house of witness, where refugees accrue the moral authority to become visible and audible to witnessing publics on their own account? *The Messenger* facilitates social connections to the public sphere in precisely this way, producing an intervention in debates about the offshore camps in the

Australian media. It creates possibilities for the camp to emerge as a 'house of witness', staking a claim to moral authority that is denied asylum seekers in official public discourse. It is no wonder that smartphones become 'things of concern' for the Australian government.

Of Hospitality

In his lectures collected in *Of Hospitality*, conducted in Paris in 1996, Jacques Derrida speculates about new technologies and, in particular, mobile telephony, email and the internet as transformations of public space at the borders between public and private, citizen and non-citizen, foreign and non-foreign. Provoked by the violent imposition of new laws on immigrants and the *sans-papiers* in France in 1996, Derrida attached thinking on hospitality to asylum seekers, and the question of what arrives at the borders in the presence of the stranger, the foreigner, as a matter of urgency at the turn of the millennium. *Of Hospitality* locates new technologies at the threshold where the possibilities of sociality and reciprocity coincide with the conditions of possibility for violence, coercion and control. New spaces of hospitality as well as militant enforcement of border control in defence of national sovereignty are facilitated by the affordances of Web 2.0 technologies. Unconditional hospitality is foundational to ethics, and yet pragmatic conditions set limits to the rights of hospitality, and these two sets of obligations remain unreconciled.

A research report on the mapping of refugee journeys and the use of smartphones in the course of the mass migration to Europe in 2015–16 demonstrates precisely this location of new technologies on a threshold, and as 'a paradoxical presence in the lives of refugees – they are both a resource and a threat' (Gillespie et al. 2016: 2). Smartphones are essential devices for refugees on the move as they negotiate their onward passage with people smugglers and handlers, exchange information about routes and borders, communicate with those left behind in their homelands, and with those they hope to meet at their destination. Refugees are constantly online – they Facebook, tweet, email and text and phone using the secure encrypted services of WhatsApp and Viber. As Alixandra Fazzina's work on African refugees suggests, in extremity, survival can depend on smartphones and their capacity to mobilise aid and rescue. Similarly on Manus, mobile phones are vital currency in the microeconomics of displacement and detention: they are traded, upgraded, bought and sold, exchanged and stolen; and, as with all currencies, access to these resources is unequal. This survey of refugees on the long journey to Europe in 2015 indicates that poverty leaves many refugees – particularly Afghans and Iraqis – with basic, cheaper mobile phones that lack essential mapping devices that access services such as Google Maps. Coverage is dominated by young male Syrians in this case study of routes into Europe, a group that is frequently well-educated and digitally literate. Network capital creates a stratified 'mobility regime', where some individuals are more mobile than others, and some are completely immobilised (Gillespie et al. 2016: 10). Inevitably, gender as well as ethnicity is embedded in these inequities: '[t]he experiences of men, women and children on the move are profoundly different, as are their demographic characteristics and ideological positions as well as linguistic, social and cultural competences and digital literacy' (Gillespie et al. 2016: 2). These devices are not only associated with freedom and mobility. They are also instruments of coercion and control: they can disclose information that places refugees at risk. They can also generate powerful life narratives that testify to experiences that remain undisclosed in conventional broadcast and print journalism.

Smartphones enabled the intimate and ubiquitous media witnessing of the mass migration across Africa, Europe and the Middle East to Europe in 2015, which researchers now identify as 'media journeys' (Gillespie et al. 2016). They are equally essential to the testimonial narratives that are emerging from detention on Manus Island. Just as video became a vital medium for documenting the testimonies of Holocaust survivors late in the last century, for example producing the Yale Fortunoff Archive of oral testimonies that has been germinal in theorising trauma narrative, the affordances of Web 2.0 technologies have been instrumental in engineering a hospitality of cyberspace for refugees. User-generated content is essential to media witnessing, and to the extraordinary intimacy and authenticity in the capture of embodied accounts produced by individual refugees on the move and in detention, as 'mortal bodies in time' (Durham Peters 2009: 31) that are recognised by name, face and personal memory. Media witnessing emphasises the historicity of these individual testimonial accounts. For example, tropes of the journey as exodus, pilgrimage and odyssey frame the migrations to Europe as *epic* events, invoking myth, ritual and cultural memory. In etic narratives this unprecedented mass migration and humanitarian crisis is translated in terms of earlier and historic journeys in the region that remain embedded in cultural memory. The prize-winning BBC documentary *Exodus: Our Journey to Europe*, for example, was pieced together from footage taken by the refugees themselves as they documented their own journey in unseaworthy boats, on foot and by rail, using mobile phones. If we understand witnessing as a distinct mode of perception – to witness an event is to be responsible in some way to it (Durham Peters 2009: 24) – this sensory evidence of refugees on the move facilitates recognition by face and proper name. At the same time, *Exodus* invokes a sacred narrative of dispossession and the search for new homelands in this region, and biblical iconography endures in media representations of refugees (Wright 2014: 462). Testifying to their own historical reality 'as both the subject and object of media witnessing' (Frosh and Pincevski 2009: 12), refugees used mobile technology to bear witness to a historic event of mass migration as it unfolded to a global audience in real time – an event told as 'the new odyssey' (Kingsley 2017) and rendered intelligible in terms of canonical and deeply familiar Western narrative tropes.

The limbo zone

The slow violence of indefinite detention does not respond to epic accounts of an exodus, or journey, that we see emerging through etic storytelling of forced migrations. It calls for a different genre of storytelling. In *The Messenger* the affordances of mobile phones enable media witnessing under conditions of extreme constraint. *The Messenger* captures this space of exception and renders it audible. The podcast bears witness to stasis in a 'limbo' zone, a journey into an underworld, and the abyssal space of Dante's *Inferno*. This is a trope in the lexicon of southern refugee testimony: men, women and children in detention on both Manus and Nauru frequently invoke 'hell' and 'limbo' in their accounts of indefinite offshore detention in correspondence. However, in *The Messenger* Aziz's interlocutor, the journalist Michael Green, cautions listeners that although Aziz may be stuck in limbo, one should not be fooled that nothing is happening: life in detention is volatile, and the men in detention on Manus resist their abjection at every opportunity (*The Messenger* #2).

By linking testimonial networks to carceral spaces and histories, we can expose more clearly the risks taken by those who bear witness from the 'outer limits of noncitizenship' (Gilmore 2017: 4). How does a carceral site become audible in *The Messenger*? Facebook Messenger and WhatsApp are free texting services that connect mobile phones. Available as a secure messenger service for smartphones since 2011, WhatsApp has been essential in communications for migrants and refugees on the move, as it secures encrypted communications transnationally. It facilitates information exchange on experiences at border crossings, the safe routes and networks that enable migration, and the smugglers and agents encountered en route.[5] The podcast takes the name of the critical component of the infrastructure that produced Aziz's digital life narrative: Facebook Messenger. The affordances of this app are essential to the construction of Aziz's identity, and to the conditions and processes mediating this identity online. So, for example, the conversations between Aziz and his interlocutor and witness Michael, who is located in Melbourne, 2,000 km to the south of Manus, are audibly mediated by Messenger as the podcast sustains the characteristic 'beep' of the digital message on its way. These exchanges are timed according to the affordances of Messenger, and so they are hostage to the vicissitudes of the digital connection – for example, Aziz's messages are stalled by the torrential rain that frequently falls at this tropical camp.

The messages that begin the encounter between Michael and Aziz commence on his 864th day in detention in March 2016 – 'it was more like writing notes for each other than having a normal conversation. I got to know him in short, 30 second bursts', Michael tells us (*The Messenger* #1). The edited podcast of these exchanges and Michael's extended commentary was uploaded serially, beginning in January 2017. This is not a conversation in real time then; it is a series of sporadic communications, and the labour of sustaining the connections between Melbourne and Manus is audible in the edited version that was subsequently posted online: the podcast.

What is mobilised here, in this assemblage of smartphone and app, is life narrative that reproduces some traditional practices of humanitarian story-telling and media witnessing – Aziz is a distant stranger and Michael bears witness to his story of suffering as a child in Sudan, and then as an asylum seeker journeying south. Aziz testifies to reclaim his name, and his humanity, in telling his life story to Michael: 'Not to have the boat number. Which is not to have these three numbers. Numbers. To have a name. Yeah. The name that I should have is Aziz. Aziz, not a boat. Not a boat number. Like QNK002' (*The Messenger* #1). In the deathworld of the camp he has been reduced to a number, dehumanised and degraded, and it is his arrival by boat in October 2013 that secures his status and indefinite detention, for since July 2013 all unauthorised arrivals by boat have been refused resettlement in Australia, even if their claims to refugee status are recognised as legitimate. The 'unfold-ing' of Aziz's story in time, episodically, is essential to the serial: 'taking you through 2016 as it happened for Aziz, I want to show you what it's been like to wait', Michael tells us (*The Messenger* #1). The trauma of time becomes audible in this podcast. The series, originally envisaged as ten episodes, was arrested when events reached a crisis point in October 2017. The camp was declared illegal by the PNG Supreme Court, and it had to be closed and the men relocated by the end of the month. They protest and resist, and a vio-lent confrontation becomes imminent. Aziz falls silent. Voice messaging is replaced by texting; surely, Michael suggests, this is a message of sorts (*The Messenger* #10). The final two episodes are filled with mourning, as Aziz presents eloquent obituaries of two men who died in detention on Manus, a grieving that bears witness to their humanity. *The Messenger* includes a series of short, strained exchanges between Michael and Aziz as the men occupy the decommissioned RPC during an extraordinary three-week period of resis-tance, when they seize control and defy their relocation to hastily constructed new camps, until their forced removal.

This assemblage of technology and subject in *The Messenger* alerts us to changing technologies of the self that occur here in this limbo zone. It is now widely understood that digital technologies are corporeally interwoven with the self (Whitlock 2007; Rak and Poletti 2014; Elliott and Urry 2010). However, little work has been done to date on what this means in the con-text of refugee life narratives, and we begin to gain insight into this and hear ways in which indefinite detention impacts upon the mind and body in Aziz's exchanges with Michael. This is not a testimonial account *describing* his experiences, it is an example of how digital devices *mobilise* affect, and become intrinsic to embodiment in refugee life narrative. We hear this corpo-really embedded sense of self mediated by new technologies in Aziz's accounts of remembering – in his voice, and his breath, as well as his words: 'What can I remember? I feel pain. My chest is beating. I wish I could describe. I have forgotten everything. My brain has been formatted by this situation' (*The Messenger* #2). In the second podcast, entitled 'I Need to Format My Memory', Dr John Zammit, a psychologist who knows Aziz from his work at the Manus medical facility and discloses details of experiences at the camp at some risk of prosecution as a whistleblower, similarly turns to new technology to describe metaphorically this damage done to memory that becomes audible in Aziz's testimonial: 'his old memories are stashed somewhere but he can't access long term memory because of daily stressors . . . I encouraged them to write their life story as a way of countering forgetfulness and loss of self' (*The Messenger* #2). Aziz trusts that the conversations with Michael, and bearing witness in the guise of the 'Messenger', will begin a therapeutic process of 'reformatting' and gaining access to memories of his past, which include traumatic events in the villages and refugee camp in Sudan (where generations of his family remain).

Messenger apps render audible new technologies of the self that have emerged via Web 2.0, and testimonial narrative in particular: devices are not only accessories carried on the body but portable technical systems that reformulate the self's relations with affect, time and space; that become intrinsic to embodiment and what Anthony Elliott and John Urry call 'portable personhood' (2010: 3). This notion of 'portable personhood' is audible here, deployed in Aziz's own conception of his memory work. In the hands of the dispossessed, smartphones and messaging apps mobilise not only intelligence on safe routes and reliable smugglers, as Gillespie's survey of media journeys in the European exodus suggests, but also painful emotions such as fear, abjection and grief, the desire for recovery from trauma, and the resources of social protest and collective activism that are available in these new assemblages which bear the weight of digital witnessing.

The articulate antagonist

On Manus, 800 men remained in indefinite detention as Aziz testified from the camp early in 2016. They were 'unauthorised maritime arrivals' claiming their human rights as refugees according to the conventions that were available to them under international law.[6] Aziz bears witness as an 'articulate antagonist' (Sharpe 2003: 45), using the limited resources available to him: tactical in his deployment of the multiple opportunities to resist detention. The podcast is one part of this series of testimonial networks and jurisdictions that mobilise his life narrative. Of all of these, the least valuable in his mind is the processing of his claim for refugee status by immigration officers. Following processing in the camp, Aziz was recognised as a refugee in early 2015. Figures tendered to the PNG Supreme Court in the course of hearings on the legality of the Manus RPC indicated that just 12.3 per cent of the detainees were found not to have valid claims for protection (Hall 2016). As his interlocutor Michael suggests, this determination of his refugee status seems a positive development: 'I would imagine that that would be such a, a relief that moment when you finally found out that they had given you a positive refugee status' (*The Messenger* #6). But this recognition of the validity of his claims to refugee status, and of his well-founded fear of persecution in Sudan, is of little value to Aziz, who will remain in indefinite detention until he accepts repatriation back to the homeland where he is at risk, or resettlement in PNG.

> Aziz: Er, actually to be honest, I don't have any feeling about having that refugee status, nothing to me . . . And because what we been through and the way that we have been treated, it's really atrocity . . . I told him that actually it doesn't bother me, so whether it is really positive or negative whatever so it doesn't bother me. At the end of the day I know myself where I have come from and what I've been through . . . and I didn't left my country with a choice because I left my country, you know, forcibly, and I have no any [*sic*] options – that's why I came and seek asylum from your country. (*The Messenger* #6)[7]

Detainees were discriminated against following the determination of refugee status on Manus. Under pressure to leave the camp and accept resettlement in PNG, their claims to asylum in Australia remained unacknowledged and their access to privileges was curtailed: 'For the authorities this is a way of making living in PNG relatively more attractive – because detention becomes worse' (*The Messenger* #6). Aziz was active in multiple acts of resistance in the camp: hunger strikes, non-compliance and boycotts, working on court cases, using every resource available to protest against this denial of human rights, culminating in the final occupation of the camp. He is in pursuit of justice, not empathy; he is a rights-bearing subject, not a victim. Producing testimonial statements using the different jurisdictions available to him is an exercise in rights-based activism. For example, Aziz was one of four detainees to make a statement to the PNG Supreme Court hearing, justifying his resistance to resettlement in PNG and appealing for his constitutional rights to personal liberty under PNG law:

> So I arrived in Australia on 17 October 2013, I had no intention of seeking asylum in PNG. I did not wish, and do not wish, to resettle in PNG. I believe that Australia has a responsibility to resettle me. I was taken by force to Christmas Island to Manus Island by Australian guards. I was humiliated and treated like a criminal. (*The Messenger* #4)

After extended deliberations and prevarications, in May 2016 this case led to the landmark finding that the detention of refugees and asylum seekers at the RPC on Manus was unconstitutional; the PNG and Australian governments were ordered to immediately begin to close the centre.

> Now when we heard this news, like, I don't know how to describe the happiness of everyone, and when I see, I walked in and I've seen like everyone is smiling and I just astonished . . . So this is really good news for us and I feel really happy that we did it . . . And I've seen every man is just smiling from his heart you know, and like, like as it someone – people like, you know thirsty, and you gave them water. (*The Messenger* #4)

In 2017 the High Court in the Australian state of Victoria recognised the legitimacy of Aziz's claims in its determination that 1,300 current and former detainees on Nauru and Manus were eligible for compensation for being illegally detained between 2012 and 2016; this is the largest human rights settlement in the Australian courts to date. The detainees alleged that the Commonwealth had breached its duty of care by holding them in conditions that did not meet Australian standards. There was also a 'glimmer of hope' for Aziz when the United States Resettlement Support Centre began to screen detainees on Manus and Nauru; however, Aziz was not one of the men selected for screening in the initial stages (Baxendale 2017). *The Messenger* is, then, one of a series of opportunities in Aziz's campaign to claim his human rights, and it enables him to seek a witnessing public, to use the devices of social media to testify for the first time to the court of public opinion. In this collaboration and exchange between Aziz and Michael, a pivotal reframing occurs: forced migration is viewed not through a state-centred meta-frame of indisputable sovereignty, but through a human-centric meta-frame of human rights discourse (Downman and Ubayasiri 2017: 87).

The house of witness

The Messenger is a component of a dense digital environment of media witnessing, as experiences of detention on Manus are rendered audible and visible by the performances of a small group of articulate and resourceful detainees who use social media creatively – to resist indefinite offshore detention, to protest against the harsh conditions at the camp, and to broadcast the traumatic experience of the men detained there. Aziz returned to the camp after an extended stay in Port Moresby for medical treatment in 2017; I must return, he tells us, 'I must report what I see' (*The Messenger* #10). As Aziz's podcast and collaboration with Michael Green makes the camp audible, so his friend Behrouz Boochani renders the camp visible. Boochani's film *Chauka: Please Tell us the Time* debuted at film festivals in Adelaide, Sydney and London in 2017. This full-length feature narrative was filmed in the camp in a series of short clips, captured on Boochani's smartphone. These clips were then sent via WhatsApp to his collaborator, the Dutch-Iranian film-maker Arash Kamali Sarvestani. Boochani, an ethnic Kurd from western Iran who was a journalist in his home country, dedicated *Chauka* to the 2,000 men, women and children detained at Nauru and Manus since 2012. The film chronicles experimentally and in excruciating detail the sensory experience of the slow passage of time in the detention centre – indeed, it records the *use* of time as an instrument of suffering and a deliberate policy in this limbo zone. Sights and sounds that generate moments of freedom are transitory, and lines of sight are curtailed as the smartphone camera pans across the camp.

Like his friend Behrouz Boochani, Aziz bears witness to the sensory experience of this camp. As the film is a practice of slow journalism that records the spatial and temporal contours of the camp visually, so the podcast captures the ambient sound of the camp to render this limbo zone audible, to capture the embodied experience of moving on foot on the phosphate surfaces within the confines of the camp – often in the dead of night. Here, as elsewhere, the smartphone and the distribution of images and sound facilitated by the messaging app enables authenticity and intimacy in accessing the experience of refugees on the move and in detention. Here on Manus, where they are immobilised and deliberately tortured by time in the course of indefinite detention, where time itself becomes a device that inflicts trauma and suffering, Behrouz and Aziz bear witness to the impact of detention on their own bodies, and intimately so. The embodied experiences of these articulate and digitally literate young men is mobilised through social media, and the affordances of smartphones and apps are as essential to their survival here as they are to those who mobilise these same technologies in their 'media journeys' across Europe.

The assemblage that mobilises *The Messenger* was disseminated by another innovation of Web 2.0 technology: the podcast. Podcasting draws on a long tradition of broadcasting life narrative in humanitarian journalism, but as a series of audio files that can be streamed to subscribers online, podcasting is unique in its capacity to enable testimonial that is set in motion and materialises serially, and on demand. It is not surprising that Salam Pax, the brilliant and inventive 'Baghdad Blogger', whose weblog created an immediate and articulate connection and online presence during the invasion of Baghdad in 2003, relished the potential of podcasting and iTunes as a new autobiographical technology in his blog in October 2005 (Whitlock 2007: 26). Podcasting has created a dynamic new genre of life narrative storytelling – an 'aural literary journalism' (McHugh 2017) that draws on the affective power of sound: we hear Aziz's voice, his distinctive, accented English, and the ambience of human and non-human sounds at this remote site. Podcasts are celebrated as intimate listening experiences; 'they suck us into places where we normally wouldn't go'; they have the ability to evoke empathy as you 'hear emotion', as McHugh suggests. Changes in technology have accelerated the uptake of podcasts by increasing the fluidity of downloads and ease of navigation: the entry of Apple into podcasting in 2005 was critical, adding the capacity to download podcasts via iTunes, and the migration of listeners to smartphones from iPods (the device that defined the medium in 2004) has been essential to the surge of podcasting in the recent past, when it has moved from a niche activity to a mainstream media platform where amateurs can compete with traditional media (Berry 2015: 4). Researchers now use the concept of 'ear-witnessing' to describe the distinctive affective power of podcasting, and the reciprocal relationship of creating, receiving and listening to sound and voice: 'podcasting has particular emotive capacities by virtue of the sonic qualities of voice and its incidental capture of the soundscape of detention, which encourages empathy in listeners' (Rae et al. 2019: 1038).

Many of these features suggest why podcasting has become part of an assemblage of communication technologies that can facilitate media witnessing and a testimonial of the camp, this space where access for journalists and human rights activists is strictly proscribed, where whistleblowers are at risk of prosecution, and where a Sudanese man with a smuggled phone under the surveillance of CCTV cameras speaks on behalf of many:

> We have been, you know, locked away in a place where is an isolated island and far away from the other world. When you cry or when you scream, no one can hear you, so, and I thought that it is a better idea for me to be the messenger – like what I mean by that, to be the voice of everyone in here. When people scream, when people cry, so that the other people will hear. (*The Messenger* #1)

The Messenger was co-produced by a production team that includes Aziz's addressee and witness, Michael Green, and it was hosted by a partnership between the Wheeler Centre, a centre for books, writing and ideas in Melbourne, and 'Behind the Wire', a volunteer-run history project that helps people who have experienced immigration detention in Australia to tell their stories.

In *The Messenger* #7 Michael travels to Manus and meets Aziz and Behrouz in person. Here, for the first time, the podcast records a conversation, an exchange not mediated by the messenger app, and we hear that Michael is at work on two 'Behind the Wire' projects that mediate refugee voices simultaneously: the podcast and an anthology. This anthology of first-person narratives from the detention centres on Manus and Nauru, *They Cannot Take the Sky*, was published as the podcast was broadcast in 2017. In their Introduction the editors begin with an anecdote related by Aziz on his smuggled phone. 'This book exists for Aziz to speak his own name', they remark, 'to tell us about his life and what is happening to him – to tell us about his toothache, about the smell of the breeze, and about the regret that fills his heart' (Green and Dao 2017: xiii). The coexistence of these different accounts in networks of human rights and narrated lives – Boochani's film *Chauka*, *The Messenger* and the anthology – indicates the different arrangements of user, story, interface and device across print, social media and film that now mediate refugee voices. Amid the proliferation of testimonial narratives on social media, a print-based literature of the humanitarian anthology continues to sustain refugee life narratives. For example, *Voices from the Jungle: Stories from the Calais Refugee Camp* (Godin et al. 2017) suggests how print remains a medium for refugee life narratives in collaboration with social activists in Europe.

Given that Aziz's voice is audible on the podcast, and that *Chauka* visualises the trauma of time in the camp graphically, what is the place of this traditional technology of the edited anthology in humanitarian activism? *They Cannot Take the Sky* suggests that print technology remains an important vehicle for life narratives. The anthology is dense with paratexts by eminent public intellectuals (J. M. Coetzee, Tom Keneally, Geoffrey Robertson) that endorse and celebrate the collection as 'illuminating', 'passionate' and 'harrowing', and in his introduction the well-known Australian author Christos Tsiolkas defines a genre of writing out of carceral spaces as 'necessary works of witnessing': *The Diary of Anne Frank*, Primo Levi's *If This is a Man* and Alexsandr Solzhenitsyn's *The Gulag Archipelago*. One other feature of *They Cannot Take the Sky* is striking: print both elicits and enables the voices of women in detention on Nauru. As Gillespie et al. (2016) found in their survey of media journeys in Europe, access to new technologies is gendered, ethnicised and privileged. It was a group of technologically savvy young men on Manus who became articulate antagonists using social media, and the friendship between Michael and Aziz is a gendered discourse that thrives on two men who share interests and habits of 'talking sports'. On Manus, as elsewhere, refugees' access to social media is gendered. The experiences of women and children in the Pacific camps are narrated in entirely different genres, forms and archives: in the Nauru Files, in Human Rights reports, in a documentary for ABC's investigative journalism programme *Four Corners*, or in repositories of letters donated by humanitarian activists in public archives.[8]

Adequate witness

Aziz testifies from Manus in multiple synchronic jurisdictions: to the PNG Supreme Court, in the course of RSD (refugee status determination) processing by Australian and PNG agencies, and in the podcast. Aziz's social activism and the multiple testimonies he creates across these different venues and jurisdictions do not invite empathy from his witnessing public. He demands justice, recognition of his human rights, and acknowledgement of the responsibility of the Australian government for the 'atrocity' of indefinite offshore detention. The bureaucratic apparatus that governs RSD is embedded in a widespread culture of disbelief, and processes that ascertain the truth of asylum seeker testimony are designed to locate inconsistencies (Sigona 2014: 375). The podcast is another opportunity to testify in Aziz's quest for 'adequate witness', an extralegal appeal offered to the court of public opinion, where the listener, in a position of judgement, can acknowledge and affirm his moral authority or deny him a hearing. The podcast is a carefully managed venue, and fit for purpose: media witnessing from within the camp that authorises the camp as a 'house of witness'.

'Adequate witness' may seem to be too modest a claim for *The Messenger*. After all, it manages to rupture a series of protocols and procedures that silence the camp and render it invisible and inaudible. Humanitarian activists have long claimed that the Pacific camps will one day be sites of conscience, and rehearse apologies to those held in indefinite detention in anticipation of that day (Wake 2015). *The Messenger* presents further evidence for this cause. However, the fact remains that as *The Messenger* is broadcast online the majority of the Australian population continues to support policies of mandatory detention and rigorous border control, and both government and opposition concur in associating citizenship with discourses of nationalism that sustain a long tradition of racialised and ethnicised population management. The concept of 'adequate witness' attaches to the testimony of those who are historically silenced and dehumanised, those whom Leigh Gilmore identifies as 'tainted witnesses' (2017: 4) such as refugees, who bear witness to atrocity in testimonial transactions where the value of their account is always open to question. In this respect, Aziz's account is in a long tradition of testimonial narrative by the undocumented and the dispossessed. However, something new happens here too, for Aziz *becomes* the Messenger in a brilliant adoption of new technologies of the self that does not transcend the camp but inhabits it, creating a voice in a register that is unique, situated and piercing.

Acknowledgements

With thanks to Alastair Blanshard, Scott Downman and Gemma King.

Notes

1. *The Messenger* was named as one of three Grand Award winners at the New York International Radio Festival's International Radio Program Awards in June 2017.
2. As of March 2019 there were 359 people left on Nauru, and 547 people (all men) left in PNG. 'Offshore processing statistics', Refugee Council Australia, https://www.refugeecouncil.org.au/operation-sovereign-borders-offshore-detention-statistics/2/ (accessed 26 June 2019).

3. http://parlinfo.aph.gov.au/parlInfo/download/legislation/ems/r5971_ ems_32fb71c4-65b9-4c64-a2c0-be0f28484c96/upload_pdf/645999.pdf;fileTyp e=application%2Fpdf#search=%22legislation/ems/r5971_ems_32fb71c4-65b9- 4c64-a2c0-be0f28484c96%22 (accessed 30 September 2017).
4. http://rapbs.org (accessed 23 September 2017).
5. http://mashable.com/2015/07/03/syrians-europe-whatsapp-refugees/#NNDbd. ZX7OqR (accessed 13 May 2019); https://www.cnet.com/au/news/whatsapp- messages-from-detention-a-thousand-miles-away-refugee-crisis/ (accessed 13 May 2019).
6. DIPS stats, http://www.aph.gov.au/About_Parliament/Parliamentary_Depart- ments/Parliamentary_Library/pubs/rp/rp1617/Quick_Guides/Offshore#_ Nationalities_of_asylum (accessed 24 May 2019).
7. In February 2019 Abdul Aziz Muhamat was allowed to travel to Geneva where he was named the 2019 Martin Ennals Award Laureate. He was granted asylum in Switzerland in June, and he continues to campaign in Europe for the human rights of the detainees of Manus.
8. *Four Corners* documentaries that draw attention to the detention of women and children include 'Asylum', broadcast on 20 October 2011; 'Bad Blood', broad- cast on 25 April 2016; and 'The Forgotten Children', broadcast on 17 October 2016. Letters written by women in detention are archived in the Elaine Smith Collection at the Fryer Library, University of Queensland. The Nauru Files, pub- lished by *The Guardian* on 10 August 2016, is a cache of over 2,000 leaked inci- dent reports written by staff in the immigration centre on Nauru, which reveal extensive evidence of assault, injury and self-harm in the Regional Processing Centre.

Bibliography

Barnes, Greg, and George Newhouse (2015), 'Border Force Act: detention secrecy just got worse', *The Drum*, 28 May, http://www.abc.net.au/news/2015-05-28/ barns-newhouse-detention-centre-secrecy-just-got-even-worse/6501086 (accessed 6 October 2017).

Baxendale, Rachel (2017), 'Refugee Abdul Aziz Muhamat, Dutton at odds over Manus resettlement', *The Weekend Australian*, 6 December, http://www.theaustralian. com.au/national-affairs/foreign-affairs/refugee-abdul-aziz-muhamat-dutton-at- odds-over-manus-resettlement/news-story/ef8ce3ab8eaebfd6852e728818625ff9 (accessed 11 January 2018).

Behind the Wire and the Wheeler Centre (2017), *The Messenger*, https://www.wheeler- centre.com/broadcasts/podcasts/the-messenger (accessed 27 August 2018).

Berry, Richard (2015), 'A golden age of podcasting? Evaluating *Serial* in the context of podcast histories', *Journal of Radio and Audio Media*, 22.2: 170–8.

Butler, Judith (2004), *Precarious Life: The Powers of Mourning and Violence* (London: Verso).

Butler, Judith (2009), *Frames of War: When is Life Grievable?* (London: Verso).

Chomsky, Noam (1967), 'The responsibilities of intellectuals', *The New York Review of Books*, 23 February, http://www.chomsky.info/articles/19670223.htm (accessed 23 September 2017).

Dao, André (2018), 'How are you today; at the Ian Potter Museum of Art', *The Monthly*, 9 October, https://www.themonthly.com.au/blog/andr-dao/2018/09/2018/1539044312/how-are-you-today-ian-potter-museum-art (accessed 26 June 2019).

Derrida, Jacques (2000), *Of Hospitality: Anne Dufourmantelle Invites Jacques Derrida to Respond*, trans. R. Bowlby (Stanford: Stanford University Press).

Downman, Scott, and Kasun Ubayasiri (2017), *Journalism for Social Change in Asia: Reporting Human Rights* (Basingstoke: Palgrave).

Durham Peters, John (2009), 'Witnessing', in Paul Frosh and Amit Pinchevski (eds), *Media Witnessing: Testimony in an Age of Mass Communication* (New York: Palgrave Macmillan), 23–48.

Elliott, Anthony, and John Urry (2010), *Mobile Lives* (London: Palgrave Macmillan).

Fazzina, Alixandra (2010), *A Million Shillings: Escape from Somalia* (London: Trolley).

Flanagan, Richard, and Ben Quilty (2017), 'Notes on the Syrian exodus: "Epic in scale, inconceivable until you witness it"', *The Guardian*, 5 March, https://www.theguardian.com/world/2016/mar/05/great-syrian-refugee-crisis-exodus-epic-inconceivable-witness-lebos-islamic-state (accessed 15 May 2019).

Frosh, Paul, and Amit Pinchevski (eds) (2009), *Media Witnessing: Testimony in an Age of Mass Communication* (New York: Palgrave Macmillan).

Gillespie, Marie, et al. (2016), 'Mapping media journeys. Smartphones and social media networks', http://www.open.ac.uk/ccig/sites/www.open.ac.uk.ccig/files/Mapping%20Refugee%20Media%20Journeys%2016%20May%20FIN%20MG_0.pdf (accessed 23 September 2017).

Gilmore, Leigh (2017), *Tainted Witness: Why We Doubt What Women Say About Their Lives* (New York: Columbia University Press).

Godin, Marie, et al. (2017), *Voices from the 'Jungle': Stories from the Calais Camp* (London: Pluto Press).

Green, Michael, and Andre Dao (eds) (2017), *They Cannot Take the Sky: Voices from Detention* (Sydney: Allen and Unwin).

Hall, Bianca (2016), 'Most people sent to Manus Island are genuine refugees, new figures show', *Sydney Morning Herald*, 30 June, http://www.smh.com.au/federal-politics/political-news/most-people-sent-to-manus-island-are-genuine-refugees-new-figures-show-20160630-gpv5ns.html (accessed 10 January 2018).

Hall, Bianca (2017), 'Lawyers representing asylum seekers are "un-Australian"', *Sydney Morning Herald*, 28 August, https://www.smh.com.au/politics/federal/lawyers-representing-asylum-seekers-are-unaustralian-peter-dutton-20170828-gy-5ci7.html (accessed 26 June 2019).

Herd, David, and Anna Pincus (eds) (2016), *Refugee Tales* (Manchester: Comma Press).

Higgins, Claire (2017), 'Australia's long history of offshore detention', *The Interpreter*, 8 September, https://www.lowyinstitute.org/the-interpreter/australia-s-long-history-offshore-detention (accessed 26 June 2019).

Kennedy, Rosanne (2014), 'Moving testimony: human rights, Palestinian memory, and the transnational public sphere', in Chiara De Cesari and Ann Rigney (eds), *Transnational Memory Circulation, Articulation, Scales* (Berlin: Walter de Gruyter), 51–78.

Kingsley, Patrick (2017), *The New Odyssey: The Story of Europe's Refugee Crisis* (London: Guardian Faber Publishing).

Lejeune, Phillippe (1989), *On Autobiography*, ed. Paul John Eakin, trans. Katherine Leary (Minneapolis: University of Minnesota Press).

McHugh, Siobhan (2017), 'Why S-Town invites empathy not voyeurism', *The Conversation*, http://theconversation.com/why-s-town-invites-empathy-not-voyeurism-76510 (accessed 23 September 2017).

The Nauru Files (2016), https://www.theguardian.com/australia-news/2016/aug/10/the-nauru-files-2000-leaked-reports-reveal-scale-of-abuse-of-children-in-australian-offshore-detention (accessed 27 August 2018).

Perera, Suvendrini, and Joseph Pugliese (2015), 'Offshore detention "black sites" open door to torture', *The Conversation*, 26 August, https://theconversation.com/offshore-detention-black-sites-open-door-to-torture-46400 (accessed 23 September 2017).

Rae, Maria, Emma K. Russell and Amy Nethery (2019), 'Earwitnessing detention: carceral secrecy, affecting voices, and political listening in *The Messenger* podcast', *International Journal of Communication*, 13: 1036–55.

Rak, Julie, and Anna Poletti (eds) (2014), *Identity Technologies: Constructing the Self Online* (Madison, WI: University of Wisconsin Press).

Schaffer, Kay, and Sidonie Smith (2014), 'E-witnessing in the digital age', in Meg Jensen and Margaretta Jolly (eds), *We Shall Bear Witness* (Madison: University of Wisconsin Press), 223–37.

Sharpe, Jenny (2003), *Ghosts of Slavery: A Literary Archaeology of Black Women's Lives* (Minneapolis: University of Minnesota Press).

Sigona, Nando (2014), 'The politics of refugee voices: representations, narratives, and memories', in Elena Fiddian-Qasmiyeh, Gil Loescher, Katy Long and Nando Sigona (eds), *The Oxford Handbook of Refugee and Forced Migration Studies* (Oxford: Oxford University Press), 369–82.

Wake, Carolyn (2015), 'Draft apology to the survivors of immigration detention', realtime 126, http://realtimearts.net/article/issue126/11919 (accessed 23 September 2017).

Whitlock, Gillian (2007), *Soft Weapons: Autobiography in Transit* (Chicago: University of Chicago Press).

Whitlock, Gillian (2015), *Postcolonial Life Narratives: Testimonial Transactions* (Oxford: Oxford University Press).

Wright, Terence (2014), 'The media and representations of refugees and other forced migrants', in Elena Fiddian-Qasmiyeh, Gil Loescher, Katy Long and Nando Sigona (eds), *The Oxford Handbook of Refugee and Forced Migration Studies* (Oxford: Oxford University Press), 460–74.

Part VIII

Home

Home: Introduction

David Farrier

There is perhaps no refugee imaginary more essential, more poignant, or with a greater capacity to shape lived experience than *home*. Home is the wound made in the act of leaving, and the hope that keeps the journey going. The experience of home for most refugees, once they have arrived in a new place, is profoundly unhomely; and it is in defence of the narrowest and least generous versions of home that the mechanisms and discourses of the detention estate operate. 'Imaginary homelands', as Salman Rushdie argued, are the fraught but compelling psychic territory that many migrants inhabit (Rushdie 1991: 10).

Mieke Bal's video installation *Nothing is Missing* explores this conflicted territory of home. In 2006 Bal filmed a series of interviews with women from the Global South whose adult children had migrated to Europe, conducted by another family member but framed so that only the mother was visible, with the camera fixed on her face. These video portraits were installed across Europe either in a domestic space or a room decorated to resemble one, and visitors were invited to sit face-to-face, as it were, with the women as they described the 'unhomeliness' of home for those who are left behind. Encouraged to take the place of the unseen family member, the visitor becomes both a trespasser in the intimate moment and a member, albeit tentatively, of a kind of transnational community. Throughout the experience, different versions of 'home' circulate, defined variously by proximity and distance, mobility and stasis, inclusion and exclusion.

In this section, the contributors endeavour to explore the various ways in which home, as a powerful form of refugee imaginary, can emerge in refugee writing. Daniel Hartley's chapter explores how definitions of legal personhood connect the concept of home with the operations of the law. World, home and legal personhood are mutually constitutive in the thinking of Hannah Arendt; however, Hartley argues in his analysis of the law in Arendt's 'We Refugees' (1943) that she overstates its autonomy while failing to properly account for its imbrication in colonial modernity. In a literary critique of Arendt, Hartley suggests that J. M. Coetzee's *The Childhood of Jesus* and Jenny Erpenbeck's *Gehen, Ging, Gegangen* provide illustrations of how impersonality and worldlessness are central to refugee experience, describing a kind of personhood that is not beholden to the legal personhood on which Arendt's analysis is based, and which is, for her, the essential route to home.

Where Hartley explores the relationship between home and the law, Mireille Rosello examines home as a haunted place. In her reading of Viet Thanh Nguyen's *The Refugees* (2017), Rosello explores how 'home' is itself spectral; when the old home is no longer available but the new home is not yet fully realised, each notion of home stalks the other. But this haunting also involves a kind of intimacy, a connection with the departed that is an essential aspect of home. Rosello shows how for refugees who have experienced trauma, real terror often comes from threats that live outside the home. Ultimately, she argues, Nguyen's story of the ghostwriter and the ghost who doesn't know she is a ghost demonstrates that learning to live between past and present involves recognising the unavoidable presence of the ghostly. Poised between here and there, then and now, horror and idyll, haunting is an integral part of being at home.

Rosello's argument is partially based on Sara Ahmed's notion of homework – homes are continually made and unmade, built and rebuilt. The final chapter also considers how home is *work*; specifically, creative and collaborative work. This is a dialogue between Misha Myers, a performance researcher and practitioner, and Mariam Issa, a visionary storyteller and community worker, who created the RAW community garden and organisation to support women's resilience through storytelling, cooking and gardening in the backyard of her own home in Melbourne. Their conversation explores Issa's experiences of resettling in Australia after leaving Somalia, and the way in which a sense of home emerges through quiet acts of making and sharing: cooking, gardening, storytelling. They describe home as a kind of meeting place; a collaborative endeavour, constructed of multiple locations and which accommodates multiple dimensions of the self. Drawing also on the critical work of Doreen Massey, bell hooks and Liisa Malkki, the dialogue between Myers and Issa testifies to the continuous creative process involved in making home, and the constructive value of a future-oriented nostalgia in this.

Bibliography

Rushdie, Salman (1991), *Imaginary Homelands: Essays and Criticism 1981–1991* (London: Granta).

Chapter 26

Home and Law: Impersonality and Worldlessness in J. M. Coetzee's *The Childhood of Jesus* and Jenny Erpenbeck's *Gehen, Ging, Gegangen*

Daniel Hartley

Home seems to belong to a different sphere of existence to that of the law.[1] Everyday phrases such as 'home is where the heart is' conjure up images of a warm domestic interior that is a far cry from the cold machinations of the law. Where 'home' seems to harbour a subjective quality, 'law' is seen as austerely objective; where the former implies a sphere of intimate personal relations, the latter connotes impersonal distance. Scholars such as Lorna Fox have noted that the law itself struggles to acknowledge these subjective aspects: 'the proposition that home can encapsulate meanings beyond the physical structure of the house or its capital value continues to present conceptual difficulties for lawyers' (Fox 2005: 25). At the same time, Marxist feminists have long argued that the notion of home as an intimate sphere, free from all social and political mediations, is a deeply ideological vision that serves to conceal women's domestic labour and the work of social reproduction (Bhattacharya 2017). During colonial modernity, these patriarchal ideologies intersected with settler-colonial visions of the home as a place of 'settlement' in the overlapping senses of 'settling down', 'arranging and organising' and 'occupation (by force)': 'home does the business of nation and carries its agendas forward in time, producing the subjects of nation and empire . . . [It is] the space designed to teach women their own imperial function' (Strehle 2008: 1). In what follows, I use the notion of the 'person', which connects home and law (the 'personal' sphere and the juridical person), to suggest that both terms are far more overdetermined and mutually imbricated than conventional wisdom might imply.

The interrelatedness of home and law becomes clear in light of recent returns to Louis Althusser's theory of interpellation. Jean-Jacques Lecercle (2016) has argued that interpellation, the process by which ideology constitutes individuals as subjects, might better be understood as a theory of 'address'. He enumerates three interconnected meanings: a place of residence, a way of addressing oneself to someone and a textual genre. 'Address' is thus a textually inscribable interpellative force that identifies a person at a fixed location. Lecercle suggests that 'person' or *persona* is preferable to 'subject' as the name for the end result of this socially contested process. This essay follows Lecercle in connecting the problematics of 'person' and 'home' as a way of teasing out the ambiguities of refugee experience presented in two contemporary novels: J. M. Coetzee's *The Childhood of Jesus* (2013) and Jenny Erpenbeck's *Gehen, Ging, Gegangen* [Go, Went, Gone] (2015). Setting out from an analysis of the mutual constitution of world, home and legal personhood in the work of Hannah Arendt, I argue that Arendt's legal and philosophical championing of the narrative structure of world and *persona* over the (perceived) anti-narrative existence of bare life is premised upon a too narrow conception of the person, an overestimation of law's autonomy from other state apparatuses, and an underestimation of its continued entanglement in the colonial discourses of modernity – all of which is surprising given her sensitivity to human rights law's connection with the nation-state. Drawing on Georg Lukács's theory of the novel, Roberto Esposito's philosophy of the impersonal and Althusser's (Lecercle-inflected) theory of interpellation, I suggest that Coetzee and Erpenbeck are consciously concerned with the exclusionary mechanisms of the *dispositif* of the person (Esposito 2014). I argue that their novels not only criticise the person, but identify – and embody – several modes of *im*personality and worldlessness at the heart of refugee experience which seem to prefigure a mode of sociality beyond the person. They thus offer a literary critique of Arendt's insistence on the continued necessity of the juridical person as a precondition of intra-worldly home making. At the extreme, they suggest that although the legal person is of immediate pragmatic importance in defending the rights of refugees, it may well also be part of the problem.

Hannah Arendt and the 'human condition': person, home and world

In her well-known 1943 essay, 'We Refugees', Hannah Arendt articulated the tripartite loss suffered by Jewish refugees who fled Nazi Germany:

> We lost our home, which means the familiarity of daily life. We lost our occupation, which means the confidence that we are of some use in this world. We lost our language, which means the naturalness of reactions, the simplicity of gestures, the unaffected expression of feelings. (Arendt 2007: 264)

Contained here *in nuce* is a constellation of figures that would be more fully developed in *The Human Condition* (1958). The latter outlines a vision of the *vita activa* [active life] consisting of three principal activities, each of which corresponds to a basic human condition and produces a specific object: labour, whose condition is life, and which (re)produces biological life as well as goods for immediate consumption; work, whose condition is 'worldliness', and which fabricates a realm of human artifice and durable and familiar things that constitute the man-made 'world' which is our earthly dwelling place; and action and speech, which are the intersubjective modes in which human beings appear to each other, whose condition is human plurality, and which produce 'stories' that become materialised in written documents or monuments. The loss of home, occupation and language suffered by Jewish refugees thus hovers between a basic empirical deprivation and the traumatic disappearance of the transcendental pre-conditions of the *vita activa*. If 'worldliness' presupposes a realm of familiar, durable things, as well as access to a realm of public appearance in which to disclose oneself through action and speech, then the situation of refugees is, strictly speaking, worldless.

Later in the essay Arendt pens a polemic against the generic figure of 'Mr. Cohen', a Jewish refugee forced constantly to flee but in continual denial of his status as Jew; in the course of his flights, he claims to have been 150 per cent German, 150 per cent Viennese, and 150 per cent French. What he seeks is 'the recovering of a new personality' (Arendt 2007: 271), a wish that Arendt brands 'hopeless' since it fails to reckon with the actuality of the political situation. At the same time, openly to admit one's status as Jew 'would mean that we expose ourselves to the fate of human beings who, unprotected by any specific law or political convention, are nothing but human beings' – an attitude she calls '[most] dangerous' (2007: 273). It is well known that this latter experience motivated Arendt's famous criticism of human rights in *The Origins of Totalitarianism* (Arendt 2004: 341–84). Less often remarked upon, however, is that it also inspired her sustained defence of legal personhood. Against the French revolutionaries who desired to tear 'the mask of hypocrisy off the face of French society' (Arendt 1963: 102), Arendt upholds the absolute centrality of legal personae that are 'affixed' by the law or 'given and guaranteed by the body politic' (1963: 102, 104).

She understands the person primarily as a legal category, but one with important phenomenological and narrative functions.[2] The 'fundamental deprivation of human rights', she explains, 'is manifested first and foremost and above all in the deprivation of a place in the world which makes opinions significant and actions effective' (Arendt 2004: 376). The worldlessness of the refugee consists in her exclusion from all legality and, by extension, from the subjective in-between of a common world that confers meaning on actions and speech. Unable to assume her public *persona*, the impersonal mask through which the distinctive voice sounds,[3] the refugee is thrust back into what Arendt problematically (and symptomatically) refers to as 'savagery' (2004: 381). This 'mere' human existence is, paradoxically, both sheer generality (human being in general) and pure difference: the sheerly *natural* individuality through which one thing can be distinguished from another. Such depersonalised individuals are subject to purely arbitrary 'blessings and doom' which are 'meted out to them according to accident and without any relation whatsoever to what they do, did, or may do' (Arendt 2004: 376). This existential arbitrariness is compounded by refugees' subsequent reliance on charity or 'the unpredictable hazards of friendship and sympathy' (Arendt 2004: 382). It is thus only in their absence that the legal, phenomenological and narrative functions of personhood become visible. Legally, the person is 'affixed' by the law to the natural individual to ensure equality before the law (personhood for Arendt is not metaphysical; it is the result of legal interpellations). Phenomenologically, personhood secures the 'respectable' interpersonal distance required for the related-but-separate worldliness of the public sphere, characterised by 'a kind of "friendship" without intimacy or closeness' (Arendt 1998: 243). Narratively, the person endows one's actions with meaning and confers unity on different aspects of one's life story (Gündoğdu 2015: 99); it is a narrativising force that counteracts the anti-narrative arbitrariness of bare life. Taken together, the institution of the person is an integral aspect of the human realm of artifice which, for Arendt, constitutes our home on earth.

Both worldliness and the person possess literary forms. As Pheng Cheah has observed, Arendt's theory presupposes that the world has a diegetic structure (2016: 151). Action within the 'web of human relationships' produces authorless 'stories' which are post-factum narrative repetitions of past deeds that endow the latter with meaning. Narration connects different stories into a larger whole – the world itself – while history is 'the storybook of mankind' (Arendt 1998: 184). The aim of this general narrative process is to enable human stories and meaning making to endure beyond the lifespan of the actors themselves. As a legal, phenomenological and relational node within the world, the person corresponds to the form of biography: 'For action and speech . . . are indeed the two activities whose end result will always be a story with enough coherence to be told, no matter how accidental or haphazard the single events and their causation may appear to be' (Arendt 1998: 97). Biography in Arendt's understanding is the narrative capacity to oppose the chaotic impermanence and tracelessness of bare life. Since for Arendt the forms of narrative and biography are literally world making, she is less concerned with their specifically literary qualities and modalities than with their basic powers of phenomenological structuration. Nevertheless, she tends towards a preference for drama 'whose very name (from the Greek verb *dran*, "to act") indicates that play-acting actually is an imitation of acting' (1998: 187). Narrative, biography and drama are thus the three principal literary forms of world making and, by extension, home making in Arendt's system. They are the symbolic formalisations of juridical personhood: narrative defences against the catastrophic effects of refugee experience.

J. M. Coetzee's *The Childhood of Jesus*

Written under very different historical circumstances, J. M. Coetzee's *The Childhood of Jesus* implicitly questions many of Arendt's presuppositions. It tells the story of David, a young boy who has lost his mother, and Simón, his adult guardian. Having crossed the sea in a boat and passed several weeks at Belstar camp, they arrive in Novilla, a Spanish-speaking city that fuses a generic Latin American socialism, the curious blandness of fictional utopias and the indeterminacy of limbo (it is often implied that those who arrive here have died). 'Washed clean' of their old lives, new arrivals are given a new name and birthday (Coetzee 2013: 24). Slowly integrating themselves into the unusual ways of this strange new world, Simón struggles to let go of his old-world desires and remains driven by the quest to find David's mother. On a trip outside the city to 'La Residencia', an ex-plantation (Coetzee 2013: 65) that is now a period-piece country home, Simón believes he has found her: Inés. The final part of the novel traces the fate of Inés, as she assumes the unexpected burden of motherhood, and David, as he struggles to submit to the conventional rules of reading, writing and counting, becoming increasingly akin to the childhood Jesus of the apocryphal Infancy Gospels. The novel ends on the road, with David, Simón and Inés fleeing the state authorities of Novilla who wish to force David to return to Punta Arenas boarding school.

In Georg Lukács's *The Theory of the Novel*, the novel is understood as an 'expression of . . . transcendental homelessness' whose chief mode is irony and whose outward form is – like Arendt's person – essentially biographical (Lukács 1971: 41). The novel is that willed form of totality inherent to a modern world devoid of the organic metaphysical 'homeliness' of Lukács's calculatedly naïve 'integrated civilisations' (1971: 29). One way of reading *The Childhood of Jesus*, I suggest, is to see Simón as a representative character of the realist novel, and hence of a 'disintegrated' civilisation, who is both literally and transcendentally homeless, transported backward (or forward) into a uniquely Coetzeean integrated civilisation. Simón embodies the contradictory common sense of classical liberal personhood, itself firmly entangled in what Agamben calls 'the anthropological machine' (2004: 37): he is sexually desirous, passionate, anthropocentric, empiricist, idealist, romantic, naturalist, sentimental, associates meat with substance and vitality, and trusts to spontaneous intuition. *The Childhood of Jesus*, like many of Coetzee's late works, might then be read as a 'de-personalising' and 'de-worlding' machine whose purpose is *theoretically* to deconstruct the specifically modern *dispositif* of the person (connecting the novel form, realism, discourses of authorship, private property, liberal individualism, and emotional regimes such as empathy) and *performatively* to enact a post-personal or *im*personal sociality characterised by a strategic inoperativity of empathy and desire (Vermeulen 2015: 51).[4] Written in the late style

that Elleke Boehmer has described as a 'language of minimalist denota-
tion' (2011: 9), and which Vermeulen calls 'weary abstractness' (2015: 49),
Novilla's bare rooms and streets match the bleakness of the style: they are
often described as 'empty', while their inhabitants are 'strangely incurious'
(Coetzee 2013: 26), 'anodyne' (2013: 76) and lack passion, thus throwing
into relief the comparatively grotesque longings of Simón. There is thus
a sense in which Coetzee has managed formally to reproduce the atmosphere of worldlessness that Arendt associates with depersonalised refugee
experience.

In her review of the novel, Joyce Carol Oates (2013) writes of Novilla that
'Nothing seems urgent here, nothing is privatized. All is generic, universal,
impersonal.' It is precisely this impersonality that irritates the person-cen-
tred Simón, just as, inversely, it is the imperative of the impersonal to which
Coetzee increasingly returns in his later works.[5] More specifically, Coetzee
seems to be engaged in a quest to discover a mode of ethico-political relation that would remain faithful to the hard-won gains of modern personhood while disentangling it from the violent legacies of colonial modernity
and the wiles of neoliberalism.[6] In doing so, he constantly revisits the ethical
terms and mores of pre-modern civilisations (from Greek *eros* and *agape* to
Christian *caritas*), juxtaposing them with more modern forms of sociality
such as the ambiguous 'care' of the modern welfare state (Coetzee 2005:
passim), the 'solidarity' of workers or the 'fraternity' of trades unions.
The Childhood of Jesus features an astonishing roll call of possible modes
of relationship: charity, friendship, comradeship, goodwill, citizenship,
abstraction, intimacy, companionship and fraternity (Coetzee 2013: 35, 41,
49, 66, 144, 148, 164, 168, 238) (not to mention its obsession with modes
of familial relation: paternity, maternity, uncle–nephew, godfather–godson).
As in the 'biologico-literary experiment' of *Slow Man* (Coetzee 2005: 114),
Coetzee seems to be testing these modes of relationship, seeking out what
Paul Rayment names the 'impersonal personal' (Coetzee 2005: 43). This is a
combination of personal intimacy and impersonal formality uncannily similar to the ontologically central relation of 'respect' in Arendt's conception of
worldliness: 'a kind of "friendship" without intimacy or closeness' (Arendt
1998: 243). It is an impersonal relation that fuses closeness with distance,
that remains provisional, emergent, yet is ever on the verge of descending
into irony, just like Paul Rayment's three kisses 'in the formal manner' at
the close of *Slow Man* (Coetzee 2005: 263). It is also an impersonality that
gestures beyond the strict distinction between humans and animals (Barney
2016). The fundamental difference between Coetzeean impersonality and
Arendtian respect, however, is that Coetzee clearly believes that the way to
the impersonal lies through the very worldlessness and depersonalisation
that, for Arendt, would render respect *a priori* impossible.

In *The Childhood of Jesus* the question of the person becomes refracted
through that of the precarious personhood of the refugee. In a moment of

realisation early on in the novel, Simón recognises that his appetites are at odds with his new surroundings:

> Is he insisting on the primacy of the personal (desire, love) over the universal (goodwill, benevolence)? . . . Is it all part of a far too tardy transition from the old and the comfortable (the personal) to the new and unsettling (the universal)? (Coetzee 2013: 68)

The person is now a figure of the past, that which Simón refuses entirely to forget – a 'memory of having a memory' (2013: 117). He is torn between the old ways of the person – desire, appetite, love and comfort – and the new ways of the 'universal': goodwill, benevolence, that which is 'unsettling'. These terms are not accidental; they constitute something like a critical philology of the bourgeois person and, by extension, of the home. 'Comfort', we are told by Franco Moretti, emerged in its modern meaning of 'everyday necessities made pleasant' (2013: 48) or 'happiness . . . being at home' (Morazé, cited in Moretti 2013: 45) in the late seventeenth century, a compromise between 'two equally contradictory sets of values . . . the ascetic imperative of modern production – and the desire for enjoyment of a rising social group' (2013: 51). Crucially, the text that inspires Moretti's excursus on this bourgeois 'keyword' (2013: 44) is Defoe's *Robinson Crusoe*, whose centrality to Coetzee's project needs no elaboration. The point here is that 'comfort' is a single node in the larger *dispositif* of the person: it connects the novel, the bourgeois individual (Marx's 'eighteenth-century Robinsonades' [1973: 83]), colonialism and the *home*. That the new world is 'unsettling' is then clearly a suggestion that any post-personal sociality must undo the interlinked notions of person and home that are imbricated with settler colonialism (Strehle 2008). Coetzee thus mobilises the transcendental and literal homelessness of the refugee to question the prevailing conceptions of person and home in a manner quite alien to Arendt's relatively naïve faith in the autonomy of juridical personhood. For what could make clearer than Defoe's *Robinson Crusoe* the fact that Arendt's *homo faber* and the durable world of things historically entailed violent practices of colonial 'unworlding' (not to mention genocide) and a concomitant mode of narrative representation (realism) that silences the 'unworlded' – the very narrativity that Arendtian 'worldliness' presupposes?

In the second half of the novel, attention turns to David's struggles at school. Likewise, the novel's concern with the person subtly shifts from exposing its imbrication in the discourses of colonial modernity to a focus on the immediate ideological production of persons. There is a remarkable confluence here between the scenes of reading, writing and counting, Louis Althusser's famous essay on ideology and ideological state apparatuses (recently reread, as mentioned above, precisely as a theory of *personification* [Lecercle 2016; Balibar 2015]), and Foucault's theory of normalisation.[7]

Under 'normal' conditions, schools teach pupils 'a certain amount of "know-how" wrapped in ruling ideology . . . or simply the ruling ideology in its pure state' (Althusser 2014: 251). In *The Childhood of Jesus* this insidious indoctrination is mediated through reading.[8] Yet David initially struggles to learn to read because he seems incapable of '[submitting] to what is written on the page', of giving up his own 'fantasies' (Coetzee 2013: 196). This, in turn, leads to 'insubordination' (2013: 248) in the classroom and his refusal to submit to authority. Ultimately, David seems incapable of becoming a 'normal person' which, by extension, threatens his ability to become a 'virtuous citizen' (2013: 255, 298). When it ultimately transpires that David has in fact successfully learned to read, one realises that it is not the rules of reading itself with which he has difficulty but 'the rules behind the rules – with the precept that language presupposes and requires a community of readers who share a common understanding both of language and of reality' (Boxall 2015: 96). Like asylum seekers forced to take citizenship tests that 'natives' themselves would invariably fail, David cleaves to the surface rules – the 'law' – but fails to recognise the law's uncanny double – the 'rules behind the rules'.[9]

These failed attempts to interpellate David, to form him into a 'normal person' (as in the *Bildungsroman*), begin to gesture towards an ambiguous zone between reality and fantasy. For Althusser, ideological interpellation implies not only the constitution of concrete individuals into concrete persons – with a 'face, first and middle names, last name, date of birth, *home address*, profession, citizenship' (Althusser 2014: 190, n. 24, emphasis added) – but also a process of misrecognition: 'Ideology represents individuals' imaginary relation to their real conditions of existence' (Althusser 2014: 181). Thus, for Althusser, common-sense reality is, strictly speaking, a web of imaginary representations. It is to this paradoxically *imaginary* reality that David refuses to submit, constantly wary of the 'gaps', 'cracks' or 'holes' in the fictional social fabric through which he fears falling; when the school psychologist suggests that David lacks the real (Coetzee 2013: 246), her diagnosis is more real than she imagines. David is drawn to those passages of Cervantes' *Don Quixote*, a children's version of which he is using to learn to read, in which 'the ideal and the real are somehow joined' (Boxall 2015: 90). It is here, in this zone of indiscernibility between fiction and the real, that Coetzee's most powerful ethico-political insights emerge. David's fidelity to Quixote's own fidelity to the fantastic is such that he sacrifices the bridges of common sense, the chains of prejudice and presupposition, that connect one thing or person to another. Consequently, when he counts he cannot conceive of numbers or things as sequential or grouped; he perceives only singularities. As Simón explains:

> 'Put two apples before him. What does he see? An apple and an apple: not two apples, not the same apple twice, just an apple and an apple . . . What is the singular of which *apples* is the plural? . . . Who is the singular of which *men* is the plural?' (Coetzee 2013: 295)

If ideological interpellation divides the world into privatised, non-singular and 'addressable' persons, David's refusal to be interpellated enables instead an *impersonal* ethics of singularity whose ontological modality coincides with the indiscernibility of the real and the fantastic. In other words, there seems to be a connection between Coetzee's implicit ethical ideal of the 'impersonal personal' and a certain subjective 'forcing' (Badiou 2005) effected through a militant fidelity to a real which, from the perspective of (ideological, imaginary) reality, appears as fantasy. Crucially, it is the figure of the refugee, with her provisional, *unheimlich* and insecure being, that Coetzee seems to associate with this fragile, yet subjectively intensive, domain of the impersonal. That the refugee here has become precisely a 'figure' is perhaps indicative of Coetzee's characteristically transversal relation to the historical immediacy of contemporary refugee experience.

Jenny Erpenbeck's *Gehen, Ging, Gegangen*

Jenny Erpenbeck's *Gehen, Ging, Gegangen* (2015) also begins with a scene of failed interpellation. Loosely based on a series of real-life events that took place in Berlin from 2012 onwards, and hence much more empirically grounded than Coetzee's spectral tribute to La Mancha, the early pages of the novel trace the fate of a set of refugees assembled in front of Berlin City Hall protesting against mistreatment and lack of access to work:

> Who are you, they are asked by the police and the officials from the [Berlin] senate who were brought here. We're not saying, say the men. But you must say, the others say, or else we won't know if you fall under the law and are allowed to stay here and work. We're not saying who we are, the men say . . . The men stay silent. (Erpenbeck 2015: 18)[10]

In what reads like a variation on the primal scene of Althusserian interpellation – the great police hail 'Hey, you there!' (Althusser 2014: 190) – the refugees fail to (mis)recognise the hail and in so doing resist interpellation. In refusing to give their names, they elude personalised inscription into the law, thus temporarily suspending the law's efficacy. They do not yet 'fall under the law' (a phrase resonant with Kafkaesque echoes) but neither is it clear that they are 'outlaws': instead, they inhabit an ambiguous legal grey zone. Such zones, I argue, are the principal object of Erpenbeck's fascination. Time and again throughout her novels, she is drawn to those figures or places in which the prevailing relations between persons, things, land and state break down or become ambiguous. If she is a writer of the uncanny, it is only to the extent that 'home' (the *heimlich*) would name the *familiar* dispensation of person, thing, land and state. The refugee is just such a figure of the uncanny, but one whose sociopolitical strangeness produces very real and tragic consequences.

The novel is narrated in free indirect style through the figure of Richard, a recently retired professor of classics and former citizen of the GDR who lives in what was formerly East Berlin. A widower at a loss as to how to fill his newly empty days, Richard encounters the protesting refugees and decides to conduct interviews with them as part of a research project ostensibly about the nature of time. Slowly integrating himself into their daily lives, though never entirely able to rid himself of residual racist prejudices, Richard befriends the refugees, helping them with transport, language skills and legal forms, buying them presents and – eventually – allowing several of them to stay in his house. A novel remarkable for its atmosphere of almost total eventlessness, this brief summary essentially resumes the entirety of the plot. Needless to say, the German press were quick to call out what *Der Spiegel* called the novel's 'bourgeois clichés' [*Wohlstandsbürger-Klischees*], an accusation which, superficially at least, seems justified (the novel even includes on its acknowledgements page the bank details of the Evangelischer Kirchenkreis Berlin Stadtmitte – the evangelical church of central Berlin – inviting readers to donate). Yet in a novel that is constantly concerned with the discrepancies between depth and surface – 'God created volume, the devil created surfaces' says the epigraph from Wolfgang Pauli – one might perhaps wish to look beyond the superficial clichés to that which lies beneath.

The basic connection between Richard and the refugees, as he sees it, is that they have both been ejected from, or imprisoned in, time (Erpenbeck 2015: 51), but that this extra-temporal condition paradoxically provides them with a more powerful insight into what time actually is. It is not simply time as such that interests Richard, but rather the metamorphosis (Ovid is mentioned four times) from one everyday temporality to another, from the 'full and structured everyday' [*ausgefüllten und überschaubaren Alltag*] to the 'open-on-all-sides, as it were "draughty" everyday of a refugee life' (2015: 52):[11] 'There, where the one life of a person [*Mensch*] borders on the other life of the same person, a transition must surely become visible which, when one looks at it closely, is actually nothing' (2015: 52).[12] In line with the fundamental socio-ontological ambiguity of the refugee traced throughout this chapter, this 'transition', 'passage' or 'crossing' [*Übergang*] from one life to another is at once subtly philosophical and brutally empirical. On the one hand, *Übergang* names the invisible spatio-temporal limit (the 'nothing') at which one thing becomes another, logically entailing that at this precise point or moment A is no longer A but not yet B – an ambiguous ontological status akin to what Roberto Esposito has described as the impersonal: 'the non-person inscribed in the person, . . . the person open to what has never been before' (2014: 151). On the other hand, the novel is full of more mundane yet no less 'metaphysical' examples of such transitions: the fall of the GDR ('In 1990 from one day to the next he became a citizen of another country; only the view out of the window stayed the same' [Erpenbeck 2015: 103]),[13] civil war in Libya, and torturous crossings over the Mediterranean. It is one of the notable features of both these novels that Coetzee and Erpenbeck are drawn to the clash of ideal and real, empirical and ontological that intersect in disconcerting ways in the figure of the refugee.

The theme of transition gradually becomes connected to that of 'world' and things. Early in the novel, echoing Arendt's *The Human Condition*, Richard ponders what will bind together his lifeless household possessions into a meaningful world when he is dead: 'will there be an invisible connection which exists insofar as [they] once belonged to him?' (Erpenbeck 2015: 16).[14] Later, in a reflection on the architectural base of Berlin's 'Fernsehturm' (TV tower), which was constructed under the GDR and whose step-like form is meant to mirror the forward march to communism, he broadens his scope from lost personal worlds to lost collective worlds: 'What actually narrates such an image, whose story has disappeared? What are the happy people advertising today? Is time at a standstill? Is there anything left to wish?' (2015: 22).[15] Just as Coetzee chose to mediate refugee experience partly through a generic Latin American socialism, so Erpenbeck connects the fate of primarily African refugees to the lost world of the GDR and, crucially, to its lost *promise*. In doing so, she connects refugee experience to a current of contemporary German literature dealing with questions of belonging, the divided legacies of *Heimat* (home) and the problems of so-called 'Ostalgie' [nostalgia for the GDR] (Pye 2013; Thompson 2009). 'Things' in Erpenbeck become pockets of hyper-temporality connecting multiple pasts, presents and possible futures; they hover between a certain Dürer-like melancholy and a material and temporal resistance potentially prefiguring alternative futures. By granting 'things' such sustained attention (she published a collection of essays on them in 2009), Erpenbeck – like Coetzee's David who 'feels sorry for old things' (Coetzee 2013: 99) – implicitly undermines the foundational distinction in Western thought between 'persons' and 'things' (Esposito 2015). In doing so, she connects the anti-personalisation of the scene of counter-interpellation, along with the impersonality of the *Übergang*, to the equally impersonal indistinction of persons and things. There thus emerges an overdetermined zone of solidarity between communist 'things' – objects and monuments which continue to endure long after the world in which they had their meaning has faded – and the refugees whose own homes and worlds are now distant memories, and who have been forced into a cruel, dysfunctional inertness.[16] When Richard utters the phrase 'Wishing as homesickness' [*Wünschen als Heimweh*] (Erpenbeck 2015: 102), he is referring both to the fact that the sheer social abjection of refugees makes wishing pointless and to the left-wing melancholy for the faded hopes of communism.

The overriding image of the novel, however, is that of intersecting histories: 'In Bach there are no surfaces, just many narratives that intersect. Crossing and crossing – at every moment, and out of all of these intersections that thing is made which, with Bach, is called music' (Erpenbeck 2015: 43).[17] This figure stands not only for Erpenbeck's vision of history but also for her *ars poetica*. Her very sentences weave together disparate times, territories and tales in a single line. Ever drawn to material configurations that spatialise time (e.g., archaeological digs in which depth becomes history), Erpenbeck connects present-day happenings to similar events in Berlin's and Germany's past. By seeking out the material residues of Germany's and Europe's colonial past, often as they emerge through urban palimpsests (such as a wall that still features the words 'Colonial Goods' alongside Second World War bullet marks and a GDR grocery sign [2015: 49]), she is clearly troubled by what Edward Said once called 'uncertainty about whether the past really is past . . . or whether it continues, albeit in different forms' (Said 1994: 1). When the protesting refugees reach an initial agreement with the city authorities, Richard remarks that from the moment it is signed, the refugees must become subject to bureaucratic management – as in colonial times when the 'colonised were smothered through bureaucracy' (Erpenbeck 2015: 64). Likewise, later in the novel, Richard returns repeatedly either to moments at which seemingly 'European' phenomena (e.g., the Greek gods) turn out to have been originally African or Middle Eastern, or to the continuing operations of (primarily European) imperial capitalism in different African nations (e.g., the French company Areva, which has a monopoly on uranium mines in Niger). What Erpenbeck is doing here, I suggest, is trying to make visible the *intersecting ties* that bind Germany to the periphery of the modern world-system through the violent histories of empire. In Erpenbeck's literary universe, the mortal sin is that which denies these ongoing, complex, racist and exploitative ties, or – alternatively – that which simply cuts them. It is no coincidence that her allegory of German law is a giant-like figure who, with an 'uncanny smile' [*unheimliches Lachen*], violently chomps through the organs and bonds of the body politic (Erpenbeck 2015: 228), just as the Tuareg body politic was once 'sliced up' [*zerschnitten*] (2015: 175) by French imperial forces. At the end of the novel, it is former East Germans – living relics of the GDR – who offer temporary homes to the refugees, while the general German populace engages in racist resentment on internet forums. Here, too, it is as if the lost promise of communism is seen as the only alternative to a conception of 'home' premised on a racist, capitalist nation-state whose imagined community represses its own historical role in the present-day abjection of refugees.

Conclusion

Coetzee and Erpenbeck associate the figure of the refugee with a precarious ontological and legal status. This precarity is a form of profound suffering, yet one through which fragile new modes of collective being – what I have called the impersonal – can be glimpsed. The distinct but interrelated modes of the impersonal can be seen to challenge Hannah Arendt's suggestive but problematic defence of the juridical person – that mode of public appearance of an individual before the law. Coetzee's *The Childhood of Jesus* suggests that the juridical person cannot be extricated from the racist and anthropocentric discourses of 'home' in colonial modernity or from its overdetermination by further 'personifications' performed by other ideological state apparatuses. Ultimately, Coetzee seeks an 'impersonal personal' mode of sociality which would deflect ideological interpellations and disentangle basic social bonds from the metaphysical baggage of empire. By the end of the novel, the impersonal becomes associated with the indiscernibility of fiction and the real, suggesting that literature itself is a space germane to the emergence of the impersonal.[18] Erpenbeck, meanwhile, implicitly questions Arendt's firm distinction between persons and things, though her emphasis on the imperialist intersection of European and African histories clearly chimes with Arendt's *The Origins of Totalitarianism*. The impersonal in *Gehen, Ging, Gegangen* ultimately comprises three moments: the ambiguous legal grey zone produced by failed interpellation, the pristine moment of 'transition', and the point at which the classical opposition between person and thing begins to break down. It is these three moments of impersonality which, together, seem to forge a tentative path through and beyond the ongoing imperialist network in which dominant conceptions of 'home' and the figure of the refugee must be understood. It is the impersonal that gestures towards a time when wishing will no longer be homesickness.

Notes

1. I am grateful to David Farrier for his comments on a previous draft of this chapter. All remaining errors are my own.
2. Ayten Gündoğdu's (2015) excellent work drew my attention to these distinct aspects of Arendt's theory of the person.
3. For Arendt's imagined etymology of *persona* as *per-sonare* see Arendt (1963: 295–6, n. 42).
4. Foucault explains the term *dispositif*: 'What I'm trying to pick out with this term is, firstly, a thoroughly heterogeneous ensemble consisting of discourses, institutions, architectural forms, regulatory decisions, laws, administrative measures, scientific statements, philosophical, moral and philanthropic propositions – in short, the said as much as the unsaid. Such are the elements of the apparatus [*dispositif*]. The apparatus itself is the system of relations that can be established between these elements' (cited in Agamben 2009: 2).
5. On Coetzee, impersonality and the 'impersonal', see Barney (2016), Piero (2014) and Attwell (2015: 1–10).
6. For a succinct history of the *dispositif* of the person, see Esposito (2014: chs 1, 2).
7. For Althusser, the educational ideological state apparatus is the dominant apparatus of 'mature capitalist social formations' (2014: 249).
8. Note, for example, the extract from one of David's schoolbooks and the manner in which it portrays the father as the figure of authority and the mother in the role of domestic labourer: 'Today Juan and María are going to the sea. Father tells them their friends Pablo and Ramona may come along. Juan and María are excited. Mother makes sandwiches for the trip' (Coetzee 2013: 264–5).

9. On the 'uncanny' or 'obscene' underbelly of the law, see Žižek (2000).
10. All translations are my own; the original text is given in footnotes. 'Wer seid ihr, werden sie von der Polizei und von Beamten des Senats, die hinzugeholt werden, gefragt. Wir sagen es nicht, sagen die Männer. Das müsst ihr aber sagen, sagen die andren, sonst wissen wir nicht, ob ihr unter das Gesetzt fällt und hier bleiben und arbeiten dürft. Wir sagen nicht, wer wir sind, sagen die Männer . . . Die Männer schweigen.'
11. 'nach allen Seiten offenen, gleichsam zugigen Alltag eines Flüchtlingslebens'.
12. 'Dort, wo man das eine Leben eines Menschen an das andere Leben desselben Menschen grenzt, muss doch der Übergang sichtbar werden, der, wenn man genau hinschaut, selbst eigentlich nichts ist.'
13. '1990 war er plötzlich, von einem Tag auf den andern, Bürger eines anderen Landes gewesen, nur der Blick aus dem Fenster war noch derselbe.'
14. 'wird es dann eine unsichtbare Verbindung geben, die darin besteht, dass [die] einmal ihm gehört hat?' Cf. Arendt (1998: 9): 'because human existence is conditioned existence, it would be impossible without things, and things would be a heap of unrelated articles, a non-world, if they were not the conditioners of human existence'.
15. 'Was erzählt eigentlich so ein Bild, dem die Erzählung abhanden gekommen ist? Wofür werbenm die glücklichen Menschen heute? Steht die Zeit? Bleibt noch etwas zu wünschen?'
16. At several points, readers are reminded of a far more literal solidarity between communist things and refugees, as tables and chairs that were once used in buildings in East Germany are now put to use by refugees in the present.
17. 'Weil es bei Bach keine Oberfläche gibt, sondern viele Erzählungen, die sich überkreuzen. Sich überkreuzen und sich überkreuzen – in jedem Moment, und aus all diesen Kreuzungen ist das Ding gemacht, das bei Bach Musik heißt.'
18. This is Maurice Blanchot's argument (cf. Esposito 2014: 125–33).

Bibliography

Agamben, Giorgio (2004), *The Open: Man and Animal*, trans. Kevin Attell (Stanford: Stanford University Press).

Agamben, Giorgio (2009), *What is an Apparatus?*, trans. David Kishik and Stefan Pedatella (Stanford: Stanford University Press).

Althusser, Louis (2014 [1995]), *On the Reproduction of Capitalism*, trans. G. M. Goshgarian (London: Verso).

Arendt, Hannah (1963), *On Revolution* (London: Faber and Faber).

Arendt, Hannah (1998 [1958]), *The Human Condition* (Chicago: University of Chicago Press).

Arendt, Hannah (2004 [1951]), *The Origins of Totalitarianism* (New York: Schocken Books).

Arendt, Hannah (2007), *The Jewish Writings*, ed. Jerome Kohn and Ron H. Feldman (New York: Schocken Books).

Attwell, David (2015), *J. M. Coetzee and the Life of Writing: Face-to-Face with Time* (New York: Viking).

Badiou, Alain (2005 [1988]), *Being and Event*, trans. Oliver Feltham (London: Continuum).

Balibar, Étienne (2015), 'Althusser's dramaturgy and the critique of ideology', *differences*, 26.3: 1–22.

Barney, Richard A. (2016), 'On (not) giving up: animals, biopolitics, and the impersonal in J. M. Coetzee's *Disgrace*', *Textual Practice*, 30.3: 509–30.

Bhattacharya, Tithi (ed.) (2017), *Social Reproduction Theory: Remapping Class, Recentring Opposition* (London: Pluto Press).

Boehmer, Elleke (2011), 'J. M. Coetzee's Australian realism', in Chris Danta, Sue Kossew and Julian Murphet (eds), *Strong Opinions: J. M. Coetzee and the Authority of Contemporary Fiction* (London: Continuum), 3–17.

Boxall, Peter (2015), 'The anatomy of realism: Cervantes, Coetzee and artificial life', *Anglistik: International Journal of English Studies*, 26.2: 89–103.

Cheah, Pheng (2016), *What is a World?* (Durham, NC: Duke University Press).

Coetzee, J. M. (2005), *Slow Man* (London: Vintage).

Coetzee, J. M. (2013), *The Childhood of Jesus* (London: Vintage).

Erpenbeck, Jenny (2009), *Dinge, die verschwinden* (Berlin: Galiani Verlag).

Erpenbeck, Jenny (2015), *Gehen, Ging, Gegangen* (Munich: Albrecht Knaus Verlag).

Esposito, Roberto (2014), *Third Person: Politics of Life and Philosophy of the Impersonal* (Cambridge: Polity Press).

Esposito, Roberto (2015), *Persons and Things: From the Body's Point of View* (Cambridge: Polity Press).

Fox, Lorna (2005), 'The idea of home in law', *Home Cultures*, 2.1: 25–49.

Gündoğdu, Ayten (2015), *Rightlessness in an Age of Rights: Hannah Arendt and the Contemporary Struggles of Migrants* (Oxford: Oxford University Press).

Lecercle, Jean-Jacques (2016), 'Adresse et interpellation', *Revue Période*, http://revueperiode.net/adresse-et-interpellation/ (accessed 14 July 2017).

Lukács, Georg (1971 [1920]), *The Theory of the Novel*, trans. Anna Bostock (Cambridge, MA: MIT Press).

Marx, Karl (1973), *Grundrisse: Introduction to the Critique of Political Economy*, trans. Martin Nicolaus (Harmondsworth: Penguin).

Moretti, Franco (2013), *The Bourgeois: Between History and Literature* (London: Verso).

Oates, Joyce Carol (2013), 'Saving grace: J. M. Coetzee's *The Childhood of Jesus*', *The New York Review of Books*, 1 September, http://www.nytimes.com/2013/09/01/books/review/j-m-coetzees-childhood-of-jesus.html?mcubz=0 (accessed 12 July 2017).

Piero, Mike (2014), 'Coetzee, Blanchot, and the work of writing: the impersonality of childhood', *MediaTropes*, IV.2: 79–97.

Pye, Gillian (2013), 'Jenny Erpenbeck and the life of things', in Valerie Heffernan and Gillian Pye (eds), *Transitions: Emerging Women Writers in German-Language Literature* (Amsterdam: Rodopi), 111–30.

Said, Edward (1994 [1993]), *Culture and Imperialism* (London: Vintage).

Strehle, Susan (2008), *Transnational Women's Fiction: Unsettling Home and Homeland* (Basingstoke: Palgrave).

Thompson, Peter (2009), '"Die unheimliche Heimat": the GDR and the dialectics of home', *Oxford German Studies*, 38.3: 278–87.

Vermeulen, Pieter (2015), *Contemporary Literature and the End of the Novel: Creature, Affect, Form* (Basingstoke: Palgrave).

Žižek, Slavoj (2000), *The Fragile Absolute* (London: Verso).

Chapter 27

Autobiography of a Ghost: Home and Haunting in Viet Thanh Nguyen's *The Refugees*

Mireille Rosello

At the beginning of her article on 'Refugees, the State and the Concept of Home', Helen Taylor regrets that 'though home is central to any understanding of displacement, the concept has not been explored as fully as possible in forced migration literature' (Taylor 2013: 130). This chapter seeks to accept this challenge and to reflect on the multiple senses of the word 'home' and equally multiple forms of homing or unhoming experienced by refugees. Regardless of whether the guardians of the 1951 Convention on Refugees agree with them or not, refugees decided, at some point, that the place they called home could no longer be home to them. To ever be home again, somewhere, anywhere, they had to leave home. This chapter focuses on the way in which homes appear and disappear around refugees, on how they shift between the present and the past, the figurative and the material, on how they come and go. This complicated game of presence–absence, I will argue, is best analysed as multiple sites of haunting. The old home is a ghostly presence and the present offers a new home that is not home yet: it is also a ghost, the ghost of a future home-to-be imagined. Refugees are confronted by an excess and a lack of home(s), a double tragedy rather than a richness: home(s) is/are now confusingly both too present and too absent, or rather not quite completely absent and never solidly present. Home(s) is/are spectral. The home that had to be left behind is both lost and still possibly the only one imaginable as home. That home, which was taken for granted as home, is no longer home, and its ghost is an energy that produces stories, images, memories and longings. The refugee's home(s) is/are both familiar and uncanny at the same time, a state reminiscent of what Homi Bhabha described as unhomeliness in *The Location of Culture*:

> To be unhomed is not to be homeless nor can the unhomely be easily accommodated in that familiar division of social life into private and public spheres. In that displacement, the borders between home and world become confused; and, uncannily, the private and the public become part of each other, forcing upon us a vision that is as divided as it is disorienting. (Bhabha 1994: 13)

At the time, Bhabha suggested that unhomeliness induced a blurring of the border between home and the world. But once 'home' splits into 'home(s)', unhomeliness will also trigger a never-ending attempt at inhabiting both kinds of homes which are impossible to completely separate, although the separation would be necessary for the refugee to be home again. The blurring occurs between home and home. Each home is haunted by the other, and the refugee will haunt both. Caught between the two extreme poles of romanticisation and demonisation, the old home as well as the new home haunt each other. Home is in the past and the future, here and there, idyllic and hideous, sending happy and sad ghosts with which the refugee needs to find a way to communicate.

Viet Thanh Nguyen's *The Refugees* offers readers an opportunity to think together the three concepts of home, refugee and haunting. This collection of short stories appeared in 2017 and focuses on the experience of the Vietnamese community in the United States. The historical events that turned all the protagonists of the stories into refugees were the wars in Vietnam, Laos and Cambodia. Nguyen's refugees are boat people who fled during the 1960s and 1970s, and the book suggests that they are now haunted subjects for whom being at home in America can never be self-evident. In a context in which Europe struggles with its lack of hospitality towards more recently exiled populations, it is worth keeping in mind that even after forced migrants have been granted the status of refugee, the work of home making never ends.

I propose to focus on the first story of the collection, 'Black-Eyed Women', in which home and haunting are defined from the perspective of the refugee. That ghosts are not universal and that the definition of haunting should be radically different from culture to culture and from period to period is easy to comprehend (Brogan 1998; Bienstock and Howard 2004). It is not the same 'spectral turn' that enables us to orient ourselves towards the medicalised and internalised ghosts of the Enlightenment (Davis 2007: 4–8), towards the ghosts of nineteenth-century British Gothic literature (Kilgour 1998) or towards the spectres summoned by Jacques Derrida's work at the end of the twentieth century (Derrida 1994). In a given time and place, dominant and minority discourses draw borders around the presence of ghosts. They create discursive houses in which ghosts can be addressed, invited, or thrown out according to radically different protocols. Ghosts will be treated differently if they haunt psychology or psychoanalysis (Freud 1975), the history of apartheid, slavery and dictatorships in South America (Bhabha 1994; Gordon 1997) or the language of queer theorists (Castle 1993).

That said, the previous paragraph is based on the assumption that discourses or theories pre-exist and will then accept the ghosts that they have constructed or made legible; yet that hypothesis fails to take into account the types of ghosts that we have not yet disciplined. Some ghosts have not yet been imagined and do not belong to any organised discourse. In other words, they are still in search of a language that they could haunt. While it is easy to distinguish between Freud's ghosts (symptoms that haunt our unconscious) and those studied by occultists (which haunted houses rather than abstract concepts), it is more challenging to imagine the kind of haunting that occurs in the absence of a (theoretical or fictional) home where the ghost may decide to appear. The question is not 'Are some ghosts homeless?' but rather 'What happens to the haunting and to the haunted when *both* ghost and the supposedly more legitimate inhabitant of the house are similarly "unhomed"' (Bhabha 1994: 13)?

In 'Black-Eyed Women', the first story of the collection, the ghost is a refugee: hybrid, American and Vietnamese, apparently integrated and yet perceived as unfamiliar as long as the reader imagines herself as a dominant ethnic subject. Deciding who is not at home in that story, regardless of whether one is a ghost or not, will be a matter of choosing the right type of storytelling: what one says to the ghost, about the ghost and what the ghost says can only be heard after the writer has found the right type of narratives, the right genre. The story unfolds as an experiment in haunting and being haunted, and cleverly maps the definition of ghosts on to the issue of writing. In what Bhabha called 'the house of fiction' (1994: 27) the refugee/ghost will be 'unhomed' but also rehomed in ways that interrogate three crucial areas: the type of homework that is necessary to live with and as a ghost, the vulnerability that comes with (gendered) agency, and (the dangers of) authorship when one is a vulnerable subject. I propose to examine the consequences of haunting from these three angles in the rest of this chapter.

Homework: ghosts making themselves at home in and out of the refugee's house

In this first part of the chapter, I use 'homework' in a very specific sense. I am referring to Sara Ahmed's definition of feminism as 'homework': in *Living a Feminist Life*, Ahmed states that feminism is a task that has to be accomplished because minority subjects such as women 'have much to work out from not being at home in a world. In other words, homework is work on as well as at our homes. We do housework' (Ahmed 2017: 7). I suggest that the work required from the refugee to rebuild a home is comparable to feminist homework to the extent that it 'does not simply clean and maintain a house. Feminist housework aims to transform the house, to rebuild the master's residence' (Ahmed 2017: 7). The refugee who rebuilds a home but also the citizen who wishes to welcome the refugee need to change the shape and function of home to make it welcoming to the ghosts that are going to live there.

In 'Black-Eyed Women', the main protagonists are a daughter and a mother who live together under the same roof in an apparently banal and traditional, middle-class American environment. As refugees go, the first-person narrator may seem to be one of the lucky ones: one of those who were not killed by the conflicts that destroyed their homes, one of those who survived the journey across miles of ocean on a raft, one of those who secured the status of refugee on arrival, but also one of those who arrived early enough to learn the language and get an education in the country where they resettled (Tran 1988; Brown, Schale and Nilsson 2010; Tingvold et al. 2012). In short, this refugee is now at home in America. Her mother has come to live with her after her husband died. She has been in the US for a long time, she talks about 'her early years in America' and about her 'American adolescence' (Nguyen 2017: 7). She has a good job and a residence. She is not homeless. The beginning of the tale describes the house where the mother and the daughter live, and all the details mentioned in passing evoke a comfortable house, a place that reflects the norms of bourgeois standards of living. There is a 'floral armchair', there is a 'carpet', there are beds and tables (Nguyen 2017: 2, 3).

The normality of this home, however, seems to include the presence of ghosts. But ghosts, in this seemingly ordinary residence, are not defined as the uncanny, because they have always been there. The details of the bourgeois house are not emphasised to better highlight the presence of the extraordinary lurking among the banal. Here the ghost is normal because ghosts (or more exactly, a certain kind of ghost) are at home in the refugees' house. And what the rest of the story is about to teach us is that what matters is not the presence or absence of ghosts but the way in which the refugees allow themselves to be haunted. What counts, it will turn out, is not whether or not ghosts exist, or even whether one believes in ghosts or not, but how to distinguish between the types of narratives that can welcome them.

At the beginning of 'Black-Eyed Women', ghosts and ghost stories have very specific characteristics: they belong to the past (before the refugees became refugees, before they came to America) and they are from the 'homeland', Vietnam (Nguyen 2017: 1). Moreover, they seem to perform a radically different function from the kinds of ghosts that we are used to encountering in the Anglo-Saxon popular culture that television and cinema exported around the turn of the century. Since the 1990s, ghosts have been famous actors; they have borrowed the features of international stars such as Patrick Swayze (*Ghost*), Nicole Kidman (*The Others*) or Bruce Willis (*The Sixth Sense*). Global Westernised spectators have learned to expect a certain kind of ghost, whose behaviour corresponds to the familiar narrative scripts. In such stories, as Colin Davis puts it:

> The dead return either because the rituals of burial, commemoration and mourning have not been properly completed (*Truly Madly Deeply*), or because they are evil and must be exorcised (*Buffy the Vampire Slayer*), or because, like the ghost of Hamlet's father, they know of a secret to be revealed, a wrong to be righted, an injustice to be made public or a wrongdoer to be apprehended (*Ghost*). (Davis 2007: 3)

Such ghosts interrupt life as usual because something is wrong and has to be fixed. At the end of the story, when they go away again, they will have fulfilled their mission and the characters' home will be normal again, by which we understand not haunted, free from the terrifying presence-absence of the living dead.

In 'Black-Eyed Women', the mother's ghosts are not demanding creatures whose haunting is a violent and frightening intrusion. These ghosts are as harmless and ordinary as a floral armchair. Part of the mother's legacy is to be absolutely sure that ghosts exist, and the absence of doubt deprives the haunting of any titillating mystery: the narrator explains that as a little girl, she was 'fed' stories (Nguyen 2017: 3). And the mother's favourite kind of story was 'the ghost story, of which she knew many, some firsthand' (2017: 3). Before they had to flee, the mother had already encountered ghosts several times. For example, 'Aunt Six' had appeared to her in her nightgown on the morning she had, it turned out, already died in her sleep. These tales are not frightening or even particularly gripping because if ghosts are a matter of fact, then ghost stories are not so ghostly after all.

At the beginning of the narrative, the narrator brackets off the ghost stories as insignificant. They are presented as a manifestation of the mother's quirky personality: she tells the same story 'once, twice or perhaps three times, repetition being her habit' (2017: 4). The narrator points out that she does not pay attention to how often the story is told, which is perhaps even more important than the repetition itself. Clearly, the fact that the stories keep 'returning' (like the revenant) does not bother her that much. The description of the mother as 'moderately forgetful' (2017: 2) is done in a respectful and loving, but still dismissive way. Neither the ghost nor the story of that ghost is striking or disturbing to her. Ghosts do not interrupt the daughter's new life and they do not really haunt the home. In the mother's story, the ghost comes and goes, leaving no trace and no message, leaving the home intact: 'her ghost simply making the rounds to say farewell' (2017: 4) she says about Aunt Six. The mother's stories, similarly, come and go, and do not alter anything. In short, those homeland ghosts are involved in a rather disappointingly banal and meaningless form of haunting. The narrator clearly invites the reader to share her indifference to such insignificant ghosts and to the mother's point of view. A generational gap opens up between the old refugee who has not adapted to the new home of Western rationality and the younger one who has grown and lived for a long time in the US, where everyone knows that ghosts don't exist. The daughter is gently but clearly rejecting one way of being at home in the world, one way of belonging.

Her mother, she explains, 'constantly fed [her] gossip and stories' (2017: 3) but she 'never took her stories seriously' (2017: 4). In other words, she stops short of dismissing the ghost stories as something that 'they' believe in over there where people are a bit backward, but the story is written as though the narrator had internalised thoughts that could, at any time, turn into a form of ethnic and cultural superiority. In other words, her relationship to ghost stories, at the beginning of her tale, makes it plausible to assume that she is a post-refugee, that she has moved on, that she is at home in a new home. She has been able to establish new forms of belonging, she has done a sort of homework that allows her to believe in the solidity of a home. Still, she cohabits with the mother who makes us imagine the possibility that in some homes, haunting is the norm rather than the exception.

That said, the role that the ghost plays in Western mythology does not disappear altogether: the ghosts inside the home are harmless, but the terror that their presence might trigger is displaced on to imaginary figures who lurk just outside the house. The narrator remembers that in her 'early years in America' (2017: 2), the borders of her new home were strictly policed in an attempt to keep terror outside. The home is a shelter whose doors protect the family from a world of horror: the rule is to not open the door to 'our young countrymen, boys who had learned about violence from growing up in wartime' (2017: 7). The neighbours are the objects of the mother's constant fear: she has heard about families held at gunpoint and tortured. Outside is occupied by barbaric and terrifying figures whom the narrators presents, to the reader, as the fictional characters of some shocking sensationalist tabloid or horror story: the daughter is told about families who were attacked when they opened the door to their house: 'They burned the baby with cigarettes until the mother showed them where she hid her money' (2017: 7). As a result, the mother treats her new home as if it were a bunker in a war-torn place. For the old refugee, the world is thus separated by a clear border between the home and the rest of the country: inside, there are ghosts who do not haunt, and outside, there are non-ghosts who haunt and terrify.[1]

The narrator's construction of the story makes it clear, however, that the imaginary reconstruction of this dangerous home in the US is not completely new: the vision of this house under siege resembles the home that the whole family had to flee. When the daughter reminisces about her youth, we realise that a bunker already existed. The mother has brought it with her. At home, in Vietnam, her husband had dug 'a sandbagged bunker whose roof was braced by timber' (2017: 6). For the narrator, who was then a young girl, the presence and absence of ghosts is also mapped on to the bunker/home/ outside, but the terror that she experiences when her mother mentions the terrifying outsiders is the kind of fear that children experience when they hear gruesome fairy tales or ghost stories. Back home, in Vietnam, she remembers that her brother told her 'tales, folklore and rumors' (2017: 6) and the storytelling would take place in the bomb shelter that was also a playground. There, ghost stories were entertaining. Paradoxically, even though the brother's tales were full of horrifying visions that grown-up readers would interpret as war crimes, the little girl received them from within a place that she considered safe, a home that was not yet haunted, but rather made entertaining by the power of ghost stories. And as a result, she 'shivered with delight in the gloom', convinced that telling ghost stories was a skill she did not have, and that she 'would never tell stories like those' (2017: 6).

When the young narrator has resettled in America, the ghost stories are a thing of the past, or rather they have stopped being interesting or pleasurable. The daughter seems to have recovered, to have created a new home, a new identity, a new vision of the world. At this point, the tale establishes a radical difference between the old and the younger refugee. The narrator has not forgotten the former home but she has established a new home that is both material and discursive, complete with values and a cosmology that reduces ghosts to the past, another country and another culture. Her new home is also based on her ability to treat the lost home as the place where ghosts existed. They have not, however, followed her. The tragic implication is that refugees like her mother will never be at home again in the present and in the US. They are ghosts themselves. The mother's 'tales of woes' (2017: 7) are an expression of her perpetual feeling of alienation: the paranoid stories are 'all of them proof of what my mother said, that we did not belong here' (2017: 7). But somehow, this 'we' has become untenable. The story proposes a generational hypothesis that presents the mother's and the daughter's home-making processes as qualitatively different.

Vulnerability and (gendered) agency: opening the door to fear

'Black-Eyed Women', however, takes a radically new spectral turn when a very different kind of ghost appears: the ghost of the narrator's brother. This ghost, whom we assume at first to be part of the mother's innocent folklore, will radically change the way in which the daughter and the reader understand the refugee's home and her subjectivity. It will prove impossible to dismiss this ghost as a figment of the mother's Vietnamese fantasy. At first, perhaps inevitably, the narrator does her best to rationalise the revenant: 'You're imagining things' (2017: 3) she says. And when the mother points to the wet carpet as evidence that her son –whose ghost swam across the Pacific – was indeed in the living room, the daughter shares her suspicion with the reader: the old woman went out in the rain and has forgotten. Her first reaction is to reject the ghost; she refuses to recognise him, disowns him: 'When she said my brother's name, I did not think of my brother. I closed my eyes and said I did not know anyone by that name' (2017: 2). The politics of visibility, recognition and naming are intricately interwoven with issues of fear, protection and denial. The problem with the brother's ghost is that he comes from the place where evil still lurks: perhaps he should be left out.

I suggest that the presence of this ghost represents the moment when the house is both undone and rebuilt because of the way in which his arrival is described. When the narrator mentions her bedroom for the first time, she only explains that 'knocking woke her' (2017: 7). We understand that the place where she sleeps is separated from the world by a door that she can lock and the text makes it clear that she needs a border as protection: 'I had locked the bedroom door just in case, and now I pulled the covers over my head my heart beating fast' (2017: 7). From the point of view of refugees who have lived in camps or 'jungles', being able to lock the door from the inside means a relief from the constant fear of being robbed, raped or killed.[2] In the short story, the lock both guarantees the right to privacy within the home but also represents the refugee's inability to forget that at any moment her female body risks being constructed as a torturable prey.

Welcoming the presence of the dead brother means acknowledging what she is willing to accept and what she still refuses. The daughter wishes to forget the brother she loves because he is undistinguishable from what he has witnessed. She grants hospitality to his ghost because she reminds herself to 'believe' (2017: 13) that he would never harm her, but she is also reluctant to let in the horrific memories that she must remember when she remembers him. The image of the house as safe bunker must now be rethought and literally deconstructed: the fear that is kept outside has to be brought inside so that the narrator can be reunited with herself as capable of writing her own story as a refugee. This rehoming entails taking responsibility for who she is, for her subjectivity as vulnerable and wounded body. For if what happened to her seems, in retrospect, to be the archetype of the female refugee's fate, her story is, until now, still untold.

In her article on 'The Use of a Novel to Discuss Vietnamese Refugee Experiences', Norma Mandel explains how she assigned Maureen Crane Wartski's novel *A Boat to Nowhere* (1981) to 'a unique group of teenagers: Vietnamese high school students who escaped from their country by boat or else left as part of an airlift of Amerasian children' (Mandel 1988: 40). And when they read chapter 8, they encountered:

> a description of Thai pirates boarding The Sea Breeze and frightening Grandfather and the children. The Vietnamese students did not know the English word 'pirates', but they understood from the story who they were. Although none had experienced pirates attacking them personally, they all had heard firsthand stories of women being raped and kidnapped and men thrown into the ocean. (Mandel 1988: 42)

The description of pirates attacking the refugees is one of those moments when home, for the students, gets split into a schizoid mixture of hyper-competence and ignorance: they do not know the English word, but they know how to insert the concept into a ready-made story which is theirs (collectively) but also not theirs. Like the narrator of 'Black-Eyed Women', these students 'have heard stories' (Mandel 1988: 42) and they know what the presence of pirates means for the women and men on the boat. And perhaps they are lying about not having experienced this violence personally; at least this is what we might suddenly fear and suspect when we realise that the ultimate goal of

'Black-Eyed Women' is precisely to create a home for a story where pirates raping women is not merely a generic script, the predictable and terrifying 'tales of woes' (Nguyen 2017: 7) that happens to others, outside, if you do not keep the doors of the new house locked.

What did happen when the 'nameless blue boat' (Nguyen 2017: 14) was attacked by pirates is a tale that can finally find a house of words and an author: the brother's ghost breaks down the reassuring opposition between the home full of familiar ghosts who do not have much to say, and the outside where murderers threaten the family. By agreeing to listen, the narrator creates a space in between the stories that her mother wants to tell and those that she is simply not able to listen to:

> For all the ghost stories she possessed, there was one story she did not want to tell, one type of company she did not want to keep. They were there, in the kitchen with us, the ghosts of the refugees and the ghosts of the pirates, the ghost of the boat watching us with those eyes that never closed, even the ghost of the girl I once was, the only ghosts my mother feared. (2017: 20)

What she narrates is a terrifying encounter between gender, embodiment and violence: she remembers what the brother did when the refugees on their small boat realised that a pirate ship was approaching. The young teenager cut off her hair with his pocket knife and smeared oil on her face. He also tore off her shirt to bind her breasts, and made her wear his clothes. He literally defaces her and regenders her as a boy. The violence of this forced transition is a predictor of the horror yet to come. Perhaps more importantly, he silences her: 'Don't speak . . . You still sound like a girl' (2017: 14). And the perversity of the moment is that in order to try and protect his beloved little sister, he needs to erase her body which is here exposed as the site of a specific type of vulnerability for the female refugee (Freedman 2015). For as a woman, she is now an object to be 'seized' like the 'gold, watches, earrings, wedding bands, and jade' (Nguyen 2017: 15) that the passengers have to hand over.

The narrator understands her act of hospitality to the ghost as a responsibility to welcome the terror of the uncanny out of gratitude. At some point, avoidance and silence (even to protect the mother) are no longer possible:

> I pulled the covers over my head my heart beating fast. I willed him to go away, but when he started rattling the doorknob, I knew I had no choice but to rise. The fine hairs of my body stood at attention with me as I watched the doorknob tremble with the pressure his grip. I reminded myself that he had given up his life for me. The least I could do was open the door. (2017: 7)

The narrator first covers her head, which makes her look like a dead body, then 'rises'. Although at this point the reader is not yet expected to understand, it is as a ghost that she will continue her tale. She must tell, differently, one of those 'stories of women being raped' that students had heard 'first-hand' (as the mother had heard about ghosts coming back or as a counsellor writing a report [Schroeder-Dao 1982]). This time, this is a woman saying 'I' and remembering what she has tried to forget and could not.

For what the brother's ghost has to tell is very simple: he has the answer to the question that has continued to silence the narrator. What she wants to know, and is incapable of asking directly, is why she lived and why he died. And to that insufferable enigma, the formulation of survivor's guilt, the ghost has the key: '"You died too", he said. "You just don't know it"' (2017: 17). The narrator's (new) home was, after all, haunted. Her mother was right and wrong all along: she was right to believe in ghosts but wrong to assume that the ghosts and terror had separate territories. For the daughter, this has radical consequences: she understands that she does not have a choice whether to believe in ghosts or not: she *is* the ghost haunting the new home.

For the reader, a new problem then arises: how are we to understand what she means. Is this ghost something we should believe in or is it another metaphor, a formal figure for guilt and gender violence. The revelation that the main protagonist is a ghost who does not know that he or she is dead is a narrative device that belongs to the repertoire of ghost stories. In *The Sixth Sense*, for example, a psychologist seeks to help a young patient deal with the supposedly pathological fact that he can see and talk to dead people. Until the very end of the movie, neither the viewer nor the protagonist is expected to understand that the child's ability to see (and show us) ghosts is the reason why the therapist is visible to us. He appeared to the child as a ghost, and even he had not noticed that he was dead. Similarly, in *The Others*, the end of the story is the revelation that the protagonists were dead all along and were disturbed, in their haunting, by the house's new tenants, who do not technically haunt them but have jurisdiction over the realm of the real. Such ghosts, however, are always supposed to be extraordinary. As Esther Peeren puts it, '[t]hat focalizing ghosts are invariably considered surprising and unusual indicates that the norm is to look *at* the specter from the outside' (Peeren 2014: 28). Therefore, in both films, the switch between the ghosts and the living is all there is to know, and the revelation of the secret is the end of the story.

If 'Black-Eyed Women' were to stop after the ghost's explanation that the sister also died and has not realised that she is a ghost, the point of the storytelling would be a desperate and nihilistic statement about the impossibility of the refugee ever finding a new home or a new form of being at home. The little girl could not have survived being raped, feeling responsible for her brother's death, for the suffering of her parents, helpless witnesses of the tragedy, and also for all the other women who were taken away and killed. But instead, that 'death' is not the equivalent of silence and disappearance. The ghost's revelation is that the narrator must rethink what it means to write and grieve.

A home of words: ghost writers and ghost stories

The story as a whole, then, is the staging of the end of a long silence, and the framing of the long-silenced voice of a little girl who, in order to protect her life, had been told not to speak, not to be a woman, and not to be in solidarity with other rape victims. And now, freed from the imperative by the ghost of the brother who had originally given the order to be quiet, she must find a way to write what Judith Butler would call 'an account of oneself' from a place that pays homage to the dead, the living and the ghosts (Butler 2005). The whole narrative is, after all, the autobiography of the ghost as ghost, of someone who says 'I am dead'. And as long as we recognise that the most important word is the 'I', the revelation does not lead to despair, silence and new forms of homelessness. Instead, the narrator must make a decision about authorship and about the point of storytelling.

At the beginning of the story, the daughter is relatively (and paradoxically) famous as a ghost writer whose name never appears anywhere. Agents know where to find her when a text needs to be written by someone whose desire to tell a story is thwarted by their inability to write. As she describes the situation, these non-authors are unfortunate victims who have been 'struck' by fame, 'usually the kind that healthy-minded people would not wish upon themselves such as being kidnapped and kept prisoners for years, suffering humiliation in a sex scandal, or surviving something typically fatal' (Nguyen 2017: 1). She does not recognise that these 'survivors' are uncannily like her and that their stories are in fact quite similar to hers: they are haunted and they, themselves, are ghosts: about Victor, the only survivor of a plane crash that killed his whole family, she writes that he believed in ghosts and 'himself seemed spectral, the heat of grief rendering him pale and nearly translucent' (2017: 10). As a ghost writer, she seems capable of empathy but not of recognition.

The difference between ghost writing and ghost stories encapsulates and mirrors the difference between the two types of ghost that the story welcomes: the mother's harmless and exotic ghosts, and the ghost of the little girl whose life has been silenced. At first, the ghost writer had 'resigned [her]self to being one of those writers whose names did not appear on book covers' (2017: 2); but before resignifying her position as that of a ghost, it is clear that she is not thrilled with the situation. When she explains that she would at the very least like to be mentioned in the 'acknowledgments' (2017: 1), she evokes once again the familiar politics of visibility and invisibility that equates the former with recognition, power and entitlement, and the latter with unfair disenfranchisement. As a ghost writer, she can never become an author.

As a ghost writer, she manifests and symbolises one of the extreme positions in the range of possibilities used by migratory subjects involved in highly visible or underground forms of home making as protest. For some, claiming the right to a new home means insisting on a politics of presence and a refusal of unhomeliness. Ilker Ataç, Stefanie Kron, Sarah Schilliger, Helge Schwiertz and Maurice Stierl point out that some migrants refuse to be ghosts and/or haunted: their home-making process involves a claim to public space, and a politics of visibility that is incompatible with the position of ghost writer adopted by the narrator of the story. They write:

> *Visible* forms of protest include those collective protest campaigns that sought to generate public attention nationally and transnationally and the visibilisation of protesters as political subjects. Examples include the struggles of the 1960s and 1970s in factories and around agricultural production, in the streets, on squares and in front of courts of law (cf. Bojadžijev 2012; Karakayali 2008; Heck 2008). From the 1980s onwards and throughout the 1990s, new forms of protest emerged: church asylum, hunger strikes, airport blockades, *No Border* camps, anti-deportation and anti-detention alliances. In Europe it was in particular the movement of the *Sans Papiers* in France since the mid-1990s which used church occupations and political strikes to leave the shadowy realm of illegality and protest criminalisation and the deprivation of rights (cf. Barron et al. 2011; McNevin 2006). (Ataç et al. 2015: 6)

For the mother, on the other hand, certain forms of ghostliness are desirable, and her strategy is the opposite of that of the *sans papiers*: she believes in invisibility as protection and she imagines the name as what exposes the daughter to the dangers that lurk outside the home. As evidence, she tells the story from the 'homeland': 'there was this reporter who said the government tortured the people in prison. So the government does to him exactly what he said they did to others' (Nguyen 2017: 1). Once again, an uncanny mirror is handed to the daughter: the reporter who disappears is supposed to teach her that she should make herself disappear for fear of that very same thing being done to her. For the mother, nothing has changed and the same strategies are still valid. The America where she lives is as dangerous as the place she had to flee. But the one story she cannot welcome is the memory of what happened on the boat, a story that precisely proves that even if the little girl were made to disappear as a girl, she was still about to be raped. Besides, the mother's belief in the power of being a ghost writer obviously does not protect her from her own memory, since even the worst paranoid urban myths that she warns her family against are in fact not as horrifying as what she experienced on the boat.

At the end of the story, when the daughter's agent, pleased with the success of her latest book, proposes a new, 'lucrative' contract to write the 'story of a soldier who lost his arms and legs trying to defuse a bomb' (2017: 19), she refuses. The dislocated, amputated body is, again, a version of her own. But this time she declines the invitation. She is, she says, 'writing a book of [her] own' (2017: 19) The next sentence is an interesting shift of perspective: we never hear the narrator state, 'I want to write ghost stories.' Instead, the text quotes the agent presumably repeating what someone (the narrator, a ghost) has said and reacting (or thinking out loud): '"Ghost stories?" Her tone was approving. "I can sell that. People love being frightened"' (2017: 19).

For the agent, ghost stories are simply another type of product and fear is a commodity. But the ghost knows that her ghost stories are not about fear because terror has precisely and finally been transformed into grief: 'My ghosts were the quiet and shy ones like my brother, as well as the mournful revenants in my mother's stories' (2017: 19). The encounter with the ghost of the brother, or rather the type of hospitality that the daughter is willing to offer, is a turning point. The relationship between the ghosts, the home and the haunting changes radically. Telling the story that was caught between the past and the present, between the new home and the old home, means accepting a reconfiguration of the haunting: when the daughter recognises that she is a ghost, the female refugee can mourn having been faced with a tragic alternative (not being a woman or dying). Worse still, after having renounced her womanhood, she had been forced to recognise that even renouncing her identity would not save her. As a ghost, she can choose to express her own survivor's guilt no longer through a form of silence or by displacing it on to her clients, other survivors whose grief and guilt are driving them to the verge of madness. Writing as a ghost who writes ghost stories means that she no longer needs to keep the doors locked to keep rapists at bay: she can now live with the ghosts she had to exclude, such as those of the other little girls who did not survive. The pirates were already inside, locked in the bunker of her memory.

Conclusion

The shift between being a ghost writer and a writer of ghost stories is both subtle and extraordinarily important, but it is also clear that it will be misunderstood and misinterpreted. On the one hand, Nguyen here takes the risk of being perceived as a bit too clever: the word 'ghost' in ghost writer and ghost stories may sound like a convenient opportunity to play with the English language. On the other hand, the radical difference between the two types of 'ghosts' in this instance is the point of the story. It is both highlighted and interrogated. The daughter's decision to reformulate her professional activity coincides with a reconfiguration of her way of being at home in the world of ghosts.

Depending on who speaks about, or for, or with, or as a refugee, home means something different. Depending on how the local context is mediated and localised or globalised, the relationship between home and what one wants, what one lacks and what one wishes to recapture, forget, remember or recreate will have to be constantly rearticulated. Sometimes the wishes and desires expressed about home will add up to incompatible and dissenting paradigms. In each context, I may have to ask again what I mean by 'home' when I observe that it is what some refugees want, but also sometimes what they do not want, or cannot afford to want, or cannot afford not to want. But all this complexity can be erased by those who shriek, 'refugees go home'.

The stories written about the ghosts who visit refugees are an example of the kind of 'homework' that refugees must constantly do. 'Black-Eyed Women' makes it clear that haunting is an integral part of homeliness. Only those 'people whose rights of residence are not under scrutiny' (Herd and Pincus 2016) can enjoy the privilege of imagining that they may choose to welcome or ignore the ghost of homelessness.

Notes

1. She thus confirms and even exaggerates the 'prevalence of associations between "family" and "home" [that] are key to the way woman asylum seekers are simultaneously included and excluded in asylum discourse, where domestic metaphors proliferate' (Farrier 2011: 106).
2. See the insistence on being able to lock the door from the inside in the testimonies cited in 'What home is for a refugee without one?' which describes the features of 'better shelters' designed by IKEA for their foundation; https://www.ikeafoundation.org/storieshome-refugee-without-one/ (accessed 26 May 2019).

Bibliography

Ahmed, Sara (2017), *Living a Feminist Life* (Durham, NC: Duke University Press).

Ataç, Ilker, Stefanie Kron, Sarah Schilliger, Helge Schwiertz and Maurice Stierl (2015), 'Struggles of migration as in-/visible politics', *Movements. Journal für kritische Migrations- und Grenzregimeforschung*, 2.1: 1–18, http://movements-journal.org/issues/02.kaempfe/01.ata%C3%A7,kron,schilliger,schwiertz,stierl--einleitung~en.pdf (accessed 15 May 2019).

Barron, Pierre, Anne Bory, Anne Sébastien Chauvin, Nicolas Jounin and Lucie Tourette (2011), *On bosse ici, on reste ici! La grève des sans-papiers: une aventure inédite* (Paris. La Découverte).

Bhabha, Homi K. (1994), *The Location of Culture* (London: Routledge).

Bienstock, Ruth Anolik and Douglas Howard (eds) (2004), *The Gothic Other: Racial and Social Constructions in the Literary Imagination* (London: McFarland).

Bojadzijev, Manuela (2012 [2008]), *Die windige Internationale. Rassismus und Kämpfe der Migration* (Münster: Westfälisches Dampfboot).

Brogan, Kathleen (1998), *Cultural Haunting: Ghosts and Ethnicity in Recent American Literature* (Charlottesville, VA: University Press of Virginia).

Brown, Chris, Codi Schale and Johanna Nilsson (2010), 'Vietnamese immigrant and refugee women's mental health: an examination of age of arrival, length of stay, income, and English language proficiency', *Journal of Multicultural Counseling and Development*, 38.2: 66–76.

Butler, Judith (2005), *Giving an Account of Oneself* (New York: Fordham University Press).

Castle, Terry (1993), *The Apparitional Lesbian: Female Homosexuality and Modern Culture* (New York: Columbia University Press).

Crane Wartski, Maureen (1981), *A Boat to Nowhere* (Harmondsworth: Penguin).

Davis, Colin (2007), *Haunted Subjects: Deconstruction, Psychoanalysis and the Return of the Dead* (Basingstoke: Palgrave Macmillan).

Derrida, Jacques (1994), *Specters of Marx: The State of the Debt, the Work of Mourning, and the New International*, trans. Peggy Kamuf (London: Routledge).

Farrier, David (2011), *Postcolonial Asylum: Seeking Sanctuary Before the Law* (Liverpool: Liverpool University Press).

Freedman, Jane (2015), *Gendering the International Asylum and Refugee Debate*, 2nd edn (Basingstoke: Palgrave Macmillan).

Freud, Sigmund (1975 [1919]), 'The Uncanny', in *Sigmund Freud. Standard Edition*, trans. James Strachey, vol. 7 (London: Hogarth Press), 219–52.

Gordon, Avery (1997), *Ghostly Matters: Haunting and the Sociological Imagination* (Minneapolis: University of Minnesota Press).

Heck, Gerda (2008), *'Illegale Einwanderung'. Eine umkämpfte Konstruktion in Deutschland und den USA* (Münster: Unrast).

Herd, David, and Anna Pincus (eds) (2016), *Refugee Tales* (Manchester: Comma Press).

Karakayalı, Serhat (2008), *Gespenster der Migration: Zur Genealogie illegaler Einwanderung in der Bundesrepublik Deutschland* (Bielefeld: Transcript).

Kilgour, Maggie (1998), *The Rise of the Gothic Novel* (London: Routledge).

McNevin, Anne (2006), 'Political belonging in a neoliberal era. The struggle of the sans-papiers', *Citizenship Studies*, 10.2: 135–51, DOI: 10.1080/13621020600633051.

Mandel, Norma (1988), 'The use of a novel to discuss Vietnamese refugee experiences', *The English Journal*, 77.5: 40–4, http://www.jstor.org/stable/818970 (accessed 15 May 2019).

Nguyen, Viet Thanh (2017), *The Refugees* (New York: Grove Atlantic).

Peeren, Esther (2014), *The Spectral Metaphor: Living Ghosts and the Agency of Invisibility* (Basingstoke: Palgrave).

Schroeder-Dao, Tu-Khuong (1982), *Study of Rape Victims among the Refugees on Palau Bidong Island: An Experience in Counselling Women Refugee 'Boat People'* (New York: United Nations High Commissioner for Refugees).

Taylor, Helen (2013), 'Refugees, the state and the concept of home', *Refugee Survey Quarterly*, 32.2: 130–52, DOI:10.1093/rsq/hdt004.

Tingvold, Laila, Anne-Lise Middelthon, James Allen and Edward Hauff (2012), 'Parents and children only? Acculturation and the influence of extended family members among Vietnamese refugees', *International Journal of Intercultural Relations*, 36.2: 260–71.

Tran, Thanh (1988), 'Sex differences in English language acculturation and learning strategies among Vietnamese adults aged 40 and over in the United States', *Sex Roles: A Journal of Research*, 19.11–12: 747–58.

Filmography

Ghost, dir. Jerry Zucker, 1990
The Others, dir. Alejandro Amenábar, 2001
The Sixth Sense, dir. M. Night Shyamalan, 1999

Chapter 28

Homing as Co-creative Work: When Home Becomes a Village

Misha Myers and Mariam Issa

Misha begins:

On an autumn day in April 2017 I had a conversation with Mariam Issa in the RAW garden, a community garden and organisation that aims to support women's resilience through storytelling, arts, cooking and gardening, created by Mariam in the backyard of the home where the Australian government had settled her and her family in the affluent Melbourne suburb of Brighton. RAW, which stands for Resilient Aspiring Women, has established distinctive strategies of inclusion and welcome forged from Mariam's personal experience of refugee migration fleeing the Somali civil war, and her inspirational determination, trust and vision to build community in a suburb that was resistant, initially, to her family's settlement. When I first stumbled upon the garden, I was inspired by the creative and radical possibilities of home making that it offers, for its proposition of what refuge and home can be when backyards are opened up and become a space to build a village (Edmanson 2014).

Originally, I had invited Mariam to walk and talk with me following my 'way from home' walk, a set of instructions that I created in 2002 that led to a series of walks and conversations with refugees and asylum seekers across the UK about their transnational experiences of home making (Myers 2009; 2011; 2017). But the conversation took a different route, as they sometimes do. As the first step of the instructions suggests, I invited Mariam to create a map of a route from a place she considered home to a special place nearby, marking significant landmarks along the way, and then we would take a walk following that map of elsewhere, perhaps here in the garden, perhaps here in the neighbourhood, wherever her map and her desires might take us. But that first step is a tricky one as the question of where is home elicits such diverse responses. I never ask this question or invite this walk lightly or with any naïve assumption that home could possibly mean the same thing for everyone, especially someone who has experienced forced migration. But this walk was one way I have found to start both a conversation about home, and a process of co-creating one together respectfully and creatively through

Figure 28.1 Issa and Myers conversing in the RAW garden, Melbourne (photograph: Iva Maria Yogini Kumaresh)

a method that promotes agency and avoids the imposition or perpetuation of ways of telling refugee experience used to determine the authenticity and validity of the claim for asylum.

On this occasion Mariam led me to a colourful mosaic map of the world (Fig. 28.1) created with members of the RAW community. With this serving as her map, she pointed to Cape Horn, and from there began tracing her finger across the colourful broken pieces of the mosaic while telling me her journey from there to Australia, telling me what home was for her and how she felt about it, how she lost it, found it and made it again and again. This conversation instigated further conversations between us about a collaboration that is still emerging and unfolding, that begins where this one leaves off. Mariam's account of her journey and creative work of home making grounds the theoretical perspectives offered here on the meanings and makings of home in the world and in action.

Home as a journey

Mariam begins:

The journey has been low and high. The low being a young woman in Africa. I went through female genital mutilation, a painful experience not only for myself but all women. Also growing up where women did not have rights to land, could not own anything for themselves. There was harsh family violence around me. When I lived in Uganda, I experienced the civil war of Idi Amin and that is when we left and came back to Kenya.

But I also experienced high moments as a curious child. I had the ability to wonder and climb trees and go around in nature and experience a freedom through having a connection to the land and seeing the people that practised that. In Kenya and Uganda the women had plots of land where they cultivated and grew their own vegetables, shambas. In these women, mama mboga, I also witnessed resilience. They would walk a marathon to sell their produce. I had the privilege of going with them sometimes. Through the walk they would cry and work through the pain of it and then by the end, when they neared the market, they were laughing as if they did not have a problem in the world. I learned so much about connection through these walks, connection not only to ourselves as people, but also to the land. All this was just something that was growing in me and I didn't realise it until my journey when I went into the Arab world in Doha in Qatar.

Misha continues:

Departing from perceptions of refuge as a state of permanent sanctuary or home as fixed place of origin, Mariam's experience of home suggests that it is something continuously made and arrived at, as in a sense of homing. Her story reveals how home is constructed through ongoing endeavour, interaction and connections made in multiple locations and through multiple dimensions of self, through a kind of creative work. That work also involves memory work that builds upon positive nostalgic feelings and attachments to past experiences and places of home, like those Mariam expresses when she speaks of the mama mboga walking to the market. So it is a work that reaches towards the past, present and future simultaneously. Understanding these aspects of refugees' creative practices of home making may complicate or offer a more nuanced recognition of how refuge or 'home' is experienced, created and can be better supported by host communities.

In formulating this notion of home making as creative work, certain theories that challenge perceptions of 'home' or refuge as a permanent, original or singular location may be helpful. In particular, Doreen Massey's definition of *place* as formed out of the specificity of interacting social relations in a particular location to constitute 'meeting places' (Massey 1994: 168, 171), bell hooks's notion of *homeplace* and of home as existing in multiple locations and affording multiple perspectives on reality and difference (hooks 1991: 149) and Liisa Malkki's critique of the 'sedentarist bias' (Malkki 1995: 16) suggest a means of approaching home and emplacement in the experience of migration and of understanding how seeking sanctuary or refuge may be a continuous creative process of home making or homing.

Whereas nostalgic longing for home is often dismissed as regressive and reactionary in its association with essentialist notions of home as fixed to a place of origin, alternative forms of nostalgia that are progressive or future-orientated suggest that situated reworkings of these feelings can act as creative strategies. Svetlana Boym's conception of forms of nostalgia that can be both retrospective and prospective (Boym 2001) and Ghassen Hage's identification of settlement strategies that seek out and employ nostalgic feelings to build a sense of being 'at home' (Hage 1997) offer ways of understanding nostalgia's creative potential. Edward Casey discerns a different kind of memory work and set of bodily skills that is necessary for inhabiting a place, whether it is establishing a new home or returning to a previous one, as habitual body memories and powers of orientation and of conceptualisation and expression of thoughts about place both to oneself and 'others who find themselves on similar journeys' (Casey 1993: 293). The telling and sharing of narratives of home, of what I have referred to elsewhere as *homing tales* (Myers 2009), such as those facilitated through 'way from home' and shared here by Mariam, enact enabling and prospective forms of nostalgia through creative discursive interactions that orient and redefine the sense of self and refuge.

When home isn't home any more

Mariam continues:

I went from Kenya to Doha because my husband was working there at the time. I married Mohammed for the freedom that I saw in his family, whereas my family was very conservative and religious. But when we came to Doha it was quite the opposite. It was a culture where women were expected to stay at home and be homemakers and men would go to work. I was brought to a two-room apartment. My husband would leave in the morning and lock the door behind him. That was not the freedom I had envisioned. I lived in that state for three years. I had two children and the only opportunity that I had to go out was to learn the language in a centre there. That is where I met with the native Arab women and realised what their culture was like and how these women, just like the African women, were nurturing each other and held this circle for each other. When I had my first baby they came to my home and took care of me.

I came back from Doha to Somalia and after we returned, I started to feel freedom again. But within the year the civil war in Somalia happened. My husband was not with me at the time. He was in the Arab world. So I had to flee alone with my children who were two and three years old. And at that time I was pregnant with my third child at 23 years old. I took a small boat from Kismayu in Somalia, where I was born, to Mombassa, the port in Kenya where I grew up. The irony is that when I came back as a refugee, Kenya would not accept me. I had a Kenyan passport, but they said, 'You can come in, but your children cannot.' Then I realised these places that I had always thought were home weren't home – one threw us out and the other rejected us. From there we were displaced for eight years. There was no place to go. It was like living in limbo and in hiding. Then after eight years of displacement and being rejected by the United Kingdom, we were finally accepted by Australia after our second attempt.

Misha continues:

The notion of home as bounded, stable and located, as 'a place called home', is one that Massey has questioned as a predominantly white/First World point of view, as she suggests that the geographical boundaries of home and the coherence of local culture would have already been disrupted for most of the world many centuries ago (Massey 1994: 165). Instead of home being associated with a geographical place, Massey conceives it as a set of social relations interacting in a 'meeting place' (1994: 154). Perhaps the way Mariam describes the circle of women in Doha and the mama mboga walking to the market qualify as such meeting places.

Relatedly, bell hooks reimagines 'home' as multiple locations, not a singular place, a notion that may speak to transnational experiences of place:

> Home is that place which enables and promotes varied and everchanging perspectives, a place where one discovers new ways of seeing reality, frontiers of difference. One confronts and accepts dispersal and fragmentation as part of the constructions of a new world order that reveals more fully where we are, who we can become. (hooks 1990: 149)

How then is this sense of home as meeting place inhabited? A set of reflective and social skills and competencies are required to navigate this dynamic space of openness, changing perspectives and fragmentation, skills that Mariam developed as she moved between different cultures and sought out the kind of connections and interaction experienced with the women in Doha and the mama mboga to create a sense of home.

Where is home?

Mariam continues:

Coming into Melbourne was an eye-opener. I had never lived with Westerners before. I didn't know much about the culture, except what I had read in books and seen on television. There was a lot of suspicion. It was a very scary moment. I came with four children all under the age of 11 and was pregnant with my fifth child. I was 30 years old. It was a complete awakening for me. The first three years I was in a depression and very vulnerable, living in a phase where I felt like a victim, a victim of war, of a culture that did not give me enough to be me. I knew nothing about myself, no individual knowledge. All I knew about myself was in the context of the culture that I had come from. Then two years after arriving, 9/11 happened and my family and I felt very unsafe again. There was such turmoil in the thought that 'Where is home, where can I be safe? Where is that space that is protecting us?'

From that experience I retreated inwardly to look for answers, to see who am I? There was an awakening moment when my daughter was four and we looked for a kindergarten for her. We had a very frosty reception. When we came out, my daughter asked me 'Mom, did they not want me because I'm black?' That for me was a time when I had to question myself as a mother – is it okay to be this fearful? What am I doing for my children? We had two options: we had to stay in Brighton or we had to go where my ethnic community lived.

When I first arrived I worked as an interpreter in hospitals, courts, different spaces, and I saw the turmoil that was going through my ethnic community in the space of finding who they are in this place. So I knew that if I went into that space, into that ethnic communal space where they were holding on to an illusion of home, I would not find the answers that I need. I knew that by being away from my community, I also had the chance to get to know the Brighton community around me. I also wanted to protect my children, to stand up and be brave for them.

Then I entered a space of anger. I became angry at my culture. I was questioning everything about the culture, about myself as a human being, and why did these things happen and why did they have to happen to me. I would see the serenity, the beauty in Brighton and I did not understand how one nation could be so rich in beauty and in abundance while another was in desperation and war. I would look at the contrasting journeys to find answers. In those days in all that turmoil, I felt like it was home, a home of chaos. That chaos was all around me. My teenagers were angry. We were finding ourselves in opposition for a space to be a part of this culture. It was a hard time.

Misha continues:

The difficult decision that Mariam faced in choosing whether to remain within her ethnic cultural community or to build a home in a community where she was unwelcome, at first, was a kind of secondary exile within exile and points to the complexities of how refuge is experienced by refugees, and the turmoil and chaos, as Mariam describes it, involved in the work of home making in this context.

The assumption that the homeland is the ideal habitat, referred to as the 'sedentarist bias' by the anthropologist Liisa Malkki, suggests that a loss of homeland equates to a loss of cultural identity (Malkki 1995: 16). Malkki suggests that 'if "home" is where one feels most safe and at ease, instead of some essentialised point on the map, then it is far from clear that returning where one fled from is the same thing as "going home"' (1995: 16). The home-place can be a perilous place, rather than one of safety and belonging, with expulsion from the homeland being the most 'dangerous displacement' (Casey 1993: 302). Casey suggests that '[w]ith literal re-inhabitation of the homeland precluded, the only way out is through re-inhabitation of another sort. That is what hooks in effect recommends: *re-inhabit the home-place*, even if it is located in a land of exile' (1993: 302).

Finding the true home

Mariam continues:

I became very curious about the Western women in Brighton in their Lycra, pushing a pram with one hand and holding the leash of a dog with another, in full make-up doing their thing early in the morning. I was witnessing her in every space – she was the teacher of my children, the doctor I visit, she was in all the administrator positions. She drew me out of this victim space, yet this was a woman I had not even met yet. I was only observing her from afar and she reminded me of the mama mboga from back home, the nurturer of the community.

   Through that chaos I went into another phase; I now call that the empowerment phase. I stopped everything and started to listen through the deep listening my mother taught me. She would walk us through nature and tell us to listen. I started becoming good friends with nature. Through that journey I became very peaceful; I had no fights in me any more. In that phase I realised that you are a creator and we do co-create with other people. We have to. So all the values I think I had lost in those times of turmoil came back to me. I started to understand how to be a co-partner in everything in life. And to look at what's calling me, what's my passion, what I want to share with the world. This phase was where I found that my true home was my heart.

Misha continues:

Similar to Massey's conception of home as a place of social relations, Boym suggests that what is most missed in the experience of displacement is not so much the past or the homeland or an actual location, but a 'sense of intimacy with the world' (Boym 2001: 251), the space of cultural experience, the context provided by culture for relationships to develop, not necessarily by continuity, but by contiguity, 'based neither on nation nor religion but on elective affinities' (2001: 53). Perhaps Mariam's recollection of mama mboga through the observation of women in Brighton can be understood as her recognition of this possibility of affinity or contiguity. The perception of this potential affinity and intimacy grew out of memory and longing for past relations or experiences and places where those intimate and nurturing relationships could thrive. This perception offers another way of understanding Casey's skills of inhabitation, the ability to conceive of and articulate the place of home, to recognise and create the conditions necessary for this inhabitation. Boym describes this kind of activation of longing for the past as a future-orientated nostalgia that 'can be retrospective but also prospective' (2001: xvi). Mariam negotiated between the values that were imposed on her to discover and understand those of her own in order to create what she considers the 'true home', a space and opportunity for future intimacy, connection and interaction with those around her.

Home is the heart

Mariam continues:

Because we are diverse communities we bring so many beautiful things into our world. But because that diversity has been suppressed and compartmentalised into boxes and every box is fighting for its rights, the world has become a place of fighting and war. I think I've been called into this space, because we are never anywhere randomly, to create those bridges between cultures, religion, gender, all the conditioning that has been happening to us. So where is home? Home is the heart.

I felt Australia welcomed me. I really feel reborn in this country. It's given me the true essence of who I am. So I felt that I had a debt to do something in this community. I was here to remember and I have remembered so much about myself and all that I brought with me from the places I called home. Remembering the women of my childhood who were so strong in their connection with the land, with their shambas, their plot of land, I realised that human connection was everything and connecting to the earth as well. So I did a permaculture course.

African women don't know themselves in closed spaces. So from that course combined with the work I have always done with women and community I had the seed of creating a garden for women. I looked around my home in Brighton and saw open space, all grass, and realised I had the space for it. So I talked to my husband and said, 'You know what, I'm going to start a community garden and I'm going to start it in our backyard.' I convinced him. In the permaculture course I connected with an incredible woman, Katrina Kons, originally from Germany, and asked if she would come on board. Also,

I had a dream about the name of the organisation. I woke up, wrote it down and went back to sleep. When I woke up and read what I'd written in the morning, I said, 'This is "RAW", but what does it mean?' Then during my meditation I got it – Resilient Aspiring Women. Three months later after we created the space, I was told 'If you read the word "RAW" backwards it's "WAR".' And literally it translated my journey. Stop the war inside; tap into your resilience and aspirations. That's how RAW talked to me.

From then on whatever war comes in – a war of doubt, a war of fear, a war of not enough – I would literally say, 'No, I'm a resilient woman, I'm aspiring to do this.' So I became a visionary storyteller. I made sure that all my stories are stories of resilience – this isn't possible now, but it's going to be.

Misha continues:

The continuous thread throughout Mariam's story of her journey is how connections with women have been a kind of home for her and the memories of these past interactions have influenced and guided her own vision and creativity in her home making. For Ghassen Hage home building is *'the building of the feeling of being "at home"'* (Hage 1997: 102, italics in original). These feelings are fostered by nostalgia, which Hage defines as 'a memory of a past experience imagined from the standpoint of the present to be homely' (1997: 105). These nostalgic feelings are triggered by direct experience and can be negative or positive 'intimations' (1997: 105). A sense of security, familiarity, community or possibility, what Hage articulates as the four 'affective blocks', combined together create a 'liveable structure' (1997: 102). Their accumulation transforms into a capacity for home making or ability to recognise and exploit nostalgic feelings to enable 'an experience of "back home"' (1997: 106).

Some of the examples Hage gives of experiences that facilitate strong intimations of home focus on food and places that trigger associations or memories of past places where particular social relationships were enacted. For Mariam, these places are the walks to the market with the mama mboga or the circle held by the women in Doha. These were powerful intimations for her that she describes as seeds that she carried with her and that guided her to find her voice and potential to go on to seek out and recreate those circles, those meeting places with women in the present, manifest as RAW (Fig. 28.2). Similar to Casey's skills of inhabitation, Hage emphasises that being at home is to be in a space where one has the most practical, spatial and communicative know-how and opportunities for advancement (Hage 1997: 102–3). Mariam has created a space where she now grows and shares food with the community around her and she invites women to sit in a circle sharing stories, art or home cooking. This creative work demonstrates the activation of experiences of nostalgia, not to return to a past home, but 'to promote the feeling of being there *here*' (Hage 1997: 108, italics in original) in order to create a

Figure 28.2 Issa with mosaic mural world map created as part of RAW garden community art activities (photograph: Iva Maria Yogini Kumaresh)

base from which to meet, come to terms with and seize opportunities from life in the present and make a difference to effect change in her community.

In addition to RAW's cooking classes and gardening, which centre around the intimations of home through food and place more explicitly, the storytelling and arts and crafts events take place in the space of an outdoor kitchen in the garden and usually involve some sharing of food as well as stories and other forms of collective creativity. Home food offers intimations of security in providing nutrition, of familiarity in the expression of practical know-how in terms of both its consumption and production, and of communality in the practices of sharing collective meals and collectively sharing personal stories.

These creative practices of home building that are core activities of RAW can also be seen in other events in Melbourne, such as Peace Meals and the Australian Intercultural Society's Ramadan home IFTAR dinners, both aimed at promoting social cohesion and interaction. All centre around sharing food production and consumption and involve some form of sharing personal stories.

At Peace Meals you are asked to sit around a shared table beside someone you do not know, not the person you came with. The cook is always someone who has recently come to Australia as a refugee and they prepare a meal from their own culture. After the meal they are invited to share their story with the guests and ask for support with anything they need to help their settlement. They also receive donations given by those attending. At the IFTAR dinner, a family volunteers to cook and host the IFTAR meal, eaten to break the fast of Ramadan, for a non-Muslim family or group. During the meal everyone is invited to go around the circle at the table to introduce themselves, saying something about their interests, work or background.

These circles are purposeful meeting places that promote openness, a sense of homeliness, familiarity and hospitality through the combination of sharing food and stories in an intentional way. They are affective structures constructed skilfully in a way that promotes and maximises social interaction, intercultural exchange, intimacy and sharing of stories amongst strangers. The openness that is offered by Mariam in making her backyard a community space, by the Peace Meal cooks in sharing their stories and home food, by the IFTAR hosts in sharing their home and the momentous occasion of breaking the day's fast with strangers encourages openness in return.

Home as open space

Mariam: The mission statement that we had for RAW was to create social environments to celebrate the uniqueness of women in their lives, communities and beyond. When we started we had to mulch the ground, cover it with cardboard. We had to create a place with intention. Every tree we planted we asked community members to adopt, because we didn't have money, and to have an intention for their tree. That apple tree is a tree of abundance. My mother-in-law was the elder present that day and she put her apple tree in the ground and it was so small. It wasn't even supposed to grow fruit that year, but it had an abundance of fruit.

Misha: How do the storytelling, cooking, art and working bee events you organise in the garden come together?

Mariam: We have four activities. The cooking is a project called 'community, culture and cuisine'. It involves inviting someone with a diverse background. It could be Italian, Greek, Maltese, African, wherever they come from. We have had so many different varieties of people, of chefs who just do a cooking class and share their stories, share the culture behind the cuisine. They talk a little about why they love cooking, or where it's originated from or how their family came to Australia, or if they were second generation or third generation.

Other activities that we run are arts and crafts. We wanted to build a feature wall for the space to block some of the air that comes into the pavilion. One of the event organisers said, 'It would look nice if we had a bottle wall.' So I knew this young Australian woman who went to California and learned about adobe structure and I asked her if she could support us with that. When we were building it we hosted asylum seekers from the detention centre at Broadmeadows. They were Tamil men, twelve of them who had not been out of the centre for five years. Their first time out was to come to the garden. That was a great privilege. Some of them were renderers and builders and they felt overjoyed to support us with building the wall. People even walked off the street to come in and contribute something. We have permaculture talks sometimes, working bees. The RAW garden is everything in one. It's about environment, about your neighbours, our connection to who we are. It's about love, trust and connection. It's a space that has given my family and me so much understanding of other people and broadened our view of the world, just being in the RAW garden (Fig. 28.3).

Figure 28.3 Plaque commemorating the founding and founders of RAW garden, Melbourne (photograph: Iva Maria Yogini Kumaresh)

Misha: How old is the mulberry tree? Was it here before?

Mariam: No, and last year we had so many mulberries.

Misha: I know, I was here eating them at the Diwali celebration! So when did you start?

Mariam: We started in 2012.

Misha: It's incredible. It was just grass? Now you have olives, apples and bananas.

Mariam: And we have apricots and nectarines.

Misha: It doesn't feel like it's trying to be a village. Like it's forced. It's just living that. You can just walk in and contribute to it. How do we create these kinds of spaces?

Mariam: Don't look for outcomes. It's registered as a not-for-profit. For instance, the kitchen is a gift from a charity organisation. I brought the CEO of this organisation, Jane, and told her my vision. It was just grass then. We didn't fill out a grant for the kitchen. I told her I'm not a project manager. I can't take responsibility for that. Can you imagine demanding that? She gave us the money and she sent someone to manage the people. That can only happen from a space of trust, a true connection of trust.

Misha: It also goes against the notion of home as a private space. That is something that touched me so deeply. This is your home and you've opened it up as a public space.

Mariam: I think that is because it's in our African culture. There's no way that I would have been able to do that if it hadn't been part of our culture. For us there is privacy. We don't see any problem with someone coming because we were neighbours and we didn't have fences. Our culture is an open culture, a giving culture in the sense that when someone comes to your home, it's something that we value, that's deeply valued in our culture. So that comes to us with ease. But it wasn't easy for the people coming. I felt that they were hesitant to come into someone else's backyard. For me what I did was create this trust for it to be both ways. I didn't want the place to become commercial. So we don't advertise, but we have a Facebook page telling about what's happened with events.[1] The other thing I ensured is that I do the work from a place of privilege, not duty. It's a lot of work. When people come in, I tell them to do what they feel comfortable doing, not to feel obliged. It's to be run like a backyard. I think I do that with intent. I want people who come to the garden to feel they are in their own home or that they are nurtured in this space. So every Tuesday when we are gardening, I make a meal. We put out the donation box. They are not asked to do it. We take out the element of money because that has become our divide. When you come in, you can find whatever you need. This is the true home. For me my need was connection, my need was trust, for people to feel loved, nurtured, listened to.

I get the privilege of hearing people's stories and every story is relative. Within each and every one of us is an incredible story. These stories come from our adversities even if that is a prick of a thorn. We collect these stories to enrich our communities so that it becomes adaptable and a liveable community.

Misha: I was struck when I came to the Diwali storytelling session that it wasn't just about the storyteller telling the story. It's about facilitating an invitation for everyone to share something that connected them through a theme established by the storyteller's own story. On that day Durgah Devi Palanisamy told the story of Diwali and then she talked about her wedding necklace and invited everyone to tell a story about a piece of jewellery that was important to them. The stories of where the jewellery came from or why it mattered both connected and revealed the differences of cultures, values, connections to family and historical periods of migration to Australia of each person in the group.

Mariam: Yes, that theme acts as a trigger. The other day it was the trigger of International Women's Day. It was 'who is the most important woman in your life?' So many different stories came out of that day; some were funny, some made us cry. There is so much energy in that space, something more than what we know, there's that common thread that connects us all.

Conclusion

Instead of being faced with an impossible choice of isolation either in cultural groups segregated from one another or in unwelcoming communities, what can host communities offer and gain in adopting a model of home making and hospitality or by getting involved in the co-creative work of home making in the ways modelled by RAW? This becomes increasingly important for social inclusion and cohesion in a context such as Australia, where communities are experiencing increased diversity and immigrant concentration as a result of immigration growth. This conversation and chapter ends with an understanding of the work of home making as a collective endeavour that relies on the powers of practical, spatial and communicative know-how and draws on the positive associations or memories of past places where positive social relationships were enacted. Those strategies of the work discussed here through this conversation suggest it involves creating places of meaning, self-growth and self-knowledge, but also intimacy, connection, empathy, exchange, conversation, communication, dialogue and meeting through intentional collective and practical activity, especially those that facilitate strong reminders of the homely.

Note

1. https://www.facebook.com/rawaustralia12/ (accessed 27 May 2019).

Bibliography

Boym, Svetlana (2001), *The Future of Nostalgia* (New York: Basic Books).
Casey, Edward S. (1993), *Getting Back into Place: Toward a Renewed Understanding of the Place-World* (Bloomington: Indiana University Press).
Edmanson, Jane (2014), *Gardening Australia*, 'Fact sheet: growing a village', Series 25, Episode 15, ABC, http://www.abc.net.au/gardening/stories/s4034618.htm (accessed 1 December 2017).
Hage, Ghassan (1997), 'At home in the entrails of the West: multiculturalism, "ethnic food" and migrant home-building', in Helen Grace, Ghassan Hage, Lesley Johnson, Julie Langsworth and Michael Symonds (eds), *Home/World: Space, Community and Marginality in Sydney's West* (Sydney: Pluto), 99–153.
hooks, bell (1990), *Yearning: Race, Gender, and Cultural Politics* (Boston, MA: South End Press).
Malkki, Liisa H. (1995), 'Refugees and exile: from "Refugee Studies" to the national order of things', *Annual Review of Anthropology*, 24: 495–523.
Massey, Doreen (1994), *Space, Place and Gender* (Cambridge: Polity Press).
Myers, Misha (2009), 'Homing Place: Towards a Participatory, Ambulant and Conversive Methodology', PhD thesis, Dartington College of Arts/University of Plymouth, https://pearl.plymouth.ac.uk//handle/10026.1/3181 (accessed 24 May 2016).
Myers, Misha (2011), 'Walking again lively: towards an ambulant and conversive methodology of performance and research', *Mobilities Journal*, 6.2: 183–201.
Myers, Misha (2017), '*way from home*: Sharing a walk elsewhere', *Livingmaps Review*, 2, http://livingmaps.review/journal/index.php/LMR/article/view/61 (accessed 1 December 2017).

Part IX

Open Cities

Open Cities: Introduction

Sam Durrant

The figure of the open city has a history as long as that of the city as defensive fortification, as citadel. Philip Marfleet has traced the idea of the city of refuge from ancient Jewish scripts and medieval Christian practices through to the rise of the nation-state and its secularisation of a religious ethos of hospitality (see Lewis and Waite in this section). One could trace similar histories of urban hospitality in other parts of the world, more or less inflected by traditions of religious observance. However, the capacity of a city to offer sanctuary to those fleeing persecution depends not only on its beliefs, customs and laws but also on its ability to protect itself: an open city must also have the ability to close itself, and the very act of opening the city gates in a gesture of welcome is determined by a prior assumption of territorial sovereignty. Indeed, this sovereignty is now almost exclusively the preserve of the nation-state rather than the city, and the modern city's ability to style itself as a place of refuge is circumscribed by its relative lack of autonomy in relation to the nation-state. This section is centrally concerned with this tension between the city and the state, openness and closedness, cosmopolitan ideals and their practical limitations.

Jonathan Darling's chapter opens the section by exploring how a range of contemporary urban movements in North America and Europe have offered sanctuary to, and solidarity with, refugees in ways that both expand and contest state forms of hospitality. On the one hand, Darling examines urban sanctuary initiatives in the US, the UK and across Europe that have sought to turn the city into a space of refuge. While such initiatives necessarily work within certain constraints, they can work towards more progressive forms of hospitality and mitigate the effects of repressive immigration controls. On the other, Darling examines activist and advocacy movements that more directly confront state policy, such as the Montreal-based Comité d'action des sans-statut, which actively disrupts attempts to deport refused asylum seekers back to Algeria, and the UK 'Dignity not Destitution' campaign, which has led to many local authorities passing motions contesting the central government policy of withdrawing all forms of support from those who have been refused asylum. Taken together, these diverse practices of hospitality, solidarity and advocacy operate as 'points of rupture and critique in relation to the politics of the nation-state', suggesting that the city can become a vital conduit for political change.

Louise Waite and Hannah Lewis's 'The Welcome City?' also explores this potential for change, asking whether the 2015 compassion spike generated by the hyper-circulated image of Alan Kurdi, the Syrian child washed up on a Turkish beach, can be translated into a truly transformative politics. The chapter contrasts this spontaneous but short-lived outbreak of public compassion with the parsimonious response of the UK government: despite some relatively small gestures of sanctuary towards select Syrian refugees, it brazenly continues its hostile environment policy towards refused asylum seekers and other irregular migrants through measures contained in the Immigration Acts of 2014 and 2016 in particular. While noting the ways in which public compassion for distant, non-threatening refugees such as Kurdi was all too easily replaced by the xenophobic fears and anxieties generated by the Brexit campaign of the following year, the chapter nevertheless draws attention to the long-standing grassroots organisations and (inter-)faith networks that continue to provide crucial forms of support to refugees and asylum seekers.

André Grahle's chapter picks up questions of refugee advocacy raised in Chapter 1, arguing that a moral society should not only recognise the justice of the asylum seeker's claim for refuge but also identify with the refugees' ongoing struggle for justice in their home countries. Grahle is primarily concerned with Syrian refugees in Germany and their attempts to form what he calls 'movements of witnesses', loose networks of Syrian refugees concerned to highlight the myriad injustices of the Assad regime. Such networks need to move beyond personal friendships to claim a space in the public sphere. Anis Hamdoun's highly acclaimed play *The Trip* shows how a refugee can become isolated within his own memories due to the lack of an audience for his testimony. However, the play itself, as a public performance, generates the very 'culture of receptivity' whose absence proves so isolating for its main protagonist. This reception of testimony serves to inscribe refugees' stories into the consciousness of the city, thereby shaping a new moral community. Implicitly reversing conservative demands for the refugee to integrate into the host culture, Grahle argues that it is the host culture that makes integration possible through the creation of public spaces in which refugee experience can be acknowledged and political solidarities affirmed.

In the final chapter, Sam Durrant takes a slightly different tack. The first two chapters broadly oppose the openness of grassroots urban movements to the nation-state's impulse to close down its borders. This chapter suggests that the seemingly open world-view of the private citizen may itself contain hidden occlusions. More specifically, cosmopolitan citizenship is reliant on structures of global privilege that function to occlude not only the refugee's experience of loss but also the threat of the citizen's own potential disenfranchisement. Teju Cole's extraordinary novel, *Open City*, demonstrates how cosmopolitanism psychically disavows both the precarious nature of its own privilege and its implication in global inequities. While cosmopolitan literature is often figured as the solicitation of sympathy for distant others such as the refugee, Durrant argues that cosmopolitanism's primary task is to produce an auto-critical account of its own precarious implication in the global structures that produce statelessness.

Chapter 29

'Another politics of the city': Urban Practices of Refuge, Advocacy and Activism

Jonathan Darling

we are dreaming of another concept, of another set of rights for the city, of another politics of the city. (Derrida 2001: 8)

In May 2017 the city of Sheffield celebrated its tenth anniversary as the UK's first official 'city of sanctuary', a city that offers welcome and hospitality to those in need of safety. Sheffield's status was confirmed following the concerted efforts of a social movement, itself called City of Sanctuary, which originated in the city in 2005. Since then, City of Sanctuary has grown into a national movement, encompassing a network of towns and cities across the UK all committed to building a 'culture of welcome' throughout society. At around the same time, the US Justice Department announced a renewed crackdown on 'sanctuary cities', threatening to remove federal grants for cities unless they give federal immigration authorities access to jails and share the citizenship status of people held in custody. As part of the Trump administration's anti-immigrant agenda, federal authorities have increasingly sought to force cities such as San Francisco and Los Angeles to cooperate with deportation efforts. To date, such efforts have been in vain as many of the country's largest cities have pledged to offer a safe haven to the estimated 11 million undocumented migrants living precariously across the US (Levin 2017).

These two events, while separated by political context, governance structures and available modes of activism, point to two notable dynamics in the contemporary politics of refuge. The first is the resurgence of a language, ethics and imaginary of sanctuary in multiple forms internationally (see Lippert and Rehaag 2012; Bauder 2017). Whether focused upon ethical demands to value and practise hospitality towards vulnerable strangers, or legislative attempts to protect the rights of irregular and undocumented migrants, sanctuary has become an important orientation point for a variety of social movements. Yet at the same time, as events in the US indicate, imaginaries of sanctuary have also become a focal point for opposition, anger and the reassertion of sovereign rights to exclude and expel unwanted others. Alongside this resurgence of sanctuary, we might note a focus on the city as the terrain on which sanctuary is practised, and through which rights are claimed. While cities have always played a critical role in shaping understandings of citizenship (Brett 2011; Isin 2002), today that role is being rewritten through the actions of asylum seekers, refugees and those advocates who work alongside them. In articulating and practising forms of 'urban citizenship' (Varsanyi 2006), 'urban belonging' (Bauder 2016) and diverse rights 'to the city' (Lefebvre 1996; Purcell 2003), these activists employ the city as a political tool to critique the nation-state. In this chapter, I explore some of these movements to consider how cities are both shaped by the politics of refuge, and may play a crucial role in supporting the rights of those seeking protection.

Focusing on the city is important not simply because of the growth of urban advocacy groups working with refugees. Cities are increasingly recognised as important destinations for refugees across the world. With more than half of the world's refugees now living in urban areas, humanitarian organisations such as UNHCR have moved to develop specific policies for supporting urban refugees (Ward 2014). The majority of these refugees are hosted informally across cities in the Global South, with the mass displacement of Syrian refugees to cities in Jordan, Lebanon and Turkey being a significant recent example. Urban environments offer opportunities for employment, autonomy and access to onward mobility, and at the same time present risks of exploitation, poverty and repressive policing (Campbell 2006; Pavanello, Elhawary and Pantuliano 2010). The issue of forced migration is therefore, increasingly, an urban concern, both in the context of mass displacements in the Global South, and in the ever more restrictive attempts to 'manage migration' that dominate policy in the Global North (Darling 2017). In this latter instance, cities have been argued to play a central role in forms of 'local border control' (Lebuhn 2013: 38), which translate policies and enforcement measures from the nation-state to specific urban contexts. Here the city is situated as a strategic location for the enforcement of border control through the use of urban networks of police, surveillance and information infrastructure to trace, detain and deport asylum seekers and undocumented migrants (Coleman 2012; Hynes 2009; Netto 2011; Zetter and Pearl 2000). Yet this is not the only story of refugees and cities. Rather, as Osborne and Rose (1999: 758) suggest, 'cities are complex multiplicities of interests, antagonisms, flows of capital, spatial constructions, moral topographies, forms of authority, and ethical stylisations', and as such they may also be incubators for dissent. Thus while efforts to regulate, monitor and manage society have been argued to reach their peak in urban environments (Graham 2010), urban features of 'density, size, and diversity' have been argued to provide 'the basic elements for contention to develop' (Uitermark, Nicholls and Loopmans 2012: 2546). It is through these features of the city that I want to examine how different imaginations of advocacy, activism and campaigns for the rights of refugees have been articulated.

In exploring these discussions, the chapter develops as follows. I begin by exploring the first of three ways in which refugee advocacy in cities has been framed, through Derrida's (2001) deconstruction of hospitality and his call to establish 'cities of refuge' that challenge the exclusions of the nation-state system. With this account of hospitality in mind, I then turn to explore the rise of movements for urban sanctuary in Europe and North America, which seek to reposition cities as sites of safety for refugees, built around narratives of urban responsibility and social justice. Following this ethical orientation, the chapter then considers a series of political campaigns by refugees and asylum seekers that use cities as strategic sites through which to make claims at national and international levels. In these cases, the city becomes a strategically important conduit for political change. In concluding, the chapter discusses how through considering these forms of advocacy together, we might unpack how cities are narrated through the agency and activism of refugees. I begin with the possibilities and limits of urban hospitality.

Hospitality and the city

Derrida's discussion of the city and its role as a potential refuge emerges as part of a wider deconstruction of hospitality and its ethico-political possibilities (Derrida 1999; 2000a). In this work, the city becomes a key context in which to imagine a renewed politics of hospitality, and to practically enact such an imagination. For Derrida, hospitality names a constant negotiation between competing demands – for welcome and for regulation at one and the same time. Hospitality is based upon the prerequisite 'that the host . . . remains the *patron*, the master of the household, on the condition that he maintains his own authority *in his own house*' (Derrida 2000b: 14, original emphasis). To be hospitable is to claim a particular space as one's own, to assume that one has the right both to welcome a stranger and, conversely, to reject such a stranger. Written into the very constitution of the hospitable are a set of conditions and expectations about who is the 'host', where the limits of this welcome lie and to whom it may be extended. It is these limits that beset the political practice of hospitality; Derrida argues that conditional hospitality

> remains a scrutinized hospitality, always under surveillance, parsimonious and protective of its sovereignty . . . That is hospitality as it is commonly understood and practiced, a hospitality that gives rise, with certain conditions, to regulated practices, laws, and conventions on a national and international . . . scale. (2003: 128)

At the same time, Derrida (1999) argues that the conditions of hospitality are always haunted by the spectre of an unconditional hospitality that marks a welcome to an unanticipated and unidentified guest. Such

> unconditional hospitality is, to be sure, practically impossible to live; one cannot in any case, and by definition, organize it . . . this concept of pure hospitality can have no legal or political status. No state can write it into its laws. But without at least the thought of this pure and unconditional hospitality, of hospitality *itself*, we would have no concept of hospitality in general and would not even be able to determine any rules for conditional hospitality. (Derrida 2003: 129, original emphasis)

The political importance of deconstructing hospitality thus lies not in rejecting or denouncing hospitality as imperfect, but rather in challenging institutions and relations of hospitality, 'calling them to something better, to more just configurations' (Smith 2005: 67). Derrida's deconstruction of hospitality seeks to focus attention on the fraught and finite negotiations of hospitality as an always imperfectly practised ethic of welcoming the unanticipated stranger, so as to ultimately find ways to 'make laws more hospitable' (Smith 2005: 70).

In considering how this philosophical account of hospitality relates to the politics of refuge, Derrida (2001) argues that the question of hospitality has too often been cynically employed to promote the conditional inclusion of only those seen as 'worthy' of protection. Thus, at the level of the nation-state a wide array of countries regularly make public statements about their hospitable nature towards refugees and their desire to welcome 'good' migrants (Rosello 2001). This language is always conditioned by the right to select, classify and limit hospitality, and it is the exclusivity of conditional hospitality that Derrida (2002) critiques most forcefully in challenging the claim by European governments that asylum seekers and irregular migrants 'abuse' the hospitality of the nation-state.

In response to such concerns, Derrida turns to the city as a site through which to envisage an alternative way of practising hospitality. Derrida argues that cities may offer a path from a conditional framework of limits to a more critical orientation in which 'disruptive narratives' are produced. Derrida (2001: 6) notes that '[i]f we look to the city, rather than the state, it is because we have given up hope that the state might create a new image for the city'. The example that Derrida draws on is that of the International Cities of Refuge Network (ICORN), a network of cities offering long-term but temporary shelter to writers and artists in need of protection. The Cities of Asylum Network, which went on to become ICORN, was founded in 1993 by the International Parliament of Writers. The network involves over fifty cities across Asia, Europe and North America, and offers shelter as a means to defend freedom of expression and democratic values. It is around the model of ICORN as an urban movement offering protection in ways not recognised by the nation-state that Derrida focuses his account of how cities may 'reorient the politics of the state' in new directions (Derrida 2001: 4). He clarifies:

> This is not to suggest that we ought to restore an essentially classical concept of the city by giving it new attributes and powers; neither would it be simply a matter of endowing the old subject we call 'the city' with new predicates. No, we are dreaming of another concept, of another set of rights for the city, of another politics of the city. (Derrida 2001: 8)

What comes to the fore here is the sense of a renewed appreciation of the urban as a space of political, and ethical, engagement and experimentation with asylum, as a space that might offer 'another' form of politics, not through simply ascribing greater powers to the city or allowing it further autonomy, but through considering how cities may offer points of rupture and critique in relation to the politics of the nation-state (Critchley 2011; Darling 2013). The actions of ICORN, in protecting writers and artists who fall outside the protections of the nation-state, offer an example of this critical position. This is not an unconditional hospitality that welcomes all strangers, nor does it evade limits and constraints, but it does offer an example of how an attempt to 'make laws more hospitable' may be put into practice. Crucially, Derrida (2001) concludes that it is only through the political position of the city, as a space tied to, but not subsumed by, the nation-state, that such experimentation is possible.

A number of theorists have followed Derrida's turn to the city and argued for the need to examine the daily realities of urban life as the grounds on which migrants' rights and claims to citizenship are articulated. Sassen, for example, suggests that the 'last two decades have seen an increasingly *urban* articulation of global logics and struggles, and an escalating use of urban space to make political claims not only by the citizens of a city's country, but also by foreigners' (2013: 70, original emphasis). Cities have thus been argued to remain 'the strategic arena for the development of citizenship' as through their 'concentrations of the nonlocal, the strange, the mixed, and the public, cities engage . . . processes which decisively expand and erode the rules, meanings, and practices of citizenship' (Appadurai and Holston 1996: 188). Cities in this imaginary are positioned as complex assemblages that gather together, coordinate and configure global flows and connections of ideas, people and materials. In the remainder of this chapter, I want to explore further examples of this form of urban experimentation, to consider how the ethical and political tensions that run through hospitality also reso-nate within urban movements for sanctuary, migrants' rights and claims to citizenship. In this context, Derrida's (2001) discussion of urban hospitality matters as it speaks to the tensions of refugee advocacy more broadly, seeking to act on present conditions and limits, while also imagining 'other' forms of political possibility beyond the present. I want now to explore two ways in which these tensions intersect with cities – first, in the case of urban sanctuary movements that draw on an ethic of hospitality, and second, in the work of refugee activists who employ the city as a strategic terrain to challenge the nation-state, akin to Derrida's politics of hospitality.

Sanctuary movements and a 'culture of hospitality'

While not reducible to hospitality, a number of social movements in Canada, the UK and the US have mobilised a language of hospitality both to shift attitudes towards refugees, asylum seekers and irregular migrants, and to advocate for the rights of those present in the city. This can be seen to varying degrees across a range of international contexts, including the work of the New Sanctuary Movement in the US and Canada, the Cities of Refuge initiative across Europe, and the UK's City of Sanctuary movement. For example, the City of Sanctuary movement explicitly seeks to inculcate a 'culture of hospitality' whereby refugees and asylum seekers are welcomed in towns and cities (Darling 2010; Squire 2011). This grassroots movement focuses on intercultural events, awareness raising and providing volunteering and training opportunities for refugee and asylum groups. In doing so, it practises a model of hospitality based on opportunities for refugees and asylum seekers to interact with the cities in which they are accommodated. City of Sanctuary is just one example of this much wider trend, with a key distinction being between the legal protections of sanctuary cities in North America, and the cultural effects of sanctuary movements in Europe.

In the first instance, the New Sanctuary Movement in North America, a network of social movements with roots in faith-based communities that focus on offering protection from deportation to individual refugees and undocumented migrants (Caminero-Santangelo 2012), coexists alongside a range of 'sanctuary cities' that have attempted to legislate for access to municipal services regardless of status and to protect residents through non-cooperation with immigration authorities (Cunningham 2012; Mancina 2012). Of these, San Francisco was an early exemplar, but the sanctuary-city designation has grown considerably over the last decade and has taken on an increasingly contentious political position since the Trump administration's threat to defund such municipalities. Examinations of 'sanctuary cities' have highlighted the opportunities to establish rights to remain through restricting the reach of federal immigration enforcement and offering services based on residency rather than status as essential elements in protecting refugees (Nyers 2011; Varsanyi 2008). From access to local healthcare services and social support, to the provision of locally bound drivers' licences for undocumented residents, the legislation on which a 'sanctuary' designation is based alters between urban jurisdictions. Yet what remains constant is a focus on protecting those already present in the city from arrest and deportation, and in doing so, foregrounding the needs of refugees and undocumented migrants as urban issues that should concern all citizens. In this sense, as Ridgley (2008: 56) argues, the sanctuary city 'is not only a space of protection from an increasingly anti-immigrant national security agenda, but also a potential line of flight out of which alternative futures can be materialized', as it serves to embed sanctuary into the very legal and social fabric of a city.

By contrast, in Europe, the growth in sanctuary-orientated movements does not carry the same legislative weight as in the North American context (Lippert and Rehaag 2012; Pyykkönen 2009). Often emerging from charitable and religious organisations, this European strand of sanctuary tends to emphasise the role of asylum seekers and refugees as contributing to the social and cultural life of their 'host' communities (Goodall 2010). Thus while in the UK, City of Sanctuary lacks the legislative authority of the sanctuary cities of North America, instead its mode of engagement strategically focuses on raising awareness of the networks of responsibility and implication that connect cities and their citizens to the lives of those displaced, both near and far (Darling 2010). Through community events, exhibitions and oral history workshops, City of Sanctuary seeks to highlight the connections of refugees in cities such as Sheffield, in both the journeys they have taken to gain protection and the struggles faced by other residents of the city, thereby offering points of identification across difference.

Similar forms of networking and advocacy are present in Sweden, where Lundberg and Strange (2017) illustrate how a range of initiatives to promote values of hospitality have been taken by different cities. For example, in Stockholm, groups wanting to align themselves with Refuge Stockholm were given a list of requirements that they had to meet before being able to be part of the movement. These included providing free or discounted services to undocumented people and not demanding social security numbers for services, in an echo of some of the requirements of North American 'sanctuary cities'. This model of gaining support from local organisations relied upon spreading the word about sanctuary events, initiatives and opportunities through everyday spaces, such as cafés, gyms, cultural associations and universities. To be part of Refuge Stockholm, organisations were required to offer opportunities for undocumented migrants and refugees to be involved in their activities (Lundberg and Strange 2017), mirroring some of the practices of City of Sanctuary in Sheffield, where volunteering was seen as a valuable resource to feel part of urban life (Darling and Squire 2012).

Furthermore, in Sweden we see a model of sanctuary practices that attempted to include both state officials and municipal representatives. For example, in Malmo, city officials worked with sanctuary groups to gain access to the library in the city and ensure that undocumented individuals could borrow books despite lacking formal status. In this context, as Lundberg and Strange argue:

> Constructive engagement with city officials complicates a simplistic image of these sanctuary initiatives as pure defiance of the state, presenting a more negotiated character in which they could be both critical of the state's migration policies but equally working with other state-employed bodies at the city level to mitigate the negative effects of the management of migration. (2017: 357–8)

This account of the need for 'constructive engagement' and negotiation with both urban and state authorities points to a wider concern running through each of these contexts of urban sanctuary – that of the limits of hospitable engagement (Bagelman 2015). The work of sanctuary movements and sanctuary cities is vitally important in trying to promote values of welcoming and hospitality within cities and in offering often piecemeal and yet important concessions to those seeking protection, from the right to borrow books to the ability to seek healthcare without risking deportation. In this way, sanctuary practices have been argued to represent actions that protect against the state (Cunningham 2012; Yukich 2012). However, such work has also been critically challenged on two key bases. First, it has been argued that sanctuary may represent a means of governing through the assertion of humanitarian intentions (Darling 2013). In legislative terms, Chavin and Garcés-Mascareñas argue that 'local incorporation practices' reflect 'regulatory imperatives and worries over public safety' (2012: 244). Through enabling undocumented migrants to access services and support, cities can be seen to 'manage' an undocumented population for the wider 'good' of the city, thereby allaying concerns over public health and public order, as Mancina (2012) argues in the case of San Francisco. Seen through this critical lens, the language of the sanctuary city becomes a means to govern the presence of irregular migrants and refugees. As a result, the question of who 'deserves' the support of the sanctuary city comes to the fore in debating the limits of urban hospitality (Houston and Morse 2016; Marrow 2012; Yukich 2013).

This question of 'deservingness' also speaks to the second basis on which sanctuary and hospitality have been critiqued – as exemplars of a humanitarian logic that can often position asylum seekers and refugees as passive recipients of support. Thus while sanctuary movements can be significant in supporting those seeking refuge, they can also risk denying agency to asylum seekers and refugees by positioning them as passively waiting for refugee status and support (Squire and Bagelman 2012). Furthermore, the temporal horizon of hospitality associated with Derrida (2000a), of a state of sanctuary that is always 'to come', may do little to promote a more assertive and agential political role for asylum seekers and refugees whereby rights are claimed *by*, and not *for*, those seeking refuge (Squire and Darling 2013; Nyers 2003).

Despite these challenges, the varied examples of urban sanctuary discussed here each reflect different political contexts and opportunity structures. Yet what they hold in common is a focus on reimagining the role of the city as a place that can offer protection to those seeking refuge. In practice, such forms of welcome may assuage the effects of repressive immigration controls. However, as noted above, the claims of sanctuary cities are also limited, most notably in that they risk the reiteration of categorical assumptions about who is 'deserving' of welcome. Distinctions such as these are central to the categorising processes that shape ideals of hospitality (Derrida 2001), and illustrate how progressive imaginaries of the city may be enfolded into state-centric logics of citizenship. The constraints of hospitality as a conditional politics still abound here, but sanctuary practices do gesture towards making such conditions 'better' in a reflection of Derrida's hopes for the city as a space to negotiate refuge with responsibility. Building on these discussions, I want now to consider a second set of attempts to rewrite the city, focusing on movements that use the city as a terrain to make claims for rights.

Migrants' rights and the strategic use of the city

Alongside the emergence of sanctuary movements, recent years have also seen campaigns organised by asylum seekers, refugees and non-status migrants that focus on the city as a strategic site through which to make claims for rights, protection and citizenship. In some cases, these campaigns draw on a language of solidarity to identify with common struggles among other marginalised groups (Maestri 2017; Swerts 2017), and in others they mobilise the notion of a 'right to the city' as a common cause, centred on asserting the right to play a role in urban decision making (Varsanyi 2006; Purcell 2003). What combines many of these approaches is a focus on the city as a point of networking, coordination and political visibility that can help make present a set of claims that would otherwise be ignored by national governments. Thus, as Sassen (2010: 9), argues, in cities 'the localization of the global creates a set of objective conditions of engagement' through which the very presence of irregular migrants, refugees and asylum seekers may be politicised in different ways (Darling 2014; 2017). This 'engagement' is twofold, reflecting both a presence to power and a presence 'vis-à-vis each other' (Sassen 2006: 317). For Sassen, presence matters because it makes claims visible to authority, but also because it makes claims visible to other interested parties and offers opportunities for identification across difference and the development of solidarities. Cities matter here as they offer a stage for such claims, and the networks of diversity and civil society that allow political movements to be sustained (Uitermark, Nicholls and Loopmans 2012). To explore this further, I shall discuss two examples.

The first comes from the work of an Algerian refugee group in Montreal who in 2002 began to contest the lifting of a moratorium on deportations to Algeria and their position as refused asylum seekers (see May 2010; Nyers 2003). The group, the Comité d'action des sans-statut (CASS), demanded the end of deportations to Algeria, the reinstatement of the moratorium and the regularisation of non-status Algerian migrants in the city. The importance attached to this group is that while CASS received support and recognition from other migrant rights groups, it was first and foremost an organisation driven by non-status migrants. CASS undertook to invade the offices of immigration officials and disrupt their work, to demonstrate publicly outside immigration buildings, to lobby, pressurise and disrupt the airlines involved in deportation flights. These acts, organised and undertaken by those without status, 'insisted that they could speak and they would be political' (Nyers 2006: 59). Nyers thus suggests that the demonstrations, protests and disruptive tactics of anti-deportation groups such as CASS work as a form of political 'interruption', through which a political subjectivity is articulated. As Nyers (2003: 1089) argues '[w]hen speechless victims begin to speak about the politics of protection, this has the effect of putting the political into question'.

CASS also had a wider resonance, for as May (2010: 40) argues, they acted to reconfigure how Montreal and its citizens saw this situation. Through the actions of CASS, individuals who were previously invisible became visible; 'through CASS they become identifiable. And once identifiable, they could become identified with.' It is precisely this identification that Sassen highlights as important in the city – offering opportunities for others to come into contact with political campaigns and claims. In this sense, *making political* the presence of asylum seekers and refugees in the city, while not without its dangers, can be an important means to gain traction for a political campaign around migrants' rights. Importantly, campaigns such as this take significant bravery, for they demand that despite the 'considerable risks that come when the non-status interrupt the public realm as speaking beings . . . people find themselves in political situations acting as political actors' (Nyers 2006: 64). These actions are political in a disruptive sense. On the one hand, they ask that fellow urban inhabitants, often in positions of privileged citizenship, take note of these exclusions and seek to act upon them. And on the other, they claim the right to political speech and visibility irrespective of such support and action. The disruptive actions of CASS do not wait to be offered hospitality or sanctuary; rather they demand rights to protection as residents of Montreal, refusing to accept a subordinate position within a given hierarchy of citizenship (Nyers and Rygiel 2012; Squire and Bagelman 2012).

The second case comes from the 'Dignity not Destitution' campaign in the UK, a campaign that seeks to challenge existing government policy on the support of asylum seekers. Asylum seekers have, since 2004, been denied the right to work while awaiting refugee status and provided with a weekly cash support capped significantly below other forms of social welfare. The 'Dignity not Destitution' campaign calls on the government to change the policy of withdrawing asylum support after decisions on status have been taken, regardless of whether or not an individual can be returned to their country of origin. As some countries do not have deportation agreements with the UK, and therefore refuse to accept returnees, this places refused asylum seekers from these countries in a legal limbo between the official refusal of status in the UK and an inability to return to the country they have fled. In such cases, refused asylum seekers are forced to rely on charities and friends for survival. Destitution in this context is less an accidental or procedural gap within the asylum system and more an intentional and insecure position imposed on those no longer wanted by the state.

In opposing the use of destitution as a deterrent within the asylum system, the 'Dignity not Destitution' campaign argues that asylum seekers who would otherwise be destitute should be provided with sufficient support so that they can meet their essential living needs, and be given permission to work if their case has not been resolved within six months. The campaign started in 2009 in Bristol and Glasgow by a mixture of asylum advocates, support groups and asylum seekers, who together attempted to gain local political support for the opposition to government policy on destitution. Following this example, the model of focusing on urban authorities was transferred to a series of other cities as local activists, social movements and support networks became aware of the 'Dignity not Destitution' campaign. The campaign not only evoked human rights claims for equality and justice via demands for basic living needs, but addressed these demands to national government *through the city* as a conduit for advancing a refugee rights agenda. Through public demonstrations, lobbying of councillors, public petitions and encouraging the public to send postcards to their elected representatives demanding 'Dignity not Destitution' for asylum seekers, the campaign was intended to encourage urban authorities to pass motions of opposition to government policy.

To date, twelve local authorities have debated and passed motions to oppose asylum destitution and to call for changes in asylum policy. The challenge beyond these local motions of support is clearly to effect an impact on central government policy. However, the importance of local authorities supporting such a cause should not be underestimated. Indeed, one of the key aims of this form of political mobilisation was to utilise multiple urban publics in order to push for change through drawing varied audiences into an awareness of destitution. In this sense, the campaign reflects how 'movements emanate from cities but also stretch outwards' (Uitermark, Nicholls and Loopmans 2012: 2546). This outward orientation in the 'Dignity not Destitution' campaign shows how the city is being employed as a site to articulate demands directed towards policy at a national level.

The work of CASS and 'Dignity not Destitution' are examples of a wider range of social movements and organisations around migrants' rights that have sought to strategically employ the city as a context from which to form networks of advocacy, dissent and campaigning. The UK's Right to Remain movement of anti-deportation activism often seeks to articulate anti-deportation struggles in a context of localised connections to specific cities and their communities, and the international No One Is Illegal movement grounds its no-borders activism in the production of a network of urban activism reaching from Berlin to Vancouver (Vrasti and Dayal 2016). In these cases, the city is imagined not simply as a target of interventions and campaigns, but as a location from which to make political claims beyond the city, be they to the nation-state, to diverse and spatially distant publics, or to networks of activists and distant campaigns. Thus, just as 'the deployment of exclusionary city ordinances are not only about shaping an *urban* public, but about shaping a *national* public as well' (Varsanyi 2008: 47, original emphasis), so too might we think of the kinds of rights claims enacted through cities as not simply affecting urban imaginaries but also affecting transnational publics. The role of the city here is both as a strategic stage for political contention (Uitermark, Nicholls and Loopmans 2012), one that takes advantage of how cities are located in networks of power and influence (Allen 2011; Sassen 2013), and as a site in which asylum seekers and refugees can find support from advocacy organisations and diverse groups of supporters. It is this mix of activism that speaks beyond the city and the piecemeal provision of support in the here and now, and has come to define how asylum seekers and refugees are rewriting the role of the city as a space of potential refuge.

Conclusion

In this chapter I have sought to highlight the varied ways in which cities have been narrated through the agency and activism of refugees and their supporters. From the promise of hospitality enshrined in the biblical 'Cities of Refuge' to the contemporary vision of 'sanctuary cities', an image of the city as a site of refuge has been a powerful part of progressive and utopian urban imaginaries. Yet alongside this desire to link the city to ethical values of hospitality and sanctuary has been a recent turn by activists and advocates to employ the strategic possibilities of the city as a conduit for political change. Such activism is, of course, not without response, for just as Uitermark, Nicholls and Loopmans (2012: 2546) argue that cities are places of contention, they also note that such practices inevitably produce new means of control as 'local states and their partners develop strategies and techniques to direct the ebbs and flows of contentiousness constantly bubbling up from the urban grassroots'. By focusing on cities as sites that often throw up the lived realities of displacement, and that place refugees in relation to other residents, activists and advocates have begun to explore how the negotiations of everyday urban life might be made more hospitable for those seeking refuge.

There are, of course, limits to the potentials of the city. As Vrasti and Dayal highlight, sanctuary politics alone often entail a tendency to reproduce 'host' and 'guest' positions in problematic ways, a potential to view access to services as the end point of migrant justice and 'the possibility that sanctuary eases and normalizes undocumented life' (2016: 998). Similarly, sanctuary and a concern with hospitality as a normative horizon 'to come' can serve to deny agency to those seeking refuge, as political questions of rights are sidelined in favour of a moral concern with forms of care and generosity. Yet it is indicative of the tensions running through accounts of sanctuary that at the same time Vrasti and Dayal argue that modalities of sanctuary, 'whether legislative or esthetic, can offer a temporary reprieve from marginalization' (Vrasti and Dayal 2016: 1008). Similarly, as I have argued through this chapter, campaigns such as 'Dignity not Destitution' provide examples of how connections have been forged in the hope of influencing government policy through incremental processes of critique, awareness raising and garnering public support. These may offer only momentary reprieves in the present, but are nevertheless important as political orientation points for further campaigns and for forging solidarities with other causes. In this way, perceptions and policies on asylum, support and entitlements are altered not immediately but incrementally, as critical questions are posed in and through the political opportunities and limits that cities provide (Darling 2017).

In this context, the role of an ethics focused on hospitality and sanctuary can never be to assert a politics of rights based around urban presence, as such an ethics can never fully escape its association with a model of 'care' and support. However, such an ethics may be significant in shaping the public and political context in which assertive claims for rights and political voice are responded to differently. This is to view the role of sanctuary and hospitality as more than simply piecemeal reprieves for those suffering the violence of the state, but as opportunities to influence the tenor and tone of debate around refuge. It is also to see the politics of advocacy, campaigning and assertion around asylum as necessarily comprised of multiple, and at times inconsistent and contradictory, political claims and positions. Within the complex mix of moral and political positions that marks contemporary advocacy, in focusing on the claims made through cities for sanctuary, rights and hospitality, refugees and advocates have increasingly begun the task that Derrida (2001) envisaged in writing of how cities would 'reorient the state' and make the laws that govern welcoming ever more hospitable. In this sense, while limited and imperfect, what we see in the diverse acts, practices and campaigns that I have explored are important attempts to reflect on, and experiment with, the role of the city. As such, they keep alive the utopian imaginary of a 'city of refuge' as 'a place for reflection – for reflection on the questions of asylum and hospitality – and for a new order of law and democracy to come to be put to the test' (Derrida 2001: 23).

Bibliography

Allen, J. (2010), 'Powerful city networks: more than connections, less than domination and control', *Urban Studies*, 47.13: 2895–911.

Allen, J. (2011), 'Topological twists: power's shifting geographies', *Dialogues in Human Geography*, 1.3: 283–98.

Appadurai, A., and J. Holston (1996), 'Cities and citizenship', *Public Culture*, 8.1: 187–204.

Bagelman, J. (2015), *Sanctuary City: A Suspended State* (Basingstoke: Palgrave Macmillan).

Bauder, H. (2016), 'Possibilities of urban belonging', *Antipode*, 48.2: 252–71.

Bauder, H. (2017), 'Sanctuary cities: policies and practices in international perspective', *International Migration*, 55.2: 174–87.

Brett, A. S. (2011), *Changes of State: Nature and the Limits of the City in Early Modern Natural Law* (Princeton: Princeton University Press).

Caminero-Santangelo, M. (2012), 'The voice of the voiceless: religious rhetoric, undocumented immigrants, and the New Sanctuary Movement in the United States', in R. K. Lippert and S. Rehaag (eds), *Sanctuary Practices in International Perspectives: Migration, Citizenship and Social Movements* (Abingdon: Routledge), 92–105.

Campbell, E. H. (2006), 'Urban refugees in Nairobi: problems of protection, mechanisms of survival, and possibilities for integration', *Journal of Refugee Studies*, 19.2: 396–413.

Chavin, S., and B. Garcés-Mascareñas (2012), 'Beyond informal citizenship: the new moral economy of migrant illegality', *International Political Sociology*, 6: 241–59.

Coleman, M. (2012), 'The "local" migration state: the site-specific devolution of immigration enforcement in the U.S. South', *Law and Policy*, 34.2: 159–90.

Critchley, S. (2011), *Impossible Objects* (Cambridge: Polity Press).

Cunningham, H. (2012), 'The emergence of the Ontario Sanctuary Coalition', in R. K. Lippert and S. Rehaag (eds), *Sanctuary Practices in International Perspectives: Migration, Citizenship and Social Movements* (London: Routledge), 162–74.

Darling, J. (2010), 'A city of sanctuary: the relational re-imagining of Sheffield's asylum politics', *Transactions of the Institute of British Geographers*, 35.1: 125–40.

Darling, J. (2013), 'Moral urbanism, asylum and the politics of critique', *Environment and Planning A*, 45.8: 1785–801.

Darling, J. (2014), 'From hospitality to presence', *Peace Review*, 26.2: 162–9.

Darling, J. (2017), 'Forced migration and the city: irregularity, informality, and the politics of presence', *Progress in Human Geography*, 41.2: 178–98.

Darling, J., and V. Squire (2012), 'Everyday enactments of sanctuary: the UK City of Sanctuary movement', in R. K. Lippert and S. Rehaag (eds), *Sanctuary Practices in International Perspectives: Migration, Citizenship and Social Movements* (Abingdon: Routledge), 191–204.

Derrida, J. (1999), *Adieu to Emmanuel Levinas*, trans. P.-A. Brault and M. Nass (Stanford: Stanford University Press).

Derrida, J. (2000a), *Of Hospitality: Anne Dufourmantelle Invites Jacques Derrida to Respond*, trans. R. Bowlby (Stanford: Stanford University Press).

Derrida, J. (2000b), 'Hostipitality', *Angelaki*, 5.3: 3–18.

Derrida, J. (2001), *On Cosmopolitanism and Forgiveness*, trans. M. Dooley and M. Hughes (London: Routledge).

Derrida, J. (2002), *Negotiations: Interventions and Interviews, 1971–2001*, trans. E. Rottenberg, (Stanford: Stanford University Press).

Derrida, J. (2003), 'Autoimmunity: real and symbolic suicides', in G. Borradori (ed.), *Philosophy in a Time of Terror: Dialogues with Jürgen Habermas and Jacques Derrida* (Chicago: University of Chicago Press).

Goodall, C. (2010), 'The coming of the stranger: asylum seekers, trust and hospitality in a British city', *New Issues in Refugee Research*, RP195, UN High Commissioner for Refugees, Geneva.

Graham, S. (2010), *Cities Under Siege: The New Military Urbanism* (London: Verso).

Houston, S. D., and C. Morse (2017), 'The ordinary extraordinary: producing migrant inclusion and exclusion in US sanctuary movements', *Studies in Social Justice*, 11.1: 27–47.

Hynes, P. (2009), 'Contemporary compulsory dispersal and the absence of space for the restoration of trust', *Journal of Refugee Studies*, 22.1: 97–121.

Isin, E. F (2002), *Being Political: Genealogies of Citizenship* (Minneapolis: University of Minnesota Press).

Lebuhn, H. (2013), 'Local border practices and urban citizenship in Europe: exploring urban borderlands', *City*, 17.1: 37–51.

Lefebvre, H. (1996), 'The right to the city', in E. Kofman and E. Lebas (eds), *Writing on Cities*, trans. E. Kofman and E. Lebas (Oxford: Blackwell), 147–59.

Levin, S. (2017), 'Trump's order to restrict "sanctuary cities" funding blocked by federal judge', *The Guardian*, 25 April, https://www.theguardian.com/us-news/2017/apr/25/trump-sanctuary-cities-funding-executive-order-blocked (accessed 27 July 2017).

Lippert, R. K., and S. Rehaag (eds) (2012), *Sanctuary Practices in International Perspectives: Migration, Citizenship and Social Movements* (Abingdon: Routledge).

Lundberg, A., and M. Strange (2017), 'Who provides the conditions for human life? Sanctuary movements in Sweden as both contesting and working with state agencies', *Politics*, 37.3: 347–62.

Maestri, G. (2017), 'Struggles and ambiguities over political subjectivities in the camp: Roma camp dwellers between neoliberal and urban citizenship in Italy', *Citizenship Studies*, 21.6: 640–56.

Mancina, P. (2012), 'The birth of a sanctuary city: a history of governmental sanctuary in San Francisco', in R. K. Lippert and S. Rehaag (eds), *Sanctuary Practices in International Perspectives: Migration, Citizenship and Social Movements* (Abingdon: Routledge), 205–18.

Marrow, H. B. (2012), 'Deserving to a point: unauthorized immigrants in San Francisco's universal access healthcare model', *Social Science and Medicine*, 74.6: 846–54.

May, T. (2010), *Contemporary Political Movements and the Thought of Jacques Rancière: Equality in Action* (Edinburgh: Edinburgh University Press).

Netto, G. (2011), 'Strangers in the city: addressing challenges to the protection, housing and settlement of refugees', *International Journal of Housing Policy*, 11.3: 285–303.

Nyers, P. (2003), 'Abject cosmopolitanism: the politics of protection in the anti-deportation movement', *Third World Quarterly*, 24.6: 1069–93.

Nyers P. (2006), 'Taking rights, mediating wrongs: disagreements over the political agency of non-status refugees', in J. Huysmans, A. Dobson and R. Prokhovnik (eds), *The Politics of Protection: Sites of Insecurity and Political Agency* (London: Routledge), 48–67.

Nyers, P. (2011), 'No One Is Illegal between city and nation', *Studies in Social Justice*, 4.2: 127–43.

Nyers, P., and K. Rygiel (eds) (2012), *Citizenship, Migrant Activism, and the Politics of Movement* (London: Routledge).

Osborne, T., and N. Rose (1999), 'Governing cities: notes on the spatialisation of virtue', *Environment and Planning D: Society and Space*, 17.4: 737–60.

Pavanello, S., S. Elhawary and S. Pantuliano (2010), *Hidden and Exposed: Urban Refugees in Nairobi, Kenya* (London: Overseas Development Institute).

Purcell, M. (2003), 'Citizenship and the right to the global city: reimagining the capitalist world order', *International Journal of Urban and Regional Research*, 27.3: 564–90.

Pyykkönen, M. (2009), 'Deportation vs. sanctuary: the rationalities, technologies, and subjects of Finnish sanctuary practices', *Refuge*, 26.1: 20–32.

Ridgley, J. (2008), 'Cities of refuge: immigration enforcement, police, and the insurgent genealogies of citizenship in U.S. Sanctuary Cities', *Urban Geography*, 29.1: 53–77.

Rosello, M. (2001), *Postcolonial Hospitality: The Immigrant as Guest* (Stanford: Stanford University Press).

Sassen, S. (2006), *Territory, Authority, Rights: From Medieval to Global Assemblages* (Princeton: Princeton University Press).

Sassen, S. (2010), 'The city: its return as a lens for social theory', *City, Culture and Society*, 1: 3–11.

Sassen, S. (2013), 'When the center no longer holds: cities as frontier zones', *Cities*, 34.1: 67–70.

Smith, J. (2005), *Jacques Derrida: Live Theory* (London: Continuum).

Squire, V. (2011), 'From community cohesion to mobile solidarities: the City of Sanctuary network and the Strangers into Citizens campaign', *Political Studies*, 59.2: 290–307.

Squire, V., and J. Bagelman (2012), 'Taking not waiting: space, temporality and politics in the City of Sanctuary movement', in P. Nyers and K. Rygiel (eds), *Citizenship, Migrant Activism, and the Politics of Movement* (London: Routledge), 146–64.

Squire, V., and J. Darling (2013), 'The "minor" politics of rightful presence: justice and relationality in City of Sanctuary', *International Political Sociology*, 7.1: 59–74.

Swerts, T. (2017), 'Creating space for citizenship: the liminal politics of undocumented activism', *International Journal of Urban and Regional Research*, 41.3: 379–95.

Uitermark, J., W. Nicholls and M. Loopmans (2012), 'Cities and social movements: theorizing beyond the right to the city', *Environment and Planning A*, 44.11: 2546–54.

Varsanyi, M. W. (2006), 'Interrogating "urban citizenship" vis-à-vis undocumented migration', *Citizenship Studies*, 10.2: 229–49.

Varsanyi, M. W. (2008), 'Immigration policing through the backdoor: city ordinances, the "right to the city", and the exclusion of undocumented day laborers', *Urban Geography*, 29.1: 29–52.

Vrasti, W., and S. Dayal (2016), 'Cityzenship: rightful presence and the urban commons', *Citizenship Studies*, 20.8: 994–1011.

Ward, P. (2014), 'Refugee cities: reflections on the development and impact of UNHCR urban refugee policy in the Middle East', *Refugee Survey Quarterly*, 33.1: 77–93.

Yukich, G. (2012), 'I didn't know if this was sanctuary: strategic adaptation in the new sanctuary movement', in R. K. Lippert and S. Rehaag (eds), *Sanctuary Practices in International Perspectives: Migration, Citizenship and Social Movements* (Abingdon: Routledge), 106–18.

Yukich, G. (2013), 'Constructing the model immigrant: movement strategy and immigrant deservingness in the New Sanctuary Movement', *Social Problems*, 60.3: 302–20.

Zetter, R., and M. Pearl (2000), 'The minority within the minority: refugee community-based organisations in the UK and the impact of restrictionism on asylum-seekers', *Journal of Ethnic and Migration Studies*, 26.4: 675–97.

Chapter 30

The Welcome City?

Hannah Lewis and Louise Waite

When we asked Jonathan, from the Survivors Speak out Network, whether he felt refugees were welcomed in the UK, he said that to answer that he would divide it into two parts. He said that the asylum system did not make him feel welcome, and that he was traumatised and angry during the five years it took him to get his refugee status. However, Jonathan told us that the welcome he got from people was very different. At a time when he was destitute and homeless while trying to get refugee status, he was supported by a church, he was given a home by a family, and welcomed into the community. (APPG on Refugees 2017: 50)

In April 2017 the All Party Parliamentary Group on Refugees published the findings from an inquiry it had conducted into refugee integration and settlement in the UK entitled *Refugees Welcome?*[1] Jonathan's account of his 'welcome' in the UK points to the heart of a paradox lived by many people who claim asylum in the UK and those who offer support to refugees: the compassion of certain parts of society and institutions towards people fleeing persecution is undermined, and often directly blocked, by hostile government immigration policies. This chapter discusses this tension between the grassroots politics of compassion that seeks to create a welcome for refugees, and a national politics that is driven by explicitly hostile asylum and immigration policies aimed at deterrence. The *Refugees Welcome?* report is contextualised with reference to the circulation from 2 September 2015 onwards of a photograph of Alan Kurdi, a drowned three-year-old boy on a Turkish beach, and the consequent public and political debate about how the UK should respond to refugees. This photograph of Alan Kurdi, one of hundreds of children who drowned in the Mediterranean in 2015, catapulted an ongoing European refugee 'crisis' into the realm of global moral concern.

The spontaneous and surprisingly compassionate response of the public in the latter half of 2015 resulted in both material outcomes for refugees (donations of clothes and personal items) and consciousness raising. Responses can be read at different scales, from the everyday involvement of individuals and civil society organisations, through to political actors and supranational bodies such as the EU. At the same time, the UK government, despite some relatively small gestures of sanctuary to selected Syrian refugees, is brazenly continuing its direction of travel to create 'discomfort and hostility' for refused asylum seekers and other irregular migrants through measures contained in the Immigration Acts of 2014 and 2016 in particular. These insidious structural and socio-spatial processes are paradoxically creating the need for the kinds of exchange, solidarity and counter-power being spearheaded by civil society under the broad 'refugees welcome' banner. Whether or not these kinds of impulses in cities can be translated into truly transformative politics is the question of the moment.

A generally negative media portrays refugees as 'exploiting' the hospitality of the UK, making it necessary for continuous awareness-raising work regarding people seeking asylum to point out that by far the majority of refugees live in countries bordering their country of origin, and few make it to cities in the Global North. The experiences of basic support, reception and longer-term settlement for refugees in complex urban environments of the Global South is an urgent and burgeoning area of research (Hoffstaedter 2015). Given this important global context, this chapter focuses on the politics of welcome in cities in the UK as a country in the Global North that received approximately 3 per cent of the asylum claims made in EU countries in 2015, making it the tenth highest recipient of asylum claims (this indicates a steady decline from 2008 figures which were about 11 per cent of EU share; Blinder 2016). Asylum seekers and refugees experience different narratives and scripts of 'welcome' in UK cities. Urban environments offer a place of welcome in which utopian and dystopian visions of the city are juxtaposed. This raises questions about whether spectacular or quotidian compassionate acts of welcome allow space for politicisation that could contribute to undermining or reshaping the vastly unequal global power dynamics of conflict and poverty that trigger (more-or-less) forced displacement in the first place, or state hostility to refugees in destination countries. If it is dependent on an image of the refugee as a needy victim, the compassionate giving of donations to refugees 'over there', outside the UK, may not only ignore the struggles of people seeking asylum in UK cities, but actually serve to cement a more draconian, exclusionary and unwelcoming xenophobic politics.

The next section explores sanctuary as a concept and practice with deep roots in the city, sketching the ancient Judaeo-Christian history of welcoming exiles and fugitives as an urban-religious phenomenon. Such a history, including the modern history of cities as places of opportunity for newcomers, paints the city as a utopian space of welcome and hospitality. The chapter then considers the converse: how cities may be dystopian, inhospitable sites for the 'other'. Following this juxtaposition, we turn to a discussion of how the 2015 crisis and 'compassion spike' was experienced in Leeds, a major refugee-receiving city in the north of England, by those individuals long immersed in welcoming activities. In a final concluding section, we question whether such forms of urban welcome can challenge a hostile national politics and argue for a 'critical compassion' that consciously builds politicised welcoming in cities and challenges hostility in national politics and local neighbourhoods.

The city as a utopian space of welcome and hospitality

The city has long been cast as an appropriate and welcoming place for the 'other', including international and rural migrants. The city has been imagined as a site of dreams and new economic opportunities for rural or international migrants perhaps more so than as a site of sanctuary for forced migrants. Yet the existence and concept of sanctuary has deep roots in the city. All of the major faiths promote welcome for those seeking sanctuary as morally necessary. Sketching the ancient and biblical history of sanctuary for exiles and refugees in Judaeo-Christian traditions, Marfleet describes how the concept and place of sanctuary can be traced back to ancient Jewish scripts that name six cities of refuge in the Jordan River region where fugitives could find protection while means of atonement were agreed. In the Greco-Roman eras, sanctuaries were sacred spaces within temples or sacred natural sites where no one could be harmed (Marfleet 2011). The fact that the lives of those defeated in war were spared on condition of them acknowledging the victor's authority and the power of its gods indicates a fascinating historical connection with contemporary policies demanding integration and declarations of citizenship from refugees granted protection. Marfleet suggests that the special status of cathedrals, abbeys, monasteries, shrines and local places of worship as sanctuaries for fugitives and victims of war and local conflict was one of the 'most consistent features of religious observance' (2011: 441) throughout the medieval period. However, the rise of the nation-state and the weakening of the religious establishment in Europe limited ecclesiastical authority, including the offering of sanctuary. Yet this process led to the emergence of sanctuary as an idea generalised to society as a whole for protecting certain groups of people (Marfleet 2011).

Both physically and figuratively, the response to Calvinist Huguenots fleeing persecution in France in the mid-seventeenth century inscribed the politics of welcome and sanctuary into British cities. King Charles II offered free denizenship to Huguenot refugees with rights to exercise trade and practise handicrafts. Collections for refugees were authorised in churches and large sums of money were raised, including grants from Parliament administered by the French Committee, a group of Huguenot aristocrats (Marfleet 2011). Huguenot and later migrations to London and other UK cities have shaped the urban geography, carving out economic niches and giving names to streets and places of residential concentration. In contemporary welcome movements, Jewish refugee populations are celebrated as providers of economic prosperity for cities through industries including, importantly for Leeds, textiles, and the foundation of the iconic high-street brand Marks and Spencer's.

The origins of the contemporary movement of cities of sanctuary in the US, Marfleet suggests, have precedents in churches providing 'sanctuaries for conscience' for conscientious objectors to fighting in the Vietnam War in the 1960s. In response to Central American refugees in the 1980s, these beginnings expanded into a more organised network of churches declaring sanctuary and engaging in political actions to challenge immigration policies, help with asylum applications and offer legal advice. This movement in the US has influenced the development in Europe of similar initiatives, including in the UK. The UK City of Sanctuary movement incorporates many activist Christians and remains strongly connected to church networks, but it explicitly claims to exceed traditional place-bound notions of sanctuary (such as churches), and to operate as a 'fluid network of practices' (Bagelman 2013: 50) to shift hostile attitudes to asylum seekers and refugees. The influence of Inderjit Bhogal – a proponent of interfaith dialogue and Methodist minister – and Craig Barnett, a Quaker colleague, as founders of the first UK City of Sanctuary in Sheffield has meant that the movement has always invited dialogue across faiths while being rooted in biblical themes of hospitality and sanctuary.[2] The extent to which an organisational interfaith outlook translates to grassroots networks across more than a hundred UK cities and towns is locally variable. In Leeds, this has manifested in strong connections with a particularly active synagogue and joint work with local Islamic charities, such as sharing an iftar, the fast-breaking meal during Ramadan. The history of welcome in cities for those fleeing persecution, then, is intertwined with the role of the religious observance of sanctuary and physical places of worship. Through the emergence of contemporary welcome movements, the origin of sanctuary in *places* within cities inside and around churches is continued through place-based *spaces* of struggle for the protection and advocacy of the rights of immigrants and refugees (Bagelman 2013).

The construction of refugees in the international political order as problematic stems, in Malkki's terms, from their position as people 'out of place' (1995a: 512) in the national order of things, a polluting force to be managed, ordered, counted and contained. In the twentieth century the refugee camp has been created as a place for the management of people fleeing conflict and persecution. Refugee camps also can be seen as places of containment and exclusion; sites envisioned as temporary spaces predicated on the notion of 'home' as the correct and acceptable place to return to. With the growth of protracted refugee situations (where people are exiled for longer than five years with no immediate prospect for the implementation of durable solutions), the city might be seen as a more welcoming site of relocation for refugees fleeing violence and persecution, for a range of economic and social reasons. However, until very recently UNHCR formally excluded urban refugees from its purview

and provision, and has been chiefly concerned with managing mass population movements and the establishment of camps. Indeed, it was only relatively
recently in 2009 that UNHCR produced its *Policy on Refugee Protection and
Solutions in Urban Areas*. Despite an enduring public and policy imagination
that fixes refugees in camps, the proportion of those living in urban areas is
now a majority. UNHCR figures indicate an ongoing growth in refugees living in urban areas from 42 per cent in 2008 to around 60 per cent in 2015
(UNHCR 2016). Zaatari refugee camp in Jordan became emblematic of the
Syrian refugee crisis (Crisp 2015), but coverage concentrating on this highly
organised and large refugee camp has deflected attention from the reality that
only an estimated 1 in 10 Syrians live in camps (UNHCR 2017). Most are
scattered across cities, suburbs and rural areas across the region. Despite this,
the emergence of urban areas as the new normal site of refugee displacement
is yet to take hold in the public imagination.

Jonathan Darling is an important contributor to the literature that
explores the city as an urban location of great significance for refugees
(Darling 2010; 2013; 2016a; 2016b; and see Chapter 29 in this volume).
He views the Global North city as the site of displacement through the
model of the 'camp-city', with associated practices of dispersal and refugee
resettlement, as a place of intensified border control, and also as a potential
space of sanctuary. Cities offer, theoretically at least, access to cosmopolitan and mixed neighbourhoods where newcomers might be welcomed and,
over time, become 'fixed' as residents. Cities offer refugees the same constrained 'opportunities' for low-wage, insecure jobs offered to other types
of newcomers such as rural migrants. However, the opportunities presented
by cities in the informal economy and for social connections with other
migrants go along with the risk of vulnerability to arrest, harassment and
abuse, highlighting a 'tension between the prospects of temporary safety
and opportunity and the risks of exploitation and marginalization' in urban
refugee experiences (Darling 2016b: 181).

We turn now to the script of the city as a dystopian place of inhospitality for outsiders, illustrating this in the first instance through the lens of
UK cities.

The dystopian, inhospitable city

A long and extended debate in sociological literature has engaged with questions of immigrant inclusion in urban communities, and lives on in contemporary UK policy debates on 'community cohesion', regarding whether minorities
live 'parallel lives'. Successive UK governments have asserted that a strong
sense of national belonging for minorities (including immigrants) is critical to
their settlement, integration and participation in civic life (Laurence and Heath
2008). Events such as the urban disturbances in northern England in 2001

were seen as critical threats to community cohesion. There has been concern from policymakers that such destabilising events are occurring because of fragilities of nationhood in spatially segregated urban neighbourhoods (Lewis and Neal 2005), which leave immigrants and other minorities feeling a sense of non-belonging to the nation which may block good relations between diverse people resident in the same place (Waite 2012). The problematising of the ethnic 'other' here is clear to see, together with a growing impulse to construct migrants as difficult and dangerous; a carving out between 'us and them' (Anderson 2013) with a frequent abjection of asylum seekers in particular (Tyler 2013). As an integral part of this, the last decade has seen security emerging as a central preoccupation of many Global North governments. States are increasingly creating a broad 'security continuum' that stretches from terrorism to action against crime and migratory flows (Walters 2004; Amoore 2006). Many states are promoting the maintenance of security as their principal contribution to the functioning of society; and immigration policies – often played out in urban contexts – are inextricably entwined in this agenda. Migration flows and migrants themselves are therefore ever more closely controlled and monitored, nowhere more so than in the realm of asylum seeking.

Key to the management of asylum seekers in the UK over the last fifteen years has been compulsory dispersal to urban centres across the country, under a rubric of 'spreading the burden' of asylum-seeker accommodation away from London and the south-east of England. Many commentators have noted the more insidious political impulses of dispersal, which is intended to deter would-be forced migrants, but most commonly maintains the marginality and impoverishment of asylum seekers in cities (Boswell 2001; Schuster 2005; Lewis 2009). Patterns of social and economic exclusion long experienced by minorities in UK cities are being mapped on to the experiences of forced migrants in urban areas. Most asylum seekers are located in the poorest parts of UK cities (Lyons and Duncan 2017) – due to accommodation being cheaply obtainable in these areas – which leaves the indelible marks of exclusion, marginalisation and poverty in the lives of forced migrants (Allsopp, Sigona and Phillimore 2014). Accommodation centres, reception centres and the characterless, sparse interiors of cheap housing can be viewed as 'non-places' along similar lines to the ways in which refugee camps have been theorised as locations that do not integrate other places, but are constructed as non-symbolised, abstract spaces (Augé 1995; Diken 2004).

Dispersal has on occasion been considered as presenting opportunities for highly disadvantaged areas of cities (Phillimore and Goodson 2006). For example, dispersal has transformed previously white estates and inner-city neighbourhoods into mixed places, with food from around the world being sold in local convenience stores, and multinational, multilingual cafés and social spaces occupying formerly abandoned or rundown shopping precincts. The extent to which asylum seekers experience the cities to which they are dispersed on a no-choice basis as 'multicultural', however, differs considerably depending on the features of the hosting neighbourhood. For those housed in neighbourhoods with a predominately white ethnic population, 'diversity' might only be glimpsed at arm's-length on trips into the city centre, rather than being a feature of everyday spaces.

For asylum seekers, undocumented migrants and increasingly all migrants, the city is also a site of surveillance and danger. The rapid growth of 'everyday bordering' (Yuval-Davis, Wemyss and Cassidy 2016) in the UK is advancing the penetration of national borders into the quotidian spaces of banks, health services, housing, schools and universities through the Immigration Acts of 2014 and 2016 (Lewis and Waite 2017). In these spaces, the prospect of deportation lies not in the hands of Home Office officials and border guards or the police, but is transmitted by bank clerks, landlords, nurses, doctors, teachers and lecturers, who are increasingly inculcated as state agents in the production of a 'hostile environment' for irregular migrants. While official policy may be aimed at facilitating the removal of those without leave to remain in the UK, the extension of border controls into multiple interactions requires everyday bureaucracies to identify potential migrants. This is likely to result in the profiling of people of colour or with any signs of a 'different' accent, features, characteristics and so on. It is axiomatic that these processes are unwelcoming, likely to be discriminatory and even xenophobic and racist (JCWI 2017; Jones et al. 2017). The result is the creation of an environment – principally in urban centres – that is hostile to all migrants and people of colour, not just those with insecure immigration status, including people seeking asylum. As Darling observes, the range of academic work on immigration enforcement makes it clear that it is through cities that 'practices of categorisation' (2016b: 184) are increasingly finding their expression in migrants' and enforcers' negotiation of status and services.

Religion has a conflicting and complex role in national political discourse around welcoming others. In response to the European refugee 'crisis', religious leadership encouraged welcoming activities in spite of continuing inhospitable statements from most major political leaders. Pope Francis called for every household in Europe to host a refugee family (Zunes 2017). Rowan Williams (former Archbishop of Canterbury), in October 2016, lamented the seemingly inhumane refusal of the UK government to bring further eligible unaccompanied minors from the about-to-be demolished Calais refugee camp to the UK under the so-called Dubs Amendment (O'Carroll and Fishwick 2016). But these examples contrast with a wider trend that poses (Muslim) refugees as a risk to Western (Christian) societies, a fear hugely inflated by President Trump's 'Muslim ban' in 2017 which was directly linked to the alleged risks posed by Muslim refugees accepted in resettlement programmes. Trump's anti-immigrant agenda extended to threatening US Sanctuary Cities with having funding removed (Buncombe 2017). Within Europe, although the scale of the grassroots compassionate response to the large number of refugees moving across Turkey and Greece and onward was impressive, there were also those who highlighted fears of Syrian (Muslim) terrorists utilising the large flow of refugees to conceal themselves and gain entry to Europe (Nail 2016). This is despite the flows being made up of a large number of well-educated professionals, while the recruiting grounds of Daesh are among the poor, unemployed and vulnerable (Zunes 2017).

This dynamic of the response to the refugee 'crisis' illustrates Derrida's analysis of the interrelationship between hospitality and hostility (Derrida 2000a). As Derrida highlighted in his discussion of hospitality, there is always a risk involved in welcoming a stranger into your home; you do not know whether the stranger will be a favourable guest or a hostile enemy. At the same time, acts of hospitality are potentially also hostile in reaffirming property rights and so on. This dangerous balance is what Derrida named as 'hostipitality' (Derrida 2000b). Hostile and host come from the same root. Hospitality cannot be assumed; it is a choice – a choice interpreted in a range of ways by different sections of UK urban populations.

Following this discussion of city scripts as utopian then dystopian, we now turn to a closer analysis of responses to the refugee 'crisis' in Leeds, a major refugee-receiving city in the north of England.

The refugee 'crisis', the compassion spike and urban welcoming in Leeds

Around the start of 2015 one man in Leeds started to network concerned individuals to explore how one urban neighbourhood in east Leeds could support Syrian refugees. Initially, efforts centred around engaging the David Young Community Academy in sponsoring Razan, a 12-year-old Syrian in a refugee camp in Jordan who needed urgent treatment for leukaemia. The local radio station Chapel FM hosted a series of 'Common Conversation' programmes in which newcomers and longer-standing residents shared their life stories and hopes for the future. From this starting point, meetings and partnerships were formed to discuss the possibilities for the direct hosting of Syrian refugees. The development of plans to host Syrian refugees directly among families in east Leeds led to meetings with the council and local refugee organisations, and a variety of awareness-raising activities. Ultimately, the lack of formal routes to secure a connection to facilitate travel and paperwork to allow the entry of Syrian refugees meant that the hosting part of the plan was not successful. However, the activities surrounding this initiative laid the ground for a much greater awareness of the urgency of the Syrian refugee issue at that time among refugee agencies, the local authority, and young people and families in the city. This groundwork was developed into a welcome pledge to promote positive engagement with refugee issues during the 2015 and 2017 general elections and 2016 local elections, signed by all leading candidates. It is almost certain that the background work to promote

Leeds as a place of sanctuary as part of the east Leeds welcome project, and among other refugee agencies during previous resettlement programmes, was fundamental in establishing a groundswell of 'welcome' that mobilised officers and leaders in Leeds City Council to be one of the first local authorities to offer to host more Syrians under the expanded Syrian Vulnerable Persons Resettlement Programme. Despite such local welcome initiatives before the Syrian refugee 'crisis' hit the press, the UK stood out in Europe as being slow to respond to the increasing humanitarian crisis of the mass movement of people across the Mediterranean to Europe.

Then, suddenly, in September, the circulation of the Alan Kurdi photograph exploded. In the space of twelve hours after the photograph was shared from a beach in Bodrum on the morning of 2 September 2015, 20 million people globally had seen the image via 30,000 tweets (D'Orazio 2015). Within a day, a viral photograph of a drowned child had transformed public interest in the issue from particular searches for 'Syrian child' or 'drowned boy' to the highest ever global search volume for the topic of 'refugees' in Google search history. Over September, the questions asked of Google reflected a dramatic change in social attitudes, with searches relating to the causes of the migrant crisis, the Syrian conflict, the reasons for migration to Europe, and how to volunteer to help refugees (Rogers 2015). In Leeds, on 3 September, the National Coordinator of City of Sanctuary wrote in an email to the local City of Sanctuary steering group:

> have been working 24/7 this week, the floodgates have broke open with lots of media interviews, new groups popping up from Orkney to a village in Sussex, hundreds of people saying 'please tell me what I can do', petitions across UK, Ireland and Europe and social media going haywire. (National Coordinator, City of Sanctuary, personal communication)

Individual charities and projects with a public profile connecting them with refugees were instantly overwhelmed with a 'revolution of generosity', as the National City of Sanctuary Coordinator later called it (City of Sanctuary Sheffield 2015). A rapid growth in donations of goods and offers to help led to the organisation of a Leeds multi-agency meeting to coordinate responses within hours:

> I am feeling a bit overwhelmed with all the offers of donations, volunteers etc in the last couple of days, which is proving tricky to coordinate. A more coordinated, multi-agency approach would be a better, more efficient way of approaching this. (Leeds City of Sanctuary coordinator, personal communication)

This was quickly usurped by a plan for a public meeting to capture the energies and interest of members of the public who were new to the issues, which was deemed more appropriate than the regular individuals used to meeting as part of the refugee and asylum multi-agency forum.

Social media was central to the coordination of the efforts of these new, grassroots groups and initiatives in cities around the UK, which largely grew out of spontaneous actions not linked to or stemming out of established small, medium or large refugee support organisations. Numerous similarly named groups sprang up on Facebook around the idea of helping or welcoming refugees. The Refugees Welcome UK group opened on 3 September 2015 and gained 2,500 members within 24 hours, later settling at around 4,000 members. An almost identically named group, Refugees Welcome – UK has 5,000 members. In these groups, people from across the UK asked for advice about where they could donate locally to convoys sending clothes and other essential items to Calais and Greece, and for ideas regarding what they could do to help. Initially, such social media groups also exposed the dichotomy between active compassion and compassionate activism in arguments between those posting articles to provoke political action against hostile UK policies or addressing the UK's complicity in the root causes of displacement, and others who rejected the 'politicisation' of the groups and wanted them to be reserved only for the exchange of information about 'helping' activities. As Mayblin (2015) points out, they also demonstrated a strange distancing or exotification of the refugee issue as something 'elsewhere', not in the UK. It was only latterly that these huge Facebook groups began to respond to the idea that there were refugees and asylum seekers on their doorsteps in the UK who also needed help. Along with all of the major UK refugee charities and local multi-agency initiatives, these social media groups worked to list, share and coordinate responses. Within a couple of days, Leeds refugee charities had produced a detailed list of what could be done in Leeds to support refugees, leading to a historic spike in volunteers coming forward for projects that usually faced perennial challenges in recruitment.

Local charities were immediately overwhelmed by donations of goods. It was beyond the scope of groups such as Leeds No Borders to deal with the rise in donations, although they had been working for months with Calais Migrant Solidarity to arrange occasional vans to take donations to 'The Jungle' in Calais. Within a few weeks, the council had offered a disused recreation centre in Richmond Hill on a temporary basis as a central site for the collection and sorting of donations. Yorkshire Aid was established to run the Richmond Hill depot and to coordinate the distribution of donations between Leeds refugee charities, and convoys to Calais and Lesbos (Figs 30.1 and 30.2). Yorkshire Aid describes itself as 'a group of individuals and organisations that work together to provide aid for refugees and asylum seekers in Leeds, Yorkshire and Europe' (Yorkshire Aid Facebook group). In the initial aftermath of the compassion spike, they had volunteers across the city with garages full of donations and wondered how they would be able to continue to manage it all, sort it, and organise distribution. However, the initial high

Figure 30.1 Richmond Hill depot, Leeds (photograph: authors)

Figure 30.2. Richmond Hill depot, Leeds (photograph: authors)

rate of donations tailed off quickly. Despite this, there has been a lasting effect, with a baseline of increased awareness of refugee issues and understanding of sites such as Calais and Lesbos as places to which goods could be donated. Everyday welcome acts have perhaps been sustained at a slightly increased level, while a majority moved on quickly from the spectacular compassion event of the autumn 2015 'revolution of generosity'.

The powerful response seen in Leeds was replicated in towns and cities across the UK and built a picture of an outpouring of support and compassion towards refugees that is unprecedented in recent decades. Thousands of individuals went out to buy toothbrushes or wet wipes destined for places receiving large numbers of new arrivals in other European countries, linking this act of giving with difficult to comprehend geopolitical issues, conflict and war on distant shores. Individuals and groups working together in local neighbourhoods connected to city-wide projects linked to key volunteers travelling to Calais and Greece to help. To a lesser extent, the surge in the desire to help refugees, and specifically Syrian refugees, extended to refugees in the UK. In Glasgow, for example, the long-established asylum and refugee rights organisation Positive Action in Housing reported that its project offering overnight shelter in people's homes went from providing 600 nights a year to 29,000 nights in the eighteen months following September 2015 (Canter, Lyons and Fidler 2017).

The default position of European states of aiming for the maximum deterrence of asylum applicants began to appear quite out of kilter with this mass outpouring of compassion. This included not only local responses in the UK as in the example of Leeds, but also the spontaneous appearance of a diverse 'volunteer army' at multiple points along the 2,000-mile-long 'refugee trail' across Europe, providing shelter, blankets, food, simple kindness (Brocklebank 2016) and much more at sites such as informal camps, roadsides and train stations (Löffler and McVeigh 2016). Only one state deviated from the hardline response revolving around deterrence. Germany – having already launched a specific Humanitarian Admission Programme for Syrians in May 2013, expanded in December 2013 and again in July 2014 – suspended the Dublin protocol in August 2015 (which requires people seeking asylum to make a claim in the first country they enter in the EU). This potentially made it easier for Syrians entering via Greece or Turkey to stay in Germany. Angela Merkel repeatedly stated that Germany 'could and would cope' with the influx of refugees (Harding 2015), while calling for a more equal distribution of refugees across EU member states as part of an agreed strategy (Nienaber 2015). In other European countries, including Hungary and the UK, the state response to the mass movement of refugees through the Turkish and Greek routes has been hostile and dominated by a powerful narrative of border control. The Hungarian Prime Minister quickly announced plans to build a massive fence at the border. Even so, Hungarians in their thousands donated food and clothing to assist refugees (Zunes 2017).

Mass petitions urging the UK government to act to protect refugees followed from the circulation of the Alan Kurdi photograph in September 2015. Only after a huge public outcry and considerable political pressure did the then Prime Minister, David Cameron, agree to take an additional – derisory – 20,000 Syrian refugees by 2020 through the highly selective Syrian Vulnerable Persons Resettlement Programme (SVPRP). This was originally launched as a more limited programme of resettlement in January 2014, intended to resettle

Syrians from refugee camps in countries neighbouring Syria. Syrians were to be prioritised from a number of specific categories considered most vulnerable, such as victims of sexual violence and torture, the elderly and the disabled. The government announced at that time that it expected several hundred refugees to arrive in the UK over three years, but did not apply a quota. The concept that the 'most vulnerable' must be 'protected' featured prominently in the UK government's rhetoric aimed at legitimising the introduction of the SVPRP. This was expressed starkly at the Conservative party conference in October 2015, when the Home Secretary, Theresa May, described the new asylum strategy. She made a distinction between the entitlements of Syrian refugees, 'deserving' by reason of their vulnerability, and spontaneous asylum seeking. Criticising the current asylum system, which she claimed rewarded 'the wealthiest, the luckiest and the strongest' people and denied support to 'the most vulnerable and most in need', a new approach to asylum was outlined:

> to offer asylum and refuge to people in parts of the world affected by conflict and oppression, rather than to those who have made it to Britain . . . to work to reduce the asylum claims made in Britain. (Theresa May, quoted in *The Guardian* 2015)

The importance placed on 'the vulnerable' in the SVPRP reflects an increasing emphasis on 'prominent and long-running social policy debates and narratives about [the] "deserving" and "undeserving"' (Brown, Ecclestone and Emmel 2017: 3). The almost paradigmatic figure of the vulnerable Syrian refugee was framed within a broader narrative of ostensible state compassion to bolster the government's identity and to pursue specialist treatment for Syrian refugees. The figure of the spontaneous asylum seeker was meanwhile left to wither on the branch of undeservingness. Hence, ultimately, accepting tiny numbers of refugees through the SVPRP – only achieved due to a massive public outpouring of welcoming compassion – arguably operated to further harden state rejection and exclusion of refugees overall.

Undoubtedly, the huge public response in cities across the UK, and the involvement of local authorities in managing this response, helped to create the political space in which pressure was brought to bear on Cameron's government, and civic leaders felt able to respond to and enthusiastically take up invitations to host Syrians as part of the SVPRP. This contrasts sharply with the decline in support for asylum seekers that had emerged across a number of local authorities since the establishment in 2000 of the National Asylum Support Service (NASS) to administer the dispersal of asylum seekers. Birmingham City Council, for example, announced in 2011 that it would no longer accept asylum seekers as part of the national dispersal programme, a decision that started the move to privatised dispersal accommodation (Darling 2016a). Indeed, the recent APPG on Refugees report (2017) forcibly notes its concern about the emerging 'two-tier system' of refugee protection whereby settlement refugees (primarily through the SVPRP) experience vastly superior support services in comparison to the spontaneous asylum seeker, who is confronted by a complete withdrawal of support following a positive decision on refugee status, patchy English-language provision, and a lack of employment and skills support. What is emerging – particularly for spontaneous asylum seekers – are contradictory experiences of reception (Smith and Waite 2018), contingent on different scales of welcome encountered across the state–civil society terrain.

By means of conclusion, we now turn to exploring whether the earlier described forms of urban welcome can challenge a national hostile politics in any meaningful way.

Conclusion: can an urban welcome challenge a national hostile politics?

In the immediate aftermath of the UK's autumn 2015 'compassion spike', many of those who had been involved long-term in the struggle for refugee rights were asking the question: will this change be sustained? Could the somewhat neocolonial outpouring of gifts and donations for refugees imagined as being 'elsewhere' be transformed into lasting social change for refugees in the UK? We echo these questions, and conclude by asking whether everyday, local, urban acts of 'welcoming' can be translated into a transformative politics to challenge national policies of hostility to asylum seekers.

If hospitality is a choice, the welcome shown towards refugees seemed largely to have been selected as a very specific type of assistance to a particular construction of the *deserving* refugee (Dhaliwal and Forkert 2015). Within the maelstrom of media and public responses, it was typically only certain types of refugee and particular refugee stories that were deemed worthy of compassion. The signs that many of the Syrians moving across Greece and the Balkans into old Europe were middle class, wore fashionable trainers and had mobile phones polluted the purity of the needy refugee victim implicit in much of the media coverage and public response (Malkki 1995b; Mayblin 2015). For one thing, the object of compassion as expressed in social media support groups and through the actions of the plethora of convoy groups established to move donations of clothes and goods to Calais and Greece seemed to have to be 'over there', somewhere else. The existence of people fleeing persecution in the UK, thousands of whom have been fighting to secure their rights while living in destitution for years with little or access to welfare and work, was, on the whole, distant from the hive of activity that surrounded the compassion spike.

The UK public has largely remained remarkably tolerant of anti-asylum policies. The sudden and dramatic shift in the autumn of 2015 from hostile to sympathetic media coverage of the refugee 'crisis' was a surprise. However, over time it began to appear only as a blip in a generally xenophobic direction of travel in national political trends and media coverage. The spectacular compassionate event post-Kurdi gave way depressingly quickly to the implicit message of unwelcome conveyed through the lack of any meaningful challenge to the anti-refugee and anti-immigrant policies being put forward in the Immigration Bill 2015, and later cemented in the boldly xenophobic EU referendum 'Leave' campaign. Immigration restrictionism and hostility to migrants has a long history from which refugees seeking protection from persecution are not exempt. While the examples of the responses to the historical migrations of Huguenot and Jewish populations fleeing persecution are commonly held up as instances of British openness and welcome to those seeking protection, they also represent the beginnings of laws to restrict the settlement of immigrants (Anderson 2013). The increasingly complex operation of border controls at points of entry to the UK, and through visa requirements, has, arguably, taken on a new dimension in recent years, however. As detailed above, the Immigration Acts of 2014 and 2016 spearheaded xenophobic and deliberately unwelcoming immigration policies, and have expanded the operation of border controls into everyday life as enforcement creeps further into public services and areas of private life (Corporate Watch 2017).

This everyday enforcement is increasingly having an impact on the practices and politics around visibility and invisibility, both for dispensers and receivers of 'welcome'. The sudden surge in public displays of compassion and welcome towards certain types of refugees brought to the fore the dedicated work of refugee organisations and their workers and volunteers, and of informal groups and religious congregations, which quietly continues in the background. Indeed, the possibilities provided by cities for *in*-visibility may be part of their attraction as a welcoming site for refugees. Being able to eschew the refugee label and become a generic ethnic 'other', newcomer or migrant can be an important mechanism for inclusion in the urban social sphere (Lewis 2014). Erkhamp and Nagel's (2014) work in this regard is highly relevant, as they have explored the support offered to undocumented migrants by churches in the southern United States, where very hostile anti-immigration stop and search policies have been enacted. They identify how the churches are able to offer support to undocumented migrants by ignoring immigration status and diverting the attention of police or even xenophobic congregants. This echoes the historic connection between churches and religious networks and practices of sanctuary in cities as sites offering material and practical support to exiles, such as the Huguenot effort. However, the benefits to refugees of invisibility in urban environments can also be seen as potentially detrimental to a wider politics of welcome and hospitality.

Downplaying or concealing refugee labels and ignoring the political context of racist immigration policies fails to provide mechanisms and spaces to challenge hostile state-level politics. By opting to quietly support undocumented migrants in their churches, the pastors in Erkhamp and Nagel's research (2014: 326), for example, simultaneously maintain social and legal boundaries between migrants and 'locals' within congregations, reproducing existing exclusion and racialised discourse. In this light, the limiting of active compassion to charitable donations could be considered to exemplify Derrida's neologism 'hostipitality': at once an act of welcome, but one strongly circumscribed by a latent hostility towards the other.

We will close by noting that the politics and practices of welcome are – of course – highly differentiated in cities. As materially witnessed through the UK's compassion spike in 2015, most of those individuals and groups expressed support and empathy by donating 'stuff'. The reaction was therefore primarily an active charitable compassion, motivated by a desire to 'help'. The great hope was that this compassion spike would lead to more impactful and transformative practices of political engagement and resistance by individuals and households against hostile national immigration politics. Yet we are not currently witnessing any broad anti-xenophobic and pro-migrants' rights mobilisation. This was devastatingly evidenced in the UK's vote to leave the EU in June 2016. The Leave side of the Brexit referendum campaign brazenly manipulated the threat of refugees massed on EU borders coupled with a generalised fear of immigration by focusing almost exclusively on the issue of free movement within Europe as a threat. These cheap points found traction in the UK electorate at that moment, *despite* coming closely after the compassion spike. The hope that this spike would facilitate a more inclusive, transformative urban politics to challenge refugee exclusion does not seem to have played out, although Leeds as a city voted very narrowly (50.3%) to remain in the EU, and an anti-xenophobia march was mobilised in the aftermath of the Brexit vote with an explicit 'Refugees Welcome' message (Fig. 30.3). Yet the welcome city, as noted above, is differentiated. There are many people – acting as individuals, in community

Figure 30.3 Refugees Welcome (photograph: authors)

organisations, migrant activism networks, faith groups and so on – who are daily engaged in the more mundane and lengthy work of influencing policy and producing change. This effort is not spectacular, so it will never create the kind of media waves that followed the Alan Kurdi photo and the associated compassion spike. However, such efforts are arguably more critical if we want truly to animate scripts of welcome and compassionate activism in our cities.

Notes

1. We would like to thank all of those we spoke to in preparation for writing this chapter. Some material was taken from the authors' own experiences of involvement in 'welcome' initiatives and networks. Thanks to the following individuals and organisations for clarifying details and for permission to include quotes or material in this chapter: Yorkshire Aid, Leeds City of Sanctuary, Tiffy Allen, Ian Martin, East Leeds Community Refugee Project and Joanna Spooner. Our thanks to Sam Durrant for helpful suggestions.
2. See, for example, https://cityofsanctuary.org/by-theme/faiths/ (accessed 27 May 2019).

Bibliography

Allsopp, J., N. Sigona and J. Phillimore (2014), 'Poverty among refugees and asylum seekers in the UK', IRiS WP Series 01.14, www.birmingham.ac.uk/Documents/college-social-sciences/social-policy/iris/2014/working-paper-series/IRIS-WP-1-2014.pdf (accessed 13 July 2017).

Amoore, L. (2006), 'Biometric borders: governing mobilities in the war on terror', *Political Geography*, 25: 336–51.

Anderson, B. (2013), *Us and Them? The Dangerous Politics of Immigration Control* (Oxford: Oxford University Press).

APPG on Refugees (2017), *Refugees Welcome? The Experience of New Refugees in the UK. A Report by the All Party Parliamentary Group on Refugees*, https://www.refugeecouncil.org.uk/assets/0004/0316/APPG_on_Refugees_-_Refugees_Welcome_report.pdf (accessed 13 July 2017).

Augé, M. (1995), *Non-places: Introduction to an Anthropology of Supermodernity* (London: Verso).

Bagelman, J. (2013), 'Sanctuary: a politics of ease?', *Alternatives: Global, Local, Political*, 38.1: 49–62.

Blinder, S. (2016), 'Briefing. Migration to the UK: Asylum', University of Oxford, Migration Observatory, http://www.migrationobservatory.ox.ac.uk/wp-content/uploads/2016/04/Briefing-Asylum.pdf (accessed 13 July 2017).

Boswell, C. (2001), *Spreading the Costs of Asylum Seekers: A Critical Assessment of Dispersal Policies in Germany and the UK* (London: Anglo-German Foundation for the Study of Industrial Society).

Brocklebank, T. (2016), 'A rebellion of kindness in Calais', *Huffington Post*, 6 October, http://www.huffingtonpost.co.uk/tina-brocklebank/a-rebellion-of-kindness-i_b_12354882.html (accessed 27 July 2017).

Brown, K., K. Ecclestone and N. Emmel (2017), 'The many faces of vulnerability', *Social Policy and Society*, 16.3: 1–14.

Buncombe, A. (2017), 'US sanctuary cities that protect illegal immigrants "cannot continue" says Trump's Attorney General Jeff Sessions', *The Independent*, 27 March, http://www.independent.co.uk/news/world/americas/us-politics/sanctuary-cities-immigrants-jeff-sessions-says-cannot-continue-donald-trump-a7652931.html (accessed 13 July 2017).

Canter, A., K. Lyons and M. Fidler (2017), '"It's like an AirBnB for refugees": UK hosts and their guests', *The Guardian*, 8 May, https://www.theguardian.com/world/2017/may/08/airbnb-for-refugees-uk-hosts-guests-in-pictures (accessed 2 July 2019).

City of Sanctuary Sheffield (2015), 'Looking back over the movement's first decade', blog post, 28 October, https://sheffield.cityofsanctuary.org/the-movements-first-decade/ (accessed 3 July 2017).

Corporate Watch (2017), 'The Hostile Environment: turning the UK into a nation of border cops', Corporate Watch, https://corporatewatch.org/sites/default/files/CW%20hostile%20environment.pdf (accessed 13 July 2017).

Crisp, J. (2015), 'Zaatari: a camp and not a city', Refugees International blog post, https://www.refugeesinternational.org/blog/zaatari-camp-and-not-city (accessed 20 April 2017).

Darling, J. (2010), 'A city of sanctuary: the relational re-imagining of Sheffield's asylum politics', *Transactions of the Institute of British Geographers*, 35.1: 125–40.

Darling, J. (2013), 'Moral urbanism, asylum, and the politics of critique', *Environment and Planning A*, 45.8: 1785–801.

Darling, J. (2016a), 'Privatising asylum: neoliberalisation, depoliticisation, and the governance of forced migration', *Transactions of the Institute of British Geographers*, 41.3: 230–43.

Darling, J. (2016b), 'Forced migration and the city: irregularity, informality, and the politics of presence', *Progress in Human Geography*, 41.2: 178–98.

Darling, J., C. Barnett and S. Eldridge (2010), 'City of Sanctuary – a UK initiative for hospitality', *Forced Migration Review*, 34: 46.

Darling, J., and V. Squire (2012), 'Everyday enactments of sanctuary: the UK City of Sanctuary movement', in R. K. Lippert and S. Rehaag (eds), *Sanctuary Practices in International Perspectives: Migration, Citizenship and Social Movements* (Abingdon: Routledge), 191–204.

Derrida, J. (2000a), *Of Hospitality: Anne Dufourmantelle Invites Jacques Derrida to Respond*, trans. R. Bowlby (Stanford: Stanford University Press).

Derrida, J. (2000b), 'Hostipitality', *Angelaki*, 5.3: 3–18.

Dhaliwal, S., and K. Forkert (2015), 'Deserving and undeserving migrants', *Soundings*, 61: 49–61.

Diken, B. (2004), 'From refugee camps to gated communities: biopolitics and the end of the city', *Citizenship Studies*, 8.1: 83–106.

D'Orazio, F. (2015), 'Journey of an image: from a beach in Bodrum to twenty million screens across the world', in F. Vis and O. Goriunova (eds), *The Iconic Image on*

Social Media: A Rapid Research Response to the Death of Aylan Kurdi (University of Sheffield: The Visual Medial Lab), 11–18.

Erkhamp, P., and C. Nagel (2014), '"Under the radar": undocumented immigrants, Christian faith communities, and the precarious spaces of welcome in the U.S. South', *Annals of the Association of American Geographers*, 104.2: 319–28.

The Guardian (2015), 'Theresa May announces drive to limit right to claim asylum in UK', 6 October, https://www.theguardian.com/uk-news/2015/oct/06/theresa-may-announces-new-plan-to-limit-right-to-claim-asylum-in-uk (accessed 2 July 2019).

Harding, L. (2015), 'Angela Merkel defends Germany's handling of refugee influx', *The Guardian*, 15 September, https://www.theguardian.com/world/2015/sep/15/angela-merkel-defends-germanys-handling-of-refugee-influx (accessed 13 July 2017).

Hoffstaedter, G. (2015), 'Between a rock and a hard place: urban refugees in a global context', in K. Koizumi and G. Hoffstaedter (eds), *Urban Refugees: Challenges in Protection, Services and Policy* (London: Routledge), 1–10.

JCWI (2017), *Passport Please: The Impact of the Right to Rent Checks on Migrants and Ethnic Minorities in England* (London: Joint Council for the Welfare of Immigrants), https://www.jcwi.org.uk/passport-please (accessed 13 July 2017).

Jones, H., Y. Gunaratnam, G. Bhattacharyya, W. Davies, S. Dhaliwal, K. Forkert, E. Jackson and R. Saltus (2017), *Go Home? The Politics of Immigration Controversies* (Manchester: Manchester University Press).

Laurence, J., and A. Heath (2008), *Predictors of Community Cohesion: Multi-level Modelling of the 2005 Citizenship Survey* (Wetherby: Communities and Local Government Publications).

Lewis, G., and S. Neal (2005), 'Introduction: contemporary political contexts, changing terrains and revisited discourses', *Ethnic and Racial Studies*, 28.3: 423–44.

Lewis, H. (2009), *Still Destitute: A Worsening Problem for Refused Asylum Seekers* (York: Joseph Rowntree Charitable Trust).

Lewis, H. (2014), 'Music, dancing and clothing as belonging and freedom among people seeking asylum in the UK', *Journal of Leisure Studies*, 34.1: 42–58.

Lewis, H., and L. Waite (2017), 'Manipulating welfare, rights and agency: UK asylum policy and susceptibility to forced labour', in Francesco Vecchio and Alison Gerard (eds), *Tracing Responsibility: Entrapping Asylum Seekers in Precarious Livelihoods* (Basingstoke: Palgrave Macmillan), 187–215.

Löffler, J., and K. McVeigh (2016), 'What's in it for them? The volunteers saving Europe's refugees', *The Guardian*, 9 June, https://www.theguardian.com/world/2016/jun/09/whats-in-it-for-them-the-volunteers-saving-europes-refugees (accessed 13 July 2017).

Lyons, K., and P. Duncan (2017), '"It's a shambles": data shows most asylum seekers put in poorest parts of Britain', *The Guardian*, 9 April, https://www.theguardian.com/world/2017/apr/09/its-a-shambles-data-shows-most-asylum-seekers-put-in-poorest-parts-of-britain (accessed 2 June 2017).

Malkki, L. (1995a), 'Refugees and exile: from refugee studies to the national order of things', *Annual Review of Anthropology*, 24.1: 495–523.

Malkki, L. (1995b), *Purity and Exile: Violence, Memory, and National Cosmology among Hutu Refugees in Tanzania* (Chicago: University of Chicago Press).

Marfleet, P. (2011), 'Understanding "sanctuary": faith and traditions of asylum', *Journal of Refugee Studies*, 24.3: 440–5.

Mayblin, L. (2015), 'Politics, publics and Aylan Kurdi', in F. Vis and O. Goriunova (eds), *The Iconic Image on Social Media: A Rapid Research Response to the Death of Aylan Kurdi* (University of Sheffield: The Visual Media Lab), 42–3.

Nail, T. (2016), 'A tale of two crises: migration and terrorism after the Paris attacks', *Studies in Ethnicity and Nationalism*, 16.1: 158–67.

Nienaber, M. (2015), 'Merkel says Germany can cope with refugees without raising taxes', Reuters world news online, http://www.reuters.com/article/us-europe-migrants-germany-merkel-idUSKCN0R50L020150905 (accessed 13 July 2017).

O'Carroll, L., and C. Fishwick (2016), 'Rowan Williams: government is "foot-dragging" over Calais child refugees', *The Guardian*, 17 October, https://www.theguardian.com/uk-news/2016/oct/17/rowan-williams-stop-foot-dragging-over-calais-child-refugees (accessed 13 July 2017).

Phillimore, J., and L. Goodson (2006), 'Problem or opportunity? Asylum seekers, refugees, employment and social exclusion in deprived urban areas', *Urban Studies*, 43: 1715–36.

Rogers, S. (2015), 'What can search data tell us about how the story of Aylan Kurdi spread around the world?', in F. Vis and O. Goriunova (eds), *The Iconic Image on Social Media: A Rapid Research Response to the Death of Aylan Kurdi* (University of Sheffield: The Visual Media Lab), 19–26.

Schuster, L. (2005) 'A sledgehammer to crack a nut: deportation, detention and dispersal in Europe', *Social Policy and Administration*, 39: 606–21.

Smith, K., and L. Waite (2018), 'New and enduring narratives of vulnerability: rethinking stories about the figure of the refugee', *Journal of Ethnic and Migration Studies*, DOI: https://doi.org/10.1080/1369183X.2018.1496816.

Tyler, I. (2013), *Revolting Subjects. Social Abjection and Resistance in Neoliberal Britain* (London: Zed Books).

UNHCR (2016), *Global Trends in Forced Displacement* (Geneva: United Nations High Commissioner for Refugees), http://www.unhcr.org/5943e8a34 (accessed 13 July 2017).

UNHCR (2017), 'Syrian Regional Refugee Response', http://data.unhcr.org/syrian-refugees/regional.php (accessed 13 July 2017).

Waite, L. (2012), 'Neo-assimilationist citizenship and belonging policies in Britain: meanings for transnational migrants in northern England', *Geoforum*, 43.2: 353–61.

Walters, W. (2004), 'Secure borders, safe haven, domopolitics', *Citizenship Studies*, 8.3: 237–60.

Yuval-Davis, N., G. Wemyss and K. Cassidy (2016), 'Changing the racialized "common sense" of everyday bordering', *Open Democracy*, https://www.opendemocracy.net/uk/nira-yuval-davis-georgie-wemyss-kathryn-cassidy/changing-racialized-common-sense-of-everyday-bord (accessed 13 July 2017).

Zunes, Stephen (2017), 'Europe's refugee crisis, terrorism, and Islamophobia', *Peace Review*, 29.1: 1–6.

Chapter 31

In the City's Public Spaces: Movements of Witnesses and the Formation of Moral Community

André Grahle

In his highly acclaimed and largely autobiographical play *The Trip*, Syrian director and playwright Anis Hamdoun portrays a group of young anti-government activists from Homs. Wrenched out of their ordinary lives, shaped by everyday problems and dreams of specific careers, the friends suddenly find themselves in the middle of revolutionary protests, aiming for the higher ends of democracy, dignity and freedom. It is 2011, the Arab Spring has reached Syria, and the regime, the downfall of which the people eventually demand, soon responds with a brutal crackdown against peaceful protesters. That crackdown develops into the war that we know has so far caused the deaths of hundreds of thousands of people and displaced half of the Syrian population. Like many at that point, the young activists portrayed by Hamdoun start documenting atrocities and help to treat the injured, but soon they become targets themselves.

Most of the play consists of the activists providing, from a place of exile, their first-person accounts of what they have witnessed through direct experience or observation: stories of enforced disappearances, rape, torture, siege and bombardment. However, towards the end of the play, it transpires that the protagonist Rami is the only one of the four who actually managed to escape the country. His friends are all dead, yet in his exile they are overwhelmingly present to him by way of their voices being inscribed on to his restless memory. Rami's exile is one of intense loneliness, pervaded by feelings of guilt, hopelessness, anger and despair; a loneliness the depth of which is made even harder to overcome by his being caught up in the memories of his dead friends. Rami is caught up in these memories, the play seems to suggest, due to his new social environment *keeping him enclosed* by way of depriving him of any meaningful method of productively engaging with his memories. The play takes place at night, and while it is never revealed to the audience which country or city Rami is in, there is no human encounter between Rami and the society in which he finds himself. In fact, other people are alluded to only schematically, as when Rami interrupts his own speech by expressing his intention to find a job at a company with a boss who remains fully abstract. It seems as if the new society is exercising power over Rami, not only through its presence and potential to act against him, but also through its absence and systematic omissions, most importantly through its utter lack of a culture of receptivity for what is on Rami's mind.

The Trip has been shown several times at Theater Osnabrück, where it had its premiere at *Spieltriebe*, a festival for contemporary theatre, in 2015. It was then read and performed in a number of other cities across Germany, including at Munich's *Kammerspiele* and Berlin's *Schaubühne* as part of a larger international theatre festival called *FIND*. Typically, performances have been followed by public discussions, with Hamdoun providing additional information about the production process, his own experience as an artist and revolutionary activist in contemporary Syria, the autobiographical aspects of the piece, and its specific political context. At that time, the question of an appropriate German and European response to the worst displacement crises since the Second World War had already received strong attention at most levels of society, including the media, political parties, activists and volunteer groups, as well as from a great number of artists, cultural networks and institutions.[1] However, it cannot be denied that acts and expressions of solidarity with refugees, as well as attempts to understand the oppression that refugees with Europe as their destination face, were primarily concerned with injustices other than those that caused these people to flee in the first place. This gave rise to an image of the plight of refugees as reducible to the risk of crossing the Mediterranean, of facing various obstacles along the Balkan route, or of later having to face racism and (other) forms of structural oppression, including the threat of deportation and detention. The injustices that refugees experienced in their country of origin, and the struggle against these injustices, have often been dealt with separately and rather insufficiently, despite it being an important field of solidarity as well.

The Trip can be seen as an early attempt to counter this prevailing tendency. It provides a basic understanding of some of the most severe injustices that have affected a great number of Syrian refugees who have recently arrived in Germany. Most crucially, however, it lays bare the harm caused by receiving societies' refusal to properly engage with refugees' testimony *about* these injustices. Yet in elegant consistency with this thought, *The Trip* does not just induce guilt in its audience, but gives it the encouraging impression that paying proper attention to the play here and now is conducive to the *prevention* of such harm. As becomes clear from media profiles (Meiborg 2016; Marcus 2016a) and from the discussions, of which I attended several over the course of a year, it is not just Rami speaking in the total absence of real human encounter, but Hamdoun speaking through his play *to his audience*. Moreover, performances and discussions have been attended by Syrians and non-Syrians alike. Occasionally, the performance served as a point of reference for other Syrians who have recently arrived in Germany, providing them with an occasion to address parts of their new social context through their own testimony without having to start from scratch. One report (Schmitt 2016) mentions a Syrian man in the audience speaking about his own time in prison, about the screams of those being tortured around him that still haunt him, as well as about the fate of his younger brother, a medical doctor who was forcibly disappeared years ago and has not been heard from since. The man is quoted as expressing his appreciation that part of his own experience has found expression in Hamdoun's play. A number of similar cases suggest that the play has indirectly benefited other Syrians in receiving acknowledgement from elements of the receiving society of their suffering and their enduring struggle for freedom and dignity in Syria.

I begin the first section of this chapter by explaining how refugees arrive as witnesses of severe injustices experienced in their country of origin, some of whom, further, are actively seeking to bear witness in exile, potentially forming what I call *movements of witnesses*. In the second section, I argue for the value of these movements making use of the city's public spaces to address the receiving society with their testimony. I argue that such giving of testimony can be a matter of inscribing one's story into the consciousness of the city and of engaging in what I call the formation of moral community. It can win over elements of the receiving society, as they morally acknowledge one's group's suffering and the rightfulness of their liberatory struggle. Moral acknowledgement, in turn, is a crucial condition for some refugees to conceive of the new society as something they can genuinely become a part of. I conclude the chapter with a few preliminary remarks on the moral duty of city communities to grant movements of witnesses more effective access to public spaces.

Witnesses and movements of witnesses

Refugees tend to arrive as witnesses of severe injustices in their country of origin. They have become such witnesses by having themselves experienced, or by having observed others nearby experiencing, such injustices. The mere fact of having been forcibly displaced is likely to count as a severe injustice already, but there is a significant chance that more has been witnessed before the event of displacement. I do not offer here a strict definition of what makes an injustice *severe*. However, we can, by relying on common sense and general knowledge of the nature of state oppression, terrorism and war today, begin an open list that would include the evils of forced disappearance, torture, rape and sexual violence, siege and starvation, mass murder, ethnic cleansing and genocide, as well as humiliation through the public denial of these crimes.

So for example, if we look at the evidence in the case of Syria, where grave crimes are committed – including the bombardment of civilian neighbourhoods, the enforced disappearance of tens of thousands, torture as a means of what the Human Rights Council of the United Nations has referred to as 'extermination', the use of starvation as a weapon against civilians living under siege, gender-based and sexual violence, as well as public mockery of victims and widespread denial of such crimes – we can estimate the likelihood of Syrian refugees arriving as witnesses of severe injustices other than forced displacement.[2] From my perspective as an activist involved with testimony projects in Germany, a country that has received about 700,000 Syrian refugees since the beginning of the war, the proportion of refugees who have been affected by these injustices is overwhelming. For many, *escaping the country* was certainly not equivalent to *escaping assaults within the country*, and loss of family members and loved ones in a conflict that goes on during exile is the rule rather than the exception.

I treat passive registration of an event to be sufficient for one to become a witness of the event. It is not up to the agent whether to become a witness at least of the fact that a certain injustice is taking place, if the injustice happens within the agent's perceptual reach.[3] The passive side of witnessing, however, is often enriched by a more active one. Witnesses can exercise their epistemic agency. I do not mean agency *en route* to witnessing, as in cases of citizen-journalists *seeking* injustices in order to systematically document them.[4] I mean that *in* witnessing, witnesses can often move beyond mere passive registration of the event.[5] They can engage with the matter in one way or another and to varying degrees. So, for example, detainees held by an unlawful regime may engage in meticulous (self-)observation as a way of trying to understand in more detail the nature of the injustice and their experience of it. Registration may be followed closely here by attempts to (actively) analyse what has been (passively) registered.[6] Moreover, in witnessing, people sometimes creatively engage with the material that their perception delivers. The accomplished Syrian painter Najah al-Bukai, who paints from personal memory his experiences of torture in Syrian detention centres, emphasises that he refused to accept passive subjection to the perception of the horror before him: 'The whole time I was in hell, I tried to not see nightmares. Instead, I forced myself to see beautiful dreams' (Alami 2018).[7] It might be possible to understand this as a matter of actively taking control over one's thought and imagination to alter the way of experiencing what one cannot avoid registering.

Another remark concerns the wider context of the injustices witnessed. The context can impact the way the injustices are experienced in the first place, which may later be reflected in the testimony communicated to others. Most significantly, it is important to note the fact that injustices are often responses to acts of rightfully resisting *other* injustices, such as when activists are detained and tortured in response to breaking laws that prevent free speech and peaceful assembly. Often the meaning of the order of events is itself reflected in experience and testimony. Frequent assertions such as 'We have been bombarded just because we asked for a little bit of freedom' or 'I have been tortured, but at least I never obeyed' capture this well. The first can be read as expressing the witness's judgement of those guilty of committing the injustice as specifically disgraceful, while the latter can be understood as an expression of a comforting pride, representing one's own resistant agency in a wider context of political struggle. Noticing these nuances is important for any potential receiver of testimony when it comes to framing an appropriate response to the testimony she listens to. We will come back to this.

I have deliberately put my focus on *refugees* as witnesses, whereas of course there are many witnesses of severe injustices linked to the same instances of oppression, or linked to the same struggle, who have not been displaced, or for whom fleeing is for the time being simply not an option. Some decide to continue with their political struggle in the country, come what may. Others would flee immediately if only they could. Witnesses may still be kept in prison, and we hear of prisoners dying under torture every day. Yet exile deserves attention as a specifically fruitful place for refugees to bear witness, and I think more should be said about why this is the case and how the desire to bear witness – to communicate one's testimony – should be better facilitated by receiving societies.

I would like to distinguish two types of witness. First, there are what I call merely *nominal witnesses*, who have acquired knowledge through direct experience and close observation of severe injustices in their country of origin, but who do not currently desire to bear witness, and hence do not seek opportunities to bear witness in exile (but perhaps engage in practices of forgetting, suppression, distraction, or personal memorisation). Secondly, there are what I call *self-identifying witnesses*, who have acquired knowledge through direct experience and close observation of severe injustices in their country of origin and do indeed have a desire to bear witness in exile. This desire can differ in strength. It can be weak or strong, sometimes so strong as to present itself to the person as the feeling that she *must* bear witness (Frankfurt 1982: 263). People with a sufficiently strong desire actively take, seek, or at least hope for opportunities to bear witness in exile. When I use the term 'witness' in an unspecified way in this chapter, I mean *self-identifying* witness.[8]

While the presence of witnesses is of specific ethical relevance for the receiving society, this is not necessarily the place where witnesses are born. So, for instance, the prospect of bearing witness after escape – of telling the world *what happened in here* – can play a central role as a motivational and justificatory source for some to fight for their own survival.[9] The desire to bear witness can even figure as a reason behind flight, as escape from one's situation – such as torture in prison – must often be followed by one's leaving a region or country to avoid repeated arrest or other kinds of assault and/or to ensure one's survival as a condition of bearing witness. This said, there are also witnesses for whom a desire to bear witness emerges during transit, or after arrival in a new area, or indeed on arrival in a new country. It can be the result of reflection on the possibilities of bearing witness and the good that can be pursued by bearing witness, of having potential listeners and of listening to other witnesses who speak about their experience of giving their testimony.

In cases of mass displacement, larger movements of refugees who arrive in countries may give rise to *movements of witnesses*. I use this term to refer to the phenomenon of a great number of witnesses beginning to bear witness under new socio-spatial conditions, by addressing parts of the receiving society with their testimony. I do not think we should make it a conceptual requirement for movements of witnesses to show much unity, especially in the early years after their arrival. Thus, the way I use the term 'movement' here allows for a social phenomenon that has a largely summative nature. They can be entities of largely unorganised structure, consisting merely of loosely connected individuals who share roughly the same fate, who have suffered from (and sometimes still are suffering from) and struggled against (and sometimes still are struggling against) the same injustices. Yet because of the unity of the source of injustice and the target of one's struggle, movements of witnesses can display a great amount of agreement in the way they evaluate these injustices, so that while they do not necessarily speak with the same voice, or have not organised some form of coordinated speaking, they can still be recognised as part of the same fragmented formation, amplifying each other's voices. Syrian witnesses in Germany who share the experience of being affected in one way or another by the oppression of the Assad regime form such a loosely associated (but quite visible) movement of witnesses.

Addressing the receiving society: public spaces in cities

Roughly, movements of witnesses have two sites in which to address elements of the receiving society with their testimony. First, there are *personal relationships*, which can be formed between newcomers and long-term members of the receiving societies. So, for example, for the vast number of citizens who volunteered in refugee support contexts during the current displacement crisis, it was far from uncommon to be offered testimony. This often remains on the level of brief encounter, but it can develop into a more solid relationship, such as a friendship. A good friend is, among other things, a person who at least tries to be a good listener, which includes a willingness to listen to testimony. Moreover, there is a distinct type of personal relationship that is more centrally constituted by practices of giving and receiving testimony. The exact nature of these relationships, which I call *witnessing relationships*, is complicated and deserves separate philosophical analysis that I provide elsewhere (Grahle n.d.).

What can be said here, however, is that virtuous listening in witnessing relationships can figure as an important source of moral acknowledgement for both the witness's suffering and the rightfulness of their liberatory struggle. In the long run, witnessing relationships can give rise to a strong moral bond between the listener and the witness that is unlikely to emerge in a less intimate social setting, and that can impose special responsibilities on the listener to offer her political solidarity. Moreover, what is distinct about witnessing relationships, and witnessing in other personal relationships, is their potential to treat testimony as confidential. This is one of the reasons why some identifying witnesses may choose personal relationships, for the time being, over any other social setting. Bearing witness frequently comes with a risk for one's own safety and the safety of family and friends (Margalit 2002: 150). That the witness operates in exile does not necessarily matter in this regard, for the witness's legal status might be unclear, and fear of deportation back into the arms of the perpetrators could be justified. Moreover, relatives and loved ones who are still in the country of origin might become a target of retaliation in place of the witness speaking out abroad. Not every witness is therefore in a position to testify about the crimes of a regime still in place in a less confidential situation than a personal relationship informed by mutual trust.

This said, beyond personal relationships there is a second site for people to bear witness. This is the focus of this chapter: public and semi-public spaces, of which plenty can be found in modern cities. To be sure, public witnessing is not confined to the realm of (semi-)public spaces. So, for instance, there is a growing amount of literature written by or giving a voice to witnesses living in exile (e.g. Yazbek 2015; Le Caisne 2015; Eid 2018; Pearlman 2017; al-Haj Saleh 2017; Hisham and Crabapple 2018), and witness accounts are regularly published by newspapers and featured on television for audiences that reach beyond any specific city. It remains the case, however, that in cities there are libraries, theatres, cinemas, schools and universities, museums and other exhibition places, parks and market places. Moreover, we have a variety of cultural networks, political groups and volunteer groups, some of which might be welcoming to witnesses. Any of these can provide witnesses with infrastructures and other resources to help them make their voices heard, especially immediately after their arrival when they cannot yet draw on their own resources.

But what, if anything, is the point of bearing witness publicly by making use of the various spaces that cities have to offer? As we have said above, only personal relationships can treat the witnesses' testimony confidentially, and we can add to this that personal relationships also figure as an important source of moral acknowledgement. This seems to suggest that the place to bear witness should be within personal relationships alone. Moreover, it could be said that if public spaces such as theatres are not used for entertainment purposes, they serve at best some general interest of certain groups in being informed, including being informed about political developments around the world, while often selecting carefully for themselves what they want to hear. This raises the question of whether witnesses operating in the city's public spaces are not necessarily reduced to an instrumental role of an epistemic source serving the interests of the long-term city dwellers who habitually attend these spaces in their free time. Those who think that public witnessing is important must therefore make a good case that witnesses can be treated as ends in themselves and, most importantly, can gain something of moral importance for themselves from telling their story to others in public. I am sceptical that for all contexts in which witnesses currently have a voice such a case can be made. However, my initial discussion of *The Trip* suggests that there is at least the *potential* for public witnessing practices to realise a good in the required sense. Often, the prospect of seeing this good realised in a public space can be sufficient for witnesses to become active, provided of course that the witness is granted access to that space.

I think we better understand this good if we pay careful attention to the fact that moral acknowledgement of somebody's suffering and rightful struggle has many layers. It makes a difference whether one receives such acknowlededgement as an individual face-to-face from another individual with whom one is in some kind of personal relationship, or whether one receives it as a group from a wider social context that one's group is now embedded in. Perhaps the kind of acknowledgement one can gain from personal relationships has a certain depth. For instance, it can provide emotional security and a greater chance to be seen as the person one is, and these things cannot be provided in the same way by an encounter in public space. And yet one can have a very good friend or be in a well-functioning witnessing relationship and still suffer from lack of moral acknowledgement on a broader social level. There is something good in its own right in receiving moral acknowledgement on a social level. In other words, there is something good about such bearing witness *in virtue* of it being done publicly.

Avishai Margalit attributes to the figure whom he refers to as the 'moral witness' – a person who has knowledge-by-acquaintance of suffering inflicted on them by an evil regime – what he describes as a 'rather sober hope', namely 'that in another place or another time there exists, or will exist, a moral community that will listen to their testimony' (2002: 155).[10] A slightly more ambitious idea, it seems to me, manifests in the way movements of witnesses address the receiving society to enliven the public spaces in the cities that the witnesses arrive in. What we can often see here is the power of witnesses to *build* some kind of moral community, however fragmented the latter may remain. Addressing parts of the receiving society with one's testimony figures as a means to achieve such an aim in the here and now. It is a project that is less reliant on hope and an attitude of waiting, but has a decisively 'presentist' character, manifesting some admirable degree of confidence in the power of one's own action, the giving of testimony that calls for the moral acknowledgement of people who often share very little of the witness's experience, but may share the conviction that what has happened to the witness – torture or any of the injustices listed above – is deeply wrong, and that resisting in some way against any instance that commits such injustices against one is justified.

I use the term 'moral community' here tentatively as a name for the social achievement of moral acknowledgement of the suffering and rightful struggle of a group within a social context that extends that very group. As Margaret Urban Walker argued, denial of moral acknowledgement for a primary injury can amount to a form of harm in its own right, one that diminishes the prospects for moral repair (Walker 2006: 34ff.), and it can have a similar impact of adding insult to injury if one has to live exclusively around people who deny the rightfulness of one's liberatory struggle (partly because it implies denying suffering). Thus, refugees who have just arrived often assign particular significance to the prospect of receiving moral acknowledgement not just from anyone, but specifically from the receiving society in which they have yet to find their place. Some witnesses may take moral acknowledgement on a wider social scale to be a condition of becoming a genuine part of the new society. We should be able to understand this even if we are not affected by similar injustices. A society that remains ignorant of the suffering and struggle of one's group cannot truly become one's own. While it might be acceptable for some to live this way temporarily, the less likely it becomes that one will be able return to one's country of origin any time soon, the more the desire for moral acknowledgement increases.[11]

Since public spaces in cities at the time of a group of witnesses' arrival are primarily inhabited by elements of the receiving society, they are attractive sites for movements of witnesses to operate. On a certain basic level, they offer an opportunity to form new relationships. In fact, the reason why the two sites – personal relationships and public spaces – figure as sources of moral acknowledgement is precisely that, structurally, they are both about encounter and mutual address, which is the condition for any kind of moral acknowledgement to take place. In public spaces, too, the audience can (unlike, for instance, the readership of a newspaper) render itself to some extent visible to the witness in its role as good listeners. Think of a discussion panel where witnesses speak. Listeners' faces can often be seen, while facial expressions, such as grief and bewilderment upon listening to the witness's suffering, reflect back to the witness that some of what they are trying to convey through their testimony has been appropriately received. The process of the audience responding to the witnesses that they have understood some of their pain itself constitutes moral acknowledgement.

Moreover, while many people hesitate to express feelings of grief in public in the same way as they might express them in personal relationships (especially crying), public spaces can help place emphasis on the more positive emotions that can be just as important to any process of moral acknowledgement. As I have said above, testimony about injustices often includes testimony to a context of resistance. 'They have tortured me, but at least I never obeyed' can be listened to as an expression of pride. An audience's response of admiration would share with the witness's pride the same intentional object (the witness's strength in refusing to obey). Such expressions of admiration can be an important form of assurance regarding the appropriateness of the witness's pride, at times where the latter might be simultaneously going through all kinds of self-scrutinising emotions, including shame and guilt.[12] Admiration for the resistant self of the witness can be a form of moral acknowledgement just as important as the acknowledgement of suffering by way of the listener responding with sympathy. A one-sided diet, that is, an address in which the listener only shows sympathy, can at worst have effects on the witness that are additionally victimising.

Bearing witness in public can have another valuable effect that goes beyond the good that is potentially realised between witnesses and their direct audiences. In personal relationships that treat testimony confidentially, the practice of bearing witness tends only to affect those who are part of the relationship. By contrast, public witnessing amounts to a form of spreading the word, which can be a desirable consequence and so one at which witnesses might aim, despite the risk it may incur. Other people who have not attended the same event can hear about testimony through word of mouth, while journalists can report it. Even where it is not the testimony as such that spreads, the mere fact of a great number of city dwellers repeatedly hearing or reading about events featuring witnesses of a certain group may be valuable in itself. It can help a broader public to gain some humility, so as at least to refrain from judgement, and perhaps further to anticipate the real possibility that a group's story is of deep moral significance. Perhaps the good that movements of witnesses pursue by going public can be understood as one of inscribing their story, and ultimately the story of their group or people, on the consciousness of the city. Public witnessing contributes to the creation of a form of social memory with which at least some segments of the city can be successfully endowed. There can be something liberating about the creation of such social memory, as it comes with the potential of setting individuals free from the permanent requirement to engage in the cognitive and emotional activities of remembering a story on their own. As Hamdoun puts it, 'the stories of war have to be told. It is only afterwards that one can focus on other things.'[13]

Finally, the building of a moral community through bearing witness in various public spaces ideally informs the agenda of political groups, most importantly refugee support groups. Having been involved in activist and volunteer contexts in a German city when most of the Syrian refugees now living in the country arrived, it is my impression that part of the experience of those non-Syrians, mostly German state citizens, in my immediate context was of a systematic broadening of perspective by way of receiving the testimony of witnesses speaking at public events that have been organised on their initiative. For us it was the EU that let people drown in the Mediterranean, but for Syrian refugees it was also – sometimes primarily – Assad being guilty of yet another crime, of pushing innocent people into the sea, knowing that many of them would die. As the dominant majority in this encounter, with the material resources of media and political networks allowing our narrative to dominate, it took us some time to realise the urgency of bringing both perspectives together. It was the witnesses who had the idea of organising public panels and solidarity events where they would give their first-hand accounts of injustices and their struggle in their own country. It was their achievement that at least some of us began to realise that either we open up to their call for solidarity, or we become guilty of committing just another form of injustice against them.

This secondary injustice, consisting of us unilaterally determining which primary injustices ought to be addressed through political campaigns, must be taken much more seriously by activists and volunteers. 'Solidarity with refugees' becomes an empty slogan if the perspective of refugees is systematically ignored because one has already decided one's aims as a group. Rather, we should see public witnessing as a chance to redistribute the power of determining political urgency. I do not mean that currently established agendas do not tackle deep injustices that affect refugees. Many of them certainly do. But still they might fail to be inclusive enough and fail to be jointly decided upon. The resulting attitude of public encounters with witnesses should be one of opening up to the possibility that the already established agendas may have to be extended given the arrival of certain groups of refugees. They might find it important to receive some form of solidarity for their struggles against severe injustices taking place in their home countries as well.

In the end, the question of the right *practice* of solidarity is, of course, much more complex. If solidarity is supposed to be more than merely expressive, it has to address the relationship between movements of witnesses and the state. I have argued elsewhere that receiving states owe to refugee groups living on their territory some degree of assistance in overcoming severe injustices in their home country (Grahle 2017). Solidarity between movements of witnesses and established refugee support networks, but also between other public groups, journalists, politicians, etc., can pressurise the state into discharging its responsibility in this regard, for example by protesting against the state's inactivity.

Public pressure can be effective. While an International Criminal Tribunal in the case of Syria is currently unrealistic, states such as Germany and Spain adhere to the principle of universal jurisdiction, which allows the prosecution of war crimes and crimes against humanity committed in another territory (Kaleck and Kroker 2018). Together with the European Centre for Constitutional and Human Rights (ECCHR), a Berlin-based NGO, Syrian lawyers and former political prisoners Mazen Darwish and Anwar al-Bunni have filed a report against six high-profile members of the Syrian regime, based on the testimony of Syrian witnesses now living in Germany. At the time of writ-ing, the highest court in Germany has decided to take up the case and has issued an international arrest warrant against Jamil Hassan, a high-ranking member of the Assad regime allegedly complicit in the death of thousands of people exterminated in prisons. Moreover, two former secret service officers from the Syrian government have been arrested in Germany on allegations of, among other things, aiding and participating in crimes against humanity in connection with torture (Connolly 2019).

Before the decision was made to take up the case, public calls for such a step were frequent and clearly audible. Sections of the public, moreover, now attend the developments with increased attention. Tina Fuchs's documentary film entitled *Zeugen gegen Assad* (Witnesses against Assad) (2018), broad-cast by Germany's largest public broadcaster ARD, featured some of the witnesses speaking about their experience under Assad and their motivation to keep on fighting for justice in exile.[14] The project is an example of a new, extended moral community rising beyond more basic expressions of moral acknowledgement in the joint attempt to make a difference in political and juridical regards.

Conclusion: another reason for cities to be open

The moral significance of the good to be realised by bearing witness in the city's public spaces strongly suggests that identifying witnesses might actu-ally have a moral right to be granted access to these public spaces. Corre-spondingly, it could be argued that the receiving society, including the state, has a duty to provide the structural conditions under which movements of witnesses can operate sufficiently freely, by avoiding interference and by organising public spaces in cities. These claims would need more philosophi-cal argument, but they are plausible enough to end this chapter with a few brief thoughts about them.

The idea is not that members of the receiving society have a duty to seek witnesses and convince them to speak. Clearly, this would be patronising: it would amount to a moral community appropriating the witnesses, rather than providing the witnesses with an opportunity to form their own moral community in exile. People should be free to determine when and how to address the new society with their testimony. This said, a duty to grant access to public spaces is no less demanding. It would at a very minimum prohibit the enforced segregation that prevents witnesses from participating in city life, which in turn prevents them from encountering members of the receiv-ing society in the first place. Therefore, the value of being able to address the receiving society with one's testimony establishes yet another argument against the current status quo of accommodating, or at worst imprisoning, refugees in camps or in remote areas of the city. Moreover, sharing public space requires more than ending directly exclusionary tendencies such as geographical segregation. It requires positive social effort: positive arrangements of sharing material resources, time and organisational effort in mutually respectful ways.

Apart from that, it is important to note that public spaces can only fulfil their purpose for witnesses if they are enlivened. More precisely, they must be spaces where people attend to each other's activities in mutually beneficial ways. Only under the conditions of witnesses receiving a sufficient amount of the right kind of attention is moral acknowledgement possible. If the duty of the receiving society is to grant witnesses access to this complex good of enlivened public spaces, discharging the duty may require significant effort in improving the social competences of virtuous listening. Questions such as how to listen appropriately to witnesses in a certain context, how to avoid reproducing epistemic injustices through continuously basing one's listening on prejudices that prevent one from granting the witness sufficient credibility (Fricker 2007: 244) and which kinds of emotions ought to be cultivated in listening to witnesses (Grahle n.d.) become relevant here.

There is, furthermore, the question of how to prevent forms of silencing, some of which need not involve direct censorship or explicit exclusion of witnesses from panels and the like. Rae Langton (1993: 315), for example, argues that the mere fact of being intimidated or believing that no one will listen anyway can cause a powerless group to remain silent. A more subtle form of silencing occurs when witnesses feel pressured into holding back their voice about certain issues, but are encouraged to speak about others. Syrian witnesses who have knowledge from experience of the tyranny of both the Assad regime and ISIS still sometimes have reason to fear an ignorant audience's suspicion, according to which giving testimony about their experience of the former implies some subtle preference for the latter. Needless to say, becoming the target of such suspicion can be extremely risky for refugees. This can cause them to bear witness only to the crimes of ISIS, with the effect of being silenced as witnesses of the crimes of the Assad regime. These cases could be understood as instances of what Kristie Dotson has called *testimonial smothering*, which is 'the truncating of one's own testimony in order to insure that the testimony contains only content for which one's audience demonstrates testimonial competence' (2011: 244).

The purpose of this chapter has been to draw attention to the general status of refugees as witnesses and to point out some central aspects of the good of bearing witness in public spaces. I have argued that this good consists of the prospect of forming some form of moral community by way of calling on parts of the receiving society to provide for some degree of moral acknowledgement of one's suffering and the rightfulness of liberatory struggle. I have also suggested that public witnessing can be a way of inscribing one's story on the consciousness of one's new city. It can be a contribution to the construction of some kind of social memory. Finally, I have argued that the practice of bearing witness can prevent refugee support groups from committing the secondary injustice of unilaterally determining which primary injustices are to be struggled against. Refugee support groups must keep their doors open and be ready to adjust their previously established political agendas in accordance with the communicated needs of newly arriving refugees.[15]

Notes

1. When I speak of the worst displacement crisis since the Second World War I mean the greatest *number* of displaced people since then, according to a UNHCR (2015) report.
2. See, for example, Amnesty International's (2015) report on enforced disappearance, and the United Nations Human Rights Council's (2016) report on torture as a means of extermination. For a report on the use of starvation as a war tactic, see the report of the Independent International Commission of Inquiry on the Syrian Arab Republic (2018a). For a report on sexual and gender-based violence, see the document of the same commission (2018b). Public denial of war crimes and mockery of the victims, in turn, has taken place on innumerable occasions. Even researchers working at Western universities have been accused of this (Ahmad 2018).
3. The passive character of witnessing, in combination with the fact that witnessing another person's devastation can itself be devastating, also means that the deliberate rendering of people into witnesses, as when an inmate is forced to witness the torture of another, can be harmful in its own right.
4. There is a link between witnessing and accountability, which also highlights the ambivalence of perpetrators' rendering of people witnesses with an intention of harming them. It can be risky for them to use this weapon.
5. Notice that I say only 'often' here. This leaves open the possibility of cases in which witnessing is confined to the passive element of registering that an injustice happened to oneself or to others, but it also allows for cases in which the impact of a traumatic event prevents people from properly registering it.
6. Jean Améry (1980: 39) describes the time after an episode of torture as having 'the urge to articulate the experience [of torture] intellectually, right away, on the spot, without losing the least bit of time'.
7. The kind of art emerging from al-Bukai's memory, though clearly informed by dreamful perception, does not transfigure reality. Rather, it makes clear to outsiders the incomprehensible degree of devastation behind the scenes, by giving rise to the thought that 'I still haven't seen reality, but what I see is terrifying. If this is a dream, then what must reality be like?' Now living in exile, al-Bukai travels through France in an effort to raise awareness about the conditions in Syria's torture dungeons.
8. The phenomenon of witnesses being endowed with a strong desire to bear witness is, of course, not confined to the context of recent refugee arrival. Primo Levi, for example, mentioned 'a need, a physiological need to break free from my experience by telling the story' (2001: 162). It should be noted, moreover, that the desire to bear witness can coexist with a number of countervailing desires *not*

to give one's testimony, because of a sense of the impossibility of communicating the scale of what happened, or because recalling one's testimony is anticipated as extremely painful (Oliver 2001: 102). There can be many obstacles to bearing witness, each of which deserves careful examination, but this discussion would go beyond the scope of this chapter.

9. I have heard versions of this more than once in conversation with refugees who have recently arrived in Europe. See also Laub (1992: 78).

10. I believe that Margalit's notion of a moral witness is in some other respects unnecessarily narrow, but that does not matter with regard to my arguments here.

11. I thank Ameen Nasir for discussing this point with me.

12. In another paper (Grahle 2019) I argue that expressions of justified admiration for an agent can amount to forms of support for that agent, including what I call *epistemic support*, akin to the above phenomenon.

13. This is my translation of a quote in Marcus (2016b), incorporated with Hamdoun's renewed approval.

14. The film has also been made temporarily available with Arabic subtitles through the broadcaster's website.

15. I am grateful to philosophical audiences at the universities of Osnabrück, York, Göttingen, Bochum, Bielefeld, UCD, HU Berlin and LMU Munich for valuable discussions of different parts of this chapter. Most importantly, however, I would like to thank Anis Hamdoun for discussing his play *The Trip* with me on numerous occasions, as well as for providing me with the manuscript at an early stage. I have, moreover, benefited from discussion with the actors of *The Trip* at Theater Osnabrück in summer 2015 and would like to thank Maria Schneider for inviting me. The term 'movement of witnesses' originates from the title of a panel on artistic testimony that I co-organised with Ma'an Mouslli for the Goethe-Institut Damascus in Exile, a series of events that took place in Berlin in 2016. I would like to thank Ulrike Gasser and Marina May for the invitation, as well as the participants in the panel, Zaina Erhaim, Zainab Alsawah, Nawar Bulbul, Sana Yazigi and Ma'an Mouslli for what I experienced as a very thought-provoking and instructive discussion. Ma'an Mouslli is to be thanked more generally for our ongoing conversation on the ethics of giving and receiving testimony in the country of arrival. Our joint projects have inspired many of the thoughts and observations in this chapter, though, of course, I am alone to blame for any errors. Last but not least, for comments and discussion I would like to thank Melanie Altanian, Monika Betzler, Christine Bratu, Sam Durrant, Anca Gheaus, Hilkje Hänel, Jan-Christoph Heilinger, Sara Höweler, Amahl Khouri, James Camien McGuiggan, Isabel Kaeslin, Natasha McKeever, Corinna Mieth, Ameen Nasir, Maria Neunteufel, Konrad Siller, Joe Saunders, Martin Sticker, Michaela Rehm, Ahmed Saleh, Anna Wehofsits, Verina Wild, and Kerri Woods.

Bibliography

Ahmad, Muhammad Idrees (2018), 'Syria: on academic freedom and responsibility', *Open Democracy*, 26 April, https://www.opendemocracy.net/north-africa-west-asia/muhammad-idrees-ahmad/syria-on-academic-freedom-and-responsibility (accessed 15 May 2019).

al-Haj Saleh, Yassin (2017), *Impossible Revolution – Making Sense of the Syrian Tragedy* (London: Hurst Publishers).

Alami, Aida (2018), 'Haunted by memories of Syrian torture, saved by art', *New York Times*, 2 February, https://www.nytimes.com/2018/02/02/world/middleeast/syria-torture-artist-najah-al-bukai.html (accessed 15 May 2019).

Améry, Jean (1980), *At the Mind's Limits – Contemplations by a Survivor on Auschwitz and its Realities*, trans. Sidney Rosenfeld and Stella P. Rosenfeld (Bloomington: Indiana University Press).

Amnesty International (2015), *Between Prison and the Grave – Enforced Disappearances in Syria*, https://www.amnesty.org/download/Documents/MDE2425792015ENGLISH.PDF (accessed 15 May 2019).

Connolly, Kate (2019), 'Germany arrests two Syrians suspected of crimes against humanity', *The Guardian*, 13 February, https://www.theguardian.com/world/2019/feb/13/germany-arrests-two-suspected-syrian-secret-service-officers (accessed 2 July 2019).

Dotson, Kristie (2011), 'Tracking epistemic violence, tracking practices of silencing', *Hypatia*, 26.2: 236–57.

Eid, Kassam (2018), *My Country – A Syrian Memoir* (London: Bloomsbury).

Frankfurt, Harry (1982), 'The importance of what we care about', *Synthese*, 53: 257–72.

Fricker, Miranda (2007), *Epistemic Injustice – Power and the Ethics of Knowing* (Oxford: Oxford University Press).

Grahle, André (n.d.), 'Two Levels of Solidarity: Witnessing Relationships and Responsibility to Act', unpublished manuscript.

Grahle, André (2017), 'Gerechtigkeit für Syrien', in Joachim Helfer, Marco Meyer and Klaus Wettig (eds), *Wenn ich mir etwas wünschen dürfte – Intellektuelle zur Bundestagswahl 2017* (Göttingen: Steidl Verlag), 71–80.

Grahle, André (2019), 'Admiration as normative support', in Alfred Archer and André Grahle, *The Moral Psychology of Admiration* (New York: Rowman and Littlefield), 149–63.

Hisham, Marwan, and Molly Crabapple (2018), *Brothers of the Gun: A Memoir of the Syrian War* (New York: One World).

Independent International Commission of Inquiry on the Syrian Arab Republic (2018a), 'Sieges as a weapon of war – encircle, starve, surrender, evacuate', https://www.ohchr.org/Documents/HRBodies/HRCouncil/CoISyria/PolicyPaperSieges_29May2018.pdf (accessed 15 May 2019).

Independent International Commission of Inquiry on the Syrian Arab Republic (2018b), '"I lost my dignity": sexual and gender-based violence in the Syrian Arab Republic', https://www.ohchr.org/Documents/HRBodies/HRCouncil/CoISyria/AHRC-37-CRP-3.pdf (accessed 15 May 2019).

Kaleck, Wolfgang, and Patrick Kroker (2018), 'Syrian torture investigations in Germany and beyond – breathing new life into universal jurisdiction in Europe?', *Journal of International Criminal Justice*, 16: 165–91.

Langton, Rae (1993), 'Speech acts and unspeakable acts', *Philosophy and Public Affairs*, 22.4: 293–330.

Laub, Dori (1992), 'An event without a witness: truth, testimony, and survival', in Shoshana Felman and Dori Laub, *Testimony – Crises of Witnessing in Literature, Psychoanalysis and History* (New York: Routledge), 75–92.

Le Caisne, Garance (2015), *Opération César – Au cœur de la machine de mort syrienne* (Paris: Editions Stock).

Levi, Primo (2001), *The Voice of Memory – Interviews 1961–1987*, ed. Marco Belpoliti and Robert Gordon, trans. Robert Gordon (Cambridge: Polity Press).

Marcus, Dorothea (2016a), 'Ratlosigkeit des Überlebens', *die tageszeitung*, 8 April, http://www.taz.de/!5293536/ (accessed 15 May 2019).

Marcus, Dorothea (2016b), 'Weg vom Leidens-Porno', Goethe-Institut, https://www.goethe.de/ins/my/de/kul/mag/20824640.html (accessed 15 May 2019).

Margalit, Avishai (2002), *The Ethics of Memory* (Cambridge, MA: Harvard University Press).

Meiborg, Mounia (2016), 'Mann, ich bin Flüchtling', *Süddeutsche Zeitung*, 6 April, https://www.sueddeutsche.de/kultur/portraet-mann-ich-bin-fluechtling-1.2936855 (accessed 15 May 2019).

Oliver, Kelly (2001), *Witnessing – Beyond Recognition* (Minneapolis: University of Minnesota Press).

Pearlman, Wendy (2017), *We Crossed a Bridge and It Trembled: Voices from Syria* (New York: Costum House).

Schmitt, Uwe (2016), 'Wütend-poetisches Stück über Syriens ermordete Träume', *Die Welt*, 23 January, https://www.welt.de/kultur/theater/article151376242/Wuetend-poetisches-Stueck-ueber-Syriens-ermordete-Traeume.html (accessed 15 May 2019).

UNHCR (2015), *Global Trends – Forced Displacement in 2015*, http://www.unhcr.org/576408cd7 (accessed 15 May 2019).

United Nations Human Rights Council (2016), 'Out of sight, out of mind: deaths in detention in the Syrian Arab Republic', A/HRC/31/CRP.1, https://www.ohchr.org/Documents/HRBodies/HRCouncil/CoISyria/A-HRC-31-CRP1_en.pdf (accessed 15 May 2019).

Walker, Margaret Urban (2006), *Moral Repair – Reconstructing Moral Relations after Wrongdoing* (Oxford: Oxford University Press).

Yazbek, Samar (2015), *Die gestohlene Revolution – Reise in mein zerstörtes Syrien*, ed. Larissa Bender (Zurich: Verlag Nagel and Kimche).

Chapter 32

Open/Closed Cities: Cosmopolitan Melancholia and the Disavowal of Refugee Life

Sam Durrant

It has long been recognised that nationalism is predicated on structures of disavowal, on a strategic forgetting of those aspects of a national culture that interrupt the purity of its nostalgic self-image. Cosmopolitanism has often been posited as an antidote to this disavowal, as a way of rendering the nation-state more open both to internal and external difference. But what if cosmopolitanism itself turned out to be structured by occlusions and disavowals, what if its posture of openness turned out to hide internal exclusions that render certain lives and deaths unavowable and hence ungrievable? My thesis is that the unfreedom of the refugee is the melancholy shadow at the heart of cosmopolitan freedom, that the cosmopolitan world-view is reliant on structures of global privilege that function to occlude the refugee's experience of destitution.

In psychic terms, refugee experience is encrypted within cosmopolitan consciousness as a disavowed memory of loss. Exceeding individual histories, this memory is as much historical as it is personal: statelessness is an ever-present threat or potentiality, a loss of status and rights that is always happening to someone and that some day, any day, may happen to you or me. What is unavowable here is the vulnerability not of the stateless but of the citizen, the possibility of her own potential ejection from the realm of privilege. The precarity of refugee life is unavowable for cosmopolitanism precisely because it threatens to reveal the precarity of the citizenship which underwrites cosmopolitan privilege, the ease with which, as Hannah Arendt and Giorgio Agamben have underlined, a citizen can become a non-citizen (Arendt 1943; Agamben 2008). And beyond this disavowal of the refugee as the unassimilable image of the citizen's own vulnerability, refugee life is also disavowed because the cosmopolitan's lifestyle is sustained by local and global structures of exploitation that never cease turning other citizens into non-citizens: regardless of the cosmopolitan's desire to open herself to the world, she is implicated in statelessness simply by virtue of belonging to a bordered state. This double disavowal of vulnerability and implication simultaneously binds and blinds cosmopolitanism to refugee life.

My debt to the work of Judith Butler throughout this essay will be obvious. In *Frames of War: When is Life Grievable?*, she writes: 'An ungrievable life is one that cannot be mourned because it has never lived, that is, it has never counted as a life at all' (2009: 38). Her project, as I read it, is to render such lives grievable by insisting on what she describes as our 'common corporeal vulnerability' (Butler 2004: 42). While such a desire is, of course, admirable, there is a danger that rendering refugee life grievable turns the refugee into the transparent, pathos-laden object of humanitarian concern without disturbing the structures of privilege that continue both to produce and occlude statelessness. I obstinately insist on the non-grievability of refugee life in the hope that we might turn cosmopolitan melancholia into a critical awareness of cosmopolitanism's structural limits, a shift that I describe as critical cosmopolitan melancholia. This slightly ungainly locution is meant to signal that there is no Archimedean position outside cosmopolitanism from which we might encounter the refugee on her own terms, that the best we can hope for is an auto-critical account of the vexed relation between cosmopolitanism and refugee life.

In what follows, I compare the self-evident disavowals that structure the exclusionary discourses of nationalism with the less evident disavowals that structure the seemingly inclusionary discourses of cosmopolitanism. I then distinguish between a normative, liberal cosmopolitanism that disavows its own limits in its assumption that refugee life is knowable and hence mournable and a melancholic cosmopolitanism for which refugee life remains ungrievable. In the second section I offer a brief analysis of how cosmopolitanism has fallen out of favour in postcolonial studies, comparing Homi Bhabha's cosmopolitan critique of nationalism (1990) with Simon Gikandi's critique of postcolonialism as a form of cosmopolitan elitism that has 'nothing in common' with refugee life (2010). Gikandi's performance of postcolonialism's non-relation to the refugee prepares the way for my third and final section, a reading of Teju Cole's extraordinary 2011 novel *Open City*, as an example of how refugee life is encrypted within cosmopolitan privilege: while the narrator, Julius, displays all the aphasic symptoms of cosmopolitan melancholia, the novel itself is an exercise in *critical* cosmopolitan melancholia in so far as it exposes the disavowed (and in this case, transgenerational) memory of 'absolute destitution' (Cole 2011: 80) at the heart of Julius's life of privilege and his violently gendered implication in the unworlding of others. The proper role of cosmopolitan aesthetics is thus, I argue, not simply to solicit sympathy for the plight of the refugee but to effect an auto-critical exposure of cosmopolitanism's implication in the global structures of oppression and exclusion that produce statelessness.

Structures of disavowal: from national to cosmopolitan melancholia

Ernst Renan famously argued that 'forgetting is a crucial factor in the creation of a nation' (Renan 1990: 11). Nationalism depends upon a collective script that leaves out anything that threatens to disrupt the fragile unity of the nation's history. This amnesia can all too easily translate itself into xenophobia. The rise of Trump, Brexit and other populist anti-immigration movements constitute belated attempts to preserve the unity of the nation by erecting various defences against the outside, from economic protectionism to tightened border controls and the expulsion of those unable to prove their right to remain.

The present wave of British nationalism is a mutation of what Paul Gilroy once diagnosed as post-imperial melancholia: 'The life of the nation has been dominated by an inability even to face, never mind actually mourn, the profound change in circumstances and moods that followed the end of Empire and consequent loss of imperial prestige' (2004: 98). This dangerous denial of Britain's implication in imperial structures of exploitation then makes it possible for a kind of imperial nostalgia to develop, evident in the Brexiteer slogan 'Make Britain Great Again', adapted from its US counterpart and curiously aphasic in relation to exactly what it was that made Britain great in the first place. While the racism of Empire is disavowed, racism directed towards those who have migrated to Britain from the ex-colonies is legitimated by a fear that Britain is losing its 'coherent and distinctive [white] culture' (Gilroy 2004: 98). The idea of a return to Britain's former greatness is only rendered compatible with the isolationism of the 'little Englander' by forgetting the expansive, even cosmopolitan, designs of empire.

This contradictory relation to the era of nation-state imperialism goes hand in hand with a disavowal of the present era of globalisation, in which the territorial sovereignty of the nation-state has been (at least partially) replaced by the deterritorialising sovereignty of capital (Hardt and Negri 2000). What Tabish Khair (2016) usefully dubs 'the new xenophobia' is coterminous with the era of finance capital. Just as capital itself now moves *invisibly* and without any border controls, the movement of labour has become increasingly *visible* and subject to various forms of control. Financial globalisation threatens national sovereignty and limits the ability of governments to defend their economies, but the anxiety generated by this increasing vulnerability is projected not on to capital but on to labour, on to the bodies whose movement is the symptom rather than cause of globalisation.

It is no coincidence that the financial crisis triggered by the 2007 banking collapse was closely followed by the so-called refugee crisis. While migrants and refugees are produced by a variety of factors, ranging from global economic inequities through to political and religious persecution, war, famine, the collapse of state infrastructures and environmental degradation, the 'refugee crisis' needs to be read as an affective phenomenon of Europe, or more broadly the Global North, a crisis that has as much to do with anxieties about national sovereignty in an era of globalisation as it does with any net increase in the actual numbers of migrants and people seeking asylum. Anxieties produced by the mobility of capital are displaced onto anxieties about the mobility of labour. Thus political arguments about the need to regain national sovereignty focus on controlling the movement of migrants as a way of disavowing the state's inability to protect its own citizens from the depradations of global capitalism. Agamben, parsing Arendt, notes that 'the citizens of advanced industrial states demonstrate . . . an evident propensity to turn into denizens, into noncitizen permanent residents, so that citizens and denizens – at least in certain social strata – are entering an area of potential indistinction' (2008: 94). It should come as no surprise that the Brexit campaign, like the Trump campaign, appealed most to those in this 'zone of indistinction', those in the lowest social strata, whose economic and political precarity renders them indistinct from the very migrants they voted to keep at bay (Becker, Fetzer and Novy 2017).

If contemporary nationalism is predicated on a complex series of disavowals, its cosmopolitan counterpart also contains its own lacunae. The first of these is the extent to which human rights law is radically dependent on the nation-state. Kant's 1795 declaration of a cosmopolitan law or right concerning the just treatment of strangers, a declaration that was later to inspire the 1948 Universal Declaration of Human Rights, must reach back into pre-history in order to make its claim: '*originally* no one had any greater right to any region of the earth than anyone else' (Kant 1983: 118, my italics). Once history begins, and especially the history of the nation-state, then questions of justice and hospitality become radically attenuated. The conditions of universal hospitality are subordinate to the laws of sovereignty, such that the stranger, even for Kant, may lay claim only to 'the right to temporary sojourn', a right to a non-hostile reception that can itself be waived 'if it can be done without destroying him' (Kant 1983: 118).

These limits to hospitality are at the bottom of cosmopolitan melancholia. Cosmopolitanism's sense of responsibility for others inevitably tips over into an irreducible or originary guilt. Not only is the hospitality one might offer to another necessarily limited, but there will be always be other others to whom one might have offered hospitality: 'Guilt is inherent in responsibility because responsibility is always unequal to itself: one is never responsible enough' (Derrida 1995: 51). Fortress Europe predictably turns this originary guilt into an alibi for inhospitality. The state's resources, we are repeatedly told, are finite, and even if we accept this or that stranger's right to asylum, then there will always be others whose entrance we must refuse – indeed, the more asylum seekers we accept, runs the logic, the more will come. Liberal cosmopolitans can critique this cynical bad faith, but they can never quite escape what Roberto Esposito describes as the 'constitutively melancholic character of community'

(2013: 30), generated by the gap between the impulse towards openness and the necessarily limited nature of any given instantiation of community.

The paradigmatically cosmopolitan space of the city thus swings compulsively between openness and closedness. As Esposito argues, the *polis* emerges from the twin impulses of *communitas* and *immunitas*. The Latin word *munus* refers the self outside of itself to an infinite 'debt, duty or obligation' to others (Esposito 2013: 3): communities are *com* (with) *munus*, formed through a common recognition of this *munus*. But communities are also formed through a negation of this *munus*, a limiting of those to whom one has an obligation or duty. Passing from the original Latin legal understanding of immunity as immunity from prosecution or taxes to the late nineteenth-century medical understanding of immunity as the ability to protect the organism from contagion, immunity comes to signify a defence system necessary to the survival of community, a system designed to protect the body politic from foreign bodies always already understood to be harmful, even while biological immunity is often paradoxically achieved through inoculation, through the controlled intake of foreign matter.

Nationalism can be readily understood as a hostile immune reaction, as an attempt to close down the borders of the body politic. But what if cosmopolitanism were also a kind of immune reaction, an attempt to present oneself as open to the world precisely in order to immunise oneself against the traumatic knowledge of cosmopolitanism's own structural inadequacy? Cosmopolitanism here becomes a mode of self-styling that wards off the traumatic knowledge of others' suffering precisely by producing a self-image of humanitarian engagement. The classically cosmopolitan figure of the philanthropist works to mask implication in the very suffering it seeks to relieve.

The reaction of those who voted 'remain' to the result of the Brexit referendum pitted the cosmopolitanism of city dwellers against the assumed parochialism and xenophobia of those who inhabited small towns and villages. There was even a brief 'Londependence' movement that sought to disaffiliate from the rest of the country (despite the fact that all of the UK's major cities voted, often by narrow margins, to remain). Theresa May's speech of 4 October 2016 in turn sought to disaffiliate Britain from the cosmopolitan ideal: 'But if you believe you're a citizen of the world, you're a citizen of nowhere. You don't understand what the very word "citizenship" means' (May 2016). Jem Eskenazi wrote to the *Financial Times* in protest:

> Anybody with an ounce of intelligence understands that climate change, pollution or epidemics know no frontiers, that extreme poverty in one region has stability implications for the whole world; that terrorism is a global problem with global solutions; that wars are not started by citizens of the world but narrow-minded people with a blind belief of [*sic*] their superiority; that some of the greatest minds in any society are descendants of immigrants and refugees. (Eskenazi 2016)

Citing a poll in which more than half of Britain 'saw themselves more as global citizens than a citizen of [their] country', Eskenazi protested that May had rendered half the UK population citizens of nowhere.

The problem with Eskenazi's response, like that of the Londependence movement, is that he speaks from within an uninterrogated position of cosmopolitan privilege, as a *beneficiary* of globalisation.[1] It should come as no surprise that Eskenazi is an international banker. As Craig Calhoun points out, capitalism is itself a form of cosmopolitanism and liberal versions of cosmopolitanism do little to challenge either local or global inequities (Calhoun 2003). Eskenazi positions himself against the 'narrow-minded people' who would deny entry to immigrants and refugees, but his pragmatic call for 'global solutions' stops short of a critique of global capitalism. His protest is that the Prime Minister has disenfranchised people such as himself who think in global terms, but this complaint erases, in a characteristically cosmopolitan gesture, the traces of those who are truly disenfranchised by the forces of globalisation.

Calhoun is part of a twenty-first-century wave of critics for whom cosmopolitanism is implicated in globalisation and thus in structures of global inequality.[2] Cosmopolitanism consistently overlooks the intractable inequities of class. As Bruce Robbins bluntly puts it, 'cosmopolitanism as it is currently conceived has to do with a "receptive and open attitude towards the other" . . . it does not have to do with economic redistribution between rich and poor' (2017a: 41). There has been a series of attempts to articulate non-elite forms of cosmopolitanism, ranging from Homi Bhabha's 'vernacular cosmopolitanism' (1996) though to Paul Gilroy's 'convivial cosmopolitanism' (2004) and Silviano Santiago's 'cosmopolitanism of the poor' (2017). But these qualified forms of cosmopolitanism necessarily abandon the universal aspirations of cosmopolitanism, introducing the antagonisms of class and race that cosmopolitanism, as the Kantian precondition for world peace, must necessarily disavow.

As a universal aspiration, the fall from idealism to disillusion is pre-programmed into cosmopolitan thought. In an unpublished article entitled 'About the End of the World: Towards a Cosmopolitanism of Loss' Mariano Siskind performs this manic flip, replacing the optimistic claims of his 2014 book *Cosmopolitan Desires: Global Modernity and World Literature in Latin America* with the apocalyptic pessimism signalled by the title of his latest essay. Siskind argues that cosmopolitanism has lost its horizon of hope: all that remains is for cosmopolitans to mourn this loss of hope, or what he describes as the loss of the world itself, the loss of our capacity to imaginatively world ourselves either in the present or the future. He goes on to prescribe a generalised mourning work, a mournful melancholia by which we might 'stay with' our loss of world.

Siskind comes close to acknowledging my sense of the encrypted relation between cosmopolitanism and the refugee in his development of Kristeva's notion of the stranger within. He speaks of 'the refugee in me as the ungrasp-able, opaque unconscious that constitutes me as a subject of loss, the end of the world as the wound that splits me, but also as the super-ego's impos-sible demand to do something about it, about the suffering that structures the non-world'. However, Siskind ultimately wants to undo Freud's opposi-tion between mourning and melancholia, while I want to insist on the classi-cally melancholic or structurally unavowable nature of the relation between the cosmopolitan and the refugee. As Abraham and Torok famously argued (1986), whereas mourning is a process of self-expansion through the introjec-tion or metaphorisation of lost love objects (expansive in the sense that we transform the other into an assimilable memory), melancholia is a process of self-partition in which the other is incorporated within the subject as if within a crypt: no metaphorisation or symbolisation takes place that would allow the loss to be acknowledged and worked through. Instead 'cryptic incorporation marks an effect of failed or impossible mourning' (Derrida 1986a: xxi).

Liberal cosmopolitanism can be described as operating according to the logic of introjection: an expansion of the self that constructs the refugee as a grievable, digestible object of pathos (e.g. Nussbaum 1998). What I am calling melancholic cosmopolitanism refuses this process of grieving, swal-lowing the refugee whole but in so doing setting up a cryptic space within the self where the refugee remains unmourned, undigested. For Derrida, this refusal of mourning is not simply pathological, as it was, at least initially, for Freud, but also has the potential to be ethical in so far as it respects the unknowability or 'infinite remove' of the other (1986b: 6). Derrida asks:

> Is the most distressing, or even deadly infidelity that of a possible mourning which would interiorize within us the image, idol or ideal of the dead and lives only in us? Or is it that of the impossible mourning, which, leaving the other his alterity, respecting thus his infinite remove, either refuses to take or is inca-pable of taking the other within oneself, as in the tomb or vault of narcissism. (1986b: 6)

Much of the literature written in response to the refugee crisis is an imagi-native interiorisation or introjection of the refugee into the realm of life.[3] Here we seem to get more or less direct access to refugee experience and the refugee seems to be included in the realm of grievable life by virtue of her common humanity or sameness. Such literature is laudable in many ways, but it has the unfortunate effect of overwriting Arendt's insistence on the refugee's exceptionality, her historical emergence as 'a new kind of human being' whose non-citizenship leaves her without access to the realm of human rights, except by assimilation within a new regime of citizenship – in which case she is no longer a refugee (Arendt 1978). To recover the refugee as the fully human subject of human rights is to deny the ever-increasing numbers of people who live and die in the various states of inhuman limbo on which earlier sections of this volume have focused. An aesthetic response that wishes to remain faithful to Arendt and to statelessness itself needs to register the refugee as that which remains *constitutively ungrievable*, as the non-citizen whose fate forever shadows the life of the citizen.

Everything depends, then, on whether or not the artwork is able to register this shadow: cosmopolitan melancholia remains pathological in so far as it is unable to register refugee life but potentially ethical if is able to recognise its own failure of registration. And this self-critical recognition acquires a specifically political valency if it can recognise the way in which its failure of registration is produced by the structures of state formation and global capital that underwrite the privileged lifestyle of the cosmopolitan and occlude the lives of the stateless. Following Ranjana Khanna's work on critical melancholia (2003), I describe this second form of awareness as *critical cosmopolitan melancholia*.

In my final section I will turn to Teju Cole's novel *Open City* (2011) as an exemplary instantiation of cosmopolitan melancholia, pathological at the level of a narrator who remains aphasic in relation to his class and gender privilege, but politically salutary, or critical, at the level of the novel itself, which exposes the aporias of the narrator and maps out the cryptological relation between cosmopolitan privilege and the destitution of the refugee. However, before I embark on this analysis, I want briefly to explore how, within my own discipline of postcolonial studies, cosmopolitanism has increasingly become the object of critique. More specifically, I want to trace how the postcolonial project has morphed from a cosmopolitan critique of imperial melancholia into an auto-critique of cosmopolitanism itself.

Baleful postcoloniality

As Calhoun notes, 9/11 and the subsequent war on terror 'made the cosmopolitan ideals articulated during the 90s all the more attractive but their realization much less imminent' (2003: 87). A 2013 special issue of the journal *Biography* usefully summed up our contemporary moment as the era of 'baleful postcoloniality', taking the adjective from Fredric Jameson's analysis of the effects and affects of late capitalism. Simon Gikandi's essay, 'Routes and Roots', published in 2010, a year before *Open City*, is very much of this baleful moment, a moment that was only to grow more baleful with the escalation of the so-called refugee crisis and the defensive responses that followed in its wake. Gikandi's (self-)critique offers a striking contrast to Homi Bhabha's (in)famous essay 'DissemiNation' (1990), published twenty years earlier in that late or post-Thatcherite moment when oppositional or minoritarian forms of cosmopolitan community seemed much more viable.

For Bhabha, as for Gilroy, melancholia is a nationalist formation that has to do with the disavowal of (the loss of) empire, a melancholia that can be alleviated by a 'vernacular cosmopolitanism' that functions to force acknowledgement of Britain's imperial history and hybridise national culture (Bhabha 1996), or by the 'convivial cosmopolitanism' produced when 'mundane encounters with difference become rewarding' (Gilroy 2004: 75). By contrast, for Gikandi, cosmopolitanism itself appears as a melancholic formation, one that needs to recognise its own implication in structures of privilege and exclusion. The point is not that nationalism is no longer a melancholic formation but that the cosmopolitan position from which postcolonialists have sought to critique nationalism also turns out to be melancholic, cryptic and structured by disavowal.

Bhabha's intoxicated identification of himself as one of the migrants who have lived 'that moment of scattering . . . that in other times and other places, in the nations of others, becomes a time of gathering' (1990: 291) occludes his own privilege as an academic soon to leave Britain for the wealth of the private US university. Gikandi, by contrast, recognises the gulf between his own privilege as an African-born but US-based postcolonial academic and the unprivilege of the refugee. Bhabha famously presents the migrant as 'the mote in the eye of history, its blind spot that will not let the nationalist gaze settle centrally' (1990: 318). Gikandi, in a phrasing that silently adapts Bhabha's formulation, presents refugees as 'a mote in the eye of cosmopolitanism' (2010: 23). This shift is a striking index of the fate of cosmopolitanism in postcolonial studies. Bhabha celebrates the capacity of the worldly migrant to undo the parochial nationalism of the metropole. For Gikandi, cosmopolitanism is no longer a sign of subaltern community, but an elitist sign of non-community. While Bhabha's migrant actively *decrypts* nationalist melancholia in order to produce a more inclusive sense of community, Gikandi's refugee remains an encrypted, unreadable figure, excluded by cosmopolitanism's inability to undo the structures of privilege by which it is constituted.

Bhabha's essay ends with a partial reading of Salman Rushdie's *The Satanic Verses* (1988), in which an Indian film producer claims that 'the trouble with the English is that their history happened overseas, so they don't know what it means' (Rushdie, quoted in Bhabha 1990: 343). The migrant is the return of this disavowed history, and Gibreel, a Bollywood movie star, takes it upon himself to incarnate, or *weaponise*, this return: 'These powerless English! – Did they not think their history would return to haunt them? "The native is an oppressed person whose permanent dream is to become the persecutor" (Fanon). He would make this land anew. He was the Archangel Gibreel – *And I'm back*' (Rushdie, quoted in Bhabha 1990: 319). Bhabha fails to see that this dream of revenge remains just that, a dream, a hallucination. Gibreel's revenge is curiously benign – the cosmopolitanisation of Englishness takes the improbably *comic* form of a heatwave that Gibreel imagines will (among other things) banish British reserve, elongate love-making and improve footballers' close control (Rushdie 1988: 355). Britain does indeed experience a heatwave, but Rushdie's novel has a darker, more melancholic side that Bhabha's essay overlooks. Gibreel's hallucinations lead, as Fanon warns, to psychosis and he eventually commits suicide in a bid to escape his visions, while his double Chamcha gives up on his attempt to become a naturalised Englishman and returns home to India. The migrant remains encrypted and disavowed by the metropolis and the dream of minority cosmopolitanism remains an unrealised fantasy.

The ensuing *fatwah* issued by the Ayatollah Khomeni in 1989 did not, of course, lead to any further decryption. Rushdie found himself the spokesperson for liberal cosmopolitanism and democratic values, while a civilisational gap appeared to open between the West and the East, fuelled by Samuel Huntingdon's thesis concerning the clash of civilisations (1993). The migrant suddenly gets overcoded as parochial, anti-modern and Muslim, as threat to Enlightenment values and, eventually, as terrorist, while cosmopolitanism morphs into an aggrieved mode of defending Western values. In this sense *The Satanic Verses* is unwittingly prophetic: Gibreel's dreams of flying over London enacting the revenge of the native stands as a compelling augury of the attacks of 9/11 and 7/7, of 'blowback' and the subsequent 'war on terror'. The oxymoronic nature of this latter phrase and its bizarre assumption of the moral high ground continues to disavow the terror of colonial history. Sivanadam's celebrated aphorism, 'we are here because you were there', needs to be updated in the light of the wars in Iraq, Afghanistan, Libya and Syria, and the various depradations of global capital that have rendered so many parts of the world uninhabitable 'death-worlds' (Mbembe 2003): we are here because you *have never ceased* to be there.

The war on terror, the financial crash and the emerging refugee crisis all contribute to Gikandi's melancholic relation to community. While Bhabha begins his essay with his own performative inscription into cosmopolitan community, Gikandi sets himself apart, positioning himself more critically as a would-be postcolonial *flâneur*, whose cosmopolitan identification with the crowd is only a pose, a delusional act of bad faith:

> In a single afternoon, strolling down the streets of the cities that I love, Nairobi, Johannesburg, Accra, I pretend to be the postcolonial flaneur [. . .] But when I board the BA flight to London and New York, I find myself in the strange company of Somali, Ethiopian and Sudanese refugees under the sponsorship of Refugees International and other charities. These are the outcasts of the civil wars in Eastern Africa and they are encountering the modern metropolis for the first time. Beneath the new garbs provided by international charities, they carry with them the look and feel of the countryside and this is what brings out the simple truth that my liberal sensibilities find hard to countenance. *I have nothing in common with these people*; we do not share a common critical discourse or set of cultural values. They are not the postcolonials with whom I have spent the last weeks, but strangers caught in the cracks of the failed state. (Gikandi 2010: 22, my italics)

The opposition Gikandi sets up between the cosmopolitan and the refugee, city and country, is hyperbolic, disavowing the possibility of cosmopolitan refugees and thus the very possibility of postcolonial community that Bhabha takes for granted.[4] Nevertheless, Gikandi is absolutely right, in the current parlance, to check his privilege, to contrast his freedom of movement with the forced migration of the refugee.

Gikandi articulates a form of cosmopolitan melancholia that echoes Siskind's lament for the lost ground of solidarity, the lost possibility of a shared imaginative world. For Gikandi, his fellow passengers, if they do succeed in gaining asylum in the Western metropole, are more likely to 'recreate locality' (i.e. ethnic enclaves) than seek out cross-cultural forms of community:

> Journeys across boundaries and encounters with others do not necessarily lead to a cosmopolitan attitude. Increasingly, the journeys that lead refugees from the war zones of the global south, processes often prompted by the collapse of those archaic, yet real, loyalties that make cultural elites uneasy, do not lead to freedom from those loyalties but to their entrenchment. (Gikandi 2010: 24–5)

The examples he cites are an uncomfortable and not quite self-aware performance of cosmopolitanism's discomfort with aspects of Islamic cultural practice:

> Indeed, even in the metropolitan spaces we perform our postcolonial identities . . . the existence of a mass of people who seem to hold on to what we consider archaic cultures (those who wear *burqas* in classrooms, or slaughter sheep in the tubs of suburban houses, or 'circumcise' their daughters in hidden alleys) seem to disturb the temporality of postcolonialism and the terms of its routing. (Gikandi 2010: 25)

While for Bhabha the temporality of postcolonialism was disruptive of modernity, for Gikandi, this temporality is itself disrupted by the (seemingly) archaic cultural values of certain migrants. Gikandi's examples betray a highly problematic Islamophobia, but he remains acute in his analysis of how the cosmopolitanism of postcolonial intellectuals is implicated in class privilege:

> Postcolonial elites are, by virtue of their class, position or education, the major beneficiaries of the project of decolonization . . . [and] of the nationalism they would later come to scorn. Indeed, quite often, these elites profited (directly or indirectly) from the inequalities and corruption of the postcolonial state. (Gikandi 2010: 29)

As we shall see, Cole's narrator was a member of the Nigerian elite and his choice to attend a military style boarding school not only enables him to gain a scholarship to Bard College in New York, but also begins the process of undoing his ties to what Gikandi calls 'locality'. The peculiar privations of boarding school life will allow him to replace such local desires with a more appropriately cosmopolitan desire for the culture of the metropolis.

Gikandi's essay is worth staying with for one last passage:

> I want to argue, then, that a discourse of cosmopolitanism remains incomplete unless we read the redemptive narrative of being global in a contrapuntal relation with the narrative of statelessness and, by reproduction, of locality, where we least expect it, in the metropolis. The refugee is the Other of the Cosmopolitan; rootless by compulsion, this figure is forced to develop an alternative narrative of global flows, functioning in a third zone between metropolis and ex-colony, producing and reproducing localities in the centres of metropolitan culture itself. (Gikandi 2010: 26)

While Bhabha's essay depicts the metropolis in the process of opening itself to the outside, of becoming cosmopolitan, Gikandi's essay depicts the city as a place that only seems to open itself to the outsider, as a cryptological formation in which subaltern ethnic groups – whether by desire or by state design – reproduce ethnic enclaves that fracture the possibility of inter-ethnic community. Much depends on what city one looks at and from whose perspective, but Gikandi's essay is salutary as the performance of a cosmopolitan *anxiety* about precisely what it means to be open to difference. Above all, it offers us a challenge: how might we conceive of a cosmopolitanism that includes those who may have no interest in the kinds of openness that cosmopolitanism habitually rehearses and which it assumes to be the indisputable marker of humanness? How might cosmopolitan aesthetics 'counter-focalise' itself (Spivak 2002), in order to render visible the 'contrapuntal narrative of statelessness?'

Open City

Teju Cole's novel *Open City* (2011) links the anxieties generated by 9/11 to the emerging refugee crisis, as part of the same immunological structure. Part of the novel's originality is to present this defensive reaction as central to the consciousness of a narrator who is himself a migrant, born in Nigeria to a Nigerian father and a German mother but now resident in New York as a trainee psychiatrist. Julius embodies Gikandi's figure of the cosmopolitan, postcolonial *flâneur*, walking the streets of the city while remaining apart from the 'strange company' he encounters.

Open City has been read first as a model and then as critique of the liberal model of cosmopolitan sympathy. Literary reviewers such as James Wood identify with Julius, the novel's seemingly cosmopolitan narrator, because they share his own blind spots. His perambulatory paragraphs offer an erudite, meditative commentary on city life that led liberal critics to forgive his 'ordinary solipsism' (Wood 2011) and, like Julius himself, pass over in silence the accusation of rape that is levelled at him by Moji, the sister of a childhood friend, a rape that Julius himself claims to have no memory of at all. Subsequent critics, by contrast, take the rape as a cue to read the novel as a *critique* of cosmopolitan privilege (Dalley 2013; Hallemeier 2013; Krishnan 2015; Vermeulen 2013). Such critics make use of Cole's public critique of humanitarianism[5] to excavate an ironic distance between narrator and author that early reviewers overlooked. In fact, we might read the novel as a mode of auto-critique analogous to Gikandi's critique of his own pretensions to postcolonial *flânerie*, an excavation of Cole's own cosmopolitan privilege as a New Yorker of Nigerian parentage who spent his childhood in Lagos, before, like Julius, attending university in the US. Cole dropped out of medical school to pursue a career in the arts, whereas Julius makes it through medical school but retains the kind of cosmopolitan aesthetic sensibility that Cole himself, at least to a degree, must share. Whereas early reviewers tend to conflate Cole with Julius in order to affirm their own cosmopolitan world-view, later, broadly postcolonial critics are keen to exaggerate the difference in order to advance their critique of cosmopolitanism. My reading of the novel as auto-critique suggests that there is no position external from cosmopolitanism from which the novel might be said to mount its critique.

The novel is the record of Julius's seemingly 'aimless wanderings', interspersed with some limited recollections of his upbringing in Nigeria. What Pieter Vermeulen dubs his 'aesthetic cosmopolitanism' manifests itself in a relation to other lives that is, like the cities he walks, simultaneously open and closed. On the one hand, Julius seems hyper-attentive, his attention turned outwards so that his diary-like entries are less the record of his interior life than the record of his immersion in the life of the city. On the other, Julius is a loner, capable of losing himself in a Mahler symphony but allergic to any form of political, especially racial, community. On the one hand, he is a compulsive recording device, a memory machine that seeks out the hidden histories of the cityscapes though which he walks. On the other, he seems to suffer from selective aphasia, ranging from the inconsequential forgetting of his ATM code to his failure to remember his rape of Moji during a drunken teenage party in Nigeria, and his inability even to recognise her when they meet again in New York a decade or so later. On the one hand, he is constantly alive to the histories of barbarity that Walter Benjamin so famously claimed underwrite the history of civilisation, and on the other, he seems dangerously unaware of his own history of barbarity.[6] His interactions with his environment are simultaneously impersonal and solipsistic, expansive and defensive, a historical materialist performance of remembrance and a carefully scored act of erasure.

In the novel's opening pages Julius stages himself, from the vantage of his high-rise apartment, as a kind of a kind of hyper-receptive diviner, watching out for bird migrations while listening to far-off classical music stations on the internet: 'on the days when I was home early enough from hospital, I used to look out the window like someone taking auspices, hoping to see the miracle of natural immigration' (Cole 2011: 4). The Freudian slip from migration to immigration suggests that he is uneasy about his own process of immigration and naturalisation, that what he wants the birds' flight to confirm is not seasonal migration but permanent settlement, the 'miracle' of US citizenship.

Julius is blissfully unaware of the ways in which the flyways of birds have been radically disrupted by the construction of skyscrapers (Berenstein 2015), imagining that the high rises might seem to the geese 'like firs massed in a grove' (Cole 2011: 4). His faux bird's-eye view of the city has the effect of naturalising both New York and his own elevated vantage point. As in Coetzee's *Disgrace* (1999), the narrative is heavily focalised through the eyes of a male rapist whose aesthetic education functions to elevate him above other people's suffering: although he leaves his high-rise apartment to pace the streets, there is a sense in which part of him remains tuned in to 'far-off classical music stations' such that his very receptiveness functions as a mode of insulation from his immediate surroundings. Tellingly, he is haunted by Coetzee's *The Lives of Animals* (1999) but makes no reference to *Disgrace*, published the same year as Coetzee's short story. Both *Open City* and *Disgrace* reveal cosmopolitanism to be a heavily *focalised* worldview, one that we must counter-focalise, *pace* Gayatri Spivak, by listening to the irruptive testimony of women such as Moji. We only hear her testimony in indirect speech, and belatedly, after Julius has walked away from the party where she has delivered it, but neither Julius nor the reader are left in any doubt as to its authenticity. The problem comes in Julius's inability to respond to her accusation. Despite its air of authenticity, it remains 'someone else's version' of his life, a version in which he is the villain rather than the hero (Cole 2011: 243) – a line that echoes Lurie's daughter's accusation that Lurie cannot see himself as anything other than the 'main character' (Coetzee 1999a: 198). Julius can admit the truth of Moji's story only as something external to his story of his life: 'each person must on some level take himself as the calibration for normalcy . . . We are not the villains of our own stories' (Cole 2011: 243). The flat, affectless tone that suggests to him the truth of her testimony is matched only by his own flatness of tone, his incapacity to respond other than though an ambulatory, aporetic prose that can only perform its own indirection, its symptomatic numbness.

Indeed, indirection is the motivating structure at the heart of *Open City*. Julius's walking is presented first as 'therapy', as 'a release from the tightly regulated mental environment of work' (2011: 7) and then as symptom, as something he finds himself 'compelled' to do for reasons that remain obscure to him. His wandering above ground is a 'reminder of freedom' in so far as Julius decides what direction to walk in, but as he enters the subway this volitional element becomes attenuated and he feels subject to a more collective compulsion: 'I felt that all of the human race were rushing, pushed by a counterinstinctive death-drive, into movable catacombs . . . all of us re-enacting unacknowledged traumas' (2011: 7). This subterranean feeling of compulsion is at least partly explained when he finds himself 'no longer heading directly home' but instead to Wall Street, to Ground Zero, to 9/11 itself, as he sardonically notes tourists have begun to refer to the site.

Although Julius claims to 'read Freud only for literary truths' (2011: 208), he deploys the Freudian distinction between mourning and melancholia, introjection and incorporation, in order to suggest that New Yorkers have cordoned off not simply Ground Zero but also their own losses: 'The neatness of the line we had drawn around 9/11 seemed to me to correspond with [the] kind of sectioning off [involved in melancholia] . . . The mourning had not been completed and the result had been the anxiety that cloaked the city' (2011: 209). Despite diagnosing this anxiety, Julius himself cannot help but mimic it: he is one of the 'we' complicit in this sectioning off, even while his narrative compulsively draws resemblances between past and present.

But there is a more obscure trauma that underwrites Julius's wandering malady. Vermeulen characterises Julius as more '*fugeur* than *flâneur*', citing Ian Hacking's study of the 'mad travellers' of nineteenth-century France who wandered far from home in what psychiatry came to describe as a 'dissociative fugue' (Vermeulen 2014: 102). Hacking describes the *fugeur*'s 'ambulatory automatism' as the flip side of the *flâneur*'s newly won mobility (Vermeulen 2014: 102). What motivates the *fugeurs*' dissociative flight is precisely the loss of home itself: they flee out of an unacknowledged sense that their home can no longer provide the sense of security once associated with home – or indeed that they, as men, can no longer furnish their homes with this sense of security. In this sense the *flâneur*'s wanderings are in fact continuous with those of the *fugeur*, in so far as the *flâneur* tries, and fails, to make himself at home in the modern metropolis: beyond their disparities in class and privilege, both are figures of an emasculated masculinity. What Cole's novel makes clear, then, is not simply Hacking's thesis that the *fugeur* is the flip side of the *flâneur* but that the statelessness of the refugee is the flip side of cosmopolitan privilege, that the former experience is encrypted with the latter.

Julius's wandering is also a symptom, an acting out, of his unmoored, estranged relation to his 'homeland', Nigeria, and his own mother's and grandmother's estranged relationship to their homeland, Germany. Just before he bumps into Moji in New York, he speaks of the past as 'mostly empty space, great expanses of nothing', and adds that 'Nigeria was like that for me, mostly forgotten except for those few things remembered with an outsized intensity' (Cole 2011: 154). What he remembers of Nigeria is not the rape but an episode of violent humiliation at boarding school, his father's funeral and his mother's attempts to talk to him about her childhood, about the 'absolute destitution' she and her mother had lived through in the immediate aftermath of the war (2011: 80). This is the last conversation they have together, and it leads to a silence that later becomes a 'rift that wouldn't heal' (2011: 81), as if Julius cannot tolerate the knowledge that behind his privileged upbringing lies an experience of destitution that he can neither own nor disown: '[Mother] had been born into an unspeakably bitter world, a world without sanctity . . . Years later, long after we became estranged, I tried to imagine the details of that life. It was an entire vanished world of people, experiences, sensations, desires, a world that, in some odd way, *I was the unaware continuation of*' (2011: 80, my italics). His realisation that his grandmother must have been raped by the Red Army in the aftermath of the war means that he is indeed the genetic continuation of this bitter history, the grandson of rape and destitution, but he remains unaware of how this history has become cryptically inverted, his grandmother's experience of gendered vulnerability 'repeating' itself in his own history of sexual violence.

While he has no desire to reconnect with his mother or indeed Nigeria, he has an obscure desire to visit his grandmother or oma, who may or may not still be living in Brussels. His connection to his oma at first appears a perverse desire to connect to someone whom his own parents seem to 'barely tolerate' (2011: 34). The only intimacy that he has ever shared with her is an hour on a trip to Olumo Rock in Yorubaland; while his parents climb the rock face, Julius spends an hour 'commun[ing] almost wordlessly' with his oma, who silently kneads his shoulder. His attempt to find her in Brussels is 'desultory' (2011: 101) and consists of more street wandering, and more random encounters with strangers. He fleetingly suggests that he, like a Rwandan woman he spots in a church, might be here in Belgium as 'an act of forgetting' (2011: 140). At one level his visit to Brussels is an act of remembrance: his wandering traces the path of his oma's disappearance, the disappearance of her citizenship, and with it, his own: encrypted at the heart of his cosmopolitan *flânerie* is her experience of absolute destitution. But at another level his trip to Brussels is indeed an attempt to forget, an attempt to forget his own violently gendered implication, as a rapist, in his grandmother's rape. In his rape of Moji he has unwittingly acted out the rape of his own oma. Like Oedipus, he is both perpetrator and victim of his own twisted family romance. However, unlike Oedipus, he never reaches that moment of *anagnorisis* in which he recognise his complicity, never reaches that moment of insight into his own blindness in which Oedipus turns his violence upon himself.

And this is the point at which we can distinguish between Julius's melancholic cosmopolitanism and the novel's *critical* melancholia. As we have noted, recent critics have read the novel as a critique of cosmopolitanism, taking Julius's blanking of Moji as the cue to separate out narrator and novelist, the cosmopolitan wrapped up in his own privileged life and the postcolonial novelist who seeks to expose the violence that underpins that privilege. The difficulty in maintaining this distinction is that Julius himself is aware of certain forms of historical violence. What he remains unaware of, and what even recent critics have largely glossed over, is the 'subterranean' link between his rape of Moji and his oma's rape by the Russians in the aftermath of the Second World War. This link suggests that his blanking of his own act of rape is an immunitary device, designed to shield him from the knowledge of the simultaneously precarious and implicated nature of his own privilege.

Browsing an exhibition of the Hungarian photo-journalist Martin Munkácsi, he comes across an image, 'at once expected and unexpected', of Goebbels and Hitler, at the same time as a young couple whom he takes to be Hasidic Jews. He recognises that he 'has no reasonable access to what being there, in that gallery, might mean for them' (2011: 154), but he has earlier had a conversation with a Berliner, presumably also a Jew but less identifiably so than the Hasidic couple, who left Germany in 1937. The man asked him if he has visited Berlin. Julius replies in the affirmative, adding that 'he enjoyed the city very much'. What he does not add is that 'my mother and my oma had been there too, as refugees near the end of the war, and that I was myself, in this distant sense, also a Berliner. If we had talked more, I would have told him only that I was from Nigeria, from Lagos' (2011: 153). His identification of himself as a Berliner must be kept at a distance, even from himself. The historical possibility that a citizen could suddenly find herself a refugee in her own country is, for Julius, a family secret, a traumatic knowledge encrypted in his very genes. Julius's distant identification of himself as a citizen of Berlin is a withheld identification with the experience of the refugee, with the 'absolute destitution' of his mother and grandmother.

The novel's title, *Open City*, thus turns out to name not cosmopolitan hospitality but radical vulnerability, the possibility that the cosmopolitan might truly find herself a citizen of nowhere. Brussels is an uncanny double of New York, in so far as Brussels, in declaring itself an open city during the Second World War, avoided aerial bombardment, while New York, which made no such declaration of surrender, was attacked by Al Qaeda. Brussels thus becomes a peculiar augur of what has already happened to New York, and Julius's compulsive pacing of both cities seems to mimic the actions of a psyche attempting to locate the source of its woundedness, of a city unable to fathom how its openness to the world has suddenly become an open wound. Just as New York is cloaked in anxiety, there is a 'palpable psychological pressure in Brussels' (2011: 98) which Julius ascribes to racial tensions and 'voter discontent about immigration' (2011: 100). Brussels, New York and Berlin are thus cities on the defensive, cities that carry memories of invasion and occupation.

Julius's melancholic identification with New York, Brussels and Berlin is an identification with cities that have ceased to offer the protection of the citadel, a disavowed identification with the *internal* failure of cosmopolitanism to offer refuge even to its own citizens. At bottom, it is not an identification with a metropolis that imagines itself under attack from a barbaric (anti-)civilisation (Al Qaeda), but rather a loss of faith in civilisation itself, what we might call a civilisational loss, whereby civilisation has revealed itself to be a front for barbarity.

It is this encrypted, or 'fenced-off', identification with civilisational loss that structures his relationships with other characters in the novel. Many critics have accused Julius of being unable to form attachments, but there a number of characters, only some of whom are his patients, towards whom Julius is drawn precisely because they offer him encrypted images of his own melancholia, of his own precarious citizenship: Professor Saito, a professor of English literature born in Japan, who commits medieval poetry to memory as a way of distracting himself from his internment as an enemy alien during the Second World War; V, a Delaware Indian historian who has written a book about the genocide of her fellow Native Americans, who consequently suffers from a depression that Julius is unable to alleviate and who eventually commits suicide; his black American friend who has escaped an 'appalling family background' of broken homes, drug-fuelled insanity, internment and suicide to become an academic (2011: 203); M, a Turkish man who feels he 'has to be responsible for the whole world' (2011: 48) after his infidelity leads to the breakdown of his marriage; and Moji herself, whose growing attractiveness may very well be the woundedness that he himself has inflicted on her. All of these attachments are cryptic in the sense that they offer images of the unacknowledged precarity of his own privilege. M and Moji offer more than this in so far as they also present him with an image of his own implication in the suffering of others – something that, as we have seen, he seems constitutively unable to acknowledge.

These identifications are matched by a similar number of *refused* identifications with those who lie outside the orbit of his precarious privilege: a Haitian shoeshine, a black taxi driver, a black post office worker and underground poet, a Liberian refugee who he visits and then neglects to visit in a detention facility in Queen's, and women marching to reclaim the streets. All of these characters lay a claim on Julius that he cannot countenance, either because they demand a compassionate attentiveness that he seems not to be able to afford (the shoeshine, the refugee), or because they seek a subaltern, oppositional form of solidarity that is at odds with the disinterested universality of Julius's cosmopolitanism (the African Americans, the women on the march). The most pivotal of these latter figures is a Moroccan migrant named Farouk whose intellectual ambitions were blocked by a racist Brussels university that refused to believe he could have written his MA thesis (2011: 128). Farouk is the rejected African that Julius himself might have been had he not had been Gikandi's 'beneficiary' of postcolonial privilege, the kind of person who, from his position on the outside of Western civilisation, might sympathise with the 9/11 attacks rather than self-identify with its victims. Troubled by Farouk's 'rage and rhetoric' (2011: 107), Julius sends him a copy of Kwame Anthony Appiah's *Cosmopolitanism*, as if Appiah's eloquent defence of liberal cosmopolitanism could defuse Farouk's rage and ward off another attack on the West by one of Farouk's more militant friends.

As I have suggested, *Open City* does not build to a moment of anagnorisis or self-recognition. Nevertheless Julius's wandering, the various 'flights of memory' that make up the novel's structure (Vermeulen 2013), has a number of bumpy landings, all of which attempt to jolt Julius out of his complacency, to remind him (or at least the reader) of both his precarity, the ease with which he too, like Farouk, might find himself on the outside looking in, and his implication.

His wandering is first brought to a halt by a mugging: two black men, with whom he had previously exchanged glances of 'quick solidarity' based on their mutual skin colour, pass him by without this gesture of recognition and then turn back to attack him (2011: 212). Although he 'trembles from the shock' afterwards, the incident does not give rise to any reflections on the motivations of his assailants or indeed any interest in their lives at all, although the chapter ends with his passing of an 'immigration crowd' (2011: 218) – a line of people queuing for documents that would legitimate their presence in the US – and a 'cordoned off monument' to what was once an African burial ground (2011: 220). As he admits, 'he has no purchase on who those people were whose corpses . . . had been laid to rest beneath his feet' (2011: 220), and the same could be said of the immigrants who, unlike him, do not have the security of American citizenship to fall back on. Like the monument, their lives remain 'cordoned off' from his.

The second moment at which his peregrinations would seem to come to a standstill is at a performance of Mahler's Ninth Symphony in Carnegie Hall. In a moment of metatextual irony, we learn that Julius was unable to get tickets for the previous night's performance of his favourite Mahler symphony, *Das Lied Von der Erde*, whose seasonal movement from autumn through winter to spring is closely mapped by Cole's novel. Julius tells us that Mahler's late symphonies were 'prolonged farewells': he was obsessed with death and was to die of a heart condition a year after completing the Ninth Symphony. But where Mahler seeks to naturalise his impending death as rebirth, Julius seeks to complete his own naturalisation as a US citizen, the securitisation of his cosmopolitan privilege, by taking up a lucrative position as a partner in a private practice. In addition, Mahler was an Ashkenazi Jew, and both symphonies were composed after 'vicious politics of an anti-semitic nature saw him forced him out of his directorship of the Vienna Opera' (2011: 249). Julius does not return to this second point but we might say that the symphonies work through, or sublimate, two forms of abjection: Mahler's antisemitic rejection by Viennese society and his impending return to *der Erde*.

Julius's reception of Mahler's symphony thus has the same cryptic structure as his relationship with Professor Saito and other precarious cosmopolitans. Before the symphony starts, he notes wearily that he is the only black person in the audience and he thinks of similar occasions when 'standing in line for the bathroom he gets looks that make him feel like Ota Benga, the Mbuti man who was put in the Bronx zoo in 1906' (2011: 252). His own, usually muted, sense of racial abjection does not prevent him getting caught up, like the rest of the audience, in the performance. In the final movement, an elderly woman gets up and walks down the aisle 'as though she had been summoned and was leaving into death': 'One of her arms was slightly raised, as though she were being led forward by a helper – *as though I was down there with my oma*, and the sweep of the music was pushing us gently forward as I escorted her out into the darkness' (2011: 253, my italics). The symphony thus provides Julius with a resolution to his desire to locate his grandmother: a peaceful, graceful death in the midst of community is Julius's belated compensation for the destitution that she experienced as a refugee, his own role as 'escort' a kind of screen memory for the violent role that men such as himself played in her destitution.

This attempt to provide a serene, non-violent ending for his oma and a sublimation of his anxieties about his own belonging is immediately disrupted by his own violent abjection from the 'all-white space' of Carnegie Hall. He mistakenly leaves by an emergency exit which then slams shut behind him, leaving him clinging to a flimsy fire escape in the rain. Moments ago, he had been 'in God's arms and in the company of many hundreds of others', in the grip of 'an impossible elation' (2011: 255), but he now finds himself ejected from this august company, on the 'unlit side' of aesthetic experience. Earlier, he described the elderly woman as 'moving so slowly that she was like a mote suspended inside the slow-moving music', but through his identification with her as his oma, he too has become a kind of mote, of the sort that obscures the vision of nationalism for Bhabha and of cosmopolitanism for Gikandi: he looks up at the stars only to find that the 'starlight was unreachable because my entire being was caught in a blind spot' (2011: 256).

The phrasing recalls his earlier critique of psychiatry as 'caught in a blind spot so big that it had taken over most of the eye' (2011: 239): 'what are we to do when the lens through which the symptoms are viewed is itself symptomatic: the mind is opaque to itself and it's hard to tell where, precisely, those areas of opacity are' (2011: 238). Julius's critique of psychiatry cannot quite turn into self-critique, into an acknowledgement of his violent, and violently gendered, privilege and the blind spots that this privilege engenders: just before he discloses Moji's accusation of rape he argues, seemingly forgetting his earlier recognition of the mind's opaqueness to itself, that 'each person must, on some level, take himself as the calibration point for normalcy, must assume that the room of his mind is not, cannot be, entirely opaque to him' (2011: 243). Satisfied that he has 'hewed close to the good', he finds it simply untenable that he could have raped her: not that he dismisses her testimony, delivered with the same 'accuracy' and 'flat affect' as his own narrative, but rather that he is completely unable to integrate the image of himself as a rapist into his own self-narrative.

The third ending to his wanderings comes as, like Melville's Ishmael, he is drawn to Manhattan's water's edge, to the islanded edge of civilisation, and finds himself invited to board a boat. The boat is a party cruiser rather than a whaler, full of college-age revellers, that sails around the Statue of Liberty. Toni Morrison famously described the unfathomable whiteness of the whale as the moment when 'whiteness became ideology': Moby Dick incarnates not the savagery of nature but the savagery of 'white racial ideology' (1992: 141–2). The Statue of Liberty would seem to be a similarly opaque symbol of whiteness, a metaphor for the free world, for civilisation, that nevertheless violently impedes 'the miracle of natural immigration'.

The final passage deflects, like so many passages before it, from his own registration of experience towards a more impersonal, historical registration, what we might call, following Freud, a *reminiscence*, that strange malady he judged peculiar to hysterics. To paraphrase: one night in 1888, 1,400 dead birds were recovered from the foot of the statue and sold off to the city's milliners and fancy stores. After that, Colonel Tassin, who had military command of the island, put a stop to this trade, decided that the carcasses should be 'retained for the services of science' and then set about recording the exact numbers of birds who met their deaths each night:

> With this strong instinct for public spiritedness Colonel Tassin undertook a government system of records, which he ensured were kept with military regularity and, shortly afterward, he was able to deliver detailed reports on each death, including the species of the bird, date, hour of striking, number striking, number killed, direction and force of the wind, character of the weather and general remarks. (Cole 2011: 259)

Julius's narrative, which simply repeats Tassin's observations, risks being a similarly dispassionate, biopolitical recording device, except that, like the tape-looping experiments of the 1960s, his splicing renders audible a ghost in the biopolitical machine, a twitch. While Tassin puts the bird deaths down to weather conditions, the novel concludes with the following, characteristically non-attributable, observation: 'the sense persisted that something more troubling was at work. On the morning of October 13, for example, 175 wrens had been gathered in, all dead of impact, although the night just past hadn't been particularly windy or dark' (2011: 259).

Gikandi, we recall, argued that 'the discourse of cosmopolitanism remains incomplete unless we read the redemptive narrative of being global in counterpoint with the narrative of statelessness' (2010: 26). Cole does not directly offer us the narrative of statelessness as such, but in this final image he offers us a memory trace of that narrative, of the violent collision of the refugee with the very system of liberties, freedoms and rights that was supposed to ensure her safe passage. And in so doing, I would suggest, Cole shows how the project of 'aesthetic cosmopolitanism' might be redirected towards its own outside: not in the liberal gesture of inclusion, whereby consciousness extends itself to imaginatively include and thus mourn the lives of others, but rather through the performance of a critical melancholia, whereby the novel gestures towards those lives, and deaths, that remain outside the ken of cosmopolitan sympathy.

Notes

1. Bruce Robbins's recent book, *The Beneficiary* (2017), argues for a 'redistributive cosmopolitanism' based on the recognition of who the beneficiaries of global capitalism are. Echoing my argument about the implication of the cosmopolitan in statelessness, Robbins argues for the recognition that 'your fate is causally linked to the fates of distant and sometimes suffering others' (2017b: 3).
2. For an up-to-date survey of cosmopolitan theory, see Robbins and Horta (2017).
3. One immediately thinks of Dave Eggers's novel *What Is the What: The Autobiography of Valentino Achak Deng* (2006) and Eggers's problematic assumption that his friendship with Deng means that he is able to tell the refugee's story from the inside, in the first person. Kate Clanchy's *Antigona and Me* (2008) is more aware of the problem of ventriloquism in that the author recognises that she 'couldn't pretend to imagine being her', and consequently elects to write 'Not Antigona's story as it happened to her, but her story as it happened to me, as I heard it, as I researched it and imagined it, as it made me think; as it changed me' (Clanchy 2008: 5).
4. Abdulrazak Gurnah goes to considerable lengths to emphasise this possibility of cosmopolitan refugees in his 2001 novel *By the Sea*, in which the refugee narrator is demonstrably more cosmopolitan than his parochial British hosts.
5. https://www.theatlantic.com/international/archive/2012/03/the-white-savior-industrial-complex/254843/ (accessed 28 May 2019).
6. Byron Caminero-Santangelo, earlier in this volume, makes a convincing case for the Benjaminian, or 'constellatory', nature of Cole's aesthetic practice.

Bibliography

Abraham, Nicolas, and Maria Torok (1986 [1976]), *The Wolf Man's Magic Word: A Cryptonymy*, trans. Nicholas Rand (Minneapolis: University of Minnesota Press).
Agamben, Giorgio (2008 [1993]), 'Beyond human rights', *Open. Cahier on art and the public domain*, 15: 86–9.
Arendt, Hannah (1978 [1943]), 'We refugees', in Ron H. Feldman (ed.), *The Jew as Pariah: Jewish Identity and Politics in the Modern Age* (New York: Grove).
Becker, Sascha O., Thiemo Fetzer and Dennis Novy (2017), 'Who voted for Brexit? A comprehensive district-level analysis', *Economic Policy*, 32.92: 601–50.
Berenstein, Nadia (2015), 'Deathtraps in the flyways: electricity, glass and bird collisions in urban North America, 1887–2014', in Kaori Nagai et al. (eds), *Cosmopolitan Animals* (Basingstoke: Palgrave Macmillan), 79–92.

Bhabha, Homi (1990), 'DissemiNation', in Homi Bhabha (ed.), *Nation and Narration* (London: Routledge), 291–322.

Bhabha, Homi (1996), 'Unsatisfied: notes on vernacular cosmopolitanism', in Laura Garcia-Morena and Peter C. Pfeifer (eds), *Text and Nation* (London: Camden House), 191–207.

Butler, Judith (2004), *Precarious Life: The Powers of Mourning and Violence* (London: Verso).

Butler, Judith (2009), *Frames of War: When is Life Grievable?* (London: Verso).

Calhoun, Craig (2003), 'The class consciousness of frequent travellers: towards a critique of actually existing cosmopolitanism', in Danielle Archibugi (ed.), *Debating Cosmopolitics* (London: Verso), 86–117.

Clanchy, Kate (2008), *Antigona and Me* (London: Picador).

Coetzee, J. M. (1999a), *Disgrace* (London: Secker and Warburg).

Coetzee, J. M. (1999b), *The Lives of Animals* (Princeton: Princeton University Press).

Cole, Teju (2011), *Open City* (London: Faber and Faber).

Dalley, Hamish (2013), 'The idea of "third generation Nigerian literature": conceptualizing historical change and territorial affiliation in the contemporary Nigerian novel', *Research in African Literatures*, 44.4: 15–34.

Derrida, Jacques (1986a), 'Fors: the Anglish words of Nicolas Abraham and Maria Torok', foreword to Nicolas Abraham and Maria Torok, *The Wolf Man's Magic Word: A Cryptonymy*, trans. Nicholas Rand (Minneapolis: University of Minnesota Press), xi–xlviii.

Derrida, Jacques (1986b), *Memoires for Paul de Man*, trans. Cecile Lindsay et al. (New York: Columbia University Press).

Derrida, Jacques (1995 [1992]), *The Gift of Death*, trans. David Wills (Chicago: University of Chicago Press).

Eggers, Dave (2006), *What is the What? The Autobiography of Valentino Achak Deng* (London: Penguin).

Eskenazi, Jem (2016), 'It's May who misunderstands world citizenship', *Financial Times*, 10 October, https://www.ft.com/content/0e175bc2-8cac-11e6-8aa5-f79f5696c731 (accessed 15 May 2019).

Esposito, Roberto (2013), *Terms of the Political: Community, Immunity, Biopolitics*, trans. Rhiannon Welch (New York: Fordham University Press).

Gikandi, Simon (2010), 'Between roots and routes: cosmopolitanism and the claims of locality', in Janet Wilson, Cristina Sandru and Sarah Lawson Welsh (eds), *Rerouting the Postcolonial: New Directions for the New Millennium* (London: Routledge), 22–35.

Gilroy, Paul (2004), *After Empire: Melancholia or Convivial Culture* (London: Routledge).

Gurnah, Abdulrazak (2001), *By the Sea* (London: Bloomsbury).

Hallemeier, Katherine (2013), 'Literary cosmopolitanisms in Teju Cole's *Every Day is the Thief* and *Open City*', *ariel: A Review of International English Literature*, 44.2–3: 239–50.

Hardt, Michael, and Antonio Negri (2000), *Empire* (Cambridge, MA: Harvard University Press).

Huntington, Samuel (1993), 'The clash of civilisations?', *Foreign Affairs*, 72.3: 22–49.

Kant, Immanuel (1983), *Perpetual Peace and Other Essays*, trans. Ted Humphrey (Cambridge, MA: Hackett).

Khair, Tabish (2016), *The New Xenophobia* (New Delhi: Oxford University Press).

Khanna, Ranjana (2003), *Dark Continents: Psychoanalysis and Colonialism* (Durham, NC: Duke University Press).

Krishnan, Madhu (2015), 'Postcoloniality, spatiality and cosmopolitanism in the *Open City*', *Textual Practice*, 29.4: 675–96.

May, Theresa (2016), 'Theresa May's conference speech in full', *The Telegraph*, 5 October, https://www.telegraph.co.uk/news/2016/10/05/theresa-mays-confer-ence-speech-in-full/ (accessed 15 May 2019).

Mbembe, Achille (2003), 'Necropolitics', *Public Culture*, 15.1: 11–40.

Morrison, Toni (1992), *Playing in the Dark: Whiteness and the Literary Imagination* (Cambridge, MA: Harvard University Press).

Nussbaum, Martha (1998), *Cultivating Humanity: A Classical Defense of Reform in Liberal Education* (Cambridge, MA: Harvard University Press).

Renan, Ernst (1990 [1892]), 'What is a nation?', in Homi Bhabha (ed.), *Nation and Narration* (London: Routledge), 8–22.

Robbins, Bruce (2017a), 'George Orwell, cosmopolitanism, and global justice', in Bruce Robbins and Paulo Lemos Horta (eds), *Cosmopolitanisms* (New York: New York University Press), 40–58.

Robbins, Bruce (2017b), *The Beneficiary* (Durham, NC: Duke University Press).

Robbins, Bruce, and Paulo Lemos Horta (2017), 'Introduction', in Bruce Robbins and Paulo Lemos Horta (eds), *Cosmopolitanisms* (New York: New York University Press), 1–20.

Rushdie, Salman (1988), *The Satanic Verses* (Dover, DE: The Consortium).

Santiago, Silviano (2017), 'The cosmopolitanism of the poor', in Bruce Robbins and Paulo Lemos Horta (eds), *Cosmopolitanisms* (New York: New York University Press), 21–39.

Siskind, Mario (2014), *Cosmopolitan Desires: Global Modernity and World Literature in Latin America* (Evanston: Northwestern University Press).

Siskind, Mario (2018), 'Towards a cosmopolitanism of loss: an essay about the end of the world' (draft MS).

Spivak, Gayatri (2002), 'Ethics and politics in Tagore, Coetzee, and certain scenes of teaching', *Diacritics*, 32.3–4: 17–31.

Vermeulen, Pieter (2013), 'Flights of memory: Teju Cole's *Open City* and the limits of aesthetic cosmopolitanism', *Journal of Modern Literature*, 37.1: 40–57.

Vermeulen, Pieter (2014), 'The biopolitics of trauma', in Gert Beulens, Sam Durrant and Robert Eaglestone (eds), *The Future of Trauma Theory: Contemporary Literary and Cultural Criticism* (London: Routledge), 141–56.

Wood, James (2011), 'The arrival of enigmas: Teju Cole's prismatic début novel, *Open City*', *New Yorker*, 28 February, https://www.newyorker.com/maga-zine/2011/02/28/the-arrival-of-enigmas (accessed 15 May 2019).

Index

Note: Page references in italics indicate images; 'n' indicates chapter notes.